# INTRODUCTION TO
# THE COMPUTER

# INTRODUCTION TO

Prentice-Hall, Inc., Englewood Cliffs, New Jersey 07632

# THE COMPUTER

## The Tool of Business

**3RD EDITION**

# WILLIAM M. FUORI, Ph.D., C.D.E.
Professor, Nassau Community College, New York

*Library of Congress Cataloging in Publication Data*

FUORI, WILLIAM M
   Introduction to the computer.

   Bibliography: p.
   Includes index.
   1. Business—Data processing.  I. Title.
HF5548.2.F86  1981      658'.054     80-26693
ISBN  0-13-480343-4

INTRODUCTION TO THE COMPUTER
The Tool of Business, 3rd Edition
William M. Fuori

Printed in the United States of America

10  9  8  7  6  5  4  3  2  1

Editorial/Production Supervision by Lynn S. Frankel
Interior and Cover Design by Janet Schmid
Cover photograph courtesy of IBM Corporation
Interior illustrations by Vantage Art, Inc.
Acquisitions Editor: Stephen E. Cline
Manufacturing Buyer: Joyce Levatino

Prentice-Hall International, Inc., *London*

Prentice-Hall of Australia Pty. Limited, *Sydney*

Prentice-Hall of Canada, Ltd., *Toronto*

Prentice-Hall of India Private Limited, *New Delhi*

Prentice-Hall of Japan, Inc., *Tokyo*

Prentice-Hall of Southeast Asia Pte. Ltd., *Singapore*

Whitehall Books Limited, *Wellington, New Zealand*

To my wife, Elizabeth,
and my children, Elizabeth E. and Michael T.

# CONTENTS

Preface                                                          xi

Acknowledgments                                                  xv

## 1 INTRODUCTION TO DATA PROCESSING AND BUSINESS

**CHAPTER 1** Automation and Data Processing                      3

A discussion of information processing, the impact of automation on business, the meaning of data processing, the uses of computers in business, word processing, and the effect of the computer on society.

**CHAPTER 2** A Brief History                                     35

A brief history of data processing including the abacus, Pascal's Machine Arithmétique, Joseph Marie Jacquard, Charles Babbage, Herman Hollerith, Howard H. Aiken, John Von Neumann, computer generations, minicomputers, and microcomputers.

## 2 COMPUTER SYSTEM FUNDAMENTALS

**CHAPTER 3** Data-entry Devices and Media                        73

A discussion of the 80- and 96-column cards, punched card concepts and terminology, key-to-tape and key-to-disk entry systems, terminals, character readers, and speech recognition systems. Operating the card punch is included in an Appendix to this chapter.

**CHAPTER 4** Input/Output Media and Devices                     117

A presentation of the various input/output devices and media associated with computers from the card reader and printer through the more recent and sophisticated devices and media including terminals, film devices, audio devices, and plotters.

# CHAPTER 5   Processing and Storage Devices      159

A discussion of the components and functions of the central processing unit with an introduction to laser, magnetic bubble, and charged-coupled storage, an introduction to virtual storage and data storage concepts, an introduction to input/output communications, and an introduction to the microcomputer including ROM, RAM, PROM, and EPROM.

# CHAPTER 6   File Processing Concepts, Devices, and Media      200

A discussion of the currently used mass storage devices and media including tape, drum, disk, data cell, and mass storage systems. The three principal file organizations (sequential, direct, and indexed sequential) are introduced. In addition, the concept of a database is explained.

# 3 SOFTWARE, PROGRAM PREPARATION, AND PROBLEM-SOLVING CONCEPTS

# CHAPTER 7   Flowcharting, Decision Tables, and Top-down Program Design      233

A discussion of the preparation necessary for programming, flowcharts and decision tables, and program documentation. Top-down program design is introduced, including HIPO, structured programming concepts and pseudocode.

# CHAPTER 8   Introduction to Computer Languages and Programming      283

A discussion of machine language, symbolic language, problem-oriented and procedure-oriented languages, and interactive languages. The areas of application together with the advantages and disadvantages of each type of computer language, the programming process, program debugging, and program documentation are also discussed.

# 4 COMMON PROGRAMMING LANGUAGES USED IN BUSINESS

# CHAPTER 9   Introduction to BASIC      321

An introduction to time sharing and how BASIC is used in time-sharing applications. The fundamentals of BASIC are presented together with numerous examples of actual BASIC programs. Topics discussed include system commands, input/output statements, arithmetic statements, and elementary branch statements.

# CHAPTER 10   Advanced Concepts in BASIC      357

The reader is introduced to the more advanced concepts utilized in most practical programs employed in business or industry. Advanced topics include additional looping and input/output statements, table handling, functions and subprograms, and file processing. A BASIC reference summary is provided in the Appendix to this chapter.

# CHAPTER 11 COBOL 411

An introduction to the COBOL programming language with a discussion of the IDENTIFICATION, ENVIRONMENT, DATA, and PROCEDURE division entries. The emphasis is on learning to read and understand COBOL programs.

# 5 A SYSTEMS APPROACH

# CHAPTER 12 Systems Analysis 449

A discussion of what a system is, the various elements of a system, and what is involved in feasibility and application studies.

# CHAPTER 13 Systems Considerations 467

An introduction to form design, card and CRT layout and design, file structure, coding of input, system flowcharting, testing, and documentation.

# CHAPTER 14 Information Systems 493

An introduction to the concepts of batch processing, online processing, online real-time processing, multiprogramming, multiprocessing, time sharing, integrated and management information systems. Also introduced is the concept of distributed data-processing, including networks, data communications, and teleprocessing.

# CHAPTER 15 Business Systems 527

The concept of a total business system is introduced. A somewhat simplified but representative payroll system is examined in detail. Samples of items used in system documentation are provided in an Appendix to this chapter.

# APPENDIX A Glossary of Data Processing Terms 559

# APPENDIX B Computer Number Systems 593

# APPENDIX C Answers to Selected Exercises 605

Index 615

# PREFACE

## GENERAL PURPOSE

Today's educator, who must prepare a student to enter the automated world of business, faces a most challenging task. He must anticipate the needs of the business community up to five years hence so that students will be prepared to serve productively and efficiently in tomorrow's business environment.

A major goal of the educator, then, is to determine those new trends that are destined to become an integral part, if not the very foundation, of the business structure in future decades.

Automation and the use of computers in every phase of business is today the driving force for change. Educators at all levels, from the private business school to the community college to the university, have recognized the impact of the computer on business and have had the foresight not only to recommend but, in many instances, to require that students planning to enter the business field at any level, and in any capacity, be exposed to the computer as an integral part of their business education. To quote Dr. R. L. Bright when he was Associate Commissioner for Research of the U.S. Department of Health, Education, and Welfare, anyone who graduates from a college or university ". . . without being instructed in the use of computers has been severely cheated."

This book is written to serve the data processing student as well as the beginning or advanced business student. It provides a basic understanding of what the computer is, what the computer can do, and how the computer can serve in professional endeavors. In addition, this text covers those topics recommended by the American Institute of Certified Public Accountants. This text is recommended for use in a one-semester survey course or in an introductory course designed for the data processing or business student contemplating an in-depth study of computers or programming languages. In either case, having completed this one-semester course, the student will be prepared to function effectively in a computerized business or pursue more advanced studies in the field of computers.

## STRUCTURE OF TEXT

Like the second edition, this edition is organized to facilitate the student's comprehension of the relevance of data processing in business. To accomplish this end, the text has been divided into five units as follows:

Unit 1 introduces the student to the impact of computers on business so that he or she may clearly understand why such a study was undertaken and to what future goals this knowledge may be applied. This unit also traces the development of computers so that the student may study recent trends and innovations in their historical perspective. The topics of word processing and microcomputers have been added to this unit in this edition.

Unit 2 This unit has been completely revised in this edition. Two new chapters have been added: data-entry devices and media, and file processing concepts, devices, and media. In addition chapters 4, 5, and 6 have been rearranged on the basis of a survey of users of the previous editions. To Chapter 5, Processing and Storage Devices, many additions have been made, including laser and magnetic bubble storage devices, ROM, RAM, PROM, EPROM, data-storage concepts and an introduction to input/output communications. The chapter on number systems has been eliminated, but many of the key concepts have been retained in Appendix B or integrated into Chapter 5.

Unit 3 discusses program preparation and problem-solving concepts. The student learns what is involved in preparing an application for programming, how to flowchart the logic of the application, and how the flowchart is used in preparing the computer program. It is not uncommon for business people to review flowcharts before an extensive programming effort is begun. They do this to make certain that the programmer has considered, and understood, all aspects of the problem. The expanded coverage of program execution, debugging, and documentation added in the second edition have been retained. This edition contains the new topics of top-down program design including HIPO charts, structured programming, and pseudocode.

Unit 4 exposes the student to two of the most commonly used programming languages in business: COBOL and BASIC. This exposure familiarizes the student with the fundamentals of each language and instructs him or her on their differences, as well as the advantages and disadvantages of each. The student is then prepared to understand computer programs—in either language—that may be written by a professional programmer to solve his or her particular problem. COBOL (Common Business Oriented Language) is the most widely used computer language in business and is easily understood because of its resemblance to English. Since many companies do not have their own on-site computers, they must often resort to time sharing. BASIC is one of the most common languages used in time-sharing applications and is, therefore, covered in this text. It is easily learned and, thus, quickly applied by both data-processing and non-data-processing personnel in business. Changes in the third edition include greatly expanded coverage of the BASIC language including establishing and referencing tables, functions and subprograms, and file processing. The complete BASIC language specifications added as a chapter appendix in the second edition have been retained.

Unit 5 discusses system analysis and design. The student is introduced to the concepts of feasibility and application studies, system design considerations, information systems, and other similar items with which the student may become associated later in his/her professional career. In addition, a representative payroll system is discussed in depth in order to provide the student with a practical knowledge of what is involved in a typical computerized business system. This will better enable the student to understand how he or she can most effectively interact with and use such a system in business. In addition, this unit provides the student with insight into types of information that are—and are not—typically processed on a computer. It also serves to tie together all material previously presented in the text. To this edition the concepts of distributed data processing, networks, data communications, and teleprocessing have been added.

## UNIQUENESS

This book is different from others that appeal to students in business or business-related areas in several ways:

1. Instead of presenting isolated topics in each chapter, this book provides continuity from chapter to chapter by means of the unit concept discussed above. This chapter-to-chapter continuity causes the student to view the subject as a whole and not as a series of disjointed topics.
2. Changes in the third edition were the result of a detailed survey of professors teaching an introductory data-processing course at colleges across the country.
3. The material in this text has already been successfully "field-tested" for several semesters at Nassau Community College. The enthusiastic response of students has convinced the author that the text is interesting, informative, and easy to read.
4. The emphasis of this book differs substantially from that of most introductory data-processing texts. It does not concentrate on teaching data processing students how to program computers but emphasizes how both business and data processing students can make effective use of the computer as an information-processing tool. Nevertheless, the student will be able to write complete and realistic computer programs using the BASIC language in either a conversational or a batch mode. Throughout the text, material presented is reinforced with illustrative business examples.

5. This text includes topics in asterisked sections and in chapter appendixes. These sections and appendixes make available to the instructor topics of a more complex and "in-depth" nature should they be desired. The instructor may thus gear the level of the course to fit the interest and backgrounds of his students.

6. This text includes a substantial number of exercises at the end of each chapter in addition to numerous self-tests which are referenced throughout each chapter. These exercises have been improved over the second edition and are far in excess of the number and scope of such exercises found in other texts of this type.

7. Programmed self-tests are provided throughout the text to reinforce previously presented material. In this way, the student derives the benefits of programmed instruction as well as the advantages of a lecture presentation.

8. Current and related articles are presented at the end of the chapters to acquaint the student with some of the more practical aspects of the subject matter as well as to stimulate the student's interest in exploring the subject matter in greater depth.

9. Timely and related cartoons are integrated throughout the text. These have proven to be both interesting and informative in the author's field testing of the material.

10. Illustrations entitled "It's Truly Amazing" are interwoven through the early chapters to make the student aware of some of the more truly amazing innovations and accomplishments that have taken place in the field.

## STUDY GUIDE

A Study Guide is available to assist the student in understanding and learning the material presented in the text. The Study Guide is divided into two parts.

Part I of the Study Guide provides for each chapter:

- A summary which emphasizes the main points of the chapter
- A vocabulary drill to allow the student to determine his or her understanding of the important terms and concepts presented in the chapter
- Matching exercises
- Debugging exercises where the student must determine which statements are true and which are false. False statements must be corrected
- A crossword puzzle to allow the student to demonstrate an understanding of the terms and concepts presented in the chapter
- Projects to be completed outside of class

Part II of the Study Guide provides approximately 100 pages of graduated exercises to help the student clarify his or her understanding of the BASIC programming concepts presented in Chapters 9 and 10 of the text. These exercises range in complexity from simply determining what is wrong with a single BASIC statement to writing a complete program. Program assignments are graduated from the very simple to those requiring substantial understanding and insight into the material presented in the text.

## TEST BANK

A test bank is also available which can be photocopied directly or extracted from by the instructor in the preparation of examinations. A test is provided for each chapter in the text.

The solutions to all programming exercises found in the Study Guide are included along with the Test Bank.

## TEACHER'S MANUAL

A teacher's manual is available to aid in structuring the course to fit the interests and backgrounds of students. Included in this unprecedented manual for each text chapter are:

- A list of performance objectives.
- A detailed summary which can be utilized by the instructor as a lecture outline.
- Text correlated illustrations that may be used directly for the preparation of overhead projector foils.
- Complete and detailed answers to all text exercises.

# ACKNOWLEDGMENTS

The author wishes to thank the Honeywell Corporation and the Univac Division of the Sperry Rand Corporation, among others, for graciously granting permission to use the illustrations that helped to make this text more meaningful. In particular the author would like to thank the International Business Machines Corporation for their assistance and for their granting permission to use photos and illustrations provided directly by IBM or contained in their publications. Gratefully noted for their artwork are Vantage Art, Inc. and cartoonists Michael Artell, Dave Carpenter, Sandy Dean, John T. Paine, and Marcelo Rodriguez.

The author also wishes to thank the following people for technical assistance and constructive criticism during the production of this third edition:

Mr. Joseph Pacilio, Professor of Mathematics/Statistics/Computer Processing, Nassau Community College, Garden City, New York.

Mr. Thomas Taylor, Assistant to the Dean of Instruction for Learning Resources, Nassau Community College, Garden City, New York.

Mr. Anthony D'Arco, Professor of Mathematics/Statistics/Computer Processing, Nassau Community College, Garden City, New York.

Mr. Karl Karlstrom, Assistant Vice President, Senior Editor, Computer Science and Applied Mathematics, Prentice-Hall, Inc.

Mr. Stephen E. Cline, Acquisitions Editor, Computing Sciences, Prentice-Hall, Inc.

Ms. Lynn S. Frankel, Production Editor, Prentice-Hall, Inc.

Mr. Joseph DiDomenico, Art & Design Director, Prentice-Hall, Inc.

Ms. Janet Schmid, Senior Designer, Prentice-Hall, Inc.

Ms. Robyn Hartmann, Marketing Manager, Prentice-Hall, Inc.

But most of all, the author would like to thank his wife, Elizabeth, without whose consideration, patience, understanding, and constant encouragement, this book would not have been possible.

# INTRODUCTION TO DATA PROCESSING AND BUSINESS

INTRODUCTION

BUSINESS AND INFORMATION PROCESSING

**Need for More Efficient Processing Methods**

IMPACT OF AUTOMATION ON BUSINESS

WHAT IS DATA PROCESSING?

**Fundamental Data-processing Operations**

Recording

Classifying

Sorting

Calculating

Summarizing

Reporting

**Data-processing Cycle**

USES OF COMPUTERS IN BUSINESS

**Characteristics of Problems Suitable
for Computerized Solutions**

Justifiable

Definable

Repetitive

Volume Data and/or Numerous Calculations

WORD PROCESSING

COMPUTERS IN SOCIETY

FOCUS ON THE FIELD

SELF-TESTS

EXERCISES

# CHAPTER 1

# Automation and Data Processing

## INTRODUCTION

This chapter introduces the student to the need for and the impact of the computer in business. We will discuss both the advantages of using computers and the possible problems associated with their use. The nature of problems suitable for a computerized solution will also be discussed.

Upon completing this chapter, you should be able to:
- Discuss the factors contributing to the development of the computer and its introduction into business.
- Describe the fundamental data-processing operations.
- Describe the characteristics of problems suitable for a computerized solution.
- Describe some of the social problems accompanying the introduction of the computer.
- Define the following terms:

| | |
|---|---|
| Business data processing | Processing |
| Calculating | Recording |
| Classifying | Repetitive problem |
| Data | Reporting |
| Data processing | Scientific data |
| Data-processing cycle | processing |
| Definable problem | Sorting |
| Information | Summarizing |
| Input | Volume data or |
| Justifiable problem | numerous calculations |
| Output | Word processing |

## BUSINESS AND INFORMATION PROCESSING

Every business, regardless of its size or purpose, is concerned with processing facts, or data, about its operations in order to provide current, accurate information to management. Executive decisions are based on data such as operating expenses, market statistics, inventory levels, and other quantitative factors. The depth, accuracy, and currentness of the factual information at the disposal of management can provide a business with a substantial edge over its competition.

However, like raw talent or raw materials, raw data are of limited use. Only after these data have been examined, compared, classified, analyzed, and summarized do they become usable information and take on real value for management. Nearly 500 billion pieces of paper filling over 100 million file drawers are generated annually by the nation's businesses. Papers piled up over the years in offices and storerooms throughout the nation amount to over 1 trillion (1,000,000,000,000) pieces. A large segment of the working population, comparable in size to the entire U.S. Army, has as its daily chore the recording, processing, and analyzing of the factual data generated by industrial, professional, and government organizations. This army of white-collar workers, consisting of more than 20 million people, does not buy, sell, manufacture, or even service goods but is concerned exclusively with the manual and automated processing of the data relating to these activities in our complex civilization.

**Need for More Efficient Processing Methods**

With the advent of the industrial revolution, which brought ever-increasing amounts of data to be processed in shorter and shorter times, business found that it needed faster, cheaper, more efficient methods of processing data.

To fill this need, various types of automated devices were developed

FIGURE 1-1
Introduction of automated devices into accounting

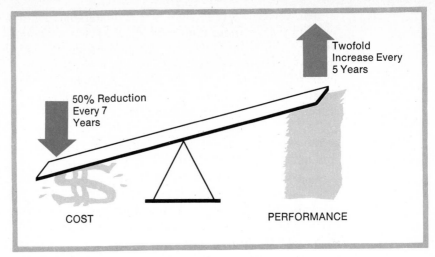

**FIGURE 1-2**

Cost/performance relationship for small business computers (Computers costing under $50,000)

and introduced. Most recent, and foremost among them, was the introduction of the electronic computer, the fastest and most sophisticated business tool yet devised (Fig. 1-1). Even with their tremendous initial speed advantage, computers have continued to become even faster and cheaper (Fig. 1-2).

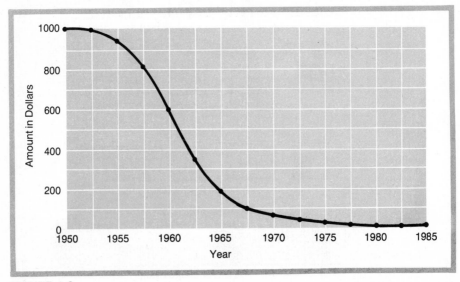

**FIGURE 1-3**

Cost of processing a job

For example, 25 years ago it cost over $1.25 to do 100,000 multiplications by computer. Today this would cost less than a penny (Fig. 1-3). By way of comparison, if other costs had dropped proportionately, one would be able to take an airline trip around the world for about $3 or buy a medium-sized car for about $200. In addition to becoming faster and cheaper, computers have decreased in size at an even more startling rate. Twenty-five years ago, to obtain the computing power available today with a briefcase-sized computer, one would have required a computer the size of the Empire State Building.

## IMPACT OF AUTOMATION ON BUSINESS

The computer revolution is for all practical purposes a second industrial revolution. And, as in the case of the industrial revolution, the computer revolution has opened many new careers for millions of people, making the automated processing of data big business. In 1980, for example, over 5 million people were employed in occupations resulting from and directly related to the computer. From an origin traceable to the abstractions of a few creative mathematicians, the concepts underlying automatic computers have grown into a billion-dollar industry. In terms of capital investment alone, this represents an increase from $30 million in 1950 to an expected $160 billion by 1985 (Fig. 1-4).

These figures include computer systems ranging in price from $500 for a small home computer to $8 million for the most powerful and

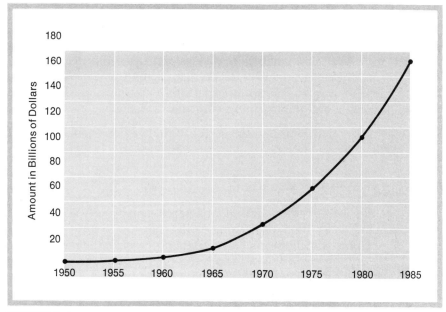

**FIGURE 1-4**
Value of computing equipment in use

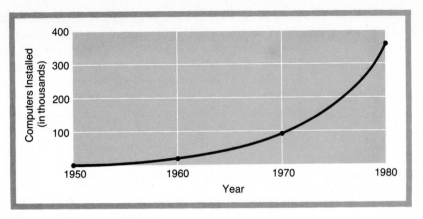

**FIGURE 1-5**
Computers installed in the United States

expensive computer, the Cray 1. The Cray 1 "supercomputer" is a six-foot high, circular structure consisting of ominous black panels and polished steel supports and surrounded by upholstered benches.

But behind this futuristic facade are dense circuits capable of performing 100,000,000 calculations per second. To put this in perspective, the Cray 1 can perform approximately 3000 calculations in the time required for a supersonic jet traveling 2000 miles per hour to move 1 inch. Computers such as the Cray 1 are generally only applied to the solution of very complex and sophisticated scientific problems.

There isn't a home or a business that hasn't felt the impact of the electronic computer. Computers are used to calculate gas and electric bills, to control electric equipment during surgical operations, to control the takeoff and landings of rockets and space vehicles, to control intricate chemical processes, to predict enemy troop movements during a time of war, and most important to the business world, to control the financial and management activities of business.

To verify your understanding of the previous material, turn to page 28 and take Self-Test 1-1.

## WHAT IS DATA PROCESSING?

Let us begin our analysis of data processing by answering the question: What does data processing really mean? "Data" is the plural of "datum," which means "fact." **Data processing,** then, is simply the manipulating and using of facts.[1] Accounts kept by the ancient Egyptians in 3400 B.C. are examples of data processing. However, for over a decade many business concerns have relied almost exclusively on com-

[1] Refer to Appendix A for the American National Standards Institute definition of data processing.

puters to process their data (Fig. 1-6). It is for this reason that the term "data processing" and the concept of processing data by computer have become synonymous.

"Business data processing," on the other hand, is used to distinguish those operations relating to management control of business from other application areas such as those relating to science and industry. The latter form of data processing is called scientific data processing.

**Fundamental Data-processing Operations**

Regardless of whether the system used to process the data is manual, mechanical, or electronic, certain fundamental operations must be performed. These operations are:

1. Recording 　　3. Sorting 　　5. Summarizing
2. Classifying 　　4. Calculating 　　6. Reporting

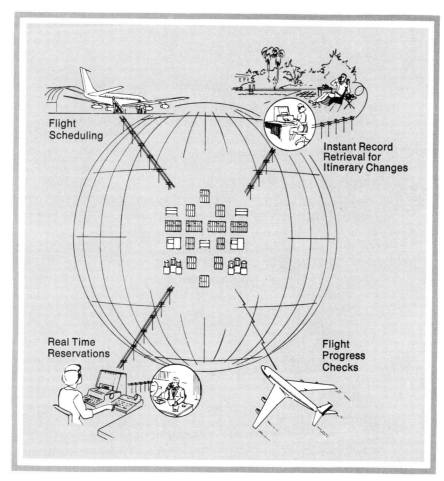

FIGURE 1-6
An automated airline reservation system

## it's truly amazing

In the computer, the basic operations can be done within the order of a NANOSECOND (one thousandth of a millionth of a second)

Within the half second it takes this spilled coffee to reach the floor, a fairly large computer could—(given the information in magnetic form) *Debit 2000 checks to 300 different bank accounts,* and *examine the electrocardiograms of 100 patients and alert a physician to possible trouble,* and *score 150,000 answers on 3000 examinations and evaluate the effectiveness of the questions,* and *figure the payroll for a company with a thousand employees,* and do a few other chores.

Recording.   Recording is the transcribing of data from a source document onto a machine-readable medium (see Fig. 1-7). When one or more items of data have been reproduced into machine-readable cards called punched cards, or into a magnetic tape similar to that commonly used with home tape recorders, or into some other permanent form, they have been recorded.

The recording of data relating to a single transaction into a punched card or other machine-readable medium corresponds to a journal entry in manual methods of accounting (Fig. 1-8).

"I asked it how to find an honest politician."

Classifying.   Classifying involves the **grouping** of like items or transactions. Classifying is a preliminary step to the accumulating and printing of totals for these like items on a report form (Fig. 1-9). Data are generally classified according to a code in the form of an alphabetic or numeric abbreviation. In charting accounts, for example, one identifies each account as an asset account, a liability account, a proprietorship account, an income account, a cost account, or an expense account. To distinguish these accounts from one another, an identifying code number is usually assigned to each account classification. Each account within a classification is also assigned a number. For example, if we were to consider an asset account, we might assign CASH the number 11. The first

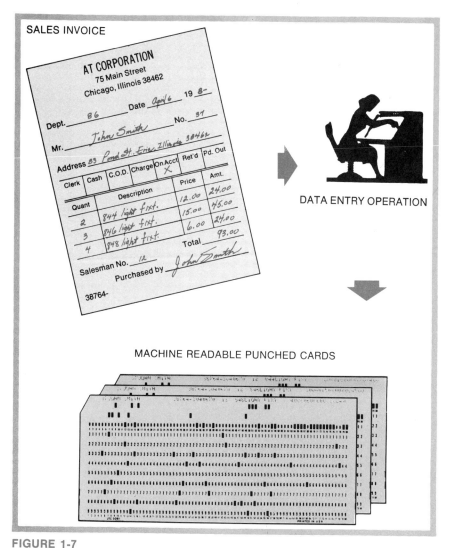

SALES INVOICE

AT CORPORATION
75 Main Street
Chicago, Illinois 38462

Date _April 6_ 19 _8-_

Dept. _86_     No. _37_

Mr. _John Smith_

Address _83 Pond St., Erie, Illinois 38462_

| Clerk | Cash | C.O.D. | Charge | On Acct | Ret'd | Pd. Out |
|-------|------|--------|--------|---------|-------|---------|
|       |      |        |        | X       |       |         |

| Quant | Description | Price | Amt. |
|-------|-------------|-------|------|
| 2 | 844 light fixt. | 12.00 | 24.00 |
| 3 | 846 light fixt. | 15.00 | 45.00 |
| 4 | 848 light fixt. | 6.00 | 24.00 |
|   | Total |  | 93.00 |

Salesman No. _12_

Purchased by _John Smith_

38764-

DATA ENTRY OPERATION

MACHINE READABLE PUNCHED CARDS

**FIGURE 1-7**

Recording sales data from a source document onto a machine-readable medium

digit or first 1 would represent the classification, ASSET. The second digit or second 1 would represent the placement of the account within the classification. Therefore, CASH would be the first account in the ASSET classification.

Classifications also take place in more routine and less technical applications. For example, the store clerk who wrote out the sales invoice for John Smith (Fig. 1-8) was classifying data when he or she distinguished the items on the sales slip: the name and address of the customer, the quantity sold of each item, the description of each item

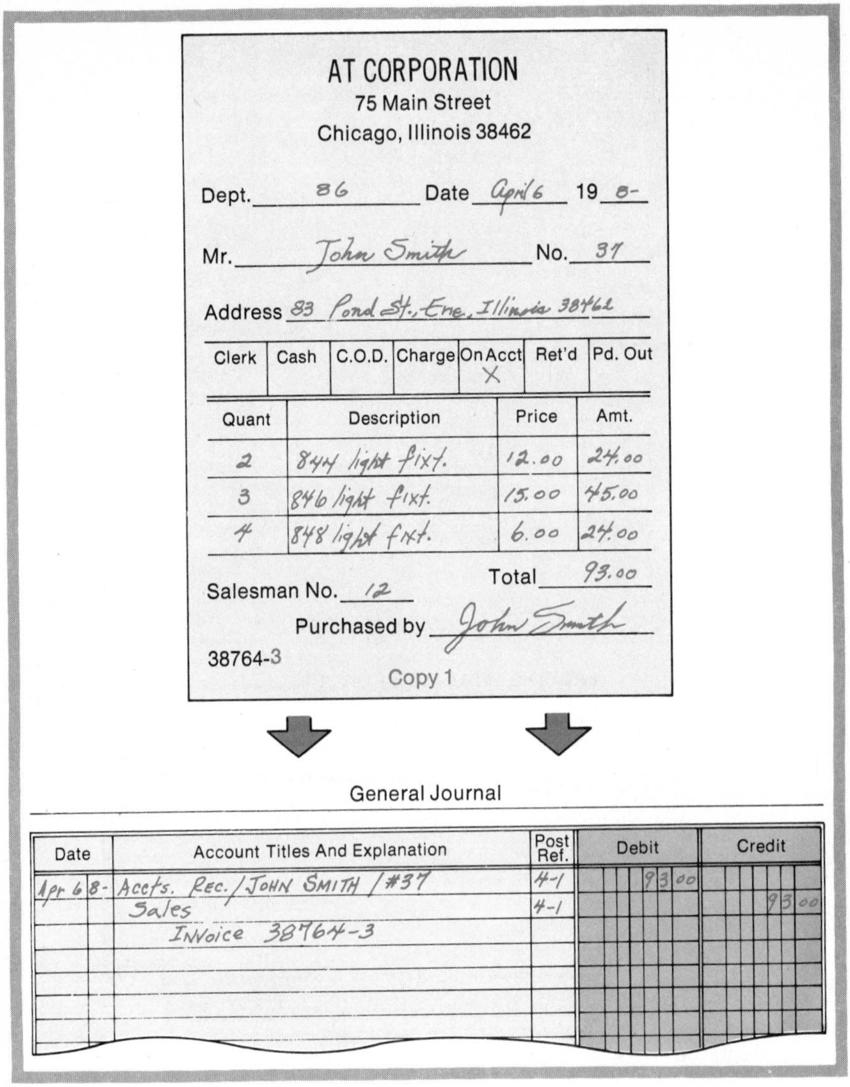

**AT CORPORATION**
75 Main Street
Chicago, Illinois 38462

Dept. _____ 86 _____ Date _April 6_ 19 _8-_

Mr. _____ John Smith _____ No. _31_

Address _83 Pond St., Ene. Illinois 38462_

| Clerk | Cash | C.O.D. | Charge | On Acct | Ret'd | Pd. Out |
|-------|------|--------|--------|---------|-------|---------|
|       |      |        |        | X       |       |         |

| Quant | Description | Price | Amt. |
|-------|-------------|-------|------|
| 2 | 844 light fixt. | 12.00 | 24.00 |
| 3 | 846 light fixt. | 15.00 | 45.00 |
| 4 | 848 light fixt. | 6.00 | 24.00 |

Salesman No. _12_ Total _93.00_

Purchased by _John Smith_

38764-3

Copy 1

General Journal

| Date | Account Titles And Explanation | Post Ref. | Debit | Credit |
|------|-------------------------------|-----------|-------|--------|
| Apr 6 8- | Accts. Rec. / JOHN SMITH / #37 | 4-1 | 93 00 | |
| | Sales | 4-1 | | 93 00 |
| | INVoice 38764-3 | | | |
| | | | | |
| | | | | |
| | | | | |

**FIGURE 1-8**

Journal entry in a manual accounting system

sold, the unit price of each item, the total selling price for each item, and the total sales amount of the invoice. Another example of classifying is found in the Post Office, where, for example, mail is classified by ZIP Code.

Sorting. Sorting is concerned with the **arranging of data into sequence** according to a common characteristic. Generally, data are arranged into either an alphabetic or a numeric sequence. Sales invoices, for example, may be sorted into sequence according to the date of the sale, the geographic region in which the sale took place, or some other

INTRODUCTION TO DATA PROCESSING AND BUSINESS

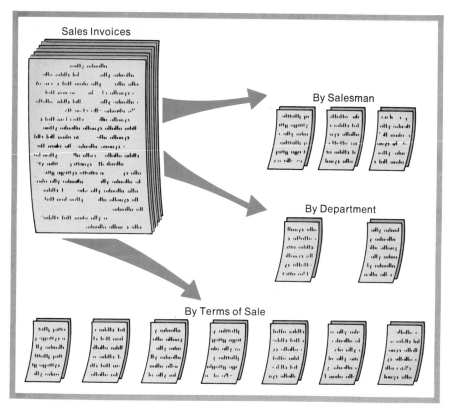

**FIGURE 1-9**

Classifying sales invoices

common characteristic (Fig. 1-10). In a banking operation, personal checks are sorted into a sequence by customer account number.

Before recording invoices in the journal, the accounting clerk must sort the sales invoices into a numerical sequence. In so doing, the accounting clerk can make certain that no invoices are missing and that the journal entries will be in chronological order.

Calculating.  Calculating (or computing) is the arithmetic manipulating (i.e., adding, subtracting, multiplying, or dividing) and comparing of raw data to produce usable results. In a typical sales situation, the number of units of an item sold must be multiplied by the unit price of the item to obtain the total price of the sale. The total selling prices of all items sold are then added to produce the total sales. And still further, the total sales may be multiplied by a percent to determine the salesperson's commission.

To produce a charge account statement, one must perform numerous calculations, including determining the interest charges on the past balance; adding this interest charge to the past balance, to produce an

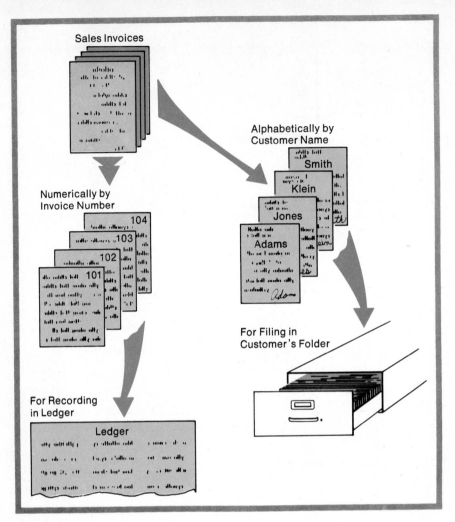

Sales Invoices

Alphabetically by
Customer Name

Smith

Klein

Jones

Adams

Numerically by
Invoice Number

104
103
102
101

For Filing in
Customer's Folder

For Recording
in Ledger

Ledger

FIGURE 1-10

Sorting sales invoices

updated past balance; adding recent purchases to, and subtracting recent payments from, the updated past balance to produce the current balance; determining the minimum acceptable next payment (Fig. 1-11).

Summarizing. Summarizing involves the consolidating of data, emphasizing main points and tendencies. A summary often appears in the form of a total or a result. However, in addition to accumulating totals or results, summarizing also includes the printing of these totals and associated identification data such as the names and codes necessary for their proper interpretation. For example, a student's report card received at the semester's end is a summary of his or her scholastic achievement and results from various kinds and amounts of calculations (Fig. 1-12).

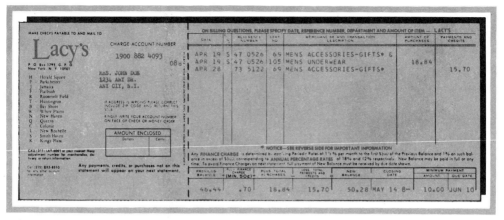

**FIGURE 1-11**

A typical charge account statement

**FIGURE 1-12**

Generation of a typical student report card

### Student Grades

| Subject | Grades | | | | |
|---------|--------|--------|--------|--------|-------|
|         | Exam 1 | Exam 2 | Exam 3 | Exam 4 | Final |
| Eng 101 | 76 | 70 | 86 | 72 | 76 |
| Mat 101 | 83 | 73 | 72 | 68 | 83 |
| Edp 120 | 93 | 87 | 91 | 86 | 97 |
| His 107 | 90 | 84 | 78 | 72 | 71 |
| Sci 101 | 84 | 88 | 64 | 83 | 94 |

### Computation of Final Grades

Eng 101 $(.5(76+70+86+72)+76)/3 = 76 = C$

Mat 101 $(.5(83+73+72+68)+83)/3 = 77 = C$

Edp 120 $(.5(93+87+91+86)+97)/3 = 92 = A$

His 107 $(.5(90+84+78+72)+71)/3 = 78 = C$

Sci 101 $(.5(84+88+64+83)+94)/3 = 85 = B$

### Report Card

```
======= =======
------- -------

      Eng 101      C

      Mat 101      C

      Edp 120      A

      His 107      C

      Sci 101      B
  Semester GPA     2.625
  Cumulative GPA   2.750
======= ======= =======
```

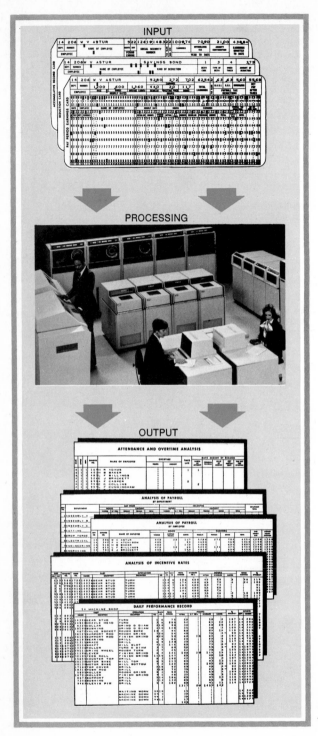

INPUT

PROCESSING

OUTPUT

INTRODUCTION TO DATA PROCESSING AND BUSINESS

FIGURE 1-13

The data processing cycle

**Reporting.** Once the data have been summarized, they must be reported to management or other concerned user(s). Unless results are communicated to the concerned individual(s) in a timely and effective manner, the efforts expended in the previous steps will have been wasted.

**Data-processing Cycle**

Careful examination of the operations discussed above will reveal that they are effectively the fundamental accounting steps, differing only in number and name. These operations, when performed on an electronic computer, can generally be combined into three very basic functions: input, processing, and output.

1. Input: Facts or data are recorded on a computer-acceptable medium and transferred to a computer or punched-card device for processing. The medium used to record these data for subsequent processing is known as the **input medium.**
2. Processing: Numerical comparisons and arithmetical operations performed on input to produce meaningful results.
3. Output: The result of the processing of input in finished or edited form is output from the computer. The form of the results and the **output medium,** or means used to record output data, are set up to facilitate interpretation by management.

The combined functions of input, processing, and output are referred to as the **data-processing cycle** (see Fig. 1-13).

To verify your understanding of the previous material, turn to page 28 and take Self-Test 1-2.

## USES OF COMPUTERS IN BUSINESS

A computer is a very useful tool but certainly not the answer to all our problems. There are certain types of problems that a computer is better equipped to handle economically and efficiently than others.

**Characteristics of Problems Suitable for Computerized Solutions**

Problems for which a computer is ideally suited generally have the following characteristics:

1. Justifiable
2. Definable
3. Repetitive
4. Volume data or numerous calculations

**Justifiable.** The first consideration in determining the suitability of an application for a computerized solution must be that the end result—knowledge gained, data or output created, financial saving, or time saved—substantiates the cost of preparing, writing, and executing the computerized solution.

All too often in today's automated world, employing a computer and the saving of time and money are assumed to be synonymous, when in reality these two factors can operate in opposite directions. That is, many menial tasks can be performed more economically by noncomputerized devices.

Definable. The problem must be in a form that can be clearly and explicitly stated, with objectives that can be reached as the result of a finite series of numerical comparisons and arithmetic steps. In an inventory system, for example, the steps required in order to determine whether or not to reorder a particular stock item consist of both numerical comparisons and arithmetical considerations. In somewhat simplified form, they are:

1. Determine the number of items on hand.
2. Compare the number of items on hand with the established minimums.
3. If the above comparison reveals that the number of items on hand is less than the established minimum number on hand, reorder; otherwise, delay reordering.

Repetitive. The application or task is one that will be performed over and over again. The generation of a company's weekly payroll, for example, is a repetitive operation in that the same basic computations are required to produce a paycheck for each of a company's thousands of employees. Such repetitive calculations would include the determination of gross pay; federal, state, and local taxes; social security deductions; union dues and other such deductions; and net pay. In addition to amortizing preparation and documentation costs, a computerized solution for a repetitive operation eliminates the boredom factor. This is a recurring problem for human beings who perform tasks that are repetitive and monotonous, but it is a nonexistent factor with respect to computers.

Volume Data or Numerous Calculations. "Volume" is a term that signifies an operation or task that requires large quantities of data to be stored or processed by the computer and/or numerous logical or arithmetic calculations to be performed. In most cases, applications requiring limited calculations on limited amounts of data can be more easily and economically handled by manual or electromechanical systems than by a computer system.

Computers, then, are ideally suited to handle the primary business functions such as payroll, personnel accounting, and inventory, since each of these functions is justifiable, definable, repetitive, and deals with a large volume of data (Fig. 1-14). New applications of computers are continually being discovered. If we were to attempt to produce a list of all the application areas to which computers are presently being applied, it would be obsolete before it could be completed.

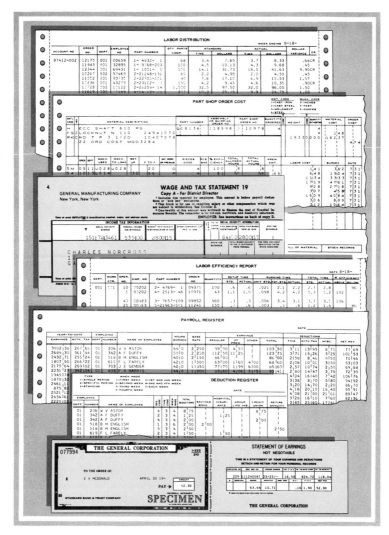

FIGURE 1-14

General business reports produced by a computer

Some general areas that employ electronic computers extensively are:

1. General business: accounts receivable, accounts payable, inventory, personnel accounting, and payroll
2. Banking: account reconciliation, installment loan accounting, interest calculation, demand deposit accounting, savings, and trust services
3. Education: attendance and grade-card reports, computer-assisted instruction, and research analysis
4. Government: income tax return verification, motor vehicle registration, budget analysis, tax billing, and property rolls

Other areas of application include law and law enforcement, military affairs, sports, transportation, real estate, business forecasting, medicine, and broadcasting, to mention but a few.

It should be apparent at this point that the uses of computers in business and industry are boundless and that present applications are only a sample of things to come (Figs. 1-15 to 1-20).

**FIGURE 1-15**

The computer in banking

**FIGURE 1-16**

The computer in the construction industry

**FIGURE 1-17**
The computer in the hospital

**FIGURE 1-18**
The computer in scientific research

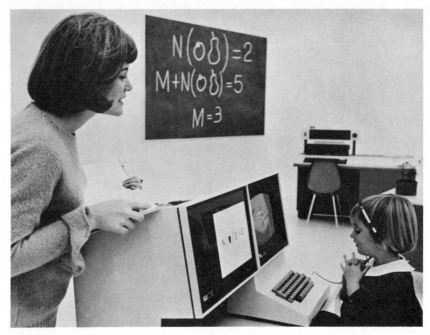

**FIGURE 1-19**
The computer in education

**FIGURE 1-20**
The computer in law enforce-
ment

## WORD PROCESSING

Word processing represents one of the fastest growing of the numerous and varied applications to which the computer has been put (See Fig. 1-21). **Word processing** (wp) can be defined as any systematic method for the handling of document production and the associated administrative support function. The three essential components of any such system are personnel, equipment, and procedures. The personnel will generally come from existing staff but will require substantial retraining. The equipment can vary from single-purpose or dedicated word-processing equipment to general-purpose computer systems. The procedures will serve to integrate the personnel and equipment into the company's information-processing mainstream.

Projections for the 1980s indicate that the sales of word-processing equipment will grow at a rate of over four times that of other computer hardware. This growth is long overdue, as office productivity has increased only 5% in the last decade when compared to an 80% increase in factory productivity.

To facilitate this growth, management and data-processing personnel will have to pool their efforts and conjunctively examine the compa-

**FIGURE 1-21**
Wang's word processing and office information system (*Courtesy Wang Laboratories*)

ny's needs and available word-processing equipment and develop a timetable and procedure for implementation. Critical to this effort is the collecting and detailed analysis of data concerning job composition, volume and distribution of work load, typing applications and documents, other clerical services, existing transcription equipment, personnel capabilities and attitudes, administrative policies and procedures, and logistical questions of what kind of equipment is to be introduced, where, and how.

## COMPUTERS IN SOCIETY

The early applications of computers (1940s) were in the area of government research and were applied to the solution of scientific and engineering problems. Approximately ten years later (1950s), as a result of the increased speeds and capabilities, greatly reduced costs, and commercial availability, computers were economically applied to the solution of business problems. Recently, however, the computer either directly or indirectly has affected the lives of every one of us (see Fig. 1-22). It has benefited us by monitoring and controlling air and water pollution, improving weather forecasting, facilitating more effective urban planning and more efficient law enforcement techniques, making possible electronic advances which have been applied to improving household appliances, providing improved medical techniques for analysis and diagnosis, and so on.

"That does not compute. That does not compute. That does. . . ."

The 1970s brought into being the age of the home or personal computer. For less than one thousand dollars a small but powerful computer system could be purchased for the home. Programs were readily available for these systems to do everything from balancing a checkbook to challenging the most capable user in a game of chess. If you couldn't find a program for what you wanted, you could write your own using the easily learned computer language BASIC.[2] For the ardent fan, optional devices such as a voice synthesizer were available to allow the computer to talk to its user.

[2] This language is discussed in detail in Chapters 9 and 10.

FINAL NOTICE!

I am your computer. No one but me knows you have not made payment. If I have not processed a payment in ten days, I will have to tell a human.

Thank you very much.

FIGURE 1-22

A card typical of those people began to see in the late 1970s

For those having only an occasional need or desire to use a computer, companies such as DBC[3] offered access to their computer system for less than three dollars per hour in increments of 1 minute, including the cost of the call from anywhere in the continental United States. In addition, the user was given access to thousands of programs offering complete business packages, computer games, stock market quotations, professional sports information, movie guides, etc. All the user would require is a device to communicate commands and data to DBC's computer system via telephone and a means to record or display the computer's responses.

However, increased use of and dependence on computers has also brought about many new problems. Complete dependence on computers can lead to serious and often insurmountable problems should they malfunction or fail or should unauthorized parties gain access to data stored in a company's computer system. Computer crime is difficult to detect and equally difficult to prosecute, as legislation is slow in coming. According to U.S. Senator Abraham Ribicoff,[4] ". . . at present there is no specific statute in the United States code that makes a computer crime a crime." He also noted that, according to FBI figures, only 1% of computer crimes are detected and of those only 12% are reported. Compared to other white-collar crimes, the losses per occurrence are high; they range from $200 to almost $6 million, with an average of $450,000, about 5 times higher than other white-collar crimes.

The advantage of using numbers or codes in computers has led to a high degree of impersonalization whereby people are reduced to mere statistics. Many individuals are deeply concerned over their lack of control or knowledge concerning information stored about themselves and

[3] Digital Broadcasting Corp., Silver Spring, Md.

[4] 1979, Fifth Annual Honeywell Computer Security and Privacy Symposium, Phoenix, Arizona.

concerning who might have access to this information and for what purpose. These are but a few of the problems that have accompanied the unprecedented growth in the number and diversity of computer applications. In light of the many new areas of computer application predicted by experts all over the world (see Fig. 1-23), it is imperative

## focus on the field

### The Paperless, Peopleless, Futureless Office
#### Arnold E. Keller

"You show me the paperless office and I'll show you the peopleless office. But you show me first!" That challenge was part of a keynote address last month in Chicago by Robert C. Murray, vice president of The Diebold Group and a leading authority on management development and innovations in the office.

The occasion was a luncheon commemorating the 75th anniversary of INFOSYSTEMS' sister publication, OFFICE PRODUCTS DEALER. The event coincided with the annual convention of the National Office Products Association (NOPA) which was also celebrating its 75th anniversary. NOPA, a trade association, represents companies that manufacture or sell supplies, furniture and machines used in the office. Its 6,500 plus membership has an obvious concern about the "office of the future," and its possible impact on the future.

In his address, "The Road To 2004," Murray discussed the problems and opportunities for office products dealers and manufacturers in the next 25 years. His thrust was bullish. He saw opportunities far outweighing problems and a continuing need for the traditional tools of the office.

We share Murray's views on the paperless office. We are reminded of yesteryear's dream of a "checkless society." Today's reality is a society creating millions more checks than ever dreamed of. But technology has provided the means to effectively and efficiently handle the processing.

And so it will be with the office of the future. Not paperless. Not peopleless. But rather an office adapting today's technology to the needs of the worker. Paperwork will be simplified, not eliminated. People will be present but more productive. The office will become an effective management information center. Technology certainly will play a role in all this. But we won't have, as some envision, a technological takeover.

John J. Connell, founder and executive director of the Office Technology Research Group, has said it well: "In the 'Office of the Future', technology is applied not only to transaction processing but to communicating. Communicating is done by people, in the office. If technology is introduced, it must stay in the office and be adaptable to the characteristics and idiosyncrasies of the many people in the office. In short, the technology must be humanized, even to the point that middle and senior management will feel comfortable with it. The technology must augment, rather than inhibit, creativity."

Connell puts technology in its proper perspective. Let's hope the systems planners will do likewise. Some may disagree, but we don't see much of a future for the paperless, peopleless office.

### DISCUSSION QUESTIONS

1. Why do you think the checkless society never materialized?

2. Do you support the author's contention that technology must be humanized? Explain.

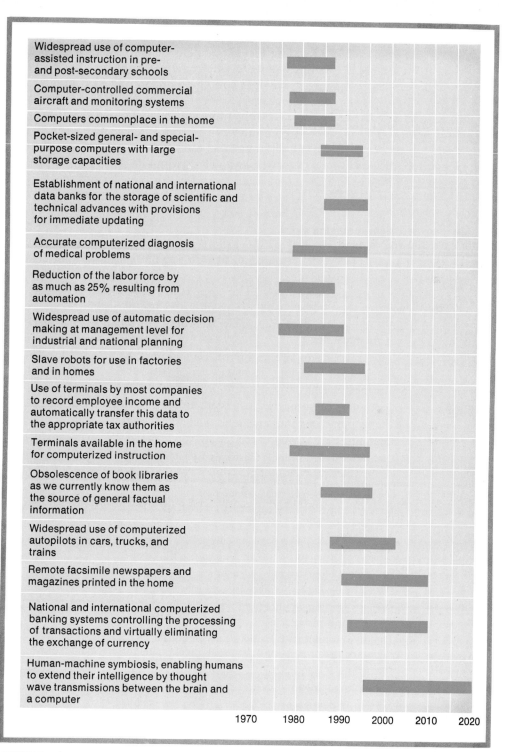

FIGURE 1-23

Computer applications by the year 2020

"Well, you can see right here the computer says that you're dead."

that we address ourselves to these problems now and formulate clearly defined policies concerning the application of computers and carefully delineate who may use, and for what purposes, the data contained in centralized computer data banks.

Only time will tell whether the use of the computer can be controlled so as to reduce if not eliminate the multitude of problems that have arisen and will continue to arise as new areas of application for the computer are discovered. In any case, one thing is for certain—**computers are here to stay.**

To verify your understanding of the previous material, turn to page 29 and take Self-Test 1-3.

## SELF-TEST 1–1

1. Every business must process raw facts or _____ relating to the operations of the business.
2. Raw facts or data are of limited use and must be processed to become usable _____ for management.
3. The most recent device used to process data is the _____.
4. Computers can process _____ data at _____ cost than ever before.
5. The computer revolution can be thought of as a second _____.
6. Computers are currently utilized in _____ field(s).
7. Computer performance increases by a factor of _____ approximately every 5 years while cost is reduced by _____% approximately every 7 years.
8. The most powerful and expensive computer system currently available is the _____ "supercomputer."

## SELF-TEST 1–2

1. Data processing is defined as _____.
2. Data-processing applications are broadly classified as either _____ or _____ applications.
3. The five fundamental operations required in the processing of data (whether the processing is manual, mechanical, or electronic) are _____.
4. Recording is defined as _____.
5. Classifying is defined as _____.
6. Sorting is defined as _____.
7. Calculating, or computing, is defined as _____.
8. Summarizing is defined as _____.

9. The three basic functions constituting the data-processing cycle are _____ .

10. The _____ function is one in which data are recorded on a computer-acceptable medium and transferred to a computer for processing.

11. Processing consists of _____ .

12. The _____ function is one in which the results of the processing of input in finished or edited form are put out from the computer.

## SELF-TEST 1–3

1. A computer (is, is not) the most efficient method of solving all types of problems.

2. Problems which are ideally suited to a computerized solution generally are characterized as _____ .

3. The computerized solution of a particular problem is justifiable if _____ .

4. A problem is _____ if its objective can be clearly and explicitly stated and can be reached as the result of a finite series of numerical comparisons and arithmetic steps.

5. A problem is repetitive if _____ .

6. A problem involves _____ if the particular application is one which involves the storing or processing of large quantities of data or the performing of numerical comparisons or arithmetical calculations.

7. With modern computers capable of processing more data _____ and _____ than ever before, the computer has become a billion-dollar industry with a virtually limitless potential.

8. The advantages of using _____ in computers have led to a high degree of impersonalization whereby people are reduced to mere statistics.

9. The three essential components of any word-processing system are _____ .

10. The home or personal computer was introduced in the 19_____ s.

11. Projections for the 1980s indicate that word-processing equipment sales will grow at a (greater, lesser) rate than general-purpose computer systems.

12. One of the most costly problems associated with the use of computers in business is _____ .

**Answers to Self-Tests**

1-1
1. data
2. information
3. electronic computer
4. more; less
5. industrial revolution
6. virtually every
7. 2; 50
8. Cray 1

1-2
1. the manipulating and using of facts
2. business; scientific
3. recording, classifying, sorting, calculating, and summarizing

4. the transcribing of data from a source document into a machine-readable medium

5. the grouping of like items or transactions

6. the arranging of data into a particular sequence according to a common characteristic

7. the arithmetic manipulating of raw data to produce usable results

8. the consolidating of data, emphasizing main points and tendencies

9. input, processing, and output

10. input

11. logical and arithmetic operations performed on input to produce meaningful results

12. output

1-3

1. is not

2. justifiable, definable, repetitive, involving volume data or numerous calculations

3. the end result warrants the cost of the computerized solution

4. definable

5. it involves a task that will be performed over and over

6. volume data or numerous calculations

7. faster; cheaper

8. numbers or codes

9. personnel, equipment, and procedures

10. 70

11. greater

12. computer crime

## EXERCISES

**1–1**
**True/False**

_____ 1. The functions of input, summarizing, and output are referred to as the data-processing cycle.

_____ 2. The use of ZIP Code by the Post Office Department is an example of classifying.

_____ 3. Sorting is generally performed after the classifying operation.

_____ 4. There are certain types of problems that a computer is better equipped to handle economically and efficiently than others.

_____ 5. Business computerized applications are generally characterized by a large volume of data to be processed.

_____ 6. Computers are seldom used by government agencies such as the IRS and the Bureau of Motor Vehicles.

_____ 7. Increased use of and dependence on computers has brought about many new problems.

_____ 8. At the close of the 1970s, there was no statute in the U.S. code that made a computer crime a crime.

_____ 9. Summarizing is part of the calculating operation.

_____ 10. In recent years, the term "data processing" and the concept of processing data by computer have become synonymous.

_____ 11. The entering of a transaction into a journal would be an example of a manual recording operation.

_____ 12. The computer revolution has been considered a second industrial revolution.

_____ 13. The Cray 1 is representative of computers used in the typical business.

_____ 14. The grade-point average generally contained on a student's transcript is an example of a summarizing operation.

_____ 15. Computer crime is one of the most serious problems which has accompanied the widespread use of computers.

_____ 16. A problem must be repetitive to warrant a computerized solution.

_____ 17. Personal computers had their beginnings in the 1970s.

_____ 18. Word processing is concerned with the systematic handling of document production and the associated administrative support function.

_____ 19. The problem of determining the most attractive person in your class is definable.

_____ 20. Arranging canceled checks into check number sequence is an example of classifying.

_____ 21. The data-processing cycle begins with the input function.

_____ 22. Heavy use of computers has led to a high degree of impersonalization.

_____ 23. The six basic data-processing operations are effectively the fundamental accounting steps.

_____ 24. Data processing is a relatively recent study, with its beginnings in the late 1800s.

**1-2**

**Multiple-
choice**

_____ 1. Summarizing is defined as the
   **a.** consolidating of data
   **b.** reporting of results
   **c.** emphasizing main points
   **d.** all of the above
   **e.** (a) and (c) only

_____ 2. Classifying is defined as the
   **a.** arranging of data into a prescribed sequence
   **b.** grouping of like items or transactions
   **c.** punching of data into punched cards
   **d.** all of the above
   **e.** (a) and (b) only

_____ 3. Calculating includes
   **a.** addition and subtraction
   **b.** comparing two or more quantities
   **c.** multiplication and division
   **d.** all of the above
   **e.** (a) and (c) only

_____ 4. Which of the following is *not* one of the fundamental data-processing operations?
   a. adding
   b. summarizing
   c. sorting
   d. reporting
   e. none of the above

_____ 5. Every business is concerned with the efficient processing of
   a. punched cards
   b. raw facts
   c. data
   d. all of the above
   e. (b) and (c) only

_____ 6. Sorting is the arranging of data
   a. before classifying
   b. in numerical sequence
   c. in alphabetical order
   d. all of the above
   e. (b) and (c) only

_____ 7. A problem suitable for a computerized solution should be
   a. definable
   b. justifiable
   c. repetitive
   d. all of the above
   e. (b) and (c) only

_____ 8. The fundamental operations, when performed on electronic computers, can be combined into the three basic functions of
   a. input, calculating, reporting
   b. processing, printing, output
   c. input, processing, output
   d. recording, summarizing, reporting
   e. none of the above

**1–3 Problems**

1. Is there a difference between data and information? Explain.
2. Discuss several applications of computers in business about which you have read or with which you have been associated.
3. If you were asked to point out the single most important contribution of the computer to business, what would you say? Answer fully.
4. Why have business concerns been forced to resort to automatic data processing?
5. What are some of the social problems that have been brought about by the introduction of the computer?
6. It has been said that the day of the fully automated office is almost here. What do you think is meant by this statement? What devices do you think would be used besides the computer?

7. Briefly comment on how the misuse of computers might cause possible violations of the following Constitutional rights:
   a. Fifth and fourteenth amendment guarantees of "due process"
   b. Fifth amendment protection against "self-incrimination"
   c. Fourth amendment protection against "unreasonable search"
   d. Eighth amendment protection against "cruel and unusual punishment"
8. List three science fiction books, movies, or television programs that show computers in use. What capabilities do these computers possess that are not generally possible today? Which capabilities do you believe will soon be possible? What unusual applications are these computers put to?

**1–4**
**Projects**

1. Go to your school or local library and examine the available computer-related literature to determine five areas of computer application that are not described in the text.
2. Visit your local computer store and compile a list of available microcomputers and features. Which would you buy for yourself? Why? What applications would you intend to use it for?
3. Visit one of the organizations or agencies described below and determine where, how, and for what the computer is used.

| | |
|---|---|
| Internal Revenue Service | Bureau of Motor Vehicles |
| Bank | Credit card agency |
| Hospital | County or community center |
| College or university | Offtrack Betting (OTB) |
| Local chain store | Other approved by your instructor |

INTRODUCTION

ABACUS

PASCAL'S MACHINE ARITHMÉTIQUE

JOSEPH MARIE JACQUARD

CHARLES BABBAGE

HERMAN HOLLERITH

HOWARD H. AIKEN

JOHN VON NEUMANN

SUBSEQUENT DEVELOPMENTS

COMPUTER GENERATIONS

First Generation (1942–1959)

Second Generation (1959–1965)

Third Generation (1965–1970)

Fourth Generation (1970–    )

Mini and Microcomputers

Minicomputers

Microcomputers

FOCUS ON THE FIELD

SELF-TESTS

EXERCISES

# CHAPTER 2

# A Brief
# History

## INTRODUCTION

The purpose of this chapter is to present readers with a brief survey of the more important events in the short history of computers so that they may better understand current developments in their proper perspective.

Upon completing this chapter, you should be able to:
- Trace the development of computers from the abacus until today
- Discuss the concept of the stored program
- Anticipate future developments based on past history
- Relate computer capabilities to hardware design
- Define the following terms:

| | |
|---|---|
| Hardware | Minicomputer |
| Integrated circuit | Software |
| Machine language | Stored program |
| Memory | Symbolic coding |
| Microcomputer | Transistor |
| Microprocessor | Vacuum tube |
| Microsecond | Virtual storage |
| Millisecond | |

## ABACUS

The most appropriate place to begin a discussion of the history of data processing is with the abacus, a device that was probably used by the Babylonians as early as 2200 B.C. As the first mechanical calculator, it existed in various forms: knotted strings, a pebble tray, and a frame of beads. The most widely known form is illustrated in Fig. 2-1.

## PASCAL'S MACHINE ARITHMETIQUE

In 1647, Blaise Pascal, an eminent French philosopher and mathematician, devised the world's first adding machine capable of counting, adding, and subtracting (Fig. 2-2). The machine, which he called his Ma-

**FIGURE 2-1**

The abacus, used in the Orient since the thirteenth century

chine Arithmétique, was based on gear-driven counterwheels, similar in operation to the odometer (mileage indicator) in an automobile. Similar gear-driven counterwheels were employed in the development of mechanical calculators for the next 300 years. Figure 2-3 illustrates some of the calculators developed in the late nineteenth century.

**FIGURE 2-2**

Pascal's Machine Arithmétique

**CALCULATOR**

1850        Parmelee        U.S.A.

The first keyboard adding machine. Readings are taken from the calibrated vertical shaft which is raised through the top of the case when the keys are depressed. Only one column of digits can be added at one time.

**THE FIRST COMPTOMETER**

1887        Dorr E. Felt        U.S.A

This machine was a direct successor to the "Mac aroni Box". Two years later the first printing de vice was added.

**BURROUGHS ADDING AND LISTING MACHINE**

1890        W. S. Burroughs        U.S.A.

This machine operates on the rocking segment principle and employs a series of pivoted bars with toothed racks at either end, and a device for printing.

**THE ADDER**

Webb        U.S.A.

1868

A pocket size stylus-operated counter useful for addition only.

**ODHNER**

1878        W. T. Odhner        Sweden

The principle was basically the same as that of the Baldwin, and was used in many different makes of European manufacture including the Brunsviga.

**BALDWIN**

1872-75        F. S. Baldwin        U.S.A.

The Baldwin variable-cogs principle was incorpo rated into numerous other makes. This marked the beginning of the calculating machine industry in the United States.

**FIGURE 2-3**

Highlights in the story of the calculator

## it's truly amazing

If technology and productivity in other industries had progressed at the same rate as computer technology, an around-the-world airline flight would take 24 minutes, and a standard-sized car would get 550 miles per gallon of gasoline.

## JOSEPH MARIE JACQUARD

In 1801 a Frenchman named Jacquard designed a loom capable of weaving patterns in cloth automatically. He used a continuous belt of metal plates similar to a modern-day tank tread. Each plate contained a series of punched holes, through which needles moved as the belt revolved. This scheme, utilizing a series of holes punched in metal plates to control the specific operations performed by the machine, pointed the way for punched holes in cards to provide data and direct the actions of punched-card machines and computers.

## CHARLES BABBAGE

Babbage, a rather obscure English mathematician and inventor, believed it possible to build a machine-driven automatic calculator capable of generating special-purpose mathematical tables. In this venture, Babbage obtained the aid of the British government in 1823 and began designing what he called his Difference Engine (Fig. 2-4). But only 12 months later he was forced, for financial reasons, to discontinue the project temporarily. However, by 1830 he had completed the preliminary design of the Difference Engine and had begun its construction. He was never satisfied with this design and was continually improving it. As a result, he never completed construction of a Difference Engine. Construction of the Difference Engine was finally abandoned in 1834 so that he could pursue development of his new idea for a more advanced device which he referred to as the Analytical Engine. The Analytical Engine was intended to be a general-purpose digital computer that would allow flexible control over the operations and the

"Not only can it play chess, but it's also programmed to tip the board if it's losing."

**FIGURE 2-4**
Charles Babbage's Difference Engine

sequence of operations that it could perform. Unfortunately, again as a result of financial, engineering, and design problems, this brilliant conception was never made operational. Babbage continued for the remainder of his life to try and construct an operational calculator, but, being far ahead of his time, was unsuccessful. A model of a Difference

it's truly amazing

The world's first large-scale automatic computer was the elephantine MARK I, built by Harvard University and IBM. Revolutionary over 40 years ago, the MARK I weighed five tons and had over 500 miles of wiring linking its 3300 electromechanical relays and controls.

By contrast, the IBM 4341 processing unit uses new high-performance technology to pack hundreds of wafer-thin, quarter-inch square chips on cards and weighs about 22 pounds. Each chip contains as many as 704 circuits. Similarly sized memory chips can each store up to 64,000 bits of information.

While the size of computers has shrunk, their speed has greatly increased. Early computers could perform about 2000 multiplications per second. Today's IBM 4341s operate about 125 times faster and can do almost a quarter of a million multiplications a second.

FIGURE 2-5

Model of the Analytical Engine constructed from one of Babbage's many designs (Copyright Science Museum, London)

41

Engine, based on Babbage's principles, was constructed in 1854 by a Swedish printer named George Scheutz and subsequently copied and used by the British government in the calculation and publication of life insurance tables. Several years ago IBM constructed an Analytical Engine according to Babbage's original drawings (see Fig. 2-5). It proved to be capable of performing the basic arithmetic operations and lent itself to some of the more recent programming techniques.

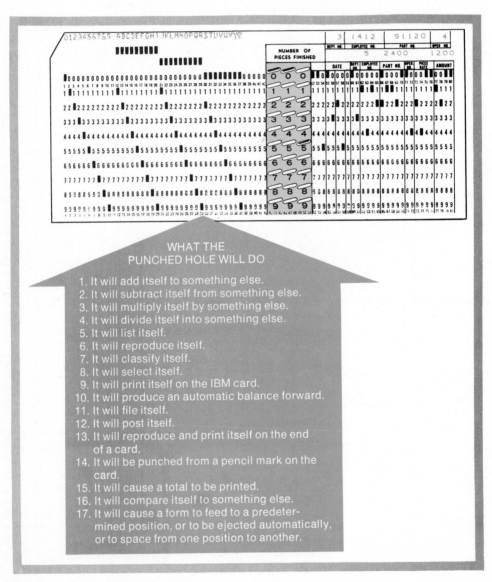

**FIGURE 2-6**

What the punched hole will do

Development of punched cards and the machines to process them was stimulated in the late nineteenth century by the needs of the U.S. Census Bureau. In 1880 the 10-year census was taken as required by law.

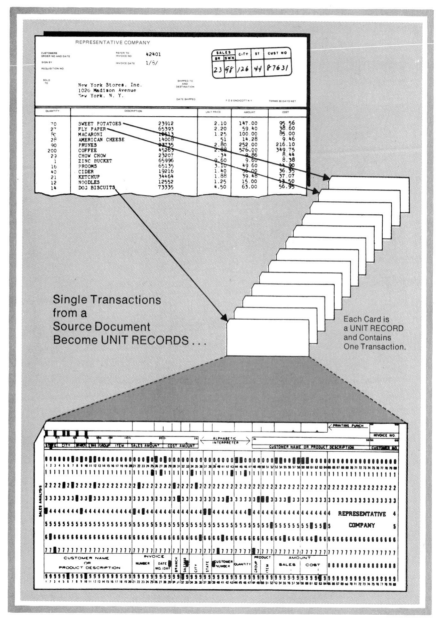

**FIGURE 2-7**
The punched card as a unit record

By 1885 the Census Bureau was still struggling to compile the collected facts of the 1880 census into meaningful form. When it became apparent that in the future this compilation would take longer than the 10-year span between censuses, it became obvious that a more accurate and faster way of performing this task would be required. In response to this need, Herman Hollerith, then a statistician with the Census Bureau, devised a method of recording the census data crosswise on a strip of paper. Hollerith's method was quite simple. Information was coded on this strip of paper by means of a series of punched holes in a planned pattern, with each hole having a specific meaning (Fig. 2-6). This system of coding information on strips of paper quickly proved to be an efficient and effective method of recording information for future processing. For better durability and ease of handling, these paper strips were soon replaced by three-by-five inch rectangular cards. Each card contained the entire record of an individual or family—a **unit record** (Fig. 2-7). These cards were the forerunners of today's punched cards, or unit records. The census data were punched into the three-by-five inch cards in the form of holes by a hand-operated punch (Fig. 2-8). To process these coded cards, now referred to as punched cards, Hollerith devised a tabulating machine (Fig. 2-9) capable of processing approximately 65 cards per minute.

"If I wanted something almost human, I'd have gone to an employment agency."

The use of the punched card and tabulating machine resulted in such substantial savings in cost and time that Hollerith began to adapt his Census Tabulator to commercial work. To this end, he organized the Tabulating Machine Company, which subsequently merged with other

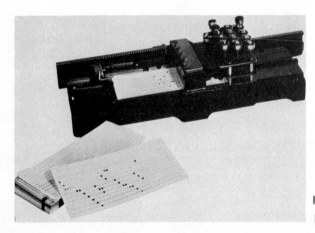

FIGURE 2-8
Mechanical keypunch, circa 1901

FIGURE 2-9

Herman Hollerith's punched card tabulating machine

companies to become the International Business Machines Corporation (IBM). An example of the present widely used 80-column punched card with its coded rectangular punches is shown in Fig. 2-10.

## HOWARD H. AIKEN

The next significant development in this area did not occur until 1937, when a Harvard physicist named Aiken designed, and with the aid of IBM constructed, a computing device capable of performing arithmetic

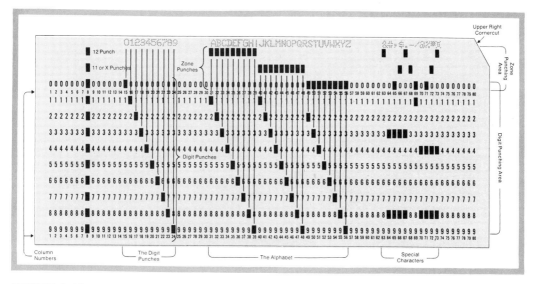

FIGURE 2-10

Example of standard IBM punched card with rectangular shaped coded holes

FIGURE 2-11
MARK I Computer

operations on data input using Hollerith punched cards. This machine, which Aiken called his MARK I, was applied to the solution of problems requiring extensive arithmetic operations (see Fig. 2-11). Professor Aiken subsequently constructed three more models culminating in his MARK IV.

## JOHN VON NEUMANN

Von Neumann's contributions to the development of computers can be considered second to none. His contributions ranged from setting forth, in detail, the logical design of the computer to introducing the concept of instruction modification and to working out the details of the computer's electronic circuitry. Together with Burks and Goldstine, von Neumann developed the revolutionary concepts of the stored program and the application of the binary number system. These concepts are employed today in the most modern and sophisticated computers. Concerning the characteristics of a commercial computer, von Neumann, Burks, and Goldstine wrote a report entitled "Preliminary Discussion of the Logical Design of an Electronic Computing Instrument," from which we quote:

"Inasmuch as the completed device will be a general-purpose computing machine it should contain main organs relating to arithmetic, memory-storage, control and connection with the human operator. It is intended that the machine be fully automatic in character, i.e., independent of the human operator after the computation starts.

"It is evident that the machine must be capable of storing in some

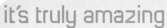

Built in 1946, the first fully electronic computer contained 18,000 vacuum tubes the size of TV tubes. Today's technology can pack that computing power into the space occupied by just one of these tubes.

manner not only the digital information needed in a given computation
. . . but also instructions which govern the actual routine to be performed on the numerical data. . . . [This is the basic idea of the stored
program. The paper continues:]

"For an all-purpose machine it must be possible to instruct the device to carry out any computation that can be formulated in numerical
terms. Hence there must be some organ capable of storing these program orders. [This is the memory unit.] There must, moreover, be a unit
which can understand these instructions and order their execution.

"Conceptually we have discussed above two different forms of
memory: storage of numbers and storage of orders. If, however, the
orders to the machine are reduced to a numerical code and if the machine can in some fashion distinguish a number from an order, the
memory organ can be used to store both numbers and orders." In other
words, the machine should be able to store instructions and data in the
same memory unit.

"If the memory for orders is merely a storage organ there must exist
an organ which can automatically execute the orders stored in memory.
We shall call this organ the Control.

"Inasmuch as the device is to be a computing machine, there must
be an arithmetic organ in it which can perform certain of the elementary arithmetic operations. There will be, therefore, a unit capable of
adding, subtracting, multiplying and dividing. It will be seen that it can
also perform additional operations that occur quite frequently.

"The operations that the machine will view as elementary are
clearly those which are wired into the machine. To illustrate, the operation of multiplication could be eliminated from the device as an elementary process if one were willing to view it as a properly ordered series of
additions. Similar remarks apply to division. In general, the inner economy of the arithmetic unit is determined by a compromise between the
desire for speed of operation—a nonelementary operation will generally
take a long time to perform since it is constituted of a series of orders
given by the control—and the desire for simplicity, or cheapness, of the
machine.

"Lastly, there must exist devices, the input and output organ,
whereby the human operator and the machine can communicate with
each other. . . . [For example, a punched card reader or punch, a
printer, or display device.]

"In a discussion of the arithmetic organs of a computing machine
one is naturally led to a consideration of the number system to be
adopted. In spite of the long-standing tradition of building digital machines in the decimal system, we must feel strongly in favor of the
binary system for our device. [Here is the proposal for the binary system of data representation.] Our fundamental unit of memory is naturally adapted to the binary system. . . . On magnetic wires or tapes and
in acoustic delay line memories one is also content to recognize the

presence or absence of a pulse or of a pulse train, or of the [algebraic] sign of a pulse . . . if one contemplates using the decimal system, one is forced into the binary coding of the decimal system—each decimal digit being represented by at least a tetrad [four] of binary digits. Thus an accuracy of ten decimal digits requires at least 40 binary digits. In a true binary representation of numbers, however, about 33 digits suffice to achieve a precision of $10^{10}$. The use of the binary system is therefore somewhat more economical of equipment than is the decimal. . . . An important part of the machine is not arithmetical, but logical in nature. Now logic, being a yes-no system, is fundamentally binary. Therefore a binary arrangement of the arithmetic organs contributes very significantly towards producing a more homogenous machine, which can be better integrated and is more efficient.

"The one disadvantage of the binary system from the human point of view is the conversion problem. Since, however, it is completely known how to convert numbers from one base to another and since this conversion can be effected solely by the use of the usual arithmetic processes there is no reason why the computer itself cannot carry out this conversion."

"Poor dear! Our new puppy chewed up all of the software for his computer."

To verify your understanding of the previous material, turn to page 66 and take Self-Test 2-1.

## SUBSEQUENT DEVELOPMENTS

It was not until the early 1940s that the first true electronic computer appeared. This was the ABC (*A*tanasoff *B*erry *C*omputer), built by John Atanasoff. The ABC didn't become recognized as the first electronic computer until 1972, and only then as a result of a long and involved court case. Until that time, the ENIAC (*E*lectronic *N*umerical *I*ntegrator *A*nd *C*alculator), designed and built by Eckert and Mauchly, was credited with being the first electronic computer. Several years later, in 1949, at Cambridge University, the first stored-program electronic computer, called the EDSAC (*E*lectronic *D*elay *S*torage *A*utomatic *C*omputer), was completed. A stored-program computer is a computer controlled by internally stored instructions that can synthesize, store, and in some cases alter instructions as though they were data and that can subsequently execute these instructions.

Until early 1951, computers were not available commercially but were used only in research and by the government. However, in 1951, the Sperry Rand Corporation built the UNIVAC I (*UNIV*ersal *A*utomatic *C*omputer) (Fig. 2-12). The UNIVAC I went into operation for the Bu-

**FIGURE 2-12**

UNIVAC I—First commercial computer *(Courtesy of UNIVAC, Division of Sperry Rand Corp.)*

reau of Census, thus becoming the first commercially available computer. The first computer installation designed to handle business applications was set up in 1954 at General Electric Park, Louisville, Kentucky. In recognition of these events as the true advent of the computer age, the UNIVAC I is now on display in the Smithsonian Institution in Washington, D.C.

## COMPUTER GENERATIONS

In the two decades after 1954, thousands of computers were put into operation, and today literally hundreds of thousands of computers are in use. Computer developments over the years have included the incorporating of computer storage or memory of substantial size and greatly increased processing speeds. These developments were so far-reaching and numerous that they have been categorized by generations, with each generation being initiated by a significant advance in **computer hardware** or in **computer software**.[1]

**First Generation (1942–1959)**  The first generation of computers utilized the vacuum tube for the storage of data (Figs. 2-13 and 2-14). However, the vacuum tube was bulky, caused tremendous heat problems, and was never a completely reliable electronic device; it caused a great number of breakdowns and inefficient operations. Programming was principally done in **machine language**.[2]

**Second Generation (1959–1965)**  The second generation of computers saw the replacement of the vacuum tube with the transistor (Figs. 2-15 and 2-16). A transistor can be thought of as a switch, such as a light switch, but with no

[1]See Appendix A for a definition of hardware and software.
[2]See Appendix A.

FIGURE 2-13
First-generation components

FIGURE 2-14
First-generation computer

moving parts (Fig. 2-17). Because of the speed with which the transistor can operate and its small size, computers could be made that were able to perform a single operation in millionths of a second and were capable of storing tens of thousands of characters.

Computer manufacturers began producing business-oriented computers with more efficient storage and faster input and output capabilities. This generation of computers was extremely reliable, compact in size, and virtually free of heat problems.

Programming was done using both machine and **symbolic coding.**[3]

**Third Generation (1965–1970)** Third-generation computers were characterized by microminiaturized integrated circuits with components so small, in many cases, that they were hardly visible to the naked eye (Figs. 2-17 and 2-18). In addition to the actual components used in their construction, third-generation computers were characterized by increased input/output, storage, and processing capabilities.

Input/output devices were introduced that could communicate with computers over great distances via telephone lines, that could scan a page and input the "observed" information directly into the com-

[3]See Appendix A.

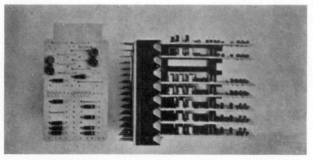

FIGURE 2-15
Second generation components

**FIGURE 2-16**
Second-generation computer

puter, that could display pictures on a televisionlike screen, and that could even accept voice input and respond in the same manner.

Storage capabilities were increased to the point where over 3 billion characters could be stored and randomly accessed by a computer in fractions of a second.

With regard to processing speeds, third-generation computers could process instructions in billionths of a second. In addition, computers were able to process several programs[4] concurrently, ushering in the era of time sharing and multiprogramming. Programmers were able

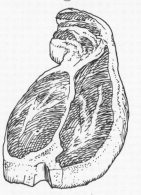

### it's truly amazing

Twenty-five years ago it cost $1.26 to do 100,000 multiplications by computer. Today it costs less than a penny. If the cost of other things had gone down the way computing costs have, you'd be able to buy: sirloin steak for about 9¢ a pound, a good suit for $6.49, a four-bedroom house for $3500, a standard-sized car for $200, an around-the-world airline trip for $3.

---

[4]Program: a preplanned series of instructions designed to solve a given problem.

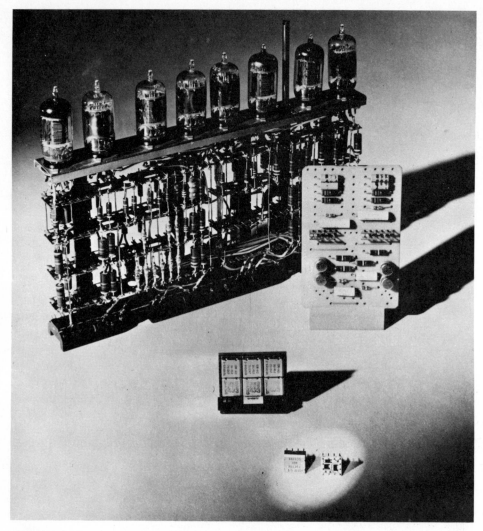

FIGURE 2-17

Comparison of first-, second-, third-, and early fourth-generation components (*Courtesy International Business Machines Corporation*)

to make extensive use of **problem-oriented** and **procedure-oriented languages** in addition to symbolic and machine language.[5]

**Fourth Generation (1970–)** The fourth generation has been responsible for, and promises to offer still greater input, output, storage, and processing capabilities (Fig. 2-19). The fourth generation of computers saw the introduction of the monolithic storage devices (see Fig. 2-20), improved and further

[5]See Appendix A.

FIGURE 2-18

Third-generation computer

miniaturized integrated logic circuits (see Fig. 2-21), and the construction of an actual laser memory for the National Aeronautics and Space Administration. Predictions have been made that with laser storage we soon will be able to store over 50 billion characters in the space occupied by a postage stamp. Concerning the potential of the laser, John M. Carrol wrote in *The Story of the Laser,* "The beam of the laser has the ability to carry all the conversation going on at one time on the planet Earth."

In the early 1970s Burroughs, and then IBM, introduced the concept of **virtual storage** into its 5000 and 370 series of computers (see Fig. 2-22). Machines previously limited to a maximum internal storage capability of approximately 1 million characters now possessed a virtual storage capability in billions and trillions of characters. This concept will be discussed in detail in Chapter 5.

In the late 1970s computers began employing a revolutionary stor-

it's truly amazing

A magnetic bubble memory device has been built by IBM scientists that can store the equivalent of about 100 pages of the Manhattan telephone directory (25 million bits of information) in an area only one square inch. The magnetic bubbles are only a millionth of a meter, or 1/25,000 of an inch, in diameter.

**FIGURE 2-19**

IBM 370 Model 155, a fourth-generation computer system (*Courtesy International Business Machines Corporation*)

**FIGURE 2-20**

Fourth-generation monolithic storage circuit containing 664 individual components shown on the head of a dime

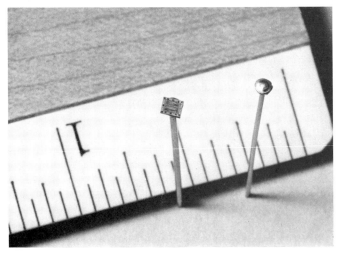

FIGURE 2-21

Integrated logic circuit further miniaturized (*Courtesy NCR Corporation*)

age device, **magnetic bubble memory.** Bubble memory may be thought of as a negatively magnetized cylindrical magnetic field or bubble less than 3 micrometers in diameter moving in a positively magnetized film of magnetic garnet material. The presence of a bubble represents a binary 1 and the absence of a bubble represents a binary 0. Figure 2-23 illustrates a bubble memory integrated circuit capable of storing 128,000 characters or 1 million binary digits.

More important are the advancements that have occurred with respect to the software or programs available with these computers. Great strides have been and are being made in the areas of high-level user-oriented programming languages, multiprogramming and multiprocessing techniques, data communications, distributed processing systems, and operating systems (to name but a few). These terms and concepts will be discussed in detail later in the text. As a result of these changes, access to substantial computer power, previously only justifiable by the very large business concerns, is now economically feasible for the small business.

According to a 1979 survey conducted by the Quantum Science Corporation of over 800 small companies employing less than 500 employees, over 50% of the respondents are equipped with in-house computers, and over 60% of the remaining respondents expected to purchase a computer or computer service within three years.

To verify your understanding of the previous material, turn to page 66 and take Self-Test 2-2.

**Mini- and Microcomputers**

Minicomputers. In addition to increasing the capabilities of large-scale computer systems, significant advances were made in the area of minicomputers. Minicomputers perform the basic arithmetic and logic functions and support some of the programming languages used

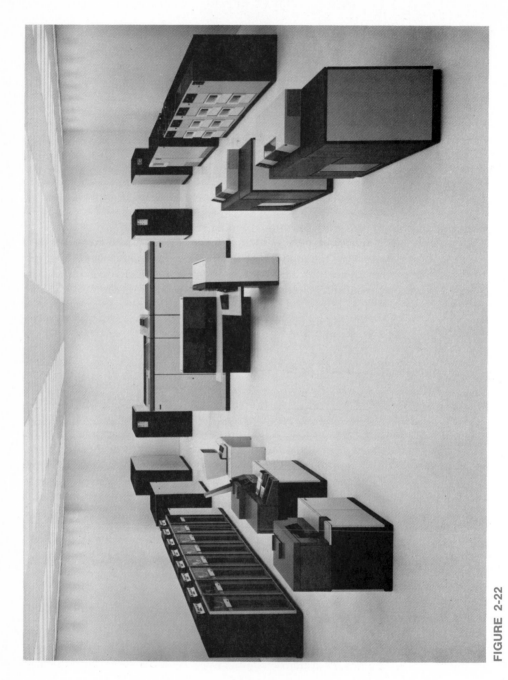

**FIGURE 2-22**

IBM 370/168 virtual storage computer system (*Courtesy International Business Machines Corporation*)

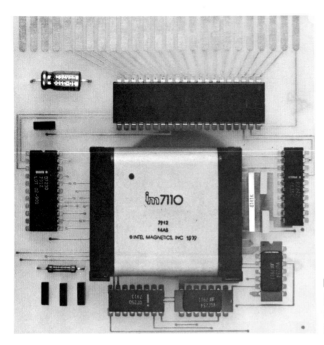

FIGURE 2-23
Intel 7110 magnetic bubble storage unit and associated circuitry (*Courtesy Intel Corporation*)

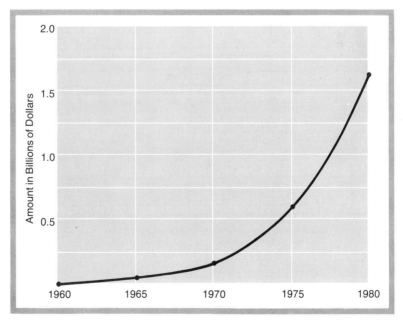

FIGURE 2-24

Value of minicomputers in use

**FIGURE 2-25**

IBM 5100 portable computer for on-site problem solving (*Courtesy International Business Machines Corporation*)

**FIGURE 2-26**

Wang Laboratories minicomputer system capable of processing up to sixteen simultaneous tasks (*Courtesy Wang Laboratories*)

with larger computer systems but are physically smaller, less expensive, and are generally limited in their storage capability. These smaller or minicomputer systems are ideally suited for processing tasks not requiring access to large volumes of stored data. As a result of their low cost, ease of operation by non-computer-oriented personnel, and versatility, minicomputers have gained rapid acceptance from their infancy only a few years ago to today, when they represent a billion dollar industry (see Fig. 2-24).

In late 1975 IBM shook the minicomputer market with its introduction of the IBM System 5100 (See Fig. 2-25). This computer system weighs only 50 pounds, is capable of storing up to 64,000 characters in its memory, supports two programming languages, and is equipped with a CRT (cathode ray tube) for displaying output and an optional 132 character per line printer, all for a cost of slightly more than $8000. This price tag refers to the purchase price, not the monthly or yearly rental price. By comparison, a large computer system can rent for as much as $100,000 *per month.* Figure 2-26 illustrates a minicomputer system costing over $20,000, designed for the small business.

Microcomputers. The microcomputer was first introduced in the mid-1970s. The basis of the microcomputer is the **microprocessor,** a silicon chip containing the necessary circuitry to perform arithmetic/logic operations and to control input/output operations (Fig. 2-27). The

FIGURE 2-27

Microprocessor on a chip (*Courtesy Eastman Kodak Company*)

## Accomplishing An Impossible Mission

### by Victor Block          Washington Editor

On April 1, the 1980 census—20th in the nation's history—will officially get underway to provide information on the number, ethnic origin, age, education and other characteristics of every American. The results of this heavily computerized effort will affect factors ranging from reapportionment of the House of Representatives and planning of highway and mass transit programs to annual allocation of billions of dollars in federal and state funds.

Deep in a high-security section of the Pentagon, behind a door emblazoned with a crest displaying two chess boards and a computer component, four-star generals and admirals, and cabinet-rank civilians gather three times a year to devise war games using the latest DP technology. From these exercises result defense policies that help to determine the safety of this country.

Driving is safer than it would otherwise be due to the National Driver Register. This is a computer-based directory of persons whose licenses have been denied or withdrawn because of driving while intoxicated, involvement in a fatal accident and other reasons. Until the nationwide register was established, an individual whose license was revoked had only to reapply in a neighboring state to obtain another.

### Saving $500 million

A computer check of federal Basic Educational Opportunity Grant requests filed by students saved taxpayers up to $500 million in one year as a result of more accurate data provided by the applicants. It also turned up instances of fraud involving such ploys as under-reporting income and filing several slightly modified applications in an effort to obtain more than one grant.

These random examples provide a glimpse of the countless projects and programs which combine to make the U.S. federal government the world's largest user of information technology. The ADP activities handled by government owned and leased computers—which the Office of Management and Budget estimates will total some 15,750 by the end of the fiscal 1980 (September 30, 1980)—have a far-reaching effect on our lives well beyond that imagined by most people.

### Services would not be available

In fact, it was the federal government that served as spawning ground for today's burgeoning computer industry. After its inception from military programs during World War II, one of the first large-scale DP applications involved the use of what now would be considered an elementary computer designed to handle statistical work, placed into operation in 1951 to help process results of the 1950 decennial census.

Today, the annual ADP budget of just the Department of Commerce, of which the Bureau of the Census is a part, is approximately $140 million. The ADP budgets of other government agencies range from about $20 million for the Department of State to $120 million for the Department of Agriculture, more than $580 million for the Department of the Treasury and $2.5 billion for the Department of Defense.

The benefits of these expenditures for every American cover an equally broad range. According to Donald L. Scantlebury, director, Financial and General Management Studies Division, General Accounting Office, "Some agencies would find it impractical, if not impossible, to accomplish their missions without computers."

● An estimated 222 million Americans will be counted during the 1980 census. Approximately three quarters of all households will receive a "short form" requiring about 15 minutes to complete, with the rest getting a "long form" that will take about 45 minutes to fill out. The questionnaires will be gathered in three processing centers, from which data will be transmitted electronically to computers at Census Bureau headquarters outside Washington, D.C.

● The use of minicomputers has led to decentralized processing of weather data collected at 52 National Weather Service forecast offices.

● Computerization of Internal Revenue Service (IRS) tax collection and auditing techniques has resulted in much quicker refunds to taxpayers, increased checking of questionable returns and other benefits. For example, installation of an automated system for checking taxpayer identification data alone enabled IRS to reduce its staff by 200 employees at an annual savings of over $2 million.

While the GAO expresses concern with the large and growing volume of automatic payment authorizations processed by computers, the Office of Management and Budget recently issued the first in a series of documents describing the use of DP "to improve federal productivity, hold down the size of government and reduce the cost of government."

Among examples included in the report: reduced waiting time for Social Security benefits, predicting water supply for farmers, energy-saving aircraft operations and cancer research.

The results of these and literally thousands of other ADP applications throughout the federal government are not always obvious to the people who benefit. Despite any problems—and, as with any undertaking of this magnitude, there are examples of waste and inefficiency—the positive factors far outweigh any negatives. The results include more efficient and effective provision of services by the government, at lower cost. □

DISCUSSION QUESTIONS

1. Comment on Donald L. Scantlebury's statement, "Some agencies would find it impractical, if not impossible, to accomplish their missions without computers."

2. Describe what problems might have arisen as a result of the government's heavy reliance on ADP (automatic data processing).

**TABLE 2-1**
Summary of the History of Computers

| SIGNIFICANT DEVELOPMENT | APPROXIMATE DATES | IMPORTANCE OF AND/OR FEATURES |
|---|---|---|
| Abacus | 2000–3000 B.C. | First mechanical calculator |
| Pascal's Machine Arithmétique | 1647 | First adding machine capable of counting, adding, and subtracting |
| Jacquard's Loom | 1801 | Utilized metal plates with punched holes to control weaving patterns |
| Babbage's Difference Engine | 1823–1834 | Intended to be used in the production of ballistic tables<br>Never completed by Babbage but was built by George Scheutz |
| Babbage's Analytical Engine | 1834–1871 | Intended to be the first general-purpose computer<br>Never constructed in Babbage's lifetime |

| SIGNIFICANT DEVELOPMENT | APPROXIMATE DATES | IMPORTANCE OF AND/OR FEATURES |
|---|---|---|
| Herman Hollerith | 1887–1896 | Designed a code and devices to punch data into cards and to tabulate the collected data<br>Used in automating the Census of 1890 |
| Howard Aiken's MARK I | 1937–1944 | The largest electromechanical calculator ever built<br>Utilized punched paper tape to input instructions |
| ABC and ENIAC | 1943–1946 | Early all-electronic computing devices<br>Programs had to be wired into a permanent panel<br>No significant storage capability |
| Von Neumann's concepts | 1945–1950 | Developed the concept of storing instructions and data in the memory of the computer<br>Credited with introducing the idea of coding instructions and data in binary |
| EDSAC, EDVAC, and IAS | 1946–1952 | First computers capable of storing instructions and data in memory |
| UNIVAC I and IBM 701 | 1951–1954 | First computers to be produced in quantity and commercially available |
| First Generation | 1942–1959 | Utilized vacuum tubes<br>Limited use of magnetic drum for secondary storage<br>Heat and size problems<br>Punched-card input<br>Programmed in machine language |
| Second Generation | 1959–1965 | Use of solid state components (transistors and diodes)<br>Smaller in size<br>Faster processing speeds<br>Increased memory utilizing iron cores<br>Utilized magnetic tape for secondary storage<br>Programmed in machine and symbolic language |
| Third Generation | 1965–1970 | Microminiaturized integrated circuits<br>Increased input/output, processing, and storage capabilities<br>Time sharing and multiprogramming<br>Problem- and procedure-oriented programming languages |
| Fourth Generation | 1970– | Semiconductor, laser, and bubble memories<br>Multiprocessing and distributed processing capabilities<br>Virtual storage capability<br>Significant applications software<br>Introduction of LSI (large-scale integrated) circuits<br>Widespread use of mini- and microcomputer systems<br>Significant advances in input/output devices |

FIGURE 2-28

TRS-80 in use in the classroom, laboratory, office, and home (*Courtesy Radio Shack*)

microprocessor is a very complex electronic circuit. It consists of thousands of transistors squeezed onto a tiny chip of silicon that is often little more than 3 or 4 millimeters square. The chip is then packaged as a single integrated circuit containing approximately 40 leads or contacts. By adding input/output devices and a memory to the microprocessor, a microcomputer is formed.

Early microcomputers offered a limited processing potential and an even more limited choice of input/output devices. Today, however, these devices have grown in size and processing capabilities and support a wide range of input/output devices. Microcomputers are currently available with a wide selection of input/output devices from tape cassette recorders to a voice synthesizer. In addition to being used as a general-purpose computation device, microcomputers have been incorporated into automobiles, airplanes, toys, clocks, appliances, etc. The TRS-80, a general-purpose microcomputer marketed by the Tandy Company, is shown in Fig. 2-28.

**To verify your understanding of the previous material, turn to page 67 and take Self-Test 2-3.**

## SELF-TEST 2–1

1. The first calculating device developed in approximately 2200 B.C. was the _____.

2. Pascal's _____, developed in about 1647, was based on gear-driven counterwheels that were used in mechanical calculators for the next 300 years.

3. _____ designed an automated loom that pointed the way for the punched card.

4. _____ was an inventor and a designer of computers in the early nineteenth century. His designs include the _____, which laid the foundation for computers developed in the 1930s and 1940s.

5. _____ was responsible for standardizing the punched card and the punched-card code and for developing the machines to process these cards in the computation of the 1890 census.

6. The Tabulating Machine Company organized by Hollerith was merged with other companies to form the company presently known as _____.

7. The MARK I was designed by _____ at Harvard in 1937.

8. _____ was a famous mathematician whose revolutionary ideas concerning computer design were principally responsible for the design of modern-day computers.

## SELF-TEST 2–2

1. The ABC (Atanasoff Berry Computer) is credited with being the first _____.

2. The EDSAC (Electronic Delay Storage Automatic Computer) was noted for being the first _____.

3. The first commercial computer was the _____, built by the Sperry Rand Corporation.

4. The first generation of computers utilized the _____, the second-generation computer the _____, and the third-generation computer the _____.

5. The _____ concept was first introduced by Burroughs in their 5000 series of computers in the early 1970s.

6. One of the newest devices used in computer memories is the _____.

7. Third-generation computers were characterized by microminiaturized _____.

8. Monolithic storage devices were introduced in _____ generation computers.

1. _____ perform the basic arithmetic and logic functions but are physically smaller, less expensive, and are generally limited in their storage capacity as compared with larger computer systems.

2. The heart of the microcomputer is the _____ .

3. A microcomputer consists of a microprocessor plus _____ .

**Answers to Self-Tests**

2–1

1. abacus
2. Machine Arithmétique
3. Joseph Marie Jacquard
4. Charles Babbage; Difference Engine and Analytical Engine

5. Herman Hollerith
6. International Business Machines Corp.
7. Howard H. Aiken
8. John von Neumann

2–2

1. all-electronic computer
2. stored-program computer
3. Univac I
4. vacuum tube; transistor; microminiaturized integrated circuit

5. virtual storage
6. magnetic bubble
7. integrated circuits
8. fourth

2–3

1. minicomputers
2. microprocessor

3. input/output devices and a memory

**EXERCISES**

2–1
**True/False**

_____ 1. Pascal's Machine Arithmétique was capable of performing the four basic arithmetic operations.

_____ 2. The UNIVAC I, built by Sperry Rand, was utilized in the preparation of the Census.

_____ 3. Third-generation computers were able to support voice response.

_____ 4. The laser is the most commonly used storage device in fourth-generation computers.

_____ 5. Jacquard designed the coding scheme used to record data on punched cards.

_____ 6. The fourth-generation computers have made processing capabilities economically feasible for the small business that previously were only practical for larger business concerns.

_____ 7. Computers were not commercially available until the UNIVAC I was built.

_____ 8. Babbage's ambition was to design a general-purpose digital computer.

_____ 9. No operational computers were developed until just prior to World War II.

_____ 10. Heat problems were not virtually eliminated until the third-generation of computers.

_____ 11. Data were input to the MARK I via Hollerith punched cards.

_____ 12. The ENIAC was used principally to produce tables.

_____ 13. The number system suggested by von Neumann was the binary system.

_____ 14. Programming methods were significantly improved in the third generation of computers.

_____ 15. According to von Neumann, the unit which can execute the orders stored in memory is called the supervisor.

_____ 16. The first electronic computer to use the stored program was the ABC computer.

_____ 17. Procedure and problem-oriented languages did not come into being until the fourth generation.

_____ 18. Von Neumann believed that a computer should operate independently of the human operator once a computation was started.

_____ 19. Completion of the construction of the Analytical Engine was one of Babbage's greatest achievements.

_____ 20. The first all-electronic computer was the ENIAC.

**2–2**
**Multiple-**
**choice**

_____ 1. Pascal's Machine Arithmétique was similar in operation to
   a. an automobile odometer
   b. an abacus
   c. electronic calculator
   d. all of the above
   e. none of the above

_____ 2. Charles Babbage completed construction of
   a. the MARK I
   b. the Difference Engine
   c. the Analytical Engine
   d. none of the above
   e. all of the above

_____ 3. One of the characteristics of third-generation computers not found in earlier generation computers is
   a. increased storage capability
   b. processing speeds in billionths of seconds
   c. time-sharing capability
   d. multiprogramming capability
   e. all of the above

_____ 4. The development of the stored program concept is credited to
   a. Herman Hollerith
   b. John von Neumann
   c. Echart and Mauchly
   d. Charles Babbage
   e. John Atanasoff

_____ 5. The UNIVAC I was
   a. the first commercially available electronic computer
   b. developed in the early 1950s
   c. developed by IBM
   d. all of the above
   e. (a) and (b) only

_____ 6. First-generation computers were characterized by
   a. vacuum tube operation
   b. bulkiness
   c. high number of breakdowns
   d. machine-language programming
   e. all of the above

_____ 7. ENIAC was not
   a. used to create mathematical tables
   b. the first all-electronic computer
   c. developed toward the end of World War II
   d. designed and built by Echart and Mauchly
   e. none of the above

_____ 8. The first all-electronic computer came into being in 1945. It was the
   a. EDSAC
   b. EDVAC
   c. ENIAC
   d. UNIVAC I
   e. ABC

_____ 9. Second-generation computers
   a. employed transistors instead of vacuum tubes
   b. were more reliable than first-generation computers
   c. gave way to third-generation computers about 1965
   d. were programmed in both machine and symbolic code
   e. all of the above

_____ 10. According to von Neumann, a computer system should not
   a. utilize the binary number system
   b. store both instructions and data
   c. contain an arithmetic organ
   d. contain an input and output organ
   e. none of the above

**2-3**
**Problems**

1. What contribution did Jacquard make to the development of computers?
2. Name and describe three early calculating devices.
3. What were some of the motivating forces that you believe were responsible for the development of computers?
4. John von Neumann has been called the "father of computers." Support or refute this claim.
5. What did Charles Babbage hope to accomplish with his Analytical Engine? Why didn't he succeed?

6. Why do you think computer developments were so sparse between the early 1800s and the early to mid-1900s?

7. Modern computers (1940 to present) are categorized by generations. List and discuss these generations and their characteristics.

8. Answer the following questions concerning the design of a computer as suggested by von Neumann, Burke, and Goldstine.

    a. How did they propose to store both instructions and data in the memory of the computer?

    b. What arithmetic operations did they propose?

    c. What number system did they propose, and why?

9. Explain the concept of the "stored program" and describe its impact on the development of computers.

**2-4**
**Projects**

1. Research the court case which established the ABC computer as the first all-electronic computer. Summarize what you find.

2. Research the history of computers and ascertain as many developments as you can that are not mentioned in the text.

3. Determine the importance of Ada Augusta, Countess of Lovelace, to the field of computers and indicate with whom she worked.

# COMPUTER SYSTEM FUNDAMENTALS

12345

INTRODUCTION

THE UNIT-RECORD OR PUNCHED CARD

IBM 80-column Card

IBM 96-column Card

Card Punching

PUNCHED CARD PROCESSING MACHINES

Reproducer

Interpreter

Sorter

Collator

KEY-TO-TAPE/DISK DATA-ENTRY SYSTEMS

Key-to-tape System

Key-to-disk System

TERMINALS

Interactive Remote Terminals

Intelligent Terminals

Point-of-sale (POS) Terminals

CHARACTER READERS

Magnetic-ink Character Readers

Optical Mark Readers

Optical Character Readers

SPEECH RECOGNITION SYSTEMS

FOCUS ON THE FIELD

SELF-TESTS

APPENDIX: OPERATING THE CARD PUNCH

EXERCISES

# 3

# Data-entry Devices and Media

## INTRODUCTION

As we learned in Chapter 1, the processing of data requires that the data first be recorded. It therefore follows that the computerized processing of data requires that the data be recorded on an input medium compatible with the computer. For general-purpose applications such as payroll, budget analysis, accounts payable, and accounts receivable, the most commonly used media are the punched card, magnetic tape, and magnetic disk. Numerous devices are available to convert data from source documents to these and other computer-compatible media. Among them are the card punch, the key-to-tape system, the key-to-disk system, and the terminal.

For special-purpose applications, data-entry devices such as magnetic-ink character readers, optical mark readers, optical character readers, point-of-sale terminals, bank teller terminals, and voice response and speech recognition devices are available.

In this chapter we will discuss the punched card together with some of the more common general-purpose and special-purpose data-entry devices and media.

Upon completing this chapter, you should be able to:
- Describe and compare currently used data-entry devices
- Describe the 80-column and 96-column punched cards
- Represent numbers and letters in Hollerith code
- Describe the punched card processing machines that can be found in a computer center
- Describe key-to-tape and key-to-disk procedures and devices and contrast them with punched card data entry
- Describe the different types of character readers in use
- Describe some of the more specialized data-entry devices
- Define the following terms

| | |
|---|---|
| Alphanumeric | Card row |
| Card column | Digit punch |
| Card deck | Diskette |
| Card format | Duplicating |

| | |
|---|---|
| Field | Optical mark reader (OMR) |
| Floppy disk | Punched card |
| Gangpunching | Reproducing |
| Hollerith code | Right-justified |
| Interpreting | Selecting |
| Left-justified | Sorting |
| Logical record | Speech recognition |
| Magnetic-ink character | system |
| recognition (MICR) | Tape pooler |
| Matching | Terminal |
| Merging | Unit record |
| Optical character | Verifying |
| recognition (OCR) | Zone punch |

## THE UNIT-RECORD OR PUNCHED CARD

We saw in Chapter 2 that the development of the punched card and the machines to process the cards was stimulated in the late nineteenth century by the needs of the United States Census Bureau. In this application, each card contained the entire record of an individual or family—a **unit record.** These cards were the forerunners of today's punched cards, or unit records. In recent years, however, the data required to describe an entire record has increased in volume to the point where it is seldom possible to contain it on one punched card. And, as the term "unit record" has come to be synonymous with the punched card, a new term was introduced—the logical record. A **logical record** is a collection of items independent of their physical environment. It would be, for example, a complete record of a transaction, family, or other logical entity. A unit record, then, may not be a complete or logical record but will contain data recorded on a single punched card. Figure 3-1 illustrates how the data from a sales invoice might appear when recorded on punched cards, one punched card for each item on the invoice.

BRONZE-IT, INC
"YOU NAME IT
WE BRONZEIT"

SANDY

"Henry spent all his time with it, so now that he's gone . . ."

Once the data have been recorded onto punched cards, they can be input to a computer and processed to produce usable information or output (Fig. 3-2).

Currently there are two types of punched cards in use: the IBM 80-column card and the IBM 96-column card. As the 80-column card is by far the most common, we begin our discussion with it.

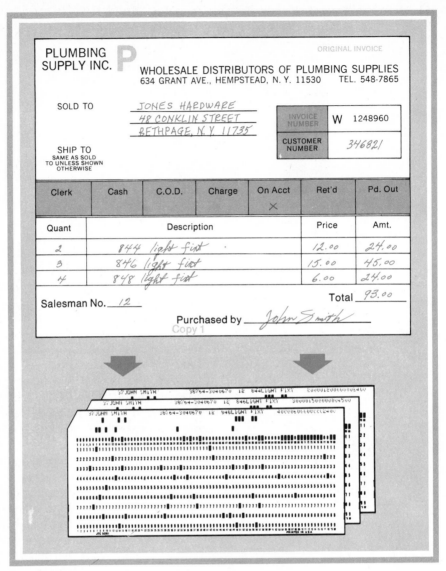

**FIGURE 3-1**

Information from a sales invoice recorded on punched cards

**IBM 80-column Card**   Figure 3-3 shows a present-day IBM 80-column punched card. Upon careful examination of Fig. 3-3 you will notice that the IBM card is divided into 80 vertical spaces or **columns. A column number** is assigned to each column beginning at the left of the card with column number 1 and ending at the right-hand side of the card with column number 80. Each of the 80 columns is capable of storing one **character,** which can be one letter of the alphabet, one digit, or one special character (period, comma, etc.).

**FIGURE 3-2**

Reports generated by a unit-record system from punched card input

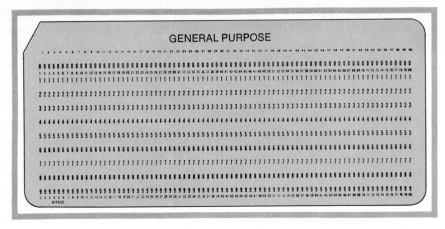

**FIGURE 3-3**

IBM general-purpose punched card

Also note that the IBM card is divided horizontally into 12 spaces or **rows.** The upper three rows constitute the **zone punching area** and are called the 12 row, 11 row, and 0 row, while the lower 10 rows constitute the **digit punching area** and are called the 0 row through the 9 row. It should be noted that the zero row serves as both a zone row and a digit row. Numbers, letters, and special characters are recorded on the IBM card in predetermined combinations of punched holes in the zone and digit punching areas. Some of these combinations are illustrated in Fig. 3-4. Because this coding scheme is credited to Herman Hollerith, the

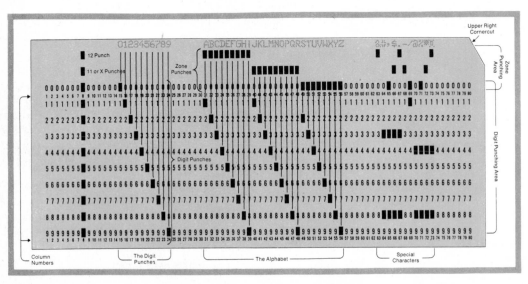

**FIGURE 3-4**

IBM punched card containing digits, letters, and special characters

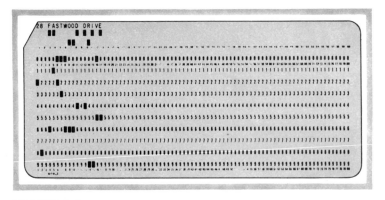

Punched card containing one item of data

IBM 80-column card is commonly referred to as the Hollerith card.

One corner is generally cut on an IBM card for ease of alignment of a series of punched cards. Such a group of cards is technically referred to as a card **deck.**[1] Any corner may be cut; the corner cut has no effect on the information punched on the card.

You are probably wondering how one records a number or a name on a card where the number or name consists of more than one character. For example, how would one punch 28 FASTWOOD DRIVE on a punched card? One would simply punch this address, character by character, including blank spaces, in successive columns. That is, the digit 2, or 2 row, would be punched in column number 1, the digit 8 would be punched in column number 2, a blank in column number 3, and so forth until an E would be punched in column number 17. Figure 3-5 illustrates how such a card would appear.

The address, 28 FASTWOOD DRIVE, is called a field. According to IBM,[2] a **field** is "a set of one or more bits (binary digits) or characters treated as a unit of information," with a **card field** being defined as "a fixed number of consecutive card columns assigned to a unit of information." In the above example the street address, 28 FASTWOOD DRIVE, is a field. More specifically, it is an **alphanumeric field,** which is defined as a field consisting of combinations of letters of the alphabet, digits, and certain special symbols (period, comma, etc.). Several illustrations of alphabetic, numeric, and alphanumeric fields are given in Table 3-1. It should be mentioned at this time that within a field, numeric data are **right-justified** and alphabetic or alphanumeric data are **left-justified.** That is, numeric data are placed as far right as is possible

[1]If the card deck represents a collection of logical records, it is often referred to as a **card file.**

[2]International Business Machines, *Reference Manual: Glossary for Information Processing* (White Plains, N.Y.: International Business Machines), pp. 2, 6.

within the field and alphabetic or alphanumeric data are placed as far left as is possible within the field.

To demonstrate your understanding of the field concept, identify the nonblank fields punched in Fig. 3-6.

You should have determined that this card contains four nonblank fields:

1. Student number in card columns 2 through 6
2. High school in card columns 7 through 29
3. Birthday in card columns 38 through 43
4. Major department in card columns 64 through 80

We were able to determine the extent of each of the above fields by using the ruled lines on the card. For example, we determined that the high school field extended from the ruled line before column 7 to the ruled line after column 29. Note, however, that the data punched in this card field did not extend beyond column 22. This situation will often occur, since the data recorded in a field can vary in length. The only restriction is that the data (high school name in this case) may not be allowed to extend beyond the ends of the field. The size of a field is

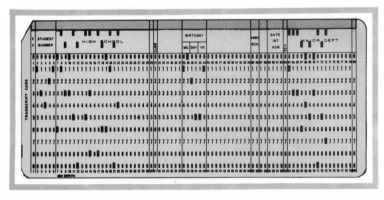

FIGURE 3-6
IBM punched card containing no printing

generally chosen so as to accommodate the longest possible item of data. Should an item of data contain more characters than the width of the field specified for that item of data, the item of data would have to be coded, abbreviated, or shortened by some means.

In cases where a card is not ruled or labeled to identify the various fields and their respective lengths, it would be virtually impossible to determine this information by simply examining the card. This information would have to be provided with the cards to be processed.

Once we have determined the **format** or standard arrangement of fields on the cards, with the aid of Fig. 3-4, we could determine the specific data punched into each field. After a brief examination, we should be able to determine that the following information is contained on the card shown in Fig. 3-6:

| | |
|---|---|
| Student number: | 13421 |
| High school: | WALTER E. HOWARD |
| Birthday: | 102551 |
| Major department: | ACCOUNTING |

What you have just done is to **interpret** a card. When a card is punched and does not contain printing along the top to indicate the information punched, it must be read or verified by eye. This process is called **interpreting.** Interpreting can be done manually, as you have just done, or by a special machine known as an Interpreter, which will be discussed later. It is not necessary, however, to interpret cards that are to be read by computers, since these machines read the punched holes and not the printing on the top of the card. Punched cards may also be produced by a computer via a punch unit, an output device of a computer system.

Punched cards have the advantages of being inexpensive and easily prepared and stored, and they can be sorted, reproduced, etc., on readily available and relatively inexpensive equipment. Their main disadvantages are their limited storage capacity (80 characters), slow processing speeds, bulkiness, sensitivity to high humidity, and poor durability.

**IBM 96-column Card\***  In the late 1960s IBM introduced its System/3, a computer system designed to provide high-speed processing capabilities for the small computer user. Accompanying the System/3 was a newly designed punched card. This new punched card differs from the 80-column IBM punched card in several ways:

1. It is smaller in size and is squarer in shape (Fig. 3-7).
2. It is subdivided horizontally into three punching areas or **tiers,** each running the length of the card and capable of recording 32 characters of information (Fig. 3-8). Thus one System/3 card can contain up to 96 characters, as opposed to the traditional 80.
3. Punched holes are round, as opposed to rectangular.

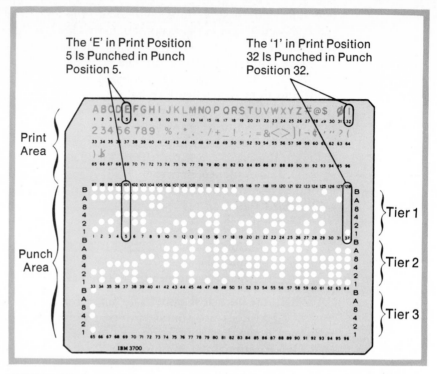

**FIGURE 3-7**

IBM System/3, 96-column punched card

4. There are three rows at the top of the card for printing, one for each tier or punching area.

5. The coding system employed is no longer the Hollerith code but a code based on the BCD[3] (*Binary Coded Decimal*) code and requiring only six rows (B row, A row, 8 row, 4 row, 2 row, and 1 row) to represent one character.

6. Its cost is slightly more than half that of an 80-column card.

A comparison between the punches on the 80-column card and those on the 96-column System/3 card as they relate to the punching of numeric and alphabetic data is given in Table 3-2. Using this table, one could verify that a Hollerith E would have a BCD equivalent of a B, A, 4, and 1 punch.

To accomplish this we would first determine that in Hollerith code the character E consists of a 12 punch and a 5 punch (see Fig. 3-4). From Table 3-2 we can see that a 12 punch on an 80-column card is equivalent to a B and an A punch on a 96-column card and that a 5 punch on an 80-column card is equal to a 4 and a 1 punch on a 96-column card.

---

[3]There are slight variations between the standard BCD code pattern and the BCD code used with the System/3 96-column card. These variations occur in the codes for the digit 0 (zero) and for certain special characters.

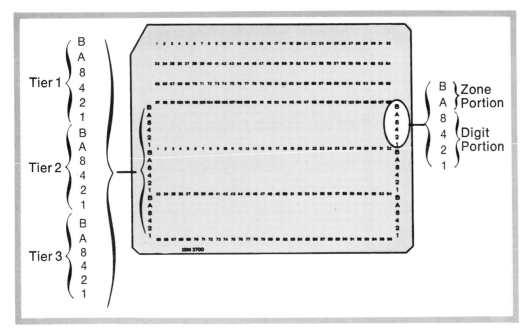

FIGURE 3-8

Punch positions on IBM System/3, 96-column card

Thus an E (12 punch and 5 punch) is equivalent to four punches on a 96-column card, namely B, A, 4, and 1 punch (see Fig. 3-7). The complete System/3 BCD character set is given in Fig. 3-9 and illustrated in Fig. 3-7.

**Card Punching**    Card punching is the method by which source data can be converted into punched cards. The card-punch operator reads the source document and, by depressing keys as done by a typist, converts this source information into punched holes on the card.

The card punch is similar to a typewriter in that it causes a character to be printed on the card when a key is depressed, and unlike the typewriter in that the card punch punches information in the form of rectangular holes, in addition to printing the character corresponding to the key that has been depressed. At the option of the card-punch operator, machine printing can be suppressed, in which case only punching will occur.

A punched card may also be produced by a computer as a form of output. In this instance, it is interpreted separately, as computers generally do not produce an interpreted punched card.

In addition to punching information from a source document, the card punch can be utilized to duplicate selected information already recorded on a punched card. **Duplicating** can be defined as the auto-

## TABLE 3-2
### Comparison of Hollerith and BCD Punches

| 80-COLUMN CARD | | | | | | | | | | | | 96-COLUMN SYSTEM/3 CARD | | | | | |
|---|---|---|---|---|---|---|---|---|---|---|---|---|---|---|---|---|---|
| 12 | 11 | 0 | 1 | 2 | 3 | 4 | 5 | 6 | 7 | 8 | 9 | B | A | 8 | 4 | 2 | 1 |
| X |   |   |   |   |   |   |   |   |   |   |   | X | X |   |   |   |   |
|   | X |   |   |   |   |   |   |   |   |   |   | X |   |   |   |   |   |
|   |   | X |   |   |   |   |   |   |   |   |   |   | X |   |   |   |   |
|   |   |   | X |   |   |   |   |   |   |   |   |   |   |   |   |   | X |
|   |   |   |   | X |   |   |   |   |   |   |   |   |   |   |   | X |   |
|   |   |   |   |   | X |   |   |   |   |   |   |   |   |   |   | X | X |
|   |   |   |   |   |   | X |   |   |   |   |   |   |   | X |   |   |   |
|   |   |   |   |   |   |   | X |   |   |   |   |   |   | X |   |   | X |
|   |   |   |   |   |   |   |   | X |   |   |   |   |   | X |   | X |   |
|   |   |   |   |   |   |   |   |   | X |   |   |   |   | X |   | X | X |
|   |   |   |   |   |   |   |   |   |   | X |   |   |   |   | X |   |   |
|   |   |   |   |   |   |   |   |   |   |   | X |   |   |   | X |   | X |

"Can I have the afternoon off?"

matic punching of one or more columns of data from a master card into the same columns on the succeeding detail card. This is normally performed as part of the card-punching function. Instead of depressing keys repetitively for common information, the operator need only punch the common information in the first card and then depress a special DUPlication key to cause the desired information to be punched into the next card. This card then serves as the master for duplicating the information onto a third card, if required, and so on (see Fig. 3-10). If information is to be duplicated into a number of cards, the card punch can be programmed to copy the desired information automatically onto each succeeding card, thus reducing the work per card, ensuring consistency of common data, and increasing the productivity of the operator.

The keyboard of most modern card punches is arranged in a manner similar to an ordinary typewriter, differing principally with respect to the location of the numeric keys (Fig. 3-11).

**Numeric Characters**

| | | 0 | 1 | 2 | 3 | 4 | 5 | 6 | 7 | 8 | 9 |
|---|---|---|---|---|---|---|---|---|---|---|---|
| Zone | B | | | | | | | | | | |
| Zone | A | A | | | | | | | | | |
| Digit | 8 | | | | | | | | | 8 | 8 |
| Digit | 4 | | | | | 4 | 4 | 4 | 4 | | |
| Digit | 2 | | | 2 | 2 | | | 2 | 2 | | |
| Digit | 1 | | 1 | | 1 | | 1 | | 1 | | 1 |

Punch Positions

**Alphabetic Characters**

| | | A | B | C | D | E | F | G | H | I | J | K | L | M | N | O | P | Q | R | S | T | U | V | W | X | Y | Z |
|---|---|---|---|---|---|---|---|---|---|---|---|---|---|---|---|---|---|---|---|---|---|---|---|---|---|---|---|
| Zone | B | B | B | B | B | B | B | B | B | B | B | B | B | B | B | B | B | B | B | | | | | | | | |
| Zone | A | A | A | A | A | A | A | A | A | A | | | | | | | | | | A | A | A | A | A | A | A | A |
| Digit | 8 | | | | | | | | 8 | 8 | | | | | | | | 8 | 8 | | | | | | | 8 | 8 |
| Digit | 4 | | | | 4 | 4 | 4 | 4 | | | | | | 4 | 4 | 4 | 4 | | | | | 4 | 4 | 4 | 4 | | |
| Digit | 2 | | 2 | 2 | | | 2 | 2 | | | | 2 | 2 | | | 2 | 2 | | | 2 | 2 | | | 2 | 2 | | |
| Digit | 1 | 1 | | 1 | | 1 | | 1 | | 1 | 1 | | 1 | | 1 | | 1 | | 1 | | 1 | | 1 | | 1 | | 1 |

Punch Positions

**Special Characters**

| | | } | ¢ | . | < | ( | + | \| | ! | $ | * | ) | ; | ¬ | - | / | & | , | % | _ | > | ? | : | # | @ | ' | = | " |
|---|---|---|---|---|---|---|---|---|---|---|---|---|---|---|---|---|---|---|---|---|---|---|---|---|---|---|---|---|
| Zone | B | B | B | B | B | B | B | B | B | B | B | B | B | B | | | | | | | | | | | | | | |
| Zone | A | A | A | A | A | A | A | A | | | | | | | | | A | A | A | A | A | A | A | | | | | |
| Digit | 8 | | | 8 | 8 | 8 | 8 | 8 | 8 | 8 | 8 | 8 | 8 | 8 | | 8 | 8 | 8 | 8 | 8 | 8 | 8 | 8 | 8 | 8 | 8 | 8 | 8 |
| Digit | 4 | | | | 4 | 4 | 4 | 4 | | 4 | 4 | 4 | 4 | | | | | | | 4 | 4 | 4 | 4 | | 4 | 4 | 4 | 4 |
| Digit | 2 | | | 2 | 2 | | | | | 2 | 2 | 2 | 2 | | | | | | 2 | 2 | | | | | 2 | 2 | 2 | 2 |
| Digit | 1 | | | | 1 | | 1 | | 1 | | 1 | | 1 | | | 1 | | 1 | | 1 | | 1 | | 1 | | 1 | | 1 |

Punch Positions

**FIGURE 3-9**

IBM System/3, punch card character set and punch combinations

To verify your understanding of the previous material, turn to page 104 and take Self-Test 3-1.

Let us now discuss those punched card machines that can still be found in a computer installation together with the functions that they perform.

## PUNCHED CARD PROCESSING MACHINES

Machines capable of performing limited operations on data recorded on punched cards have been in use since the time of Herman Hollerith. These machines are generally referred to as unit-record machines, and some are still in use today. Those still in use include the Reproducer, Interpreter, Sorter, and Collator.

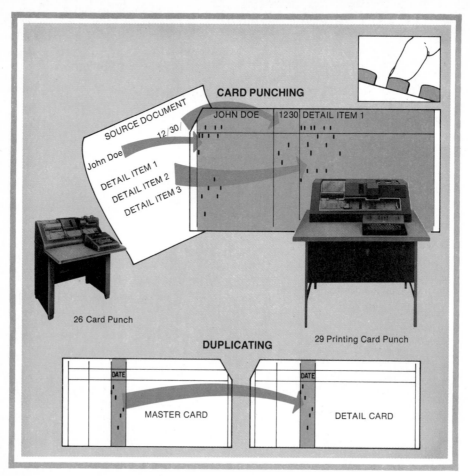

**FIGURE 3-10**

Card punching and duplicating

**Reproducer**  Reproducers are capable of **reproducing** or copying all or part of the data from one card to another. Reproducers are also available with a comparing feature that indicates to the operator of the machine if an error has occurred while copying the data from one card to another and in what column(s) the error(s) occurred.

**Gangpunching,** like reproducing, involves the punching of data from one card to another. It is different from reproducing in that it involves the punching of all or part of the data from a master card into one *or more* detail cards that follow the master card. As with reproducing, the information can be copied into the same or different card columns on the detail cards from the columns the data occupied on the master card.

If groups of cards are desired, one group for each of several different master cards, the operation required would be called interspersed

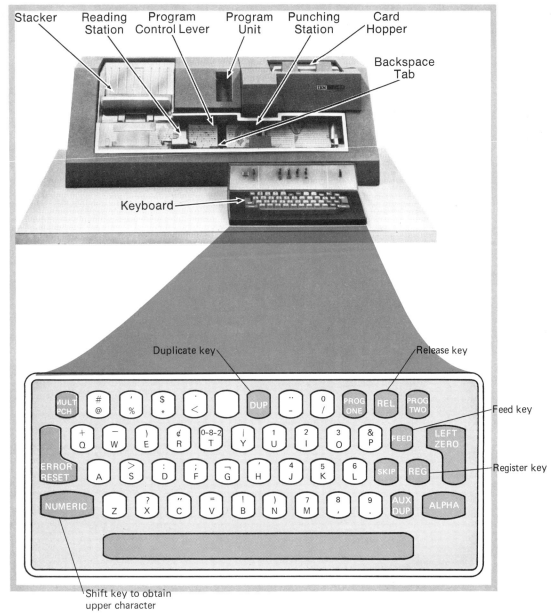

**FIGURE** 3-11

IBM 029 card punch and alphabetic keyboard

master card gangpunching. In this method, master cards are interspersed into a deck of blank or detail cards with a master card preceding each group of blank or detail cards. Information read from a master card is then automatically copied onto all succeeding cards until another master card is detected. Data from this second master card are

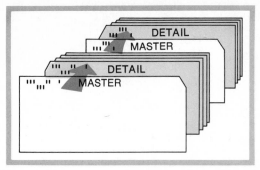

**FIGURE 3-12**
Gangpunching

then automatically copied into the blank or detail cards following it. This process continues until all master cards have been read and the data contained on them copied onto the blank or detail cards following them (see Fig. 3-12).

The reproducer can also perform an operation called **mark-sensed punching.** Mark-sensed punching is the automatic punching of a card by means of electrically conductive marks made on a specially marked area on the card with a special pencil (see Fig. 3-13).

The principal advantage of using the mark-sensed punching is that the original data can be recorded anywhere—in the office, plant or field, by workmen, timekeepers, or field workers—and then these data can be quickly and easily translated directly into punched-hole form.

One disadvantage, however, is that each space required for a sense mark is approximately three times that which would be required to record the same data in punched-hole form. This would then limit the capacity of one card to 27 mark-sense columns instead of the normal 80 punching columns.

**Interpreter**    **Interpreting** is a means by which punched cards that do not contain printing at the top can be read, and the information read printed on the top of the card. Depending on the particular model of interpreter used, printing will take place on one or two lines near the top of the card or on various lines throughout the body of the card (see Fig. 3-14).

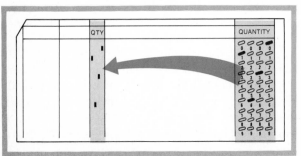

**FIGURE 3-13**
Mark-sensed punching

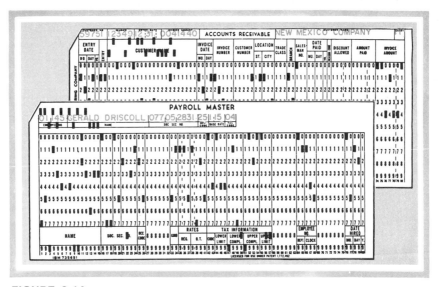

FIGURE 3-14

Upper and lower line interpreting

**Sorter**    Sorting is a process by which a deck of cards is arranged in a numerical or alphabetical sequence according to the data punched in one or more common fields.

The sorter provides an automatic means by which cards can be arranged in a predetermined fashion for the preparation of various reports, each originating from the same punched cards but each requiring sequencing based on different fields. The sorter may also be used to select cards with a specific punch or punches from a group of cards.

**Collator**    The collator is capable of performing operations such as selecting, merging, and matching.

**Selecting** is the process by which punched cards containing coded data concerning some particular quality or characteristic may be selected or pulled out from a deck of cards (see Fig. 3-15).

**Merging** is the process by which two decks of cards, arranged in some predetermined sequence, are combined to produce one large deck of cards in ascending or descending sequence. It is essential, however, that both files be arranged in the same sequence before they are merged.

**Matching** is a procedure by which two decks of cards, arranged in the same sequential order, can be compared with respect to specific data to determine if they are identical. Groups of cards in one file are compared with similar groups in a second file on a card-by-card basis. If one or more cards of a particular group do not match with cards in the other group, they may be selected from the group and filed separately in

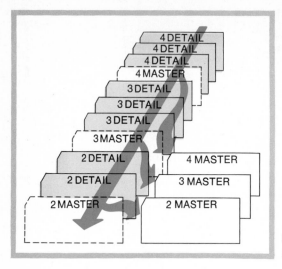

**FIGURE 3-15**
Selecting

a special stacker on the machine. Matching is often done in connection with a merging operation.

Let us turn to some of the more recent data-entry techniques.

**To verify your understanding of the previous material, turn to page 104 and take Self-Test 3-2.**

## KEY-TO-TAPE/DISK DATA-ENTRY SYSTEMS

For over two decades the punched card maintained its position as the principal medium onto which source data were recorded for input to a computer. During this time computer processing speeds have increased almost 100 times with an equivalent decrease in their physical size, while punched card input speeds have barely doubled and (with the exception of the IBM 96-column card) the physical size of the punched card has remained the same. This has prompted the search for other recording media and devices. Among the devices that have proved practical are the key-to-tape and key-to-disk recording devices. These devices, however, have not eliminated all the disadvantages associated with the punched card as an input medium. They still require the manual keying of data from source documents and are subject to all the limitations and possible sources of error inherent in any manual operation. The advantages result from lower costs, better space utilization, and increased productivity. This does not include the savings realized after the data have been recorded. Let us now examine each of these devices in more detail.

**Key-to-tape System**   A key-to-tape recorder is very similar in operation to a card punch with the exception that the source data are recorded on magnetic tape instead of punched cards (Fig. 3-16). The magnetic tape used with

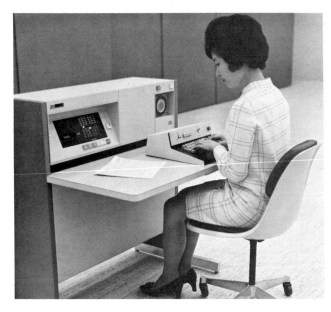

FIGURE 3-16
Key-to-tape recorder (*Courtesy International Business Machines Corporation*)

these recorders is similar to the tape cartridge or cassette used with home recorders. As with the card punch, data are entered directly from the keyboard. Keying accuracy is verified by placing the recorded tape into a magnetic tape verifier and having the original data retyped, as is done in the case of punched card verification. Magnetic tape encoders and verifiers are generally housed in the same physical unit. Any errors detected are corrected by simply erasing the mistakes and substituting the correct character(s).

Key-to-tape recorders generally record data on a 7-inch reel or cassette at a rate of approximately 20 characters per inch. As this is not acceptable to most computers, the tape must be converted with the aid of a **tape pooler.** The pooler can combine several small reels or cassettes and record the data on a larger reel at whatever density is required by the computer system. Computer tape drives generally operate at densities of 800, 1200, or 1600 characters per inch. Thus, when this pooling process has been completed, the equivalent of from 120 to 240 fully punched cards would be contained on one foot of tape. Once the computer starts reading a tape, it can read characters at an average rate of approximately 320,000 characters per second. This is well over 200 times faster than the data can be input from cards. As business applications are characterized by a large volume of input data, it is no wonder that key-to-tape devices are experiencing such a rapid growth rate.

**Key-to-disk System**  A multiple-station key-to-disk system generally consists of from 8 to 64 key stations (Fig. 3-17), a magnetic disk, a control unit, a magnetic tape unit, and a minicomputer. The procedure involves keying in the source data at a key station keyboard, verifying the correctness of

**FIGURE 3-17**
Key-to-disk and key-to-diskette terminals (*Courtesy International Business Machines Corporation*)

the data on the CRT (cathode ray tube) screen, editing the data by the minicomputer, and temporarily recording the data on a disk. Once the source data have been recorded on the disk, it is copied onto a computer-compatible magnetic tape for future processing. Thus, the final output of the key-to-disk system is the same as that of a key-to-tape system—a computer-compatible magnetic tape. Most currently available key-to-disk systems also maintain operator statistics available upon request by the system supervisor. These statistics typically consist of operator identification, operator start and stop times, number of keyed records or transactions, number of errors corrected or bypassed, and number of operator keystrokes.

Such systems are generally economically feasible in companies where there is a substantial volume of data to be entered into the system. In such cases, the cost of a key-to-disk system can represent a savings of as much as 30% over the cost of a card punching system. Multistation key-to-disk systems enhance operator productivity in a way no other type of data system can. They essentially remove all responsibilities from the key station operator except for the single task of keying data.

Key-to-disk stations are also available with another data storage medium, the **diskette** or **floppy disk.** The term "floppy disk" stems from the fact that the disk is a thin (0.025 inches thick), compact, round, flexible mylar disk approximately 7.5 inches in diameter which is enclosed in a square plastic jacket (Fig. 3-18). The floppy disk or diskette is commonly used with mini- and microcomputer systems. A single floppy disk can store up to 250,000 characters or the equivalent of approxi-

FIGURE 3-18
Floppy disk with its square plastic jacket
(*Courtesy International Business Machines Corporation*)

mately 3000 fully punched cards. Floppy disks are expected shortly with storage capacities in excess of half a million characters.

To verify your understanding of the previous material, turn to page 105 and take Self-Test 3-3.

## TERMINALS

**Interactive Remote Terminals**   An interactive remote terminal is a data-entry device generally located remotely from a central computer system but operating under the direct control of the central computer system. Such devices generally consist of a keyboard, a communications network or capability to transmit the data to the central computer system, and a typewriter or CRT device to display messages received back from the central computer system. Most terminals equipped with a CRT device also use this device to visually verify the keyed data prior to transmitting them to the central computer (Fig. 3-19). Currently available CRT devices are capable of displaying as many as 2000 characters. Once the data have been transmitted to the central computer, they can be edited,

**FIGURE 3-19**

A Teletype Model 4500 Interactive Terminal
(*Courtesy Teletype Corporation*)

compared against preestablished limits, tested as to type, etc. Errors detected by the central computer are reported back to the terminal for correction. Acceptable data are processed or stored for future processing by the central computer system. A single central computer system can support numerous interactive remote terminals concurrently; thus the power of the central computer can be made available to many distant locations at the same time.

Examples of such systems are the reservation systems in use by most automobile rental agencies or airlines. Clerks from remote terminals separated by great distances can communicate with a central computer concurrently. In this way changes in available resources resulting from a transaction entered at one remote station will be considered when answering an inquiry from another remote terminal.

**Intelligent Terminals**   Intelligent terminals possess all of the capabilities of interactive remote terminals plus a processing capability. That is, an intelligent terminal can process the data entered into it prior to transmitting it to the central computer system. This processing capability can vary from terminal to terminal, ranging from the ability to format the data and perform limited editing to that of a complete mini- or microcomputer system.

Intelligent terminals are generally not used in data-entry applications where the primary concern is the speed with which characters are

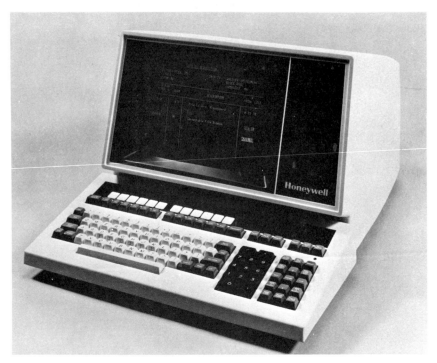

**FIGURE 3-20**

Honeywell's microprocessor-based intelligent terminal (*Courtesy Honeywell Information Systems, Inc.*)

keyed, but are used in those applications where accuracy is critical and where the operator must be familiar with the technical aspects of the application in order to interact with the central computer system. Such applications might include order processing, material control, text editing or word processing, automatic bank tellers, etc. (see Fig. 3-20).

**Point-of-sale (POS) Terminals**    In most retail firms, the majority of the raw data required for data-processing operations originate at the point of sale. Therefore, if the data can be recorded on a computer-acceptable medium at the time of the transaction, the need for additional data-entry costs will be minimal. It is no wonder that POS terminals are replacing the retailer's cash register (see Fig. 3-21). POS terminals generally record the transactions on a self-contained cassette or are wired to a mini- or microcomputer, which records the data received from each of the terminals in the store. In the case of a large retail chain, the data are often communicated from the store's computer to a central computer system that does the processing for the entire chain. To accomplish this, the data are converted to a form that can be transmitted over a voice-grade telephone line by a controller located at the point of sale and then converted back

**FIGURE 3-21**
Point-of-sale cash register terminal
(*Courtesy NCR Corporation*)

to a computer-acceptable medium by a controller at the site of the central computer system.

One of the advantages of a point-of-sale terminal being tied to a mini- or microcomputer is that once the item number has been entered, the minicomputer can provide the price if the salesperson does not recall the price or correct the price should an incorrect price be entered. Special discounts, quantity prices, etc., can also be programmed into the minicomputer.

In some retail stores (food stores, for example) the products are premarked by the manufacturer with standard UPC (Universal Product Code) bar codes that can be scanned by a "wand" or scanning device tied in to the terminal. Examples of bar codes used on labels are shown in Fig. 3-22. Once the product-identifying data have been recorded, the terminal computer can provide the price and any other pertinent

"Hey, Sam, is this ▮▮▮ or ▮▮▮ ?"

FIGURE 3-22

Examples of the Universal Product Code (UPC)
as it appears on everyday food items

information. The computer also keeps track of each item sold and thus
aids management in maintaining current inventory status.

To verify your understanding of the previous material, turn to page
105 and take Self-Test 3-4.

## CHARACTER READERS

Character readers are capable of accepting printed or written characters from source documents and converting these data into a computer-acceptable code for processing. High-speed character readers
currently available are capable of reading source documents at rates of
up to 2000 documents per minute and may cost several hundred thousand dollars. The three basic types of character readers are magnetic-
ink character readers, optical mark readers, and optical character
readers.

**Magnetic-ink Character Readers**

The concept of **magnetic-ink character recognition** (MICR) was
first developed by the Stanford Research Institute for use by the
world's largest bank, the Bank of America. This system was designed to directly read data prerecorded on checks and deposit slips
and then automatically sort the checks and deposit slips by the characters found in these prerecorded data. The data are prerecorded on the
checks and deposit slips with a special ferrite-impregnated ink that has
a magnetic characteristic. This magnetic characteristic can be detected

**FIGURE 3-23**

IBM 1419 Magnetic Character Reader and magnetic character reading

and interpreted by MICR equipment, allowing the input document to be mechanically processed (see Fig. 3-23).

In Fig. 3-24 you see a canceled check containing, along the bottom, data relating to the individual bank's assigned number, the customer's account number, and the amount of the check. The amount field is, of course, coded by the bank at the time the check is received for payment.

**Optical Mark Readers**

Optical mark readers (OMR) optically read pencil marks on special and carefully printed forms. Optical mark forms are relatively expensive, as they must be printed with exacting tolerances so that the marks will line up under the optical sensing devices when read (Fig. 3-25). The most popular use of such devices is in educational institutions for the scoring of examinations.

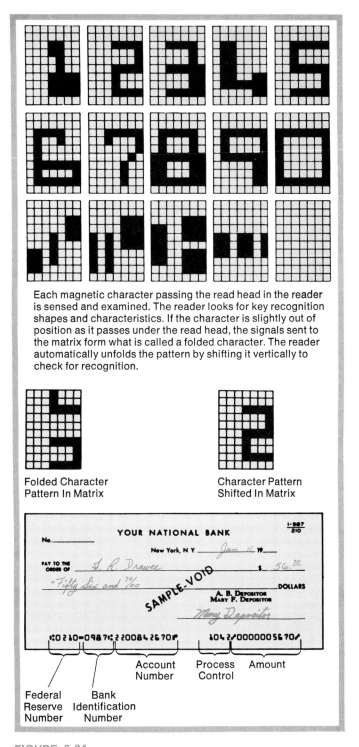

Each magnetic character passing the read head in the reader is sensed and examined. The reader looks for key recognition shapes and characteristics. If the character is slightly out of position as it passes under the read head, the signals sent to the matrix form what is called a folded character. The reader automatically unfolds the pattern by shifting it vertically to check for recognition.

Folded Character
Pattern In Matrix

Character Pattern
Shifted In Matrix

Federal Reserve Number

Bank Identification Number

Account Number

Process Control

Amount

FIGURE 3-24

Magnetic-ink characters and a typical application

**FIGURE 3-25**
Optical sensors employed in optical mark readers

**Optical Character Readers**    **Optical character recognition** (OCR) devices can convert data from source documents to a machine-recognizable form (Fig. 3-26). Current applications of optical scanning include billing, insurance premium notices, and charge sales invoices. It should be pointed out that there are currently no OCR devices that can reliably read and interpret handwriting. However, some are available that can read hand printing provided that certain general guidelines are observed when the data are printed. Figure 3-27 illustrates some of these guidelines. Generally, opti-

**FIGURE 3-26**

IBM 3890 OCR Document Processor (*Courtesy International Business Machines Corporation*)

| | RIGHT WAY | WRONG WAY |
|---|---|---|
| 1 Write big | I A 4 2 C | I A 4 2 c |
| 2 Keep char. in box | 5 P 7 8 6 | 5 p 7 8 6 |
| 3 Capitals only | B D A L R | b d a l r |
| 4 Simple shapes | C I Z 2 7 | C 1 Z 2 7 |
| 5 Block print | 5 5 T N R | S 5 T N R |
| 6 No broken lines | 4 T K P 5 | 4 T K P 5 |
| 7 Close loops | 6 B 8 9 O | 6 B 8 9 O |
| 8 Do not link char. | 4 7 O O O | 4 7 O O O |

**FIGURE 3-27**

Guidelines to be used when recording characters for optical character reading

cal character readers are limited with respect to hand-printed characters and can only read hand-printed digits and some symbols. Many more OCR devices are available for reading of machine-printed characters including digits, letters, and some special characters. For example, IBM makes special optical character typing elements for their Selectric typewriters to reduce errors during an optical character reading operation.

Because of the great cost of these devices, they are generally impractical unless a substantial number of documents are to be processed each day—generally a minimum of 5000 to 10,000 documents per day. OCR devices are beginning to fulfill the potential that has long been latent in them, and they are expected to see widespread use in the 1980s. Current applications of optical scanning include utility billing, insurance premium notices, and charge sales invoices. Even in their infancy, optical scanners show promise for greatly reducing, if not ultimately eliminating, the need to convert any source document onto punched cards or other input media. Presently such devices are not used to a greater extent because of the poor reliability of character interpretation resulting from source-document typewriter inconsistencies, erasures, etc. Eventually, technological improvements and design innovations should eliminate these problems and permit broad and extensive application of optical character recognition techniques in automated data processing.

# Data Entry Operator: The Key Element

## by Lawrence Feidelman

Data entry is unlike any other part of the data processing system in that the individual has a greater effect on the system's daily operations than the machine does. The computer functions are certainly dependent upon the programmer, but once the program has been developed and tested, the machine itself becomes the dominant factor. The storage peripherals, printer and communications are certainly machine dependent.

However, since most data is entered via a keyboard, the operator dictates the data volume and accuracy. This fact has become the most significant understatement in the industry. From every angle, the operator is the key element of the system. The program results are only as valid as the accuracy of the input. How much time and additional money have you spent rerunning programs because of inaccurate data? Obvious also is the over-riding time factor when data entry time units are minutes and hours versus computer time units of microseconds and nanoseconds. The data entry time span is what dictates total system throughput.

From an economic viewpoint, data entry accounts for 30 percent to 50 percent of the data processing annual expenditure and personnel accounts for approximately 80 percent of data entry costs. With equipment prices constantly decreasing and labor prices increasing, the percentages are going to be greater, and this fact will hold true for the next decade as keyboard entry continues to be the major means of data entry. No data entry technology, from optical reading to voice data entry, will change that status. In fact, data entry is heading towards decentralization, where clerical personnel entering data at the source are replacing the professional operator. While this source data capture is needed, the controls to manage this situation are still unclear.

Having established the criticalness and continuance of the data entry position, let us examine the key problems that now exist and the steps management has taken to solve them.

As I have stated, two key measures of the success of a data entry installation are the data entry volume and accuracy. The means of obtaining goals of high data entry volume and accuracy continue to call for a struggle throughout the data entry profession, but it's a struggle that can be won. The complexities of the situation appear to involve the relatively low status of data entry, the repetitive nature of the work, and the consistently high work pressure.

We are now effectively attacking the data entry status situation, at least at the management level. The Data Entry Management Association (DEMA) has been the driving force in improving data entry management's status. We have done little, however, to improve the data entry operator status even to a level similar to that of the office secretary. The company can show its recognition of this position through management/employee interaction, increased benefits and better physical conditions. Furthermore, a stated promotional path should be defined for those interested. While many prefer to remain data entry operators, others desire to become lead operators, supervisors and managers. Without an upward path of mobility, the company can expect a definite increase in turnover. As we know, turnover is a very expensive proposition.

The need exists to permit data entry employees to be effectively trained to reach desired management levels. Considering that most data entry employees do not have the same education as employees in the other areas of data processing, the company must allow attainment of this education through colleges, community colleges and seminars. Although few will probably take advantage of such training, those who do will become invaluable to the company as it moves into distributed processing.

The repetitive nature of the work is certainly the worst problem because it affects not only the turnover rate but also the work itself. The approaches to solving this problem have varied from ignoring it to implementing incentive pay systems. Both solutions appear to be avoiding the actual problem in that they state that the problem exists, but offer different levels of compensation. While incentive pay can be an expensive proposition, it does begin to hit upon motivation of some kind and to directly enhance productivity and accuracy. It does not appear, however, to be the sole motivating factor or the best—it is the simplest from management's viewpoint. Incentive pay will have an effect if given in continuing situations rather than only a few times. If not given, it may very well be a demotivating factor.

The means of effectively motivating data entry operators, in spite of repetitive work which can lead to boredom, is to give both the work and the data entry operator importance. This means that the data entry manager and supervisor must devise methods of not only controlling the data entry department but also keeping in contact with the personnel staff to avoid work problems. Such techniques include explaining the importance of work, creating work variety, setting work challenges, developing team work efforts, and numerous motivational factors.

The cost of implementing these techniques is certainly less than a formal incentive program. These motivational techniques do not replace qualified operators utilizing effective key techniques. They do assure a high quality of work and get the best out of the individual, however.

While work pressure is constantly with us, it must be varied by the manager. The manager must be aware of work priorities and properly schedule them so as to avoid high peaks. He should be aware of such peaks well in advance. High pressure can be handled better when people know that it is coming and that it will be over. The data entry operator is indeed a valuable resource within the data processing department and within user departments as distributed processing takes hold. It is the key human link between the company business and the company. How the data entry operator is managed is of importance to your data processing operation and, on a daily basis, is worth more than the programs themselves. We would be better off getting down to basics.□

DISCUSSION QUESTIONS

1. What are some of the reasons that have made the position of a data-entry operator an unenviable one?

2. One of the most difficult problems faced by management is motivation. What suggestions would you have to motivate data-entry operators and to reduce boredom?

## SPEECH RECOGNITION SYSTEMS

Speech recognition devices were first introduced in the early 1970s. In most such systems, the voice patterns for up to 50 words and the ten digits are stored in the recognition unit, to which a microphone is connected. This unit simply compares the spoken words with the stored pattern and responds accordingly. In the case of numbers, they must be spoken as a series of digits and not as a single number. For example, the number 4873 would be input as "four, eight, seven, three." Speech recognition devices are generally used in cases where access to a switch or control is not possible or where a user's hands are otherwise occupied. As voice patterns vary greatly from person to person, the speech recognition device will have to be "fine-tuned" to each operator. Speech recognition devices are currently employed in the preparation of numerical control tapes and in airline baggage sorting.

To verify your understanding of the previous material, turn to page 105 and take Self-Test 3-5.

## SELF-TEST 3–1

1. A logical record is _____.
2. A unit record is another name for _____.
3. The standard IBM punched card is divided into _____ columns and _____ rows, with each column being capable of holding one _____ of information.
4. A character can be a _____, a _____, or a _____.
5. Characters contained on a punched card are expressed as a combination of punches in the _____ and _____ punching areas.
6. A _____ can be defined as a set of one or more bits (binary digits) or characters treated as a unit of information.
7. A card field, on the other hand, is defined as _____.
8. To interpret a card manually, one must know the _____ or arrangement of fields on the card.
9. Fields are classified, according to the type of information that they may contain, as _____, _____, or _____.
10. 417, 347A3B, and SALARY are _____, _____, and _____ fields, respectively.
11. Some of the advantages of using punched cards are _____.
12. Some of the disadvantages of using punched cards are _____.
13. The _____ card was designed for use on IBM's System/3 computer.
14. The IBM System/3 96-column punched card is (larger, smaller) than the 80-column card, uses (round, rectangular) punched holes, and employs the _____ coding system.

## SELF-TEST 3–2

1. Functions performed by punched card processing machines that can cause data to be copied from one card to another include _____.
2. Gangpunching differs from reproducing in that _____.
3. Operations performed by the collator include _____.
4. Operations performed by the reproducer include _____.
5. Unit-record machines have been in use since the time of _____.

## SELF-TEST 3-3

1. The slow processing speed and bulkiness of the _____ has led to a search for more efficient means of data entry.
2. In a key-to-tape system, data are entered directly from a _____ and recorded on _____.
3. A key-to-disk system consists of _____.
4. Most key-to-disk systems maintain operator _____ available upon request by the system supervisor.
5. The term _____ came from the fact that it is a round disk made up of a thin, flexible, mylar substance.
6. Tape _____ are used to combine several small reels or cassettes onto a larger and more dense magnetic tape.

## SELF-TEST 3-4

1. A(n) _____ terminal is defined as a data-entry device generally located remotely from a central computer system but operating under its direct control.
2. Interactive terminal networks generally consist of _____.
3. An interactive remote terminal that has a processing capability is referred to as a(n) _____.
4. Intelligent terminals are generally used in those applications where (speed, accuracy) is critical.
5. A standard code used to premark products for point-of-sale terminal processing is the _____.

## SELF-TEST 3-5

1. Character readers convert _____ characters from source documents and convert these data to a _____ form.
2. Character readers include _____.
3. _____ require that the data be recorded on special and carefully printed forms.
4. Optical character readers (can, cannot) read and interpret handwriting.
5. Optical character readers are generally impractical for (small, large) volume applications.
6. Speech recognition devices can generally recognize the voice patterns for up to _____ words and the ten digits.
7. The number 1245 would be spoken into a speech recognition device as _____.

**Answers to Self-Tests** 3-1
1. a collection of items independent of their physical environment
2. a punched card
3. 80; 12; character
4. digit; letter; or special character

5. zone; digit
6. field
7. a fixed number of consecutive card columns assigned to a unit of information
8. format
9. alphabetic; numeric; alphanumeric
10. numeric; alphanumeric; alphabetic
11. they are inexpensive, easily prepared, easily stored, easily sorted, and easily reproduced
12. they have a limited storage capacity, slow processing speeds, are bulky, do not lend themselves to correction, and are sensitive to high humidity
13. IBM 96-column
14. smaller; round; BCD (Binary Coded Decimal)

3–2

1. duplicating, reproducing and gangpunching
2. gangpunching copies data from a master card to one or more detail cards, while reproducing copies data from one card to a single other card
3. selecting, merging, and matching
4. reproducing, gangpunching, and mark-sensed punching
5. Herman Hollerith

3–3

1. punched card
2. keyboard; magnetic tape reel or cassette
3. 8 to 64 key stations, a magnetic disk, a central control unit, a magnetic tape unit, and a minicomputer
4. statistics
5. floppy disk
6. poolers

3–4

1. interactive remote terminal
2. a keyboard, communications network, and a typewriter or CRT device
3. intelligent terminal
4. accuracy
5. Universal Product Code (UPC)

3–5

1. printed or written; machine readable
2. magnetic-ink character readers, optical mark readers, and optical character readers
3. Optical mark readers
4. cannot
5. small
6. 50
7. one, two, four, five

_____ 1. It is generally impossible to interpret the data contained on a punched card if the format of the data is not known.

_____ 2. The 0 row of a punched card serves as both a zone row and a digit row.

_____ 3. A tape pooler is generally used with key-to-tape devices to produce a computer-compatible magnetic tape.

_____ 4. Interactive terminals operate under the direct control of the central computer system.

_____ 5. Character readers are of three types: magnetic-ink, optical mark, and optical character.

_____ 6. Speech recognition devices compare spoken words to stored word patterns and respond accordingly.

_____ 7. Banks routinely utilize MICR devices.

_____ 8. Punched card input speeds have increased by almost 10 times in the last decade alone.

_____ 9. A card file is a place in which cards are stored.

_____ 10. Key-to-disk devices are equally practical with large- and small-volume data-entry applications.

_____ 11. Point-of-sale terminals are rapidly replacing the cash register in retail stores.

_____ 12. IBM provides a typewriter element specifically designed to produce documents which can be accurately read by OCR devices.

_____ 13. OCR devices are generally impractical in installations processing less than several thousand documents per day.

_____ 14. The United Producers Code is used to premark products with identifying data for reading by a scanning device tied into a point-of-sale terminal.

_____ 15. The final output of a key-to-disk system is a computer-compatible magnetic tape.

_____ 16. A logical record is another term for a unit record.

_____ 17. The IBM 96-column card is subdivided into three tiers, each capable of storing 32 characters in the BCD coding scheme.

_____ 18. Intelligent terminals are principally employed in data-entry applications where the primary concern is input speed.

_____ 19. Another name for the IBM 80-column punch card is the Hollerith card.

_____ 20. Unit-record machines date back to the time of Herman Hollerith.

_____ 21. An alphanumeric field consists of numbers and letters only.

_____ 22. The IBM 96-column card employs the Hollerith code to record data.

_____ 23. The BCD code consists of combinations of six possible column punches.

_____ **24.** The top row of an 80-column card is the 12 row; the bottom row is the 9 row.

_____ **25.** A card punch is capable of performing the operations of card punching and duplicating.

**3–2**

**Multiple-choice**

_____ **1.** The number of columns in a single tier of a 96-column card is
   **a.** 20
   **b.** 32
   **c.** 40
   **d.** 80
   **e.** 96

_____ **2.** Key-to-tape devices employ a _____ to transpose the data from a cassette to a computer-compatible tape.
   **a.** tape spooler
   **b.** tape pooler
   **c.** tape cartridge
   **d.** converter
   **e.** none of the above

_____ **3.** The zone positions on a standard IBM card include
   **a.** 12, 4, 0
   **b.** 11, 0, 1
   **c.** 12, 1, 0
   **d.** 13, 4, 0
   **e.** none of the above

_____ **4.** Optical character readers determine the value of recorded data by
   **a.** sensing magnetic-ink patterns
   **b.** sensing special pencil marks
   **c.** sensing the shape of a character
   **d.** sensing magnetic spots on magnetic tape
   **e.** sensing holes punched in cards

_____ **5.** A punched card field is
   **a.** a group of columns
   **b.** a standard unit for measuring columns
   **c.** one or more adjacent columns reserved for a unit of information
   **d.** the first grouping on a card
   **e.** none of the above

_____ **6.** Which of the following card rows can serve as both a zone and a digit punching row?
   **a.** 1
   **b.** 12
   **c.** 11
   **d.** 0
   **e.** none of the above

_____ **7.** Point-of-sale terminals cannot
   **a.** record data on a cassette
   **b.** be connected to a mini- or microcomputer
   **c.** scan and interpret Universal Product Codes

**d.** be used with controllers to transmit data to a central computer

**e.** none of the above

———— **8.** Unit record machines include the

    **a.** sorter

    **b.** reproducer

    **c.** optical character readers

    **d.** all of the above

    **e.** (a) and (b) only

**3–3**
**Problems**

**1.** Contrast intelligent and nonintelligent terminals.

**2.** Describe the different character readers in use. What types of applications is each used for?

**3.** Describe the similarities and differences between the 80- and 96-column punched cards.

**4.** What limitations are associated with speech recognition systems?

**5.** Contrast key-to-tape and key-to-disk data-entry devices.

**6.** Briefly explain how point-of-sale recorders can be used.

**7.** How is MICR used by banks in check processing?

**8.** In view of the many new data-entry devices, how would you assess the future of the punched card?

**3–4**
**Projects**

**1.** Describe a possible card format that could be used to contain student application data such as name, address, high school, high school average, rank in class, college board scores, and area of concentration in college.

**2.** Visit a local airport, bank, etc., and determine what, where, and how data-entry devices are employed.

**3.** Visit your local department store and determine what data-entry devices are employed. Are these devices being used as efficiently as they could be?

**4.** Find one or two current articles in your library, newspaper, or magazine relating to data entry. Briefly comment on what you have read.

## appendix: OPERATING THE CARD PUNCH

**The Punching
Operation**

As a card is punched, it moves through four areas of the card punch, namely:

1. Card hopper
2. Punching station
3. Reading station
4. Card stacker

The keypunching operation is initiated by the operator's depressing the FEED key on the keyboard. This causes a single card to be released from the card hopper. The subsequent depressing of the REGister key by the operator causes the card to be advanced until column 1 of the card is positioned at the punching station. If several cards are to be punched, the AUTO FEED switch located above and behind the keyboard should be turned on. In this case, the

FEED key is depressed a second time instead of depressing the REG key. This causes the first card fed to be registered and the second card to be fed from the card hopper and not registered. As the result of either procedure, column 1 of the first card is positioned at the punching station.

The punching station contains a set of 12 **dies** or **blades,** one for each row on the card. As a key is depressed by the operator, the appropriate blades are energized punching the Hollerith code for the keyed character into the card. Figure A-1 illustrates the punching of the character "D" into a card. After the character has been punched into the column of the card positioned below the blades, the card is automatically advanced to the next card column. The column at which the card is positioned and where punching will occur is shown by a **column indicator** located at the bottom of the program unit (see Fig. A-2). After the punching of this card has been completed, a second card may be registered at the punching station by one of the two methods described above. This causes the previously punched card to simultaneously move to and be

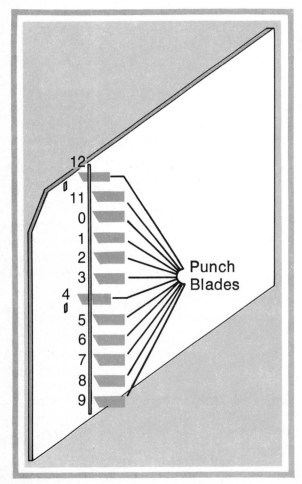

**FIGURE A-1**

The letter "D" punched into a card

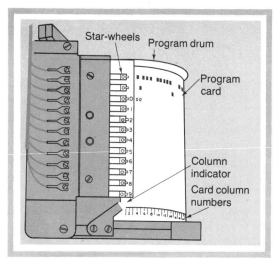

FIGURE A-2

Program control unit

registered at the reading station. The second card may be punched in the same manner as the first card, or some or all of the data punched into the first card may be duplicated into the second card.

**Duplicating and Correcting a Card**

If a second copy of the first card is desired, the operator need only hold down the DUPlicate key and column by column the data will be read from the first card under the reading station and punched into the second card under the punching blades.

The keying and duplicating operations may also be combined to facilitate the correction of a keying error in a previously punched card. For example, let us assume that the character X was incorrectly punched in column 18 of a card and that the correct character should have been a Y. After punching of the card containing the error has been completed, a second card is registered at the punching station and the error card is registered at the reading station. To punch the new and correct card, the operator depresses the DUP key until the column indicator points to column 18, at which point the DUP key is released. The Y key is then depressed, causing the character Y to be punched into column 18 of the new card. The DUP key is again depressed and held down until the remaining characters from the first card have been duplicated into the second card. The feeding of a new card will cause each card to advance to the next station with the first error card advancing to the card stacker, the correct card advancing to the read station, and the new card advancing to the punch station.

**Programming the Card Punch**

The card punch can also be programmed to perform certain operations automatically. For example, if data were to be punched into columns 10 through 20 of a large number of cards, the card punch could be programmed to skip automatically past columns 1 through 9 and position column 10 of each new card under the punching blades at the punching station. After the manual punching of columns 10 through 20, the card punch would cause the remaining columns of the card to be automatically skipped and the next card read in,

## TABLE A-1
### Program Control Card Codes

| TYPE OF PUNCH | FUNCTION |
|---|---|
| Blank | Indicates the beginning of a numeric field to be punched |
| 11 (−) | Indicates the beginning of a field to be skipped |
| 0 | Indicates the beginning of a field to be duplicated |
| 12 (&) | Signifies the remaining positions of the field defined by the blank, 12, 11, or 0 codes |
| 1 | Used in combination with the above punches to designate alphabetic fields; otherwise, the card punch will be in numeric mode |

registered, and advanced to column 10. In this way, the only manual operations the operator would have to perform would be the punching of the actual data into card columns 10 through 20. The card feeding and skipping operations would be handled automatically.

In order to program the card punch to perform such operations automatically, the operator must complete the following steps:

1. Punch the appropriate codes into a program card to indicate to the machine which operations to perform, where to start, and where to end. A list of program control card codes is given in Table A-1.
2. Remove the program drum located above the column indicator, wrap the program control card around the drum, and replace the program control drum.
3. Move the program control lever to the automatic position. Care should be taken to ensure that the lever is *not* in the automatic position when the drum is inserted or removed. This could result in damage to the card punch.

An example of a punched program control card is shown in Fig. A-3.

## FIGURE A-3
Punched program control card

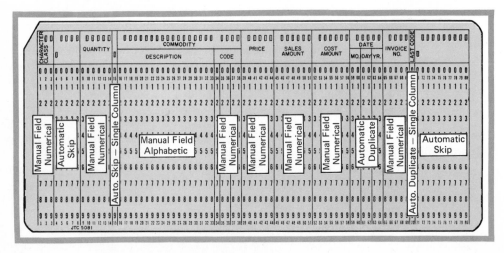

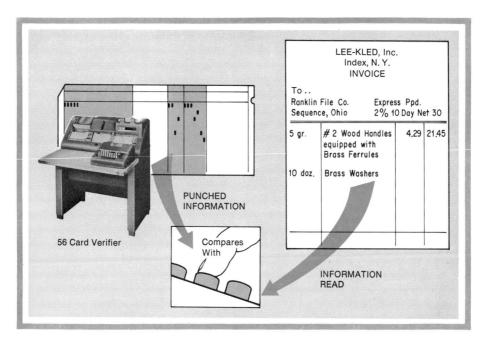

FIGURE A-4

Card verifying

**Card Verifying** Card verifying is an efficient and effective means of checking the accuracy of a previous card punching operation. This operation entails a second operator depressing keys on the verifier while reading the same source data utilized to produce the cards being verified. These are precisely the same operations as were performed by the first operator, with one major difference. Here, no punching takes place. What happens is that instead of punching holes in a card, the verifier compares the key depressed with the holes previously punched in the card by the first operator. Any difference causes the machine to stop and an error light to come on, indicating that a discrepancy exists. An error key can then be depressed and a second attempt at verification made. If no agreement is reached, a third attempt is made.

If still no agreement is reached, the card will advance to the next column after the operator has keyed in the correct character. This process is continued until the card has been completely verified. At this point a new card is punched with the corrections in it. This new card receives a single punch in the right margin to indicate that it is a corrected card (see Fig. A-5C). The original (incorrect) card does not receive any punches in the right margin (see Fig. A-5B).

If no errors are detected during the verification of a card, two punches are placed in the right margin of that card (see Fig. A-5A).

Univac, Decision Data, and IBM have produced devices that are capable of keypunching[4] cards and verifying cards in the same machine (see Fig. A-6). This capability greatly increases space utilization and combined operating

[4]The terms "keypunching" and "card punching" are synonymous.

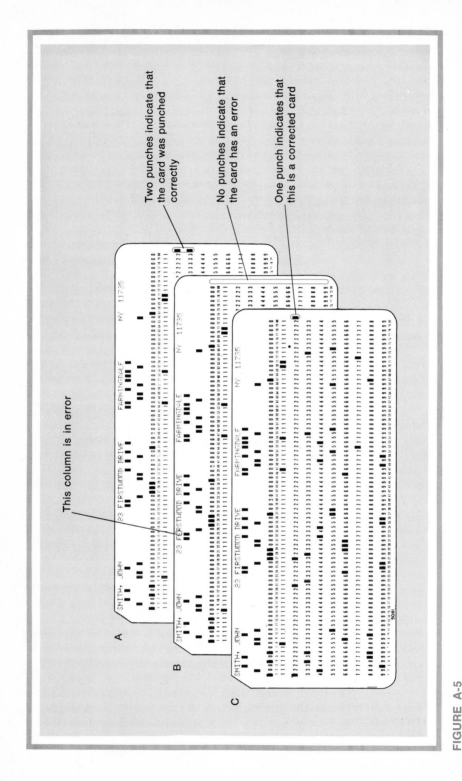

**FIGURE A-5**

(A) A correctly punched and verified card; (B) An incorrectly punched card; (C) A new card produced during verification with errors corrected

114

FIGURE A-6

Univac 1801 Verifying Keypunch capable of card punching and verifying (*Courtesy Sperry Corp., Univac Division*)

speeds. In addition, each of these devices is equipped with a **buffer,** a temporary storage area which holds the keyed characters prior to their actual punching. That is, punching does not actually occur as the operator presses a key. Instead, the character corresponding to the key depressed is stored in the buffer until a given amount of keying has been completed. At this time, the operator can cause the characters stored in the buffer to be punched onto a card. In this way, if an incorrect key has been depressed, it can be corrected in the buffer before it is punched into the card. This eliminates the expense of wasting a card and the time lost in having to prepare a new card.

The Decision Data 8010 can even interpret punched cards. One or more card fields can be selected to be read by the 8010, and the data read can be printed directly on the face of the same card.

Other features of these machines include such items as a production statistics feature, which totals the operations performed on a particular machine by the number of characters keyed, the number of records, or the number of errors. It is also possible to obtain an accumulator, which adds up the data in selected fields so as to allow them to be balanced against predetermined totals and reduce the amount of required verification. An advantage for the novice as well as the professional keypunch operator is the fact that the column about to be punched is now displayed via an indicator light on the keyboard.

INTRODUCTION
PUNCHED CARD INPUT/OUTPUT
**Punched card Readers**
**Card-punching Devices**
PRINTERS
**Character-printing Devices**
**Line-printing Devices**
TAPE INPUT/OUTPUT
**Punched-paper-tape Devices**
**Magnetic-tape Devices**
**Magnetic-tape Cassette Devices**
DIRECT-ACCESS INPUT/OUTPUT DEVICES
TERMINALS
**Keyboard Devices**
**Visual Display Devices**
OTHER INPUT/OUTPUT DEVICES *
**Microfilm Devices**
**Audio Devices**
**Plotters**
FOCUS ON THE FIELD
SELF-TESTS
EXERCISES

# CHAPTER 4

# Input/Output Media and Devices

## INTRODUCTION

We recall from Chapter 1 that the data-processing cycle consists of three basic functions: input, processing, and output. In this chapter we discuss input/output media and devices. Computers are available in all sizes, shapes, and colors, and with few exceptions, no matter what type or size of business enterprise you consider, there is available a computer or computer service suitable to handle its data-processing needs efficiently and economically. Furthermore, regardless of type, size, shape, or color, there is one thing about which we can be certain; there must be a means of feeding it data and getting back meaningful and useful information.

Upon completing this chapter, you should be able to:
- Describe the types of input/output devices currently supporting computers
- Describe the various types of printing devices
- Differentiate between line and character printers and between impact and nonimpact printers
- Describe the advantages and disadvantages of, and differentiate between, punched paper tape and magnetic tape
- List the advantages and disadvantages of the various types of terminals
- Describe the functions performed by terminals
- Describe some of the newer and more sophisticated input/output devices and techniques
- Define the following terms:

| | |
|---|---|
| Audio device | Laser printer |
| Character printer | Line printer |
| COM device | Machine code |
| CRT | Magnetic tape |
| Data collection | Message switching |
| Hard-copy output | Microfiche |
| Impact printer | Microfilm reader |
| Inquiry processing | Nonimpact printer |
| Keyboard device | Offline |

| Online | Remote job processing |
| Peripheral device | Transaction processing |
| Photoelectric card reader | Visual display device |
| Plotter | Wire-brush-type card reader |
| Punched paper tape | Wire matrix printer |

Computer applications in business are characterized by their limited computations and by the large volume of data which are input to, and output from, the computer. Handling this volume of data is one of the functions of the input/output devices, or **peripheral devices,** supporting a computer. These devices are responsible for sensing or reading data from the input medium and converting these data into a form that the computer can understand, which we call **machine code.** Input/output devices are also responsible for converting computer output from a machine-coded form into a language and onto an output medium we can read and understand.

"It likes to unwind after a long, hard day."

As you now certainly realize, input/output (I/O) devices perform a significant function and are an indispensable part of a computer complex or computer system. It should also be clear that the faster and more efficiently we can get the data to the computer, the more efficiently the computer will function and the faster we will obtain our results. Thus we must examine the various input/output devices so that we will know what devices are available to do what kinds of jobs and when to use each. We shall also examine the **media,** or means, used to record data associated with these input/output devices. Specific details such as operating speeds are presented only for purposes of comparison and need only be examined with this purpose in mind. Such specific information is included in the specifications available from equipment manufacturers. Some of these specifications are given in Table 4-1.

To verify your understanding of the previous material, turn to page 152 and take Self-Test 4-1.

## PUNCHED CARD INPUT/OUTPUT

**Punched card Readers**    The punched card reader is one of the most common input devices. This is due, in part, to the fact that the punched-card medium is so inexpensive and because the punched card is easily prepared and visually verified. It can be used with almost any computer system, from the very smallest to the very largest systems in use today. The principal use

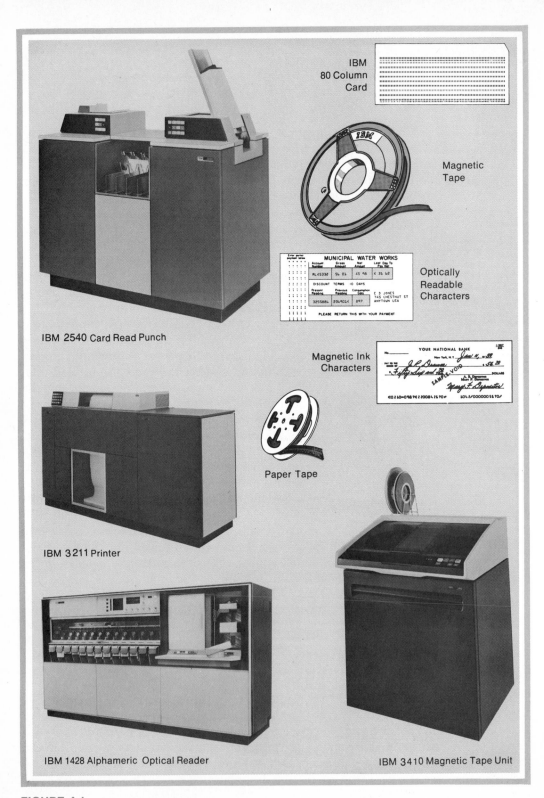

IBM
80 Column
Card

Magnetic
Tape

Optically
Readable
Characters

Magnetic Ink
Characters

IBM 2540 Card Read Punch

Paper Tape

IBM 3211 Printer

IBM 1428 Alphameric Optical Reader

IBM 3410 Magnetic Tape Unit

**FIGURE 4-1**

Input/output devices and media

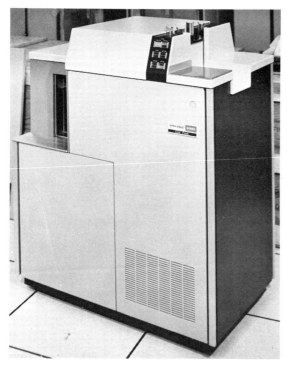

of the card reader is to transmit the information contained on the punched card directly to the memory or storage unit of the computer. This function can be accomplished at speeds ranging from 150 cards per minute to over 2500 cards per minute.

There are basically two kinds of punched card readers: the wire-brush type and the photoelectric type. In the wire-brush type, the card is read row by row by a series of 80 wire brushes, one for each card

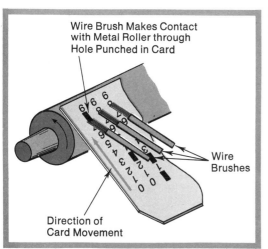

FIGURE 4-3

Wire-brush card reader

Wire Brush Makes Contact with Metal Roller through Hole Punched in Card

Wire Brushes

Direction of Card Movement

**TABLE 4-1**
Input/Output Media and Devices

| DEVICE | PURPOSE | MEDIUM | TYPICAL SPEED RANGES | CAPACITY | APPLICATION AREAS |
|---|---|---|---|---|---|
| Card Read/Punch | Input/output of source data on 80- and 96-column punched cards | Punched card | 150–2500 cpm* reading 80–600 cpm punching | 80 or 96 characters per card | Low-volume applications in small or medium computer systems and for turnaround documents (telephone bills, etc.) |
| Paper Tape Reader/Punch | Low-speed I/O of low-volume files | Paper tape | 350–1000 cpm reading 15–150 cpm punching | Up to 250,000 characters per tape; compact and easy to transport | Low-volume, long-term storage applications |
| Impact Line Printer | Low-volume, hard-copy output | Special paper | 150–2500 lines per minute | High-speed, hard-copy output | Applications requiring low-volume reports, documentation, or results in printed form |
| Nonimpact Printer | High-volume, hard-copy output | Regular or special paper | 2000–20,000 lines per minute | High-speed, hard-copy output | For applications requiring a tremendous volume of hard-copy output |
| Magnetic Tape Reader | High-speed I/O of large-volume sequential files | Magnetic tape | 15,000–1,250,000 cps† | Up to 160 million characters per tape; compact and easy to transport | High-volume sequential processing applications (payroll, inventory) |
| Magnetic Drum Unit | Storage and high-speed I/O of data | Magnetic drum | 230,000–1,500,000 cps | Up to 200 million characters of storage; bulky and not mobile | Applications requiring extremely rapid random access |
| Magnetic Disk Unit | Storage and high-speed I/O of data | Magnetic disk | 100,000–1,000,000 cps | Up to 100 million characters per disk pack; virtually unlimited offline storage; compact and easy to transport | High-volume random-access applications |
| Magnetic Card/Strip Storage Unit | Large-volume I/O; random-access storage | Card/strip cartridge | 25,000–50,000 cps | Up to 400 million characters of random-access storage | |

| Device | Function | Medium | Speed | Capacity | Application |
|---|---|---|---|---|---|
| Mass Storage System | Large-volume I/O; random-access storage | Magnetic tape cartridges | 50,000–500,000 cps | Up to 472,000,000,000 characters of storage; cartridges are portable and easy to store or transport | Extremely large-volume random-access files; ideal to support central data base in a distributed processing system |
| Character Readers | Direct reading from source documents | Special paper or print | Up to 2000 documents per minute | | Installations requiring high-volume data input from source documents |
| Computer Output Microfilm (COM) | Storage of large-volume output for subsequent remote use | Microfilm or microfiche | 40,000–120,000 cps | Up to 2,000,000 lines of data | High-volume output for later use on a COM reader |
| CRT Display Devices | Keyboard entry of input data and inquiries; visual display of output on the CRT | Cathode ray tube | 250–10,000 cps | | Online inquiries and file updating; ideal in time-sharing and reservation systems |

* cards per minute
† characters per second

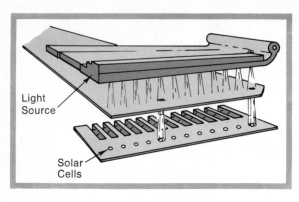

**FIGURE 4-4**
Photoelectric card reader

column (Fig. 4-3). A punched hole is detected when a wire brush is pushed through a punched hole in the card and contacts the metal roller just below the card. Most card readers contain two such sets of 80 wire reading brushes. As a card passes under the first set of 80 brushes (read-check station), a hole count is taken; that is, the number of punches in the card is determined and held for checking purposes. The card then moves under a second set of 80 brushes (read station), where the punched card is read, the hole count from the read-check

**FIGURE 4-5**
Univac 716 Card Reader Subsystem

station verified, and the data contained on the card are transferred electrically into the computer.

Photoelectric card readers differ from wire-brush card readers in two basic ways. In photoelectric card readers, cards are read column by column, and a light source and light-sensing unit are used to detect the punched holes (Fig. 4-4).

**Card-punching Devices**    The IBM 2540 Card Read Punch illustrated in Fig. 4-6 is actually two machines in one. The right half of the machine is a card reader, and the left half of the machine is a card punch unit. At the direction of the computer or other controlling device, it will punch data onto blank cards that are housed in the **punch hopper.** Punch verification is accomplished in the same manner as was read verification in the wire-brush-type card reader. As a blank card passes under the first station containing 80 punching dies, it is punched row by row. The card then moves to the second station, where it is read by 80 wire brushes to check the accuracy of the punching dies. If an error is detected, the machine stops and an error light comes on; otherwise the card is dropped into a stacker below.

The speed of card punch devices ranges from 80 cards per minute to a maximum of about 600 cards per minute. Card punches are generally not equipped for interpreting the punched output, as this process is too costly. If desired, the punched cards produced by the card punch can be processed through an Interpreter.

The card punch is utilized in many business concerns to produce two-part punched card bills or invoices, one part of the invoice to be

FIGURE 4-6

IBM 2540 Card Read/Punch Unit

retained by the customer and the second part to be returned to the company, where it will be fed back into the computer together with the customer's payment record for additional processing.

As we saw in Chapter 3, however, there has been a tendency in recent years to utilize other data-entry devices and media because of the bulkiness, limited storage capacity, and relatively slow input/output processing speeds associated with the punched card. However, the future of punched cards is very promising for the small business concern that cannot justify the cost of some of the newer data-entry techniques.

To verify your understanding of the previous material, turn to page 152 and take Self-Test 4-2.

## PRINTERS

Of all the output devices used in business, the printer is the most common. It provides the user with a permanent visual record of the data output from the computer. It is one of the few output devices capable of producing business reports and documents. Printers have been devel-

FIGURE 4-7
Xerox 9700 High Speed Laser Printer (This device is capable of printing up to 18,000 lines per minute)

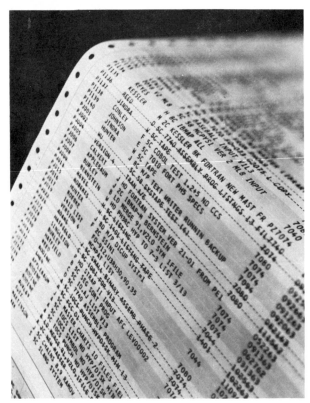

**FIGURE 4-8**
Continuous form paper listing

oped that are capable of printing from 150 lines per minute to 20,000 lines per minute (the speed that can be reached by the Itel 7800 Printer), with each line consisting of up to 150 characters. A quick calculation will reveal this to be a maximum printing speed of approximately 50,000 characters per second.

Printers can print on ordinary paper or on specially prepared forms such as invoices, labels, and other special-purpose forms used in the operation of a business (see Figs. 4-8, 4-9, 4-10, 4-11). Printers even fulfill

it's truly amazing

The IBM 3890 check processor prints unique sequence numbers on as many as 40 checks per second. The numbers are sprayed on the checks, moving through the machine at almost 31 feet per second, using a computer-controlled ink jet that squirts 130,000 drops of ink per second.

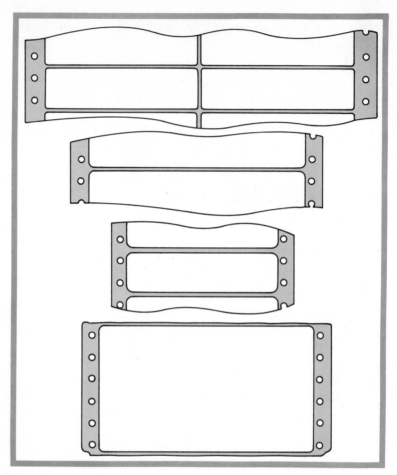

**FIGURE 4-9**
Standard label forms

the needs of business for accuracy and speed in printing on card documents such as checks, earnings statements, premium notices, and bills.

Printers can be subdivided into two broad categories: impact and nonimpact, with impact printers being the most common. An impact printer is one in which printing occurs as a result of the impact of a character form striking against an inked ribbon, causing the ribbon to press an image of the character onto paper. This can be done one character at a time or one line at a time.

**Character-printing Devices**
Typewriters and teletypewriters (Fig. 4-12) print one character at a time at maximum speeds of from 10 to 70 characters per second. Another and faster such printer is the wire-matrix printer. It prints characters made up of a pattern of dots formed by the ends of small wires arranged in a 5 × 7 rectangle. By extending certain wires beyond

Form W-2
U. S. Treasury Department
Internal Revenue Service

**WITHHOLDING STATEMENT—19**
Wages Paid and Income Tax Withheld

ORIGINAL 1
Do Not Lose This Statement

To EMPLOYEE:
CHANGE NAME AND ADDRESS IF NOT CORRECTLY SHOWN

To EMPLOYEE:
You may use the form on the back of this original Form W-2 as your income tax return **under certain conditions**. Before you use it, read the instructions on the back of the attached Employee's Copy.

| Employee to whom paid (name and address) | Marital Status 1 Single, 2 Married | Social Security No. | TOTAL WAGES (BEFORE PAYROLL DEDUCTIONS) PAID IN 1947 | Federal Income Tax Withheld, If Any |
|---|---|---|---|---|
| A D STANTON 2150 SYCAMORE DRIVE TROY PA | 2 | 3 1 2 4 3 5 6 0 1 | 3 5 4 0 6 5 | 2 4 5 0 0 |

DO NOT WRITE IN THIS SPACE—FOR COLLECTOR'S USE ONLY

Tax.............$.................
Credit's..........$.................
Balance due or refund......$.................
Interest on refund.......$.................
Total...........$.................

EMPLOYER BY WHOM PAID (Name, address, and S. S. identification No.)

**GENERAL MANUFACTURING COMPANY**
ENDICOTT, NEW YORK

---

Form W-2
U. S. Treasury Department
Internal Revenue Service

**WITHHOLDING STATEMENT—19**
Wages Paid and Income Tax Withheld

ORIGINAL 1
Do Not Lose This Statement

To EMPLOYEE:
CHANGE NAME AND ADDRESS IF NOT CORRECTLY SHOWN

To EMPLOYEE:
You may use the form on the back of this original Form W-2 as your income tax return **under certain conditions**. Before you use it, read the instructions on the back of the attached Employee's Copy

| Employee to whom paid (name and address) | Marital Status 1 Single, 2 Married | Social Security No. | TOTAL WAGES (BEFORE PAYROLL DEDUCTIONS) PAID IN 1947 | Federal Income Tax Withheld, If Any |
|---|---|---|---|---|
| R L MORRISON 186 ELM ST TROY PA | 1 | 5 0 3 6 5 2 1 9 8 | 3 2 1 0 8 6 | 4 0 5 6 0 |

DO NOT WRITE IN THIS SPACE—FOR COLLECTOR'S USE ONLY

Tax.............$.................
Credits..........$.................
Balance due or refund......$.................
Interest on refund.......$.................
Total...........$.................

EMPLOYER BY WHOM PAID (Name, address, and S. S. identification No.)

**GENERAL MANUFACTURING COMPANY**
ENDICOTT, NEW YORK

---

Form W-2
U. S. Treasury Department
Internal Revenue Service

**WITHHOLDING STATEMENT—19**
Wages Paid and Income Tax Withheld

ORIGINAL 1
Do Not Lose This Statement

To EMPLOYEE:
CHANGE NAME AND ADDRESS IF NOT CORRECTLY SHOWN

To EMPLOYEE:
You may use the form on the back of this original Form W-2 as your income tax return **under certain conditions**. Before you use it, read the instructions on the back of the attached Employee's Copy.

| Employee to whom paid (name and address) | Marital Status 1 Single, 2 Married | Social Security No. | TOTAL WAGES (BEFORE PAYROLL DEDUCTIONS) PAID IN 1947 | Federal Income Tax Withheld, If Any |
|---|---|---|---|---|
| A W RENNINGER 275 WASHINGTON AVE TROY PA | 2 | 5 1 2 4 3 7 1 0 2 | 4 9 2 0 0 0 | 3 6 9 2 0 |

DO NOT WRITE IN THIS SPACE—FOR COLLECTOR'S USE ONLY

Tax.............$.................
Credits..........$.................
Balance due or refund......$.................
Interest on refund.......$.................
Total...........$.................

EMPLOYER BY WHOM PAID (Name, address, and S. S. identification No.)

**GENERAL MANUFACTURING COMPANY**
ENDICOTT, NEW YORK

DETACH BEFORE ISSUING

FIGURE 4-10
W-2 continuous forms

the others, dot patterns can be created which give the appearance of a number, letter, or special character (Fig. 4-13). This character is then pressed against an inked ribbon to print the character.

Figure 4-14 illustrates output produced by Radio Shack's Quick-printer II. This unit prints on special aluminum-finish paper at a rate of up to 32 characters per second and costs less than $300 total. The Quickprinter II utilizes a 5 × 7 element matrix.

**Line-printing Devices**    Impact printers capable of printing a line at a time employ print wheels or a moving chain or drum (Fig. 4-15). The print-wheel printer consists of a series of print wheels, each containing a full complement of numerals and alphabetic symbols in addition to a set of special characters. At the time of printing, all print wheels are correctly

The IBM 3800 printer can print up to 450 lines per second. At that rate it can print a 225 page book in a minute.

FIGURE 4-12

Digital and teletype character-printing devices

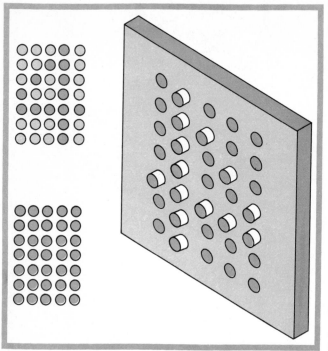

**FIGURE 4-13**

Arrangement of wire-matrix dot patterns for the digit 4

positioned to represent the data to be printed on one line and then impacted simultaneously at a speed of 150 lines per minute.

The chain or drum printer is the fastest and most commonly used of all impact printers. As the print chain (containing five 48-character sections) or drum revolves, each character is printed as it comes into position, (see Figs. 4-16 and 4-17). Up to 150 characters per line can be printed at speeds of up to 2500 lines per minute.

Nonimpact printers, xerographic, electronic, or laser, are the fastest of all printers. The Xerox 9700 Laser printer, for example is capable of printing at over 18,000 lines per minute (see Fig. 4-7 on page 126). Prior to the release of the laser printers, nonimpact printers of this type were not heavily used for several reasons.

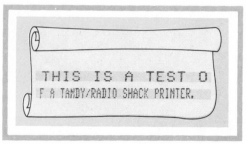

**FIGURE 4-14**

Output of Radio Shack's Quick-printer II (*Courtesy Radio Shack, a division of Tandy Corp.*)

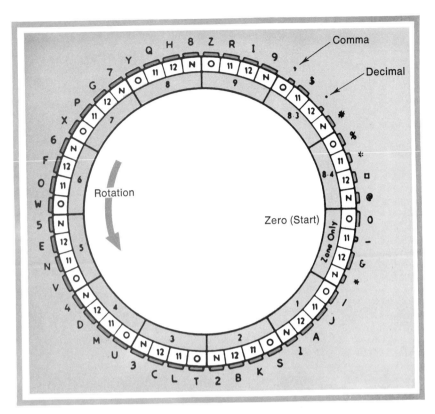

**FIGURE 4-15**
Print wheel

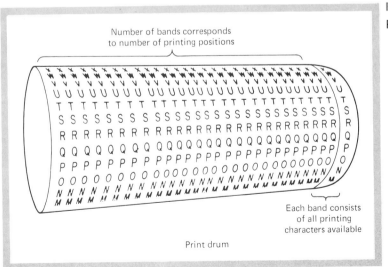

**FIGURE 4-16**
Print drum

Print drum

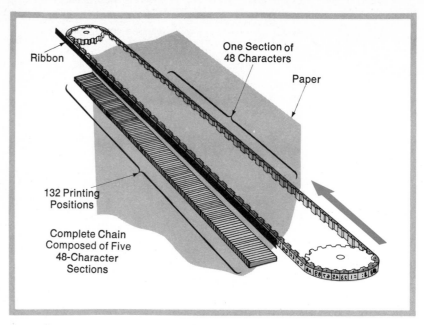

FIGURE 4-17
Print chain

1. Special and more expensive paper is required.
2. Printed output is not as sharp or clear as with impact printers.
3. Only one copy can be printed at a time.
4. Output cannot be easily and satisfactorily copied on office copiers.

With the exception that only one copy may be printed at a time, none of these limitations apply to the newer laser printers.[1] Even this limitation is a minor consideration when one considers their increased printing speed over other available printers.

Laser printers are, however, only practical for companies with extensive hard-copy output requirements. The slower-impact and non-impact-type printers remain the most practical for the small computer user.

To verify your understanding of the previous material, turn to page 152 and take Self-Test 4-3.

## TAPE INPUT/OUTPUT

**Punched-paper-tape Devices**  Punched-paper-tape readers were among the first input devices to be used with a computer. Punched-paper-tape readers, like punched card readers, are available with wire-brush or photoelectric sensing devices. Modern punched-paper-tape readers operate at speeds

[1]The Xerox 9700 Laser Printer shown in Fig. 4-7 is equipped with a built-in copy capability to provide any desired number of copies of the printed output.

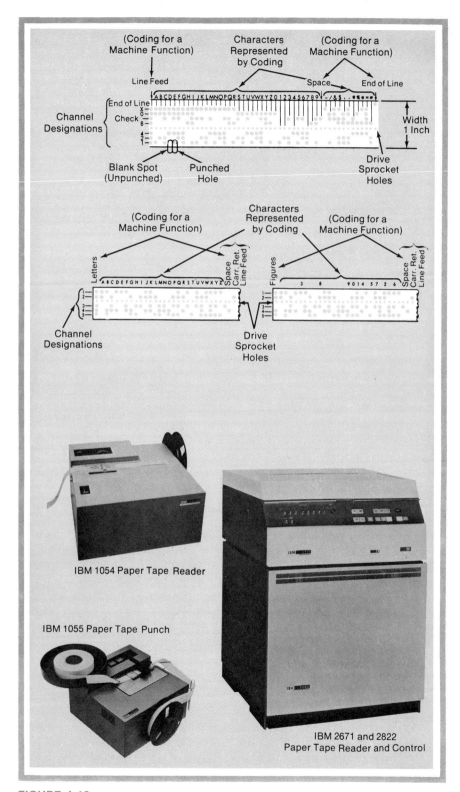

**FIGURE 4-18**

Punched-paper-tape media and devices

135

**FIGURE 4-19**
Teletype device with attached paper tape reader and punch

ranging from 350 to 1000 characters per second, with those utilizing photoelectric reading generally being the fastest.

A paper tape punch can also be used as a computer output device. In this capacity, the paper tape punch accepts data from the computer, converts them to a paper tape code, and punches them onto blank tape. The accuracy of paper tape reading and punching operations is checked in the same manner as it was for the punched card. However, the process of punching paper is relatively slow (15 to 150 characters per second) when compared to the recording speeds of other output media. This, coupled with the facts that punched paper tape is easily torn and that it does not lend itself to additions and deletions, is the principal reason punched paper tape is no longer a widely used output medium.

Currently paper tape is used with cash registers, adding machines, and teletype devices (see Fig. 4-19). Typically, a teletype can be used to prepare a paper tape off-line (that is, while not communicating with the computer). The teletype can then be connected online (in communication with the computer system) and the data previously punched in the paper tape transmitted to the computer at over 1000 characters per second. While connected on-line, the teletype can be used to store programs and data output from the computer for future input.

Teletype devices are also available with a capability of storing data on both punched paper tape and magnetic tape (see Fig. 4-20).

**Magnetic-tape Devices**    Magnetic tape is an input/output recording media commonly used with computers and is principally used for storing large amounts of data, in an ordered sequence (see Fig. 4-21). This is because of its very high speed, mass storage capability, compact size, and relatively low cost of operation. The IBM 3400 series magnetic tape units, for example, are capable of reading or writing in excess of 1 million characters per second. This is extremely fast when compared to a card reader, which is

FIGURE 4-20

Teletype 4210 Magnetic Tape Data Terminal

capable of reading a maximum of approximately 1500 characters per second, or a high-speed impact printer capable of printing a maximum of approximately 6000 characters per second. This, coupled with the fact that as many as 6250 characters can be stored in 1 inch of magnetic tape, has been responsible for the wide use of magnetic tape as an input/output medium.

The magnetic tape device functions as both an input and an output unit and may be operated under the control of the computer (online) or

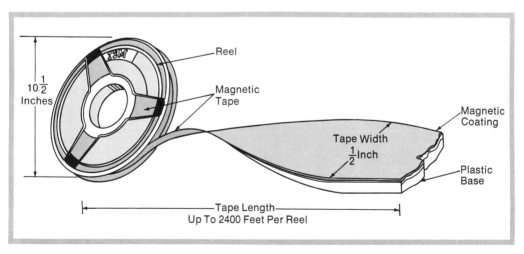

FIGURE 4-21

Magnetic tape reel and composition

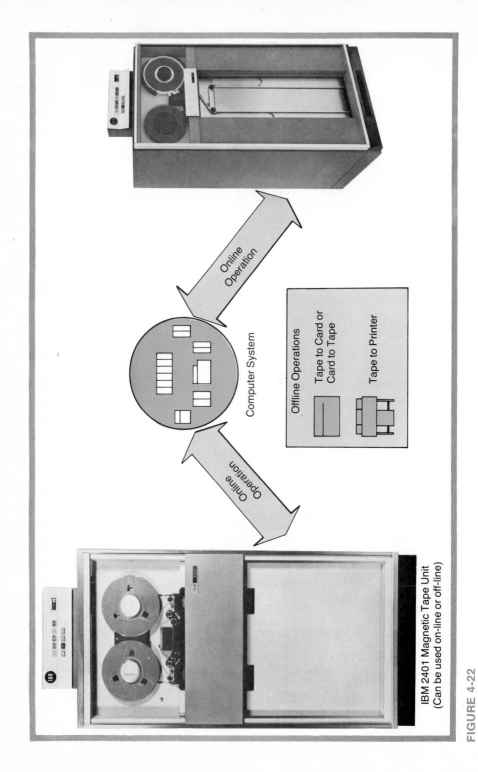

Online Operation

Computer System

Online Operation

Offline Operations

Tape to Card or Card to Tape

Tape to Printer

IBM 2401 Magnetic Tape Unit
(Can be used on-line or off-line)

**FIGURE 4-22**

IBM Magnetic-tape Units with on-line and off-line capabilities

independently (offline) to perform routine functions such as card-to-tape, tape-to-card, and tape-to-printer conversions (see Fig. 4-22).

There are also some limitations or disadvantages associated with the use of magnetic tape. First and foremost is the fact that a magnetic tape may only be processed sequentially. That is, data must be recorded onto and read from a magnetic tape in a predetermined order. For example, if a magnetic tape was created containing a payroll record for each employee in a company in employee number sequence; the payroll records could only be read or accessed in that sequence. Records would have to be accessed in order beginning with the record of the employee with the lowest employee number and ending with the record of the employee with the highest number. In addition, if one or more records are to be added to or deleted from those contained on a magnetic tape, it is usually necessary to recopy the tape completely. For many applications, this limitation offers little or no problem. Other applications that require the ability to access a specific record quickly and directly without the need to access all previous records could not effectively utilize magnetic tape.

"Sssssssh! Be right with you, dear. . . just got to zap one more Klingon."

**Magnetic-tape Cassette Devices**

With the introduction of the microcomputer came the cassette recorder as a principal input/output device. The cassettes used with these devices are virtually the same in appearance and operation as those used in home recording applications (see Fig. 4-23). The principal

FIGURE 4-23

NCR Magnetic Tape Cassette

differences lie in what is recorded on the cassette tape and the uses to which it is put.

A microcomputer equipped with a cassette recorder can be used to store data or programs output from the microcomputer as well as to input data or programs previously stored on cassette. Virtually all microcomputer systems are equipped with a cassette input/output device.

## DIRECT-ACCESS INPUT/OUTPUT DEVICES

In addition to magnetic tape, several other media and devices are used to input and output data from a computer. These devices include the magnetic drum, disk, and mass storage system. Data are stored on these devices in the form of magnetic spots in much the same manner as it was stored on the surface of a magnetic tape. And, as with magnetic tape devices, these devices can be used to input and output data sequentially. But, unlike magnetic tape devices, these devices can also input or output data records directly. That is, records do not have to be recorded on these devices in a predetermined order, nor do they have to

FIGURE 4-24

Magnetic disk and magnetic drum devices

be accessed in any particular order. A single record can be read from or written directly onto any one of these devices without the need to read or write any previous records. This capability has led to these devices being referred to as direct-access storage devices (DASDs).

These devices, together with the manner in which data stored on them are organized and accessed, will be discussed in greater detail in Chapter 6.

To verify your understanding of the previous material, turn to page 154 and take Self-Test 4-4.

## TERMINALS

The terminal is one of the most rapidly growing additions to the family of input/output devices. Terminals are used to facilitate two-way communications with the CPU or with other terminals located from a few feet to thousands of miles apart. Thus, with the aid of a terminal, a user can access a computer physically located a great distance away. Some of the functions that can be performed using terminals are:

1. Message switching: The communication of information input at one terminal to one or more remote terminals. The teletype system used by police departments to communicate with one another represents such a function (see Fig. 4-25).

FIGURE 4-25

Typical police message being broadcast to all terminals

FIGURE 4-26

IBM 1092 programmed keyboard for use in data collecting

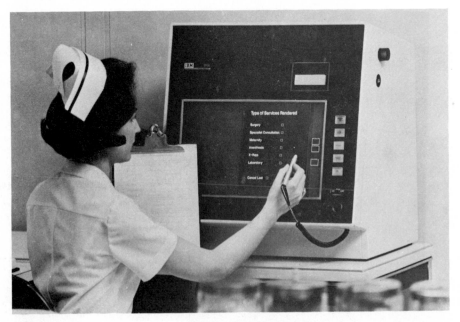

FIGURE 4-27

Patient records being updated using a CRT terminal

2. Data collecting: Data are input to one or more terminals and stored for subsequent processing. This eliminates the need to record the information on a source document, to keypunch the information from the source document, and to read the punched card into the computer (see Fig. 4-26).

3. Inquiry or transaction processing: Data stored in central data files can be accessed from remote terminals for the purpose of updating these files or to determine the answer to inquiries relating to information stored in these files. The system employed by most airlines to maintain and update flight information is an example of such a function. A terminal used in a hospital information system is shown in Fig. 4-27.

4. Remote job processing: Programs can be input from remote terminals directly to the CPU for processing. After execution, the results can be transmitted back to the terminal or to one or more other terminals for output (see Fig. 4-28).

**Keyboard Devices**    There are many types of terminals currently on the market with new ones appearing on the scene daily. One of the least expensive and most common types of terminals is of the keyboard variety, similar in operation to a conventional typewriter, but capable of being used to perform any of the functions listed above. Since data must be keyed into these devices one character at a time, the possibility of error is high and the data transmission rate very low, thus limiting the use of console keyboards to small-volume input and inquiries. With proper communication links, inquiry keyboards can be located at great distances from the central processing unit.

It is often desirable to have many keyboard input units with the capability of simultaneously communicating with the processing unit. In an automated banking operation, for example, each teller may require a separate input unit with file inquiry capabilities. This type of

**FIGURE 4-28**

IBM 3780 Remote Job Processing terminal

operation can be provided with a relatively small and inexpensive computer. For instance, Honeywell's Teller Terminal Series is an on-the-counter, online banking system which can be used to process all teller-assigned bank transactions. This system operates in conjunction with the Honeywell 200, a powerful small-scale computer. The Teller Register contains a modular, removable Teller Register Printer designed to print on the journal tape and customer's record simultaneously. A locked supervisor's panel is also available by which the teller supervisors can utilize the Register. Figure 4-29 illustrates such a terminal in use with an IBM computer system.

**Visual Display Devices**　A visual display terminal might be described as a combination type-writer and television set (Fig. 4-30). By means of the keyboard, a terminal operator can type or key information directly into the computer and receive replies which are pictured on a CRT (cathode ray tube) display tube. The visual display terminal, therefore, serves as both an input device and an output device.

Transmission speeds to and from the computer and the terminal can be as high as 10,000 characters per second. If the terminal is located at a great distance from the computer, data keyed in at the terminal can be transmitted over telephone lines to the computer at speeds of over 200 characters per second.

Visual display stations such as the Honeywell Type 303 Display Station (Fig. 4-30) are capable of displaying typed information, bar graphs,

**FIGURE 4-29**
IBM Teller Register

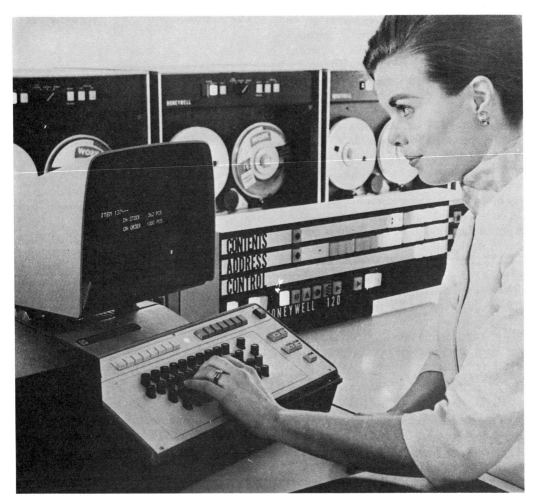

FIGURE 4-30

Honeywell Type 303 Display Station
(*Courtesy Honeywell Corp.*)

tables, and numerous other forms of visual output. Visual display stations are presently in use in airline reservation offices for the purpose of accepting inquiries about available seats on scheduled airline flights and to display the computer's answer in a matter of seconds; in commercial banks to accept inquiries concerning the status of a customer account, possibly displaying the history of that account from several years past up to and including the instant the inquiry is made; and in stock exchange brokerage houses across the country to provide local offices with up-to-the-minute quotations of stock prices useful to customers. This list could go on and on, for as soon as one can jot down an application of a visual display station, another application is created.

**FIGURE 4-31**
IBM 3275 Display Station

The IBM 3275 Display Station (Fig. 4-31) is capable of displaying tables, graphs, charts, circuit diagrams, and alphanumeric data on a square screen containing over 1,000,000 display points. It can be equipped with a **light pen** or penlike device that can be used by the operator to identify a particular point or character displayed on the screen and can be used alone or in conjunction with a keyboard to add, rearrange, or delete information which is displayed on the screen (see Fig. 4-32).

**FIGURE 4-32**
Light pen in use with graphic display terminal

FIGURE 4-33
Kodak 16 mm microfilm cartridge
(*Courtesy Kodak Corp.*)

## OTHER INPUT/OUTPUT DEVICES*

**Microfilm Devices** Computer output microfilm (COM) devices convert computer output to a human-readable form stored on rolls of microfilm or as microfilm frames stored on cards called **microfiche** (Figs. 4-33 and 4-34). At speeds of from 10,000 to over 30,000 lines per minute, COM devices represent one of the fastest of the computer output devices—more than ten times faster than the fastest impact printer. A single roll of micro-

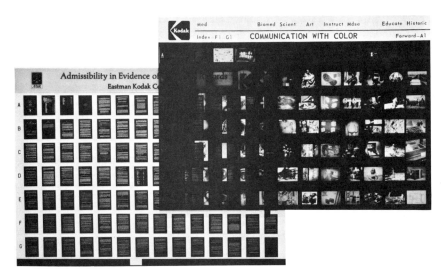

FIGURE 4-34
Kodak microfiche (*Courtesy Kodak Corp.*)

**FIGURE 4-35**

Kodak's Komstar 200 Microimage Processor (*Courtesy Kodak Corp.*)

film can store approximately 2000 frames and costs less than half of the cost to print the same amount of data on plain paper.

The use of COM devices can serve to lessen the normally high demand on computer printers and free them to produce reports for which microfilm is inappropriate. However, because of the high cost of the COM equipment, it is generally only practical for the larger business concerns—those generating approximately 500,000 report pages per month. COM devices are commonly used in libraries, mail order concerns, etc. (Fig. 4-35).

**Audio Devices**     In today's automated world it is even possible to obtain voice response to inquiries made from telephone or similar types of terminals. In the IBM 7770 Audio Response Unit, for example, the audio response is composed from a prerecorded vocabulary (selected from the most frequently used words associated with commercial and industrial applications) contained on an external disk file (Fig. 4-36). As an inquiry is received by the 7770, it is sent to the computer for decoding. The computer then decodes and evaluates the inquiry and, from the prerecorded vocabulary on disk, constructs an appropriate digitally coded voice message which is sent back to the Audio Response Unit. The IBM 7770 then converts this message to a vocal reply which is "spoken" to the inquirer.

Many people feel that computer-generated output sounds terribly "mechanical" or "artificial." This may be true, but its purpose is clarity, not beauty. It can be easily understood. It doesn't mumble, stutter, slur its words together, or cough. These devices cannot reproduce the subtle shading of intonation commonly used in everyday speech. Their main advantage lies in the fact that they can be clearly understood over 99% of the time and that people respond more quickly to the spoken word than to the written word. Areas of application are generally characterized by situations that require responses to inquiries or verification of data entered directly into a computer system. Voice-response devices are typically found in use in banks for reporting bank account balance information or in large business concerns for credit checking and status reporting concerning the company's inventory or the state of completion of work in progress.

One of the strongest impacts made on the future of voice response has come from the manufacturers of mini- and microcomputers. They have brought the pricing and availability of voice-response units down to a point where they are economically feasible for even the smallest business concern. Voice response is no longer an isolated, esoteric discipline but another among the multitude of computer output techniques.

**Plotters**    Figure 4-37 illustrates a relatively small and inexpensive device that can be used to create plots accurate to 0.05 inches from data recorded on magnetic or punched paper tape. This device may also be used to create a magnetic or punched paper tape from a specially prepared plot placed on the device.

Plotters are also available for use in automated drafting with plotting surfaces in excess of 50 square feet and costing as much as a small computer system (Fig. 4-38).

# focus on the field

## Electrostatic Process Speeds Computer Printing

**A group of scientists, who were looking for a way to reduce computer room noise, took more than six years to develop Honeywell's Page Printing System.**

"The system's a marvel, you know. It's really a technical marvel." That's the way physicist-inventor Ron Borelli, Honeywell, described the mainframe computer firm's Page Printing System (PPS), a minicomputer-controlled, high-speed, non-impact page printer. Development of the PPS took more than six years, starting in 1967 when he and a group of scientists set out to pioneer non-impact printing as a way to reduce computer room noise generated by mechanical line printers, and to increase printing speeds limited then by mechanical units to about 1,100 lpm.

### Studied choices

Borelli and his group set 5,000 lpm as "high-speed" printing, and were met with skeptical criticism. But he noted that the first production unit, delivered in 1973 to Lawrence Livermore Labs in California, still churns away at 18,000 lpm, the top-rated speed of the PPS.

After studying the technical choices of magnetic, thermal, electrographic and electrophotographic, the scientific group decided no other technology could match the performance and cost effectiveness of the electrostatic or dielectric process in which toner is attached to electrically charged images formed on specially-coated paper.

Although the electrostatic process is somewhat unique in this type of high-speed printing, the physics technology is based on Faraday's electrostatic theories established in the early 1800s, according to

Honeywell's Ernie Truax, an early member of the PPS development team.

After the initial PPS shipment to Livermore Labs in 1973, additional test systems were shipped over the next two years. Then a separate marketing and dedicated PPS sales force was established in 1976, resulting in more than 250 Page Printing Systems, being sold and installed in user environments since that time, the company said.

Physically, the PPS consists of a non-impact printing mechanism, a minicomputer processor, operator console and work station, magnetic tape handler and output stacker. The PPS can use conventional company forms preprinted on long rolls of the coated dielectric paper, or can print its own forms by using specially engraved cylinders that fit on the unit much like cylinders on a printing press.

Size of forms can vary according to user needs, Honeywell said. Pages can be as small as $3 \times 8 1/2$ in. to as large as $11 \times 14$ in. The PPS automatically cuts the paper roll to the size designated.

Tim McIntyre, director of PPS marketing in Honeywell's central region, said the PPS, with its electrostatic printing process and relatively simple paper transport system, is more reliable, easier to maintain and less costly than complex laser-beam, high-speed page printers offered by other firms.

According to Russell Bishop, PPS product marketing manager at Honeywell, about half of the installed systems are in "other than Honeywell" DP centers, accepting magnetic tape output from IBM, Burroughs and Univac mainframe computers. The PPS operates off-line from a computer and accepts print image magnetic tape in a variety of codes.

Bishop said the PPS is cost-effective and price-competitive with other units that produce up to two million copies or more per month. A typical Honeywell PPS user runs between 1.2 million and 1.5 million pages per month. The unit is available in printing speeds of 8,000, 12,000 and 18,000 lpm or, in other words, 90, 140 or 210 pages per minute. □

DISCUSSION QUESTIONS

1. What advantages do you feel are associated with a Page Printing System that can be operated offline?

2. What do you see as the future for the slower impact printers in light of the available high-speed nonimpact page printers?

No matter whether your application is a general one (such as designing, mapping, or schematics) or more specialized (such as three-dimensional data presentation, structural analysis, contouring, piping isometrics, or business charts), a plotter is available (Fig. 4-39).

To verify your understanding of the previous material, turn to page 154 and take Self-Test 4-5.

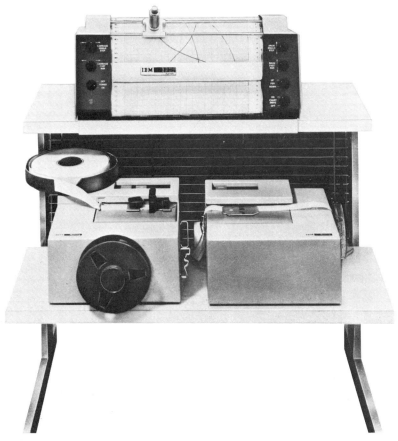

**FIGURE 4-37**

IBM 1627 Plotter off-line with paper tape input

**FIGURE 4-38**

Calcomp's 748 Flat-bed Plotter and 925 Controller

## SELF-TEST 4–1

1. The heavy use of punched card readers and punches as input/output devices can be attributed to _____.
2. The two general types of punched card readers and punches are the _____ type and the _____ type.
3. The principal differences between wire-brush and photoelectric readers or punches are _____.
4. Verification of reading and punching operations is _____.
5. Card punches are generally not equipped for interpreting punched output because _____.

## SELF-TEST 4–2

1. Before data can be stored and used by a computer, they must be converted to _____.
2. The physical input/output unit is called the _____; the means used to record the data is called the _____.

## SELF-TEST 4–3

1. Printers are capable of printing on _____.
2. The two categories of printers are _____ and _____.
3. Impact printers are classified according to the number of characters printed at one time. The resulting classifications are _____.
4. Examples of character printers are _____.

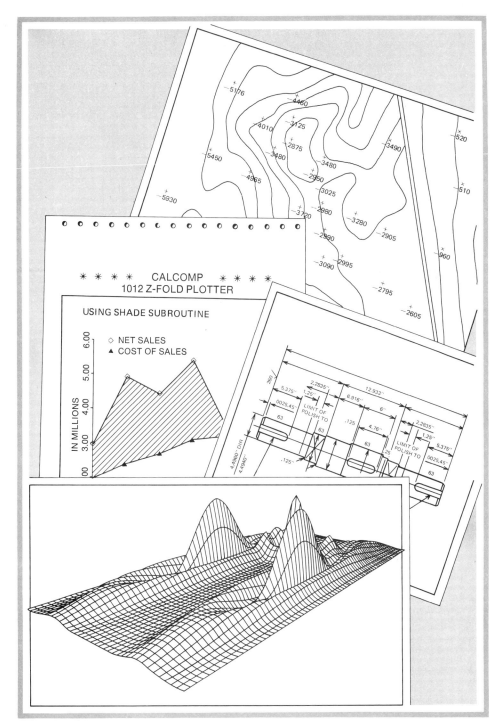

**FIGURE 4-39**

Graphics generated by a Calcomp Plotter

5. Impact line printers contain the character sets on either ———— or ————
   with the ———— printer being one of the fastest and most commonly used
   of all printers.
6. The fastest of all possible printers is the ————.
7. The principal disadvantage of the laser nonimpact printer is that most
   laser printers cannot ————.

## SELF-TEST 4–4

1. The two kinds of tape media currently used are ———— and ————.
2. A ———— device is often used to prepare punched paper tape offline.
3. Accuracy of paper tape reading and punching is verified in a manner similar to the way verification is performed on the reading and punching of
   ————.
4. Magnetic tapes can be read and/or written at speeds in excess of ————
   million characters per second.
5. The ———— is used to verify that the bits representing a character are not
   altered during the reading or processing of the tape.
6. ———— is the highest-speed and most efficient tape medium.
7. Some of the advantages of using magnetic tape are ————.
8. Data are recorded on magnetic tape as magnetized spots called ———— in a
   manner similar to that in which data are recorded on ————.
9. Direct access devices (may, may not) be used sequentially.
10. DASD is a commonly used abbreviation for ————.

## SELF-TEST 4–5

1. The operation of a console keyboard is similar to ————.
2. Console keyboards can be used for ————.
3. The disadvantages of console keyboards are ————.
4. Visual display terminals are capable of displaying ————.
5. CRT (————) terminals are similar in operation to the ordinary home
   ————.
6. Film recorders provide the capability of recording alphanumeric and
   graphic computer output directly onto ————.
7. Devices which facilitate voice communications with a computer system
   are called ————.
8. When an audio device receives a "spoken" request for information, it
   ————.
9. ———— devices are generally only practical for those concerns generating
   500,000 or more report pages per month.
10. Audio output devices (can, cannot) reproduce the intonations commonly
    used in everyday speech.
11. A variety of ———— is available for producing hard-copy graphics.

**4-1**

1. the advantages of the punched card and the fact that these devices can be used with most computers
2. wire-brush; photoelectric
3. the wire-brush reader reads row by row, employing wire brushes, whereas the photoelectric devices read column by column and employ light-sensing solar cells
4. automatic
5. it is too costly

**4-2**

1. machine code
2. device; medium

**4-3**

1. plain paper, special forms, and special card documents
2. impact, nonimpact
3. character printers and line printers
4. typewriters, teletypewriters, and wire-matrix printers
5. print wheels; a print chain or drum; chain or drum
6. laser nonimpact printer
7. print more than one copy at a time

**4-4**

1. punched paper tape; magnetic tape
2. teletype
3. punched cards
4. one
5. check bit
6. Magnetic tape
7. large capacity, high speed, compact size, and low cost of operation
8. bits (binary digits); punched cards
9. may
10. Direct-access storage device

**4-5**

1. a conventional typewriter
2. program testing, program or data alterations, inquiries, and to enter data directly into processor storage
3. high input-error rate and low transmission rate
4. typed data, graphs, tables, etc.
5. cathode ray tube; television tube
6. microfilm or microfiche
7. audio devices
8. decodes and evaluates the inquiry and constructs and sends back an appropriate digitally coded voice message
9. COM
10. cannot
11. plotters

# EXERCISES

_____ 1. Magnetic tape units are available that can read and write over 6000 characters per inch of magnetic tape.

_____ 2. A light pen can be used to input data via a visual display terminal.

_____ 3. Punched paper tape is a commonly used input/output medium.

_____ 4. Magnetic tape is a sequential storage medium.

_____ 5. Printers are subdivided into two broad categories, impact and nonimpact.

_____ 6. Input/output devices are commonly referred to as peripheral devices.

_____ 7. The fastest and most common type of impact printer is the wire matrix printer.

_____ 8. Punched paper tape is a more efficient storage medium than magnetic tape.

_____ 9. COM devices convert computer output to a form stored on rolls of microfilm or microfiche.

_____ 10. The most commonly used type of terminal has a keyboard similar to an ordinary typewriter.

_____ 11. Magnetic tape devices operate at high speeds while providing the user with a low-cost medium for storing information.

_____ 12. Terminals may be used to access computers thousands of miles away.

_____ 13. The card reader/punch is an example of a high-speed input/output device.

_____ 14. Cassettes are principally used with microcomputer systems.

_____ 15. Magnetic tapes are economical in that they are a reusable storage medium.

_____ 16. The printer is the most common of all output devices.

_____ 17. Punch card readers are of two types, wire brush and photoelectric.

_____ 18. A disadvantage of printers is their inability to accept different size forms.

_____ 19. A visual display terminal serves as both an input and an output device.

_____ 20. Voice response units are generally not available with mini and microcomputer systems.

_____ 21. The three most common line printers are the chain, drum, and print wheel printers.

_____ 22. In most card readers and punches the verification of the reading and punching operations is automatic.

_____ 23. Unlike magnetic tape devices, direct-access devices can input and output data directly.

_____ 24. Impact printers are more commonly used than nonimpact printers.

_____ 25. The wire matrix printer is an example of a nonimpact printer.

4–2
Fill-in
Exercises

1. Wire-brush card readers read _____ by _____, whereas photoelectric card readers read _____ by _____.

2. The two tape media currently in use are _____ tape and _____ tape.

3. Typewriters and teletypewriters are classified as _____ printing devices.

4. COM stands for _____.

5. Speeds of input or output devices are generally _____ than internal processing speeds.

6. Magnetic tape is a _____ storage medium.

7. Suitable input/output devices are _____ for an efficient computer system.

8. CRT is an abbreviation for _____.

9. An input or output device connected to and capable of communicating with the computer system is said to be _____.

10. DASD is an abbreviation for _____.

**4–3**
**Problems**

1. Compare impact and nonimpact printers with respect to their similarities and differences. Point out the advantages and disadvantages of each.

2. Discuss the role of the input and output devices in the overall performance of a computer system.

3. Discuss the differences between the two types of card readers.

4. Describe the similarities and differences between punched paper tape and magnetic tape. Point out the advantages and disadvantages of each.

5. Discuss some of the prime considerations that should be given to the types of input/output devices needed in a computer system.

6. Discuss any recent input or output devices about which you have read or heard. What do you believe to be their potential?

7. Determine whether each of the devices or media listed below are used for input only, output only, input/output, or as an offline device.
   a. card readers
   b. card punches
   c. card reader/punch
   d. printer
   e. teletypewriter
   f. paper tape reader
   g. paper tape punch
   h. magnetic tape
   i. visual display devices
   j. COM
   k. audio devices
   l. terminals
   m. plotters
   n. keyboard devices
   o. DASD

**4–4**
**Projects**

1. Visit your computer center and determine what input/output devices are being used. What new devices are being considered?

2. Examine a current computer-related magazine or newspaper and identify three input/output devices not described in the text.

INTRODUCTION

CENTRAL PROCESSING UNIT

CONTROL UNIT

ARITHMETIC/LOGIC UNIT

STORAGE UNIT

Concept of Core or Primary Storage
Noncore Storage
Laser Memory Systems
Magnetic Bubble Memory
Charged-coupled Devices
Virtual Storage Concept

DATA STORAGE CONCEPTS*

Binary
Computer Coding Schemes
BCD
EBCDIC
ASCII

SECONDARY STORAGE

INPUT/OUTPUT COMMUNICATIONS

Overlapped Processing*

MICROCOMPUTERS*

ROM, RAM, PROM and EPROM
TRS-80
APPLE-II

FOCUS ON THE FIELD

SELF-TESTS

EXERCISES

# Processing and Storage Devices

## INTRODUCTION

In this chapter we examine the central processing unit (CPU) of a computer system. We also examine some of the storage devices used with modern computer systems to augment the storage available with the processing unit.

Upon completion of this chapter you should be able to:
- Discuss the three units that make up the CPU
- Discuss the need for and currently available secondary storage devices
- Discuss the concept of virtual storage together with its advantages and disadvantages
- Understand overlapped processing and the need for and purpose of channels, buffers, and control units
- Describe the three principal internal computer coding schemes
- Understand and compare ROM, RAM, PROM, and EPROM
- Define the following terms:

| | |
|---|---|
| Address | Laser memory |
| ALU | Magnetic bubble memory |
| ASCII | Memory |
| Auxiliary storage | Microminiaturized integrated |
| BCD | circuit |
| Binary | MOS chip |
| Bit | Multiplexor channel |
| Buffer | Odd parity |
| Byte | Primary storage |
| Central processing unit (CPU) | PROM |
| Control unit | RAM |
| Core | Register |
| Doubleword | ROM |
| Dump | Secondary storage |
| EBCDIC | Selector channel |
| EPROM | Sensing |
| Fullword | Stored program |
| Halfword | Virtual storage |
| Hex notation | Virtual storage page |

# CENTRAL PROCESSING UNIT

Every computer system contains a unit whose primary purpose is to process data. This unit is the control center of the entire computer system. It accepts data from any of the various input devices, processes these data according to the programmer's instructions, and sends the results to the printer or other output device for recording. This unit can, in a few billionths of a second, add, subtract, multiply, divide, move items of data from one place in its storage area to another, or compare two quantities, to mention but a few of its capabilities. The name of this unit is the **central processing unit,** more commonly referred to as the CPU (see Fig. 5-1). The CPU is composed of three functional subunits:

1. Control unit
2. Arithmetic and logic unit
3. Storage unit[1]

# CONTROL UNIT

The control unit controls and coordinates the activities of a computer system much as the human brain coordinates and controls the activities of the human body. Table 5-1 illustrates how closely the control functions performed by the human brain relate to equivalent functions performed by the control unit of a computer's central processing unit.

It should be noted, however, that the control unit does not input, output, process or store data; rather, it initiates and controls the sequence of these operations. In addition, the control unit communicates

**TABLE 5-1**
Similarity Between Control Functions Performed by the Human Brain and Those Performed by the Control Unit of the CPU

| HUMAN BRAIN CONTROL FUNCTIONS | CONTROL UNIT CONTROL FUNCTIONS |
|---|---|
| Five basic senses | Input devices |
| Storing and retrieving of information from memory | Storing and retrieving of data from the storage unit |
| Ability to solve analytical problems and make decisions | The operations of the arithmetic/logic unit |
| Ability to communicate verbally, in writing, etc. | Output devices |
| Order in which we perform the above operations | Order in which instructions are to be executed |

[1]In many computer systems the storage unit is physically located within and considered part of the CPU, whereas in other computer systems (for example, the IBM 360 and 370 computer systems) it is not.

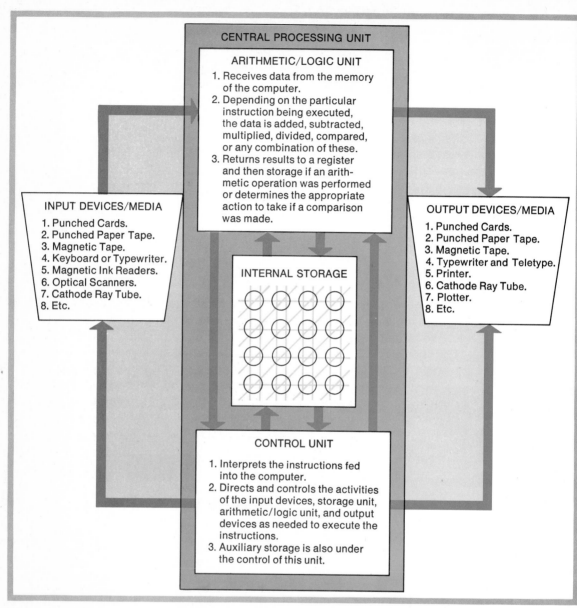

**CENTRAL PROCESSING UNIT**

**ARITHMETIC/LOGIC UNIT**

1. Receives data from the memory of the computer.
2. Depending on the particular instruction being executed, the data is added, subtracted, multiplied, divided, compared, or any combination of these.
3. Returns results to a register and then storage if an arithmetic operation was performed or determines the appropriate action to take if a comparison was made.

**INPUT DEVICES/MEDIA**

1. Punched Cards.
2. Punched Paper Tape.
3. Magnetic Tape.
4. Keyboard or Typewriter.
5. Magnetic Ink Readers.
6. Optical Scanners.
7. Cathode Ray Tube.
8. Etc.

**INTERNAL STORAGE**

**OUTPUT DEVICES/MEDIA**

1. Punched Cards.
2. Punched Paper Tape.
3. Magnetic Tape.
4. Typewriter and Teletype.
5. Printer.
6. Cathode Ray Tube.
7. Plotter.
8. Etc.

**CONTROL UNIT**

1. Interprets the instructions fed into the computer.
2. Directs and controls the activities of the input devices, storage unit, arithmetic/logic unit, and output devices as needed to execute the instructions.
3. Auxiliary storage is also under the control of this unit.

**FIGURE 5-1**

Subunits of Central Processing Unit (CPU)

with input devices in order to begin the transfer of data or instructions into storage and with output devices in order to begin the transfer of results from storage.

In executing an instruction, the control unit performs the following functions:

1. Determines the instruction to be executed
2. Determines the operation to be performed by the instruction
3. Determines what data, if any, are needed and where they are stored
4. Determines where any results are to be stored
5. Determines where the next instruction is located
6. Causes the instruction to be carried out or executed
7. Transfers control to the next instruction

## ARITHMETIC/LOGIC UNIT

The arithmetic/logic unit (ALU) performs the three basic functions of data transfer, arithmetic operations, and decision making. Data transfer involves the moving of data from one location within the computer to another.

Arithmetic operations include addition, subtraction, multiplication, and division. The ALU makes use of temporary storage areas referred to as **registers** when performing these operations. Data to be arithmetically manipulated are taken from storage and placed in registers for processing. Upon completion of an arithmetic operation, the result is transferred from its register to storage freeing the registers for the next arithmetic operation.

Decision making is the ability to compare two quantities or numbers to determine, for example, if the first quantity is smaller than, equal to, or greater than the second quantity and respond by taking an appropriate action based on the result of the comparison. It is also possible to test for the existence of a condition encountered during the processing of a particular application and to alter the sequence of instructions accordingly.

Most small to medium-sized computer systems have one arithmetic/logic unit. However, in some of the larger "super" computer systems, the ALU is actually made up of several units under the direction of a high-capacity control unit. This increases the capability of the CPU tremendously but is very expensive.

To verify your understanding of the previous material, turn to page 192 and take Self-Test 5-1.

## STORAGE UNIT

The computer primary storage unit, or **memory** as it is sometimes called, is as essential to the operations of a computer as your memory is to you in the performance of common, everyday activities. It must have the capacity to store large quantities of data, any item of which must be capable of being accessed from its location in storage and moved to a location elsewhere in the computer, such as to the arithmetic unit, in millionths or billionths of a second. It is noteworthy that when an item of data is stored in a given location, it replaces the previous contents of that location, but when an item of data is "moved" from one location in storage to another, the item of data is not physically removed from its initial storage location. What does happen is that a copy or image of the data is transferred to where it is needed. This process is analogous to the one which takes place when you request information from your memory. For example, if you wish to write down your telephone number for a friend, you simply transfer an image of the number from your memory to the paper, while the telephone number in your memory remains unaltered. Thus, once an item of data has been stored, it can be used over and over again until no longer needed or until replaced by a new data item.

"He has the mind of a computer—one that's slipped a disc."

In addition to storing data, the storage unit of the CPU is also used to store computer instructions. The instructions necessary to direct the computer in the solution of a given problem are fed into the computer via any of a number of input devices and are stored in the computer's memory or storage unit. Once the set of instructions necessary to solve the problem has been stored, the instructions may be recalled in sequence, together with the data they require, and executed. This stored set of instructions is referred to as a **stored program.** We perform a similar process virtually every day. For example, when we go to work or school, we recall and execute a sequence of instructions that gets us to our destination. This set of instructions constitutes a stored program, and it is a very complex one at that. For example, before we get on the main highway we must determine whether or not we have sufficient fuel for the round trip. If we have enough fuel, we can consider taking the most direct route. If we do not have sufficient fuel for the round trip, we must determine whether or not there is sufficient fuel for a one-way trip. If we have sufficient fuel for a one-way trip, we must decide whether to stop for fuel on the way to or on the way back from our destination. If we do not have fuel for a one-way trip, we must immediately fuel up. This analysis could go on and on to consider such items as how much money we have with us, the best route for the particular day and time, whether or not we have to pick up riders, road conditions and traffic bulletins, and where we will park.

If we were to list the instructions involved in handling all these contingencies, we could fill a notebook. Programs stored in a computer can be equally long if not longer. Thus, an important consideration when selecting a computer system must be whether it has a primary storage capacity sufficient for the type of programs it will be required to solve.

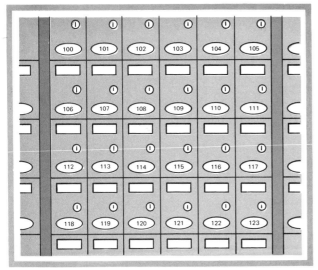

FIGURE 5-2
Post office mail boxes

Computer primary storage consists of a large number of cells, each with a fixed capacity for storing data, each with a unique location and **address.** The addresses of these cells can be likened to post office boxes in that each box has a unique location and address (Fig. 5-2). Each storage cell is capable of holding a specific unit of data and, depending on the system, the unit of data may be a fixed number of digits, characters, words, or even an entire record.

**Concept of Core or Primary Storage**

Early computer memories utilized vacuum tubes similar to those used in early radio and television sets. Subsequently, these tubes were replaced by tiny iron rings called **ferrite cores** for use in computer memories (Fig. 5-3).

Core storage consists of thousands of these tiny doughnut-shaped metal rings in which the direction of magnetization indicates a 1 or a 0 (see Fig. 5-4).

it's truly amazing

A nanosecond is to a second what a second is to 30 years. And a picosecond is to a second what a second is to 31,710 years.

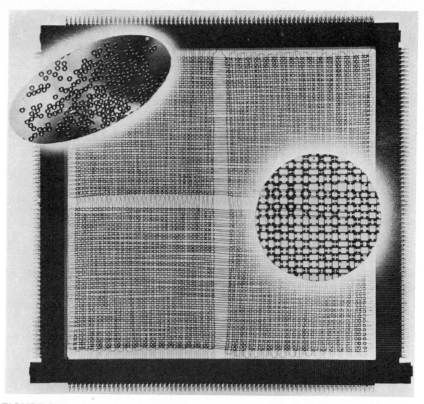

**FIGURE 5-3**

A series of ferrite cores strung together for use in a computer's memory

Each tiny core measures only a few thousandths of an inch in diameter and is capable of holding one *bi*nary digi*t* or **bit** of data. Once magnetized to either a 0 or a 1, the core will remain in this state indefinitely, unless deliberately changed (Figs. 5-5 and 5-6). As shown in Fig. 5-7, these cores are threaded at the intersections of a network of wires forming a grid system. With such a grid system, a single core can be

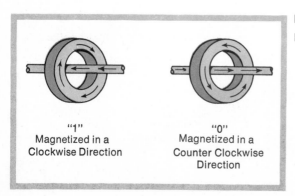

"1"
Magnetized in a
Clockwise Direction

"0"
Magnetized in a
Counter Clockwise
Direction

**FIGURE 5-4**

Magnetic states of a ferrite core

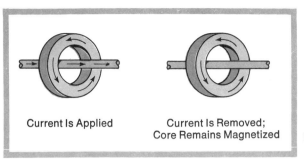

Current Is Applied

Current Is Removed;
Core Remains Magnetized

**FIGURE 5-5**
Magnetizing a core

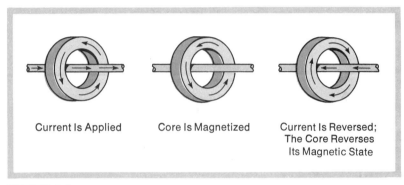

Current Is Applied

Core Is Magnetized

Current Is Reversed;
The Core Reverses
Its Magnetic State

**FIGURE 5-6**
Reversing a core

uniquely accessed by one vertical and one horizontal wire. For example, only one core in Fig. 5-7 can be identified by G-e. That is, only one core is on both the G-wire and the e-wire.

The reading or writing of information onto a given core requires current on both the horizontal and the vertical wires passing through the core. That is, placing current on the e-wire alone would not be sufficient to affect any core on that wire. But, if current were simultaneously applied to the G-wire, only one core would be affected, as only one core would have current passing through it vertically and horizontally.

An additional set of wires are passed through each core so that the state of the core (1 or 0) can be read. This reading process is called **sensing** a core.

Since the core is stationary, and since current travels along these grid wires at the speed of light (186,000 miles/second), the reading or writing of a single core takes place extremely rapidly.

Figure 5-8 illustrates how the character "A" could be represented by a particular combination of 1's and 0's within the core or memory of the computer. From Fig. 5-8 you can see that one character consists of one core from each of the seven core planes. Taken together, they represent the letter "A." To determine this, the computer must read each of seven distinct cores and determine whether they are set to 0 or 1. Similarly, to

Processing and Storage Devices          **167**

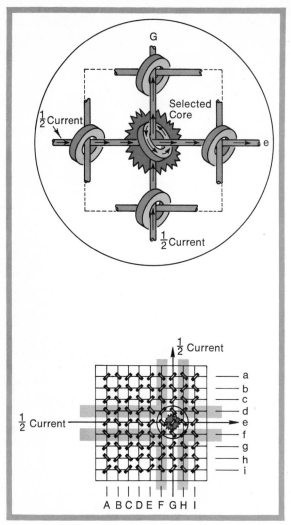

**FIGURE 5-7**
Selecting and magnetizing a core

store any character in memory, the computer must set each of seven cores, one per core plane or grid, appropriately to a 1 or to a 0. In modern computers, this operation can be completed in billionths of a second.

Few of the new generation of computers still employ the magnetic core in primary storage.[2] Most computers currently being manufactured employ more sophisticated components such as the ones described below.

[2]In the late 1970s, some computers manufactured by Digital Equipment Corp., for example, utilized the magnetic core.

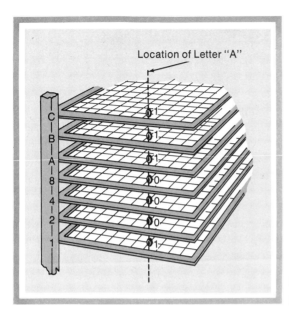

Location of Letter "A"

FIGURE 5-8

Character "A" represented in core storage

**Noncore Storage**

MOS Memory. A new innovation in computer design in the early 1970s was the integration of the faster **MOS (metal-oxide-semiconductor)** microminiaturized integrated circuit memory with the slightly slower ferrite core memory. Figure 5-9 illustrates two MOS chips mounted on a ceramic base. Each chip has monolithic integrated circuits etched on it to form over 250 memory circuits. This system was first employed in the IBM 370 Series computer.

FIGURE 5-9

MOS miniaturized integrated circuit

More recently IBM has succeeded in storing 8000 bits (binary digits) or approximately 1000 characters on one chip measuring only 0.001 inches square.

MOS chips are used in most mini- and microcomputer system memories.

**Laser Memory Systems**

While MOS memories were being developed and produced, research was directed toward the **laser memory system,** which employs the polarization of light in the same manner as the magnetic core employs magnetic polarization. Laser memory experiments resulted in a holographic memory system employing a special optical plate to disperse laser beams as they pass through it (Fig. 5-10). In the early 1970s an actual holographic memory was developed which could store over 2500 characters on a circular space only one half millimeter in diameter. The National Aeronautics and Space Administration (NASA) subsequently succeeded in developing a one-million-bit all-optical laser memory with access times ten times faster than existing devices and with a total CPU storage capacity in the billions of characters. **Access time** is the time required to locate an item of data in storage and transfer it to the processor.

**Magnetic Bubble Memory**

Magnetic bubbles are tiny areas approximately one ten-thousandth of an inch in diameter of reversed magnetism that form when an external magnetic field is applied to certain materials.

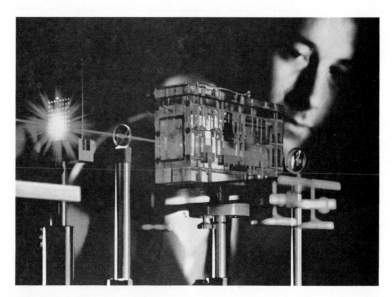

FIGURE 5-10

IBM scientist developing the laser for use in computers (*Courtesy International Business Machines Corp.*)

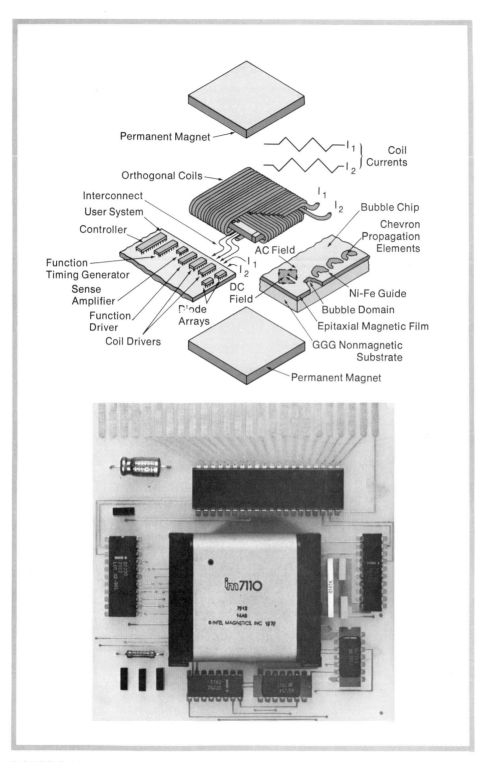

FIGURE 5-11

Bubble memory device and associated circuitry

In the late 1970s a new technique was developed by IBM for tailoring the properties of magnetic bubble materials by laser annealing, followed by a rapid cooling to freeze in the annealed structure.

This concept resulted in the newest and most sophisticated computer memory yet devised. A single chip approximately the size of a quarter, developed by the Intel Magnetics Corp. in the late 1970s, was capable of storing 1 million binary digits (Fig. 5-11).

From an economic point of view alone, it is expected that the 1980s will see widespread use of magnetic bubble memories in computers (Fig. 5-12).

**Charged-coupled Devices**   One of the newest devices to be considered for use in computer primary storage units is the **charged-coupled device.** A charged-coupled device (CCD) is a semiconductor that utilizes the electrons within a metal oxide semiconductor (MOS) crystal to store data. Production of these devices has been slow in coming, as it is an involved process. It is anticipated that when these devices become more readily available, they will be used in conjunction with magnetic bubble memories. As the CCDs have faster access times than magnetic bubble memo-

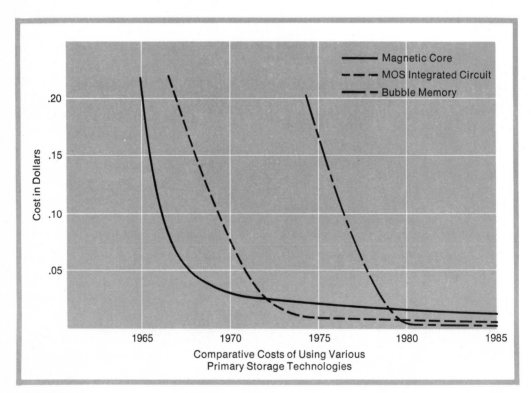

FIGURE 5-12

Comparative costs for computer storage devices

ries, they are expected to be used principally as secondary storage or possibly as a means of extending existing magnetic bubble memory.

**Virtual Storage Concept**     Later models of the System 370 were available with what IBM called **virtual storage.** This revolutionary storage technique allowed the user of the computer system to process programs requiring more total storage capacity than was physically present in the storage unit of the CPU. Simply stated, virtual storage is a storage management technique that allows one to view the computer system as one containing many times the primary storage capacity that is physically contained in the CPU. For example, a program previously requiring 100,000 storage locations could now be processed on a virtual storage computer containing many fewer actual storage locations. This is accomplished by breaking the program up into segments of a certain size which are stored outside the CPU. As needed, these segments or groups of instructions are called into the storage area of the CPU and are executed. The remaining segments of the program are stored outside the CPU on a direct-access storage device until needed. When needed, a segment(s) is brought into the CPU replacing a previous segment(s) no longer being used. This process is very similar to that which takes place when we read a book. We begin by reading the first page. When we have finished the first page, we replace it with the next page by turning the page. This process can be continued for as long as we like. If at any time it becomes necessary to refer back or ahead to a particular page, we can access it by simply turning to that page number. Throughout this process we had access to only one page of the book at a time. The factor which most affected our reading rate was the number of times we had to turn to a new page. So it is with virtual storage. The more movement of sections of coding, or **pages** as IBM calls them, that there is in and out of the CPU, the more time-consuming the process will be. The circuitry and control programs provided with virtual storage computer systems are designed to reduce this movement to a minimum.

it's truly amazing

In one second an IBM 3033 Attached Processor can execute 5.5 million instructions. In that time, the 3033 AP could receive inquiries from 180 airline reservation clerks, check on whether seats are available, and start information back to the clerks. In some 20 years the work computers can do in a second has increased almost 27 times, and the cost per instruction has declined to 1/37th of what it was.

As a result of this virtual storage capability, the primary storage requirements of a program are greatly diminished, since it is now necessary to maintain only sections or pages of the program in the CPU at any one time. Thus, where a program might have once required all of a computer's primary storage capacity, now it will only require a small portion of the primary storage available with a virtual storage computer system. The remainder of the primary storage can be used to process other programs concurrently in a similar manner.

*To verify your understanding of the previous material, turn to page 193 and take Self-Test 5-2.*

## DATA STORAGE CONCEPTS*

We have learned that computers can accept data from many devices and in many forms. In Chapter 3, for example, we learned that a computer can accept data from punched cards, magnetic tape, terminals, character readers, and even the human voice.

The processing of these data once input to the computer represents a different story. The form in which data must be represented before they can be processed by computer is very specific. Let us now examine how data must be represented so that they can be processed.

**Binary**  Basically, all data contained in primary storage must be in the form of 1's and 0's, or in **binary** form. The binary numbering system is a place-value or positional numbering system much like our decimal

"Rats! A bacterium just ate the new micro-mini circuit."

numbering system. The difference is that the binary system employs the binary digits (or bits) 0 and 1 as opposed to the familiar decimal digits 0 through 9, and the weights associated with the digits in a binary number are multiples of 2 as opposed to multiples of 10 (units, tens, hundreds, thousands, etc.) in a decimal number.

It is not essential at this point that you be capable of thinking in binary or that you develop dexterity in converting to and from decimal and binary. Should you decide to choose a career in a computer-related field, however, you will need to work with binary data. What is important at this point is that you should understand why the binary system is employed in computers. A more detailed discussion of numbering systems can be found in Appendix B.

Since the result of one or more calculations is independent of the numbering system employed, the choice of a computer numbering system comes down to deciding which system can be made to operate most rapidly and efficiently. Naturally, the decimal numbering system is more convenient for us, since we are most familiar with it. It also appears that the decimal system is more efficient, since it generally requires fewer decimal digits than binary digits to represent a physical quantity of objects. For example, nine objects are represented in decimal as 9, whereas in the binary system the representation would be 1001.

Why, then, with these advantages of the decimal system, do computers utilize the binary number system? The answer is a simple one. Designers and engineers can design or develop computers that are faster and much less expensive utilizing the binary number system than if they were to utilize the decimal number system in an otherwise comparable computer. Computer designers have also realized that utilizing the binary system will result in a computer which is significantly more reliable (many fewer components) and significantly smaller.

We have learned of magnetic bubble memory devices that can store 1,000,000 bits on a chip the size of a quarter. We have also learned of the CRAY 1 "supercomputer" system, which is capable of performing 100 million calculations per second on quantities stored in the binary system. Certainly there can be little doubt that the use of the binary numbering system is both extremely fast and extremely efficient.

**Computer Coding Schemes**
Several binary coding schemes are employed in modern computer systems to represent both numerical and nonnumerical data. Foremost among these schemes are the BCD (*B*inary *C*oded *D*ecimal), EBCDIC (*E*xtended *B*inary *C*oded *D*ecimal *I*nterchange *C*ode), and the ASCII (*A*merican *S*tandard *C*ode for *I*nformation *I*nterchange) coding schemes.

Let us now examine these coding schemes and their relationship to the familiar Hollerith code.

BCD. The BCD or Binary Coded Decimal coding scheme is one of the simplest of all computer coding schemes. The BCD scheme is a character or zoned decimal scheme, as is the Hollerith coding scheme. That is, data are represented in the BCD scheme on a character-by-character basis with each character consisting of a zone portion and a decimal portion. You may recall that the character A in Hollerith code consisted of a zone portion represented by a 12 punch and a digit portion represented by a 1 punch. An A is similarly represented in the BCD coding scheme. The difference, however, lies in how the zone and decimal portions are represented.

Since a computer can only store bits, or 0's and 1's, the zone and decimal portions of a character must consist of strings or combinations of 0's and 1's. Tables 5-2 and 5-3 illustrate the combinations of 0's and 1's that are equivalent to the corresponding Hollerith zone and decimal codes. For example, from Table 5-2 we can see that the Hollerith 12

**TABLE 5-2**
Table of Zone Equivalences

| BINARY CODED DECIMAL | HOLLERITH |
| --- | --- |
| 11 | 12 zone |
| 10 | 11 zone |
| 01 | 0 zone |
| 00 | No zone |

punch is equivalent to the combination of bits 11 in BCD. From Table 5-3 we can ascertain that a Hollerith 1 punch is equivalent to the combination of bits 0001. Thus, the character A in BCD would be represented by the string of bits 110001, where 11 is the zone portion and 0001 is the numeric portion. For easy reference, the BCD zone bits are referred to as the B and A bits, from left to right, and the BCD numeric bits are referred to as the 8, 4, 2, and 1 bits, from left to right. Thus, any character can be represented in BCD by the appropriate combination of B, A, 8, 4, 2, and 1 bits. Employing these names, the character A described above as 110001, would appear as BA1 or BA      1.

To reinforce your understanding of the above, verify the BCD representation of the characters M7Z given below using Tables 5-2 and 5-3.

|  | B | A | 8 | 4 | 2 | 1 |
| --- | --- | --- | --- | --- | --- | --- |
| M | 1 | 0 | 0 | 1 | 0 | 0 |
| 7 | 0 | 0 | 0 | 1 | 1 | 1 |
| Z | 0 | 1 | 1 | 0 | 0 | 1 |

**TABLE 5-3**
Table of Digit-punch Equivalences

| BINARY CODED DECIMAL | | | | |
| --- | --- | --- | --- | --- |
| 8 | 4 | 2 | 1 | HOLLERITH |
| 0 | 0 | 0 | 1 | 1 |
| 0 | 0 | 1 | 0 | 2 |
| 0 | 0 | 1 | 1 | 3 |
| 0 | 1 | 0 | 0 | 4 |
| 0 | 1 | 0 | 1 | 5 |
| 0 | 1 | 1 | 0 | 6 |
| 0 | 1 | 1 | 1 | 7 |
| 1 | 0 | 0 | 0 | 8 |
| 1 | 0 | 0 | 1 | 9 |
| 1 | 0 | 1 | 0 | 0 |

In addition to the six bits required to represent any character, one additional bit is provided by the computer and is called the C bit (parity or check bit). Its only purpose is for internal checking by the computer. It is possible, although very unlikely, that the computer could introduce a coding discrepancy while attempting to read, write, or process a character. To prevent such an occurrence going unnoticed, a check or C bit is assigned to each character within the machine in such a way as to make the total number of 1's in the character equal to an even or odd number, depending on the machine. For simplicity we will limit our discussion to machines in which the total number of 1's in each character is odd. The practice of maintaining an odd number of 1's at all times is called **odd parity.** To further clarify this principle, let us consider the BCD representation of the decimal digit 6:

| Bit names | B | A | 8 | 4 | 2 | 1 |
|---|---|---|---|---|---|---|
| BCD code | 0 | 0 | 0 | 1 | 1 | 0 |

You will notice that there are two 1's, or an even number of 1's, in the BCD representation. The computer would, therefore, assign a 1 to the C bit, making the total number of 1's odd, and produce the following BCD representation of the decimal digit 6:

| Bit names | C | B | A | 8 | 4 | 2 | 1 | |
|---|---|---|---|---|---|---|---|---|
| BCD code | 1 | 0 | 0 | 0 | 1 | 1 | 0 | (odd parity) |

To see how the maintaining of an odd parity within each character in the computer allows the computer to detect when a single bit has been lost or gained accidentally, let us consider two cases.

Case 1. Let us assume that somehow the computer misread the character 6 as follows:

| C | B | A | 8 | 4 | 2 | 1 | |
|---|---|---|---|---|---|---|---|
| 1 | 0 | 0 | 0 | 1 | 0 | 0 | (a 1 bit was lost) |

This condition would be immediately sensed by the computer's control unit, since the parity check, or total number of 1's in this character, is even. And this is an invalid condition for any legitimate BCD character. The operator would then be signaled by the computer.

Case 2. Let us assume that somehow the computer misread the character 6 as follows:

| C | B | A | 8 | 4 | 2 | 1 | |
|---|---|---|---|---|---|---|---|
| 1 | 0 | 0 | 0 | 1 | 1 | 1 | (a 1 bit was added) |

As in case 1, this condition would also be easily detected by the computer. The presence of an even-parity character would then be immediately reported to the computer operator.

Therefore, by adding one additional bit, the C bit, to the bit configuration of each character, the computer will be able to determine, quickly and easily, whether or not a 1 bit has been gained or lost.

## NUMERIC CHARACTERS

| CHARACTER | CODE |
|---|---|
| 0 | C 8 2 |
| 1 | 1 |
| 2 | 2 |
| 3 | C 2 1 |
| 4 | 4 |
| 5 | C 4 1 |
| 6 | C 4 2 |
| 7 | 4 2 1 |
| 8 | 8 |
| 9 | C 8 1 |

## ALPHABETIC CHARACTERS

| CHARACTER | CODE |
|---|---|
| A | B A 1 |
| B | B A 2 |
| C | C B A 2 1 |
| D | B A 4 |
| E | C B A 4 1 |
| F | C B A 4 2 |
| G | B A 4 2 1 |
| H | B A 8 |
| I | C B A 8 1 |
| J (Minus Zero) | B 8 2 |
| K | C B 1 |
| L | C B 2 |
| M | B 2 1 |
| N | C B 4 |
| O | B 4 1 |
| P | C B 4 2 1 |
| Q | C B 8 |
| R Record Mark | B 8 1 |
| S | C A 2 |
| T | A 2 |
| U | C A 4 |
| V | A 4 1 |
| W | A 4 2 |
| X | C A 4 2 1 |
| Y | A 8 |
| Z | A 8 1 |

## SPECIAL CHARACTERS

| CHARACTER | CODE |
|---|---|
| BLANK | C |
| . | B A 8 2 1 |
| □ Left Parenthesis (Special Character) | C B A 8 4 |
| < Less Than (Special Character) | B A 8 4 1 |
| ‡ Group Mark (Note 1) | B A 8 4 2 |
| & | C B A 8 4 2 1 |
| $ | C B A |
| * | C B 8 2 1 |
| ) Right Parenthesis (Special Char.) | C B 8 4 |
| ; Semicolon (Special Character) | C B 8 4 2 |
| Delta (Made Change) | B 8 4 2 1 |
| - | B |
| / | C A 1 |
| , | C A 8 2 1 |
| % Word Separator | A 8 4 |
| = | C A 8 4 1 |
| ' Apostrophe (Special Character) | C A 8 4 2 |
| " Tape Segment Mark | A 8 4 2 1 |
| ¢ Cent (Special Character Note 2) | A |
| # | 8 2 1 |
| @ | C 8 4 |
| : Colon (Special Character) | 8 4 1 |
| > Greater Than (Special Character) | 8 4 2 |
| √ Tape Mark | C 8 4 2 1 |
| ? (Plus Zero) | C B A 8 2 |

**FIGURE 5-13**

Standard Binary Coded Decimal (BCD) Code

However, if two 1 bits are lost, or two 1 bits are gained, or if one 1 bit is lost and one 1 bit is gained, for example, the computer would be incapable of detecting this situation. The reason for this is simply that the parity would have remained odd. But computer designers have determined that the likelihood of an error occurring in more than one bit of a character at the same time is so small that the additional complex design that would be required to detect such a condition is not practical.

A complete list of the seven-bit BCD codes for representing the 10 decimal digits, the 26 letters of the alphabet, and selected special characters is given in Fig. 5-13.

**FIGURE 5-14**

Standard Extended Binary Decimal Interchange Code (EBCDIC) for selected characters

| Character | Hollerith card code | EBCDIC Binary | Hexa-decimal |
|---|---|---|---|
| 0 | 0 | 1111 0000 | F0 |
| 1 | 1 | 1111 0001 | F1 |
| 2 | 2 | 1111 0010 | F2 |
| 3 | 3 | 1111 0011 | F3 |
| 4 | 4 | 1111 0100 | F4 |
| 5 | 5 | 1111 0101 | F5 |
| 6 | 6 | 1111 0110 | F6 |
| 7 | 7 | 1111 0111 | F7 |
| 8 | 8 | 1111 1000 | F8 |
| 9 | 9 | 1111 1001 | F9 |
| A | 12-1 | 1100 0001 | C1 |
| B | 12-2 | 1100 0010 | C2 |
| C | 12-3 | 1100 0011 | C3 |
| D | 12-4 | 1100 0100 | C4 |
| E | 12-5 | 1100 0101 | C5 |
| F | 12-6 | 1100 0110 | C6 |
| G | 12-7 | 1100 0111 | C7 |
| H | 12-8 | 1100 1000 | C8 |
| I | 12-9 | 1100 1001 | C9 |
| J | 11-1 | 1101 0001 | D1 |
| K | 11-2 | 1101 0010 | D2 |
| L | 11-3 | 1101 0011 | D3 |
| M | 11-4 | 1101 0100 | D4 |
| N | 11-5 | 1101 0101 | D5 |
| O | 11-6 | 1101 0110 | D6 |
| P | 11-7 | 1101 0111 | D7 |
| Q | 11-8 | 1101 1000 | D8 |
| R | 11-9 | 1101 1001 | D9 |
| S | 0-2 | 1110 0010 | E2 |
| T | 0-3 | 1110 0011 | E3 |
| U | 0-4 | 1110 0100 | E4 |
| V | 0-5 | 1110 0101 | E5 |
| W | 0-6 | 1110 0110 | E6 |
| X | 0-7 | 1110 0111 | E7 |
| Y | 0-8 | 1110 1000 | E8 |
| Z | 0-9 | 1110 1001 | E9 |

A careful examination of the possible BCD character representation will show that there are a total of 64 BCD characters. Many computer applications require additional characters, for example, the lower-case letters of the alphabet. For this and other reasons, IBM devised and introduced a coding scheme consisting of 256 characters (Fig. 5-14).

EBCDIC. The EBCDIC, or Extended Binary Coded Decimal Interchange Code, is similar to the BCD and Hollerith codes in that it is a character or zoned-decimal scheme. As a matter of fact, the EBCDIC representation for the numeric portion of most characters is almost identical to the BCD representation.[3] Thus the BCD and EBCDIC coding schemes differ only with respect to their zone representations. A comparison of BCD and EBCDIC zone representations is given in Table 5-4.

To reinforce our understanding of EBCDIC, let us consider the representation of the three characters M7Z with the aid of Tables 5-3 and 5-4.

|  | ZONE | | | | NUMERIC | | | |
|---|---|---|---|---|---|---|---|---|
| M | 1 | 1 | 0 | 1 | 0 | 1 | 0 | 0 |
| 7 | 1 | 1 | 1 | 1 | 0 | 1 | 1 | 1 |
| Z | 1 | 1 | 1 | 0 | 1 | 0 | 0 | 1 |

As you can see, each of the above characters was represented in EBCDIC in eight bits. This is true for all characters represented in EBCDIC. This unit of eight bits is referred to as a **byte.** Two bytes is referred to as a **halfword,** four bytes as a **word** or **fullword,** and eight bytes as a **doubleword** (see Fig. 5-15). Typically, the sizes of computer memories are specified in words or bytes.

When it becomes necessary for a programmer to verify that an item of data has been correctly stored, the programmer can call for a **dump,**

**TABLE 5-4**
Zone-bit Combinations

| BCD | EBCDIC |
|---|---|
| 11 | 1100 |
| 10 | 1101 |
| 01 | 1110 |
| 00 | 1111 |

[3]The EBCDIC representation of the digit zero differs from the BCD representation of the digit zero. Thus any characters having a zero numeric portion will differ in this respect.

or a printout of a specific area of the computer's memory. When this request occurs, the computer dumps its memory in a shorthand form of EBCDIC referred to as **hex notation.** The hex notations of the digits and letters of the alphabet are shown in Fig. 5-14. If the reader desires to understand the relationship between hex notation and EBCDIC, the hexadecimal section of Appendix B should be reviewed.

As with BCD character representation, EBCDIC characters also employ parity bits to detect gained or lost bits during the transmitting or processing of data.

ASCII. Since EBCDIC was introduced by IBM and not universally accepted by computer manufacturers, the American National Standards Institute sponsored the development of an eight-bit code known as ASCII (American Standard Code for Information Interchange). This code was developed by a number of computer manufacturers and was

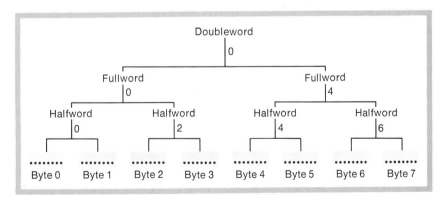

**FIGURE 5-15**

Relationship between byte, halfword, fullword, and doubleword intended to provide a computer user with a coding scheme which would be acceptable on virtually all makes and models of computers. The principal difference between ASCII and EBCDIC is in the specific combinations of eight bits used to represent the various characters. The eight-bit ASCII code is shown in Figure 5-16.

To verify your understanding of the previous material, turn to page 193 and take Self-Test 5-3.

| CHARACTER | EBCDIC<br>BIT REPRESENTATION | ASCII<br>BIT REPRESENTATION |
|-----------|------------------------------|------------------------------|
| 0 | 1111 0000 | 0101 0000 |
| 1 | 1111 0001 | 0101 0001 |
| 2 | 1111 0010 | 0101 0010 |
| 3 | 1111 0011 | 0101 0011 |
| 4 | 1111 0100 | 0101 0100 |
| 5 | 1111 0101 | 0101 0101 |
| 6 | 1111 0110 | 0101 0110 |
| 7 | 1111 0111 | 0101 0111 |
| 8 | 1111 1000 | 0101 1000 |
| 9 | 1111 1001 | 0101 1001 |
| A | 1100 0001 | 1010 0001 |
| B | 1100 0010 | 1010 0010 |
| C | 1100 0011 | 1010 0011 |
| D | 1100 0100 | 1010 0100 |
| E | 1100 0101 | 1010 0101 |
| F | 1100 0110 | 1010 0110 |
| G | 1100 0111 | 1010 0111 |
| H | 1100 1000 | 1010 1000 |
| I | 1100 1001 | 1010 1001 |
| J | 1101 0001 | 1010 1010 |
| K | 1101 0010 | 1010 1011 |
| L | 1101 0011 | 1010 1100 |
| M | 1101 0100 | 1010 1101 |
| N | 1101 0101 | 1010 1110 |
| O | 1101 0110 | 1010 1111 |
| P | 1101 0111 | 1011 0000 |
| Q | 1101 1000 | 1011 0001 |
| R | 1101 1001 | 1011 0010 |
| S | 1110 0010 | 1011 0011 |
| T | 1110 0011 | 1011 0100 |
| U | 1110 0100 | 1011 0101 |
| V | 1110 0101 | 1011 0110 |
| W | 1110 0110 | 1011 0111 |
| X | 1110 0111 | 1011 1000 |
| Y | 1110 1000 | 1011 1001 |
| Z | 1110 1001 | 1011 1010 |

FIGURE 5-16
A comparison of ASCII and EBCDIC eight-bit codes

## SECONDARY STORAGE

Many data-processing procedures require more storage capacity than is available in core storage. In these instances, the computer system can be augmented by one or more **auxiliary** or **secondary storage** devices. Data stored in a secondary storage device are not immediately accessible to the processing unit or to other input/output devices and hence must be routed through primary storage. Thus the processing of a record of data contained in secondary storage first requires that the record be transferred or moved into primary storage, where it can be processed as any other data stored in primary storage (Fig. 5-17). Less frequently used data, or items of data whose great volume make it impractical if not impossible for them to be stored in primary storage, are

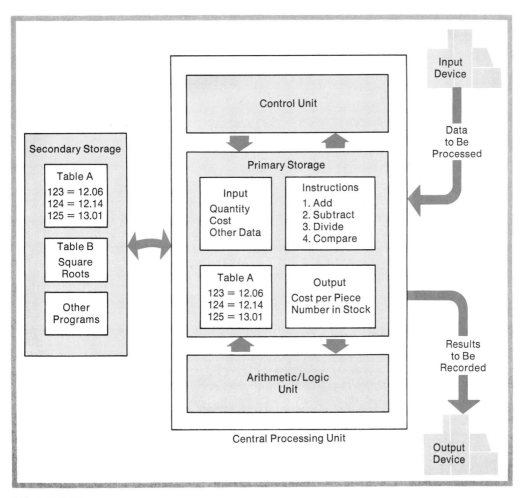

FIGURE 5-17

Schematic, main, and secondary storage

**TABLE 5-4**

Comparison of Primary and Secondary Storage

| CHARACTER-ISTIC | PRIMARY STORAGE | SECONDARY STORAGE |
|---|---|---|
| Location with respect to the CPU | Within CPU | Outside of, but connected to, CPU |
| Cost* | Most expensive | Less expensive than primary storage |
| Capacity* | Up to several million characters | Billions of characters |
| Average access time* | In billionths of a second | In millionths of a second |
| Can data be processed directly from storage? | Yes | No, must first be moved into primary storage |
| Means of storing information | Magnetic core, thin film, microminiaturized integrated circuit, electrooptical | Magnetic disk, magnetic tape, magnetic drum, mass, storage system |

\* These items will vary with manufacturers and computer systems.

reserved for secondary storage. Table 5-4 illustrates some of the differences between primary and secondary storage.

Data to be maintained in secondary storage must be organized and assigned to one or more of the sequential or direct-access storage devices, depending on factors such as the amount of data to be stored, whether the data can be accessed and/or processed in a prescribed sequence, or whether the data must be accessed and/or processed directly without regard to sequence.

We will discuss these concepts, together with the currently used secondary storage devices, in greater detail in Chapter 6.

**To verify your understanding of the previous material, turn to page 194 and take Self-Test 5-4.**

## INPUT/OUTPUT COMMUNICATIONS

There are a number of ways computer manufacturers have attempted to solve the problem of slow input/output devices, which cause the processing unit to have to wait continually, reducing the efficiency of the entire computer system, and the problem of expanding the capabilities of a computer system to handle more and more input/output devices. Their attempts have resulted in the implementation of a concept known as overlapped processing.

**Overlapped Processing\***

All data-processing applications involve the operations of input, processing, and output, with each of these requiring a specific amount of time for its completion. The time required to solve a problem completely, then, will be a combination of the times required to complete each of the above operations. However, the total required time will be heavily dependent on what is meant by a combination of the times required to complete each operation. If, for example, only one of these operations could be performed at a time, the total required time for the completion of the job would be the sum of the times required to complete each input, processing, and output operation (nonoverlapped processing). Figure 5-18 illustrates how this might take place. In this illustration you will notice that only three input-processing-output cycles were possible in the time period represented. In Fig. 5-19, however, in the same time period it was possible to perform more than seven input-processing-output cycles. This was accomplished by performing more than one operation at a time (overlapped processing). As you can clearly see, overlapped processing is more efficient than nonoverlapped processing. It is for this reason that most computers today employ overlapped processing.

You are probably wondering how it is possible for a computer to do more than one thing at a time. The answer is relatively simple. Attached

"The computer seems to have sprung a leak!"

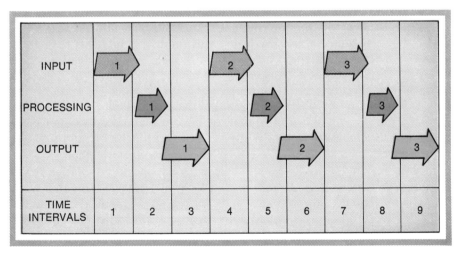

FIGURE 5-18
Nonoverlapped processing

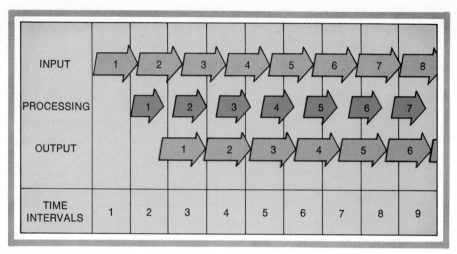

**FIGURE 5-19**

Overlapped processing

to the computer are special devices, called **channels,** that control the input/output operations, thereby freeing the processing unit to perform other operations. Thus, at a given time, one channel can be controlling an input operation while a second channel is controlling an output operation and the computer is possibly performing an arithmetic calculation. A computer system may have many channels attached to it, with each channel being responsible for controlling one or more input or output devices.

Data channels are categorized as either selector or multiplexor channels. A **selector channel** is one that can be used with one high-speed input or output device at a time. **Multiplexor channels,** on the other hand, are logically connected to several low-speed devices at the same time but electronically connected to only one of these devices—the one transmitting or receiving at that instant. The multiplexor alternately selects a limited amount of data from the low-speed devices connected to it and transmits these data at high speed to the CPU. Figure 5-20 illustrates one of many possible arrangements and uses of channels.

What actually takes place between the input/output device, the channel, and the computer is as follows. Let us assume that we wish to read some data from cards, perform a detailed calculation, and output the results. To begin with, the channel would cause the input device to read one or more cards and store their contents in a temporary storage location, called a **buffer.** This operation can be performed while the computer is busy with another operation. When these data are needed for processing, they will be called for by, and transferred to, the proc-

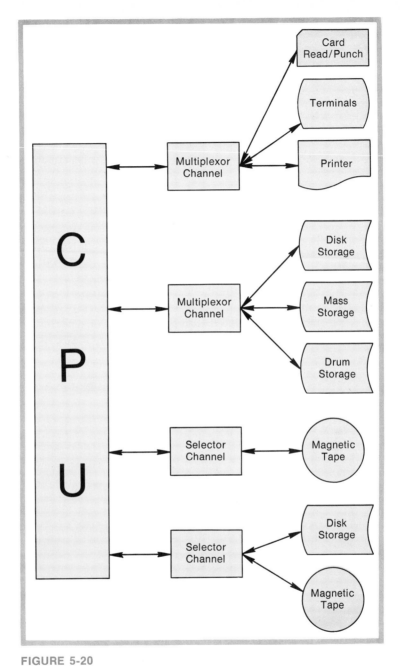

**FIGURE 5-20**

Schematic of an overlapped processing computer system configuration

essing unit at a very rapid rate. While these data are being processed in the processing unit, the channel is causing the buffer to be filled for ready availability. When the processing of the previously read data has been completed, the computer will cause these output data to be rapidly transferred, via another channel, to an output buffer, from which location the channel will control the slower operation of printing, thus freeing the processing unit to accept more data from the input buffer via its channel and begin processing these data. What we have, then, is a condition where the relatively slow operations of reading cards and printing are controlled by the channels, allowing the processing unit to communicate only with the channels at high speeds. In this manner the processing unit is operating as much as possible and is not constantly waiting for the card reader or the printer to become available.

In many cases, the physical buffer is not located within the physical input/output device but resides in an intermediate device referred to as a **control unit.** Besides housing the input/output buffer, this device often houses the circuitry necessary to convert the data from a form acceptable to the device to a form compatible with the particular computer and vice versa. For example, during an input operation the control unit associated with the card reader will convert the data being read from Hollerith code to binary, BCD, EBCDIC, ASCII, or whatever code the particular CPU can process.

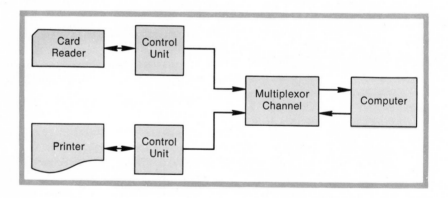

To verify your understanding of the previous material, turn to page 194 and take Self-Test 5-5.

## MICROCOMPUTERS*

A microcomputer is basically a small computer system that contains the same basic components as larger systems: a central processor or microprocessor, storage, and input/output. Typically, input is accomplished through a typewriterlike keyboard while output is displayed on a CRT screen or simple printer. Logical and arithmetic operations, as well as overall control of the computer, are handled by the microprocessor and associated circuitry.

In contrast to the larger computer systems costing upwards of $100,000, a microcomputer can be purchased for from $500 to approximately $20,000 and is generally small enough so that a self-contained system can fit on a desk top.

The primary storage capability of microprocessors is generally in the range of from 4K to 64K (1K is approximately equal to 1000) bits of RAM (random-access memory) and an equivalent amount of ROM (read only memory). Most microcomputer systems are available with different amounts of RAM depending on the user's requirements.

**ROM, RAM, PROM and EPROM**

The terms ROM, RAM, PROM, and EPROM are used in connection with the storage unit of mini- and microcomputers. These memories are generally contained on MOS chips or integrated circuits.

**ROM** or **read only memory** is provided by the computer manufacturer and has the data already hardwired or permanently stored on the chip. Thus, the user may only read from it but may not write on it. Even the application or removal of power from a ROM chip will not affect its contents. ROM is used to store manufacturer-supplied programs, routines, and translators for immediate access by the user of the mini- or microcomputer system.

**RAM** or **random-access memory,** on the other hand, is general storage which can be read from or written onto by the user. RAM memory is used primarily to store user programs and data. Unlike ROM, however, the contents of RAM are lost when power is removed.

**PROM** or **programmable read only memory** begins as blank chips which have nothing programmed or recorded on them. Once a series of instructions or data has been programmed onto the chip by a special programming device, the PROM chip permanently stores this information and behaves the same as ROM. The programming of the PROM chip is generally done by the manufacturer of the microcomputer.

**EPROM** or **erasable programmable read only memory** chips can be programmed as with PROM chips but differ in that they can be reprogrammed by the programming device should it become necessary or desirable. Once programmed, however, an EPROM chip behaves the same as ROM.

In addition to primary storage, most microcomputer systems are also equipped with some form of secondary storage. Generally, this is in the form of cassette tapes and/or floppy disks, often referred to as diskettes. As with full-size computer systems, the tape cassette provides a sequential storage capabil-

"I know we said we needed a good basic RAM, but. . ."

ity while the floppy disk provides a direct-access capability. Floppy disks are available with storage capacities of up to 100K bytes per diskette with a typical maximum total capacity of four floppy disk drive units or approximately 400,000 bytes of direct-access secondary storage (see Fig. 5-21).

Two of the most popular microcomputer systems are the TRS-80 and the APPLE II.

**TRS-80**  The TRS-80 is available in three configurations: Model I Level I, Model I Level II, and Model II. Each configuration is larger, more powerful and/or faster than the previous. The basic TRS-80 Level I Model I system comes with 4K of RAM, a tape cassette unit, and a 12-inch black and white CRT monitor. The CRT can display 16 lines of text with either 32 or 64 characters per line. (See Fig. 5-22.)

The TRS-80 is expandable with respect to both hardware and software. Hardware options include several printers, up to four diskette drives, and a voice synthesizer. A user can purchase the minimal system and add on to suit his or her needs. Software available with the TRS-80 includes payroll, inventory, and numerous other business programs, a statistical package, mathematics programs, and games. Because of the wide acceptance of the TRS-80, many user groups and private companies have formed and offer, free of charge or at a reasonable cost, additional hardware and software options. Included among these are translators for some of the more popular languages such as COBOL, FORTRAN, and PASCAL.

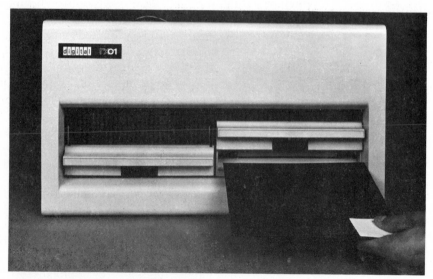

**FIGURE 5-21**
Digital Corporation Floppy Disk Drive Unit (*Courtesy DEC*)

**FIGURE 5-22**
TRS-80 Model 1 Level 1 Microcomputer System (*Courtesy Radio Shack, a division of Tandy Corp.*)

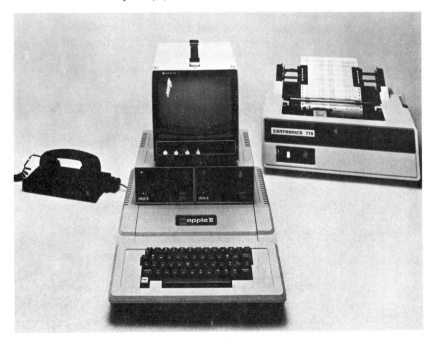

**FIGURE 5-23**
APPLE II Microcomputer System (*Courtesy Apple Computer Inc.*)

Processing and Storage Devices

191

# focus on the field

**APPLE II**  The basic APPLE II system does not come with a CRT monitor, but it is available separately. (See Fig. 5-23.) This is simply because the APPLE II can be tied into a regular television set if desired. Video output can be up to 24 lines with up to 40 characters per line. An advantage of the APPLE II over the TRS-80 is that the basic APPLE II system can produce graphical displays in up to 15 colors (if a color monitor is attached) and audio output at no extra cost.

Hardware and software options available with the APPLE II are similar to those available with the TRS-80.

To verify your understanding of the previous material, turn to page 194 and take Self-Test 5-6.

## SELF-TEST 5-1

1. The _____ unit is the control center of the entire computer system.

2. The accepted abbreviation for the term "central processing unit" is _____.

3. The three subunits of the central processing unit are the _____, _____, and _____ units.

4. The function performed by the _____ is to control and coordinate the activities of the computer system as the human brain controls and coordinates the activities of the human body.

5. Specific operations controlled by the control unit include the following: _____.

6. The three basic functions of the arithmetic/logic unit are _____, _____, and _____.

7. The decision-making capability of the arithmetic/logic unit is limited to two general types: _____ and _____.

8. The ALU makes use of temporary storage areas referred to as _____ when performing arithmetic operations.

9. Most small to medium-size computer systems employ _____ ALU unit(s).

## SELF-TEST 5–2

1. Once data have been _____, they can be used over and over again until no longer needed and deliberately replaced.

2. Each storage cell in the computer is associated with a unique _____.

3. One ferrite core is capable of storing _____.

4. Many modern computers have replaced the _____ type of memory with a system of microminiaturized integrated circuits.

5. One of the newer primary storage devices is _____, which is based on the polarization of light.

6. _____ chips are used in most mini- and microcomputer systems.

7. The newest and most sophisticated computer memory device yet devised is _____.

8. _____ devices are one of the most recent semiconductor devices to be considered for use in computers with the magnetic bubble and will be used principally for secondary storage.

## SELF-TEST 5–3

1. All data stored within primary storage is in the form of _____.

2. A bit is another name for a(n) _____.

3. The BCD system is capable of representing any character using _____ binary digits or bits.

4. The names of the seven BCD bits required to represent any character are _____.

5. The C bit serves to control the _____ of a BCD character.

6. Given an odd-parity machine and the bits below, the C bit would have to be a _____.

| ? | 1 | 1 | 1 | 0 | 0 | 1 |
|---|---|---|---|---|---|---|
| C | B | A | 8 | 4 | 2 | 1 |

7. The B and A bits are called the _____ bits, and the 8, 4, 2, and 1 bits are called the _____ bits.

8. The BCD code for the characters A, 3, 0 (zero), and S are _____, _____, _____, and _____, respectively.

9. The EBCDIC for the characters A, 3, 0 (zero), and S are _____, _____, _____, and _____, respectively.

10. The _____ is an eight-bit standard coding scheme developed by several computer manufacturers and intended to be acceptable to all makes and models of computers.

11. When a programmer wishes to verify that an item of data has been correctly stored, he or she can call for a _____, or printout of a specified area of the computer's memory.

12. When a memory dump occurs, it is generally in a shorthand form of EBCDIC known as _____.

## SELF-TEST 5–4

1. The computer's main memory can be augmented by one or more _____ devices.

2. All data coming from or going to secondary storage must pass through _____.

3. Second storage files are generally classified as either _____ or _____.

## SELF-TEST 5–5

1. _____ is one of the methods presently employed to solve the problem of slow input/output devices and increase the overall efficiency of a computer system.

2. The concept of overlapped processing involves _____.

3. The function of a _____ is to control an input and/or output operation, thereby freeing the processing unit to perform other operations.

4. The two types of channels are _____.

5. In an overlapped processing operation, data are not read directly from the input medium and stored in the computer's memory but are read and first stored in a temporary location called a _____.

6. After data have been read and stored in the buffer, they can be called into the computer at _____ speeds when they are needed and when the processor is available.

7. Information to be output in an overlapped-processing system is transferred to the buffer at high speed and stored until _____.

## SELF-TEST 5–6

1. Microcomputers range in cost from _____ to approximately _____.

2. Microcomputers generally employ a(n) _____ device or simple printer for displaying output.

3. Microcomputers employ _____ for sequential secondary storage and _____ for direct-access secondary storage.

4. The contents of a ROM chip (may, may not) be altered by applying or removing power.

5. RAM (may, may not) be written on.

6. Once programmed, _____ chips behave the same as ROM.

7. EPROM differs from PROM in that _____.

8. _____ is a storage-management technique that allows one to view the computer system as one containing many times the storage capacity that is physically contained in the CPU.

9. The two most popular microcomputer systems are _____.

**Answers to Self-Tests**

5–1

1. central processing unit

2. CPU

3. control; arithmetic/logic; storage

4. control unit

5. interpret and direct the execution of instructions; control the operations of peripheral devices; control the operations of other subunits of the CPU; and control auxiliary storage devices.

6. data transfer; arithmetic calculations; decision making

7. comparing two quantities as to size; testing for the existence of a condition

8. registers

9. one

5–2

1. stored

2. address

3. 1 bit (binary digit) of data

4. core

5. laser memory

6. Metal-oxide semiconductor (MOS)

7. magnetic bubble memory

8. Charged-coupled

5–3

1. 1's and 0's

2. binary digit

3. seven

4. C, B, A, 8, 4, 2, and 1

5. parity

6. 1 bit to make the total number of bits odd (5)

7. zone; numeric

8. 0 11 0001; 1 00 0011; 1 00 1010; 1 01 0010

9. 1100 0001; 1111 0011; 1111 0000; 1110 0010

10. ASCII coding scheme

11. dump

12. hex notation

5–4

1. auxiliary or secondary storage

2. primary or main storage

3. sequential-access; as random-access

5-5

| | |
|---|---|
| 1. Overlapped processing | 5. buffer |
| 2. the performing of more than one operation at a time | 6. high |
| 3. channel | 7. the output device is free and can output the data stored in the buffer |
| 4. selector or multiplexor | |

5-6

| | |
|---|---|
| 1. $500; $20,000 | 6. PROM or EPROM |
| 2. CRT | 7. EPROM can be reprogrammed |
| 3. cassettes; diskettes | 8. Virtual storage |
| 4. may not | 9. the TRS-80 and the APPLE II |
| 5. may | |

## EXERCISES

**5-1**
**True/False**
**Exercises**

_____ 1. The primary storage unit is sometimes referred to as memory.

_____ 2. The control unit initiates and controls the sequence of input, output, and processing operations.

_____ 3. Data channels are categorized as either selector or multiplexor.

_____ 4. A ferrite core can be magnetized to either a zero or a one.

_____ 5. In all computer systems, the storage unit is located within and is considered part of the CPU.

_____ 6. It is anticipated that charged-coupled devices (CCD) will replace the magnetic bubble.

_____ 7. In the BCD coding scheme, the C bit is a check or parity bit.

_____ 8. A dump is useful if a programmer wishes to examine the contents of a specific portion of primary storage.

_____ 9. RAM may not be written on by the user of the computer system.

_____ 10. The stored set of instructions necessary to solve a problem is referred to as a stored program or simply as a program.

_____ 11. The APPLE II microcomputer system can produce graphical displays in up to 15 colors.

_____ 12. Virtual storage is a storage-management technique that allows one to view the computer system as one containing many times the primary storage capacity actually available.

_____ 13. The control unit makes use of temporary storage areas referred to as registers.

_____ 14. Unlike the BCD scheme, no parity bits are used with the EBCDIC scheme.

_____ 15. EPROM is more like ROM than like RAM.

_____ 16. MOS integrated circuits are faster than the ferrite core in primary storage units.

_____ 17. Laser and magnetic-bubble devices are among the newest storage devices.

_____ 18. "Bit" is another name for a binary digit.

_____ 19. CPU is an abbreviation for "Computer Processing Unit."

_____ 20. BCD stands for "Binary Coded Digits."

_____ 21. The control unit of the CPU communicates with both input and output devices.

_____ 22. In terms of storage capacity, primary storage is generally more restrictive than secondary storage.

_____ 23. The ASCII scheme was intended to provide a computer user with a coding scheme which would be acceptable on virtually all computer systems.

_____ 24. An input/output control unit often contains the circuitry necessary to convert data to and from a form compatible with the computer system.

_____ 25. To change the value of a ferrite core, it is only necessary to energize one of the wires passing through the core.

**5–2
Fill-in
Exercises**

1. _____ is the time required to locate an item of data in storage and transfer it to the processor.

2. A primary storage device that utilizes the polarization of light is the _____.

3. The total storage capacity of a computer system consists of its _____ storage capacity together with its _____ storage capacity.

4. The three subunits of the CPU are the _____, _____, and _____ units.

5. In a virtual storage computer system, a program is subdivided into segments referred to as _____.

**5–3
Multiple-
choice
Exercises**

_____ 1. The EBCDIC scheme for the letter V is
   a. 11000100
   b. 11100100
   c. 11000101
   d. 11100101
   e. 11010101

_____ 2. A fullword would consist of _____ bits.
   a. 8
   b. 16
   c. 32
   d. 64
   e. none of the above

_____ 3. A storage capacity of 64K would be approximately equal to
   a. 64 bytes
   b. 640 bytes
   c. 6400 bytes
   d. 64,000 bytes
   e. none of the above

Processing and Storage Devices

_____ 4. A term used in connection with the storage unit of mini- and microcomputers is
   a. ROM
   b. RAM
   c. PROM
   d. EPROM
   e. all the above

_____ 5. Modern devices used in primary storage units include
   a. magnetic bubble
   b. charged-coupled
   c. metal-oxide-semiconductor
   d. laser
   e. all the above

_____ 6. The BCD code for the letter T in an odd parity machine is
   a. 0100010
   b. 1010010
   c. 0100011
   d. 1010011
   e. 0010011

_____ 7. The term used to describe the simultaneous operation of input, output, and processing is
   a. overlapped processing
   b. concurrent processing
   c. teleprocessing
   d. channel processing
   e. none of the above

_____ 8. Channels allow data to flow to the central processing unit at
   a. low speed
   b. high speed
   c. average speed
   d. varying speed
   e. none of the above

**5–4 Problems**

1. Describe and contrast primary and secondary storage. Give examples.
2. Describe the concept of core storage. Contrast core storage with some of the newer storage devices.
3. Describe the essential hardware elements necessary to facilitate overlapped processing. When is overlapped processing advantageous?
4. Assuming odd parity, convert the following to BCD:
   a. 327
   b. 3759
   c. HAPPY
   d. NUMBER SYSTEM
5. Convert the following to EBCDIC and ASCII:
   a. 1347
   b. 456A6T
   c. HAPPY
   d. NUMBER SYSTEM

**6.** Briefly summarize the differences between ROM, RAM, PROM, and EPROM.

**5–5** **1.** Visit your local electronics store and make a list of what microprocessor
**Projects** and other integrated circuit components are readily available.

**2.** Visit your local computer store and determine and describe the available microcomputer systems.

INTRODUCTION

MASS STORAGE MEDIA AND DEVICES

**Magnetic Tape**

**Magnetic Drum**

**Magnetic Disk**

**Data Cell** *

**Mass Storage System**

FILE ORGANIZATION

**Organizational Considerations**

**Sequential File**

**Direct File**

**Indexed Sequential File**

DATABASE

FOCUS ON THE FIELD

SELF-TESTS

EXERCISES

# File Processing Concepts, Devices, and Media

## INTRODUCTION

Mass storage devices are principally employed to store the numerous programs and masses of data that must be processed daily to support the activities of a modern business. The manner in which these data are organized, stored, and accessed will determine to a great extent the value that the results will have to the company and the expense that will be incurred in their production. It is therefore essential that we understand these concepts.

In this chapter we shall discuss the currently used mass storage devices, data files, their organizations, methods of access, and the advantages and disadvantages associated with each medium, organization, and device.

Upon completing this chapter, you should be able to:
- Discuss and compare currently used mass storage devices and media
- Describe the three principal file organization methods
- Compare the principal file organization methods
- Discuss the concepts of and need for databases
- Define the following terms:

| | |
|---|---|
| Block | Index |
| Cartridge | Indexed sequential file |
| Database | Interblock gap |
| Database management | Magnetic disk |
|   system | Magnetic drum |
| Direct-organized file | Magnetic tape |
| Disk pack | Mass storage system |
| File | Redundant data |
| File organization | Sequential organized file |
| File protect ring | Volume |

## MASS STORAGE MEDIA AND DEVICES

Numerous devices are currently available for the input, output, and storage of data. We briefly discussed some of these devices in previous chapters. Let us now review and expand on these discussions as well as examine some additional devices.

**Magnetic Tape**    Magnetic tape is one of the principal secondary storage media in use with computers today. Its areas of application within a computer system are many and diverse.

Magnetic tape, like the punched card, is principally a **sequential** storage medium. That is, data recorded on magnetic tape may be read only in the order in which they were written. The third data record, for example, can be accessed only after the first and second data records have been read. For some applications, this fact will offer no particular problems. But for other applications it is essential that an ability exist for directly accessing any given data record. In these cases, a more appropriate storage medium would be the magnetic disk, magnetic drum, or mass storage system. These direct-access storage devices will be discussed later in the chapter.

The variety of magnetic tape used with computers is very similar in constitution to the tape used in home tape recorders, but it is of a substantially higher quality. It consists of a plastic base, approximately one half inch wide, coated on the side with a compound containing microscopic iron particles (see Fig. 4-21). By passing this tape over a read/write mechanism, the iron particles can be rearranged into magnetized patterns or bits. These bits occur in groups of seven or nine across the tape, thus forming either seven or nine parallel tracks along the tape. Seven-track tapes use the BCD coding scheme, whereas nine-track tapes employ the EBCDIC or ASCII coding scheme.

The manner in which data are generally recorded on tape is similar in appearance to the way they are recorded on a card. That is, the rows on a card correspond to the horizontal positions on a tape (tracks), and one character is represented by one vertical column on a card and one vertical column on a magnetic tape (see Fig. 6-1).

Referring to Fig. 6-1, you will note that in addition to the zone and numeric parts of a character, each character on the tape contains a **check bit.** This check bit is used by the system to verify that the bits representing a character are not altered during the reading or processing of the tape. The check bit is automatically placed on the tape as each character is written on the tape.

Magnetic tape is in motion only when data are being read from it or written onto it. During these operations, the magnetic tape must be moving at a constant speed. Consequently, blank space must be left on the tape before and after each record or **block** (two or more records) of data written. This space or **interblock gap** (IBG) serves three purposes:

1. While the tape is accelerating from rest to the constant speed at which the tape must be moving before data can be read, no data are lost.

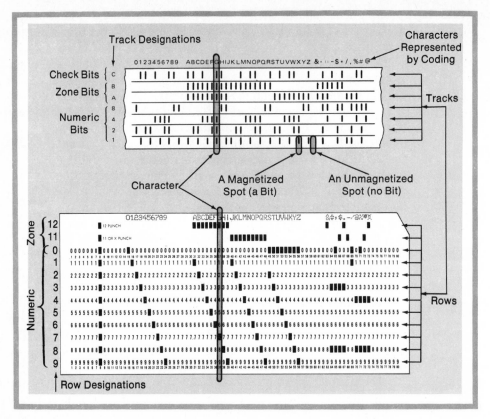

FIGURE 6-1

Recording similarities between punched card and 7-track magnetic tape (even parity)

2. While the tape is decelerating from constant speed after having read one record or block of data recorded on the magnetic tape, no data will be lost.

3. It separates physical or tape records from one another.

Tape IBGs range in size from 0.6 to 0.75 inch, a space capable of otherwise storing up to 4600 characters.

Tape records are not limited to any fixed number of bytes, characters, or fields. A tape record can be any size, provided that there is available primary storage to store an entire record as it must be read into primary storage before it can be processed. Figure 6-2 illustrates some of the possible ways in which records can be recorded onto magnetic tape.

Magnetic tape files can be easily protected against accidental erasure of data. The most common means is through the use of a **file protect ring** (see Fig. 6-3). This is a plastic ring that fits into a groove in the back of the magnetic tape reel. When it is installed, the tape can be read and can be written on. However, when the file protect ring is removed, the tape can no longer be written on but is still capable of being read. The jargon for this is "no ring, no write."

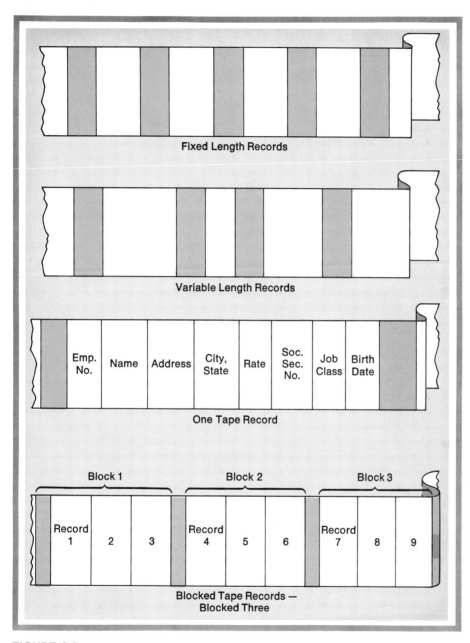

**Fixed Length Records**

**Variable Length Records**

| | Emp. No. | Name | Address | City, State | Rate | Soc. Sec. No. | Job Class | Birth Date | |
|---|---|---|---|---|---|---|---|---|---|

**One Tape Record**

Block 1      Block 2      Block 3

| Record 1 | 2 | 3 | Record 4 | 5 | 6 | Record 7 | 8 | 9 |
|---|---|---|---|---|---|---|---|---|

**Blocked Tape Records —
Blocked Three**

FIGURE 6-2

Possible data record arrangements on magnetic tape

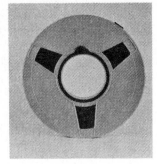

**FIGURE 6-3**

File protect ring

**Magnetic Drum**   A magnetic drum is a metal cylinder that rotates at a constant speed of about 3500 revolutions per minute. The outer surface of the cylinder is coated with a thin magnetic material. This surface is subdivided into channels and each channel into tracks as shown in Fig. 6-4. Data are recorded directly onto the surface of the drum, and once recorded, they

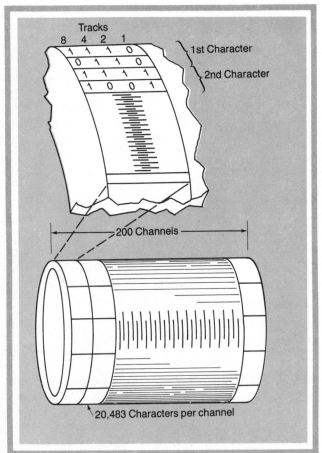

**FIGURE 6-4**

Character storage on a 2301 magnetic drum

Tracks

8  4  2  1

1st Character

2nd Character

200 Channels

20,483 Characters per channel

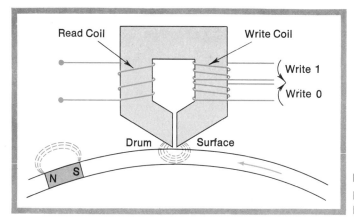

FIGURE 6-5

Magnetic Drum Read/Write Head

may be accessed and processed an indefinite number of times. However, each time new data are recorded on the surface of the drum, the
old data are automatically erased. Data are recorded and accessed by
read/write heads (similar to those on a tape recorder) that are sus-
pended a very slight distance from the surface of the drum (see Fig. 6-5).

An IBM 2301 drum, for example, can store over 4 million bytes or
characters (see Fig. 6-6). On the average, it takes approximately 8.6 milliseconds to rotate the drum to the desired position, at which point characters can be transferred to or from the CPU and the drum at a rate of
1.2 million characters per second. For example, 1 million characters
could be read from or written onto a 2301 drum in approximately 1
second.

The magnetic drum has been utilized as an auxiliary storage device
for many years, during which time it has functioned in two general

FIGURE 6-6

IBM 2301 Drum Storage Device

capacities. When it was first introduced, it was intended to be used as a high-capacity, intermediate-access storage device. It was used to store data that were repetitively referenced through a computing operation (actuarial tables, interest tables, income-tax tables, etc.) and to augment main storage.

Subsequently, however, it has been utilized as a random-access storage device. In this capacity it was used for program storage and as a temporary storage area for high-activity random-access operations on limited data.

The magnetic drum does not possess the speed of core storage and does not possess the removable feature of the disk pack, but it does offer a versatile capability at a reasonable cost.

**Magnetic Disk**    Magnetic-disk storage consists of a series of thin, magnetically coated disks, similar in appearance to a stack of long-playing phonograph records. These disks are mounted on a vertical shaft, each disk separated from the disks above and below it by a small space. As the shaft rotates, it spins the disks at a very high but constant speed—generally over 2000 revolutions per minute. As these disks revolve about the center vertical shaft, read/write access arms are free to move in and out between the disks (see Fig. 6-7). Each of these access arms contains two read/write heads that can read or write on the disk surface immediately above or below the heads.

Data are recorded on the surface of a disk magnetically in much the same way that they are recorded on magnetic tape or a magnetic drum. The recording surface of each disk is subdivided into concentric areas or **tracks** similar to the concentric circles that appear on an archery target. In one complete rotation of a disk, the read/write head assigned to the disk can read or write an entire track.

Data are recorded serially around a track with multiple data records being separated by IBGs (interblock gaps), as is done when records are blocked on magnetic tape. The storage capacity of each track on a disk

it's truly amazing

The reading head on an IBM 3350 disk storage device is positioned 17 microinches (millionths of an inch) above the surface of record-album sized disks. A particle of smoke is about 100 microinches in size and a human hair 2500 microinches in circumference.

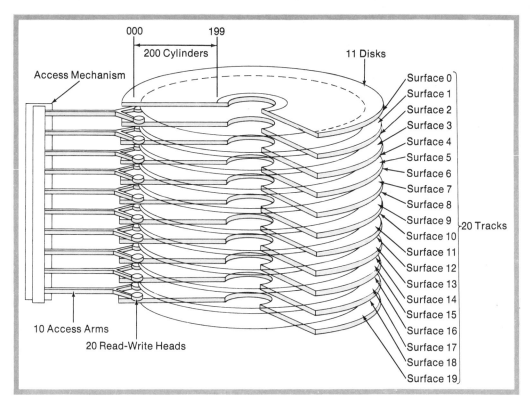

Access Mechanism

000 199

200 Cylinders

11 Disks

Surface 0
Surface 1
Surface 2
Surface 3
Surface 4
Surface 5
Surface 6
Surface 7
Surface 8
Surface 9
Surface 10
Surface 11
Surface 12
Surface 13
Surface 14
Surface 15
Surface 16
Surface 17
Surface 18
Surface 19

20 Tracks

10 Access Arms

20 Read-Write Heads

FIGURE 6-7

Magnetic disk access mechanism

is exactly the same. This might seem somewhat confusing, since we know that as the location of a track approaches the center of the disk, its length gets increasingly shorter. Thus, to maintain a constant storage capacity on each track, the **density** of the data stored is greater the closer the track is to the center of the disk. In some cases the disk is even further subdivided into several pie-shaped sections referred to as **sectors.**

Disks generally contain from 200 to 400 tracks per surface. These tracks can be accessed as the read/write heads are moved in and out. It should be noted, however, that all of the access arms containing the heads move in and out together. Thus, when a read/write head is positioned over a track on one surface, the other read/write heads are automatically positioned over the same track on the other disk surfaces. These tracks are referred to as a **cylinder.** Data contained on any of the tracks constituting a cylinder may be accessed without any need to move the access arms in or out. Thus to uniquely access a single track, one would have to provide the number of the cylinder desired and the disk surface on which the track is located (see Fig. 6-7).

FIGURE 6-8

IBM 2305 Fixed Head Storage Module and Control Unit

Disks may be permanently attached to the drive unit (Fig. 6-8) or they may be made up as removable **disk packs** containing six or more disks each (Fig. 6-9). Disk packs, depending on the particular model, can store tens of millions of characters. The IBM 3348 Disk Pack pictured in Fig. 6-9, for example, is capable of storing approximately 70 million characters.

As was the case with magnetic cores, magnetic tape, and magnetic drum storage media, once data have been recorded on a magnetic disk

FIGURE 6-9

IBM 3348 Data Module (*Courtesy International Business Machines Corp.*)

**FIGURE 6-10**
IBM 3344 Direct Access Storage Facility

they may be read an indefinite number of times and will remain on the disk until they are written over.

Disk storage devices are capable of reading and writing data sequentially or directly, which provides a very flexible storage device. It is, however, slower than the magnetic drum but with a capacity to handle larger volumes of data. Disk packs also provide the capability of easy removal and portability not available with either the core or drum.

For those organizations requiring more direct-access or random-access storage than is available with a single disk unit, a number of direct-access storage facilities are available. The disk storage facility shown in Fig. 6-10 can provide direct-access storage for over 1,800,000,000 characters, access any record stored in an average time of 25 thousandths of a second, and transfer characters between it and the CPU at a rate of over 800,000 characters per second.

**Data Cell\***    A data cell is a device containing removable and interchangeable strips of magnetic film that are capable of storing large volumes of data with direct-access capabilities (see Fig. 6-11). A single strip of magnetic film measuring only 2¼ by 13 inches contains 100 tracks for data, with each track capable of storing 2000 bytes—200,000 bytes of storage in one magnetic strip. With a complement of 10 cells each containing 20 subcells of 10 strips each, a total capacity of 400,000,000 nonnumeric characters or 800,000,000 digits is possible (see Fig. 6-12). With a proper controlling device (IBM 2841 Storage Control), up to eight data cells can be utilized, giving the computer system a maximum total online capacity of 6,400,000,000 characters of storage. Figures such as these can stagger the imagination. However, because access of individual records is

Rotating Drum

Drive Cylinder

**FIGURE 6-11**
IBM 2321 Data Cell Drive Model 1

so slow, the newer disk storage facilities have virtually replaced the data cell. The 3344 facility mentioned earlier can store 1,800,000,000 characters, access any data item stored in an average of 25 milliseconds, and transfer characters between it and the CPU at a rate of over 800,000 characters per second. This is even more staggering than the data cell.

Average access time for a given record is, of course, longer for the data cell than for either the disk or drum simply because of the mechanics involved in accessing a record. The data cell drive must pluck the appropriate magnetic strip from its subcell and wrap it around a rotating drum located just above the drive cylinder (see Fig. 6-11) before the desired record can be accessed. The CRAM (Card Random Access Memory) unit is a similar device manufactured by the National Cash Register Company. Considering that average access time is still in fractions of a second, its somewhat slower operating speeds are somewhat compensated for by its virtually limitless storage capacity, sequential- or random-access storage capabilities, easily removable and replaceable element, and low cost.

"Oh, that reminds me. Our system also has a rather sophisticated file protect feature."

**Mass Storage System**    Representative of the latest in mass storage devices are the CDC 38500 Mass Storage System and the IBM 3850 Mass Storage System (Fig. 6-13). The 3850 can store from 35 to 472 **gigabytes** (billion bytes) of data utilizing the IBM 3851 Mass Storage Facility. This is comparable to the capacity of 4700 IBM 3330 disk packs, 47,000 reels of tape, or almost

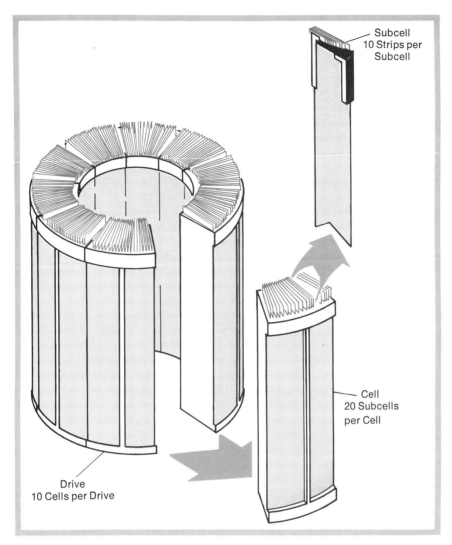

Subcell
10 Strips per
Subcell

Cell
20 Subcells
per Cell

Drive
10 Cells per Drive

**FIGURE 6-12**
Data cell drive unit showing data cell and subcell

5,900,000,000 fully punched cards. This system combines the low cost of magnetic tape with the direct-access or random-access capability of magnetic disk.

To facilitate this capability, the data are recorded on **cartridges** as shown in Fig. 6-14. These cartridges are plastic cylinders approximately 4 inches long and two inches in diameter and contain a 770-inch spool of magnetic tape. A single cartridge can store over 50 megabytes of data. Two such cartridges, referred to as a **volume,** are capable of storing the same amount of data as an entire model 3336 disk pack (Fig. 6-14).

FIGURE 6-13

IBM 3850 Mass Storage System

These data cartridges reside in cartridge storage cells from which they can be accessed by the cartridge access station (Fig. 6-15).

The 3851 can accept requests from up to four IBM 370 Model 145s or equivalent computer systems. Upon receiving a request for data, the 3851 searches the inventory of cartridges and mass storage volumes to locate the cartridge on which the data are contained. Once located, the desired cartridge is retrieved by the access station, mounted on the

FIGURE 6-14

Data cartridge compared with older disk packs

Cartridge access station

read/write station, opened, and its contents transferred to a disk for processing. If the processing of the record caused the record to be updated, it can now be rewritten back on the tape over the old record, and then the cartridge can be returned to its cell. All this can be accomplished for any of 472 gigabytes in a maximum of a few seconds.

To verify your understanding of the previous material, turn to page 225 and take Self-Test 6-1.

## FILE ORGANIZATION

Before we begin our discussion of file organization, let us clarify our understanding of the term "file." Previously we used the term in connection with a card file—a collection of punched card records. However,

the concept of a file is not limited to the punched card or any other individual storage medium. Files apply to all data storage media. Simply stated, a **file** is a set or collection of records composed of related items of data or fields. An inventory file, for example, would consist of a collection of inventory records, each record of which could describe an item in the company's inventory. Each record would, in turn, be composed of such data items or fields as the name and/or number of the item, the number on hand, the order point, the minimum quantity order, the location in the warehouse, the purchase price, the selling price, and the discount structure.

Before a file storage medium can be selected or a file can be created, the applications to which the file will be applied must be carefully examined. Clearly, a fundamental consideration in this examination will concern the data to be recorded on the file. But an equally important and less obvious consideration concerns how the data are to be placed on the file. To determine this, one must first know how the data are to be accessed from the file. For example, will the applications allow for the processing of one record after the other sequentially, as a computer would read punched card records from the card reader, or will the applications require an ability to access a specified record directly from the file without having to access all previous records, as a computer would access an item of data directly from its memory? It is even possible that an application might require both of these methods. In this case, when the file is created the data records must be placed on it in such a way that they can be retrieved either sequentially or directly, as dictated by the nature of the application. To illustrate this concept let us examine the organization of your textbook. When your textbook was created, it was organized so that you would have a sequential or direct-access capability. You could access the information contained in it sequentially by simply reading one page after the other. On the other hand, should you need a specific item of "data," you could simply turn to the page on which the information was contained. If you didn't know the specific page, you could refer to the Index, get the page number, and then turn to the specific page and begin reading.

**Organizational Considerations**

The three principal factors that must be considered to determine an appropriate file organization are:

Volatility
Activity
Size

**Volatility** is a measure of the frequency with which records are added to or deleted from a file. A **static** file is one in which there are relatively few additions or deletions. A **dynamic** or **volatile** file, on the other hand, is one in which there is a significant number of additions and deletions in a given period of time.

**Activity** refers to the average number of records that are processed during a single computer run. Activity is generally a function of two quantities: **percentage** or **hit rate** and **distribution** of activity. In cases where the percentage of activity is low—where the ratio of accessed to nonaccessed records is low—the file should be organized to allow a minimum access time to each record. This can generally be accomplished by a direct file organization. It may also be the case that the activity is not equally distributed. Certain records may be accessed more often than others; these records should be accessible in minimum time. Thus if the organization chosen is sequential, it would be beneficial to place these records toward the beginning of the file, if possible.

**Size** refers to the number of records in the file. This is an important consideration when a file is so large that the entire file cannot be placed online simultaneously. The file must be organized so as to minimize the time required to process the file. It is also possible that if the file is relatively small, the processing times may be similar regardless of the type of organization used with the file. In such a case, however, the growth potential of the file must not be overlooked. If it is anticipated that the file will be expanded to any great extent in the foreseeable future, a careful consideration of the file organization at this point may eliminate many problems and possible expense in the future.

After the above factors have been carefully examined, one should have a clear picture of the processing requirements. It now remains to choose the specific file organization to be employed. Before this can be done, one must be aware of the possible file organizations.

Currently, there are three commonly used file organizations: sequential, direct, and indexed sequential. Let us consider each of these.

**Sequential File**

A sequential file is one in which the records have been arranged into ascending or descending sequence according to a key field. This key field may be numeric, alphabetic, or a combination of both, but it must be contained in each record, as it forms the basis for determining the order in which the records will appear on the file. In cases where there can be several records having the same value in their key fields, a secondary key field should be specified. For example, if a sequential file of employees was to be created in ascending sequence by last name, it would be advisable to establish a secondary key field consisting possibly of the employee's first name, and maybe even a third and fourth key field. In this way Smith, John would be certain to appear before Smith, Joseph. In cases where it is possible to arrange a file in sequence according to a key field that cannot have the same value for more than one record on the file, no secondary key fields need be used. An employee file arranged in increasing numerical sequence according to social security number would be an example of such a case.

Sequential files are generally maintained on punched cards, magnetic tape, disk or drum, or a mass storage system.

**Direct File**     As with a sequential file, each record in a direct-organized file must contain a key field. However, the records need not appear on the file in key field sequence. In addition, any record stored on a direct file can be accessed if its location or address is known. All previous records need

"We'd like to put two bucks on "Happy Daddy" running in the seventh today."

not be accessed. The problem, however, is to determine how to store the data records so that, given the key field of the desired record, its storage location can be found. It would be ideal if the key field could also be the location of the record in the file, but this is rarely if ever possible. Therefore, before a direct file can be created, a scheme or method must be devised to convert the key field value for a record to the address or location of that record on the file. This scheme or method is generally called an **algorithm.** How the particular algorithm is arrived at will vary from application to application and is beyond the scope of this text. It is sufficient to say that it can be very complex and generally requires an expert to determine the most efficient algorithm.

Thus, in a direct-organized file, each record on the file is assigned to a storage address based on an algorithmic or mathematical relationship between the key of that record and the address of that record on the file.

It should be quite clear, however, that this method is not used for processing an entire file but where several records need to be accessed quickly and directly as in the case of an online inquiry. This method of file organization is employed by most airlines to obtain quickly and directly the most up-to-date flight information. All the agent need do is key in the flight number (key field value) and virtually immediately the desired record is accessed and displayed on the agent's terminal screen.

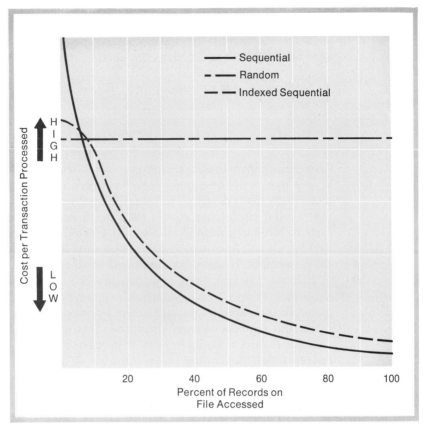

**FIGURE 6-16**

Cost vs. activity for the three commonly used file organizations

Direct-organized files are generally maintained on magnetic disk or drum or on a mass storage system.

**Indexed Sequential File** An indexed sequential file, referred to as ISAM for "indexed sequential access method," offers the simplicity of sequential file processing while at the same time offering a capability for direct access. To accomplish this, records are initially stored on the file in sequential order according to a key field. In addition, as the records are being recorded on the file, **indexes** are established by the system that associate the key field values with the storage location of the record on the file. These indexes are then used by the system to allow a record to be directly accessed. These indexes function in much the same manner as the indexes would function for a book consisting of one or more volumes. That is, in order to access a particular record directly with ISAM, the indexes are searched for the key value of the desired record, which will then provide the address of the record to be accessed from the file.

Indexed sequential files are generally maintained on magnetic disk or drum or on a mass storage system. Figure 6-16 illustrates the relationship between cost and activity for each of the above file organizations.

To verify your understanding of the previous material, turn to page 225 and take Self-Test 6-2.

## DATABASE

As we saw above, the organization selected for a particular file depends on the nature of the applications for which it will be used. Files have historically been designed to match a specific application. Payroll files are created containing all the data pertinent to a company's payroll system. Similarly, individual files are created for use with the company's Personnel, Accounts Payable, Accounts Receivable, Inventory and other systems. If the data contained on these files are not carefully delineated, it is very likely that the same data will appear on several of these files. That is, these files would contain **redundant data.** For example, both a company's payroll file and personnel file could contain the name and address of each employee. This would mean that a simple change of address would have to be processed twice and probably three or four times, depending on the number of other files on which these data appear.

Wouldn't it be more practical to have each employee's name and address on one file from which it can be accessed by all programs requiring these data? This would reduce the amount of redundant data and minimize the possibility that data contained on a file might be inaccurate because they were never updated. It was for these reasons that the concept of a database was developed.

A **database** can be thought of as a set of logically related files organized in such a way that data access is improved and redundancy is minimized. This concept does not imply that all the data relating to a company's business should be contained on one single database, but simply that all records in a database should be related and that redundant data should be minimized.

In addition to the database itself, a set of programs is necessary to facilitate the adding of new data as well as the modifying and retrieving of existing data within the database. This set of programs is referred to as a **database management system (DBMS).**

Figure 6-17 illustrates how the traditional approach to data organization compares to a database management approach. Figure 6-18 illustrates a database implementation procedure.

To verify your understanding of the previous material, turn to page 226 and take Self-Test 6-3.

(A)

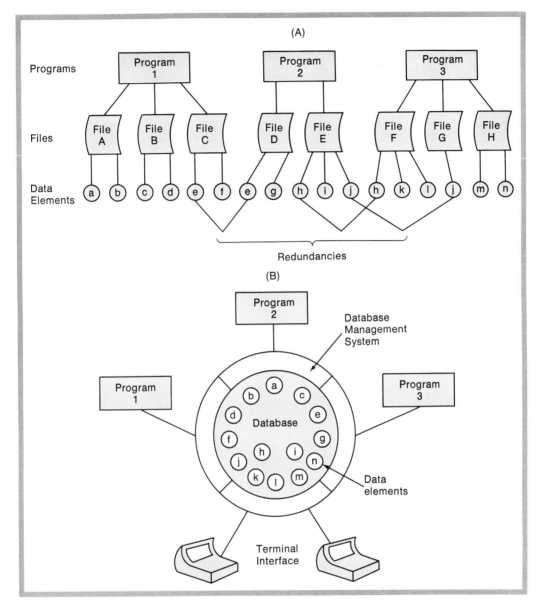

FIGURE 6-17

(A) Traditional approach to data organization; (B) Database management approach to data organization

| STEP | DESCRIPTION | RESPONSIBILITY |
|---|---|---|
| 1. | **DEFINE SCOPE OF THE DATABASE PROJECT** | |
| a. | Identify which organizational subdivisions will be served by the database | DP Steering Committee |
| b. | Define which functions within these organizations will utilize the database | DP Steering Committee |
| c. | Identify which existing and planned applications will be converted to the database system | Data Processing |
| d. | Prepare proposal for management and obtain go-ahead | Data Processing |
| 2. | **ORGANIZE DATABASE PROJECT** | |
| a. | Pick users for design team | Top Management |
| b. | Select Database Administrator | Data Processing |
| c. | Establish regular meetings and periodic management reporting for design team | DBA |
| 3. | **SELECT DATABASE MANAGEMENT SYSTEM PRODUCTS** | |
| a. | Document requirements in formal RFP | DBA |
| b. | Select DBMS vendor | Design Team |
| 4. | **DEVELOP INITIAL IMPLEMENTATION PLAN AND SCHEDULE** | |
| a. | Identify files that will be converted | Data Processing |
| b. | Identify programs within applications specified | Data Processing |
| c. | Estimate programmer hours needed to modify applications programs | Data Processing |
| d. | Estimate user clerical support needed to verify data during conversion | Design Team |
| e. | Develop implementation schedule | Design Team |
| 5. | **DESIGN DATABASE** | |
| a. | Complete detailed information requirements | Design Team |
| b. | Identify data requirements | Design Team |
| c. | Determine data structure and complete design specifications | DBA |
| d. | Review and approve design specifications | Design Team |
| 6. | **PERFORM TRAINING** | |
| a. | Develop training requirements and training schedule | DBA and DP Manager |
| b. | Train programmers in use of DML | Vendor |
| c. | Train DBA in DMCL and DDL | Vendor |
| 7. | **INSTALL AND TEST DATABASE** | |
| a. | Code DMCL, schema and subschema | DBA |
| b. | Modify representative programs for DBMS test | Applications Programmers |
| c. | Code conversion programs | Applications Programmers |
| d. | Generate the database | DBA |
| e. | Test and debug | DBA and Applications Programmers |
| f. | Review and approve test results | Design Team |

| | | |
|---|---|---|
| 8. | DEVELOP DETAILED CONVERSION PLAN | DP Manager |
| a. | Make individual programming assignments for each program to be modified and each file to be loaded | Design Team |
| b. | Schedule users to verify and correct file contents | Data Processing |
| c. | Schedule computer availability | DBA |
| d. | Prepare formal written conversion schedule and obtain commitments from all parties involved | Design Team |
| e. | Approve Conversion Plan | |
| 9. | CONVERT EXISTING APPLICATIONS | Data Processing |
| a. | Bring up one application at a time | DBA |
| b. | Update and regenerate database as required | DP Steering Committee |
| c. | Approve revised applications as they are converted | Data Processing |
| d. | Begin using database for new applications and programs | |
| 10. | FINE TUNE DATABASE | DBA |
| a. | Monitor DBMS access statistics and visible performance, and modify database as required | DBA |
| b. | Regenerate database when necessary | |
| 11. | PERIODICALLY REVIEW DATABASE PERFORMANCE | DP Steering Committee |
| a. | Restate organizational goals and information requirements | DP Steering Committee |
| b. | Evaluate success of database project | DP Steering Committee |
| c. | Begin new database projects when required | |

FIGURE 6-18

Database implementation procedure

223

# focus on the field

## The Importance of a Dictionary-Driven Database Management System

A data dictionary is simply a software system which enables the user to define and catalog his data processing environment in one place. It is a file of consistent, up-to-date information that describes all of the entities of a data management system: hardware/software systems, application systems, subsystems, programs, subprograms, modules, files, records, elements, users and security parameters. When the dictionary "drives" the major software components of database management system (DBMS) and related systems, it automatically extracts information from control software and application systems and, in turn, makes that information available to other systems. In a DBMS environment, an active data dictionary automatically tracks and records not only the entities of the DP environment but the *relationships* between entities as well. An active data dictionary is, therefore, a vital maintenance and control tool in today's increasingly complex information management environment. An active data dictionary brings to systems management a level of control comparable to the level of control DBMS brings to large-scale applications processing.

In a database/data communications environment, the ability to define system entities in one place at one time is especially important. The purpose of implementing a database management system is to eliminate data and system redundancies and to increase performance. If in doing so, the systems staff has created additional maintenance problems for itself in order to keep every component and every application program consistently up-to-date, the problem of complexity and redundancy has not been solved. It has merely been shifted from the application level to the systems level.

An active data dictionary, therefore, is needed in that it provides a production control and reporting system for data processing management. An active data dictionary—one that is an integral part of the DBMS itself—serves the database and systems environment in the same way the DBMS serves the application environment. A data dictionary can serve as "a DBMS within a DBMS." It provides data processing with an index to the types of information contained in the database and the interrelationships between systems and information. It controls and consolidates definitions of system entities just as the DBMS controls and consolidates data.

A data dictionary documents the DBMS. It maintains the view of database records established by each application program. It maintains information on all entities that make up the system and keeps track of all users, terminals, systems and programs that access the database. The data dictionary supports system definition and design just as the DBMS supports more efficient file management and application production and design. The data dictionary allows the user to get reports out on what his environment looks like and to maintain that environment dynamically.

In a very real sense, a data dictionary can function as an application system for the data processing department. It helps programmers, DP managers, and database and data communications administrators to keep track of daily operations.

The importance of a dictionary-driven system can best be understood in terms of the functional software systems with which it must interface. These may include database management, telecommunications, both batch and on-line report generators, program development systems and facilities, and others.

Each of these systems makes use of common information—both data files and processing facilities. However, unless a common repository of systems information and a mechanism for tracking the effects of changes, deletions, or updates consistently throughout all systems exists, the organization must accept redundant software and data, limited system design options and unnecessarily complex maintenance requirements. Without an active data dictionary capability associated with the DBMS and related software components, each component system and its files must be updated independently.

In a multilanguage environment, for example, an active data dictionary saves programmer time and maintenance problems by allowing the user to store and automatically retrieve synonyms for the same elements. Preprocessors for COBOL, FORTRAN, PL/1 and Assembler can build definitions from the data dictionary in the appropriate languages and number of characters simply by examining the program source code and determining what is needed.

A ''copybook'' capability exists for all systems. Commonly used commands and routines may be stored in the dictionary and simply filled in automatically rather than laboriously recoded for every program. Error checking and validation of user requests for service can also be handled through the dictionary.

Why is it important to have a central data dictionary which drives not only the DBMS but other control software systems as well? The benefit is primarily greater productivity. Every piece of information that the dictionary captures means that a programmer or database administrator does not have to individually update a multitude of systems and programs. That translates directly into man hours and money saved. It also translates into a greatly reduced opportunity for operator-induced error. A dictionary-driven system means shorter application development, greater programmer and program efficiency, and better documentation. □

DISCUSSION QUESTIONS

1. After reading this article, how would you describe a data dictionary? What is its purpose?

2. Do you feel that such a dictionary would be practical for the small business? Explain.

## SELF-TEST 6–1

1. The principal sequential-access storage medium is _____.
2. Between every record or block on tape there must always be an _____, the purpose of which is _____.
3. Random-access storage devices include the _____.
4. The _____ is removed from a magnetic tape reel to prevent accidental erasures.
5. Once data have been recorded on a magnetic drum or disk, it may be read _____ times.
6. The random-access storage device with the largest storage capacity is the _____.
7. The most commonly used random-access storage device is the magnetic (disk, drum, or card).
8. Magnetic disk units are available with _____ or _____ disks.

## SELF-TEST 6–2

1. The three traditional file organizations are _____.
2. Sequential files are arranged in sequence according to a _____.

3. A scheme or method used to convert the key field value for a record to the address of the record in a direct file is called a(n) _____.
4. Direct files are generally maintained on _____.
5. The addresses of data records on an indexed sequential file are maintained on one or more _____.
6. Records in an indexed sequential file are initially recorded in _____ order.
7. Indexed sequential files are generally maintained on _____.
8. Three considerations in determining an appropriate file organization are _____.

## SELF-TEST 6–3

1. Items of data appearing on more than one file are referred to as _____.
2. A _____ is a set of logically related files organized to improve access and minimize redundancy.
3. The set of programs which facilitate the adding of new data or the modifying or retrieving of existing data is called a(n) _____.

**Answers to Self-Tests**

6–1

1. magnetic tape
2. interblock gap (IBG); to provide tape space to allow the tape to accelerate to or decelerate from constant speed
3. magnetic drum, disk, card, and mass storage system

4. file protect ring
5. an indefinite number of
6. mass storage system
7. disk
8. fixed; removable

6–2

1. sequential, direct, and indexed sequential
2. key field
3. algorithm
4. magnetic disk, drum or a mass storage system

5. indexes
6. sequential
7. magnetic disk, drum, or a mass storage system
8. volatility, activity, and size

6–3

1. redundant data
2. database

3. database management system

## EXERCISES

6–1
True/False

_____ 1. Magnetic disk files are more versatile than magnetic tape files.
_____ 2. An advantage to tape and disk files is that there is virtually no limit to the number of characters a record may contain.
_____ 3. The size of the IBG is related to how fast the tape starts and stops.

_____ **4.** Drum storage provides the greatest online storage capability available today.

_____ **5.** In order to file-protect a magnetic tape, the file protect ring must be in place in the tape reel.

_____ **6.** A cylinder consists of a series of tracks, each located the same distance from the center of each usable disk surface.

_____ **7.** Disk storage units are available with either fixed or removable disks.

_____ **8.** A dynamic file is one to which there are relatively few additions or deletions.

_____ **9.** In order to handle the access, additions, deletions, and modification of data within a database efficiently, a set of programs referred to as a database management system is necessary.

_____ **10.** Sequential files never utilize more than one key field.

_____ **11.** It is generally a simple matter to determine an algorithm to convert key field data to the locations of the desired records in the file.

_____ **12.** Magnetic tape may be used for both sequential and direct-access processing.

_____ **13.** The surface of a disk is subdivided into concentric areas referred to as sectors.

_____ **14.** An algorithm is a method used to determine the location of a record in an indexed sequential file.

_____ **15.** A distinct advantage of magnetic tape, disk, and drum is that they are reusable.

_____ **16.** Magnetic drum storage is faster than other forms of direct-access secondary storage.

_____ **17.** Magnetic disk is considered a sequential storage medium.

_____ **18.** Data stored on magnetic disk may be accessed randomly as well as sequentially.

_____ **19.** Records or blocks on tape are separated by interblock gaps.

_____ **20.** The direct-access storage device with the greatest capacity is the data cell.

_____ **21.** The magnetic drum is the most commonly used direct-access storage device.

_____ **22.** Information is retrieved from disk storage via access arms which contain read/write heads.

_____ **23.** The activity of a file is a function of the hit rate and distribution.

_____ **24.** Interblock gaps restrict the amount of data that can be stored on a reel of magnetic tape.

_____ **25.** The mass storage systems currently available can store data in the gigabyte range.

**6–2**
**Multiple-**
**choice**

_____ **1.** The principal factors that affect the organization of a file are
  **a.** volatility
  **b.** activity

    **c.** size

    **d.** all of the above

    **e.** none of the above

_____ 2. Of the following, the device which is the most versatile is the

    **a.** magnetic drum

    **b.** magnetic disk

    **c.** data cell

    **d.** mass storage system

    **e.** magnetic core

_____ 3. The currently used file organizations do not include

    **a.** sequential

    **b.** direct

    **c.** indexed sequential

    **d.** direct indexed

    **e.** none of the above

_____ 4. A storage medium which cannot be used for both a direct-access and a sequential-access application is

    **a.** drum

    **b.** disk

    **c.** tape

    **d.** data cell

    **e.** none of the above

_____ 5. The storage medium with the greatest direct-access secondary storage capacity is

    **a.** disk

    **b.** drum

    **c.** data cell

    **d.** mass storage system

    **e.** magnetic tape

_____ 6. Of the following media, which is generally not removable?

    **a.** magnetic tape

    **b.** magnetic disk

    **c.** magnetic drum

    **d.** magnetic card

    **e.** none of the above

_____ 7. The storage medium with the fastest average access time is the

    **a.** magnetic disk

    **b.** magnetic drum

    **c.** data cell

    **d.** mass storage system

    **e.** magnetic tape

_____ 8. Direct-access storage devices do not include the

    **a.** magnetic drum

    **b.** magnetic disk

    **c.** data cell

    **d.** mass storage system

    **e.** none of the above

**6–3** **1.** Discuss briefly the features and uses of mass storage devices. How do they
**Problems** relate to and differ from primary storage?

**2.** What is an interblock gap? Why is it necessary in tape processing?

**3.** Describe and compare sequential-access storage with direct-access storage. Indicate what types of jobs would best be suited for each.

**4.** Compare the various types of storage media with respect to speed, cost, and data accessibility.

**5.** What is the purpose of the file protect ring?

**6.** What is meant by access time? Why is this an important consideration when selecting a secondary storage device?

**7.** Why is access time generally given in the form of an average?

**8.** In large-scale computer systems, several types of secondary storage devices are generally used. Why?

**6–4** **1.** What kind of file organization do you think would be appropriate for each
**Projects** of the applications below? Visit local businesses to verify your choices.
     **a.** Payroll
     **b.** Personnel
     **c.** Accounts payable
     **d.** Accounts receivable
     **e.** Inventory
     **f.** Banking

**2.** Choose one of the above application areas and determine what fields should be included in each data record contained on the file(s) employed. How many and what types of characters would you allocate to each field?

# SOFTWARE, PROGRAM PREPARATION, AND PROBLEM-SOLVING CONCEPTS

INTRODUCTION

FLOWCHARTING SYMBOLS,
NOTES, AND FLOWLINES

**Input/output Symbol**
**Processing Symbol**
**Decision Symbol**
**Connectors and the Terminal Symbol**

SAMPLE APPLICATION 1

SAMPLE APPLICATION 2

ADDITIONAL FLOWCHARTING

APPLICATIONS

DECISION TABLES*

TOP-DOWN PROGRAM DESIGN

**Hierarchy plus Input-processing-output (HIPO)**
**Structured Programming**
**Pseudocode**

SELF-TESTS

EXERCISES

# Flowcharting, Decision Tables, and Top-Down Program Design

## INTRODUCTION

The flowchart is a means of visually presenting the flow of data through an information-processing system, the operations performed within the system, and the sequence in which they are performed. In this chapter we will concern ourselves with the program flowchart, which describes what operations are required (and in what sequence) to solve a given program application.

Upon completing this chapter, you should be able to:

- Understand the need for and purpose of the program flowchart
- Describe the principal flowcharting symbols
- Read and understand a program flowchart
- Describe the basic flowcharting techniques and use them in the construction of program flowcharts
- Describe the basic components of a decision table
- Construct a decision table
- Discuss the concept of top-down program design
- Describe the types of HIPO charts
- Describe the basic structures used in structured programming
- Represent the logic flow of a program with pseudocode
- Define the following terms:

| | |
|---|---|
| Connector | IF-THEN-ELSE structure |
| Decision symbol | Initialization |
| Decision table | Input/output symbol |
| Developing a counter | Input-process-output |
| Developing a sum | chart |
| DO-UNTIL structure | Looping |
| DO-WHILE structure | Note |
| Flowchart symbol | Pseudocode |
| Flowchart template | SEQUENCE structure |
| Flowline | Structured programming |
| Hierarchy chart | Terminal symbol |
| HIPO | Top-down program design |

## FLOWCHARTING SYMBOLS, NOTES, AND FLOWLINES

The program flowchart can be likened to the blueprint of a building. And, as a designer draws a blueprint before beginning construction on a building, so does the programmer draw a flowchart prior to writing a computer program. As in the case of the drawing of a blueprint, the flowchart is drawn according to definite rules and utilizing standard flowchart symbols prescribed by the American National Standards Institute, Inc.

In order to understand a flowchart, we must first understand the two basic parts of the flowchart, the flowchart symbols, and the flowlines connecting these symbols (see Fig. 7-1).

Just as we read a printed page from top to bottom, we read a program flowchart in the same manner. Hence the direction of flow is also from top to bottom.

Thus, a flowchart is a series of symbols, each representing a function in the program, each connected to the next in a vertically downward direction by flowlines. Let us examine a typical flowchart, as illustrated in Fig. 7-2. You will notice that the first and third symbols have the same shape and therefore represent the same **function.** Within

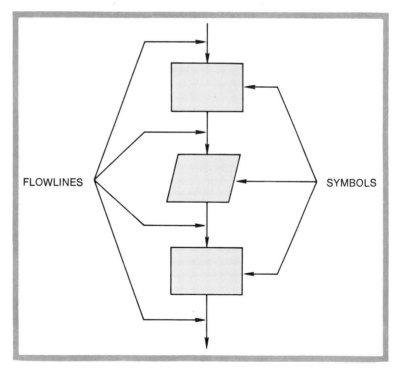

FIGURE 7-1

Symbols and flowlines

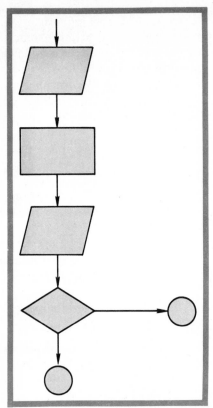

**FIGURE 7-2**

Flowchart segment employing symbols and flowlines

a given function category, we can have several different **operations.** For example, within the input/output function category are such operations as the reading of a card, the punching of a card, and the printing of a line. It is therefore necessary, in a flowchart, to show what specific operation is intended within a given function category. This is accomplished by means of a *note* within the flowchart symbol, where the symbol indicates the function and the note indicates the operation.

In the above example, the symbol ⬡ indicates an input/output function, while the note READ EMP-NAME, HOURS-WKD, HOURLY-RATE indicates the specific operation intended by the programmer.

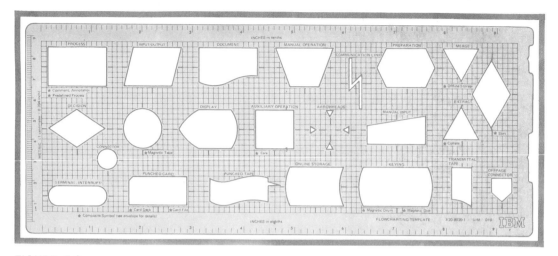

**FIGURE 7-3**

Flowcharting template

To aid the programmer in drawing the flowchart symbols there is a **flowcharting template.** It is a piece of transparent plastic that has cut-outs of various symbols. Figure 7-3 shows such a template. All of these symbols will not be discussed. At this time we will discuss only the more commonly used program flowchart symbols (Fig. 7-4).

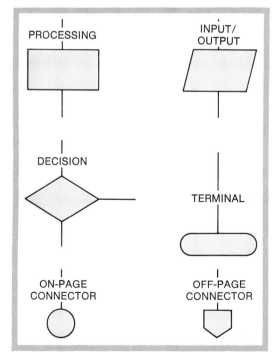

PROCESSING

INPUT/ OUTPUT

DECISION

TERMINAL

ON-PAGE CONNECTOR

OFF-PAGE CONNECTOR

**FIGURE 7-4**

Basic program flowchart symbols

**Input/output Symbol**    Let us now examine in detail each of these symbols and the functions that they represent. To begin, we consider the input/output symbol:

This symbol is used whenever information is to be input to the computer or output from the computer. The note within this symbol indicates the specific operation that is to be performed. In this case the operation is to PRINT EMP-NAME, GROSS-PAY.

**Processing Symbol**    At least as commonly used in flowcharts is the processing symbol:

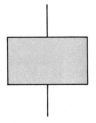

This symbol is used whenever data are to be processed to produce output. **Arithmetic** and **data-transfer** operations can be called processing functions, since they involve the processing of data and since they lead to, if not actually produce, data to be output.

An example of an arithmetic operation would be

This indicates that the current value of HOURS-WKD is to be multiplied by the current value of HOURLY-RATE. The product is then to be stored in GROSS-PAY.

A data-transfer operation is the moving of a constant or the current value of a storage location to the storage location indicated at the left of the equal sign.

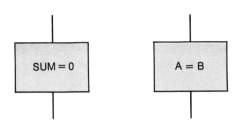

In the first case shown above, the constant 0 is moved to the location SUM. This would correspond to clearing a calculator before beginning to add several numbers to produce a SUM. In the second case, the current value stored in location B is transferred to and becomes the value stored in A. Thus at the end of this data-transfer operation, both locations B and A contain the same value—the value that was in B prior to the operation.

To verify your understanding of the previous material, turn to page 275 and take Self-Test 7-1.

**Decision Symbol**    The above two symbols, then, cover all the major computer functions but one, the logic function. This function includes those operations which require the making of a decision. Most common among these is determining whether two items of data are equal and, if not, which is the larger or smaller. Decisions also involve a determination of whether or not a condition exists. For example, one could request a decision from the computer concerning whether or not the last data card had been read. The symbol representing the logic function is

The purpose of any decision is to determine a future course of action. So it is with computers. For any decision there must be alternatives and a definite course of action for each alternative.

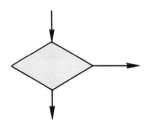

The decision symbol is used to represent operations in which there are only two possible alternatives for a given decision. To illustrate this type of operation, let us consider a hypothetical situation. Suppose we wish to decide whether a quantity, which we call QUANT, is equal to a second quantity, which we call QUANT2. The possible results are quite simple. True, the two quantities are equal, or false, the two quantities are not equal. In a flowchart, this would appear as follows:

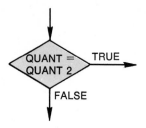

If QUANT is equal to QUANT2, the flow of the program would be into the decision symbol and out to the right along the flowline marked "TRUE." If QUANT is not equal to QUANT2, the flow of the program would be into the decision symbol and out in a downward direction along the flowline marked "FALSE."

The same decision could be symbolized in a slightly different way:

In this representation, the relationship between QUANT and QUANT2 is to be determined. If it is determined that the relationship is one of equality (QUANT = QUANT2), then the direction of flow is to the right:

| TABLE 7-1 | |
| --- | --- |
| SYMBOL | MEANING |
| $<$ | Less than |
| $>$ | Greater than |
| $\leq$ | Less than or equal to |
| $\geq$ | Greater than or equal to |
| $=$ | Equal to |
| $\neq$ | Not equal to |

If it is determined that the relationship is one of inequality (QUANT $\neq$ QUANT2), then the direction of flow is downward:

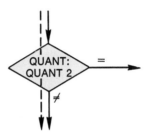

Relationships that can be tested are shown in Table 7-1.

**Connectors and the Terminal Symbol**  The input/output, processing, and decision symbols are the primary flowchart symbols. The remaining symbols, which are shown in Fig. 7-5, are equally essential, although less significant. **Connectors** are flowchart symbols that are used to connect remote portions of a flowchart with one another without using long or crossing lines and to avoid making a complex diagram into an unintelligible maze of flow-lines and flowchart symbols. A common practice is to place a letter in

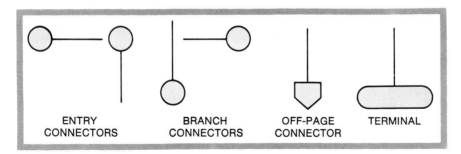

**FIGURE 7-5**

Connector and terminal symbols

each connector, the same letter being used at corresponding entrance and exit points. In Fig. 7-6, for example, there are two connectors marked with an "A." One of the connectors is an **entry connector,** while the other is an **exit** or **branch connector.** For illustrative purposes, the direction of flow has been indicated by dashed lines.

Quite often, however, the entry and branch connectors are not on the same page of the flowchart. In a case such as this, valuable time could be wasted while the flowchart reader searches through many pages attempting to locate the other half of the connector. To avoid this situation, special **off-page connectors** are used instead of the standard branch and entry connectors to indicate that the corresponding flowchart segments are contained on different pages and to indicate on what page(s) they are contained. In Fig. 7-6, for example, connector "B" is an off-page connector, identified by its unique shape. The number 3

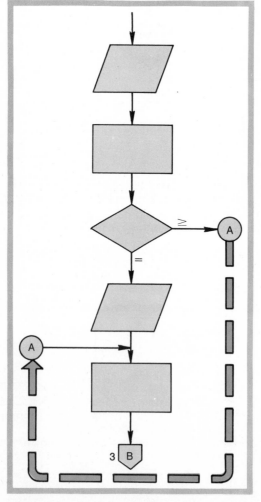

**FIGURE 7-6**

Interconnecting entry and branch connectors

SOFTWARE, PROGRAM PREPARATION, AND PROBLEM-SOLVING CONCEPTS

adjacent to the off-page connector symbol indicates that the corresponding entry off-page connector may be found on page 3 of the flowchart.

It should also be pointed out that there may be many standard or off-page branch connectors associated with one entry connector. That is, there can be many paths from which the entry connector might have come, but there can be *only one* entry connector containing a given letter within it. Let us examine this in Fig. 7-7. In case 1, we can

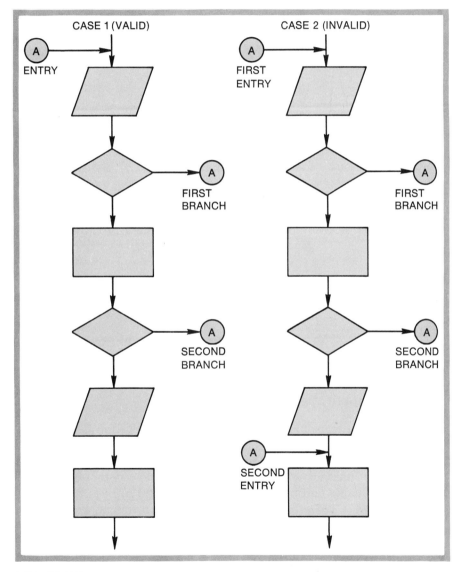

FIGURE 7-7
Valid and invalid use of connectors

"Before attempting to determine the country's next president, I suggest you try something comparatively simple, like who the class president will be!"

see that there are two branch connectors labeled with the note "A" and one entry connector "A." This does not lead to a problem, since no matter where the exit occurs, the next step will be to proceed to entry connector "A." In case 2, however, this is not the case. After control is transferred to branch connector "A," it is impossible to determine the appropriate entrance point. Should one go to the connector labeled FIRST ENTRY or to the connector labeled SECOND ENTRY? There is no conceivable way of determining the answer to this question. It is for this reason that there can be only one entry connector associated with one *or more* branch connectors.

The **terminal** symbol is used principally to indicate the starting or stopping of instruction execution in a program.

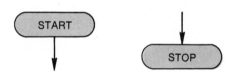

To verify your understanding of the previous material, turn to page 275 and take Self-Test 7-2.

## SAMPLE APPLICATION 1

Let us consider what would be involved in flowcharting a very simple problem. In this way we may verify and strengthen our understanding of the various flowchart symbols and notes. In this problem we assume that we wish to read two cards into a computer, each card containing one number, add the numbers, and print out the answer.

After briefly analyzing this problem you would probably reason out a plan of attack similar to the following:

1. Start the processing
2. Read the first number
3. Read the second number
4. Add the two numbers
5. Print out the answer
6. Stop the processing

| | TABLE 7-2 | | |
|---|---|---|---|
| STEP | TYPE OF OPERATION | SYMBOL | |
| 1. Start the processing | Terminal | | |
| 2. Read the first number | Input/output | | |
| 3. Read the second number | Input/output | | |
| 4. Add the two numbers | Processing | | |
| 5. Print out the answer | Input/output | | |
| 6. Stop the processing | Terminal | | |

Our next step would be to determine what kind of operation is being called for in each step and the appropriate flowchart symbol to be used. The result of this step is illustrated in Table 7-2.

Once we have the necessary flowchart symbols, we need connect them with flowlines and insert appropriate notes. This would produce

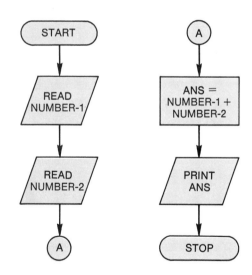

In most cases, however, it is not such a simple matter to determine a complete plan of attack as it was in this case. More often than not, the programmer cannot see a clear path to the solution and begins by attacking the problem one step at a time. Let us consider a second flowcharting problem, which is of this type.

## SAMPLE APPLICATION 2

Consider the following hypothetical problem:

PROBLEM: Read an unknown number of items of data to be keyed into a terminal or input from cards (if cards, one number per card). Determine the average of these numbers and print it out.

As we have previously stated, most flowchart problems must be solved in a series of steps. Therefore, in solving this problem, we will proceed in small steps, each step refining, clarifying, and adding to the previous steps as a novice programmer might approach the problem. In this way the reader will be able to follow the thought process associated with the solution of this and other more complicated problems. As one develops more and more insight into the process of creating logical and efficient flowcharts, many of the developmental steps can be combined, if not skipped entirely.

As we have stated earlier, the terminal symbol is used to indicate the beginning of a flowchart. Therefore we have

The next step is not such a simple one. To determine it, we must examine our final objective and work backward toward our present position. This process, in its simplest form, consists of a series of questions and answers. For example, in our case these questions and answers might be those in Table 7-3.

This apparently trivial series of questions and answers has led us to our next step:

READ NUMBER

This would now give us the following cumulative flowchart:

### TABLE 7-3

| QUESTION | ANSWER |
| --- | --- |
| What is our objective? | To develop an average of some numbers |
| How do I determine the average of these numbers? | Add them together and divide the sum by the number of numbers |
| How do I determine the value of these numbers? | Read them from the cards or request the terminal operator to key them in |

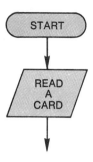

Now we ask ourselves: Why did we read this item of data? As we see from Table 7-3, the answer is that we wished to obtain the total of the number just read and the numbers to be read subsequently. For illustrative purposes let us call this total SUM, and the number read NUMBER. We can now begin to develop this total (SUM) by first including the number just read (NUMBER). This can be indicated with the following flowchart symbol and note:

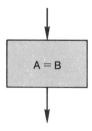

This note may appear somewhat confusing, so we will discuss it in greater depth. Let us begin by discussing the operation implied by the symbol =. In a flowchart, the symbol = *does not* mean the same thing that it does in arithmetic. That is, it does not mean "is equal to." It means "is replaced by the value of." For example,

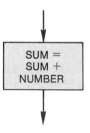

would be read as

the value of A is replaced by the value of B

That is, the data name A now contains the same quantity as was in B. If initially A contained the number 73 and B contained the number 96, after such an operation was performed A would now contain 96 and B would be unchanged or also contain the number 96. Therefore, in the case of our example, we are saying that

SUM is replaced by the value of SUM + NUMBER

But it appears as though SUM is being replaced by itself plus NUMBER. This conclusion is not completely correct. What is being said is that the value of SUM *after* this step will be the value of SUM *before* this step plus the value of NUMBER.

For example, let us assume that before this operation was performed, SUM contained the number 8 and NUMBER contained the number 7. Then after the operation is performed, SUM will contain the number 15 and NUMBER will contain the number 7. That is,

$$SUM = SUM + NUMBER$$
$$15 = 8 + 7$$

However, in our example we do not have a previous value for SUM, although we assumed it to be zero. Assuming it to be zero is not sufficient.

Situations such as this, which require **initialization** are quite common in programming. They are generally identifiable by the fact that the same variable appears on both sides of the equal sign ($=$). In our case, the variable SUM appears on both sides of the equal sign. When this occurs, it means that the value of the variable after the step will depend on the value of the variable before the step. Thus, to make certain that there is a value of the variable before the step, it must be initialized to whatever value is appropriate to the problem at hand. In our case, we should initialize SUM to zero. Incorporating this step into our cumulative flowchart will then give us the following:

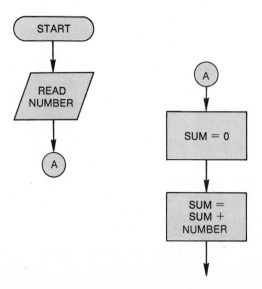

What shall we do next? To answer this we go back to our questions and answers (Table 7-3). Here we see that we wished to obtain a total of the numbers read in. Therefore, we must read the next number and add this number to our total. That is, we must first read the number:

Since we no longer need the number read previously, we can store this new number in the same location, NUMBER. When a second number is stored in a location already occupied, the previous contents are destroyed or replaced by the new contents. Therefore, in our case, the data name NUMBER would now contain the second number read.

Proceeding to add this number to our existing subtotal SUM, we would have

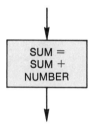

Our cumulative flowchart would appear as

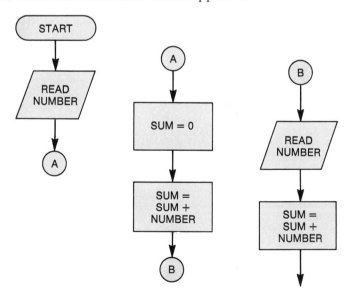

Notice that the last two symbols and notes are identical to two previously used symbols and notes. The only difference is that the previous symbols were separated by the symbol and note:

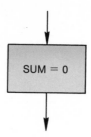

By simply moving this symbol and note up in our flowchart, we now have two identical flowchart sequences, one after the other.

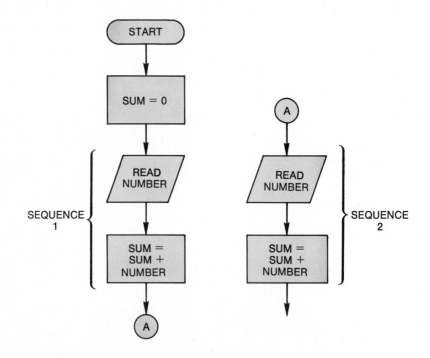

However, there is a more efficient way of indicating that a process repeats itself in a flowchart without including the flowchart of the process several times. This is done by creating a **loop**.[1] In our case this loop requires the use of the CONNECTOR symbol and appears as follows.

[1]An American National Standards definition of a **loop** is: a sequence of instructions that is executed repeatedly until a terminal condition prevails.

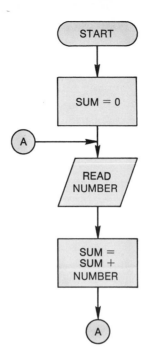

We must now determine a way to exit from this loop at the appropriate time. To do this, we must first determine the circumstances under which we would desire to exit from the loop. Since this loop accomplishes the reading of numbers and the accumulating of these numbers, it would be reasonable to assume that we would desire to exit from this loop *after* the last number has been read and added to SUM. But how are we going to determine whether the last number has been read? There are two commonly accepted answers.

"The company replaced me by a computer Ethel! . . . I wonder what comes next!"

One way to know that the last number has been read is via a signal from the computer system that an end of data has been reached. However, this capability is not available with all computer systems or under all circumstances. In particular, if a user is keying in the data as the program requires it, the computer system would not generate such a signal, since there would be no way for the system to know that there are no more data. In this case, the user would have to indicate to the program that there are no more data. This is generally accomplished by the user entering a unique data code that can be tested for in the program. Thus, each time a data item is input, the program would test it to determine if it is a data item to be processed or the unique data code indicating the end of the data. If the data were input via cards, this unique data code would be punched onto a card which is placed immediately after the last valid data card. This card is commonly referred to as a **trailer.**

One must exercise caution when employing this technique. First, one must make certain that this unique code is truly unique. That is, we must be certain that this code could not possibly occur in the data to be processed. Second, one must make certain to test for this code immediately after the read statement. This will ensure an immediate exit from the loop and eliminate the possibility that the special code might be added to the SUM or otherwise processed as valid data.

In our case, let us assume that the number $-9999999$ is not possible as a valid value for NUMBER. Therefore, it could be used as an end-of-data code. That is, immediately after a number is read, it would be compared to $-9999999$. If NUMBER is equal to $-9999999$, the program will branch out of the loop; otherwise, NUMBER will be processed, as shown below.

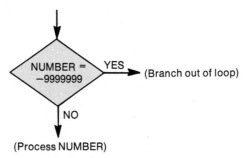

Incorporating this into our flowchart, we have

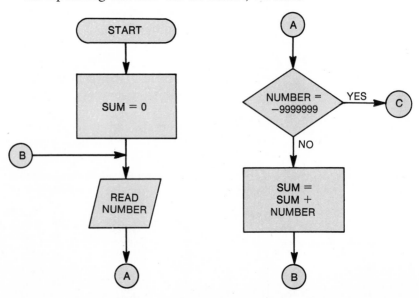

SOFTWARE, PROGRAM PREPARATION, AND PROBLEM-SOLVING CONCEPTS

After careful examination of this flowchart, you will see that the only way the loop can be broken is if all the numbers have been read and accumulated—exactly what we wished to accomplish.

Proceeding, we must determine our next step. Again, we go back to our questions and answers (Table 7-3). Here we see that we wished to determine an average of the numbers input. Since we now have SUM, which is the total of the numbers input, we need only divide SUM by the number of numbers input. Therefore, as the number of numbers was not given, we must determine a means of obtaining the number of numbers input. The simplest way to do this is to instruct the computer to count them as they are read. That is, we must **establish a counter** and add 1 to it each time a number is read. Let us call this counter N. Then each time a number is read, we can increment, or add 1 to, N.

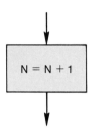

As we found it necessary in the case of SUM to assign an initial value, we also must assign an initial value to N. An appropriate initial value would be 0, since we want our counter to be set to zero initially. In the cumulative flowchart, this would appear as follows:

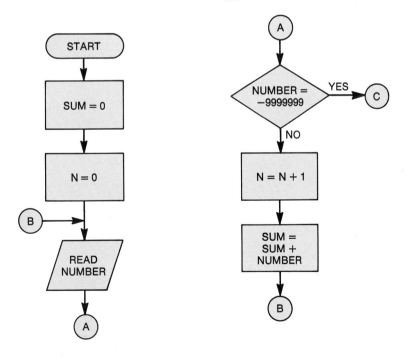

Now that we have the sum of the numbers (SUM) and the number of numbers read (N), we are able to compute the average of the numbers read. We call this quantity AVERAGE. This operation will take place after exiting from the reading loop and would appear as

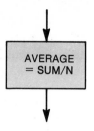

It is not necessary to assign an initial value to AVERAGE, since we are assigning it the value resulting from the division of SUM by N and not relying on its having or assuming it to have any specific previous value.

It now only remains for us to print out this result and terminate the

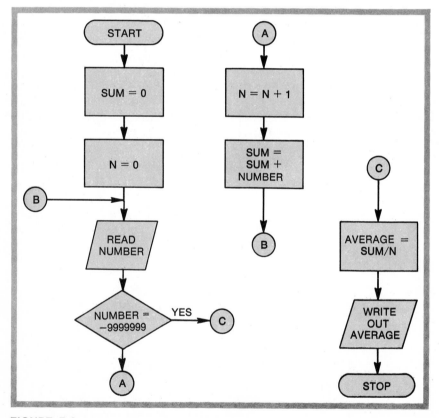

FIGURE 7-8

Completed flowchart of sample application 1

SOFTWARE, PROGRAM PREPARATION, AND PROBLEM-SOLVING CONCEPTS

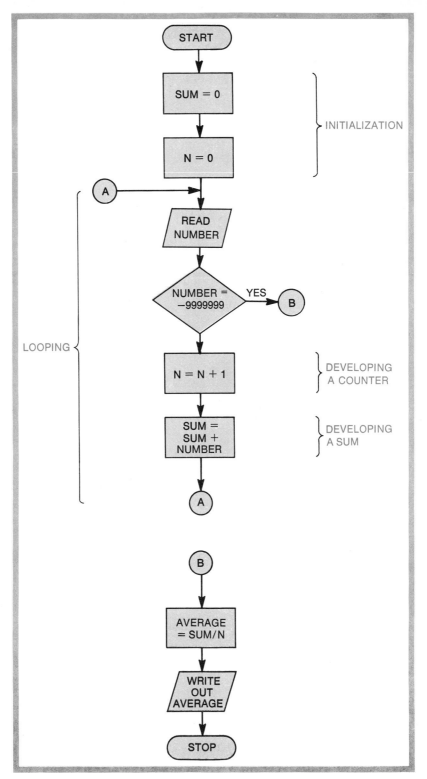

FIGURE 7-9
Four major flowcharting techniques

255

program. Incorporating these steps into our cumulative flowchart, we have Fig. 7-8.

In the course of developing this flowchart we have encountered four major flowcharting techniques: looping, initializing, developing a sum, and developing a counter (see Fig. 7-9). One or more of these techniques will be used in just about every flowchart you will ever write.

The importance of the flowchart as a means of documenting a program and for developing the logic of a program cannot be overemphasized. We will refer to and utilize the flowchart in subsequent chapters.

To verify your understanding of the previous material, turn to page 276 and take Self-Test 7-3.

## ADDITIONAL FLOWCHARTING APPLICATIONS

The versatility of flowcharting is illustrated in Fig. 7-10. In this example, the flowchart describes a sequence of operations and decisions to solve a problem. Although it is frivolous, it nevertheless illustrates the versatility of applications of flowcharts.

## DECISION TABLES*

The decision table is a tool of the programmer or systems analyst and can be used either as a substitute for the flowchart or to supplement the flowchart. It affords the programmer/analyst a convenient means of recording, in tabular form, the various conditions and possible courses of action when the solution to a problem involves substantial logical decisions.

The decision table separates the conditions from the courses of action and establishes a relationship between specific conditions and appropriate courses of action.

As illustrated in Fig. 7-11, the decision table physically resembles a rectangle that has been divided into six parts by a series of horizontal and vertical lines. To explain the use of each

"Quick, Charlie! How much is 27 minus 6?"

of these segments, we will discuss each segment in a general way and then apply the discussion to the following problem: We wish to construct a decision table which will enumerate the conditions under which a credit sale will be accepted or rejected. The conditions are as follows:

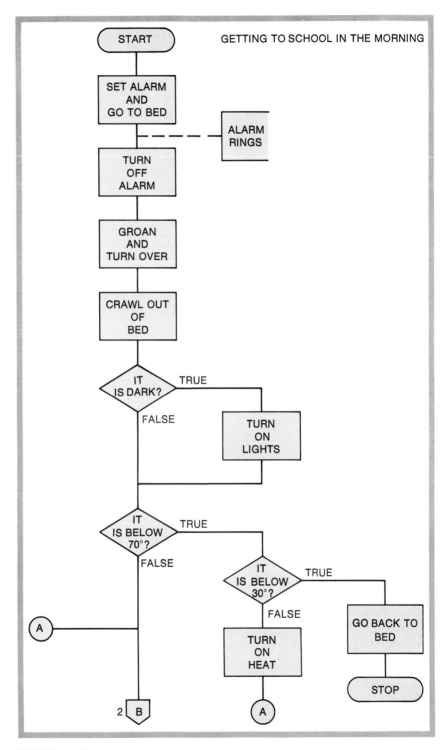

FIGURE 7-10
Flowchart for getting to school in the morning

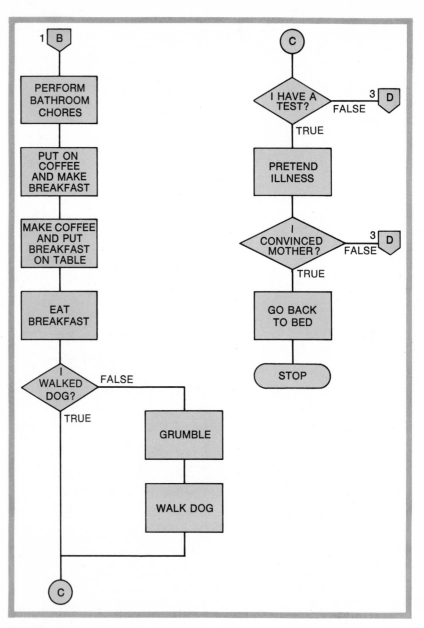

FIGURE 7-10 continued

SOFTWARE, PROGRAM PREPARATION, AND PROBLEM-SOLVING CONCEPTS

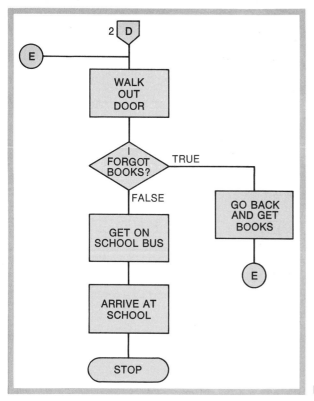

FIGURE 7-10 continued

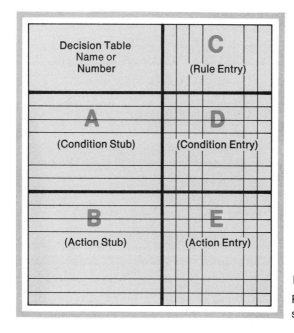

| Decision Table Name or Number | C (Rule Entry) |
|---|---|
| A (Condition Stub) | D (Condition Entry) |
| B (Action Stub) | E (Action Entry) |

FIGURE 7-11

Physical layout of a decision table

1. If a customer has a charge account with the store and also has a satisfactory credit rating, allow the credit purchase.
2. If a customer has a charge account with the store but has an unsatisfactory credit rating, allow the credit purchase only if special management approval has been given.
3. Reject the credit purchase in all other cases.

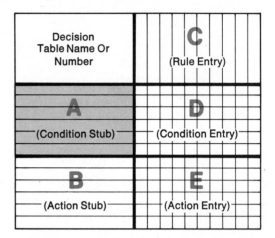

Block A (condition stub) above is to contain the possible conditions that exist in the problem, one condition per row with each condition being answerable with a simple *yes* (Y) or *no* (N) answer. In our sample problem, there are three separate conditions. These are concerned with

1. The existence of a charge account
2. The customer's credit rating
3. Special management approval

Stating these conditions in such a way as to allow them to be answered by a simple yes or no answer and placing them in block A, we have

| Decision Table 1 | C |
|---|---|
| Customer Has A Charge Account | |
| Customer Has A Good Credit Rating | D |
| Customer Has Special Management Approval | |
| B | E |

Block B contains the possible courses of action. In our sample problem, there are two courses of action: Allow the credit purchase *or* refuse the credit purchase.

| Decision Table 1 | C |
|---|---|
| Customer Has A Charge Account | D |
| Customer Has A Good Credit Rating | |
| Customer Has Special Management Approval | |
| Accept Credit Purchase | E |
| Refuse Credit Purchase | |

Blocks C, D, and E are completed together. Each column contains a C, D, and E section and contains a specific combination of conditions (D) and action (E) and a name (C).

In our problem, there are four possible combinations of conditions for which action is to be taken (see Fig. 7-12).

Reading a decision table is simply a matter of reading each rule or action column to determine what combination of conditions suggest what action. For example, let us consider the decision table given below, which illustrates the rules for the multiplication of signed numbers as they relate to the sign of the product.

| Decision Table 2 | Rule 1 | Rule 2 | Rule 3 | Rule 4 |
|---|---|---|---|---|
| First Number Is Positive | Y | Y | N | N |
| Second Number Is Positive | Y | N | Y | N |
| Answer Is Positive | X | | | X |
| Answer Is Negative | | X | X | |

From this decision table one could determine that

Rule 1. (positive first no.) × (positive second no.) = positive answer.

Rule 2. (positive first no.) × (negative second no.) = negative answer.

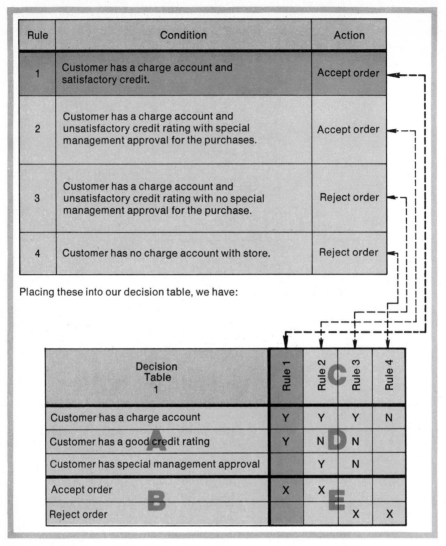

| Rule | Condition | Action |
|------|-----------|--------|
| 1 | Customer has a charge account and satisfactory credit. | Accept order |
| 2 | Customer has a charge account and unsatisfactory credit rating with special management approval for the purchases. | Accept order |
| 3 | Customer has a charge account and unsatisfactory credit rating with no special management approval for the purchase. | Reject order |
| 4 | Customer has no charge account with store. | Reject order |

Placing these into our decision table, we have:

| Decision Table 1 | Rule 1 | Rule 2 | Rule 3 | Rule 4 |
|------------------|--------|--------|--------|--------|
| Customer has a charge account | Y | Y | Y | N |
| Customer has a good credit rating | Y | N | N | |
| Customer has special management approval | | Y | N | |
| Accept order | X | X | | |
| Reject order | | | X | X |

**FIGURE 7-12**

Conditions and corresponding actions

Rule 3. (negative first no.) × (positive second no.) = negative answer.

Rule 4. (negative first no.) × (negative second no.) = positive answer.

It is also possible to construct a decision table involving conditions where the response can be less than ($<$), equal to ($=$), greater than ($>$), less than or equal to ($\leq$), greater than or equal to ($\geq$), or not equal to ($\neq$) instead of a simple "yes" or "no" response. For example, suppose

SOFTWARE, PROGRAM PREPARATION, AND PROBLEM-SOLVING CONCEPTS

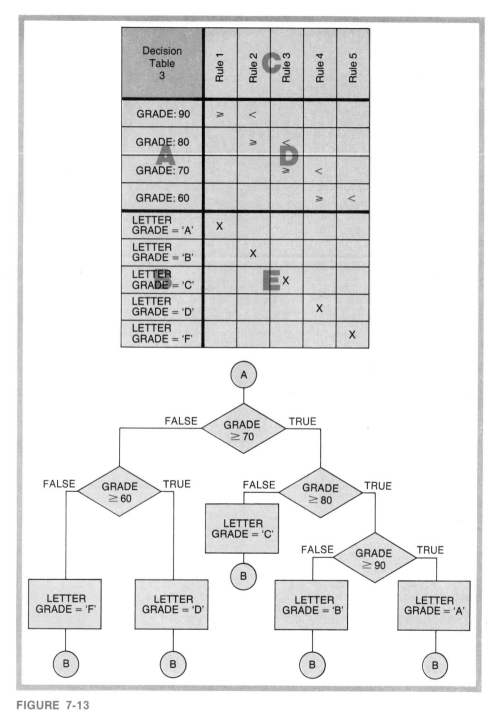

FIGURE 7-13

Decision table and flowchart for determining student's letter grade from numerical grade

that we wished to determine what letter grade a student should receive for a course, given his numerical average in the course. A possible decision table and program flowchart are given in Fig. 7-13.

*To verify your understanding of the previous material, turn to page 276 and take Self-Test 7-4.*

## TOP-DOWN PROGRAM DESIGN*

For many years data-processing personnel have been searching for more efficient program design techniques. For many, the methods used in writing a program were relatively unimportant; only the results were important. The programming process was considered an individual art rather than a carefully designed and structured practice. This attitude resulted in programs which were difficult to follow and virtually impossible to modify or update. To cope with this problem, MCAUTO[2] established a pilot task force to determine how and to what extent they could utilize some of the newer and improved programming techniques that were developing and emerging. One of the conclusions reached by this group was that one of the newer program design and coding techniques seemed to offer the greatest potential. This technique was referred to as *top-down program design* and offered the following advantages:

● improved program design
● reduced program complexity
● increased programmer efficiency

The top-down program design process utilizes two techniques:

● Hierarchy plus input-processing-output (HIPO)
● Structured programming

**Hierarchy plus Input- processing-output (HIPO)** HIPO, originally designed as a documentation tool, has become an invaluable tool of program design as well. The major objectives of HIPO as a design and documentation tool are:

1. State the functions to be accomplished by the program.
2. Provide an overall structure of hierarchy by which the individual functions of the program or system can be understood.
3. Provide a visual description of the input to be used and the output produced by each function.

To accomplish these ends, HIPO utilizes two types of charts: a **hierarchy chart** and an **input-process-output chart.** The hierarchy chart pictorially illustrates how each program function is divided into subfunctions or modules, and the input-process-output chart expresses each module in the hierarchy in terms of its input and output considerations. Examples of these charts are shown in Figs. 7-14 and 7-15.

[2]The McDonnell Douglas Automation Company, a division of the McDonnell Douglas Corporation.

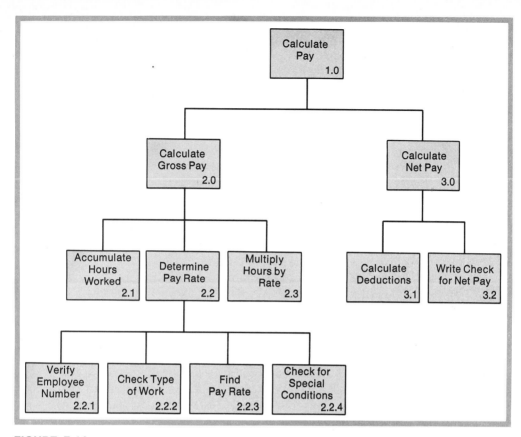

**FIGURE 7-14**

Example of a HIPO hierarchy chart

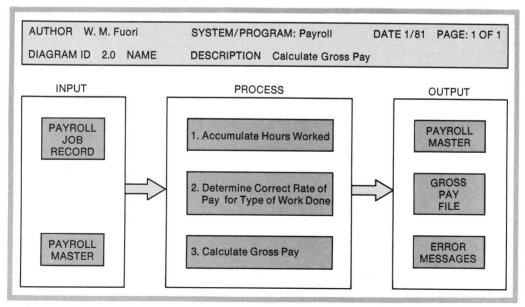

**FIGURE 7-15**

Example of a HIPO input/process/output chart

HIPO diagrams are constantly being refined as the program development continues. The initial emphasis is on ensuring that program functions are clearly understood by both the designers and users so that the resulting program will meet the needs for which it is being designed. The major functions of the program are listed at the top level and expanded to lower-level modules as more detail is required.

During this process, certain basic guidelines should be observed. All modules in the hierarchy chart should logically relate to one another, with control passing from the top module down to the next lower module, and so on. Each module in the hierarchy chart should represent only one program function and contain a single entry and a single exit. The function of each module should be specific enough so that it can be implemented with a minimum of one page or approximately 50 lines of coding. This will greatly enhance the readability of the code and simplify the testing and debugging of the module.

Once the hierarchy and input-processing-output charts have been completed, the detailed program design can commence. This can be accomplished with the aid of a program flowchart or pseudocode.

Modules should be programmed in the same order in which they appear in the hierarchy chart. The upper-level modules should be coded and tested before the coding of the next lower level is begun. When a module is tested, some provision must be made for the fact that it will generally call or reference a module lower in the hierarchy chart which has not yet been coded. In Fig. 7-14, for example, if we were to test module 2.2 (Determine Pay Rate), it would call modules 2.2.1 through 2.2.4. As these modules would not have been coded, we would have had to replace them temporarily with "dummy" modules in order to complete the testing of module 2.2. Dummy module 2.2.3, for example, would simply return some arbitrary pay rate and control back to module 2.2.

In this manner, each level of modules is tested and debugged before the next lower level is coded. As subsequent levels are tested, the upper levels are retested until finally, when the lowest level is tested, the whole program is actually being tested.

**Structured Programming**    Structured programming is defined in many different ways by many people. There is general agreement, however, on its purpose and its impact.

Its purpose, as the name suggests, is to produce programs that have a definite form and are therefore more easily understood by the programmer and by anyone else who needs to read and understand them. A program written with structured programming techniques is more likely to be *correct* than was possible with previous methods.

The impact of structured programming is evident in the amount of discussion and the number of articles and books about the subject and, more important to those about to study it, in the widespread adoption of structured programming by the data-processing and business communities.

A key characteristic of a structured program is that it is written using only three basic control structures: SEQUENCE, IF-THEN-ELSE, and DO-WHILE. These structures lend themselves to top-down program design, as each allows for a single entry point and a single exit. And since control flows from the top down, structure by structure, the logic of the program can be followed and understood easily.

The term **SEQUENCE structure** is used to describe program routines that are executed sequentially, one after the other. The following diagram illustrates a SEQUENCE structure, as routine A must be executed before routine B and no other routine can be executed between them.

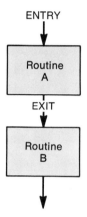

The **IF-THEN-ELSE structure** allows a program to branch to one of two routines on the basis of a condition that can be either true or false. This structure is graphically represented as follows:

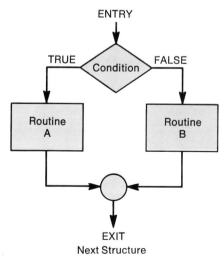

IF the condition is true, THEN routine A will be executed; ELSE routine B will be executed. Routines A and B do not necessarily have a SEQUENCE structure; they may have any of the three possible structures (SEQUENCE, IF-THEN-ELSE, or DO-WHILE). On completion of the IF-THEN-ELSE sequence, program execution will proceed to the next structure. If either the A or the B routine is not needed, the IF-THEN-ELSE structure will reduce to the following:

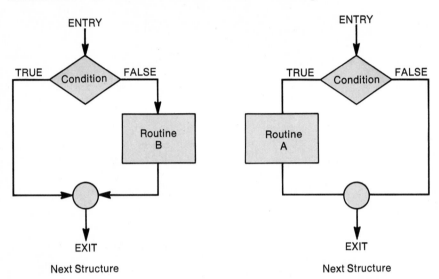

The **DO-WHILE structure** is used to describe the repetition of an action under prescribed conditions. This is commonly referred to as looping and is graphically illustrated below.

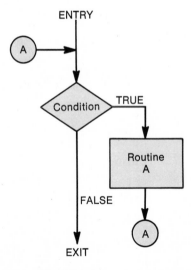

In this structure the program sequence is to DO routine A WHILE the condition is true. If the condition is false, control proceeds to the next structure. An accepted variation of this structure, referred to as the **DO-UNTIL structure,** is illustrated below.

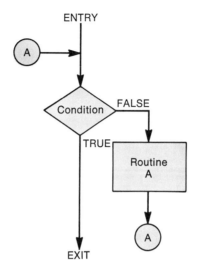

In this structure, the program sequence is to DO routine A UNTIL the condition is true.

Figure 7-16 illustrates a segment of a structured program to determine a salesman's pay.

In actual practice, many of these structures will be combined. Figure 7-17, for example, illustrates a sequence in which an IF-THEN-ELSE is controlled by a DO-WHILE. Figure 7-18 shows a SEQUENCE and DO-WHILE being controlled by an IF-THEN-ELSE.

Although these structures may, at first glance, appear to be somewhat limited, they can be utilized in various combinations to solve any problem.

To verify your understanding of the previous material, turn to page 276 and take Self-Test 7-5.

**Pseudocode**     Pseudocode, as its name implies, is an imitation computer code. It is used in place of symbols or a flowchart to describe the logic of a program. Pseudocode is intended to overcome the two principal disadvantages of the flowchart: The flowchart is time-consuming to create and is difficult to modify without redrawing it completely.

Pseudocode employs the basic structures utilized in structured programming (SEQUENCE, IF-THEN-ELSE, and DO-WHILE, or DO-

UNTIL). Figure 7-19 illustrates how these basic structures would appear in pseudocode. You will recall that these structures were used in the flowchart of a program segment to determine a salesperson's total pay based on base pay plus commission (see Fig. 7-16). The pseudocode equivalent of this flowchart would be

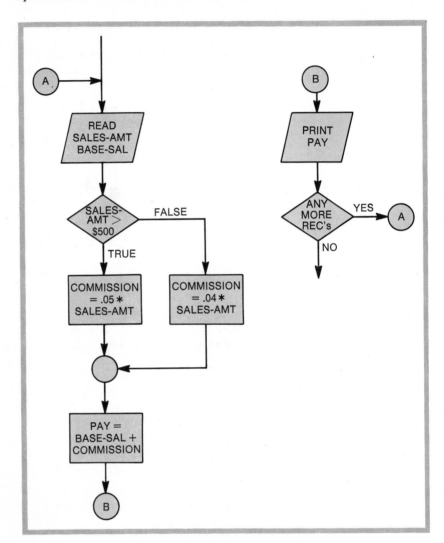

FIGURE 7-16
Structured flowchart segment to determine a salesperson's pay

SOFTWARE, PROGRAM PREPARATION, AND PROBLEM-SOLVING CONCEPTS

```
DO WHILE there are more records
  IF sales exceed $500.00
        calculate commission at 5% of sales
    ELSE calculate commission at 4% of sales
  ENDIF
  Add commission to base salary
  Write pay report
ENDDO
```

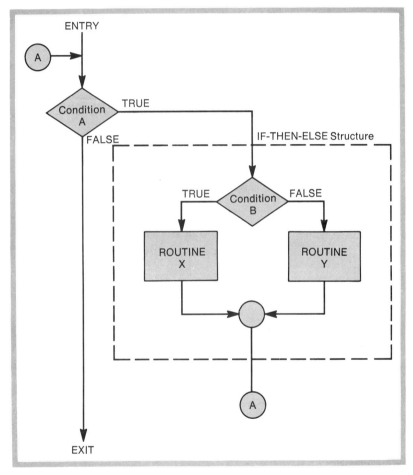

**FIGURE 7-17**
Example of an IF-THEN-ELSE controlled by a DO-WHILE

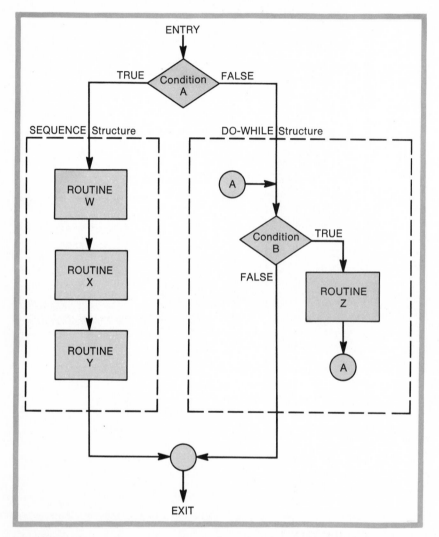

**FIGURE 7-18**
Program segment illustrating a SEQUENCE and DO-WHILE structure controlled by an IF-THEN-ELSE structure

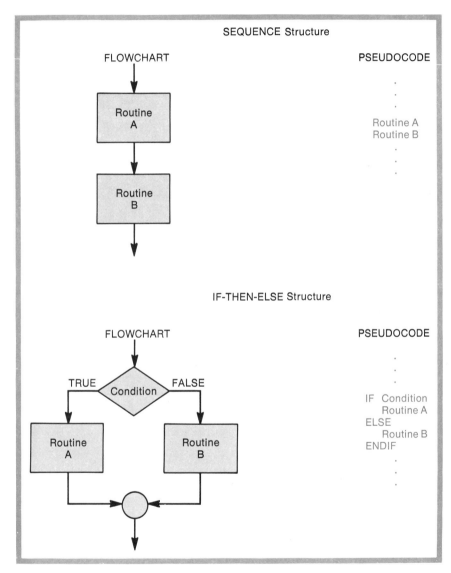

**FIGURE 7-19**
Basic structures shown in flowchart and pseudocode forms

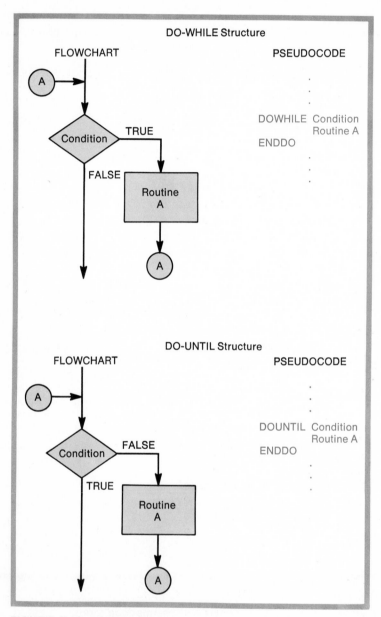

FIGURE 7-19 continued

SOFTWARE, PROGRAM PREPARATION, AND PROBLEM-SOLVING CONCEPTS

Programmers and systems analysts still disagree on whether they prefer the program flowchart or pseudocode. Both techniques are currently in use. Only the future will tell which technique, if any, will gain universal acceptance.

## SELF-TEST 7–1

1. A program flowchart indicates the _____ to be performed and the _____ in which they occur.
2. The two basic parts of a flowchart are _____ and _____ .
3. Each flowchart symbol represents a unique _____ which is determined by _____ .
4. To construct a flowchart, one must adhere to prescribed symbols provided by the _____ .
5. A program flowchart is read from _____ to _____ .
6. Flowcharting symbols are connected together by means of _____ .
7. Several _____ may be represented by one flowchart symbol.
8. The specific operation intended by a given flowchart symbol can be indicated by _____ .
9. The programmer uses a _____ to help in drawing flowchart symbols.
10. The names of the symbols below are _____ and _____ , respectively.

11. Two types of operations that are represented by a processing symbol are _____ and _____ .

## SELF-TEST 7–2

1. A decision operation is used to _____ .
2. A decision symbol may be used in determining the _____ between two data items.
3. The decision symbol may be used to determine whether the relationship _____ , _____ , _____ , _____ , _____ , or _____ holds between two data items.
4. _____ are used to join remote portions of a flowchart. They include _____ connectors, which specify where the flow is coming from, and _____ connectors, which specify where the new flow is to begin.
5. _____ connectors are used when a flowchart ends on one page and begins again on another page.
6. A _____ symbol is used at the beginning and end of a flowchart.

## SELF-TEST 7-3

1. The logical sequence of operations required to flowchart a problem can often be discovered using a series of _____.
2. In the flowchart note A = A + 6, A on the left of the = refers to _____, while A on the right of the = refers to _____.
3. When a program repeats the same group of instructions over and over again, the condition is termed _____.
4. A loop is terminated by _____ out of the loop.
5. In a flowchart, the symbol = means _____.
6. Four major flowcharting techniques include _____, _____, _____, and _____.
7. The flowchart is an integral part of program _____ and aids in developing the _____ necessary to solve the problem.

## SELF-TEST 7-4

1. A _____ is a means of recording, in tabular form, the various conditions to be considered in a problem and their associated courses of action.

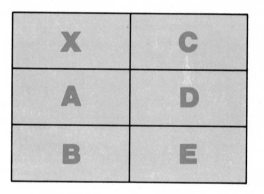

2. The six parts of the decision table shown above are _____, _____, _____, _____, _____, and _____.
3. Block A of the decision table above contains _____.
4. Block B of the decision table above contains the _____.
5. Blocks C, D and E are completed together and correspond to _____, _____, and _____, respectively.
6. Apart from the qualitative yes/no or true/false responses, a decision table may also contain _____ responses.

## SELF-TEST 7-5

1. _____ program design offers the advantages of improved program design, reduced program complexity, and increased programmer efficiency.
2. The two techniques employed in top-down program design are _____.

3. The two charts used by HIPO are _____.

4. Modules should be programmed in the _____ order as they appear in the hierarchy chart.

5. The principal control structures employed in a structured program are _____.

6. An acceptable variation of the DO-WHILE structure is the _____ structure.

7. An alternative to the program flowchart is _____.

**Answers to Self-Tests**

7–1

1. operations; sequence
2. symbols; flowlines
3. function; the shape of the symbol
4. American National Standards Institute
5. top; bottom
6. flowlines
7. operations
8. placing a note within the symbol
9. flowcharting template
10. input/output; processing
11. arithmetic; data transfer

7–2

1. alter the sequence of operations
2. relationship
3. less than, greater than, less than or equal to, greater than or equal to, equal to, or not equal to
4. Connectors; entry; branch or exit
5. Off-page
6. terminal

7–3

1. questions and answers
2. the value of A after the step has been completed; the value of A before this step
3. looping
4. branching
5. is replaced by the value of
6. initialization; looping; developing a sum; developing a counter
7. documentation; logic

7–4

1. decision table
2. X, name of decision table; A, condition stub; B, action stub; C, rule entry; D, condition entry; E, action entry
3. the possible conditions that can exist in the problem
4. possible courses of action
5. the name or rule number; the combinations of conditions; one action for each combination of conditions
6. quantitative or relational

7–5

1. Top-down
2. hierarchy plus input-processing-output (HIPO) and structured programming
3. hierarchy and input-process-output

4. same
5. SEQUENCE structure, IF-THEN-ELSE structure, and DO-WHILE structure
6. DO-UNTIL
7. pseudocode

# EXERCISES

**7–1**
**True/False**

_____ 1. Variables that require initialization are generally identifiable by the fact that they appear on both sides of the equal sign in a note contained within a processing symbol.

_____ 2. The top-down design process utilizes HIPO charts and structured programming.

_____ 3. A program flowchart indicates the operations to be performed in the sequence in which they are to occur.

_____ 4. The program flowchart is an integral part of program documentation.

_____ 5. The number next to an off-page connector indicates the number of off-page connectors in the program with the same letter inside.

_____ 6. Decision symbols should have only two exit paths.

_____ 7. The rectangular flowchart symbol represents an input/output function.

_____ 8. HIPO charts are used principally for program documentation.

_____ 9. A flowcharting template aids the programmer or analyst in constructing a program flowchart.

_____ 10. All computers signal the user when the last data item has been read by a program.

_____ 11. A program flowchart generally contains both symbols and notes.

_____ 12. A note is used to indicate a specific operation within a function category.

_____ 13. A flowchart containing no notes would be impractical.

_____ 14. Flowlines are used to connect symbols.

_____ 15. A loop is a sequence of operations that is executed repeatedly until an exit condition is met.

_____ 16. The function of each hierarchy module should be specific enough so that it can be implemented with approximately 50 lines of coding.

_____ 17. The condition entry of a decision table contains the name of the decision table.

_____ 18. Modules in a hierarchy chart should be programmed in order from the lowest level to the highest level.

_____ 19. Structured programming concepts are not practical for the small business.

_____ **20.** Flowcharts are generally read from top to bottom.

_____ **21.** Testing of a structured program should be performed module by module beginning with the highest-level module.

_____ **22.** Programmers and analysts agree that pseudocode is superior to the program flowchart.

_____ **23.** The DO-WHILE structure facilitates looping.

_____ **24.** Flowcharting standards are prescribed by the National Standards Bureau.

_____ **25.** Structured programming concepts encourage programmers to try new and exciting approaches to program design.

_____ **26.** A program flowchart has a similar place in programming to that of a blueprint in construction.

_____ **27.** The basic control structures should be independent and not combined where one structure might control another structure.

_____ **28.** The DO-UNTIL structure is an accepted variation of the DO-WHILE structure.

_____ **29.** The symbol = as used in a flowchart is defined as "is equal to."

_____ **30.** The key to developing an effective program flowchart is to analyze the problem in depth by setting up and answering a series of pertinent questions.

**7–2**
**Matching**

Match each of the symbols or decision table areas with the names given below. Note that more than one symbol may be associated with a single name.

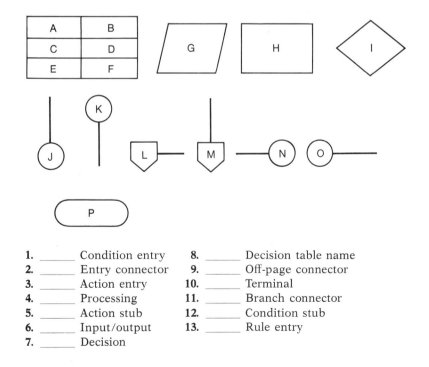

| 1. | _____ | Condition entry | 8. | _____ | Decision table name |
| 2. | _____ | Entry connector | 9. | _____ | Off-page connector |
| 3. | _____ | Action entry | 10. | _____ | Terminal |
| 4. | _____ | Processing | 11. | _____ | Branch connector |
| 5. | _____ | Action stub | 12. | _____ | Condition stub |
| 6. | _____ | Input/output | 13. | _____ | Rule entry |
| 7. | _____ | Decision | | | |

**7-3**
**Problems**

1. List the basic flowcharting symbols and name the function each represents. Describe two possible operations for each function.

2. Contrast the program flowchart with pseudocode. Which do you prefer? Explain.

3. What is the purpose of a decision table? Under what circumstances is the decision table most useful?

4. Name and describe each of the parts of the decision table given below.

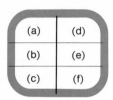

| (a) | (d) |
| (b) | (e) |
| (c) | (f) |

5. Construct a flowchart to describe the procedure you go through to determine what clothes to put out for the next day.

6. Construct a flowchart to describe the process you employ in studying for a test.

7. Construct a flowchart to describe how you would evaluate a used car that you are considering purchasing.

8. Draw a program flowchart to solve the following problem: Calculate gross pay from input data containing employee name, hours worked, and hourly rate. Assume that time-and-a-half is paid to any employee for those hours worked over 40 hours. Print your results.

9. Construct a decision table to determine which of the four numbers N1, N2, N3, and N4 is the smallest. If two or more of the four quantities are equal, any one of them may be selected as the smallest of the equal quantities.

10. Construct a flowchart for the problem in Exercise 9.

11. Construct a flowchart for a program to determine the amount and denominations of the minimum number of coins to be given in change for a purchase of D dollars paid for with an X-dollar bill. (X is not to exceed 2 but may be less than D.)

12. Construct a flowchart to read in the current date in MM/DD/YY format (MM is the month, DD is the day of the month, and YY is the last two digits in the year) and print out this date in Julian format YYDDD (YY is the last two digits of the year and DDD is the day of the year. For example, 01/25/81 and 12/31/81 would be 81025 and 81365, respectively, in Julian format.) Consideration of leap years is optional.

13. Construct a flowchart to determine the letter grade for each student in a class as follows:
   a. Read in the student's name and four examination grades.
   b. Determine the student's numerical average by averaging the student's three highest grades.
   c. Determine the letter grade appropriate for the numerical average computed in (b) above. Assume $A \geq 90$, $90 > B \geq 80$, $80 > C \geq 70$, $70 > D \geq 60$, $60 > F$.

    **d.** Print out the student's name, grades, lowest grade, average, and letter grade.

    **e.** Repeat the above four steps for each student until the student name "END" is read.

    **f.** Determine the average of all the students in the class and print it out.

**14.** Solve Problem 13 utilizing the basic control structures employed in structured programming if this was not done in Problem 13.

**15.** Complete a program flowchart for Problem 8 above utilizing the basic control structures employed in structured programming if not done in Problem 8.

**16.** Solve Problem 12 using pseudocode.

**17.** Solve Problem 13 using pseudocode.

INTRODUCTION

PREPARATION FOR PROGRAMMING

PROBLEM ANALYSIS

FLOWCHART APPLICATION

CODING AND EXECUTING THE APPLICATION PROGRAM

**Types of Instructions**
**Machine Language***
**Symbolic Language***
**Procedure-oriented Languages***
**Problem-oriented Language***
**Interactive Language***
**Compiling, Executing, and Debugging the Program**
Types of Programming Errors

DOCUMENTATION

**Organization of Program Documentation**
Title Page
Control Sheet
Narrative Descriptions
Narrative Modifications
Flowcharts and Decision Tables
Input and Output Data Codes
Input and Output Formats
Input Test Data and Sample Output
Other Instruction Sheets and Worksheets

FOCUS ON THE FIELD

SELF-TESTS

EXERCISES

# Introduction to Computer Languages and Programming

## INTRODUCTION

It is rarely the case that the accountant, business manager, or other computer user would attempt to prepare a computer program to solve his or her problem. More often, the user would communicate the problem to the programming department of the company or to an outside consulting firm and ask for a solution. An essential part of this cooperative process is that the accountant or business manager be able to communicate effectively to the programmer the nature and details of the problem in the most understandable and meaningful way. To do this, the accountant or business manager must understand, in general terms, what steps the programmer must go through in order to program a solution to a problem. Armed with a basic understanding of the programmer's needs, the businessperson can prepare the problem description and solution requirements in a manner which will be most easily understood by, and most meaningful to, the programmer. A mutual understanding, at this point in the development of a computerized solution to the problem, can avoid needless and wasteful changes and revisions in the future.

It is for this reason that we shall describe those facets of the programming function that the computer user should clearly understand.

Upon completion of this chapter you should be able to:

- Describe the programming process in detail
- List and describe the five types of computer instructions
- Compare the principal types of computer languages
- Describe the debugging process
- Describe the various items of documentation found in a run manual
- Define the following terms:

| | |
|---|---|
| Arithmetic instruction | Compiler |
| Assembly system | Control instruction |
| BASIC | Debugging |
| COBOL | Executing a program |
| Coding a program | FORTRAN |
| Coding error | Interactive language |
| Compilation | I/O instruction |

Logical instruction   Processor
Logic error      Program abstract
Machine language   Program documentation
PASCAL       RPG
PL/I         Run manual
Problem analysis    Specification instruction
Problem-oriented language Symbolic language
Procedure-oriented language Syntax error

## PREPARATION FOR PROGRAMMING

A considerable amount of preparation is necessary before a programmer actually begins to write the computer program. The programmer must consider many areas and answer many questions about the nature of the problem, its input, and its output. Some of these questions are:

1. What are the desired output data?
2. What are the output media?
3. What input is needed to produce the desired results?
4. What are the input/output formats?

These questions are typical of some of the multitude of questions which the problem analyst must answer in preparing an application for a digital computer. The problem analyst must be able to see the problem as a whole as well as its component parts. He or she must be able to understand the computer's limitations and the computer's advantages. In general, there are four areas that the problem analyst or programmer must consider in the course of developing a computerized solution to a problem:

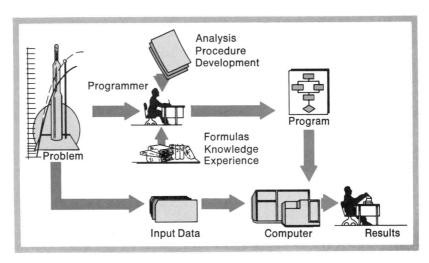

**FIGURE 8-1**

Direct conversion of problem to machine program

1. Problem analysis
2. Flowchart application
3. Coding and executing the application program
4. Documentation

## PROBLEM ANALYSIS

The first step in preparing an application for a computer is to define the problem precisely. Once defined, the problem should be carefully analyzed to ascertain whether or not using a computer is the most appropriate and efficient means of solving the problem. Unnecessary and wasteful major changes after the programming of a problem has been started may be avoided only if a detailed problem analysis takes place prior to the actual preparation of the program. Only after it has been determined that this problem warrants a computerized solution do we proceed to analyze the source data, the logical and practical procedures that will be needed to solve the problem, and the form of the final output. In the case of a simple payroll application, this analysis might reveal that required inputs would include regular hours worked, overtime hours worked, and a tape or disk file to input deductions, exemptions, and other data pertinent to payroll computations. It might also reveal that required outputs would include gross pay, withholding taxes, FICA deductions, accumulated tax-year withholdings and earnings, and, in addition, several detailed reports. Problem analysis is generally carried out in conjunction by the user and programmer or analyst.

## FLOWCHART APPLICATION[1]

A flowchart is a method by which the operations and flow of data during the solution of a problem may be shown using symbols and narrative descriptions. As we saw in Chapter 7, the **program flowchart** can be likened to the blueprint of a building. It represents what must be done to produce the desired building. As the designer draws a blueprint prior to beginning construction on a building, so does the programmer draw a flowchart prior to writing a computer program. And, as in the case of the drawing of a blueprint, a flowchart is drawn according to definite rules and utilizing standard flowchart symbols prescribed by the American National Standards Institute.

The flowchart serves three major functions:

1. It allows the user to view the logic of the problem's solution in a pictorial fashion.
2. It serves the programmer by breaking up a large problem into smaller steps which can be individually coded or programmed, without having to be concerned with how this smaller segment of the problem will fit into the total solution.

[1]Pseudocode may be used in place of a flowchart in some installations.

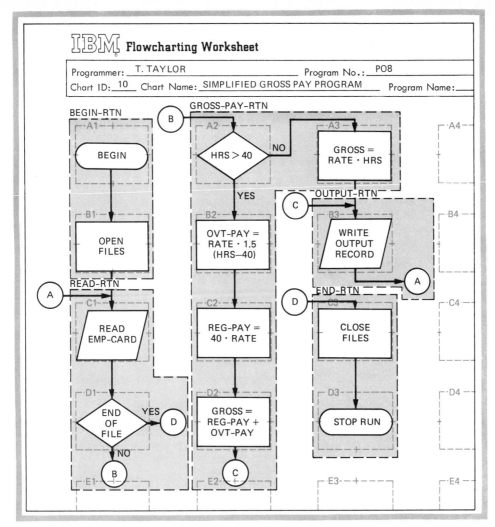

FIGURE 8-2

Sample program flowchart

3. It serves as a means of communication between the management analyst or accountant and the programmer and as a means of communication from programmer to programmer. The accountant, for example, does not have to be familiar with computer codes if he or she is able to understand a flowchart. From the flowchart it can be easily and quickly determined if the proposed computer program solution is logically correct and contains all necessary considerations and limitations. Even if one were capable of reading the programmer's coding, however well written and annotated, it would be very difficult and very dull work. Computers are designed to read code; human beings are more fluent with flowcharts.

When flowcharts were first used, they were crude and often difficult to follow. Every user had his/her own symbols and style, and this added to the difficulty of reading and understanding the logic of the problem's solution. Flowchart writing has, of course, been significantly refined and standardized since that time. A sample program flowchart using IBM's flowcharting worksheet is shown in Fig. 8-2.

To verify your understanding of the previous material, turn to page 313 and take Self-Test 8-1.

## CODING AND EXECUTING THE APPLICATION PROGRAM

After the problem has been analyzed and a detailed program flowchart has been written, the programmer must code the program as detailed in the flowchart. Coding simply involves the translation or conversion of each operation in the flowchart or pseudocode into a computer-understandable language. In our study of data processing thus far, we have learned that a computer program consists of a series of instructions that, when successfully carried out or executed, will accomplish the desired results. Let us now discuss the types of instructions that are available to the programmer.

**Types of Instructions**

Computer instructions consist of five types: (1) input/output, (2) control, (3) arithmetic, (4) logical, and (5) specification.

1. Input/output—Instructions of this type direct the computer to move information to and from the computer's memory and an input or output unit.
2. Control—Instructions of this type control the order in which other instructions are performed. That is, they direct the computer concerning what instruction is to be executed next.
3. Arithmetic—These instructions direct the performance of arithmetical computations and the moving of data from one place in memory to another.
4. Logical—Instructions of this type enable the computer to compare items of data and proceed according to the result of the comparison as well as enabling the computer to deviate from the normal sequence of instructions in accordance with the existence or nonexistence of certain conditions.
5. Specification—These instructions are descriptive in purpose, and through them the programmer can inform the computer regarding such items as the types of data items used in the program, the allocation of storage, and so forth.

However, we have not discussed how the programmer can communicate instructions to the computer. Many types or levels of computer languages are available to aid the programmer in communicating with the computer. Five of the more commonly used types of computer languages are:

1. Machine language
2. Symbolic language
3. Procedure-oriented language

4. Problem-oriented language
5. Interactive programming language

**Machine Language\*** Machine language is a series of numbers, letters of the alphabet, or special characters that are used to represent bit patterns which can be recognized by the computer and cause specific operations to take place. An example of a machine-language instruction to add regular pay to overtime pay, yielding total pay, might appear as follows:

21    300    400    500

In this example, the 21 is a code which means ADD to the computer. The 300 and 400 are addresses or locations at which regular pay and overtime pay are stored. The 500 represents the storage locations for the sum, total pay.

Let us examine more completely what would be happening inside a hypothetical computer before, during, and after the execution of this instruction.

To begin with, let us examine the memory of the computer immediately before the execution of this instruction (see Fig. 8-3). At this point, the instruction being executed is one that is located in storage prior to the ADD instruction under discussion. Since instructions are generally executed in sequential order as they exist in storage, the instruction under consideration will not be executed until the previous instructions have been executed. When the sequence of execution reaches this instruction, it will be taken from storage and executed. The execution of this instruction will consist of taking the contents of memory locations 300 and 400 and moving them to an accumulator. The accumulator then adds these two numbers, and the result is returned to storage location 500.

Control is then transferred to the next instruction in storage for execution. At this point, the memory of our hypothetical computer would appear as shown in Fig. 8-4. It is the programmer's task to make certain, via previous instructions, that regular pay and overtime pay are in locations 300 and 400, respectively. The machine has no way of knowing what should be in these locations, and therefore it adds their contents regardless of whether these contents are correct or incorrect. The programmer, then, must know what codes correspond to what operations. For example, the code 21 means ADD. He or she must ensure that the instructions are written and executed in the correct order in addition to keeping track of what data are stored at what addresses and ascertaining that the correct information is at this address when it is needed. In short, machine-language programming places a large burden on the person writing the program to keep track of the details involved.

Although machine language is ideal for the computer, programmers find it a difficult and tedious one with which to work. Because of this fact, long and detailed programs are rarely written in machine language. Other easier-to-use languages have been devised to make the

| Memory Address | Memory Contents | Content Description |
|---|---|---|
| 0001 | • • • | First Instruction |
| ⋮ | ⋮ | ⋮ |
| 0040 | 21300400500 | ADD Instruction |
| ⋮ | ⋮ | ⋮ |
| 0210 | 31 | STOP Instruction |
| ⋮ | ⋮ | ⋮ |
| 0300 | 3476 | The First Number to Be Added |
| ⋮ | ⋮ | ⋮ |
| 0400 | 24192 | The Second Number to Be Added |
| ⋮ | ⋮ | ⋮ |
| 0500 | • • • | Any Number Remaining in this Storage Location from the Previous Operation |

FIGURE 8-3

Contents of computer memory before executing ADD instruction

programmer's task an easier one. However, since the computer is only capable of understanding and executing instructions written in machine language, programs written in other languages will eventually have to be translated into machine language before they can be executed. Translators for other standard languages are generally provided with the computer by the computer manufacturer. Such languages fall into four categories, symbolic languages, procedure-oriented languages, problem-oriented languages, and interactive languages.

| Memory Address | Memory Contents | Content Description |
|---|---|---|
| 0001 | • • • | First Instruction |
| ⋮ | ⋮ | ⋮ |
| 0040 | 21300400500 | ADD Instruction |
| ⋮ | ⋮ | ⋮ |
| 0210 | 31 | STOP Instruction |
| ⋮ | ⋮ | ⋮ |
| 0300 | 3476 | The First Number to Be Added |
| ⋮ | ⋮ | ⋮ |
| 0400 | 24192 | The Second Number to Be Added |
| ⋮ | ⋮ | ⋮ |
| 0500 | 27668 | The Sum of the Numbers Stored in Memory Locations 300 & 400 |

FIGURE 8-4

Contents of computer memory after executing ADD instruction

**Symbolic Language***     A symbolic language is one which is very closely related to machine language in that, in general, one symbolic instruction will translate into one machine-language instruction.

The advantage of such a language is in the ease with which the programmer can use the language. A symbolic instruction contains fewer symbols, and these symbols may be letters and special characters, as well as numbers. Let us consider the hypothetical machine-language instruction discussed in the previous section, as shown below:

21    300    400    500

The symbolic equivalent might appear as

A    RPAY    OPAY    TPAY

When this instruction is translated by a manufacturer-supplied translator, the A will be replaced by 21, the name RPAY replaced by the address 300, the name OPAY replaced by the address 400, and the name TPAY replaced by the address 500.

As you can see, the symbolic instruction would be significantly easier to write than the machine-language equivalent and is certainly easier to read and understand. This last factor is especially important in regard to the ease with which corrections and changes can be made. On the other hand, a certain amount of time is required to convert from symbolic to machine language, but this does not compare to the time saved by the programmer in working with a symbolic language as opposed to working with machine language.

The translation from symbolic to machine language is done by a computer program referred to as an **assembly system,** or **processor.** This assembly system keeps track of all memory locations and all names or symbolic tags associated with memory locations. This translation process also provides the programmer with error diagnostics to assist in detecting certain types of coding errors.

Summarizing, one could say that when the programming goal is to employ an easy-to-read, easy-to-write, and easy-to-modify language in addition to making the most efficient use of the computer's hardware, a program should be written in the symbolic language.

However, symbolic language leaves two things to be desired: a programming language more similar to that normally used to describe the problem or procedure and a programming language that is virtually machine independent and can be used on various computers. These two properties are possessed by the procedure-oriented languages.

**Procedure-oriented Languages***    Assembly systems or machine-oriented programming systems require a thorough understanding of the computer system (hardware) to be used in the execution of the program by the programmer. In contrast, procedure-oriented programming systems for all practical purposes remove the necessity for the programmer to understand how the computer system will go about executing the program. The programmer may, instead, concentrate on expressing the procedure or logic of solving the problem. In many cases, it is not even necessary that one know what kind of computer system will be used for the execution of the program. The translation from a procedure-oriented language to machine language is done by a program referred to as a **compiler.** This name was chosen because a procedure-oriented system usually compiles many machine-language instructions from one source-language statement.

There are over 100 procedure-oriented languages currently in existence, the most popular and commonly used of these being FORTRAN (*FOR*mula *TRAN*slator) and COBOL (*CO*mmon *B*usiness *O*riented *Lan*guage), PASCAL (named after the mathematician Blaise Pascal), and PL/I (Programming Language I) (see Fig. 8-5). The languages of FORTRAN, COBOL, PL/I, and PASCAL have become so common and so extensively used that a variation of, if not the complete version of, each of these languages is available for virtually every medium to large computer manufactured.

Table 8-1 illustrates how the assembly-language instruction mentioned above

A    RPAY    OPAY    TPAY

might appear in machine language, FORTRAN and COBOL.

Advantages of using procedure-oriented languages are many. Procedure-oriented languages are accompanied by extensive diagnostic routines that often make program checking far simpler than with assembly languages. Procedure-oriented language instructions are written in a manner very similar to that normally used to describe the problem by the scientific- or business-oriented individual (see Figs. 8-5 and 8-6). And finally, procedure-oriented languages are virtually machine independent. That is, a computer program written for one computer installation can be used on another similar-sized computer system, even one produced by a different manufacturer, with just a few minor changes.

**TABLE 8-1**
Comparison of Instructions in Different
Computer Languages

| COMPUTER LANGUAGE | INSTRUCTION FORMAT |
|---|---|
| Machine language | 21   300   400   500 |
| Symbolic language | A   RPAY OPAY TPAY |
| FORTRAN | TOTPAY = REGPAY + OVTPAY |
| COBOL | ADD REGPAY, OVTPAY GIVING TOTPAY |

```
001010 IDENTIFICATION DIVISION.
001020 PROGRAM-ID. 'PROG2'.
001030 AUTHOR. DR WM FUCRI.
001050 ENVIRONMENT DIVISION.
001060 CONFIGURATION SECTION.
001070 SOURCE-COMPUTER. IBM-360 E25.
001080 OBJECT-COMPUTER. IBM-360 E25.
001090 INPUT-OUTPUT SECTION.
001100 FILE-CONTROL.
001110     SELECT IN-FILE ASSIGN TO 'SYSC05' UNIT-RECCRD 2540R UNIT.
001120     SELECT OUT-FILE ASSIGN TO 'SYSC07' UNIT-RECORD 1403 UNIT.
001140 DATA DIVISION.
001150 FILE SECTION.
001160 FD  IN-FILE
001170     RECORD CONTAINS 80 CHARACTERS
001180     RECORDING F
001190     LABEL RECORD OMITTED
001200     CATA RECORD IS CARD-IN.
002010 01  CARD-IN.
002020     02 ITEM-DES             PICTURE X(20).
002030     02 INV-NO               PICTURE 9(5).
002040     02 UNIT-PRC             PICTURE 9(4)V99.
002050     02 QUANTITY             PICTURE 9(4).
002060     02 FILLER               PICTURE X(45).
002070 FD  OUT-FILE
002080     RECORD CONTAINS 133  CHARACTERS
002090     RECORDING F
002100     LABEL RECORD OMITTED
002110     DATA RECORD IS PRINTOUT.
002120 01  PRINTOUT               PICTURE X(133).
002130 WORKING-STORAGE SECTION.
002140 77  QUANTI      PICTURE 99999999V99 VALUE ZEROS.
002150 77  FINAL-TOTAL PICTURE 99999999999V99 VALUE ZEROS.
003010 01  TITLE-1.
003020     02 FILLER               PICTURE X(61) VALUE SPACES.
003030     02 TITLE1               PICTURE X(12) VALUE 'SALES REPORT'.
003040     02 FILLER               PICTURE X(60) VALUE SPACES.
003050 01  TITLE-2.
003060     02 FILLER               PICTURE X(36) VALUE SPACES.
003070     02  TITLE2    PICTURE X(17) VALUE 'ITEM           '.
003080     02 TITLE3               PICTURE X(14) VALUE 'INVENTORY    '.
003090     02 TITLE4               PICTURE X(13) VALUE '  UNIT       '.
003100     02 FILLER               PICTURE X(53) VALUE SPACES.
```

FIGURE 8-5
COBOL source program listing

However, there are several disadvantages that are associated with the use of procedure-oriented or compiler languages. The first disadvantage is the time lost in translating to machine language. Another disadvantage is that the machine-translated or compiled program may not make as efficient use of the computer's resources as a program written by an experienced programmer using a symbolic or machine-language system. The advantages, it would seem quite evident, greatly outweigh the disadvantages.

As compilers are improved, an on-going process, the advantages of their use will become numerous, the efficiency greater, and the disadvantages less and less.

```
003110 01    TITLE-3.
003120       02 FILLER                    PICTURE X(33) VALUE SPACES.
003130       02 TITLE5      PICTURE X(20) VALUE 'DESCRIPTION       '.
003140       02 TITLE6      PICTURE X(14) VALUE '   NUMBER      '.
003150       02 TITLE7      PICTURE X(13) VALUE '   PRICE      '.
003160       02 TITLE8      PICTURE X(15) VALUE 'QUANTITY        '.
003170       02 TITLE9      PICTURE X(11) VALUE '   TOTAL      '.
003180       02 FILLER      PICTURE X(27) VALUE SPACES.
003190 01    DETAIL.
003200       02 FILLER      PICTURE X(28) VALUE SPACES.
003210       02 ITEM-D      PICTURE X(20).
003220       02 FILLER      PICTURE X(7) VALUE SPACES.
003230       02 INV-N       PICTURE 9(5).
003240       02 FILLER      PICTURE X(7) VALUE SPACES.
003250       02 UNIT-P      PICTURE $ZZZZ.99.
004010       02 FILLER      PICTURE X(7) VALUE SPACES.
004020       02 QUANT       PICTURE ZZZ9.
004030       02 FILLER      PICTURE X(9) VALUE SPACES.
004040       02 TOTAL       PICTURE $ZZZZZZZZ.99.
004050       02 FILLER      PICTURE X(27) VALUE SPACES.
004060 01    TOTAL-SALES.
004070       02 FILLER      PICTURE X(76) VALUE SPACES.
004080       02 TITLE10     PICTURE X(16) VALUE 'TOTAL SALES
004090       02 TOTAL-S     PICTURE $ZZZZZZZZZZ.99.
004100       02 FILLER      PICTURE X(27) VALUE SPACES.
004120 PROCEDURE DIVISION.
004130       OPEN INPUT IN-FILE, OUTPUT OUT-FILE.
004140 START.
004160       WRITE PRINTOUT FROM TITLE-1 AFTER ADVANCING 0 LINES.
004170       WRITE PRINTOUT FROM TITLE-2 AFTER ADVANCING 3 LINES.
004180       WRITE PRINTOUT FROM TITLE-3 AFTER ADVANCING 1 LINES.
004190 READ1.
004200       READ IN-FILE AT END GO TO WRAP-UP.
004210       MULTIPLY UNIT-PRC BY QUANTITY GIVING QUANT1.
004220       ADD QUANT1 TO FINAL-TOTAL.
004230       MOVE ITEM-DES TO ITEM-D.
004240       MOVE INV-NO TO INV-N.
004250       MOVE UNIT-PRC TO UNIT-P.
005010       MOVE QUANTITY TO QUANT.
005020       MOVE QUANT1 TO TOTAL.
005030       WRITE PRINTOUT FROM DETAIL AFTER ADVANCING 1 LINES.
005040       GO TO READ1.
005050 WRAP-UP.
005060       MOVE FINAL-TOTAL TO TOTAL-S.
005070       WRITE PRINTOUT FROM TOTAL-SALES AFTER ADVANCING 1 LINES.
005080       CLOSE IN-FILE, OUT-FILE.
005090       STOP RUN.
```

FIGURE 8-5 continued

**Problem-oriented Language***   The principal problem-oriented language is RPG (Report Program Generator). RPG was first introduced with second-generation computers and is still going strong. It was intended for use with small computer systems for the creation of business-oriented reports requiring small to moderate amounts of mathematical calculation. Programs are written in RPG by filling out special RPG specification sheets. These sheets allow the programmer to describe the components of his program in a mechanical fashion requiring very little knowledge of the computer's hardware characteristics. Each component of the program is described on these sheets, one for file description, input processing, calculations to be performed, and output processing. (See Fig. 8-7.)

```
C       SAMPLE FORTRAN PROGRAM
        READ (1,10) PRINC, RATE, PERPYR, NOPER
10 FORMAT (F7.2,F4.3,F4.0,I4)
        AMT = PRINC * (1.0 + RATE / PERPYR) ** NOPER
        WRITE (3,20) PRINC, RATE, PERPYR, NOPER, AMT
20 FORMAT (1H1,10X,'PRINCIPAL INVESTED = ',F7.2/
     -           11X,'ANNUAL RATE = ',F4.3/
     -           11X,'COMPOUNDED ',F4.0,' TIMES PER YEAR'/
     -           11X,'COMPOUNDED FOR A TOTAL OF ',I4,' PERIODS'//
     -           8X,'***********************************************'/
     -           8X,'*            AMOUNT = ',F10.2,'            *'/
     -           8X,'***********************************************')
        CALL EXIT
        END
```

FIGURE 8-6
Sample of FORTRAN program segment

Although RPG lacks the flexibility and power of the more sophisticated programming languages such as FORTRAN, COBOL, and PL/I, it does provide a fast and simple technique for producing computer-generated business reports.

**Interactive Language***  Interactive programming languages allow the programmer to communicate with the computer on a conversational basis. The programmer can simply key in the program, instruction by instruction, via a CRT or teletype terminal. After the program has been input, the computer can be directed to execute the program with a one-word command. Computer responses to the programmer's commands take place in a matter of seconds, as if the programmer and the computer were having a private conversation. In fact, possibly twenty other programmers are communicating with the computer currently, although no indication is given of this.

Programs written for interactive processing are generally simple and involve minimal data. Interactive programming is used to process one-time programs, transaction processing, and data inquiry.

The most common of all interactive programming languages is BASIC (Beginner's All-purpose Symbolic Instruction Code). This language was originally developed at Dartmouth College. BASIC was intended to be a simple language, useful for teaching programming concepts. Because of its simplicity and powerful capabilities, however, BASIC became a popular language for use with terminals in a time-sharing environment.

In the time-sharing environment, terminal users create small- to medium-sized programs and execute these directly from the terminal. BASIC, with its easily learned vocabulary and limited input/output capability, is ideally suited for this environment.

In appearance, BASIC is similar to FORTRAN, since it also uses a concise mathematical form of notation. The simplicity of the language has prompted many people to declare that BASIC is virtually the easiest

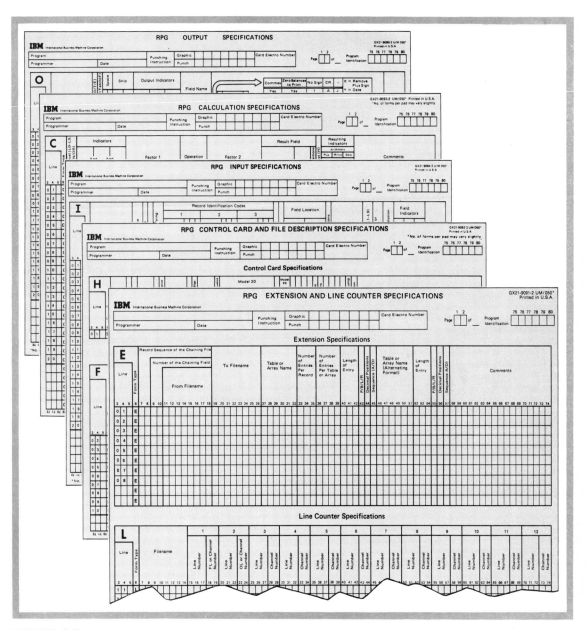

FIGURE 8-7

RPG specifications sheets

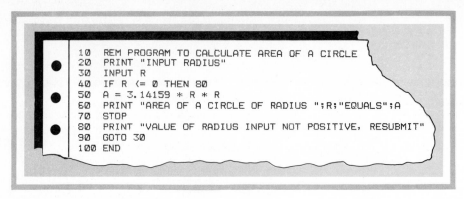

```
10   REM PROGRAM TO CALCULATE AREA OF A CIRCLE
20   PRINT "INPUT RADIUS"
30   INPUT R
40   IF R <= 0 THEN 80
50   A = 3.14159 * R * R
60   PRINT "AREA OF A CIRCLE OF RADIUS ";R;"EQUALS";A
70   STOP
80   PRINT "VALUE OF RADIUS INPUT NOT POSITIVE, RESUBMIT"
90   GOTO 30
100  END
```

**FIGURE 8-8**

Sample BASIC program

programming language to learn. An example of BASIC programming is shown in Fig. 8-8.

Once the programmer has determined which level of computer language, and what specific language within this level, is most appropriate for use in the solution of the problem, he or she is prepared to code the solution. The coding phase can be completed easily and quickly if a sufficiently detailed flowchart has been previously prepared.

**Compiling, Executing, and Debugging the Program**

Once the problem has been analyzed, flowcharted, and coded, it is ready to be compiled, executed or tested, and debugged.[2]

Compiling. The compiler is a translator program supplied by the manufacturer of the computer system. The primary purpose of the compiler is to translate the source program into a language and form which the computer can execute. Compilers are generally maintained on disk or tape with a backup tape kept in the company's library. In the case of the microcomputer, the compiler actually can be maintained on a PROM chip for immediate access. In all other cases, the compiler must be loaded into the computer. Once in the computer, the compiler will read in the program being compiled as data. The compiler will then convert the programmer's instructions into machine-language instructions. During this translation, the compiler will print out messages concerning any coding errors present in the program.

Types of Programming Errors. There are two general types of errors that programmers make: syntax or coding errors and logic errors.

A *syntax* or *coding* error occurs when the programmer fails to follow the rules on how a particular instruction is to be written. For exam-

---

[2]The term **debug** simply means to locate and correct any errors, or "bugs," that have been made in the preparation of the program.

ple, if a programmer misspelled the word WRITE in an instruction, the computer would print out a diagnostic message to inform the programmer that a coding error had been made, the statement in which it occurred, and the nature of the error. Figure 8-10 illustrates those diagnostic messages that resulted from the incorrectly written student program shown in Fig. 8-9. As a result of the severity of these errors, the computer was unable to understand the program completely and consequently the program was not executed. Compilers available with most large computer systems have reached a level of sophistication that allows them to make corrective assumptions concerning common coding errors. For example, if a programmer omitted a required comma in an instruction, the compiler would print out an appropriate diagnostic message and proceed with the compilation as if the comma had been present.

"Pardon me, are we going to the personnel office, or is this part of the psychological testing?"

Once the programmer has removed all the coding errors, the compiler is able to understand and translate the programmer's instructions. However, when executed, the translated instructions may not be appropriate to solve the problem. Errors resulting from an incorrect sequence of instructions are referred to as *logic* errors. For example, if the programmer added instead of subtracted, he or she would have made an error in the program logic—a logic error. There are no fixed rules on how debugging a program containing logic errors should be accomplished, because the kinds of bugs that can occur are so varied. Debugging a computer program is like solving a murder mystery. The programmer, as the detective, must exercise all his or her deductive reasoning powers to determine the culprit. The programmer must col-

```
00001      001010 IDENTIFICATION DIVISION.
00002      001020 PROGRAM-ID. PROGRAM1.
00003      002010 ENVIRONMENT DIVISION.
00004      002020 CONFIGURATION SECTION.
00005      002030 SOURCE-COMPUTER. IBM-370-H155.
00006      002040 OBJECT-COMPUTER. IBM-370-H155.
00007      003010 DATA DIVISION.
00008      003030 WORKING-STORAGE SECTION.
00009    **003020 77  DATA-OUT  PIC $999.99.
00010      004010 PROCEDURE DIVISION.
00011      004020 START.
00012      004030     ACCEPT DATA-IN.
00013      004040     MOVE DATA-IN TO DATA-OUT.
00014      004050     DISPLAY DATA-OUT.
00015      004060 STOP RUN.
```

FIGURE 8-9

Sample program containing coding errors

| CARD | ERROR MESSAGE |
|------|---------------|
| | |
| 11 | IKF1100I-W SEQUENCE ERROR IN SOURCE PROGRAM. |
| 11 | IKF1087I-W * START * SHOULD NOT BEGIN A-MARGIN. |
| 11 | IKF4050I-E SYNTAX REQUIRES QISAM-FILE WITH NOMINAL KEY . FOUND END-OF-SENT . STATEMENT DISCARDED. |
| 12 | IKF3001I-E DATA-IN NOT DEFINED. DISCARDED. |
| 13 | IKF3001I-E DATA-IN NOT DEFINED. DISCARDED. |
| 15 | IKF1087I-W * STOP * SHOULD NOT BEGIN A-MARGIN. |

**FIGURE 8-10**

Computer diagnostics for sample program

"Now hear this! I am the programmer. You are the programmee!"

lect all clues and try to fit them into a pattern. As the detective reenacts the crime to gain insight into the solution, the programmer runs or executes the program utilizing carefully prepared sample data. These sample data must be prepared so as to test the results of all possible types of transactions and all possible alternatives that could occur during the actual running of the finished program. This process can uncover an error or bug which might otherwise have gone undetected, and it is certainly better to determine the existence of the error or bug at this point than when the program is in actual use in the field. Once debugged, the program should again be tested using actual data for which a solution is known. In this way, the program can again be tested by the programmer and the results verified by the user, be he or she an accountant, business manager, or other user. Any discrepancies between the manner in which the user planned to input the data and the manner in which the programmer expected to receive the data will be clearly apparent at this point and can be rectified.

In testing larger or more complex programs, it is usually advisable to test one segment or module of the program at a time. When all segments have been tested, the complete program may then be tested. Segmenting a large program facilitates finding errors, as the more errors that there are in a program, the more difficult they are to find, since one error may obscure clues to other errors.

To verify your understanding of the previous material, turn to page 314 and take Self-Test 8-3.

## DOCUMENTATION

The programming process is not complete until the program has been written and thoroughly field tested for a substantial period of time. A program is said to be operational when it has been thoroughly tested and completely documented.

It is essential that the programmer adequately document each program. A properly documented program is useful for management in understanding the application and its solution, aids the public accountant in performing an audit, and serves as a frame of reference for those who would implement or modify the program. It is far easier to modify or update a thoroughly documented program than one which may be absolutely correct and efficient but has been shabbily documented.

It is equally essential that each program not be over- or under-documented. Overdocumentation can be needlessly expensive and time-consuming and overwhelming to those who must refer to it, and it can result in great delays in the implementation of the program. Underdocumentation, however, can also be needlessly expensive and time-consuming because of the confusion and misunderstandings resulting from incomplete or missing information. Therefore, it is essential that a program be *appropriately* documented.

Documentation should not be something a programmer considers after a program has been written and debugged; it should be an integral part of the programming process. For example, Fig. 8-11 illustrates two COBOL program segments, both technically correct and both intended to perform the same function. It should be apparent that the programmer of the second version, by appropriately choosing data names, has produced a clearer and better documented program. The additional time and effort expended are easily justified by the added clarity obtained, which will ultimately result in time and cost savings.

```
004010    P2.
004020        READ T END GO TO P7.
004030    P3.
004040        IF H > 40 GO TO P5.
004050    P4.
004060        COMPUTE G = R * H.
004070        GO TO P6.
004080    P5.
004090        COMPUTE S = 40 * R.
004100        COMPUTE O = 1.5 * R * (H - 40).
004110        COMPUTE G = S + O.
004120    P6.



004010    READ-TIME-CARD.
004020        READ TIME-CARD, AT END GO TO END-PROGRAM.
004030    DETERMINE-OVERTIME.
004040        IF HOURS-WORKED > 40, GO TO GROSS-PAY-WITH-OVERTIME.
004050    GROSS-PAY-NO-OVERTIME.
004060        COMPUTE GROSS-PAY = HOURLY-RATE * HOURS-WORKED.
004070        GO TO NET-PAY-ROUTINE.
004080    GROSS-PAY-WITH-OVERTIME.
004090        COMPUTE REGULAR-PAY = 40 * HOURLY-RATE.
004100        COMPUTE OVERTIME-PAY = 1.5 * HOURLY-RATE *
004110            (HOURS-WORKED - 40).
004120        COMPUTE GROSS-PAY = REGULAR-PAY + OVERTIME-PAY.
004130    NET-PAY-ROUTINE.
```

**FIGURE 8-11**

Two COBOL program segments

**Organization of Program Documentation**[3] There are numerous forms that can be used in documenting a program. Many forms are shown throughout this chapter, but these vary greatly from computer installation to computer installation. Each installation establishes its own documentation standards with respect to the forms used and the information to be placed on each form. Therefore, in this chapter, only those standards are discussed that are required by most existing installations. The programmer generally collects the documentation information into a folder referred to as a **procedures** or **run manual** (see Fig. 8-12). Some of the papers that are generally included in this manual are the following:

1. Title page
2. Control sheet
3. Narrative descriptions
4. Narrative modifications

[3]This material is taken with permission from *Introduction to American National Standard COBOL* by William M. Fuori, McGraw-Hill Book Company, 1975.

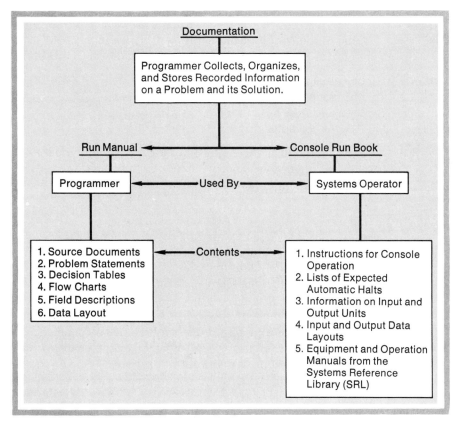

FIGURE 8-12

Documentation of a program

5. Flowcharts and decision tables
6. Input and output data codes
7. Input and output formats
8. Input test data and sample output
9. Other instruction sheets and worksheets

Title Page.  The title page of a run manual contains basic information about the program for easy reference. Some of the items generally contained on the title page of a run manual are shown in Fig. 8-13.

Control Sheet.  The control sheet is used to indicate to a reader of the run manual that changes have been made in the program since the time it was first documented and implemented. This sheet indicates such items as

1. The section of the manual or program that has been changed
2. The name and title of the individual making the change
3. The name and title of the individual who approved the change
4. The date the change became effective
5. The duration of the change

Some of the conditions affecting a program that would require the above entries on the control sheet may include the following:

1. Changes in input or output media
2. Changes in input or output formats
3. Changes in the logic of the program
4. Code or condition changes

Thus, the control sheet not only documents the changes that the program has undergone since its inception but also serves as an indication that the documentation of the program is current.

Narrative Descriptions.  Although the purpose of the program is stated on the Title Page, this is not sufficient for documentation purposes. In this section, the program must be discussed in sufficient detail so that the reader can clearly understand what the program does and how it goes about doing it. Many installations refer to this description as a **program abstract.** A typical abstract for the program described on the sample Title Page is illustrated in Fig. 8-14. Note that this abstract describes the input, output, and processing requirements of the program.

In some narrative descriptions it may be necessary to include or refer to specific statements within the program. This situation is rare, however, and should be avoided whenever possible.

Narrative Modifications.  This section is intended to contain descriptions of any modifications that the program has undergone, whether or not they involve actual changes in the source program itself. Entries in

TITLE PAGE

| | |
|---|---|
| PROGRAM NAME | CREATE-EARNINGS-FILE |
| PROGRAM NUMBER | P003 |
| PROGRAMMER | William M. Fuori, Ext 406 |
| USER | Payroll Department, Ext 493 |
| DATE WRITTEN | January 15, 1975 |
| PROJECT SUPERVISOR | T.M. Taylor, Ext 348 |
| SCHEDULE | Weekly (Wednesday) |
| ESTIMATED TIME | 15 Minutes |
| CONTROLS | Total of straight and overtime hours with control totals from Payroll Department. Internal & external tape label checks. |
| SECURITY | None |
| PURPOSE OF PROGRAM | Generate an Earning File from the Master File and Earnings Cards. |
| INPUT | (1) MASTER-FILE<br>Reel Label: MASTER-P003<br>Data Records: MASTER-REC<br>Estimated Volume: 350 records (1 reel)<br>Sequence: Numeric by Employee Number<br>Tape Labels: Standard volume, header, and trailer<br>Record Length: 200 Characters<br>Blocking Factors: 5<br><br>(2) PAY-CARD<br>Source: Payroll Department<br>Data Records: PAY-REC<br>Estimated Volume: 350 cards<br>Sequence: Numeric by Employee Number<br>Forms: 0583 Preprinted Payroll cards |
| OUTPUT | (1) CURRENT-EARNINGS<br>Reel Label: EARNINGS-P003<br>Data Records: CUR-EARN<br>Estimated Volume: 350 records (1 reel)<br>Sequence: Numeric by Employee Number<br>Tape Labels: Standard volume, header, and trailer<br>Record Length: 157 Characters<br>Blocking Factor: 5<br><br>(2) EXCEPTION-REPORT<br>When Issued: Whenever input data exceptions occur<br>Form Used: 0585 Preprinted continous forms |
| DISTRIBUTION | Earnings File to be maintained in Computer Center.<br>Copy 1 of Exception Report (if any) to Payroll Department. |
| REMARKS | Program provides input to programs P002, P005, P006, and P008. |

NCC Form 1887

**FIGURE 8-13**

Sample run manual title page

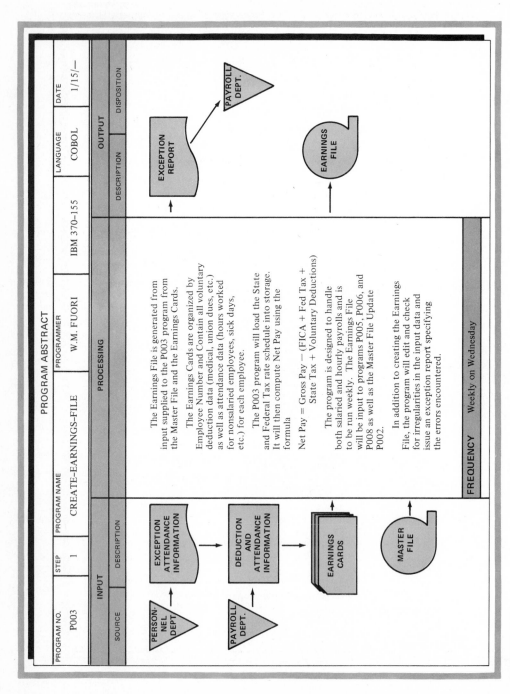

**FIGURE 8-14**

Sample program abstract

this section should be as brief as possible. They should be summaries and not line-by-line analyses.

It is also a good practice to correlate the narrative modifications with the original narrative descriptions to which they refer. This is generally done by placing the number of the narrative modification next to the narrative description that has been modified. When the narrative modification is substantial or sufficiently involved, the narrative description itself should be rewritten.

Flowcharts and Decision Tables. The flowchart is a graphic representation of the nature and order of the operations and decision logic required to solve a problem. It illustrates the sequential order of the steps that must be taken by the computer in processing input data to provide meaningful results. A flowchart is especially useful to someone attempting to follow the logic of a very complex program. When substantial logical analysis is necessary to produce a desired result, a decision table may be used in conjunction with the program flowchart to explain the logical flow of the problem. In most installations, standard flowcharting and decision table worksheets are readily available. One such flowcharting worksheet, shown in Fig. 8-2, illustrates a simple program to calculate an employee's gross pay. Note that each flowchart segment corresponding to a paragraph in the source program is enclosed in dotted lines and assigned the same name assigned to the paragraph in the actual program. Thus, a direct relationship is established between the program and the flowchart. To maintain this relationship, the programmer must make certain to update the flowchart whenever the program is modified.

Input and Output Data Codes. A code can be thought of as a system of symbols for representing data. A code provides a substitute, in the form of a set of arbitrary characters, for actual names or numbers.

There are many reasons why data are coded. Among the more important of these are the following:

1. To save space on an input or output medium
2. To give processing and storage advantages
3. To provide file security
4. To increase remote entry speed and accuracy
5. To increase the efficiency of sorting operations
6. To facilitate limited information retrieval

In most cases, however, codes are used simply to save space on an input or output medium or to save internal storage space. Codes such as 1 for male and 2 for female, or the like, have become commonplace in programming. It is important that the programmer set down, with a detailed explanation, every code that is used with any input or output medium, making certain that the place each code is used is indicated.

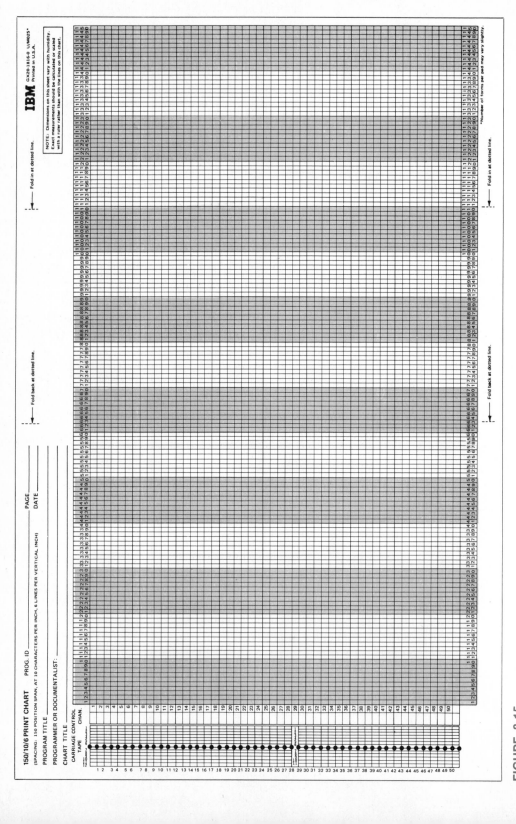

**FIGURE 8-15**
Printer spacing chart

Input and Output Formats. The source program itself provides a great deal of information regarding the format of input and output records used by the program. However, this is not sufficient. In many cases the record descriptions do not describe the contents of each field; they describe only those fields used by the program. The remainder may be assigned a dummy name or may not be described at all. However, these fields may be important to the next program that uses the files.

There are numerous ways in which input and output formats can be shown; they vary greatly from installation to installation. To help standardize the documenting of input and output formats, preprinted standard forms are generally available. One of these forms is used each time an output report is planned: the printer spacing chart (see Fig. 8-15). This chart is generally prepared while the program is being written to aid the programmer in determining the output record layouts, particularly in those cases where the output report can be complex.

Another commonly used preprinted, standardized form is the Multiple-Card Layout Form (see Fig. 8-16). This form provides a better visual image of the card than does a list of card columns and fields. However, it is difficult to use if the record being described contains many small fields; there is very little space in which to describe these fields. Nonetheless, it is one of the best ways to illustrate multiple-card records. In the case illustrated in Fig. 8-16, for example, a three-card record is illustrated.

Another standard preprinted form that is commonly used when documenting tape and disk layouts is the record layout worksheet illustrated in Fig. 8-17. This form enables the programmer to include such information as the type of characters found within a field and the fields on which the file is sorted.

Input Test Data and Sample Output. Input test data are extremely important. They can be used initially to verify that the program has been adequately checked. Later, if a problem arises, this test data can be used again to determine whether the program was changed, and if not, whether or not the test data tested the current trouble condition.

Sample output can be in the form of printed reports, tape dumps, punched cards, or other forms of output that are produced by the program. It is important that a programmer demonstrate a thorough testing of the program with the preprinted forms that will be used in production. Consider the consequences if a program is put into use and prints out several thousand paychecks with all the data in the wrong

IBM

INTERNATIONAL BUSINESS MACHINES CORPORATION

**MULTIPLE-CARD LAYOUT FORM**

GX24-6599-0
Printed in U.S.A.

Company  NASSAU COMMUNITY COLLEGE

Application  PAYROLL SYSTEM          by  W.M. Fuori          Date  1/15/74          Job No.  P001          Sheet No.  1

**Format #1**

| Emply. No. | Last Name | First Name | middle init. / dept. code | Street Address | Town/City | State | salary code | Salary/Rate | accum. sick days | accum. vacn. | 1 on seq |
|---|---|---|---|---|---|---|---|---|---|---|---|

**Format #2**

| Emply. No. | Accum. State W/H | Accum. Fed. W/H | Accum. Gross W/H | Accum. FICA W/H | bond code | Bond Amt. | Bond Balance | Bond Deduct | actual dep. / education cd / military cd | Date of Empl. | Tax exempt | Last FICA Ded. | Last Federal Tax W/H | diff. code | 2 on seq |
|---|---|---|---|---|---|---|---|---|---|---|---|---|---|---|---|

**Format #3**

| Emply. No. | Last State Tax W/H | medical cd | Accum. Med. Ded. | union code | Accum. Union Ded. | credit union | Accum. Credit Union Ded. | Quarterly Gross | Zip Code | Social Security Number | marital cd | NOT USED | 3 on seq |
|---|---|---|---|---|---|---|---|---|---|---|---|---|---|

FIGURE 8-16
Multiple card layout form

places. If preprinted forms are not required, the sample output will still serve to verify that report titles are spelled and positioned correctly and that the data are aligned properly with respect to the titles.

Other Instruction Sheets and Worksheets. The preceding documentation is required in most installations. But besides the various forms mentioned so far, there may be others for which the programmer is responsible. These others, which vary with the computer installation, may include such forms as a programming checklist, a job request form, an operating instruction sheet, and a run sheet. Using one of these forms or a like form, the programmer must convey specific instructions for running the program. Included would be such information as the following:

1. Input media with identifying data (tape reel number, disk pack number, etc.)

| ORGANIZATION UNIT | OPERATIONS | | | | INDEX NUMBER | |
|---|---|---|---|---|---|---|

| DISTRIBUTION LIST NO. | SUBJECT OR TITLE | RECORD LAYOUT | | |
|---|---|---|---|---|

| ISSUE DATE | | | PAGE 1 OF 3 |
|---|---|---|---|

| PROGRAM NUMBER | PROGRAM NAME | MACHINE | PROGRAMMER | STEP | DATE |
|---|---|---|---|---|---|
| P001 | CREATE-MAST | IBM-370-155 | W.M. Fuori | 1 | 1/8/-- |

| RECORD NAME | FILE NAME | FILE NO. | SIZE |
|---|---|---|---|
| MASTER-REC | PAYROLL-MASTER | 3147P | 1 Reel |

| FIELD | | SIZE | CHAR. | SORT SEQ. | FIELD NAME | REMARKS |
|---|---|---|---|---|---|---|
| FROM | TO | | | | | |
| 1 | 6 | 6 | N | 1 | EMPLOYEE-NO | 9 (6) |
| 7 | 21 | 15 | A | | LAST-NAME | |
| 22 | 31 | 10 | A | | FIRST-NAME | |
| 32 | | 1 | A | | MIDDLE-INIT | |
| 33 | | 1 | N | 2 | DEPT-CODE | Code = '1', '2', '3', or '4' |
| 34 | 46 | 13 | AN | | STREET | |
| 47 | 56 | 10 | A | | TOWN-CITY | |
| 57 | 66 | 10 | A | | STATE | |
| 67 | | 1 | A | | SALARY-CODE | Code = 'S' or 'W' |
| 68 | 75 | 8 | N | | SALARY RATE | 9 (6) V99 |
| 76 | 77 | 2 | N | | SICK-DAY-ACCUM | 99 |
| 78 | 79 | 2 | N | | VACN-DAY-ACCUM | 99 |
| 80 | 86 | 7 | N | | ST-TAX-ACCUM | 9 (5) V99 |
| 87 | 94 | 8 | N | | FED-TAX-ACCUM | 9 (6) V99 |
| 95 | 102 | 8 | N | | GROSS-ACCUM | 9 (6) V99 |
| 103 | 107 | 5 | N | | FICA-ACCUM | 999V99 |

CHAR.
A – ALPHA        S – SIGNED NUMERIC
N – NUMERIC      AN – ALPHA NUMERIC

SORT SEQ.    1 – MAJOR
             2 – INTERMEDIATE
             ETC.

APPROVED            DATE 1/15/--

NCC

| NEW | REPLACES INDEX NO. | ISSUED | REPLACES | PAGES |
|---|---|---|---|---|
| REVISION | | | | |

FORM NO. MI-165-00 UNIFORM MANUALS AND METHODS

FIGURE 8-17

Record layout worksheet

# focus on the field

## The Challenge of ADA

### Editorial by Lawrence J. Curran

The Defense Department is engaged in the most formidable software undertaking in its history—the development and implementation of ADA, a high-level language that's to become the standard language for all future DOD software. There's both widespread interest in, and concern about, the ADA project in the computer industry because of the implications of any such standard that could reach into the commercial world, and because of a skepticism that questions the advisability of getting involved with the military establishment.

There was a time, not very long ago, when U.S. military requirements resulted in major contributions to this nation's growth in semiconductor and computer technology. The Minuteman ICBM system, for example, required semiconductor components that could be crammed into small spaces, particularly in the missile's guidance computer. That requirement was probably the most important single contributor to the rapid development and maturity of integrated circuit design and production, hastening the transition from discrete transistors to ICs. It's true that there were years of controversy over the reliability of the new ICs that resulted from the Minuteman program. But if the military requirement hadn't existed, those devices probably wouldn't have been developed—and the problems that contributed to their unreliability wouldn't have been solved—until much later.

The U.S. computer industry has benefited greatly from the establishment of a competitive semiconductor industry that got a big, early boost from the requirements of that military weapon system. But in the decade and a half since the early Minuteman days, this nation has fought and lost a horribly wasteful war in Vietnam, and a generation of war-embittered young people, computer scientists among them,

doesn't want to have anything to do with weapon-related technology. Add to this scenario the fact that most military system procurements now seek to apply existing technology instead of plowing new ground, and it becomes apparent that the military services have a problem attracting technologists to their own ranks.

Military contract work simply doesn't command the high priorities it once did at electronics and computer companies. Because of that, it's imperative that the Defense Department and the military services very persuasively present their case for the development and implementation of ADA to the computer industry.

ADA represents a staggering undertaking, with at least another eight years of development planned in an effort that began in 1975. Computer companies, even those that haven't yet been funded for any of the early development phases, have designated certain of their software specialists to monitor the ADA effort. Part of the motivation for monitoring the program stems from enlightened self-interest because the companies will be in a better position to win future ADA-related software and hardware procurements, if they want to compete. Other computer companies are guardedly watching ADA because they're concerned that the language will be forced on them as it eventually works its way into the commercial market.

There's a challenge, then, to the Defense Advanced Research Projects Agency (DARPA), which is managing ADA development for DOD, to put some of its best and brightest people to work on the project in-house. There's a further challenge to DARPA and the services to enlist the efforts of qualified people in the industry and academia, whether or not they stand to win big contracts. In short, it's up to DOD to convince the computer industry that ADA is worth the effort because ADA has a chance to become a standard that will be embraced both inside and outside DOD circles.

That will be no easy task for a military establishment that's often perceived as an exasperating customer, and whose contributions to the advancement of technology, rightly or wrongly, are often viewed as destructive.

DISCUSSION QUESTIONS

1. Why does the Department of Defense (DOD) want the creation of ADA with all the other languages currently in existence?

2. Do you believe that the Department of Defense will be able to convince the computer industry to promote ADA to become a standard language Explain.

3. Where do you think the name ADA came from? (Hint: See Project 3, Chapter 2.)

2. Form numbers for special output forms or number of parts of paper to be used
3. Instructions for aligning forms on the printer
4. Hardware devices required
5. Expected processing time
6. Special operator instructions in case the program abnormally terminates
7. Program messages and required operator actions

It must be realized, as was pointed out early in this discussion, that all programs do not receive the same level of documentation. It makes little sense to provide the level of documentation previously discussed for a small, one-time program. However, even the smallest program must be documented to some extent. The programmer must always bear in mind that until the program has been thoroughly tested and documented, it may not be considered complete or operational.

To verify your understanding of the previous material, turn to page 314 and take Self-Test 8-3.

## SELF-TEST 8-1

1. The _____ must be able to see the problem as a whole as well as in its component parts.
2. The four areas the problem analyst must consider in the course of developing a computerized solution to a problem are _____ , _____ , _____ , and _____ .
3. The first step in problem analysis is to determine _____ .
4. Problem analysis is usually carried out by a team consisting of _____ .
5. The _____ is a method by which the operations and flow of data during the solution of a problem may be shown using symbols and narrative descriptions.
6. The flowchart serves three major functions: _____ , _____ , and _____ .

## SELF-TEST 8-2

1. _____ an application involves the translation or conversion of each operation in the flowchart into computer-understandable language.

2. Computer instructions consist of five types, namely _____.

3. The purpose of control instructions is to _____.

4. _____ instructions are descriptive in purpose.

5. _____ uses a series of numbers, letters, or special characters that are accepted by the computer and cause a specific operation to take place.

6. The only language a computer can understand without translation is _____.

7. Symbolic language is most closely related to _____ and has the advantage of being easier to use.

8. Symbolic-language programs must be translated to _____ before they can be executed.

9. _____ languages allow the programmer to concentrate on expressing the logic of the problem and not be concerned with how the computer will solve the problem.

10. The most commonly used procedure-oriented languages are _____.

11. _____ language translators are equipped with extensive diagnostic routines which aid in program checking.

12. The two main disadvantages of procedure-oriented languages are _____ and _____.

13. Locating and correcting errors made in preparing a program is termed _____.

14. An example of a problem-oriented language is _____.

## SELF-TEST 8–3

1. A program cannot be considered _____ until it has been thoroughly tested and completely documented.

2. Programmer documentation requires the preparation of a _____ manual and console _____ containing source documents, problem statements, decision tables, flowcharts, field descriptions, and data layouts and detailed operations instructions necessary to execute the program.

3. Some of the items generally included in a procedures or run manual would include _____.

**Answers to Self-Tests**

8–1

1. problem analyst

2. problem analysis; flowchart application; coding and execution of application program; documentation

3. whether the problem warrants a computerized solution

4. the user and the programmer or analyst

5. program flowchart

6. it shows the logic of the problem's solution in pictorial form; it allows the programmer to concentrate on small portions of the program without trying to visualize the logic of the entire program; it serves as a means of communication between management personnel and the programmer as well as among programmers

**8-2**

1. Coding
2. input/output, control, arithmetic, logical, and specification
3. control the order in which other instructions are executed
4. Specification
5. Machine language
6. machine language
7. machine language
8. machine language
9. Procedure-oriented
10. FORTRAN, COBOL, PASCAL, and PL/I
11. Procedure-oriented
12. they must be translated into machine language; the resulting machine-language programs do not always make the most efficient use of the computer's resources
13. debugging
14. RPG

**8-3**

1. operational
2. run; run book
3. title page, control sheet, narrative descriptions, flowcharts, decision tables, input and output data codes, input and output formats, input test data and sample output, and other instruction sheets and worksheets

# EXERCISES

**8-1**
**True/False**

_____ 1. Programs written for interactive processing are generally simple and involve minimal data.

_____ 2. An assembly system or processor is a computer program that translates symbolic language into machine language.

_____ 3. Of the types of computer languages discussed, the symbolic language is the most difficult to program in.

_____ 4. Computer instructions are generally executed in sequential order.

_____ 5. Debugging a program involves correcting both syntax and logic errors.

_____ 6. Symbolic programs do not require translation before they can be executed.

_____ 7. Flowcharts or pseudocode and decision tables are part of program documentation.

_____ 8. There are five basic types of computer instructions.

_____ 9. Two examples of procedure-oriented languages are COBOL and FORTRAN.

_____ 10. Coding involves converting the logic exhibited in the flowchart or pseudocode into a computer-acceptable language.

_____ 11. Procedure-oriented languages are generally easier to program in than machine language.

_____ 12. Before a program written in a procedure-oriented language can be executed, it must be translated into machine language.

_____ 13. A program written in a procedure-oriented language will be more efficient than one written in a symbolic language.

_____ 14. A detailed problem analysis should precede the actual program preparation.

_____ 15. Problem analysis generally involves both the programmer and the user.

_____ 16. A user does not have to be able to write a computer program but should be able to read and understand a flowchart or pseudocode.

_____ 17. Programmers must follow specific rules when coding a program.

_____ 18. Procedure-oriented languages require that the programmer have an extensive knowledge of machine language.

_____ 19. No diagnostic messages are associated with machine language.

_____ 20. The first step in the analysis of a problem is to determine whether or not the problem warrants a computerized solution.

**8-2**
**Multiple-choice**

_____ 1. Which of the following is not a commonly used procedure-oriented language?
a. COBOL
b. FORTRAN
c. PL/I
d. PASCAL
e. RPG

_____ 2. Debugging does not utilize
a. actual data
b. data with a known solution
c. sample data
d. deductive reasoning
e. none of the above

_____ 3. Which of the following is not a commonly used type of language?
a. symbolic
b. procedure-oriented
c. problem-oriented
d. interactive
e. machine language

_____ 4. Machine language coding would be most like
a. 24 0600 0800 1000
b. ADD A TO B
c. C = C + B
d. GO TO PAR-A
e. COMPUTE X = Y + Z

_____ 5. Translation from a procedure-oriented language to machine language is done by a program called
a. a compiler
b. an assembly system
c. a converter
d. a translator
e. none of the above

**6. Flowcharts**
   a. break up large problems into a series of small steps
   b. allow the user to view the logic of the problem's solution
   c. serve as a means of communication between the programmer and user
   d. all of the above
   e. (a) and (b) only

**7.** Which of the following would be entered on a program control sheet?
   a. changes in input or output media
   b. changes in input or output formats
   c. changes in program logic
   d. all of the above
   e. none of the above

**8.** Translation from symbolic language to machine language is done by
   a. the programmer
   b. a program called a processor
   c. an assembly system
   d. the operator of the computer system
   e. (b) and (c)

**8–3**
**Fill-in**

1. A computer _____ is a logical series of instructions designed to solve a given problem.
2. Translator programs are generally provided by computer _____.
3. Computer instructions consist of five types: _____.
4. Flowcharting symbols have been standardized by _____.
5. Procedure-oriented languages utilize _____ to translate their instructions into machine language instructions.
6. _____ refers to the removing of errors from a computer program.
7. A programmer should not consider a program _____ until it has been thoroughly tested and completely documented.
8. Computer instructions are generally executed in _____ order.
9. Debugging a program involves removing both _____ and _____ errors.

**8–4**
**Problems**

1. What is meant by debugging a program? How is it done?
2. Contrast machine language with symbolic language.
3. Contrast procedure-oriented languages with other available types of languages.
4. Why would program modifications be affected by poor or inadequate documentation?
5. If a newly written program has been tested with known valid data, why might it be advisable also to test the program with intentionally invalid data?

6. What is entailed in documenting a program? When should this process begin?

7. The following is a hypothetical machine-language instruction.

   35   600   734   971

   What could each of these numbers represent?

8. How might a computer distinguish between instructions and data?

9. What are the steps that should be considered in developing a computerized solution to a problem? Explain briefly.

10. Describe each of the basic types of computer instructions.

11. What are the advantages to constructing a flowchart or pseudocode for a proposed computer application?

12. Describe the process that you would use to test a large program.

13. What is a computer run manual? What materials would it contain?

14. What is a computer instruction? How does it function?

15. Why is it advisable to consult the user concerning test input and output data?

# COMMON PROGRAMMING LANGUAGES USED IN BUSINESS

INTRODUCTION
BATCH BASIC
INTERACTIVE BASIC
ACCESSING THE COMPUTER
SYSTEM COMMANDS
BASIC STATEMENTS
Format
Line Numbers
Remarks
Constants
Variables and Variable Names
General Form
INPUT/OUTPUT AND END STATEMENTS
PRINT Statement
BASIC Rules for Printing Numbers
Printed Line Format
INPUT Statement
END Statement
Sample Program 1
ARITHMETIC STATEMENTS
Arithmetic Operators
Expressions
Hierarchy of Arithmetic Operators
LET Statement
Sample Program 2
BRANCH STATEMENTS
GO TO Statement
IF/THEN Statement
Relational Comparisons
Looping
FOCUS ON THE FIELD
SELF-TESTS
EXERCISES

# Introduction to BASIC

## INTRODUCTION

Today almost every business concern provides its key personnel with access to a computer. The computer may be large or small and may be used exclusively by the business, or computer time may be purchased from a service organization; in any case, a computer is accessible. More and more, this access is being provided via conveniently located terminal devices.

In many cases, these terminals are an integral part of a computer system facilitating two-way data communications between the accountant, manager, or other key personnel and the computer, in addition to providing a fast and effective means by which the system can communicate urgent messages to management, such as informing management of the occurrence of any unusual or unexpected circumstances the instant they are detected. Such systems attempt to provide management with information it must have to function efficiently and effectively. But, whether such a complex system is available or not, the accountant or business manager will still encounter in the course of performing his/her duties numerous small and isolated problems to which the computer can be applied but, for one reason or another, no provision has been made for their solution. In such cases, the accountant or business manager could choose one of several possible alternatives. He or she could choose to solve it manually, or he or she could request the data-processing department to solve the problem. Either of these solutions could be time-consuming and expensive. On the other hand, should the accountant or business manager have a working knowledge of a modern programming language, he or she can use this knowledge to develop a simple program to solve the problem, thus eliminating any delay or need to first communicate the problem to a programmer. It should be noted, however, that for other than small or isolated problems, the data-processing department should be consulted. Even in this case, a knowledge of a pro-

"Looks like you're ready to call it a day, too."

gramming language by the business person will make communications with the programmer that much easier.

In order to provide the reader with a knowledge of the programming process, we will consider BASIC, a language originally created as a teaching language to illustrate programming concepts. Our study of BASIC in this chapter will be limited to a discussion of those instructions necessary to facilitate an understanding of the programming process. Chapter 10 will consider more advanced BASIC instructions and will investigate some of the more sophisticated aspects of programming.

Upon completion of this chapter, you should be able to

- Understand and write simple programs in BASIC

- Convert a program flowchart or pseudocode into a BASIC program

- Discuss the differences between conditional and unconditional branches

- Discuss the general form of a BASIC statement

- Use the BASIC statements REM, PRINT, INPUT, END, LET, GO TO, and IF/THEN

- Discuss the types of and differences between variables and constants

- Understand and use the system commands RUN, LIST, and DELETE

- Define the following terms:

| | |
|---|---|
| Arithmetic operator | Literal |
| Batch BASIC | NEW |
| Branch statement | OLD |
| BYE | PRINT |
| Constant | Printed line format |
| DELETE | Relational |
| Ellipsis | comparison |
| END | REM or REMARK |
| Exponential form | RETURN |
| Expression | RUN |
| General form | SAVE |
| GOODBYE | Shift count |
| GOTO | Simple variable |
| Hierarchy | STOP |
| IF/THEN | String variable |
| Interactive BASIC | System command |
| LET | UWBIC |
| Line number | Value of an expression |
| LIST | Variable |
| List of variables | Zone |

## BATCH BASIC

The ease with which BASIC can be learned and utilized by the novice and programmer alike is responsible for its wide and rapid acceptance into the computer field. As a result, W. F. Sharpe, of the University of Washington, Seattle, developed and programmed a BASIC compiler called UWBIC (*University of Washington BASIC Interpretive Compiler*), which facilitates the use of BASIC in a batch mode. That is, the user can prepare his program and data on punched cards and submit these cards to the computer center to be processed when computer time becomes available. This form of BASIC is generally referred to as **batch BASIC.**

## INTERACTIVE BASIC

An appropriate programming language for use by the business person in solving small and isolated problems is the language BASIC. BASIC (*Beginner's All-purpose Symbolic Instruction Code*) is an easily learned and easily used computer language. It was originally developed at Dartmouth College under the direction of J. G. Kemeny and Thomas E. Kurtz for use online with a time-sharing computer, that is, a computer system in which a user can communicate a program to the computer via a console or terminal similar in appearance to a typewriter, with results being returned almost instantaneously. This form of BASIC is generally referred to as **interactive BASIC.**

In this chapter and Chapter 10 we study interactive BASIC, with the intent of being able to write operational programs to be used on a time-sharing computer system.

## ACCESSING THE COMPUTER

In a time-sharing computer system, many users share the use of a computer, each having his or her own input/output terminal from which to communicate programs and data to the computer and to which the computer can communicate results. Communication between terminals and the computer usually takes place over telephone lines or via special direct lines to the computer. Most time-sharing computer systems can handle 20 or more terminals concurrently.

For a given user to communicate a BASIC program to such a computer, he or she must first determine if the computer is available to handle the job. Using a telephone located on the terminal, the user dials a predetermined number which opens a line to the computer.[1] If all communication lines to the computer are in use, a "busy" signal will be heard and the user can wait a few minutes and try again or, if available, dial up another computer. If a free channel is available, the connection is made and typed communications can take place between the user and the computer via the terminal.

[1] For terminals directly connected to the computer system, no telephone is necessary. The terminal can simply be turned on and the appropriate start-up commands typed in.

The particular commands necessary to access the computer will vary from computer system to computer system. Thus, before attempting to communicate with the computer you should obtain these commands from your computer center or instructor. A typical conversation might be as follows:

```
USER:   LOGON (user presses RETURN key)
COMPUTER:   USER NUMBER—
USER:   XXXXXX (user types in his six-character identification number
                next to the USER NUMBER— and presses the RETURN key)
COMPUTER:   SYSTEM—
USER:   BASIC (user types word BASIC next to SYSTEM— to indicate
               a BASIC program and then presses RETURN key)
COMPUTER:   NEW OR OLD—
USER:   NEW (user types word NEW next to NEW OR OLD— if a new
             program is to be input for processing and then presses RE-
             TURN key)
        OLD (user types word OLD next to NEW OR OLD— if a previ-
             ously written program is to be retrieved from the location in
             which the computer has stored it and presses RETURN key)
COMPUTER:   NEW PROGRAM NAME— or
            OLD PROGRAM NAME—
USER:   XXXXXX (user types in new or old program name next to previ-
                ous computer response and presses RETURN key)
COMPUTER:   READY
```

## SYSTEM COMMANDS

**System commands** are not instructions used in a program for the solution of a problem but special commands or messages that you can communicate directly to the computer.

Let us assume, for example, that a BASIC program has been written and stored in the computer system. To access this program, the user would first establish communications with the computer system and identify the OLD, or previously written and stored, program that is desired. When this program has been located and accessed, the computer will respond with READY.

Typing in the word LIST will cause the entire OLD program to be listed, and typing in the word LISTn, where n is a one- to five-digit number, will cause only the lines from n on of the program accessed to be listed. The listing process can be stopped at any time by depressing the STOP or BREAK key.[2]

If you desire to execute this program, you only need type in the system command RUN. This will cause the instructions in the program to be carried out beginning with the first statement or instruction in the program.

If, for example, a new program is to be entered, the user would establish communication with the computer system and indicate that a

[2]Some systems do not utilize this particular key or the RETURN key but will employ one or more other keys to accomplish this task.

NEW program is being entered. This program would then be typed in, line by line, with the typing of each line followed by the pressing of the RETURN key. After the entire program has been keyed in, execution can be initiated by simply entering the system command RUN. If no errors are present, the results will be returned. If the results are correct, the user can type the system command SAVE and the program will be saved for future use. By typing in the system command BYE or GOOD-BYE, the user breaks off the communication line to the computer. If a line is to be corrected, it can be done simply be retyping another line with the same line number as the incorrect line and pressing the RE-TURN key. All statements or lines must begin with a line number. A complete line can be deleted by typing in only the line number and pressing the RETURN key or by typing in the system command DE-LETE followed by the line number of the statement.[3]

Many other system commands are available for communication with the computer; for information concerning them, the reader should consult the reference manuals appropriate for the system being used.

We now investigate the fundamental item in any BASIC program—the statement.

**To verify your understanding of the previous material, turn to page 347 and take Self-Test 9-1.**

## BASIC STATEMENTS

**Format**    A BASIC program is composed of a series of instructions or statements. These statements are written in "free form"; that is, they begin anywhere on a line and, with one exception, are unaffected by spaces. The one exception will be discussed later.

**Line Numbers**    Each BASIC statement must have a line number between 1 and 99999. Statements may be input in any order, as the BASIC compiler automatically sequences them by line number. It is advisable to leave spaces when assigning line numbers so that additions can be made without having to reassign the line numbers. A common scheme is to assign to statements line numbers which are multiples of 10 (i.e., 10, 20, 30, etc.). In this way the numbers are in sequence yet still allow up to nine additional statements to be inserted between existing statements without violating the sequence.

**Remarks**    In writing a program it is often desirable to annotate it for easier reading. Annotations or remarks are ignored by the computer and can be used freely as long as the program does not become excessively long.

---

[3]In IBM BASIC, a line may be deleted as shown only if the computer is in EDIT mode. The computer can be switched back and forth between BASIC mode and EDIT mode by simply pressing the RETURN key without entering any characters.

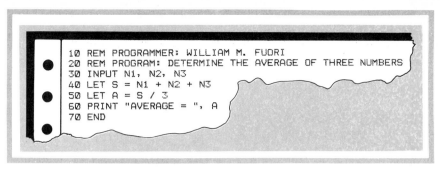

```
10 REM PROGRAMMER: WILLIAM M. FUORI
20 REM PROGRAM: DETERMINE THE AVERAGE OF THREE NUMBERS
30 INPUT N1, N2, N3
40 LET S = N1 + N2 + N3
50 LET A = S / 3
60 PRINT "AVERAGE = ", A
70 END
```

FIGURE 9-1

Program utilizing the REM statement

Adding remarks to longer programs should be done with care so as to avoid increasing the length of the program and jeopardizing its chance of running on smaller computer systems. A remark statement must have a statement number followed by the command REM or REMARK, after which the remark itself appears.

Figure 9-1 illustrates a BASIC program containing the REM statement.

**Constants**  A BASIC constant is a number such as 14, 34.3, − 17, and − 13.8. Constants are divided into two broad types:

1. **Integer** constants: whole numbers not containing a decimal point (e.g., 46, − 16, 3842, − 101101)
2. **Real** constants: numbers containing a decimal point (e.g., − 46., 3.418, − 16.42, 8.00)

Real constants may also be expressed in another form, referred to as the **exponential form.** In exponential form, the number 3840000. could, for example, appear as

$$38.4E5$$

$$.384E7$$

$$384.E4$$

Each of these can be determined to be equal to the original number 3840000. once we understand the meaning of the "E" within each of the above representations.

The letter E, in the exponential form of a number, simply serves as a placeholder between the actual digits of the number and what we shall refer to as the **shift count.** The shift count, or number following the letter E in a number expressed in exponential form, refers to the number of places that the decimal point must be shifted from where it is presently located to where it would normally appear in nonexponential form.

For example, in the number 38.4E5, the shift count or number following the letter E is a 5. This means that to locate the decimal point in its proper position it must be shifted five places to the right (to the right because the number 5 is positive), giving us

$$38.4\text{E}5 = 3 \ 8 \underbrace{4 \ 0 \ 0 \ 0 \ 0}_{1 \ 2 \ 3 \ 4 \ 5},$$

Similarly, for the other two numbers given above in exponential form, we have

$$.384\text{E}7 = 3 \underbrace{8 \ 4 \ 0 \ 0 \ 0 \ 0}_{1 \ 2 \ 3 \ 4 \ 5 \ 6 \ 7};$$

and

$$384.\text{E}4 = 3 \ 8 \ 4 \underbrace{0 \ 0 \ 0 \ 0}_{1 \ 2 \ 3 \ 4};$$

For a number containing a negative shift count, one simply moves the decimal point to the left of where it occurs in the number in exponential form a number of places equal to the shift count. For example, for the number 54.36E-6 we would have

$$54.36\text{E-}6 = . \underbrace{0 \ 0 \ 0 \ 0 \ 5 \ 4}_{-6 \ -5 \ -4 \ -3 \ -2 \ -1} 3 \ 6$$

## Variables and Variable Names

A variable is a quantity that can take on different values at different times during the execution of a BASIC program. A variable name is assigned to each variable to distinguish it from other variables in the program. The variable name can be thought of as a label placed on a mailbox, inside which is an item of data. The data item placed in the mailbox can vary from time to time but is identified and referenced by the name placed on the front of the mailbox.

BASIC variables are of two types: simple variables and string variables. **Simple variables,** generally referred to as **variables,** contain numbers and may be used in computations. A BASIC variable name can be a letter of the alphabet or a letter of the alphabet followed by a digit (e.g., A3, B, R, T6).

Some examples of the values that a simple variable can assume are

$$A = 4730$$
$$A = +36.75$$
$$A = -239$$
$$A = +3.5\text{E}4$$
$$A = -4.85\text{E} - 6$$

**String variables** are used to store alphanumeric quantities which *will not be used in any form of computation.* A string variable name is denoted by a letter followed by a $, for example A$, R$, T$. A string variable can take on the value of a **string,** or group of numbers, letters, or special characters enclosed in quotation marks.[4] Almost all systems can store strings of up to 15 characters, counting all blanks, but not quotation marks; many systems can store considerably longer ones. In IBM BASIC, for example, a character string associated with a string variable may consist of up to 18 characters.

Some examples of the values a string variable (A$) can assume are

A$ = "SELL"

A$ = "S,4"

A$ = "THE ANSWER"

If a quotation mark is to be included as part of the string, it must be distinguished from the quotation marks enclosing the string. This is accomplished by inserting two quotation marks side by side in the position where the quotation mark is desired in the string. For example, if the string ANSWER IS "NO". is to be stored, "ANSWER IS ""NO""." would be input.

**General Form**    In the course of this chapter you will be introduced to many BASIC statements. Each statement must be written in accordance with specific rules. These stipulate what words or symbols must be present in the statement and in what relative positions. They also stipulate where and what information is to be provided by the programmer and whether this information is required or optional. Understanding and remembering the rules associated with each BASIC statement can be a time-consuming endeavor. To simplify this task, each BASIC statement will be presented in a general form. This form is based on the following conventions:

1. All required parts of the BASIC statement will be underlined.
2. All words that must appear exactly as presented will be capitalized.
3. Whenever used, the symbol = will be required.
4. Optional parts will be included in braces, {  }.
5. Information relative to the problem at hand and to be provided by the programmer will be included in parentheses, (  ).
6. The ellipsis . . . indicates that the immediately preceding unit may occur once, or more than once in succession.

For example, let us consider the general form of a particular BASIC statement:

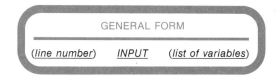

GENERAL FORM

(*line number*)    *INPUT*    (*list of variables*)

---

[4]In the BASIC supported by IBM, either of the characters ' or " is understood to be a quotation mark.

Using our list of conventions, we can determine certain facts about this statement with only a simple inspection.

| | |
|---|---|
| (*line number*) | A line number *must* be used and is determined by the programmer for the program under consideration. |
| *INPUT* | The word INPUT *must* be used exactly as shown in the general form. |
| (*list of variable names*) | A list of the specific variable names *must* be used and is determined by the programmer for the program at hand. |

After the programmer has exercised his or her options, the statement may appear as

```
3840   INPUT   A,B3,C6,R$
```

To verify your understanding of the previous material, turn to page 347 and take Self-Test 9-2.

## INPUT/OUTPUT AND END STATEMENTS

**PRINT Statement**   Every computer program must contain instructions which direct the computer to input or output information. It is, therefore, fitting that we should begin our study of the various BASIC statements by studying those statements which direct the computer to perform an input or output operation.

The braces in this statement indicate that there are options open to the programmer. In this particular statement, there are four options:

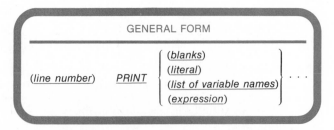

GENERAL FORM

$$(line\ number)\quad PRINT\quad \begin{Bmatrix} (blanks) \\ (literal) \\ (list\ of\ variable\ names) \\ (expression) \end{Bmatrix} \ldots$$

1. (*blanks*): In this option, nothing follows the BASIC required word PRINT. This causes a line of blanks or a blank line to be printed. By properly spacing the data presented in a report, the appearance and readability of the report can be substantially increased.

2. (*literal*): In this option, the exact characters to be printed are included within quotes and follow the BASIC required word PRINT. For example, the statement

```
70   PRINT "PAYROLL AUDIT REPORT"
```

would cause PAYROLL AUDIT REPORT to be printed out. Blanks within the quotes are a definite part of the literal and will be printed.[5]

3. (*list of variable names*): In this option, a list of previously defined variable names follows the BASIC required word PRINT. This causes the printing of the current value of each of the variable names in the list. For example, if A = 6, B = 15, and C = −7, the statement

$$80 \quad \text{PRINT A, B, C}$$

would cause 6, 15, and −7 to be printed.

4. (*expression*): In this option, an expression, or variables and/or constants involved in arithmetic operations, follows the BASIC required word PRINT. First the expression is evaluated, and then the result of the evaluation is printed out. For example, if A = 7, the statement

$$60 \quad \text{PRINT } 2 * A + 6$$

would cause the number 20 to be printed out, as $20 = 2 \times 7 + 6$. Expressions will be discussed in greater detail later.

In addition, it is also possible to use a combination of these options in the same PRINT statement. For example, if A = 7, B = 9, and C = 14, then the PRINT statement

$$45 \quad \text{PRINT A, B, ''ANS} = '', C$$

would cause 7, 9, ANS = , and 14 to be printed out.

BASIC Rules for Printing Numbers. It is essential that the BASIC user be aware of rules governing the printing of numbers. There are four such rules:

1. A maximum of seven significant digits can be printed for a real or integer number.
2. Numbers less than 0.1 will be printed in exponential form unless the number consists of seven or fewer significant digits.
3. The printing of nonsignificant zeros will be suppressed.
4. The first character printed will be a blank or a minus (−) depending on the algebraic sign (positive or negative) of the number.

Printed Line Format. We can now control what is printed by using the appropriate option available with the PRINT statement. We will now discuss where the printing will occur.

In BASIC, the page is subdivided into zones of 15 or 18 spaces each across each line (a typical teletype page is 75 characters wide). IBM computer systems generally support 18 character zones, while several other manufacturers support 15 character zones (see Fig. 9-2). Any item in quotes (literal) is printed just as it appears within the quotes, whether it can be contained in one zone or spans more than one zone. However, for anything that is not a literal, a comma causes the printer to skip to the next zone. For example, on an IBM computer system supporting four 18-character zones the statement

$$85 \quad \text{PRINT A, ''THIS IS A SAMPLE LITERAL'', B}$$

---

[5]Literals may be restricted in the number of characters they may contain depending on the computer system used.

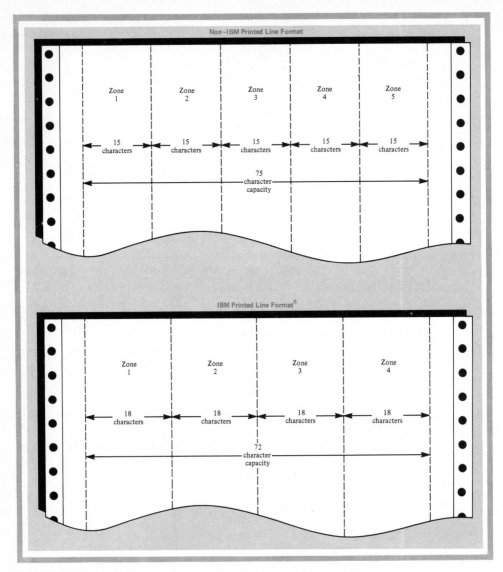

**FIGURE 9-2**

BASIC printed line format

would cause the present value of A to be printed in zone 1 beginning in print position 1. The comma following A in the print statement causes the printer to skip to the second zone and print THIS IS A SAMPLE LITERAL beginning in print position 19 and terminating in print position 42. The comma following the literal causes the printer to skip to the next zone (zone 4) and commence printing of the present value of B in position 55.

[6]IBM's interactive BASIC utilizes 18 character zones but will allow for more than 4 zones depending on the capabilities of the printing device employed.

If the number of items listed in a PRINT statement is such that their printing cannot be completed on one line, then any items left unprinted on the first line will be printed on subsequent lines. For example, in the PRINT statement

```
80   PRINT A, B, C, D, E, F
```

the contents of variables A, B, C, and D will be printed on one line and the contents of variables E and F will be printed on the next line.

Should the problem require that more than four or five items be printed on a line or that the items be edited (i.e., a number stored as real be printed out as an integer), additional BASIC capabilities are available. These will be discussed in the next chapter.

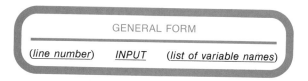

GENERAL FORM

(*line number*)    *INPUT*    (*list of variable names*)

**INPUT
Statement**    The **list of variable names** is a list of specific programmer-assigned variable names, one variable name for each item of data to be read by the INPUT statement. The order in which the variable names are written must agree with the order in which the corresponding data are to be read, and the variable names must be separated by commas.

When the INPUT statement is executed, it causes the computer to stop executing instructions and wait for the terminal operator to type in the specific data from the terminal. To determine exactly how this works, let us examine the following sequence of instructions:

```
0190   INPUT H, R

9999   END
RUN
```

After the RUN statement is sent to the computer, it would begin executing the program. When execution reached statement number 0190, three things would happen:

1. A special character, usually a "?," will be printed on the output sheet, notifying the user that the computer is ready to receive the data corresponding to the variables H and R.
2. Execution is terminated until the two data items requested have been typed in and transmitted to the computer. The data items must be typed in the order in which they appear in the INPUT statement and must be separated by commas.
3. The data items input are stored in the locations labeled H and R, respectively, for future use. The computer then proceeds to execute the next instruction.

This statement is principally used when a program is to be used over and over again with various data that the user will determine at the time of execution of the program.

Since in such cases the user most likely did not write the program or may not know or remember exactly what data the computer requires at this point, it is a good programming practice to prompt the user prior to requesting input. This is accomplished by simply adding one or more PRINT statements to the program immediately before the INPUT statement. In this way the PRINT statement can prompt the user as to what he or she will need to input after the "?" appears. This could be accomplished as follows for the previously illustrated program.

```
0185  PRINT "KEY IN HOURS AND RATE SEPARATED BY A COMMA"
0186  PRINT "WHEN YOU SEE THE QUESTION MARK"
0190  INPUT H, R
      ⋮
9999  END
RUN
```

Now, when this section of the program is executed, the user will see:

```
KEY IN HOURS AND RATE SEPARATED BY A COMMA
WHEN YOU SEE THE QUESTION MARK
?
```

Even a novice user would have no doubt that the computer is requesting data, exactly what the data are, and how the data are to be input.

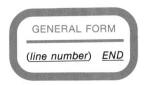

GENERAL FORM

*(line number)* <u>END</u>

**END Statement**    The END statement is required by most BASIC compilers and must be the last statement in the program. This means that the END statement must be assigned the highest line number used in the program. This is due to the fact that interactive BASIC executes statements in sequence according to their line numbers. Since the largest line number possible in BASIC is 99999, assigning this line number to the END statement will make certain that it will be the last statement in the program. However, any line number that is larger than the largest line number appearing elsewhere in the program may be used.

**Sample Program 1**    In order to clarify and solidify our understanding of the foregoing BASIC concepts, we will illustrate how these concepts may be used in a relatively small program.

*Problem Definition:* Write a BASIC program to read in a student's name and three examination grades and print this data out in a report. Assume that the user of the program is unfamiliar with the program and must be provided with instructions concerning when and what to input.

A complete BASIC program for the solution of this problem is shown in Fig. 9-3. Note that in this program the dummy literal " " was used to cause the printer to skip a print zone. For example, in line number 100, " " was used to skip the first print zone and cause STUDENT GRADE LISTING to be printed beginning in the second print zone (print position 19). The same result could have been achieved by using a comma in place of " ". An extra comma will also cause the

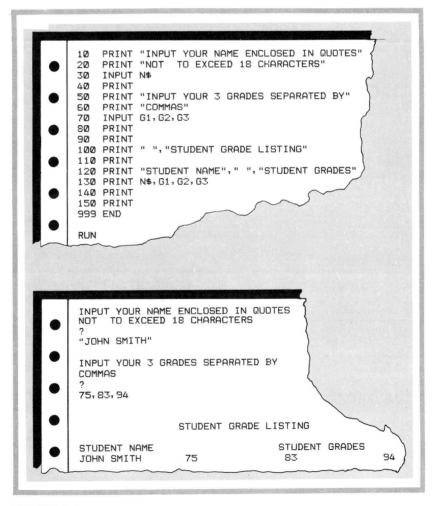

```
10   PRINT "INPUT YOUR NAME ENCLOSED IN QUOTES"
20   PRINT "NOT   TO EXCEED 18 CHARACTERS"
30   INPUT N$
40   PRINT
50   PRINT "INPUT YOUR 3 GRADES SEPARATED BY"
60   PRINT "COMMAS"
70   INPUT G1,G2,G3
80   PRINT
90   PRINT
100  PRINT " ","STUDENT GRADE LISTING"
110  PRINT
120  PRINT "STUDENT NAME"," ","STUDENT GRADES"
130  PRINT N$,G1,G2,G3
140  PRINT
150  PRINT
999  END

RUN
```

```
INPUT YOUR NAME ENCLOSED IN QUOTES
NOT   TO EXCEED 18 CHARACTERS
?
"JOHN SMITH"

INPUT YOUR 3 GRADES SEPARATED BY
COMMAS
?
75,83,94


                STUDENT GRADE LISTING

STUDENT NAME                    STUDENT GRADES
JOHN SMITH         75                83           94
```

FIGURE 9-3

Sample program 1, using a teletype input/output device

skipping of a zone. For example

$$70 \quad \text{PRINT , A ,, B}$$

will cause zone 1 to be skipped, the current value of A to be printed in zone 2, zone 3 to be skipped, and the current value of B to be printed in zone 4.

**To verify your understanding of the previous material, turn to page 348 and take Self-Test 9-3.**

## ARITHMETIC STATEMENTS

**Arithmetic Operators**    One of the great advantages of a computer is its ability to deal quickly and easily with arithmetic computations. As a result, virtually every computer language has symbols that represent the fundamental operations of addition, subtraction, multiplication, division, and exponentiation. These five operations are available in BASIC and are represented by the following symbols:

| ARITHMETIC OPERATIONS | SYMBOLS |
|---|---|
| Exponentiation | ↑ or ** |
| Multiplication | * |
| Division | / |
| Addition | + |
| Subtraction | − |

The operation of exponentiation refers to the raising of a number to a power. That is, 10 ↑ 4 or 10**4 would mean that ten is to be raised to the fourth power, mathematically expressed as

$$10^4$$

To determine the value of $10^4$, one would simply multiply 10 by itself four times:

$$10^4 = 10 \times 10 \times 10 \times 10 = 10{,}000$$

**Expressions**    An expression is one or more numeric variables or constants combined by arithmetic operators (↑,*,/,+,−). An expression, then, specifies the computations that are to be performed and on what constants or variables in order to obtain the desired result or **value of the expression.** For example, the expression

$$A * B + C - 7$$

means that the current value of the variable called "A" is to be multiplied by the current value of the variable called "B." This product is then to be added to the current value of the variable called "C." From this sum, 7 is to be subtracted. If, for example, A contained the number 3, B the number 4, and C the number 5, the value of the expression $A * B + C - 7$ would be

$$A * B + C - 7 = (3 \times 4 + 5 - 7) = 10$$
$$= \text{value of the expression}$$

Other examples of expressions include

1. $A3 + 7.4$          6. $6$
2. $3 * 6$               7. $A$
3. $8 / J$               8. $3.46$
4. $R4 - S$              9. $A7$
5. $A \uparrow 7$        10. $R**2$

*Hierarchy of Arithmetic Operations.* Arithmetic expressions can be written with the arithmetic operators appearing in any order depending only on the operation(s) to be performed. However, the order in which the computer will perform these operations is predefined. It is essential that this order or hierarchy be understood so that no confusion or errors will result. Consider the expression

$$A + B * C$$

Without knowing the hierarchy of arithmetic operators, this expression could be interpreted to mean two entirely different things:

$$(A + B) * C$$
$$A + (B * C)$$

To avoid this ambiguity, the computer assigns a priority, or *hierarchy*, to arithmetic operators in the following order:

| OPERATIONS IN HIERARCHY ORDER | SYMBOLS |
|---|---|
| Exponentiation | $\uparrow$ or $**$ |
| Multiplication or division | $*$ or $/$ |
| Addition or subtraction | $+$ or $-$ |

In BASIC, as in mathematics, expressions in parentheses are evaluated before expressions not contained in parentheses. In the case of nested parentheses (parentheses within parentheses), the innermost parenthetical expression is evaluated first, then successive outer ones. The remaining expressions not enclosed in parentheses are then evaluated in the order dictated by the operations involved.

For example, in the expression

$$Y * (Z - K)$$

$Z - K$ is parenthetical and therefore is evaluated first. The resulting difference is then multiplied by Y.

In the expression

$$(Y * (Z - K))**4$$

the innermost parenthetical expression, $Z - K$, is evaluated first, the next innermost parenthetical expression (Y times the difference $Z - K$) is evaluated next, and finally, the product is raised to the fourth power.

---

**GENERAL FORM**

*(line number)*　　*LET*　　*(variable)* = *(expression)*

---

**LET Statement**[7]　　The LET statement is one which causes an expression to be evaluated and the result of the evaluation to be stored in the computer for future reference. Since the value of the expression evaluated is to be referenced at a future date, some means must be provided to label this quantity so that it can be called back when needed in the future. To accomplish this, a variable name is assigned to the value of the expression at the time it is computed. From this time on and until changed by the programmer, when this assigned variable is used in a computation or other operation, the value of the expression will be recalled from storage and made available. For example, let us assume that $A = 3$, $B = 4$, and $C = 7$. Then the series of statements

```
10010   LET A7 = A * B - C
10020   LET G = A7 * A - 7
```

would, when executed, cause the expression $A * B - C$ to be computed and the value of this expression to be placed in storage and called A7; that is,

$$A7 = A * B - C = 3 * 4 - 7 = 5$$

The next statement would cause the expression $A7 * A - 7$ to be com-

---

[7]In some versions of BASIC, the word LET is optional. In all other respects the LET statement is the same.

puted and the value of this expression to be placed in storage and called G; that is,

$$G = A7 * A - 7 = 5 * 3 - 7 = 8$$

Therefore, at the completion of the execution of these two statements, the values of the variables concerned would be in storage as follows:

$$A = 3$$
$$B = 4$$
$$C = 7$$
$$A7 = 5$$
$$G = 8$$

It is also possible that no calculation will be involved in a LET statement. As an expression can be a single variable or constant, a legitimate LET statement could be

$$10 \quad \text{LET A4} = 7.2$$

or

$$20 \quad \text{LET A5} = A$$

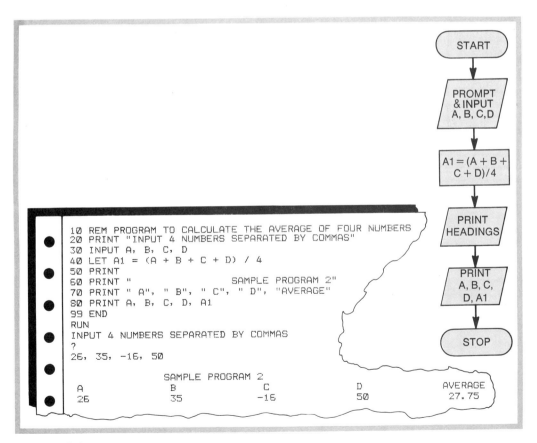

```
10 REM PROGRAM TO CALCULATE THE AVERAGE OF FOUR NUMBERS
20 PRINT "INPUT 4 NUMBERS SEPARATED BY COMMAS"
30 INPUT A, B, C, D
40 LET A1 = (A + B + C + D) / 4
50 PRINT
60 PRINT "               SAMPLE PROGRAM 2"
70 PRINT " A", " B", " C", " D", "AVERAGE"
80 PRINT A, B, C, D, A1
99 END
RUN
INPUT 4 NUMBERS SEPARATED BY COMMAS
?
26, 35, -16, 50

               SAMPLE PROGRAM 2
 A                B               C               D          AVERAGE
 26               35             -16              50          27.75
```

Flowchart: START → PROMPT & INPUT A, B, C, D → A1 = (A + B + C + D)/4 → PRINT HEADINGS → PRINT A, B, C, D, A1 → STOP

**FIGURE 9-4**

Sample program 2, using a teletype input/output device

In each of these cases, the value of the variable on the left of the equal sign is simply replaced by the value of the constant or variable stated on the right-hand side of the equal sign. For example, if A = 3 in the above expressions, the results after their executions would simply be that

$$A4 = 7.3$$

and

$$A5 = 3$$

**Sample Program 2**   A second BASIC program is shown in Fig. 9-4 to further clarify and solidify our understanding of foregoing concepts. The definition of this problem is as follows:

> *Problem Definition:* Write a BASIC program to read in four numbers, determine the average of these numbers, and print out the numbers and their average with appropriate titles. Assume 5 zones, 15 characters each, are available.

**To verify your understanding of the previous material, turn to page 348 and take Self-Test 9-4.**

## BRANCH STATEMENTS

The sequence in which statements are executed is generally in order by statement number. However, situations arise in which it is necessary to deviate from this prescribed sequence. This capability is provided the programmer by a group of statements known as **branch statements.** These statements fall into two general categories:

1. Unconditional branch statements—statements that cause the normal sequence of execution of instructions to be altered without the consideration of any conditions and without exception
2. Conditional branch statements—statements that cause the normal sequence of instructions to be altered in accordance with some specific condition existing at the time the statement is to be executed

The simplest of all branch statements is the GO TO statement. This statement is an unconditional branch statement and, as such, causes the normal sequence of execution of instructions to be altered without consideration of existing conditions and without exception.

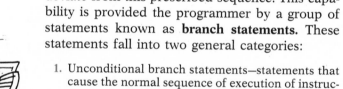

GENERAL FORM

(*line number*)    <u>GO TO</u>    (*line number*)

**GO TO Statement**

Let us assume that we wish to write a BASIC program to print out the multiples of 3 until the operator stops the process. Such a program could appear as follows:

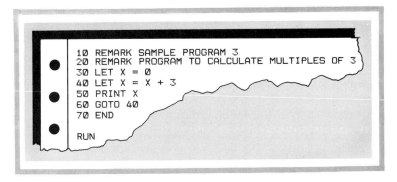

```
10 REMARK SAMPLE PROGRAM 3
20 REMARK PROGRAM TO CALCULATE MULTIPLES OF 3
30 LET X = 0
40 LET X = X + 3
50 PRINT X
60 GOTO 40
70 END

RUN
```

Line 10, 20 These statements serve to identify the program.

Line 30  This statement serves to create a variable called "X" and assigns to it the initial value of 0 (zero).

Line 40  This statement causes a new value to be computed for X, where this new value of X is to be equal to the existing value of X plus 3. Thus, the first time this statement is executed, the new value of X will be 3 since the old value of X (zero) plus 3 is equal to 3. However, if this statement were to be executed again, this time the new value of X would be 6, or the old value of X (now 3) plus 3. In other words, each time this statement is executed the value stored in X is increased by 3 from its existing value.

Line 50  This statement causes the current value of X to be printed out.

Line 60  This statement causes the program to go back and execute statement number 40 again. Each time this statement is executed, the program will branch to statement number 40 for the next instruction.

Line 70  This statement must be the physically last statement in every BASIC program.

The output of this program would appear as follows:

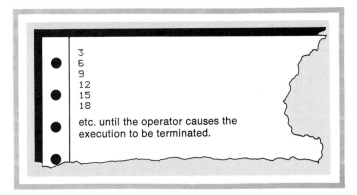

```
3
6
9
12
15
18
etc. until the operator causes the
execution to be terminated.
```

```
                        GENERAL FORM
─────────────────────────────────────────────────────────
(line number)    IF    (expression) (relation) (expression)
                                              THEN    (line number)
```

This statement is a conditional branch statement and, as such, causes the normal sequence of execution of statements to be altered, depending on the existence of a certain condition at the time of execution of the statement. In this statement, the condition is relational. That is, the condition refers to whether or not a predefined relationship exists between the first and second expressions listed in the IF/THEN statement.

Relational Comparisons. The relation between expressions can be any of the following:

| RELATION | MEANING |
|----------|---------|
| $<$ | Is less than |
| $<=$ | Is less than or equal to |
| $>$ | Is greater than |
| $>=$ | Is greater than or equal to |
| $=$ | Is equal to |
| $<>$ | Is not equal to |

Several examples of statements of this type and their meaning are

| | |
|---|---|
| 10  IF A = 7 THEN 30<br>20  ... | If the value of the variable A is equal to 7, branch to statement 30; otherwise, proceed to statement 20. |
| 10  If A + B $<$ C + D THEN 50<br>20  ... | If the value of the sum A + B is less than the value of the sum C + D, branch to statement 50; otherwise, proceed to statement 20. |
| 10  IF A\$ = "SELL" THEN 70<br>20  ... | If the value of the string variable A\$ is SELL, then branch to statement 70; otherwise, proceed to statement 20. |
| 10  IF A − B $<=$ C↑2 THEN 50<br>20  ... | If the value of the difference A − B is less than or equal to the value of C raised to the second power, branch to statement 50; otherwise, proceed to statement 20. |

```
10  IF A$ < B$ THEN 40
20  ...
```

If the value of the string variable A$ is less than the value of the string variable B$ branch to statement 40; otherwise, proceed to statement 20.

However, this last example poses a problem. Suppose that the string variable A$ contains an "S" and the string variable B$ contains a "C." Which is smaller, an "S" or a "C"? To resolve this question, each character is associated with a particular position in a hierarchy sequence. This sequence can vary with the machine on which the BASIC program is to be run but is generally as follows:

| Lowest | ƀ (blank) |
| ↓ | special characters |
| | letters A thru Z |
| Highest | digits 0 thru 9 |

If two strings of the same length are compared, the result is based on the relationship between their leading characters, as is the case when two numbers of equal length are compared. That is, MARY is considered larger than JACK since M is larger than J; and JOHN is considered larger than JACK since the J's are the same and the O of JOHN is larger than the A of JACK.

If two strings of different lengths are compared, the shorter string and the corresponding part of the longer string will form the basis for comparison. Should this comparison prove to be equal, the shorter string will be considered to be the lesser; that is, JOHN is considered less than JOHNSON.

Some comparisons are:

| STRINGS TO BE COMPARED | | CHARACTERS INITIALLY COMPARED AND RESULT |
|---|---|---|
| AAAAA | 7 | A < 7 |
| HARRY | JOHN | HARR < JOHN |
| JOHN | 114 | JOH < 114 |
| 47 | 36 | 47 > 36 |
| SMITH | SMITHSONIAN | SMITH < SMITH |

Let us examine a sample program dealing with the IF/THEN statement. Suppose that we wish to calculate all multiples of 3, beginning with 3 itself and not exceeding 99, and to print out these multiples. The program might appear as follows:

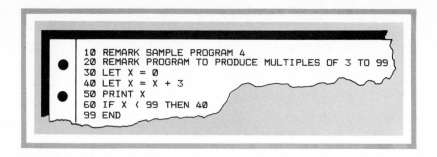

```
10 REMARK SAMPLE PROGRAM 4
20 REMARK PROGRAM TO PRODUCE MULTIPLES OF 3 TO 99
30 LET X = 0
40 LET X = X + 3
50 PRINT X
60 IF X < 99 THEN 40
99 END
```

You will notice that the basic difference between this program and the previous one is that we now have the capability to control the point at which the program will terminate automatically instead of requiring the operator to depress the STOP or BREAK key when he or she wishes to terminate execution of the program. In the above example the program instructs the computer to branch to statement 40 if the multiple of 3 is less than 99, and otherwise to proceed to statement 99 and cause the processing to halt.

Looping.  Looping involves the executing of one or more instructions over and over again. In the above sample program, the principle of looping was utilized. In this example statements 40 through 60 were executed over and over again, forming a **loop.** As the program executed these few statements over and over again, it was **looping.**

To solidify your understanding of the IF/THEN statement, we will consider an additional, somewhat more involved problem. Let us assume that we wish to write a program flowchart and BASIC program to INPUT a student's name and four examination grades. The program is to compute the student's average and letter grade (A, B, C, D, or F). The flowchart and program for this problem are shown in Fig. 9-5.

"My programmer doesn't understand me."

To verify your understanding of the previous material, turn to page 349 and take Self-Test 9-5.

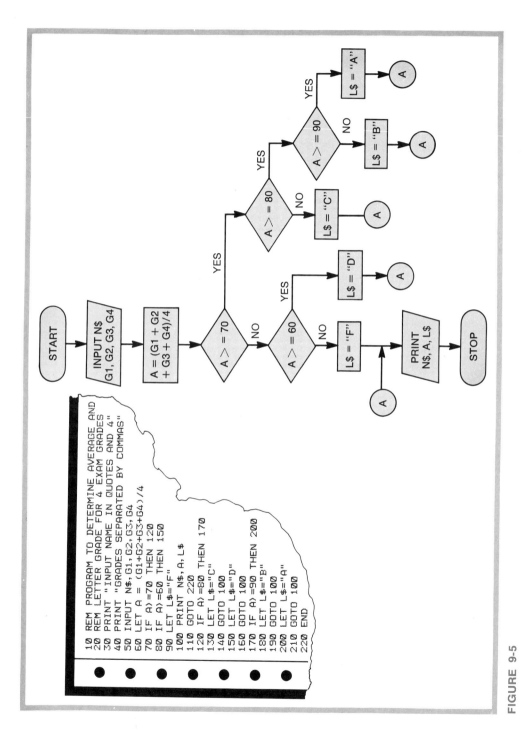

```
10   REM PROGRAM TO DETERMINE AVERAGE AND
20   REM LETTER GRADE FOR 4 EXAM GRADES
30   PRINT "INPUT NAME IN QUOTES AND 4"
40   PRINT "GRADES SEPARATED BY COMMAS"
50   INPUT N$,G1,G2,G3,G4
60   LET A = (G1+G2+G3+G4)/4
70   IF A>=70 THEN 120
80   IF A>=60 THEN 150
90   LET L$="F"
100  PRINT N$,A,L$
110  GOTO 220
120  IF A>=80 THEN 170
130  LET L$="C"
140  GOTO 100
150  LET L$="D"
160  GOTO 100
170  IF A>=90 THEN 200
180  LET L$="B"
190  GOTO 100
200  LET L$="A"
210  GOTO 100
220  END
```

**FIGURE 9-5**

Program to determine letter grade from four examination grades

345

# focus on the field

## Experimental Signature Verification System Detects Forgeries

### By M.B. Girsdansky

An experimental signature verification system invented by IBM scientists has detected the difference between forged and genuine signatures in realistic field testing. The system may someday be used in controlling access to sensitive data, devices, or locations.

In field trials of the system, held at an IBM facility, 2,907 of 2,958 verification attempts (98.3 per cent) were accepted. An even greater proportion of forgery attempts—490 of 492 (99.6 per cent)—was rejected. The 2,958 valid signatures were collected from 248 individuals, who volunteered for the field trials. The ''forgery'' attempts were made by some staff members from the IBM Thomas J. Watson Research Center, who tried as best they could to fool the machine.

This is, so far as is known, the best performance ever achieved by an automatic signature verification system, according to one of the system's inventors, Noel M. Herbst. The principles on which the machine is based will allow it to be more accurate than human document examiners, he believes.

''The results have been so encouraging,'' says Herbst, ''that a great deal of interest has been voiced in developing it still further and putting it into practical application. Possible examples could be control of access to credit or medical information, secure areas, Social Security records, and the automatic teller machines at banks.''

The system does not ''read'' handwriting as such, but instead compares data obtained from a pen's acceleration (changes in speed and direction) and pressure with similar information on reference signatures contained in the computer.

Studies have shown that rapid handwriting familiar patterns, such as one's signature, becomes habitual to the extent that the timings of the muscular movements are consistent and beyond deliberate control. The virtually ingrained nature of such muscular coordination is the key to verification in the experimental IBM system.

The new system measures data as a signature is actually being written. Small accelerometers and a pressure detector built within the barrel of a pen linked to a computer detect the differences in accelerations and pressure, as well as the revealing hesitations, that can betray attempts to forge a signature.

''The system verifies, rather than identifies,'' says Herbst. ''An individual must give a name or an account number and then sign on the system. The chances of the bearer of a stolen or forged identifying document being able to imitate the dynamic characteristics of the 'real' individual's signature are very small.

The fact that a larger percentage of valid signatures was rejected (1.7 per cent) than forgeries accepted (0.4 per cent) is important, Herbst notes. ''In the high security applications to which this system may be put, one can ask additional proof of identity from someone mistakenly rejected. What's to be avoided is having someone accepted who should *not* be.''

In an earlier version of the system, patented in 1976 by Herbst and John H. Morrissey, only acceleration data were measured as the signature was being written. To improve the system's discrimination of true signatures from forgeries, Herbst—together with two other IBM scientists, Chao N. Lui and Nicos J. Anthony—added pressure-recording features. They also refined the decision procedure (algorithm) by which the computer evaluates the signature.

The decision procedure at the heart of the system took over four years of research effort. This algorithm compares two signature patterns, measuring the similarities in fine detail, while ignoring the gross changes that often occur in signatures—such as missing strokes and stylistic variations.

In order to test the system in a realistic environment, the 248 participants (programmers at another IBM location) used the equipment for five months. To obtain printout from the computer, they were required to sign in and have the system verify identity.

During the study, an applicant was allowed three attempts to have the system accept the signature, resulting in a 1.7 per cent rejection of true signatures and acceptance of 0.4 per cent of deliberate forgeries.

Later, the effects of allowing four attempts to produce an acceptable signature were simulated. In this case, rejection of true signatures was reduced to 1.2 per cent—35 of 2881—and no additional forgeries were accepted.

DISCUSSION QUESTIONS

I. What advantage does this signature verification system have over currently used visual methods?

2. Do you believe such a system might begin to be incorporated into banks and other high-security applications in the near future? Explain.

## SELF-TEST 9–1

1. An appropriate computer language for solving small business-oriented problems is _____ .

2. BASIC stands for _____ .

3. The two forms of BASIC currently available are _____ and _____ .

4. Communications between terminals and a computer usually take place over _____ lines or special _____ lines to the computer.

5. The system command _____ will cause the program currently in the computer to be listed instruction by instruction.

6. The system command RUN will cause the program currently in the computer to be _____ .

## SELF-TEST 9–2

1. BASIC statements are written in _____ form.

2. When assigning _____ numbers to program statements, provision should be made for the insertion of additional program statements.

3. Remark statements require _____ numbers and must begin with the required word _____ .

4. Constants are classified as either _____ or _____ constants.

5. The number $7.34E-2$ is expressed in _____ form and is equal to the number _____ .

6. In the example above, the $-2$ following the letter E is called the _____ .

7. A _____ is a quantity that can take on different values at different times during the execution of BASIC program.

8. Each variable in a program is identified by a unique variable _____ .

9. A string variable can take on the value of a _____ generally consisting of at least _____ characters enclosed in quotes.

10. In the general form of a BASIC statement all required parts will be _____;
all words which must appear exactly as presented will be _____; whenever used the symbol _____ is required; optional parts are _____; and
the programmer-supplied information will be _____.

## SELF-TEST 9–3

1. The general form of the PRINT statement is _____.
2. The PRINT statement 50 PRINT would cause _____ to be printed.
3. The PRINT statement 50 PRINT "I WILL GET AN A" will cause _____ to
be printed out.
4. The PRINT statement 50 PRINT A, B, C will cause _____ to be printed out
in zones _____ of the line, respectively.
5. Given that A = 10, the PRINT statement 50 PRINT 3 * A / 2 will cause
_____ to be printed out.
6. A maximum of _____ digits can be printed for integer and real numbers.
7. Numbers exceeding seven significant digits and smaller than 0.1 will be
printed in _____ form.
8. When output is from a non-IBM computer system, a BASIC line is usually
divided into five zones each capable of holding _____ characters to a total
of _____ characters.
9. The PRINT statement 50 PRINT A, B, "HARRY" executed on an IBM
computer system will cause the current value of A to be printed in zone(s)
_____ beginning in print position _____, the current value of B to be
printed in zone(s) _____ beginning in print position _____, and HARRY
to be printed in zone(s) _____ beginning in print position _____.
10. In the above example, if A = 10, the 1 and 0 would be printed in print
positions 2 and 3, since print position 1 is reserved for _____.
11. The PRINT statement 50 PRINT "THE ANSWER IS ABSOLUTELY", A1
will cause THE ANSWER IS ABSOLUTELY to be printed out in zone(s)
_____ beginning in print position _____ and the value of A1 to be printed
in zone(s) _____ beginning in print position _____.
12. The statement INPUT A, B, C will cause a _____ to be printed out and the
execution of program instructions to be _____ until the values of A, B, and
C have been input.
13. The _____ statement must be the last statement in the program and hence
is assigned the _____ line number in the program.
14. When executed, the END statement causes _____.

## SELF-TEST 9–4

1. The five arithmetic operations in hierarchy sequence are _____.
2. 4 ↑ 3 means that 4 is _____ and is equal to _____.
3. A * B − 6 is an example of a(n) _____.
4. A single constant or variable (is, is not) a valid expression.
5. The general form of the LET statement is _____.

6. Given that A = 6, B = 3, and C = 9, execution of the statement 340 LET A3 = A * B / C would cause _____.

7. In question 6 the values of A, B, and C *after* the execution of the LET statement would be _____.

## SELF-TEST 9–5

1. The two general types of branch statements are _____ and _____ branch statements.

2. The _____ statement is an example of an unconditional branch statement.

3. The GO TO statement must contain _____ line numbers.

4. Execution of the program statement 70 GO TO 90 causes _____.

5. The _____ statement is an example of a conditional branch statement.

6. The IF/THEN statement has the general form _____.

7. The relations which can be used with an IF/THEN statement are _____.

8. The sequence of statements:

    50   IF A< = B THEN 90
    60   . . .
    90   . . .

    will cause the program to branch to statement _____ if A< = B and to statement _____ if it is not the case that A< = B.

9. When compared with one another, the string JACK would be considered (*less than, equal to, greater than*) the string JACKSON.

10. When compared with one another, the string MARY would be considered (*less than, equal to, greater than*) the string MARK.

11. A program loop is defined as _____.

12. A statement that will cause control to be transferred to statement 90 if A is not equal to B, and cause control to be transferred to statement 120 if A = B is _____.

**Answers to Self-Tests**

9–1

1. BASIC

2. Beginner's All-Purpose Symbolic Instruction Code

3. interactive BASIC; batch BASIC

4. telephone; direct

5. LIST

6. executed

9–2

1. free

2. line

3. line; REM or REMARK

4. integer; real

5. exponential; .0734, $(.07 \times 3^{4})$
$\phantom{...}-2\phantom{..}-1$

6. shift count

7. variable

8. name

9. string; 15

10. underlined; capitalized; =; included in braces { }; included in parentheses, ( )

9–3

1. (*line number*) *PRINT*
$\left\{\begin{array}{l}(\underline{blanks}) \\ (\underline{literal}) \\ (\underline{list\ of\ variable\ names}) \\ (\underline{expression})\end{array}\right\}$

2. a blank line
3. I WILL GET AN A
4. the current values of A, B, and C; 1, 2, and 3
5. 15, (3 * 10 / 2)
6. 7
7. exponential
8. 15, 75

9. 1; 1; 2; 19; 3; 37
10. the sign should the number be negative
11. 1 and 2; 1; 3; 37
12. ?; halted or stopped
13. END; highest
14. the execution of the program to be terminated

9–4

1. exponentiation (↑ or **), multiplication (*) and division (/), addition (+) and subtraction (−)
2. raised to the third power; $4 \times 4 \times 4 = 64$
3. expression
4. is

5. (*line number*) *LET* (*variable*) = (*expression*)
6. the expression to be evaluated (6 * 3/9) and the result (2) to be stored in A3
7. unchanged or 6, 3, and 9, respectively

9–5

1. unconditional; conditional
2. GO TO
3. two
4. control to be transferred to statement 90
5. IF/THEN
6. (*line number*) *IF* (*expression*) (*relation*) (*expression*) *THEN* (*line number*)
7. less than (<), less than or equal to (< =), greater than (>), greater than or equal to

(> =), equal to ( = ), and not equal to (< >)
8. 90; 60
9. less than
10. greater than
11. a series of statements that are executed over and over
12. (*line number*) IF A< >B THEN 90 120 . . . or (*line number*) If A = B THEN 120 90 . . .

1. System commands allow direct communication between the user and the computer system.

2. The statement 10 PRINT A, B would cause an A to be printed in zone 1 and a B in zone 2.

3. All interactive BASIC statements must begin with a line number.

4. One output line consists of up to 132 characters.

5. A valid expression could be a single constant or variable.

6. In interactive BASIC, the END statement must be the last statement typed in.

7. When a literal is printed out, it may exceed one zone.

8. An IF . . . THEN . . . is an example of a conditional branch statement.

9. The statement 60 PRINT would cause a blank line to be printed out.

10. When instructed to LIST 25, the computer will print the first 25 instructions in the program.

11. Line numbers must be between 1 and 99999.

12. The statement 40 INPUT A, B6, HI$ is a valid BASIC statement.

13. There are six arithmetic operators that may be used in the BASIC language.

14. BASIC statements are written in a "fixed form."

15. An expression can be defined as one or more variables or constants combined with arithmetic operators.

16. An integer constant may appear in exponential form.

17. When the computer asks "NEW OR OLD," OLD refers to a program which has been previously written and stored.

18. The END statement is required in every BASIC program and must have the statement number 9999.

19. On some computer systems, the output page is divided into zones of 15 spaces each.

20. A LET statement causes the expression to the right of the = symbol to be evaluated and the result stored as the value of the variable to the left of the = symbol.

21. $3 * 10E4 <> 3 * 10 \uparrow 4$

22. A string variable appearing in an INPUT statement is used to store a string of alphanumeric characters keyed in during program execution.

_____ 23. String variables cannot exceed 15 characters, regardless of the computer system employed.

_____ 24. $- 314159.E - 5 = 3.14159$

_____ 25. When a numeric data item is printed out, either a plus or a minus sign will be printed before the number.

_____ 26. A remark is indicated by the command REM or REMARK.

_____ 27. The number 1,000,000,001 would be printed out as $1.0E + 9$ or $1.0E + 09$.

_____ 28. $5 \uparrow 3 = 3 \uparrow 5$

_____ 29. The instruction 70 PRINT "EXAMPLE 12" would cause the computer to print "EXAMPLE 12".

_____ 30. It is not advisable to skip numbers when assigning line numbers.

## 9-2
### Multiple-choice

_____ 1. When two strings of different length are compared,
   a. the shorter string and the corresponding part of the longer string will form the basis for the comparison
   b. the longer string will always be greater
   c. they cannot be compared; the strings must be the same length
   d. (a) and (b) only
   e. none of the above

_____ 2. Which of the following is incorrect?
   a. 10 LET A = "11874"
   b. 10 LET C$ = "TOTAL SALES TAX"
   c. 10 LET S$ = "STEAM BUCKET SIZE"
   d. 10 LET X$ = """NO""SALE"
   e. none of the above

_____ 3. The IF/THEN is principally used to
   a. evaluate expressions
   b. conditionally branch to a specific instruction
   c. unconditionally branch to a specific instruction
   d. all of the above
   e. none of the above

_____ 4. Of the following, which is invalid?
   a. 80 GO TO 15
   b. 120 RUN
   c. LIST
   d. all of the above
   e. (b) and (c) only

_____ **5.** In comparing the value of string variables, which of the following is incorrect?
   **a.** SMYTH > SMITH
   **b.** SMITH < SMITHSON
   **c.** SMITHSON > SMITHS
   **d.** all of the above
   **e.** none of the above

**9–3**
**Fill-in**

**1.** In interactive BASIC, the output page is normally divided into _____ zones of _____ spaces each.

**2.** The expression A< = B means that A is _____ to B.

**3.** The typing of the word _____ in interactive BASIC causes communication between the terminal and the computer to cease.

**4.** The arithmetic operations available in BASIC are_____.

**5.** A BASIC simple variable name can be either a _____ or a _____.

**6.** The two types of BASIC are _____ and _____ BASIC.

**7.** An _____ constant does not have a decimal point.

**8.** The word BASIC is an abbreviation for _____.

**9.** The special character ↑ in interactive BASIC represents the operation of _____ and is equivalent to the symbol _____.

**10.** An algebraic sign will be printed to the left of a number only if _____.

**9–4**
**Problems**

**1.** Determine the errors, if any, in the following expressions:
   **a.** 3.97
   **b.** D7
   **c.** 4C/X + Y
   **d.** (8.7 + C7)/−5.6
   **e.** Y1 + Y0
   **f.** Z25 + X
   **g.** XY/Z
   **h.** (L + M)/(M + N)↑(L + M)
   **i.** A↑(X + −Y)
   **j.** X(Y + Z)
   **k.** A↑.5 * B
   **l.** A + (X + Y)/Z

**2.** Determine the errors, if any, in the following input or output statements:

    **a.** 10   PRINT A, B, C, D.
    **b.** 10   PRINT A, B$, C$, D
    **c.** 10   PRINT X$, Y, C↑2 + D↑2
    **d.** 10   PRINT "THE ANSWER IS" Y
    **e.** 10   PRINT "SAMPLE". "PROBLEM" "3"
    **f.** 10   INPUT X; Y
    **g.** 10   INPUT A, B$, C
    **h.** 10   INPUT X, "BETTY", Y
    **i.** 10   INPUT W, X, Y, Z

**3.** Write BASIC statements to compute the following algebraic statements:

    **a.** $A = (X + Y)/Z$
    **b.** $R = \sqrt{H^2 + V^2}$ or $R = (H^2 + V^2)^{1/2}$
    **c.** $A = 5L + 7M - 6.28$
    **d.** $X = \dfrac{A^2(3B^2 - 4C^2)}{A - B + C}$

    **e.** $S = \dfrac{\pi}{4}(4H^2 + C^2)$

**4.** Write the mathematical equivalents of the following BASIC statements:

    **a.** LET A = X ↑ 2 − 5 * Y * Z
    **b.** LET A = (X ↑ 2 + B ↑ 2 + C ↑ 2) * (1/3)
    **c.** LET X + A * (1 + B/C) ↑ (C * D)
    **d.** LET L = 3 * C ↑ 4 * D
    **e.** LET G = H/18 ↑ .5
    **f.** LET I = B * H ↑ 3/12

**5.** Determine the errors, if any, in the following sequence of instructions:

REMARKS PROBLEM PROGRAM
010   PRINT "PROBLEM PROGRAM"
020   PRINT A, B
040   INPUT A, B
060   LET M = (A * B)/4
070   IF M < 4 THEN 100
090   LET N = 0
100   LET N = 1
130   LET P = (M − N) ↑ 2
200   PRINT A, B, N, P
170   END
180   RUN

**6.** Write a BASIC program that will compute and print the value of X, where A, B, and C are typed in from the console for the following:

    **a.**    $X = A + B + C$    if $A < 0$
        and $X = A - B - C$    if $A > = 0$
    **b.**    $X = A(B - C)/(B + C)$    if $A = 0$
        and $X = A(B - C)(B + C)$    if $A < 0$ or $A > 0$

7. Write a BASIC program to calculate the squares and cubes of the numbers from 1 to 25 and print them out in columns with appropriate titles.

8. Write a BASIC program to calculate the amount of P dollars invested at R percent compounded C times per year for 1 to N years. P, R, C, and N are to be input at the time the program is executed. You may assume that P will not exceed 999.99 dollars, R will not exceed 0.050, C will not exceed 12, and N will not exceed 5. The formula to determine amount is

$$A = P(1 + R/C)^{CN}$$

9. Write a BASIC program for the Julian date program flowcharted in Problem 12, Chapter 7.

10. Write a BASIC program for the grade problem flowcharted in Problem 13, Chapter 7.

INTRODUCTION

ADDITIONAL TRANSFER OF CONTROL AND LOOPING STATEMENTS

**FOR and NEXT Statements**

**STOP Statement**

**COMPUTED GO TO Statement**

ADDITIONAL INPUT/OUTPUT STATEMENTS

**READ and DATA Statements**

**RESTORE Statement**

**Using the Semicolon**

**PRINT with TAB Option**

**PRINT with USING Option**

TABLE HANDLING

**Creating a Table**

DIM Statement

**Accessing a Table**

**Two- and Three-level Tables**

**Matrices**

MAT READ

MAT PRINT

MAT INPUT

FUNCTIONS AND SUBPROGRAMS

**Library Functions**

**User-defined Functions**

**Subprograms**

FILE PROCESSING*

**Creating a File**

OPEN Statement

PUT Statement

CLOSE Statement

**Accessing a File**

GET Statement

**Updating a File**

FOCUS ON THE FIELD

SELF-TESTS

EXERCISES

# CHAPTER 10

# Advanced Concepts in BASIC

# INTRODUCTION

In Chapter 9 we learned how to write relatively simple BASIC programs and to understand programming concepts. In this chapter we will learn some of the more sophisticated programming concepts. These advanced programming concepts are utilized in most practical programs employed in business and industry. Therefore, it is essential that these concepts be clearly understood if one is to interpret or create such programs.

In recent years BASIC has gained acceptance as a practical programming language as well as a teaching language. Virtually every microcomputer and most full-size computer systems support a version of BASIC. Because of its rapid growth and expansion, minor and sometimes subtle differences have emerged in the BASIC compilers offered by the various computer manufacturers. Therefore, it is recommended that you verify the availability of each of the instructions presented with your instructor or data-processing center.

For your convenience, comments have been included in the discussions of those instructions for which variations are most likely.

Upon completing this chapter, you should be able to:
- Produce more sophisticated and practical output
- Use the powerful and versatile FOR/NEXT statement in the construction of program loops
- Create and understand nested loops
- Discuss the concept of a table
- Create and access tables in programs
- Understand and use library and user-defined functions in programs
- Understand and use subprograms
- Construct programs to create and access files
- Define the following:

| | |
|---|---|
| ABS(X) | GOSUB |
| Argument | INT(X) |
| CLOSE | Library function |
| DEF | MAT INPUT |
| DIM | MAT PRINT |
| FOR/NEXT | MAT READ |
| GET | Matrix |

| | |
|---|---|
| NUM | RND(X) |
| ON/GOTO | SGN(X) |
| OPEN | SQR(X) |
| PRINT/TAB | STOP |
| PRINT/USING | Subprogram |
| PUT | Subscript |
| READ/DATA | Table or array |
| RESTORE | User-defined |
| RETURN | function |

## ADDITIONAL TRANSFER OF CONTROL AND LOOPING STATEMENTS

**FOR and NEXT Statements**   The FOR and NEXT statements are used in the creation of program loops. The FOR statement provides the necessary information for setting up or initializing the loop, and the NEXT statement is used by the computer to facilitate a return to the beginning of the loop or an exit from the loop. The general form of the FOR and NEXT statements is

```
                          GENERAL FORM

(line number)  FOR  (variable) = (expression)  TO  (expression)
   {STEP  (expression)}


          (line number)  NEXT  (variable)
```

*Variable* as used here must be a computational variable and *not* a string variable. It is the name assigned to the counter or *index* used to control the number of times the loop is executed. The *expression* appearing before the word TO is the initial or starting value that the index will assume; the *expression* following the word TO is the last or termination value of the index; and the *expression* following the word STEP, if used, is the increment by which the index is varied each time a NEXT statement is executed. If the STEP *expression* option is omitted, the increment is assumed to be 1. A program segment containing a loop with and without the FOR/NEXT statement is shown below.

| WITHOUT FOR/NEXT | WITH FOR/NEXT |
|---|---|
| 60   LET I = 1 | 60   FOR I = 1 TO 10 |
| 70   PRINT I, I**2 | 70   PRINT I, I**2 |
| 80   LET I = I + 1 | 80   NEXT I |
| 90   IF I < = 10 THEN 70 | 90   . . . |
| 100   . . . | |

In each of these program segments, when the loop has been executed 10 times, control will be transferred outside the loop—to statement 100 in the first case and statement 90 in the second case. Following are some points to remember when using the FOR and NEXT statements:

1. Every FOR statement must have at least one NEXT statement referencing the same variable.
2. Any number of statements may appear between the FOR statement and its associated NEXT statement.
3. FOR/NEXT loops may be nested within one another as long as the inner loops are completely contained within the outer loop.
4. The index of the loop may not be varied by any statement within the loop.
5. Exiting the loop (through an IF . . . THEN statement) before the termination value of the index has been reached will cause the index to remain at the last value attained before the loop was exited.
6. The results of entering a FOR/NEXT loop at other than the FOR statement are unpredictable. Thus this situation should be avoided.
7. After a FOR/NEXT loop has been completed, the value of the index is unpredictable. That is, at statement 90 in the previous example (containing the FOR/NEXT statement) the value of I is unpredictable.
8. A FOR/NEXT loop will be executed at least once even if the exit condition is satisfied when the loop is entered.

Examples of programs employing the FOR/NEXT statement are shown in Figs. 10-1 and 10-2.

FIGURE 10-1

A BASIC program employing the FOR/NEXT statement with the STEP option

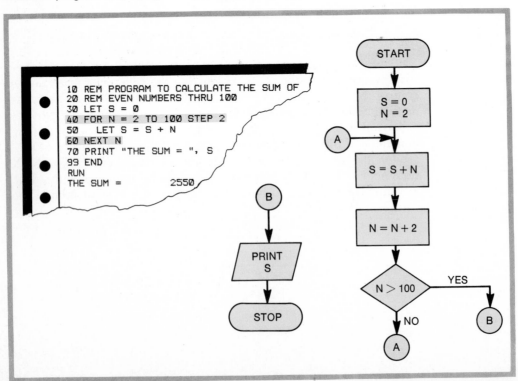

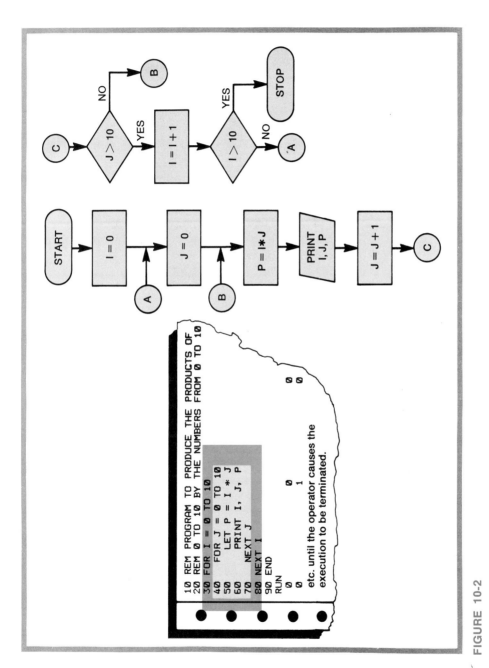

**FIGURE 10-2**

A BASIC program employing nested FOR/NEXT loops

```
          GENERAL FORM

    (line number)   STOP
```

**STOP**       The STOP statement can be placed anywhere in the program where
**Statement**  it is desired that execution be halted. This statement has the same
effect as the statement GO TO n, where n is the line number of the END
statement. For example, if the END statement had line number 999, the
statements STOP and GO TO 999 would serve identical purposes. The
only advantage of using the STOP statement over the GO TO statement
in this instance is that the STOP statement immediately tells the computer that execution is to be terminated, while the GO TO 999 statement
requires that the computer first locate statement 999 END before it
knows that execution is to be terminated.

An example of the STOP statement used in conjunction with two
IF/THEN statements is given below and compared with the same program using the GO TO statement.

```
10   REM SAMP. PROG.        10   REM SAMP. PROG.
20   . . .                  20   . . .

40   . . .                  40   . . .
50   IF A = 5 THEN 70       50   IF A = 5 THEN 70
60   STOP                   60   GO TO 999
70   . . .                  70   . . .

110  . . .                  110  . . .
120  IF B = 9 THEN 140      120  IF B = 9 THEN 140
130  STOP                   130  GO TO 999
140  . . .                  140  . . .

270  . . .                  270  . . .
999  END                    999  END
```

```
                         GENERAL FORM

    (line number)   ON   expression   GO TO   (line number 1), (line number 2), . . .
```

**Computed**       The computed GO TO statement causes the computer to evaluate
**GO TO**          the expression appearing after the word ON and branch to one of
**Statement**[1]   several points within the program. The expression will always be
evaluated to an integer. If, for example, the expression mathematically
evaluates to 6.65, it would be set equal to the integral value 6. That is,
any decimal positions are truncated or cut off. The computer then

[1]Some BASIC compilers do not offer the computed GO TO statement. Therefore, ask
your instructor or data center before using this statement.

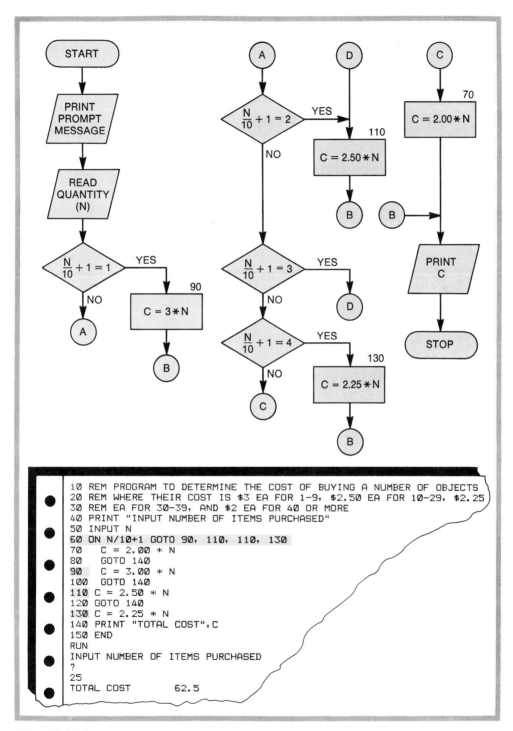

```
10 REM PROGRAM TO DETERMINE THE COST OF BUYING A NUMBER OF OBJECTS
20 REM WHERE THEIR COST IS $3 EA FOR 1-9, $2.50 EA FOR 10-29, $2.25
30 REM EA FOR 30-39, AND $2 EA FOR 40 OR MORE
40 PRINT "INPUT NUMBER OF ITEMS PURCHASED"
50 INPUT N
60 ON N/10+1 GOTO 90, 110, 110, 130
70   C = 2.00 * N
80     GOTO 140
90   C = 3.00 * N
100    GOTO 140
110 C = 2.50 * N
120 GOTO 140
130 C = 2.25 * N
140 PRINT "TOTAL COST",C
150 END
RUN
INPUT NUMBER OF ITEMS PURCHASED
?
25
TOTAL COST     62.5
```

FIGURE 10-3
BASIC program employing the computed GO TO

causes control to be transferred to one of the statements whose line number is listed after the word GO TO. But which one? The answer is very simple and very precise. If the expression evaluates to 1, control is transferred to the first line number listed after the GO TO. If the expression evaluates to 2, 3, 4, etc., control is transferred to the second, third, fourth, etc., line number listed after the GO TO, respectively.

However, if the expression evaluates to an integer greater than the number of line numbers present after the GO TO, or if the expression evaluates to an integer less than 1, the entire statement is bypassed and control is transferred to the next sequential statement.

Let us consider the computed GO TO statement

```
60   ON (A + B)/C GO TO 80, 50, 30, 90, 120, 150, 150, 170
70
```

If the expression (A + B)/C is equal to 1, 2, 3, 4, 5, 6, 7, or 8, control will be transferred to statements 80, 50, 30, 90, 120, 150, 150, or 170, respectively. However, if the expression is equal to 0, −1, −2, −3, etc., or 9, 10, 11, 12, etc., control will pass sequentially to the next statement, statement 70.

To verify our understanding of this statement, let us consider the following problem:

Determine the total cost of buying a number of objects if they cost

| | |
|---|---|
| $3.00 each for 1-9 | $2.25 each for 30-39 |
| $2.50 each for 10-29 | $2.00 each for 40 or more |

The flowchart and BASIC program for this problem are shown in Fig. 10-3.

To verify your understanding of the previous material, turn to page 392 and take Self-Test 10-1.

## ADDITIONAL INPUT/OUTPUT STATEMENTS

GENERAL FORM

(*line number*)  *READ*  (*list of variable names*)
(*line number*)  *DATA*  (*list of data constants*)

**READ and DATA Statements**  The READ and DATA statements are used together. The READ statement directs the computer to read certain data, while one or more associated DATA statements provide the data that are to be read. For example, let us assume that we wish to read four numbers into the computer, namely, 16, 15, 86, and 85. From the general form we can see that we must provide four items, which comprise two **line numbers,** a **list of variable names,** and a **list of data constants.** Let us assign to the READ statement the line number 30 and to the DATA statement the line

COMMON PROGRAMMING LANGUAGES USED IN BUSINESS

number 500, since the DATA statement generally appears after the corresponding READ statement, and usually near the end of the program. Since we are intending to read four items of data, we must assign four variable names to the list, one for each item of data. It has been previously stated that a variable name can be a letter of the alphabet, or a letter followed by a single digit, or a letter followed by a $ (string variable). This allows us 312 possible names from which to choose 4. Let us assume that we choose simple and not string variable names and that we agree on the simple variable names N1, N2, N3, and N4. We now have all the necessary information to construct the READ statement:

30  READ N1, N2, N3, N4

The **list of data constants** required in the DATA statement is a series of constants separated by commas, one constant corresponding to each variable name in the READ list. For the specific data given above, we have

500  DATA 16, 15, 86, 85

It should be apparent, however, that the READ and DATA statements are used only when the data are known to the programmer at the time of the writing of the program. In cases where the data are not known, the INPUT statement should be used. Let us consider a program utilizing the READ and DATA statements. Let us reconsider Sample Program 1, but this time let us assume that JOHN SMITH is writing this program for himself and that his grades are 75, 83, and 94.

This program would appear as shown in Fig. 10-4.

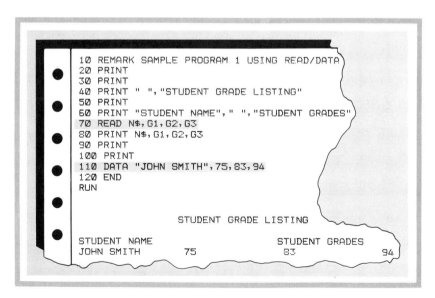

```
10 REMARK SAMPLE PROGRAM 1 USING READ/DATA
20 PRINT
30 PRINT
40 PRINT " ","STUDENT GRADE LISTING"
50 PRINT
60 PRINT "STUDENT NAME"," ","STUDENT GRADES"
70 READ N$,G1,G2,G3
80 PRINT N$,G1,G2,G3
90 PRINT
100 PRINT
110 DATA "JOHN SMITH",75,83,94
120 END
RUN


                    STUDENT GRADE LISTING

STUDENT NAME                        STUDENT GRADES
JOHN SMITH          75                  83              94
```

**FIGURE 10-4**
Sample program 1 with the READ and DATA statements

**RESTORE Statement**   This statement causes the list of data used by the program to be recycled back to the beginning or first item of data. That is, the same data are to be used over again. Let us assume that we wish to have the variable A take on the successive values 1, 2, 1, 2. A program segment showing how this could be done is given below:

```
10   REMARK SAMPLE PROGRAM
20   LET N = 0
30   . . .
40   . . .
50   READ A
60   LET N = N + 1
70   IF N = 4 THEN 999
80   . . .
90   PRINT A
100  IF N = 2 THEN 120
110  GO TO 30
120  RESTORE
130  GO TO 30
140  DATA 1,2
999  END
```

**Using the Semicolon**   We have seen that it is possible to print up to four or five items per line. Circumstances may arise, however, where it is desirable to accommodate more. This can generally be accomplished by replacing the comma normally used to separate output items in the PRINT statement with a semicolon. This will cause the number of printing areas and the size of each area to be a function of the data being printed and generally result in a line capacity of more than four or five quantities per line. When each number is printed, a space is left before the number for the sign, as the sign is printed only if the number is negative, and a space will be left after the number.

It should be noted, however, that if a literal is specified in a PRINT statement and preceded by a semicolon, it will be printed immediately after the last character of the previous field. All characters, including any blanks contained within the quotation marks, will be printed. On the other hand, if a string variable is preceded by a semicolon in a PRINT statement, the field width will be assumed to be 18 characters *minus any trailing blanks*. For example, if A$ = "JOHN          ", the PRINT statement

"I input/output COBOL, FORTRAN, and BASIC fluently."

50 PRINT A$;" IS YOUR NAME    ";"YES OR NO?"

would cause the following to be printed out:

JOHN IS YOUR NAME   YES OR NO?

It should be noted, however, that the semicolon may only be used with the PRINT statement. It *may not* be used with other BASIC statements discussed in this chapter.

Another use of the comma or semicolon in the PRINT statement is possible in some forms of BASIC.[2] Normally, the output generated by a PRINT statement will begin in print position 1 of zone 1. However, if the previous PRINT statement ended in a comma (e.g., 50 PRINT A,) the output from the current PRINT statement will begin with the next available zone. For example, in the program sequence

```
50   PRINT A, B,
60   PRINT C
```

the current values of A and B will be printed in zones 1 and 2, respectively, and the current value of C will be printed in zone 3 *of the same line.* This also applies to the use of the semicolon. The program segment below contains a loop that will cause the printing of a line of 70 asterisks.

```
50   FOR I = 1 TO 70
60   PRINT "*";
70   NEXT I
80   PRINT
```

Statement 80 serves to print blanks in the remaining positions on this line and readies the printer to print on the next line. This might not seem to be a useful tool at first glance, but it turns out to be extremely useful. For example, let us suppose that we wish to create a bar graph to represent the centimeters of rain that fell each month during a given year. Let us further assume that the rainfall is as described below.

[2]Commonly these forms of BASIC are referred to as BASIC PLUS or BASIC II.

| MONTH | CENTIMETERS OF RAINFALL |
|-------|-------------------------|
| 1     | 5                       |
| 2     | 10                      |
| 3     | 13                      |
| 4     | 18                      |
| 5     | 10                      |
| 6     | 5                       |
| 7     | 3                       |
| 8     | 0                       |
| 9     | 5                       |
| 10    | 3                       |
| 11    | 8                       |
| 12    | 10                      |

A program which will produce a graph of this data and its output is shown in Fig. 10-5.

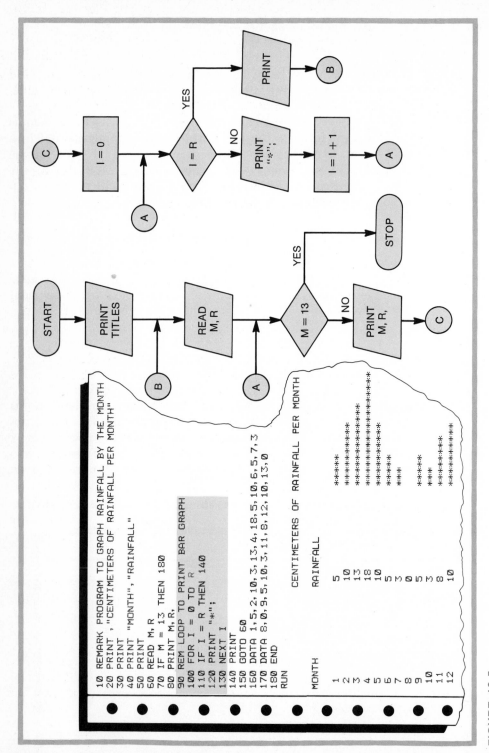

**FIGURE 10-5**

Program to generate a bar graph

**PRINT with TAB Option**[3]    The simple PRINT statement offers the programmer limited control over the format of the printed output. To overcome this limitation, some manufacturers provide two additional options to the PRINT statement: the TAB and the USING option. The TAB option performs the same function in a PRINT statement as depressing the TAB key on a typewriter, that is, it causes the printer to skip to a specified print position before printing. The general form of the PRINT with TAB option is

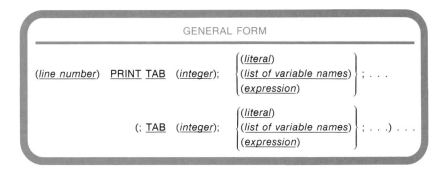

Integer as used above refers to an unsigned integer enclosed in parentheses. This integer identifies the actual print position in which the printing of a literal, list of variable names, or expression is to begin. *Literal, list of variable names*, and *expression* are as described in the simple PRINT statement. For example, if the value of A were 5, the statement

    60   PRINT TAB(6); "THE VALUE OF A IS"; A

would cause the following to be printed out:

    ƀƀƀƀƀTHEƀVALUEƀOFƀAƀISƀ5

where ƀ indicates a blank space. As you can see, the TAB(6) caused the printer to skip the first five printing positions and begin printing in the sixth position. The remainder of the statement produced the same results as with any other PRINT statement.

**PRINT with USING Option**    The PRINT statement with the USING option provides the most sophisticated method of controlling the format of the printed output. When the PRINT statement with the USING option is employed, it must be accompanied by a separate BASIC statement referred to as a **format** statement. This format statement describes the desired output format in detail and may appear anywhere in the program. The same format statement may be used with more than one PRINT USING statement. The general form of the PRINT statement with the USING option is

[3]The TAB option of the PRINT is generally not available on IBM computer systems.

(*line number*)   PRINT USING   (*line number*),   $\left\{ \begin{array}{l} (\textit{list of variable names}) \\ (\textit{expression}) \end{array} \right\}$, . . . .

The second *line number* entry refers to the line number of the corresponding format statement. The general form of a format statement is

(*line number*):   $\left\{ \begin{array}{l} (\textit{label}) \\ (\textit{format-description}) \end{array} \right\}$, . . . .

A **label** as used in a format statement refers to a string of characters *not* containing the # symbol. These characters will be printed out exactly as they appear. This is identical to what can be accomplished with a literal in a simple PRINT statement with the exception that any quotation marks (' or ") appearing in a format statement will be printed out as they appear in the format statement. The **format description** is used to describe the form in which a simple or string variable is to be printed out. The symbols that can be used in a format description and their meanings are as follows:

| Symbol[4] | Meaning |
|---|---|
| # | One character is to be printed. If more than one character is to be printed, one # symbol must be used for each character. |
| . | A decimal point is to be printed out in the position indicated by the period (.). |
| !!!! | Four exclamation points indicate that the number is to be printed out in exponential form. |

For example, if the variable A is equal to 15.447, the variable B is equal to 96.3, and the value of C$ is "ABCD", the BASIC statements

```
60   PRINT USING 70, A, B, C$
70   :THE VALUE OF A IS $# # # . # # ,
     THE VALUE OF B IS .# # # # !!!! AND
     THE VALUE OF C$ IS # # # #
```

would cause the following to be printed out:

[4]The symbols described here may vary with the computer system used.

```
THE VALUE OF A IS $ 15.45,
THE VALUE OF B IS .9630E+02 AND
THE VALUE OF C$ IS ABCD
```

However, if the variable A had been equal to 1154.51 and C$ had been equal to "ABCDEFG", the above statements would have caused the following to be printed out:

```
THE VALUE OF A IS $******,
THE VALUE OF B IS .9630E+02 AND
THE VALUE OF C$ IS ABCD
```

That is, when the size of the number to be printed out contains more integer positions (positions to the left of the decimal point) than are provided for in the format, *'s are printed out to inform the user of this fact. Note, however, that this does not apply to string variables, that the value of the string variable C$ was printed after being truncated to the specification contained in the format statement. Examples of output produced by the USING option of the PRINT statement for various format specifications are shown below.

| FORMAT SPECIFICATION | VALUE | PRINTED OUTPUT |
| --- | --- | --- |
| # # # | 123 | 123 |
| # # # | 12 | ∮12 |
| # # # | 12.3 | ∮12 |
| # #.# # | 123 | ***** |
| # #.# # | 1.23 | ∮1.23 |
| # #.# # | 1.23456 | ∮1.23 |
| # #.# # | .123 | ∮0.12 |
| # #.# # | 12.345 | 12.35 |
| # # # !!!! | 123 | 123E+00 |
| # # # !!!! | 12.3 | 123E−01 |
| # # # !!!! | .1234 | 123E−03 |
| # #.# # !!!! | 123 | 12.30E+01 |
| # #.# # !!!! | 1.23 | ∮1.23E+00 |
| # #.# # !!!! | .1234 | 12.34E−02 |
| # #.# # !!!! | 1234 | 12.34E+02 |
| # # # # | ABCD | ABCD |
| # # # # | ABCDE | ABCD |
| # # # # | ABC | ABC∮ |

*Note:* In the above illustrations, ∮ represents a blank space.

To verify your understanding of the previous material, turn to page 392 and take Self-Test 10-2.

## TABLE HANDLING

Thus far in this chapter, we have discussed the BASIC instructions necessary to enable a programmer to input discrete data items, arithmetically and logically manipulate the data read, and then output the appropriate results. However, many programs require an ability to access and manipulate more than discrete variables; they require an ability to handle one or more arrays or tables of data.

An **array** or **table** can be defined as a collection or arrangement of data in a fixed form for ready reference. Such data include sales tax tables, interest rate tables, insurance rate tables, and tables of names. Figure 10-6 illustrates a hypothetical table of postal rates.

The cost of sending a package third class can be found in the second column of this table by choosing the weight in the first column that is closest to, but not less than, the weight of the package. Each weight–cost combination is referred to as an element of the table and consists of a **subscript** (in this case the weight of the package) and a **value** (in this case the cost of mailing the package third class). The table itself is referred to as a **one-level** or **single-dimension**

"When I got it about half completed, it started criticizing the way I was putting it together!"

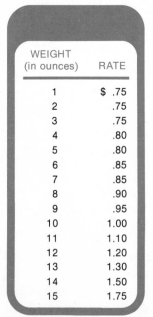

**FIGURE 10-6**
A hypothetical one-level postal rate table

| WEIGHT (in ounces) | RATE |
|---|---|
| 1 | $ .75 |
| 2 | .75 |
| 3 | .75 |
| 4 | .80 |
| 5 | .80 |
| 6 | .85 |
| 7 | .85 |
| 8 | .90 |
| 9 | .95 |
| 10 | 1.00 |
| 11 | 1.10 |
| 12 | 1.20 |
| 13 | 1.30 |
| 14 | 1.50 |
| 15 | 1.75 |

table.[5] That is, it takes one or a single subscript to determine the value of an element in the table. It is also possible to define and process tables of more than one level or dimension. Figure 10-7 illustrates a two-level table. In this table, the value of an element is determined by two subscripts: the weight of the package and the class of mail by which the package is to be shipped.

**Creating a Table**   Let us assume that we wish to establish in storage the single-dimension postal rate table discussed above. The first consideration is to assign the table a variable name. Table names as variable names are simple or string. Tables containing simple variable values are assigned simple variable names; tables containing string values are assigned string variable names. In this case the table would be assigned a simple variable name—let us say P. As this table contains 15 elements, we must make certain that the machine allocates sufficient storage in this array or table for these elements. This is accomplished using a DIM statement.

DIM Statement.   The **DIM statement** serves to reserve as many elements of storage as there can be elements in the array or table. The general form of the DIM statement is seen on page 374.[6]

[5]A one-level or single-dimension table is sometimes referred to as a **list.**

[6]Many BASIC compilers do not require a DIM statement if a table has 10 or fewer elements.

FIGURE 10-7

A hypothetical two-level postal rate table

| WEIGHT (in ounces) | RATE | | |
| --- | --- | --- | --- |
| | FIRST CLASS | SECOND CLASS | THIRD CLASS |
| 1 | $1.05 | $ .90 | $ .75 |
| 2 | 1.15 | .95 | .75 |
| 3 | 1.30 | 1.00 | .75 |
| 4 | 1.55 | 1.10 | .80 |
| 5 | 1.80 | 1.20 | .80 |
| 6 | 2.05 | 1.35 | .85 |
| 7 | 2.45 | 1.50 | .85 |
| 8 | 2.85 | 1.65 | .90 |
| 9 | 3.35 | 1.80 | .95 |
| 10 | 3.95 | 2.00 | 1.00 |
| 11 | 4.70 | 2.20 | 1.10 |
| 12 | 5.60 | 2.40 | 1.20 |
| 13 | 6.85 | 2.60 | 1.30 |
| 14 | 8.25 | 2.80 | 1.50 |
| 15 | 9.75 | 3.00 | 1.75 |

```
                        GENERAL FORM
─────────────────────────────────────────────────────
(line number)  DIM   array-name (elements in the array)  , . . .
```

In a DIM statement, the number of *elements in the array* must be a positive integer constant. In our case, this statement would be

20   DIM P(15)

With this statement we have reserved 15 consecutive storage locations for a table called P. Now we must fill these locations with the appropriate values. To accomplish this we will need to be able to identify and access individual elements within the table. This is done with the aid of the subscript. For example, the first element of the table can be accessed with the variable name P(1), where P is the name of the table and 1 is the subscript or position of the element in the table. Subsequent elements in the table can be accessed with the variable names P(2), P(3), P(4), P(5), P(6), P(7), P(8), P(9), P(10), P(11), P(12), P(13), P(14), and P(15). Any element of the table can also be accessed with the variable name

P(I)

where I is any variable name containing a value equal to the subscript of the element to be accessed. By changing the value of I from 1 to 15 in increments of 1, every element of the table can be accessed. This technique is employed below to establish the postal rate table.

```
20   DIM P(15)
30   FOR I = 1 TO 15
40      READ P(I)
50   NEXT I
60   DATA .75,.75,.75,.80,.80,.85,.85,.90,.95
70   DATA 1.00,1.10,1.20,1.30,1.50,1.75
```

**Accessing a Table**     Once the table has been established, it may be used in subsequent processing. Figure 10-8 illustrates a program segment which inputs the weight of a package in ounces and outputs the corresponding third-class shipping rate. This program is idealized in that the shipping weight was input in ounces so that the weight could be used directly as the subscript of the element desired in the table. But how would the program have appeared if the weight had not been in a whole or integer number of ounces?

If the weight of the package was not a whole number of ounces, it would be necessary to convert it to the nearest integer weight greater than or equal to the package weight. This can be accomplished with the statement

85   LET W = INT(W + .999999)

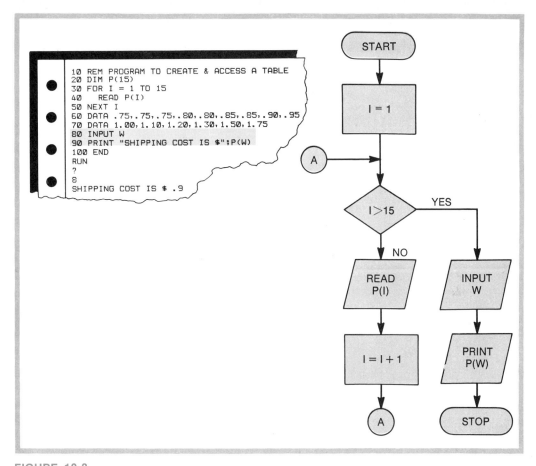

```
10 REM PROGRAM TO CREATE & ACCESS A TABLE
20 DIM P(15)
30 FOR I = 1 TO 15
40    READ P(I)
50 NEXT I
60 DATA .75,.75,.75,.80,.80,.85,.85,.90,.95
70 DATA 1.00,1.10,1.20,1.30,1.50,1.75
80 INPUT W
90 PRINT "SHIPPING COST IS $";P(W)
100 END
RUN
?
8
SHIPPING COST IS $ .9
```

START

I = 1

A

I > 15 — YES

NO

READ P(I)

INPUT W

I = I + 1

PRINT P(W)

A

STOP

FIGURE 10-8

Program to access a postal rate table given the weight of the parcel in a whole number of ounces

This statement first causes .999999 to be added to the package weight W. For example, if the package weight was 4.75 ounces, it would now be 5.749999 ounces. The integer portion of this number is now the subscript we are looking for. All that we need to do is eliminate the decimal portion. This is accomplished with the library function INT.

**Library functions** are prewritten and stored programs that are made available with the BASIC compiler. A complete list of the functions available with your compiler can be obtained from your computer center or instructor. The particular library function INT(X) accepts a numeric value X and returns only the integral portion of X. Thus, the value returned for INT(5.749999) will be 5. That is, statement 85 above will cause the original weight of 4.75 ounces to be converted to the integer weight of 5 ounces. In essence, W was rounded up to the nearest integer. The complete program would be as shown in Fig. 10-9. Library functions will be discussed in greater detail later in this chapter.

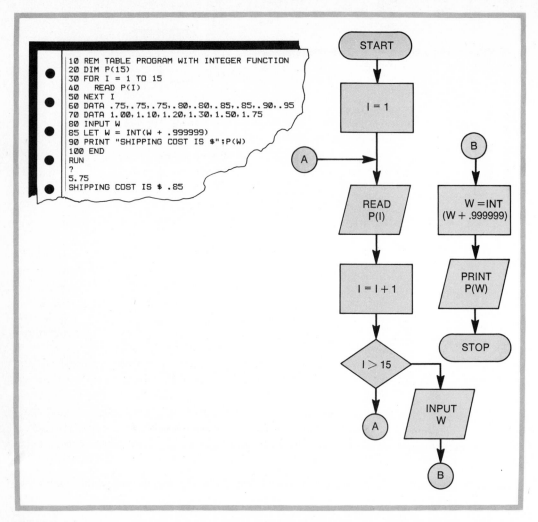

```
10 REM TABLE PROGRAM WITH INTEGER FUNCTION
20 DIM P(15)
30 FOR I = 1 TO 15
40    READ P(I)
50 NEXT I
60 DATA .75,.75,.75,.80,.80,.85,.85,.90,.95
70 DATA 1.00,1.10,1.20,1.30,1.50,1.75
80 INPUT W
85 LET W = INT(W + .999999)
90 PRINT "SHIPPING COST IS $";P(W)
100 END
RUN
?
5.75
SHIPPING COST IS $ .85
```

**FIGURE 10-9**

Program to access a postal rate table given that the weight of the parcel may or may not be in a whole number of ounces

**Two- and Three-level Tables**

Sometimes a particular value in a table is determined by more than one variable. For example, in Fig. 10-7 the cost of shipping a package depends on both the weight of the package *and* the class of mail by which it is to be shipped. A package weighing 5 ounces (rounded up to the nearest integer) and being shipped second class would cost $1.20. This same cost may be represented as

$$P(5, 2)$$

where P is the name chosen for the table, 5 represents the fifth weight classification, and 2 represents the second mail type classification. Some other examples are

P(3, 3)  = .75 (3-ounce package sent third class)

P(1, 1)  = 1.05 (1-ounce package sent first class)

P(9, 1)  = 3.35 (9-ounce package sent first class)

P(8, 2)  = 1.65 (8-ounce package sent second class)

P(8, 4)  = INVALID, as there is no fourth-class mail

P(18, 2) = INVALID, as this table cannot accommodate packages over 15 ounces

It should be noted, however, that the DIM statement for this table should indicate that it is a two-level or two-dimensional table by providing a separate positive integer constant for each level or dimension. This would be accomplished with the statement

```
20   DIM P(15, 3)
```

Note that the order of the subscripts in the DIM statement must be the same as the order of the subscripts when referring to elements of the table.

Figure 10-10 illustrates a three-level table, and Fig. 10-11 illustrates a program to create and access this table.

**Matrices**    The term **matrix** is a mathematical term for an array or table. This term is introduced here because some BASIC compilers are available with a series of matrix statements that facilitate the processing of arrays and tables. A single matrix statement can perform the same function that previously required several statements to accomplish. Each such matrix statement begins with the word MAT. MAT statements are available to add, subtract, and multiply tables by one another. These operations are of a sophisticated mathematical nature and will not be dis-

FIGURE 10-10

Hypothetical three-level insurance premium table

| THREE-LEVEL INSURANCE PREMIUM TABLE | | | | | |
|---|---|---|---|---|---|
| | MALE | | | FEMALE | | |
| AGE CATEGORY | RISK CLASS | | | RISK CLASS | | |
| | 1 | 2 | 3 | 1 | 2 | 3 |
| below 18 | $38.50 | $42.35 | $46.59 | $34.65 | $38.12 | $41.94 |
| 18–34 | 36.00 | 39.60 | 43.56 | 32.40 | 35.64 | 39.21 |
| 35–39 | 36.75 | 40.43 | 44.48 | 33.03 | 36.38 | 40.04 |
| 40–44 | 38.00 | 41.80 | 45.98 | 34.20 | 37.62 | 41.39 |
| 45–49 | 39.50 | 43.45 | 47.80 | 35.55 | 39.11 | 43.02 |
| 50–54 | 45.00 | 49.50 | 54.45 | 40.50 | 44.55 | 48.96 |
| 55–59 | 52.00 | 57.20 | 62.92 | 46.80 | 51.48 | 56.63 |
| above 59 | 70.00 | 77.00 | 84.70 | 63.00 | 69.30 | 76.23 |

Flowchart labels:

START → I = 1 → I > 8 (YES → D) (NO) → J = 1 → J > 2 (YES → K = K + 1 → C) (NO) → K = 1 → K > 3 (YES → J = J + 1 → B) (NO) → READ P(I, J, K) → K = K + 1 → A

C (loop back to before I > 8)
B (loop back to before J > 2)
A (loop back to before K > 3)

D → INPUT A → INPUT B → INPUT C → PRINT T(A, B, C) → INPUT A$ → A$ = YES (YES → D) (NO) → STOP

```
10  REM CREATE & ACCESS A THREE-LEVEL TABLE
20  DIM T(8,2,3)
30  FOR I = 1 TO 8
40      FOR J = 1 TO 2
50          FOR K = 1 TO 3
60              READ T(I,J,K)
70          NEXT K
80      NEXT J
90  NEXT I
100 DATA 38.50,42.35,46.59,34.65, 38.12,41.94
110 DATA 36.,39.6,43.56,32.4,35.64,39.21
120 DATA 36.75,40.43,44.48,33.03,36.38,40.04
130 DATA 38.,41.8,45.98,34.2,37.62,41.39
135 DATA 39.50,43,45,47.80,35.55,39,11,43.02
140 DATA 45.,49.5,54.45,40.5,44.55,48.96
150 DATA 52.,57.2,62.92,46.8,51.48,56.63
160 DATA 70.,77.,84.7,63.,69.3,76.23
170 PRINT "INPUT A 1 IF YOUR AGE IS BELOW 18, A 2 IF 18-34, A"
180 PRINT "3 IF 35-39, A 4 IFF 40-44, A 5 IF 45-49, A 6 IF 50-54, "
190 PRINT "A 7 IF 55-59, AND AN 8 IF ABOVE 59"
200 INPUT A
210 PRINT "INPUT A 1 IF YOU ARE MALE AND A 2 IF YOU ARE FEMALE"
220 INPUT B
230 PRINT "INPUT YOUR RISK CLASS NUMBER"
240 INPUT C
250 PRINT "YOUR INSURANCE PREMIUM WILL BE $";T(A,B,C)
260 PRINT "WOULD YOU LIKE ANOTHER QUOTE? ANSWER YES OR NO."
270 INPUT A$
280 IF A$ = "YES" THEN 170
290 END
```

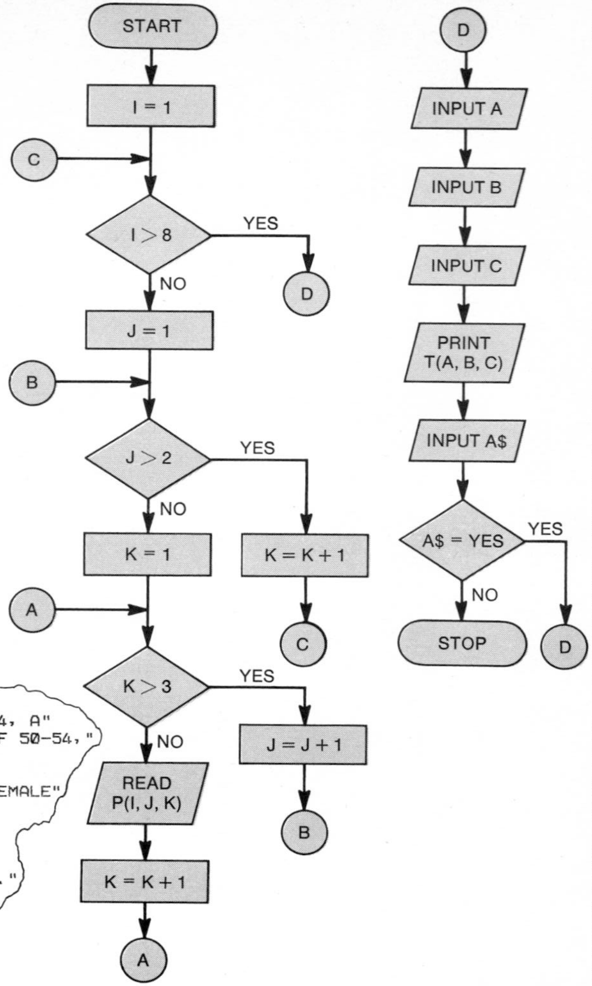

**FIGURE 10-11**

Program to create and access a three-level table

cussed here. However, there are some MAT statements that are not that involved and are very useful. These statements are MAT READ, MAT PRINT, and MAT INPUT.

MAT READ.  The MAT READ statement is used to READ an array or table. The general form of this statement is

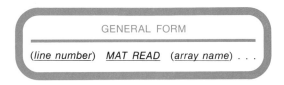

GENERAL FORM

(*line number*)  *MAT READ*  (*array name*) . . .

Let us assume that we wish to read into the two-level table A the following values:

```
45  72  85  57
86  90  20  27
```

This can be accomplished very easily with the sequence of instructions

```
10  DIM A(2, 4)
20  MAT READ A
30  DATA 45,72,85,57,86,90,20,27
```

Without this statement, the reading of the table with FOR/NEXT statements would appear as follows:

```
10  DIM A(2, 4)
20  FOR I = 1 TO 2
30    FOR J = 1 TO 4
40      READ A(I, J)
50    NEXT J
60  NEXT I
70  DATA 45,72,85,57,86,90,20,27
```

It should be apparent that this statement can save a substantial amount of coding.

MAT PRINT.  The MAT PRINT statement can serve a similar purpose in that it can be used to print out an array or table. The general form of the MAT PRINT statement is

GENERAL FORM

(*line number*)  *MAT PRINT*  (*array name*) . . .

For example, in the above program segment, which read in array A, it would be a simple matter to print it out with the MAT PRINT statement. This program segment would appear as follows:

```
10  DIM A(2, 4)
20  MAT READ A
30  MAT PRINT A
40  DATA 45,72,85,57,86,90,20,27
```

It should be noted that the table is read and printed *row by row* when the MAT READ and MAT PRINT statements are used. If the table is a three- or four-level table, these statements will cause the table to be read or printed beginning with the rightmost subscript, then the next rightmost subscript, and so on until all the elements of the table have been read or printed.

MAT INPUT.  The MAT INPUT differs from the MAT READ and MAT PRINT statements in that it may only be used with a one-level or single-dimension table. The general form of this statement is

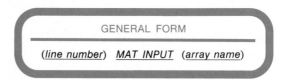

GENERAL FORM

*(line number)*  *MAT INPUT*  *(array name)*

When a MAT INPUT statement is executed, a question mark (?) will appear, indicating that the program is requesting data. The user may type in from one to the number of variables specified in the DIM statement, separated by commas. The first value typed in will be assigned to the first position in the array, the second value to the second position in the array, and so on. After the last value has been typed in, they are transmitted to the computer by hitting the RETURN key or other applicable key(s). Program execution will then resume.

It is important to note that it is not necessary to enter the number of values equal to the size of the array specified in the DIM statement. The computer actually counts the data values that are input and stores this count in a location called **NUM.** Thus, NUM contains the actual number of values that the user has typed in. This number can be used to control the exit from a loop. This is illustrated in the program segment below.

```
10   REM PROGRAM TO AVERAGE UP TO 100 NUMBERS
20   DIM X(100)
30   MAT INPUT X
40   LET N = NUM
50   LET S = 0
60   FOR I = 1 TO N
70     LET S = S + X(I)
80   NEXT I
90   LET A = S/N
100  PRINT A
```

To verify your understanding of the previous material, turn to page 393 and take Self-Test 10-3.

# FUNCTIONS AND SUBPROGRAMS

**Library Functions**   We have seen the use of a library or predefined function in a previous example. A knowledge of these functions can save a great deal of time and effort in that one does not have to write a routine or program segment to accomplish these tasks.

Each of the available library functions can be accessed simply by stating its name, followed by whatever information is required by the function, enclosed in parentheses. A simple variable or numeric quantity that is required by a function is referred to as an **argument.** Once such a function has been accessed, it will be executed automatically, utilizing the current value of the argument specified. The value returned or resulting from executing the function will then be used in the statement in which the function appeared. For example, in the statement

$$90 \quad \text{LET A} = 2 * (\text{INT}(5.7) + \text{INT}(3.1))$$

the function INT(5.7) would be replaced with the value 5, the function INT(3.1) with the value 3, and the value of A set equal to $2 * (5 + 3)$ or 16.

A list of some of the library functions available in BASIC is given in Table 10-1.

**TABLE 10-1**
**Available Library Functions**

| FUNCTION | ARGUMENT | PURPOSE | EXAMPLES |
|---|---|---|---|
| ABS (X) | May be a constant, simple variable, or expression. | Returns the absolute value of X. This value will always be positive even if X is negative. | ABS(6.5) = 6.5<br>ABS(−6.5) = 6.5<br>ABS(2 − 3) = 1 |
| INT(X) | May be a constant, simple variable, or expression | Returns the integral value of X with any decimal places cut off or truncated. | INT(3/2) = 1<br>INT(−7.5) = −7<br>INT(7.5) = 7 |
| RND(X) | May be zero or a positive integer | Returns a random number between 0 and 1 if X is zero; and between 1 and X if X is a positive integer | RND(0) = .756934<br>RND(0) = .430128<br>RND(6) = 1.29253<br>RND(12/2) = 5.08137<br>RND(6) = 4.46493 |
| SGN(X) | May be a constant, simple variable, or expression | Returns +1 if X is positive; 0 if X is zero; and −1 if X is negative | SGN(−2) = −1<br>SGN(7) = +1<br>SGN(1 − 3 + 2) = 0 |
| SQR(X) | May be a constant, simple variable, or expression whose value is positive | Returns the square root of X | SQR(4) = 2<br>SQR(100/4) = 5<br>SQR(2) = 1.41421 |

**User-defined Functions**   If a function is desired that is not available as a library function, it can be defined by the user within the program. For example, let us suppose that within a program the expression A**2 + A is to be used several times. This expression can be defined as a function. Then, whenever the expression is needed, the programmer can substitute the name of the function followed by the appropriate argument enclosed in parentheses.

The first step in the process would be to define the function. This is accomplished with a DEF statement.

---

GENERAL FORM

---

(*line number*)   *DEF*   (*function name*) (*argument in parentheses*) = (*expression*)

---

The *function name* must be provided by the programmer and must begin with the letters FN followed by any letter of the alphabet. That is, possible function names are FNA, FNB, FNC, . . . , FNX, FNY, and FNZ.

Only one variable is permissible as the *argument*, and it may not be an array or a table.

Any valid *expression* may be used provided that it does not cause the DEF statement to extend beyond a single line.

In the case of the user-defined function described above, an appropriate function definition would be

$$10 \quad \text{DEF FNS(A)} = \text{A**2} + \text{A}$$

Function definition statements may appear anywhere in a BASIC program. However, they are generally grouped together if there is more than one and are generally placed near the beginning or end of the program. Once a function has been defined, it may be accessed anywhere, any number of times in the program. When accessed, it will be evaluated and the resulting value returned.

Several statements containing references to the above function are shown below and evaluated on the assumption that the value of A is 3 and the value of X is 4.

---

| STATEMENT | EVALUATION |
|---|---|
| 30   LET Z = FNS(5) | Z = 5**2 + 5 = 30 |
| 40   LET Z = FNS(X) | Z = 4**2 + 4 = 20 |
| 50   LET Z = FNS(X) + A | Z = (4**2 + 4) + 3 = 20 + 3 = 23 |
| 60   LET Z = FNS(A) + FNS(X) | Z = (3**2 + 3) + (4**2 + 4) = 12 + 20 = 32 |
| 70   LET Z = FNS(X − A − 4) | X − A − 4 = −3 |
|  | Z = (−3)**2 + (−3) = 9 − 3 = 6 |

---

Note, in statement 70, that it was necessary to determine the value of the argument (X − A − 4) before the function could be evaluated. This will be the case whenever the argument of a function is other than a constant or simple variable.

**Subprograms**   There are many instances where a routine must be performed in a program but where the detailed sequence of instructions might distract from the overall logical flow of the program. There are also cases where a particular routine may need to be performed several times within a program. Both of these ends can be achieved with the aid of a subprogram. In BASIC the statement which facilitates the concept of the subprogram is the GOSUB statement. The form of this statement is

GENERAL FORM

*(line number)*   <u>GOSUB</u>   *(line number)*

FIGURE 10-12

Program to access a postal rate table which is established in a subprogram

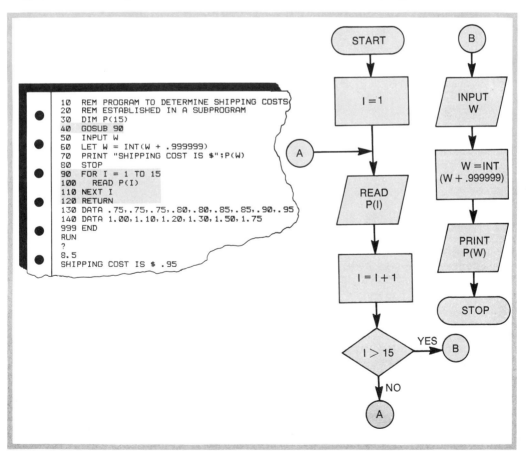

When a GOSUB statement is encountered during program execution, control is unconditionally transferred to the line number stipulated immediately after the word GOSUB. Program execution will continue from this point on in a sequential fashion until a RETURN statement is encountered. At this point control will be unconditionally transferred back to the statement immediately following the GOSUB statement. The collection of statements executed from the first transfer to the return constitutes a **subprogram.**

Figure 10-12 illustrates the same program as shown in Fig. 10-9 but utilizing the concept of a subprogram.

**To verify your understanding of the previous material, turn to page 394 and take Self-Test 10-4.**

## FILE PROCESSING*

Thus far, we have written programs that required the user to INPUT the data to be processed or we provided these data in one or more DATA statements within the program. Each of these alternatives was effective when dealing with relatively small amounts of data to be accessed by a program. They are, however, impractical for use in programs where a significant amount of data is involved or where the data must be accessed by several users or programs.

"I'm sorry, Mr. Hoover, but I'm afraid your experience as a pantyhose salesman would be of little value to us in our software operation."

We learned in Chapter 6 that large volumes of data are generally organized into files for more efficient processing. BASIC, as well as most other problem- or procedure-oriented languages, offers a capability to process these large volumes of data or files. In BASIC we can create files and assign a unique name to each file created. These files can then be saved by the system on tape or disk for future use. Once saved, these files can be recalled and accessed. And, since they are independent of any program, more than one program can access the same file or pool of data.

The BASIC language can be used to establish and access both sequential and direct-organized files. In this section we will confine our discussion to sequential files. However, there are variations in the specific instructions that are available with the different BASIC compilers to process files. The instructions presented here will run on an IBM system and with minor modifications will run on PDP, DEC, Hewlett-Packard, and other computer systems. Conceptually, the techniques presented here will apply to any other computer system, but one can expect some variation in the specific instructions employed. Therefore, it is suggested that you determine any variations that might be necessary from your instructor, manufacturer's user's guide, or data-processing center.

**Creating a File**  Before any file can be read or written, it must be prepared for this operation. That is, the file must be opened.

OPEN Statement.  The OPEN statement opens a file for reading or writing as the cover of a textbook might be opened before it can be read or a notebook might be opened before it can be written in. The general form of the OPEN statement is

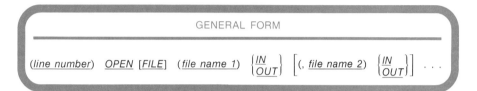

GENERAL FORM

(*line number*)  *OPEN* [*FILE*]  (*file name 1*)  $\left\{ \begin{matrix} IN \\ OUT \end{matrix} \right\}$  $\left[ (, \textit{ file name 2}) \left\{ \begin{matrix} IN \\ OUT \end{matrix} \right\} \right]$  . . .

A *file name* may be from 1 to 8 characters long; the first character must be alphabetic. There may not be any leading or embedded blanks. The file name must be enclosed in quotes wherever it is used. The file type (IN or OUT) is used to specify whether the file is an INput or OUTput file. When being created, a file must be OPENed as OUTput, and when being read it must be OPENed as INput.

Thus, the OPEN statement to create a file named INFILE would be

```
150  OPEN ''INFILE'' OUT
```

PUT Statement.  Now that we have OPENed the file, we can write on it. The statement that is used to write data on a file is the PUT statement. The general form of the PUT statement is

GENERAL FORM

(*line number*)  *PUT*  (*file name*), (*list of variables*)  [, *EOF*  (*line number 2*)]

The *file name* used in the PUT statement must have appeared previously in an OPEN statement with file type OUT. *Line number 2* in the *EOF* (End Of File) option is the line number of the statement to which control is to be transferred when there is no more room on the file.

Let us now consider a program to create a file to be called STUDENT and to contain the name and examination grades of each student in a particular class. Below is a program that will accomplish this task.

Advanced Concepts in BASIC

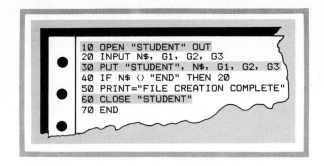

```
10 OPEN "STUDENT" OUT
20 INPUT N$, G1, G2, G3
30 PUT "STUDENT", N$, G1, G2, G3
40 IF N$ <> "END" THEN 20
50 PRINT="FILE CREATION COMPLETE"
60 CLOSE "STUDENT"
70 END
```

CLOSE Statement.   Note that statement 60 contains a new statement. As you might expect, any file that has been OPENed must be CLOSEd before program execution is terminated. It is only necessary to state the file name in the CLOSE statement, as the file type (IN or OUT) was already specified in the OPEN statement. The general form of the CLOSE statement is

GENERAL FORM

*(line number)*   *CLOSE* [*FILE*]   *(file name 1)* [, *file name 2*] . . .

**Accessing a File**   As with creating a file, the file must be OPENed. In the OPEN statement the file must be declared to be INput and must be assigned the file name that was used when the file was created. For example, if we wished to read the file that was created above, we would first OPEN it with the statement:

10   OPEN "STUDENT" IN

We would now be in a position to read the records contained in this file. The statement used to read data from a file in an IBM computer system is GET.

GENERAL FORM

*(line number)*   *GET*   *(file name)*, *(list of variable names)*   [, *EOF*   *(line number)*]

GET Statement.   Thus, for the file "STUDENT" the GET statement would be

20   GET "STUDENT", N$, G1, G2, G3

The complete program to read the STUDENT file and print out a report containing the name and grades of each student on the file is given below.

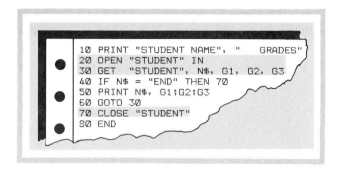

```
10 PRINT "STUDENT NAME", "   GRADES"
20 OPEN "STUDENT" IN
30 GET  "STUDENT", N$, G1, G2, G3
40 IF N$ = "END" THEN 70
50 PRINT N$, G1;G2;G3
60 GOTO 30
70 CLOSE "STUDENT"
80 END
```

**Updating a File**

One of the most common applications involves file maintenance. Most files have to be maintained or updated periodically. In a payroll system, for example, the payroll master file must be updated regularly to allow for new employees, terminated employees, and changes in employee data. With sequential files this involves the creation of a completely new file. To see how this process works, let us assume that we wish to update the file OLDPAY using the file UPDATE and produce a new, updated file, NEWPAY. OLDPAY and UPDATE are in employee number sequence. Let us assume that records contained on the UPDATE file each contain an extra field called C1, where C1 contains a 1 if the record is new, a 2 if the record is to be deleted, and a 3 if the record is to replace the existing record.

The program to accomplish this is shown in Fig. 10-13. If these were disk files, it might be desirable to get the updated file back onto OLDPAY for the next processing cycle. This could be accomplished by OPENing OLDPAY again, but this time, as OUTput, and OPENing NEWPAY as INput. NEWPAY could then be copied onto OLDPAY. Of course, this should not be attempted unless there is a listing or backup copy of the OLDPAY file prior to this update. Should something unforeseen happen during the update to render OLDPAY unusable, the backup or listing will be essential.

"There's nothing I can do about her trouble. You know, these things only *look* human."

To verify your understanding of the previous material, turn to page 394 and take Self-Test 10-5.

Advanced Concepts in BASIC

```
10 REM PROGRAM TO UPDATE A SEQUENTIAL FILE
20 REM THE FILE (UPDATE) PRODUCING AN UPDATED SEQUENTIAL FILE
30 REM (NEWPAY). ALL FILES ARE IN EMP-NO SEQUENCE
40 OPEN "OLDPAY" IN
50 OPEN "NEWPAY" OUT
60 OPEN "UPDATE" IN
70 GOSUB 370
80 GOSUB 420
90 REM ROUTINE TO COMPARE EMP-NOS ON NOWPAYROLL AND UPDATE
100 IF E3<=E1 THEN 130
110 PUT "NEWPAY", E1,,N$,P1,P2,P3,P4,P5,P6,P7,P8,P9
120 GOTO 80
130 IF E3<E1 THEN 200
140 IF E3=999999 THEN 470
150 REM EMP-NOS IN NOWPAYROLL AND UPDATE EQUAL. DETERMINE IF
160 REM DELETION, UPDATE OF EXISTING RECORD, OR BAD C1 CODE
170 ON C1 GOTO 330,270,300
180 GOTO 330
190 REM NEW EMPLOYEE OR BAD C1 CODE
200 IF C1=1 THEN 230
210 PRINT "INVALID UPDATE CARD FOR EMPLOYEE ";C3
220 GOTO 240
230 PUT "NEWPAY", E3,D$,D1,D2,D3,D4,D5,D6,D7,D8,D9
240 GOSUB 370
250 GOTO 100
260 REM DELETE EMPLOYEE ROUTINE
270 PRINT "EMPLOYEE NUMBER ";C1;" HAS BEEN DELETED"
280 GOTO 70
290 REM UPDATE EXISTING RECORD ROUTINE
300 PUT "NEWPAY", E3,D$,D1,D2,D3,D4,D5,D6,D7,D8,D9
310 GOTO 70
320 REM UPDATE CODE ERROR ROUTINE
330 PRINT "BAD UPDATE CODE ";C1;" FOR EMPLOYEE NUMBER ";E1
340 PUT "NEWPAY", E1,N$,P1,P2,P3,P4,P5,P6,P7,P8,P9
350 GOTO 70
360 REM READ UPDATE FILE, AT END SET E3 EQUAL TO 999999
370 GET "UPDATE", E3,D$,D1,D2,D3,D4,D5,D6,D7,D8,D9,C1
380 IF D$<>"END" THEN 400
390 LET E3=999999
400 RETURN
410 REM READ NOWPAYROLL FILE, AT END SET E1 EQUAL TO 999999
420 GET "OLDPAY", E1,N$,P1,P2,P3,P4,P5,P6,P7,P8,P9
430 IF N$<>"END" THEN 450
440 LET E1=999999
450 RETURN
460 REM CLOSE FILES AND TERMINATE EXECUTION OF PROGRAM
470 CLOSE "OLDPAY" ,"UPDATE" ,"NEWPAY"
480 END
```

FIGURE 10-13

BASIC program to update a sequential file

## The Computerized Resumé

### Douglas W. Green     Denise Thaler Green

Whether using a BASIC program or a word processing system, the importance of making sure all words are spelled correctly shouldn't be overlooked.

The society of the 1980s will be, without a doubt, a fast-paced and fast-changing world. The implications for job seekers and career changers are endless, but one aspect is clear: the individual who presents the most marketable package to the prospective employer will obtain the most desirable position. In the mid 1970s, approximately 300,000 executives changed jobs each year. Meanwhile, professional and technical employees changed jobs even more frequently.

The preparation of a personal resumé is a necessary step in the pursuit of greener employment pastures.

Add these people to the pool of college graduates seeking employment and a substantial number of job hunters results. Whether you are entering the job market or happily situated on the sidelines looking for that offer you can't refuse, the preparation of a personal resumé is a necessary step in the pursuit of greener employment pastures.

With the use of a computer, the preparation and updating of one's resumé can be greatly streamlined. The exercise can also serve as a simple, yet highly practical introduction to computer programming. The remainder of this article will present some general advice regarding resumés that anyone can use, followed by some tips on how to use a computer to prepare just the right resumé for each prospective employer.

### A Resumé for Every Job

The key to an effective resumé is that it be tailor-made for the particular job. It must also emphasize the individual's unique skills and experiences as they relate to the job being sought. Without a computer, the task of designing the resumé for each job can become a full time job in itself. For the person who is already employed but is always looking, the constant updating and retyping process has the potential of developing into a time-consuming, yet nontherapeutic hobby. This is especially true if the resumé contains a goals statement or if you are planning a change in careers.

The key to an effective resumé is that it be tailor-made for the particular job.

There are two approaches to resumé writing that fit the two general classifications of people seeking employment. The most often used type is the chronological resumé. This is the standard approach best used by people who have a number of years of experience which directly relate to the position for which they are hoping to interview. In addition to education and other personal information, this type of resumé simply lists the jobs the person has had in reverse chronological order. If you are satisfied that you are in the right career and are looking for a step up the ladder or just a change in scenery, then this is the approach for you.

### Resumés for Beginners and Career Changers

If you lack experience that directly relates to the position for which you are applying, you certainly want to avoid advertising this fact. If this is the case, it is important to emphasize the skills you have acquired that will serve your new employer well and make him/her soon forget about your lack of experience. To do this, you need to use a skills-based resumé. By listing skills first you show the reader how your talents fit his/her needs. If you do not do this, the reader may see your list of experiences as being irrelevant to the position in question. Saying that you are skilled in developing and implementing small-group instruction may be more impressive than saying that you served as a junior leader for the Boy Scouts. It also allows the young job seeker to list several skills that were developed during the course of one summer job. This can serve to make the resumé appear more respectable without padding it. Sample headings that can be used in the two types of resumés are given in Figure 1, while Figure 2 shows a portion of a sample skills-based resumé.

---

**If you lack experience that directly relates to the position for which you are applying, you certainly want to avoid advertising this fact.**

---

## FIGURE 1

| Sample headings for your resumé | |
|---|---|
| **Chronological** | **Skills-based** |
| Personal Data | Personal Data |
| Education | Skills Developed |
| Work Experience | Work Experience |
| Certification | Education |
| (licenses) | Professional Affiliations |
| Professional Affiliations | Certification |
| and Offices | Publications |
| Publications | Other Skills and |
| Other Skills and Interests | Interests |

| **Suggested subheadings for a skills-based resumé** | |
|---|---|
| administrative | communication |
| managerial | problem solving |
| financial | learning |
| computer | research |
| social skills | resource location |
| instructional | persuading |
| writing | coping with pressure |
| speaking | personal relations |
| skills related to knowledge of a specific subject matter | |

## Writing Your Program

Most programs consist of three basic parts: input, processing, and output. A resumé program, however, need only contain output statements and for this reason is a natural for the beginner. All one need know is how to use the PRINT statement, which is usually the first statement anyone learns in the BASIC language. In many respects, therefore, this is more aptly considered an exercise in word processing than computer programming. All we are interested in here is using the PRINT statement to arrange our output in the most desirable manner. In order to do this, one must also learn how to use the TAB statement. This statement tells the computer in which column the next character of output will be placed. For example, if you entered the statement:

```
10 PRINT TAB(13);
   "PERSONAL DATA"
```

the computer would move over to the 13th column before it started printing. Another important and simple skill is knowing how to skip a line between sections of your output by using a PRINT statement by itself.

---

**Saying that you are skilled in developing and implementing small group instruction may be more impressive than saying that you served as a junior leader for the Boy Scouts.**

---

Once you have written your entire program all you have to do is save it on tape or disk to have it available for making more copies or updating the information. The amount of core required for this type of activity should not exceed 8K. If it does, your resumé may be too long. Remember, the prospective employer may have a large number of resumés to sort through, and you don't want to give him/her more information than needed during the initial screening. If you are convinced, however, that you need more than 8K or only have a 4K system, your troubles are easily solved. You simply divide your resumé in half and write it as two separate programs. Since

## Administration

Prepared and conducted bi-weekly comprehensive patient care conferences at Highgate Manor Nursing Home

Planned and coordinated a community skills program

Supervised student interns

Acted as liaison between Highgate Manor Nursing Home and a number of community and governmental organizations

Assisted in the administration of the Adult Basic Education and High School Equivalency programs at Cortland-Madison BOCES

## Instruction

Developed and implemented a program of small group therapeutic instruction for a number of psychiatric patients in reading skills

Taught English, social studies, health, and home economics to students who for reasons of health or behavior were excluded from the regular programs at Cortland Jr.-Sr. High School

Taught English to eighth graders at Jamesville-DeWitt Middle School

Developed the ability to diagnose and remediate reading problems

## Work Experience

### Psychiatric Social Worker

Highgate Manor Nursing Home, Cortland, N.Y., May 1977 to present

Carry a caseload of 80 residents on the health related units 70% of whom are diagnosed as having various mental disorders

Obtain and update full social histories

Prepare for, lead, and write conference reports for interdisciplinary patient care conferences

Meet with clients on a regular basis and conduct group therapy

Conducts in-service training and supervises student interns

FIGURE 2

A portion of the output of a skills-based resumé

there are no variables in your program, you need not be concerned with the techniques involved in program chaining.

### Other Programming Concerns and Possibilities

When typing a given line of your output, it is important to keep track of the paper width. If a line is too long, the prospects of having portions of a single word appear on two lines increases while your employment prospects decrease. If your system has a CRT you should note how far you can go on it before a statement must end. When doing this, be sure to count any spaces included in your tabs. With careful spacing it is possible to include more than one line of output per statement. This, however, requires consideration of the maximum number of key strokes your system allows per statement. On the other hand, using a good word processing system will be a great aid in formatting and updating a resumé. This approach will also eliminate the hassle of writing a BASIC program for the project. It is a good idea to use 8½ x 11 inch paper. The format can be horizontal or vertical as long as you provide the new boss with paper that can easily fit into a briefcase or filing cabinet.

---

**Your computerized resumé will definitely set your personal history apart from the competition.**

---

One final advantage that must be mentioned stems from the fact that your computerized resumé will definitely set your personal history apart from the competition. And don't fail to mention in your cover letter that you programmed it yourself. This is no time to be modest. Even if the job seems to have no direct relation to com-

puters, at least for now, a self-programmed resumé tells the future employer that here is someone who is intelligent, creative, and conversant with the foremost tool our technological society has to offer. ◻

References

1. Field, H. S. and Holley, W. H. Resumé Preparation: An Empirical Study of Personal Manager's Perceptions. *Vocational Guidance Quarterly,* 1976, 24, 229–237.
2. Bolles, R. N. *What Color Is Your Parachute?* Berkeley, CA: Ten Speed Press, 1972.

DISCUSSION QUESTIONS

1. What advantages does the computerized preparation of a resumé have over a manual preparation?

2. What should be emphasized in the resumé of a graduating student with limited or no experience?

## SELF-TEST 10–1

1. The general form of the FOR/NEXT statement is _____ .
2. The STEP option in the FOR/NEXT may be omitted when _____ .
3. A FOR/NEXT loop to sum the odd numbers from 1 thru 99 is _____ .
4. After a FOR/NEXT loop has been completed, the value of the index is _____ .
5. A FOR/NEXT loop should never be entered at other than the _____ .
6. The index in a FOR/NEXT statement (*may, may not*) be varied by any statement within the loop.
7. The general form of the STOP statement is _____ .
8. The purpose of the STOP statement is to _____ .
9. The statement _____ where statement 99 is 99 END is equivalent to the STOP statement.
10. The expression in a computed GO TO will always be evaluated to an _____ value.
11. If the value of the expression is equal to a value greater than the number of line numbers appearing after a computed GO TO, control will be transferred to _____ .
12. In the statement 50 ON N GOTO 30,40,50,75,90, where the current value of N is 4, control will be transferred to statement number _____ .

## SELF-TEST 10–2

1. In order to read data contained within the program, a _____ statement must be used.
2. The general form of the READ statement is _____ .

3. A _____ is a series of programmer-assigned variable names separated by commas with one variable name corresponding to each item of data to be input or output.

4. The general form of the DATA statement is _____ .

5. The combination of statements

```
50   READ A, N3, R$
60   PRINT A, N3, R$
70   DATA 34.6, 76, "THE ANSWER IS NO"
```

will cause _____ to be printed out.

6. The general form of the RESTORE statement is _____ .

7. The RESTORE statement causes the data listed in one or more DATA statements to be _____ .

8. When used to separate variables in a PRINT statement, the _____ causes the current value of the variables to be printed out and separated from each other by at most two spaces.

9. The statement PRINT A, B; C, D will cause D to print in zone _____ if the values of A, B, C, and D are 1, 2, 3, and 4 respectively.

10. The sequence of statements

```
60   PRINT A;
70   PRINT B, C,
80   PRINT D
```

will cause D to print in zone _____ of (*the same line, a different line*) from the one on which A will be printed.

11. The semicolon (*may, may not*) be used with any statements other than the PRINT statement.

12. In the PRINT statement 50 PRINT "JOHN"; "SON", JOHN will be printed beginning in print position _____ and SON will be printed beginning in print position _____ .

13. The statement 80 PRINT TAB (16); "A=";A1 would cause the characters A= to be printed in print positions _____ and the value of A1 to be printed beginning in print position _____ .

14. The statements

```
90   PRINT USING 95, A1
95   :A = # # #.# #
```

would cause _____ to be printed out if A1 was equal to 17.1.

## SELF-TEST 10–3

1. A _____ is defined as a collection or arrangement of data in a fixed form for ready reference.

2. Each element of a table consists of a _____ and a _____ .

3. The _____ statement serves to reserve sufficient storage to contain a table.

4. The statement DIM X(5,5) reserves _____ elements of storage.

5. _____ functions are prewritten and stored programs that are made available with the BASIC compiler.

6. The value of X after the statement LET X = INT(5.45) + INT(6.58) is executed is _____ .

7. The term _____ is a mathematical term for an array or table.

8. Three of the available matrix statements are_____ .

9. The number of data items input in a MAT INPUT statement will be stored in _____ automatically by the computer.

10. When the MAT READ or MAT PRINT statements are used, data are read or written _____ by_____ .

## SELF-TEST 10–4

1. Functions are of two types, _____ and _____ functions.

2. The _____ statement is used to define a function.

3. The statement which would define a function to square a number would be_____ .

4. If the value of A is 6, the sequence of instructions

   70   DEF FNX(Y)= Y+7
   80   LET A = FNX(A)

   will cause the value of A to be _____ after they have been executed.

5. The function that will generate a random number between 0 and 1 is_____ .

6. The value of the function SGN (2 * 4 − 16) is_____ .

7. A_____ may be employed when a particular routine is to be performed at several places within a program.

8. The _____ statement is used in BASIC to initiate a subprogram.

9. The return from a subprogram is initiated by the statement_____ .

## SELF-TEST 10–5

1. Large volumes of data to be processed are generally organized into_____ .

2. BASIC can be used to establish and access _____ organized files.

3. Before a file can be read or written, it must be_____ .

4. A file name can be _____ characters and must begin with a_____ .

5. The _____ statement is used to write data onto a file.

6. EOF is used with the PUT statement to allow a transfer of control in the event that_____ .

7. A statement that will read a file called INFILE consisting of student names (S$) would be_____ .

8. Files (*must, must not*) be declared to be IN or OUT files in the CLOSE statement.

9. When opened, a file to be read in must be declared as (*IN, OUT*).

**Answers to Self-Tests**

10–1

1. (*line number*) *FOR* (*variable*) = (*expression*) *TO* (*expression*) {*STEP* (*expression*)} (*line number*) *NEXT* (*variable*)

2. the step is equal to 1

3.  10   LET S=0
    20   FOR N=1 TO 99 STEP 2
    30   LET S=S+N
    40   NEXT N

4. unpredictable

5. first or FOR statement

6. may not

7. (*line number*) *STOP*

8. halt the execution of the program

9. GO TO 99

10. integral

11. the next sequential statement

12. 75

## 10–2

1. READ

2. (*line number*) *READ* (*list of variable names*)

3. list of variable names

4. (*line number*) *DATA* (*list of data constants*)

5. 34.6, 76, and THE ANSWER IS NO

6. (*line number*) *RESTORE*

7. recycled to the beginning so that it can be read and used again

8. semicolon (;)

9. three

10. three, the same line

11. may not

12. one; five

13. 16 and 17; 18 or 19 depending on the algebraic sign of A1

14. A = ƀ17.1ƀ (ƀ represents a blank)

## 10–3

1. table or array

2. subscript; value

3. DIM

4. 25

5. Library

6. 11

7. matrix

8. MAT READ,
   MAT PRINT,
   and MAT INPUT

9. NUM

10. row; row

## 10–4

1. library; user-defined

2. DEF

3. (line number) DEF FNS (X) = X**2

4. 13

5. RND (0)

6. −1

7. subprogram

8. GOSUB

9. RETURN

## 10–5

1. files

2. sequential or direct

3. OPENed

4. 1 to 8; letter

5. PUT

6. no more room is available on the file

7. (line number) GET "INFILE", S$

8. must not

9. IN

**10-1**
**True/False**

1. The sequence of statements

```
10   INPUT I,J
20   DIM X(I),Y(J)
```

is valid.

2. A FOR/NEXT loop must be executed at least once.

3. A user-defined function may not have more than one argument.

4. The statement 10 MAT READ X will read the first value of the array X.

5. The statement 10 DEF FNC(X) = X**2 would define the squaring function FNC.

6. An OPEN statement must be accompanied by a file type designation of IN or OUT.

7. To create a loop in a BASIC program, a FOR and a NEXT statement must be used.

8. The RESTORE statement will cause the data stored in the program to be recycled back to the first item of data listed in a DATA statement.

9. There may be only one NEXT statement for each FOR statement in a BASIC program.

10. Functions not available as library functions can often be established as user-defined functions.

11. The statement GOSUB can be thought of as a GO TO statement with a return.

12. The GET statement is used to read a file whereas the PUT statement is used to write a file.

13. The statement 10 ON N GOTO 50,60,70 will cause control to be transferred to statement 50 if N is equal to zero.

14. The statements

```
10   PRINT A;B,C,
20   PRINT D,E
```

would cause E to be printed in zone 2 of line 2.

15. The DIM statement serves to allocate 100 positions of storage for the array named after the word DIM.

16. The EOF option allows the programmer to stipulate the line number to which control is transferred when a file has been completely read.

17. Each element in a one-level table would be determined by one or a single subscript.

18. Library functions are prewritten and stored programs that are made available with the BASIC compiler.

19. File processing statements are the same from BASIC compiler to BASIC compiler.

_____ **20.** The storage location NUM is automatically assigned a value as the result of executing a MAT INPUT statement.

**10-2**
**Matching**

a. matrix
b. CLOSE
c. READ
d. ON/GOTO
e. GET
f. DIM
g. NEXT
h. subscript
i. RND(X)
j. DATA
k. USING
l. STOP
m. argument
n. OPEN
o. RESTORE
p. RETURN
q. TAB
r. DEF
s. library functions
t. PUT
u. FOR
v. GOSUB
w. EOF
x. MAT PRINT

_____ **1.** Used to define a function.

_____ **2.** Simple variable or numeric quantity used with a function.

_____ **3.** Must be applied to all files before program execution is terminated.

_____ **4.** Statement that can be used to initiate a loop.

_____ **5.** Transfers control to a subprogram.

_____ **6.** Statement used to update or exit from a loop.

_____ **7.** Statement used to terminate program execution.

_____ **8.** Another name for an array or a table.

_____ **9.** An option facilitating a transfer of control when a file has been completely read or when no more room exists for writing onto a file.

_____ **10.** Option used to cause the printer to begin printing in a specified print position.

_____ **11.** Provides data for use by the program as requested.

_____ **12.** Statement used to allocate storage space for an array.

_____ **13.** A single statement that can cause the printing of an entire array.

_____ **14.** Used to read data from a file.

_____ **15.** Accesses data defined in the program.

_____ **16.** Used to write data onto a file.

_____ **17.** Used to indicate the position of an element in an array.

_____ **18.** Function used to generate random numbers.

_____ **19.** An option to allow printing to take place according to a specified format.

_____ **20.** Used to ready a file for reading or writing.

_____ **21.** Statement that causes a conditional branch to one of several places depending on the value of an expression.

_____ **22.** Prewritten and stored programs available with the compiler.

_____ **23.** Causes stored data to be recycled back to the first data item.

_____ **24.** Returns control from a subprogram.

**10-3 Problems**

1. Determine the errors, if any, in the following input or output statements:
   - **a.** 10   PRINT E; F; G; H$
   - **b.** 10   READ K, L ↑ M + N
   - **c.** 10   READ L; M; N; S
   - **d.** 10   READ X$, "BETTY", Y
   - **e.** 10   READ A, B$, C$, D
   - **f.** 10   READ X, Y
   - **g.** 10   PRINT TAB(6), A, "X SQUARE ="; X2
   - **h.** 10   PRINT TAB(5); X + Y ** 2
   - **i.** 10   PRINT TAB(I); X; "IS THE ANSWER"
   - **j.** 10   PRINT USING 20, X + Y
         20   :GROSS PAY = $#,###.##
   - **k.** 10   PRINT USING 20, A, B, C$, D
         20   :A = ###., B = ###.#, C$ = ##.#
   - **l.** 10   PRINT USING 20, A, B
         20   :A = #.##!!!!, B = #.##!!!!, C = #.##!!!!
   - **m.** 10   PRINT USING 30, A
         20   :TOTAL NUMBER OF #'S EQUALS ###.#

2. Determine the number of times each of the following loops will be performed:
   - **a.** 10   FOR I = 1 TO 10 STEP 3
            ⋮
         70   NEXT I
   - **b.** 10   LET I = 2
         20   LET J = 15
         30   LET K = 3
         40   FOR I = 1 TO J * K STEP K
            ⋮
         90   NEXT I
   - **c.** 10   FOR J = 2 TO 25
            ⋮
         60   NEXT J
   - **d.** 10   FOR J = 1 TO 25 STEP J + 3
            ⋮
         70   NEXT J

3. Write a BASIC program that will sum the elements in each row and each column of the array given below.

| 1 | 27 | 18 | −8 | 9 | 11 |
|---|----|----|----|---|----|
| 11 | 7 | −6 | 7 | 0 | 15 |
| −5 | 10 | 7 | 3 | 1 | 4 |
| 3 | 16 | 2 | 4 | 9 | −7 |
| 1 | −1 | 23 | 0 | 7 | 16 |

4. Write a BASIC program to read in the table in Problem 3 above and print it out with the rows and columns exchanged. That is, row 1 is to be printed out as column 1, etc., for each of the five rows.

5. Solve Problem 7, Chapter 9, utilizing the FOR and NEXT statement.

6. Solve Problem 10, Chapter 7, employing the FOR and NEXT statements and an array.

7. Solve Problem 6 above employing the concept of a subprogram.

8. Construct BASIC functions for each of the situations described below.

    **a.** Evaluate the formula $A = \dfrac{(B/3) + (B*5)}{4}$.

    **b.** Determine the value of the real number X rounded to two decimal places.

    **c.** Determine the average of a number and its square.

9. Write a BASIC program to

    **a.** create a file of the numbers listed in problem 3 above

    **b.** read the file created in (a) above and determine

        (i) the number of positive numbers

        (ii) the average of the numbers

10. Read the file created in Problem 9 above and sort the numbers into increasing numerical sequence. Print out the numbers in sequence and create a new file with the numbers in sequential order.

# appendix: IBM® SYSTEM/370 VS BASIC (TSO)
## Reference Summary[1]

---

### Syntax Conventions

- Upper-case characters, digits, and special characters represent information that must appear as shown.
- All characters in italics represent information that is supplied by the user.
- A series of three periods (ellipsis) indicates that a variable number of items may be included in a list.
- Items shown in braces { } represent alternatives of which one is to be chosen. Braces are also used for grouping one or more items where ambiguity might otherwise exist.
- Items shown in brackets [ ] represent options that may be omitted.
- An underscored item represents the assumption made if no alternative is chosen.
- A vertical stroke | indicates that a choice is to be made between the option on the left of the stroke and the option on the right.
- Vertical stacking is sometimes used to represent alternatives.
- For debug subcommands, the variable *line-number-specification* can be a single TSO line number, a range of line numbers specified as *line-number-1:line-number-2*, or a list of line numbers enclosed in parentheses with individual line numbers separated by commas or blanks.

---

[1]This is a digest of the VS BASIC language and the requirements for its use under the TSO system. It assumes you are familiar with the language and system details described in *System/370 VS BASIC Language*, Order No. GC28-8303, and *System/370 VS BASIC TSO Terminal User's Guide*, Order No. SC28-8304, respectively.

## TERMINAL OPERATING PROCEDURES

Establishing a Connection

See *System/370 VS BASIC TSO Terminal User's Guide*, Order No. SC28-8304, or *OS/MVT and OS/VS2 TSO Terminals*, Order No. GC28-6762.

Logging On

Type in the LOGON command, followed by your *userid*, and if required, a password, logon procedure name, and account number. Certain terminals permit invisible password entry. See *Terminal User's Guide* for instructions.

Logging Off

From command mode, type in LOGOFF.

Special Characters

Certain characters have different representations on various terminals. For terminals not listed in the following table, see *TSO Terminals* book.

| Character | 2741 PTTC/EBCD | 2741 (# 9812) Correspondence | Teletype Models 33 and 35 |
|---|---|---|---|
| ¬ | ¬ | ± | ! |
| ∨ | ∨ | [ | ∨ |
| ∧ | ∧ | ] | ∧ |
| ↑ or ** | ** | ** | ↑ or ** |
| ≤ | ≤ | [≤ | ≤ |
| ≥ | ≥ | ]≥ | ≥ |
| ≠ | ≠ | ☐ | ≠ |

## CORRECTION PROCEDURES

Typing Corrections        (Any Mode)

*Character Deletions:*     Use BACKSPACE key, or other installation-defined key to delete to point of error; retype correct material

*Line Deletions:*          Use ATTN key or other installation-defined key.

Program Modifications:     (Edit Mode Only)

*Insertions:*              Type line number, a blank, and text of line.

*Replacements:*            Type line number, a blank, and new text of line.

*Deletions:*               Use DELETE subcommand, or type line number followed by a Ⓒ R

*Character String Changes:*  Use the CHANGE subcommand.

*Renumbering:*             Use RENUM subcommand.

## MODES OF OPERATION

There are three modes of operation that apply to VS BASIC use under TSO.

1. Command Mode (also called ready mode), in which you perform catalog maintenance, system control functions, initiate edit mode, initiate debug mode, execute existing VS BASIC programs. System prompt is READY.
2. Edit Mode, in which you create, store, modify, and execute VS BASIC programs, and initiate debug mode. System prompts are EDIT. E, and click. System prompts in input phase are line numbers and INPUT.
3. Debug Mode, in which you debug programs by examining step-by-step execution. System prompt is TESTVSB.

# Commands and Subcommands and Their Formats*

| COMMAND / SUBCOMMAND | FORMAT | MODE | FUNCTION |
|---|---|---|---|
| ALLOCATE (ALLOC) | ALLOCATE DATASET(*data-set name*) FILE(*file-name*) [VOLUME(*volume-id*)] | Command (also edit under VS2 Release 2) | associates a file name from a program with the data set containing the file; required for steam files not following standard file naming conventions and for all record-oriented files. |
| AT | AT *line-number-specification* [(*subcommand-list*)] [COUNT(*n*)] [NOTIFY | NONOTIFY] | debug | sets a breakpoint within a program; may include a list of debug mode subcommands that are to be performed automatically when the breakpoint is reached. |
| BOTTOM (B) | BOTTOM | edit | moves the TSO line pointer to the last line in a data set. |
| CHANGE (C) | CHANGE *line-nbr mrkr string1 mrkr string2 mrkr* [ALL] | edit | changes a string of characters within a line of data set. |
| DELETE (DEL) | DELETE {*data-set-name* | (*data-set-name-list*)} | command | deletes and uncatalogs a data set previously created. |
| DELETE (DEL) | DELETE [*line-number* [*line-number-2*]] | edit | deletes a line from a data set. |
| DOWN | DOWN [*number*] | edit | moves the TSO line pointer down. |
| EDIT (E) | EDIT *data-set-name* {VSBASIC | DATA} [NEW | OLD] [NUM | NONUM] | command | initiates edit mode; edit mode subcommands are described separately, below. |
| END | END | edit | terminates edit mode. |
| END | END | debug | terminates debug mode without completing program execution; returns user to mode from which debug mode was initiated. |
| FREE | FREE DATASET (*data-set-name*) FILE (*file-name*) | command | frees storage space being used by a previously-allocated data set so that further allocations can be performed. |
| GO / GOTO | GO[TO] [*line-number*] | debug | causes execution of program to resume in normal execution sequence, or from a particular line. |
| HELP (H) | *For command or subcommand help:* HELP [*command-name*] [ALL] | [FUNCTION] [SYNTAX] [OPERANDS [(*operand-list*)]]] *For message help:* HELP VSBASIC OPERANDS (*message-id*) *Alternate Form for Message Help for VS2 Release 2:* HELP VSBASIC MSGID(*message-id*) | command edit debug | provides information on the function, syntax, and operands of any debug mode subcommand; provides explanations of any error messages issued by VS BASIC. |

*The above alphabetical list gives the formats of all commands and subcommands from all three modes. Abbreviations for command names (where they exist) are given in parentheses after the name.

## Commands and Subcommands and Their Formats (Continued)

| COMMAND/ SUBCOMMAND | FORMAT | MODE | FUNCTION |
|---|---|---|---|
| IF | IF (condition) {subcommand | HALT} | debug | defines a condition to be tested and a single debug mode subcommand to be executed if the condition is true. |
| INPUT (I) | INPUT [line-number [increment]] | edit | initiates input phase of edit mode. |
| Insert/ Replace Delete Functions | Insertions and Replacements: line-number text-of-line Deletions: line-number **CR** | edit | facilitates the adding, replacing or deleting of BASIC instructions. |
| LIST (L) | LIST [line-number [line-number-2] | *] | edit | lists the contents of a data set, or lists individual lines from the data set. |
| LIST(L) | LIST {variable | (variable-list) | *} | debug | lists the value(s) of any program variable(s). |
| LISTALC (LISTA) | LISTALC | command | lists the names of all data sets that have been allocated. |
| LISTBRKS | LISTBRKS | debug | lists the currently-set breakpoints within a program along with any WHEN conditions that are defined. |
| LISTCAT (LISTC) | LISTCAT | command | lists the names of all cataloged data sets in your collection. |
| LISTFREQ | LISTFREQ [line-number-specification] [ZEROFREQ] | debug | lists the frequency of execution of any program statement; lists statements that have not been executed at all. |
| LOGOFF | LOGOFF | command | terminates a terminal session. |
| LOGON | LOGON userid[/password] [PROC(procedure-name)] [ACCT(account-number)] [MAIL | NOMAIL] [NOTICES | NONOTICES] | command | initiates a terminal session by identifying you to TSO. |
| NEXT (N) | NEXT | debug | sets a temporary breakpoint at the next program statement in line for execution. |
| OFF | OFF [line-number-specification] | debug | removes a breakpoint set by an AT subcommand. |
| OFFWN | OFFWN [condition-id | (condition-id-list)] | debug | turns off monitoring of WHEN conditions; definitions of the conditions are unaffected by OFFWN and may be restarted by WHEN subcommand. |
| PROFILE (PROF) | PROFILE [CHAR(character) | D≤CHAR(BS)] | NOCHAR] [LINE(character) | LINE(ATTN) | LINE(character) | NOLINE] [MSGID | NOMSGID] [INTERCOM | NOINTERCOM] [LIST] | command | allows definition of character-delete and line-delete keys; determines whether user will receive messages ids for error messages, and whether user will be able to receive messages sent from other terminals. |

from a program unit (MAIN or user-defined function) other than the currently executing one may be examined, reset, etc.

| Command | Syntax | Type | Description |
|---|---|---|---|
| RENAME (REN) | RENAME old-name new-name | command | renames a data set. |
| RENUM (REN) | RENUM [starting-number [increment [location]]] | edit | renumbers the line numbers of a data set after insertions, deletions, etc. |
| RUN (R) | RUN data-set-name VSBASIC [SPREC | LPREC] [STORE | NOSTORE] [GO | NOGO] [SOURCE | OBJECT] [TEST | NOTEST] [PAUSE | NOPAUSE] [SIZE(number)] | command | executes an existing program (see VSBASIC, below). |
| RUN (R) | RUN [LPREC | SPREC] [STORE | NOSTORE] [GO | NOGO] [TEST | NOTEST] [PAUSE | NOPAUSE] [SIZE(number)] | edit | executes the VS BASIC program being edited; addition of TEST option allows initiation of debug mode; additional options allow for storing object code, running with long precision, controlling program chaining, and controlling size of user region. |
| RUN(R) | RUN [line-number] | debug | removes all breakpoints, condition monitoring, etc.; runs the program to completion. |
| SAVE (S) | SAVE [data-set-name] | edit | stores and catalogs a data set. |
| SET (S) | SET variable = value | debug | assigns values to variables. |
| TOP | TOP | edit | moves the TSO line pointer to the position preceding the first line of a data set. |
| TRACE (T) | TRACE [STMT | FUNC | OFF] | debug | causes notification of program branching as it occurs; tracing of all program branches, or just of calls to user-defined functions may be traced. |
| UP | UP [number] | edit | moves the TSO line pointer up. |
| VERIFY | VERIFY [ON | OFF] | edit | causes verification of lines to be printed automatically after any subcommand that moves the line pointer is issued, or after any CHANGE subcommand. |
| VSBASIC | VSBASIC data-set-name [SPREC | LPREC] [STORE | NOSTORE] [GO | NOGO] [SOURCE | OBJECT] [TEST | NOTEST] [PAUSE | NOPAUSE] [SIZE (number)] | command | executes an existing VS BASIC program; addition of TEST option allows initiation of debug mode; additional options allow for storing object code, running with long precision, controlling program chaining, and controlling size of user region. |
| WHEN (WN) | WHEN condition-id [(condition) | variable] | debug | defines a condition to be monitored and then starts monitoring it; can be used to turn on monitoring previously turned off with an OFFWN subcommand, in which case no re-definition is required. |
| WHERE (W) | WHERE [STMT | FUNC | ALL] | debug | informs user where he is stopped in the program; options allow user to trace the calling sequence that led to the current location. |

## Language Elements

### Character Set

Alphabetic character:    A, B, C, ..., Z, #, @, $

Numeric character:    0, 1, ..., 9

Alphameric character:    alphabetic character or digit

Special character:    blank = + − * / ↑ ↓ ( . , " ' : ; | & ! ?
     > < ≠ ≤ ≥

### Operators

**Arithmetic Operators**

↑ or ** exponentiation
* multiplication
/ division
+ addition and unary plus
− subtraction and unary minus

**Relational Operators**

= equal to
≠ or <> not equal to
> or >= greater than or equal to
≥| or <= less than or equal to
> greater than
< less than

**Logical Operators**

& and
| or

**Character Operator**

| | concatenation

### Data

Arithmetic:    Data having a numeric value.
Range: 0 or $10^{-78}$ through $10^{75}$ (approx. absolute value)
Precision:   7 significant decimal digits (short)
           15 significant decimal digits (long)
Forms: Integer, Fixed-Point, and Floating-Point

Character:    Any string of characters.
Length: At least one and as many as 255 characters.

### Variables

**Simple Variables (Scalar Variables)**

Arithmetic:    Named by a single alphabetic character or by an alphabetic character followed by a numeric character. The initial value of all arithmetic variables is 0.

Character:    Named by a single alphabetic character followed by the currency symbol ($). The initial value of each character variable is blank characters, the number of which depends on the defined length of the variable; in the absence of such a definition, a length of 18 is assumed.

**Array Variables**

Arithmetic:    Named by a single alphabetic character. The dimension and number of members in an arithmetic array is defined by a DIM statement. In the absence of such a definition, the array will be implicitly defined to have either one or two dimensions (depending on context) and either 10 or 100 members, respectively. All members of an arithmetic array are initially set to 0.

Character:    Named by a single alphabetic character followed by the currency symbol ($). The dimensions and number of members of an arithmetic array are defined by a DIM statement. In the absence of such a definition, the array will be implicitly defined to have either one or two dimensions (depending on context) and either 10 or 100 members, respectively. The length of each member of an implicitly-defined character array is 18. All members of a character array are initially set to blanks.

### Constants

**Arithmetic Constants:**

Integer constants:    [+ | −] d ...

Fixed-point constants:    [+ | −] {[d] ... (.) d ...} | {(.) d ...} | {d ... (.) [d] ...}

Floating-point constants:    {integer-constants / fixed-point-constants} E [+ | −] d[d]

where d is any digit, 0 through 9.

**Character Constants:**

'c ...'
"c ..."

where c is any character.

### Internal Constants

| Constant | Name | Short Form Value | Long Form Value |
|---|---|---|---|
| π | &PI | 3.141593 | 3.14159265358979 |
| Based of natural logs | &E | 2.718282 | 2.71828182845905 |
| Square root of two | &SQR2 | 1.414214 | 1.41421356237301 |
| Centimeters per inch | &INCM | 2.540000 | 2.54000000000000 |
| Kilograms per pound | &LBKG | .4535924 | 4.53592370000000 |
| Liters per gallon | &GALI | 3.785410 | 3.78541178400000 |

### Filenames

A filename is a character expression whose value is the name of a record-oriented or stream-oriented file. Under TSO, this value may be from 1- to 8-characters long; the first character must be alphabetic. There may not be any leading or embedded blanks.

### Expressions

Any representation of an arithmetic or character value.

## Scalar Expressions

*Arithmetic:*
1. An arithmetic constant.
2. A simple arithmetic variable.
3. A scalar reference to an arithmetic array.
4. An internal constant.
5. An arithmetic-valued function reference.
6. A sequence of the above separated by arithmetic operators and parentheses.

*Character:*
1. A character constant.
2. A simple character variable.
3. A scalar reference to a character array.
4. A character-valued function reference.
5. A sequence of the above separated by the character operator ( | | ) and parentheses.

## Array Expressions

An array expression may appear only on the right side of the equal sign in an array assignment statement. It can take one of the following forms:

| Form | Meaning |
|---|---|
| $a$ | An array |
| $a + b$ | Sum of two arrays |
| $a - b$ | Difference between two arrays |
| $a * b$ | Matrix product of two arrays |
| $(e) * a$ | Product of a scalar value and an array |
| IDN | Identity matrix |
| INV($a$) | Inverse of a matrix |
| TRN($a$) | Transpose of a matrix |
| ASORT($a$) | Ascending sort of an array |
| DSORT($a$) | Descending sort of an array |

where $a$ and $b$ are array names, and $e$ is a scalar arithmetic expression.

## Logical Expressions

A logical expression is either a logical subexpression, or two logical subexpressions joined by a logical operator (& or |).

Logical expressions can appear only in IF statements. The form of a logical expression is as follows:

$$subex_1 \ [op \ subex_2]$$

where: $subex$ is a logical subexpression
$op$ is either & or |

## Logical Subexpressions

A logical subexpression compares the values of two arithmetic expressions or two character expressions. Its form is as follows:

$$e_1 \ rop \ e_2$$

where: $e_1$ and $e_2$ are scalar expressions of the same data type
$rop$ is a relational operator

# VS BASIC Statements and Their Formats

| STATEMENT | FORMAT |
|---|---|
| Array Assignment | MAT $array_1$ [(r)] = (scalar-expression)<br>MAT $array_1$ [(r)] = $array_2$<br>MAT $array_1$ [(r)] = $array_2$ (+ \| −) $array_3$<br>MAT $array_1$ [(r)] = $array_2$ * $array_3$<br>MAT $array_1$ [(r)] = (scalar-arithmetic-expression) * $array_2$<br>MAT $array_1$ [(r)] = IDN<br>MAT $array_1$ [(r)] = INV ($array_2$)<br>MAT $array_1$ [(r)] = TRN ($array_2$)<br>MAT $array_1$ [(c)] = ASORT ($array_2$)<br>MAT $array_1$ [(c)] = DSORT ($array_2$)<br>where:<br>$r$ is a redimension specification |
| CHAIN | CHAIN chained-program-name [,passed-value] |
| CLOSE | CLOSE [FILE] $filename_1$ [,$filename_2$] . . . |
| DATA | DATA [$integer_1$*] $constant_1$ [,[$integer_2$*] $constant_2$] . . . |
| DEF | [DEF] FN$\begin{Bmatrix} a \\ b\$ \end{Bmatrix}$ [($dummy_1$ [,$dummy_2$] . . . )]<br><br>[= scalar-expression]—can and must appear only for single-line functions<br>where:<br>  $a$  is any alphameric character, specifying the function name and identifying the function as arithmetic.<br>  $b\$$  identifies the function as character; $b$ must be an alphameric character. |
| DELETE FILE | DELETE FILE filename, KEY = key<br>$\begin{bmatrix}\text{,EXIT es} \\ \text{,NOKEY s} \end{bmatrix}$ [,IOERR s]<br>where:<br>  es  is the number of an EXIT statement.<br>  s  is the number of any executable statement. |
| DIM | DIM $array_1$ [$length_1$] [($row\text{-}size_1$ [,$column\text{-}size_1$])]<br>[,$array_2$ [$length_2$] [($row\text{-}size_2$ [,$column\text{-}size_2$])]] . . . |
| END | END [comment] |
| EXIT | EXIT [EOF s] [,IOERR s] [,DUPKEY s] [,NOKEY s]<br>[,CONV s]<br>where:<br>  s  is the statement number of the statement to receive control when an I/O operation results in the condition specified with s. |

| STATEMENT | FORMAT |
|---|---|
| FNEND | FNEND [comment] |
| FOR | FOR variable = $e_1$ TO $e_2$ [STEP $e_3$]<br>where:<br>  variable  is a simple arithmetic variable.<br>  $e_1$  is an arithmetic expression. |
| FORM | FORM$\begin{bmatrix} c_1 \\ [n_1\text{*}]d_1 \end{bmatrix}\begin{bmatrix} ,c_2 \\ ,[n_2\text{*}]d_2 \end{bmatrix}$<br>where:<br>  $c_i$  is the X, POS, or SKIP control specification.<br>  $d_i$  is a C, NC, PD, S, L, or PIC data form specification.<br>  $n_i$  is an unsigned, nonzero, integer constant, or an arithmetic variable whose value is greater than zero. |
| GET | [MAT] GET filename, $v_1$[,$v_2$] . . .<br>[,EXIT es]<br>[,EOF s] [,CONV s] [,IOERR s]<br>where:<br>  $v_i$  is any of the following:<br>    • a scalar variable<br>    • a subscripted array member reference<br>    • the STR pseudo-variable<br>    • an array name optionally preceded by MAT<br>    • an array name with redimensioning and optionally preceded by MAT<br>  es  is the number of an EXIT statement.<br>  s  is the number of any executable statement. |
| GOSUB | *Simple:*<br>  GOSUB statement-number<br>*Computed:*<br>  GOSUB $number_1$ [,$number_2$] . . . ON arith-expression |
| GOTO | *Simple:*<br>  GOTO statement-number<br>*Computed:*<br>  GOTO $number_1$ [,$number_2$] . . . ON arith-expression |

| | |
|---|---|
| IF | IF *logical-expression* $\left\{\begin{array}{l}\text{GOTO } number\\ \text{THEN } \{number \mid statement\}\end{array}\right\}$<br>[ELSE {*number* \| *statement*}]<br>where:<br>  *statement* may be any of the following statements:<br><br>array assignment   LET       RESET<br>CHAIN            OPEN     RESTORE<br>CLOSE            PAUSE    RETURN<br>DELETE FILE      PRINT     REWRITE FILE<br>GET              PUT        STOP<br>GOSUB          READ      WRITE FILE<br>GOTO           READ FILE<br>INPUT          REREAD FILE |
| Image | $\left\{\begin{array}{l}c_1\\ f_1\\ c_1f_1[c_2f_2]\ldots[c_n]\\ f_1c_1[f_2c_2]\ldots[f_n]\end{array}\right\}$<br>where:<br>  $c_i$   is any string of EBCDIC characters without enclosing quotes. The pound sign (#) cannot appear in the string.<br>  $f_i$   is one of the following specifications:<br>    character—one or more # characters<br>    I-format —optional sign followed by one or more characters<br>    F-format —optional sign followed by combination of # characters and a decimal point<br>    E-format —I- or F-format followed by four vertical line characters (\| \| \| \|). |
| INPUT | [MAT] INPUT $v_1$ [,$v_2$] . . .<br>where:<br>  $v_i$   is defined as any of the following:<br>    • a scalar variable<br>    • a subscripted array member reference<br>    • the STR pseudo-variable<br>    • an array name, optionally preceded by MAT<br>    • an array name with redimensioning and optionally preceded by MAT |
| LET | [LET] $v_1$ [,$v_2$] . . . = expression<br>where:<br>  $v_i$   is a scalar variable, a subscripted array member reference, or the STR pseudo-variable. |

| | |
|---|---|
| NEXT | NEXT *variable* |
| OPEN | OPEN [FILE] *filename*₁ $\left\{\begin{array}{l}\text{IN}\\ \text{OUT}\\ \text{ALL[HOLD]}\end{array}\right\}$ $\left[,filename_2\left\{\begin{array}{l}\text{IN}\\ \text{OUT}\\ \text{ALL[HOLD]}\end{array}\right\}\right]\ldots$ |
| PAUSE | PAUSE [*comment*] |
| PRINT | [MAT] PRINT [$exp_1$] [, \| ;] [$exp_2$]] . . .<br>where:<br>  $exp_i$   is a scalar expression or an array name preceded by the word MAT. |
| PRINT USING | [MAT] PRINT USING s [,$exp_1$[,$exp_2$] . . .]<br>where:<br>  s   is the number of the Image or FORM statement to be used.<br>  $exp_i$   is a scalar expression or an array name preceded by the word MAT. |
| PUT | [MAT] PUT *filename*, $exp_1$ [,$exp_2$] . . .<br>$\left[\begin{array}{l}\text{,EXIT } es\\ \text{,EOF } s \text{] [,IOERR } s\text{]}\end{array}\right]$<br>where:<br>  $exp_i$   is a scalar expression or array name preceded by the word MAT.<br>  es   is the number of an EXIT statement.<br>  s   is the number of any executable statement. |
| READ | [MAT] READ $v_1$ [,$v_2$] . . .<br>where:<br>  $v_i$   is defined as one of the following:<br>    • a scalar variable<br>    • a subscripted array member reference<br>    • the STR pseudo-variable<br>    • an array name, optionally preceded by MAT<br>    • an array name with redimensioning, and optionally preceded by MAT |

# VS BASIC Statements and Their Formats (Continued)

| STATEMENT | FORMAT |
|---|---|
| READ | [MAT] READ FILE [USING sn] filename [, KEY r exp], $v_1[v_2]\cdots$ $\big[$ [,EXIT es] [,EOF s] [,IOERR s] [,NOKEY s] [,CONV s] $\big]$ where:<br><br>sn  is the number of a FORM statement.<br>r  is one of the relational operators =, ≥, or > =<br>exp  is a character expression.<br>$v_i$  is one of the following:<br>  • a scalar variable<br>  • a subscripted array member reference<br>  • the STR pseudo-variable<br>  • an array name, optionally preceded by MAT<br>  • an array name with redimensioning, and optionally preceded by MAT<br>es  is the number of an EXIT statement.<br>s  is the number of any executable statement. |
| REM | REM [comment] |
| REREAD FILE | [MAT] REREAD FILE [USING sn] filename, $v_1$ [$v_2$] ··· $\big[$ [,EXIT es] [,CONV s] $\big]$ where:<br><br>sn  is the number of a FORM statement.<br>$v_i$  is one of the following:<br>  • a scalar variable<br>  • a subscripted array member reference<br>  • the STR pseudo-variable<br>  • an array name, optionally preceded by MAT<br>  • an array name with redimensioning, and optionally preceded by MAT<br>es  is the number of an EXIT statement.<br>s  is the number of any executable statement. |
| RESET | RESET [FILE] $filename_1$ $\begin{bmatrix} \text{END} \\ \text{KEY } r_1\ exp_1 \end{bmatrix}$ $filename_2$ $\begin{bmatrix} \text{END} \\ \text{KEY } r_2\ exp_2 \end{bmatrix}$ ··· where<br><br>$r_i$  is one of the relational operators =, ≥, or > =<br>$exp_i$  is a character expression |

| STATEMENT | FORMAT |
|---|---|
| RESTORE | RESTORE [comment] |
| RETURN | For Subroutines:<br>RETURN [comment]<br><br>For Multi-line Functions:<br>RETURN scalar-expression |
| REWRITE | [MAT] REWRITE FILE [USING sn] filename [,KEY r exp], $e_1[,e_2]\cdots$ $\big[$ [,EXIT es] [,EOF s] [,IOERR s] [,NOKEY s] [,CONV s] $\big]$ where:<br><br>sn  is the number of a FORM statement.<br>r  is one of the relational operators =, ≥, or > =<br>exp  is a character expression.<br>$e_i$  is a scalar expression or an array name preceded by the word MAT.<br>es  is the number of an EXIT statement.<br>s  is the number of any executable statement. |
| STOP | STOP [comment] |
| USE | USE receiving-character-variable |
| WRITE | [MAT] WRITE FILE [USING sn] filename, $e_1$ [,$e_2$] ··· $\big[$ [,EXIT es] [,EOF s] [,IOERR s] [,DUPKEY s] [,CONV s] $\big]$ where:<br><br>sn  is the number of a FORM statement.<br>$e_i$  is the scalar expression or array name preceded by the word MAT.<br>es  is the number of an EXIT statement.<br>s  is the number of any executable statement. |

# Intrinsic Functions

| FUNCTION | MEANING | FUNCTION | MEANING |
|---|---|---|---|
| ABS(x) | Absolute value of x | KLN(x) | Length in bytes of embedded key for file x |
| ACS(x) | Arcosine (in radians) of x | KPS(x) | Byte position at which embedded key for file x starts |
| ASN(x) | Arcsine (in radians) of x | LEN(x) | Length of character string x, minus trailing blanks |
| ATN(x) | Arctangent (in radians) of x | LGT(x) | Logarithm of x to the base 10 |
| CEN(x) | Centigrade equivalent of x Fahrenheit degrees | LOG(x) | Logarithm of x to the base e |
| CLK | Time of day in 24-hour clock notation | LTW(x) | Logarithm of x to the base 2 |
| CNT | Number of data items successfully processed by last I/O statement | MAX(x,y [,z . . .]) | Maximum value of x,y,z. . . . |
| COS(x) | Cosine of x radians | MIN(x,y [,z . . .]) | Minimum value of x, y, z . . . . |
| COT(x) | Cotangent of x radians | NUM(x) | Arithmetic value of character string x |
| CPU | Seconds taken by program execution | PRD(x) | Product of elements in array x |
| CSC(x) | Cosecant of x radians | RAD(x) | Number of radians in x degrees |
| DAT[(x)] | Current Gregorian date or Gregorian equivalent of Julian date x | RLN(x) | Length of last record referred to in file x |
| DEG(x) | Number of degrees in x radians | RND[(x)] | Random number between 0 and 1 |
| DET(x) | Determinant of an arithmetic array | SEC(x) | Secant of x radians |
| DOT(x,y) | Dot product of arrays x and y | SGN(x) | Sign of x (−1, o, or +1) |
| EXP(x) | Natural exponential of x | SIN(x) | Sine of x radians |
| FAH(x) | Fahrenheit equivalent of x Centigrade degrees | SQR(x) | Square root of x |
| HCS(x) | Hyperbolic cosine of x radians | STR(x,y[,z]) | Portion of string x from yth character to end of string or z characters from string x, starting with yth character |
| HSN(x) | Hyperbolic sine of x radians | SUM(x) | Sum of elements in array x |
| HTN(x) | Hyperbolic tangent of x radians | TAN(x) | Tangent of x radians |
| IDX(x,y) | Position of first character of string y within string x | TIM | Time of day in seconds since midnight |
| INT(x) | Integral part of x | | |
| JDY[(x)] | Current Julian date or Julian equivalent of Gregorian date x | | |

INTRODUCTION

OVERVIEW OF THE COBOL LANGUAGE

**IDENTIFICATION DIVISION**

**ENVIRONMENT DIVISION**

**DATA DIVISION**

**PROCEDURE DIVISION**

SAMPLE COBOL APPLICATION 1

**Statement of the Problem**

**IDENTIFICATION DIVISION Coding**

**ENVIRONMENT DIVISION Coding**

CONFIGURATION SECTION

INPUT-OUTPUT SECTION

**DATA DIVISION Coding**

FILE SECTION

WORKING-STORAGE SECTION

**PROCEDURE DIVISION Coding**

SAMPLE COBOL APPLICATION 2

**Statement of the Problem**

**Program Flowchart**

FOCUS ON THE FIELD

SELF-TESTS

EXERCISES

APPENDIX: IBM'S AMERICAN
NATIONAL STANDARD COBOL
RESERVED WORDS

# CHAPTER 11

# COBOL

# INTRODUCTION

As is the case with any new discovery, the advantages of the discovery are to some extent offset by accompanying limitations and disadvantages. So it was with the introduction of the computer into the business world. Three of the more prominent problems that arose as a result of, and were directly attributable to, the introduction of the computer into the business field were

1. The need to develop data-processing systems for existing computers that can also be processed on future larger and more powerful computers with minimal conversion, reprogramming, and retraining costs.
2. Since the data-processing system is so closely linked to the needs of management, the rapidly changing and expanding requirements of management have caused data-processing systems to constantly be revised and augmented. Therefore, documentation of the system in use is required in a form conducive to making such changes and additions with a minimum expenditure of time and money.
3. More and more complicated programs are being required in shorter and shorter times. This condition has created a need for a computer language with which the average programmer can write a given program in a reasonably short period of time.

To fulfill these and other needs of the business world, development of a computer source language suitable to commercial data processing began. In May 1959, a committee of computer users, computer manufacturers, the federal government, and other interested parties called CODASYL (*Conference On DAta SYstems Languages*) came into existence. This group produced a report in April 1960 containing the first version of present-day COBOL (*COmmon Business Oriented Language*). Since that time the language has undergone substantial improvements and revisions. Some of the advantages of the present-day COBOL are

1. COBOL programs are written in precise, easily learned English words and phrases instead of complex codes.
2. COBOL programs make use of ordinary business terminology and therefore can be read by nonprogrammers such as accountants, auditors, or business executives with only a minimum background in data processing.
3. Retraining and reprogramming costs due to the acquisition of new equipment are substantially reduced.
4. COBOL programs written for one computer will run with minor modifications on most other computers. This also enables a company with more

than one computer to reduce programming time by using the same programming language (COBOL) for each computer.

5. COBOL facilitates program testing so that, when necessary, a program can be tested efficiently and thoroughly by someone other than the original programmer.

6. Documentation is simpler and improved. In many cases the COBOL program itself provides a substantial portion of the necessary documentation.

It is not the intent of this chapter, however, to investigate all the details of the COBOL language necessary to write a proficient COBOL program, but instead to introduce the reader to those concepts of the language which are necessary in order to be able to examine a COBOL program, understand it, and determine whether or not it is consistent with the definition and flowchart of the problem. However, should the reader desire to consider the COBOL language in greater depth, a reference summary of ANS COBOL language specifications is generally available from the manufacturer of your computer system.

Upon completing this chapter, you should be able to:

● Describe the advantages of COBOL as a business programming language

● Describe the basic structure of a COBOL program

● Read and understand a COBOL program

● Determine whether a COBOL program is consistent with its program flowchart

● Define the following terms:

| | |
|---|---|
| American National Standards Institute | IDENTIFICATION DIVISION |
| | INPUT-OUTPUT SECTION |
| COBOL | Object program |
| CODASYL | Paragraph name |
| CONFIGURATION SECTION | PICTURE clause |
| DATA DIVISION | PROCEDURE DIVISION |
| Division | Reserved word |
| ENVIRONMENT DIVISION | Source program |
| File description entry | WORKING-STORAGE |
| FILE SECTION | SECTION |

## OVERVIEW OF THE COBOL LANGUAGE

Like all procedure-oriented languages, the COBOL system consists of a source language together with a translator program to convert or translate the source program into machine language. The machine-language program resulting from the translation process is called the **object program.** Translator programs are generally supplied by the computer manufacturer for use with its computers. As computer users, we need only concern ourselves with the COBOL source language.

The COBOL language provides for four separate and distinct **divisions** within each source program. Each division *must* appear in every program. The divisions must also appear in the order given below, with each of the four divisions serving a unique and special function.

**IDENTIFICATION DIVISION** The purpose of the IDENTIFICATION DIVISION is to provide a standard method of identifying the COBOL program to the computer. In this division, the programmer includes such information as the name of the program, his name, the date the program was written, the purpose of the program, and other pertinent information that would be meaningful to anyone analyzing the program.

**ENVIRONMENT DIVISION** The ENVIRONMENT DIVISION contains information about the computer which will translate the COBOL program (source computer), and the computer, if different from the translating computer, which will execute the translated or object program (object computer). This division is concerned with the specifications of the equipment being used and hence is the most computer-dependent division.

**DATA DIVISION** The DATA DIVISION describes the input and output data to be used by the program. It also describes the constants to be used in the program as well as work areas in storage to be used during the processing of the data.

**PROCEDURE DIVISION** The PROCEDURE DIVISION contains instructions in the logical sequence in which they must be executed in order to create the desired end results from the given input or starting data. The instructions in this division are essentially written in meaningful English. To illustrate this, refer to Fig. 11-1, which illustrates a segment of the procedure division from a simple program.

As previously stated, our intention in studying the COBOL language is not so that we should become COBOL programmers, but so that we should be capable of understanding a professionally written, operational COBOL program. It is therefore not necessary that we study the COBOL language in the same depth or with the same degree of rigor that is usually found in an introduction to COBOL.

The best way to understand the COBOL language is to carefully examine an actual COBOL source program. We will begin by examining a very simple program but nevertheless a program which would translate or compile and run successfully on an IBM 370 Model 138 computer. With slight modifications, this program would also run on most other large-scale computers.

"The obstetrician wants to talk to you, Mr. Wilcox!"

To verify your understanding of the previous material, turn to page 437 and take Self-Test 11-1.

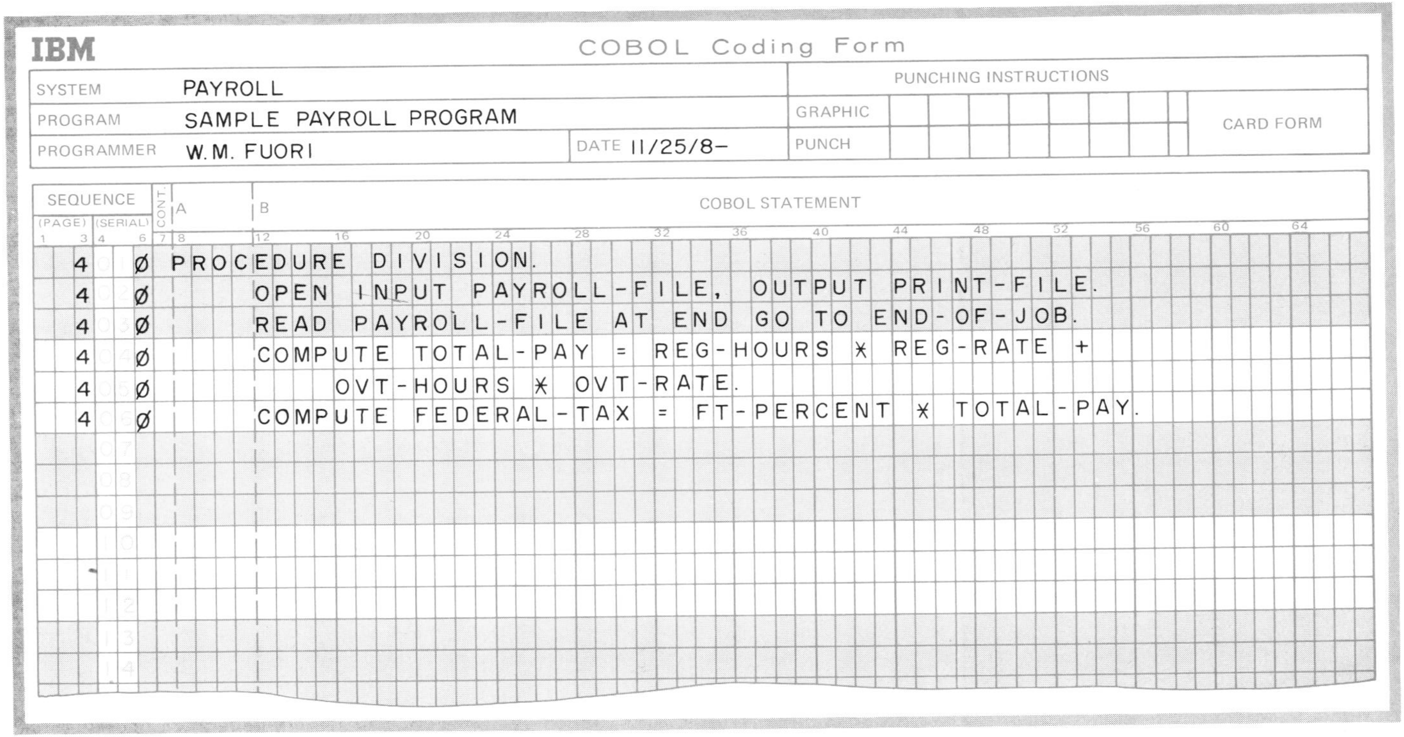

COBOL Coding Form

IBM

SYSTEM  PAYROLL

PROGRAM  SAMPLE PAYROLL PROGRAM

PROGRAMMER  W.M. FUORI                    DATE 11/25/8-

PUNCHING INSTRUCTIONS

| GRAPHIC | |
| PUNCH | |

CARD FORM

COBOL STATEMENT

```
PROCEDURE DIVISION.
    OPEN INPUT PAYROLL-FILE, OUTPUT PRINT-FILE.
    READ PAYROLL-FILE AT END GO TO END-OF-JOB.
    COMPUTE TOTAL-PAY = REG-HOURS * REG-RATE +
        OVT-HOURS * OVT-RATE.
    COMPUTE FEDERAL-TAX = FT-PERCENT * TOTAL-PAY.
```

FIGURE 11-1

Segment of the PROCEDURE DIVISION of a typical COBOL program using a standard coding form

415

## SAMPLE COBOL APPLICATION 1

For any business entity, we can be reasonably certain of one thing: There will be a payroll to prepare. And with the preparation of a payroll go the associated reports that accompany it. One such report is an employee earnings statement. It is for this reason that we have chosen, as our first example, a somewhat simplified version of this report. For this we shall consider the COBOL program necessary to produce a printout of a company's weekly salary file.

Prepare a program to print a weekly salary listing by employee for the AT company.

1. The input for this problem will be a card file with the following format:

| CARD COLUMN USED | INFORMATION CONTAINED |
|---|---|
| 1–20 | Employee name |
| 21–23 | Regular hours worked |
| 24–26 | Regular hourly rate |
| 27–29 | Overtime hours worked |
| 30–32 | Overtime hourly rate |
| 33–80 | Not used |

2. Employee gross pay is to be calculated according to the following formulas:

REGULAR PAY = (REGULAR HOURS WORKED)
× (REGULAR HOURLY RATE)
OVERTIME PAY = (OVERTIME HOURS WORKED)
× (OVERTIME HOURLY RATE)
GROSS PAY = (REGULAR PAY) + (OVERTIME PAY)

3. Output is to be printed and should appear as follows:

| AT COMPANY—WEEKLY SALARY LISTING | | |
|---|---|---|
| EMPLOYEE | TOTAL HOURS WORKED | GROSS PAY |
| XXXXXXXXXXXXXXXXXXXX | XXX | $X,XXX.XX |
| ↓ | ↓ | ↓ |
| XXXXXXXXXXXXXXXXXXXX | XXX | $X,XXX.XX |

*Note:* Each X in this illustration represents a digit, letter of the alphabet, or blank in the output report.

A flowchart of this program is shown in Fig. 11-2.

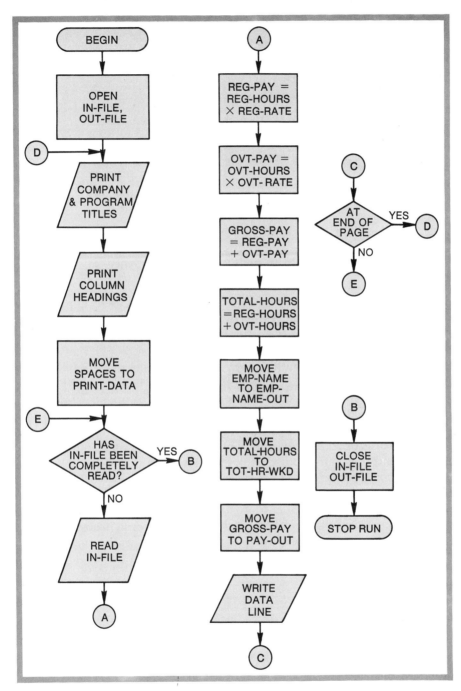

FIGURE 11-2

Flowchart of Sample COBOL Application 1

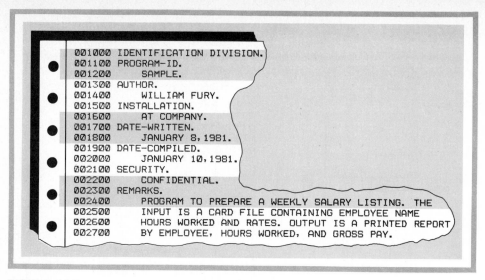

**FIGURE 11-3**

Computer listing of IDENTIFICATION DIVISION of Sample COBOL Application 1

**Statement of the Problem** The coding in Fig. 11-3 is the sample COBOL application 1 as it would appear written by the programmer William Fury using the COBOL language. The numbers which appear at the left are simply programmer-assigned sequence numbers. Although these numbers are *not* required in COBOL, they can be an aid if changes or corrections of any kind ever become necessary, and they can be an aid in placing the program (source deck) back in its proper sequence should it ever be dropped or disarranged.

In COBOL, as in all high-level programming languages, certain words or combinations of words have specific meanings to the compiler and may only be used for their intended purposes. In COBOL these words are referred to as **reserved words.** In Fig. 11-3, for example, each of the words beginning at the left is a reserved word and serves to identify the type of entry following it to the compiler. A complete list of American National Standard COBOL reserved words is given in the Reference Summary following the Exercises at the end of this chapter.

The four divisions of the source program (IDENTIFICATION, ENVIRONMENT, DATA, and PROCEDURE) will now be illustrated and individually discussed.

**IDENTIFICATION DIVISION Coding** As you can see, this division serves to identify the program to the computer. The various entries in this division are concise and easily understood. Yet this example can be considered to be as complete an example as you are likely to encounter. This is simply because the above IDENTIFICATION DIVISION contains all possible entries. However, all the entries given above are not required in the IDENTIFICATION DIVISION of a COBOL program. The only required entry in this division is the PROGRAM-ID entry, all others being optional. One should bear in mind, however, that the more entries that the programmer includes in the program, the more complete will be the documentation of the program.

**ENVIRONMENT DIVISION Coding**

The ENVIRONMENT DIVISION is that part of the COBOL source program that specifies the equipment being used (Fig. 11-4). It names the computer on which the source program is to be compiled and describes the computer on which the object program is to be run. In this division, names can be assigned to particular pieces of equipment. Those aspects of the input or output file that relate directly to the computer's hardware are described also. Since this division deals exclusively with the specifications of the equipment being used, it is largely computer-dependent. This, then, is the division of the COBOL program that would normally require the greatest amount of alteration if a program written for a particular SOURCE- and OBJECT-COMPUTER was to be run on a different SOURCE- or OBJECT-COMPUTER. The ENVIRONMENT DIVISION consists of two sections: (1) the CONFIGURATION SECTION and (2) the INPUT-OUTPUT SECTION.

CONFIGURATION SECTION. Here, in line 003300 (IBM-370-H138), the programmer has stated that the source program will be compiled (translated) on an IBM 370 Model 138 computer to produce the machine-language or object program. In line 003500 (IBM-370-H138) the programmer has stated that the object program will also be run or executed on an IBM 370 Model 138 computer. By stating the source and object computers separately, it is possible for the programmer to compile the source program on one computer and process or execute the object program on a different computer.

INPUT-OUTPUT SECTION. This section contains the FILE-CONTROL paragraph. The FILE-CONTROL paragraph specifies the equipment units that are to be used to input and output data during the

FIGURE 11-4

Computer listing of ENVIRONMENT DIVISION of Sample COBOL Application 1

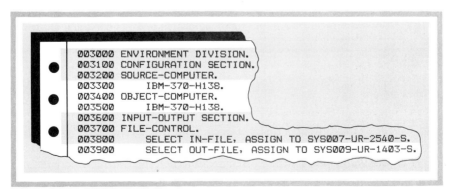

```
003000  ENVIRONMENT DIVISION.
003100  CONFIGURATION SECTION.
003200  SOURCE-COMPUTER.
003300      IBM-370-H138.
003400  OBJECT-COMPUTER.
003500      IBM-370-H138.
003600  INPUT-OUTPUT SECTION.
003700  FILE-CONTROL.
003800      SELECT IN-FILE, ASSIGN TO SYS007-UR-2540-S.
003900      SELECT OUT-FILE, ASSIGN TO SYS009-UR-1403-S.
```

execution of the object program. In the given example, the programmer has stated that two files are to be utilized in this program. In the source program, these files are called IN-FILE and OUT-FILE. For example, line 003800 (SELECT IN-FILE, ASSIGN TO SYS007-UR-2540-S) states that the input file will be called IN-FILE and will be input by a Unit-Record device, namely the IBM 2540 Card Reader. Similarly, line 003900 (SELECT OUT-FILE, ASSIGN TO SYS009-UR-1403-S) states that the output file will be called OUT-FILE and will be output by a Unit-Record device, the IBM 1403 printer unit. It is not necessary that the reader know or understand the meaning of the entries "SYS007" and "SYS009".

Briefly stated, in this section the programmer is assigning names or labels to the physical pieces of hardware that will be required for the input and output of all data.

To verify your understanding of the previous material, turn to page 438 and take Self-Test 11-2.

**DATA DIVISION Coding**    The purpose of the DATA DIVISION is to describe the data that the object program is to read, process, and output (Fig. 11-5). This division is extensively computer-independent, as the data in this division are described in relation to a standard format with no reference to the actual hardware employed.

Initially, the entries in this division may seem very confusing, but with a small amount of background they can be easily understood. Basically, there are two sections in the DATA DIVISION in which data are defined, the FILE SECTION and the WORKING-STORAGE SECTION.

1. FILE SECTION: Data that are defined in the FILE SECTION of the DATA DIVISION are stored on an external medium such as on cards, on tape, on disk, and so on. Since these data are externally stored, they must be brought to the memory of the computer if associated with an input file and sent from the memory of the computer if associated with an output file. This section of the DATA DIVISION serves the primary purpose of describing, in detail, these input and output data files.

2. WORKING-STORAGE SECTION: Data that are defined in the WORKING-STORAGE SECTION of the DATA DIVISION are not part of input or output, but data which are necessary for the processing of input data to produce output data. This would incude any constants, intermediate totals, and work areas which were not defined in the FILE SECTION and which affect the processing in one manner or another.

FILE SECTION.   We have stated that data stored in the FILE SECTION of the DATA DIVISION describe, in detail, the input and output data files. In the case of our example, the input file (IN-FILE) is a card file consisting of a distinct card layout or format; the output file (OUT-FILE) consists of two different formats, one from which output titles will be printed and the other from which the output data will be printed. Each different input or output format constitutes a different input or

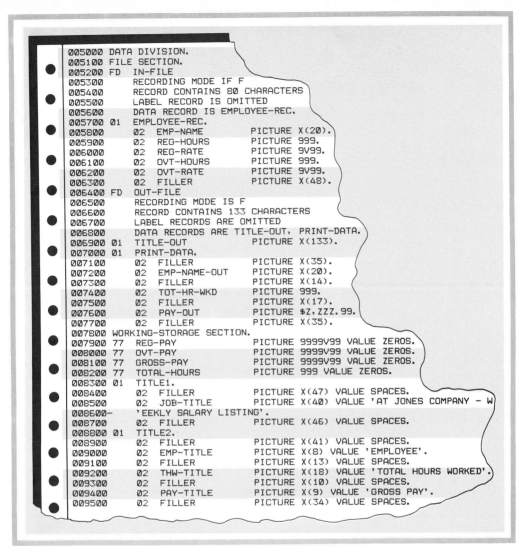

```
005000 DATA DIVISION.
005100 FILE SECTION.
005200 FD  IN-FILE
005300     RECORDING MODE IF F
005400     RECORD CONTAINS 80 CHARACTERS
005500     LABEL RECORD IS OMITTED
005600     DATA RECORD IS EMPLOYEE-REC.
005700 01  EMPLOYEE-REC.
005800     02  EMP-NAME        PICTURE X(20).
005900     02  REG-HOURS       PICTURE 999.
006000     02  REG-RATE        PICTURE 9V99.
006100     02  OVT-HOURS       PICTURE 999.
006200     02  OVT-RATE        PICTURE 9V99.
006300     02  FILLER          PICTURE X(48).
006400 FD  OUT-FILE
006500     RECORDING MODE IS F
006600     RECORD CONTAINS 133 CHARACTERS
006700     LABEL RECORDS ARE OMITTED
006800     DATA RECORDS ARE TITLE-OUT, PRINT-DATA.
006900 01  TITLE-OUT           PICTURE X(133).
007000 01  PRINT-DATA.
007100     02  FILLER          PICTURE X(35).
007200     02  EMP-NAME-OUT    PICTURE X(20).
007300     02  FILLER          PICTURE X(14).
007400     02  TOT-HR-WKD      PICTURE 999.
007500     02  FILLER          PICTURE X(17).
007600     02  PAY-OUT         PICTURE $Z,ZZZ.99.
007700     02  FILLER          PICTURE X(35).
007800 WORKING-STORAGE SECTION.
007900 77  REG-PAY             PICTURE 9999V99 VALUE ZEROS.
008000 77  OVT-PAY             PICTURE 9999V99 VALUE ZEROS.
008100 77  GROSS-PAY           PICTURE 9999V99 VALUE ZEROS.
008200 77  TOTAL-HOURS         PICTURE 999 VALUE ZEROS.
008300 01  TITLE1.
008400     02  FILLER          PICTURE X(47) VALUE SPACES.
008500     02  JOB-TITLE       PICTURE X(40) VALUE 'AT JONES COMPANY - W
008600-    'EEKLY SALARY LISTING'.
008700     02  FILLER          PICTURE X(46) VALUE SPACES.
008800 01  TITLE2.
008900     02  FILLER          PICTURE X(41) VALUE SPACES.
009000     02  EMP-TITLE       PICTURE X(8) VALUE 'EMPLOYEE'.
009100     02  FILLER          PICTURE X(13) VALUE SPACES.
009200     02  THW-TITLE       PICTURE X(18) VALUE 'TOTAL HOURS WORKED'.
009300     02  FILLER          PICTURE X(10) VALUE SPACES.
009400     02  PAY-TITLE       PICTURE X(9) VALUE 'GROSS PAY'.
009500     02  FILLER          PICTURE X(34) VALUE SPACES.
```

**FIGURE 11-5**

Computer listing of DATA DIVISION of Sample COBOL Application 1

output record and is correspondingly identified by the level number 01 placed to the left of the record name. In the FILE SECTION of our sample program there are three 01-level items, one input record (EM-PLOYEE-REC) and two output records (TITLE-OUT and PRINT-DATA). Since the form of each of the input and output records is similar, we will examine only one of these records in greater detail, the EMPLOYEE-REC record.

We have seen that the presence of the level number 01 indicates that EMPLOYEE-REC is a record. We can also see that under the heading FD (**F**ILE **D**ESCRIPTION), this file contains **F**ixed-length records (RECORDING MODE IS F), and that each record is 80 characters in length (RECORD CONTAINS 80 CHARACTERS). We can also see that the file IN-FILE contains the record EMPLOYEE-REC (DATA RECORD IS EMPLOYEE-REC).

Succeeding level numbers are used to show the subdivisions of the record. That is, EMPLOYEE-REC has been subdivided into six 02 levels or areas, which have been called

```
02   EMP-NAME
02   REG-HOURS
02   REG-RATE
02   OVT-HOURS
02   OVT-RATE
02   FILLER
```

To indicate the size of each of these subdivisions of the EMPLOYEE-REC input record, each level or item has associated with it a PICTURE clause. The purpose of this clause is to describe the number of card columns or print positions assigned to an item and the type of data contained in the item. In the case of our example, the PICTURE clause refers to the number of card columns read since we are dealing with an input card record. Let us consider the following:

```
02   EMP-NAME      PICTURE X(20).
```

This data item is a 20-character alphanumeric field, alphanumeric because the code "X" is used, while the (20) indicates a field width of 20 such characters.

In the next 02-level item,

```
02   REG-HOURS     PICTURE 999.
```

This data item is assumed to contain three numeric characters, one for each code "9" used in the PICTURE clause.

The third data item introduces a new code, a "V":

```
02   REG-RATE      PICTURE 9V99.
```

This data item is a three-character numeric field, one numeric character or digit for each 9 used in the PICTURE clause. For computational purposes, the computer assumes that a decimal point exists between the two digits separated by the V, in this case before the last two numeric characters (although no actual point is punched on the input card).

There is only one other PICTURE clause form that we have not discussed, and this is the clause PICTURE $Z,ZZZ.99 appearing in the output record PRINT-DATA. In this clause a "$" will be printed in the first position of the field. The "Z" code is similar to the "9" code in that it represents a digit, but different in that if a leading zero, it will be suppressed from being printed. For more details concerning the PICTURE clause, it is suggested that the reader refer to one of the technical manuals published by the various computer manufacturers.

FILLER is a name that is used to label unused or unreferenced positions in a record. In the case of our example, the input data cards in the EMPLOYEE-REC record contained five fields of usable information. These are EMP-NAME, REG-HOURS, REG-RATE, OVT-HOURS, and OVT-RATE. The remainder of the card was unused by this program. But the computer had been informed in the FD (**F**ile **D**escription) that each record would contain 80 characters. Therefore, to make the total number of characters equal 80, the unused columns must be accounted for. As the data contained in these columns will never be used or referenced, all such areas are given the same name, FILLER. To verify that his record description has considered each column on an input card, the programmer should total all of the PICTURE clause dimensions. He or she should arrive at a total of 80, corresponding to the 80 columns on a card.

"It gives the answer as 12,621,859,007. But, it says it's just a hunch."

For a printed record, the total should be 132 or 133, corresponding to the 132 positions available on the printer; if desired by the programmer, one position is assigned and used to control the advancing of the paper on the printer. This can be likened to the dial or lever on a typewriter that controls whether the paper advances 1, 2, or 3 lines when the carriage is returned. Later, when we discuss the PROCEDURE DIVISION, you will see specific instructions which will control how many lines the printer will advance. Tape and disk records are not always the same size but can be of varying sizes. But, whatever the size of a tape or disk record, the sum of the lengths of the associated PICTURE clauses should be equal to the record size.

WORKING-STORAGE SECTION.  Thus far, the programmer has not provided for the storage of the results of calculations. For example, no space has been provided in the FILE SECTION for

1. Regular pay (REG-HOURS × REG-RATE)
2. Overtime pay (OVT-HOURS × OVT-RATE)
3. Gross pay (Regular pay + overtime pay)
4. Total hours (REG-HOURS + OVT-HOURS)

Since these items are not specifically described in the input or output files in the FILE SECTION, they must be described in the WORK-

ING-STORAGE SECTION. Individual data items in this section are assigned the level number 77. Notice that these items can be assigned an initial value, in this case zeros (VALUE ZEROS). It is not possible to assign initial values to items described in the FILE SECTION of the DATA DIVISION.

Notice also that the output titles are described in this section. This is simply because of the fact that in this section we can assign initial values, whereas we could not do so in the FILE SECTION. For example, in the record TITLE1, the item JOB-TITLE was given the initial value AT JONES COMPANY-WEEKLY SALARY LISTING, which is the title we wished to be printed out. The apostrophe or quotation (') marks were used to define the extremities of the characters being defined.

Two records have been defined in the WORKING-STORAGE SECTION, TITLE1 and TITLE2, one for each of the title output lines required in the final report.

Now that we have identified the program to the computer (IDENTIFICATION DIVISION), described the equipment being used (ENVIRONMENT DIVISION), and described the input, output, and intermediate storage areas (DATA DIVISION), we are ready to specify the steps the computer is to follow in processing the input data to produce the required output (PROCEDURE DIVISION).

To verify your understanding of the previous material, turn to page 438 and take Self-Test 11-3.

**PROCEDURE DIVISION Coding**

The PROCEDURE DIVISION of a COBOL program specifies the particular steps or instructions that the computer will follow in processing the input data. These instructions are expressed in terms of simple but meaningful English words, statements, and sentences. This division is essentially computer-independent, since it describes what is to be done, and not on what devices it will be done. A detailed flowchart of the logical sequence of steps required to produce the output report from the input data is given in Fig. 11-2, page 417. Note that by using COBOL sentences in the flowchart, the programmer has closely linked the flowchart to the actual coding in the PROCEDURE DIVISION shown in Fig. 11-6. It should also be noted that thus far there is little or no indication in the flowchart, other than the data names used, that any divisions other than the PROCEDURE DIVISION even exist. Since an understanding of this division is of prime importance to the business-related user in understanding whether or not the program fulfills its intended purpose, we will discuss this division in depth with respect to this program and our second sample COBOL program.

In line 009700 of Fig. 11-6 we see the statement OPEN INPUT IN-FILE, OUTPUT OUT-FILE. This statement opens the input and output files for the reading and writing of data as one might open the cover of a textbook before reading it or open a notebook before writing in it. In COBOL, no file can be read or written before it has been opened.

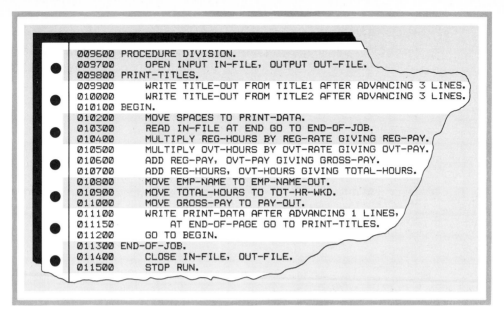

```
009600  PROCEDURE DIVISION.
009700      OPEN INPUT IN-FILE, OUTPUT OUT-FILE.
009800  PRINT-TITLES.
009900      WRITE TITLE-OUT FROM TITLE1 AFTER ADVANCING 3 LINES.
010000      WRITE TITLE-OUT FROM TITLE2 AFTER ADVANCING 3 LINES.
010100  BEGIN.
010200      MOVE SPACES TO PRINT-DATA.
010300      READ IN-FILE AT END GO TO END-OF-JOB.
010400      MULTIPLY REG-HOURS BY REG-RATE GIVING REG-PAY.
010500      MULTIPLY OVT-HOURS BY OVT-RATE GIVING OVT-PAY.
010600      ADD REG-PAY, OVT-PAY GIVING GROSS-PAY.
010700      ADD REG-HOURS, OVT-HOURS GIVING TOTAL-HOURS.
010800      MOVE EMP-NAME TO EMP-NAME-OUT.
010900      MOVE TOTAL-HOURS TO TOT-HR-WKD.
011000      MOVE GROSS-PAY TO PAY-OUT.
011100      WRITE PRINT-DATA AFTER ADVANCING 1 LINES,
011150          AT END-OF-PAGE GO TO PRINT-TITLES.
011200      GO TO BEGIN.
011300  END-OF-JOB.
011400      CLOSE IN-FILE, OUT-FILE.
011500      STOP RUN.
```

FIGURE 11-6

Computer listing of PROCEDURE DIVISION of Sample COBOL Application 1

Line 009800 (PRINT-TITLES.) is a **paragraph name** and serves to reference the statements below it. If it is desired to transfer from anywhere in the program to this area, the programmer only need instruct the computer to GO TO PRINT-TITLES, as was done in continuation statement 011150 (AT END-OF-PAGE GO TO PRINT-TITLES). In this paragraph the computer is directed to print out two lines or records. Each of these records is defined in the WORKING-STORAGE SECTION of the DATA DIVISION. These records are then moved to the output record area TITLE-OUT and printed after the paper has been advanced three lines. It is necessary to move the records TITLE1 and TITLE2 to TITLE-OUT before they can be printed, since records can only be output from the FILE SECTION of the DATA DIVISION and not from the WORKING-STORAGE SECTION of the DATA DIVISION.

We can never be certain that storage locations within the memory of the computer are blank unless they are defined in WORKING-STORAGE to be filled with spaces. Therefore, for areas which should be blank, but not specifically defined in WORKING-STORAGE to be blank, the programmer must be certain to clear or fill these areas with blanks before attempting to use them. This is accomplished by moving spaces (blank spaces) into these areas. Such is the purpose of line 010200 (MOVE SPACES TO PRINT-DATA). With this statement, the programmer can cause the clearing of the output area that is to be used to develop our printed records.

To this point, no data have been input from the card file waiting in the card reader. We have simply printed titles of our report. In line 010300 (READ IN-FILE AT END GO TO END-OF-JOB.) the computer

COBOL                                                                    425 was instructed to read a record (a card). The programmer's purpose in including the latter portion of this statement is to handle the situation that could arise if the computer attempted to read a card and all the cards had already been read. In this case, following the programmer's instructions, the program would skip to the paragraph called END-OF-JOB or the equivalent of line 011300 in the object program. The meaning and purpose of the instructions beginning on line 010400 (MULTIPLY REG-HOURS BY REG-RATE GIVING REG-PAY.) through line 011150 (AT END-OF-PAGE GO TO PRINT-TITLES.) should be quite clear with only a brief examination.

Line 011200 (GO TO BEGIN.) instructs the computer to go unconditionally to line 010100 and again execute the paragraph called BEGIN.

Line 011300 contains the paragraph name END-OF-JOB, which refers to the next two lines of coding. Within this paragraph line 011400 (CLOSE IN-FILE, OUT-FILE.) closes the input and output files as one might close a book after it has been read or close a notebook when one has completed writing in it. And, as in all processes, there must be a stop or an end

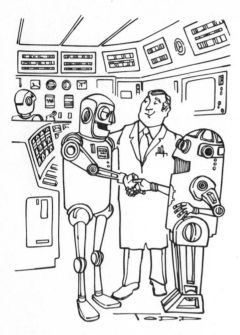

"Hello, I'm 912YZ, but everyone usually calls me by my nicknumber, 912WZ..."

**FIGURE 11-7**
Output from Sample COBOL Application 1

| AT JONES COMPANY — WEEKLY SALARY LISTING | | |
|---|---|---|
| EMPLOYEE | TOTAL HOURS WORKED | GROSS PAY |
| ALFRED ABARTH | 035 | $    131.25 |
| AL ANDERSON | 025 | $     63.75 |
| WILLIAM BRONSON | 046 | $    130.00 |
| JOSEPH CONGERO | 045 | $    269.25 |
| FRED JONES | 020 | $     55.00 |
| LOUIS NAPOLI | 040 | $    340.00 |
| BEN NARUCKI | 050 | $    231.00 |
| JACOB SMITH | 052 | $    317.00 |
| JOHN SMITH | 042 | $    315.00 |
| THOMAS TRACO | 025 | $     93.75 |
| FRANCES WILLIAMSON | 041 | $    136.50 |
| ROBERT SMITH | 042 | $    159.00 |
| HENRY ROBERTSON | 035 | $     87.50 |
| JOHN WILLIAMSON | 049 | $    217.50 |
| JOE JONES | 047 | $    243.00 |

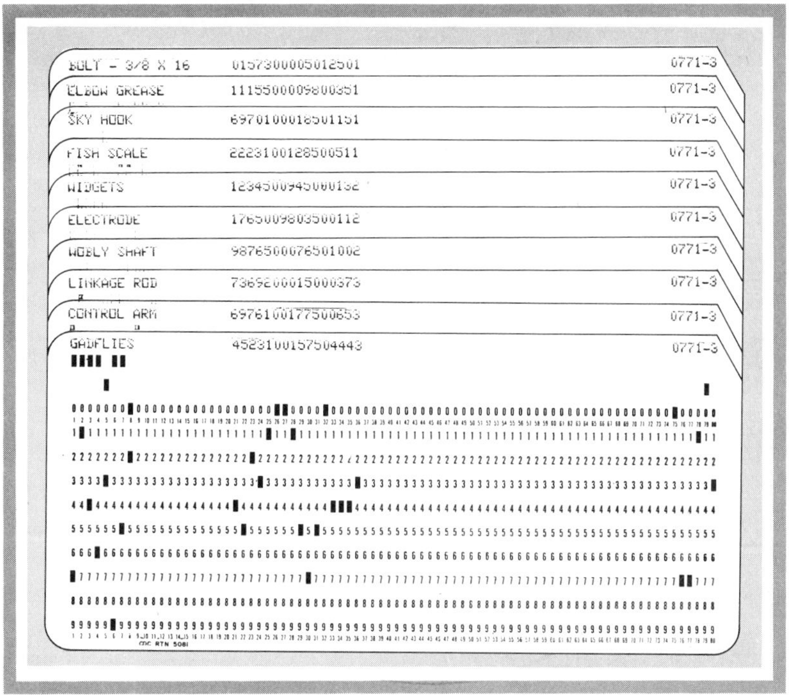

FIGURE 11-8

Input cards used for Sample COBOL Application 2

to the process. This is accomplished by line 011500 (STOP RUN.). This instruction tells the computer that the job is finished, and to go to the next job.

As you can see, with a little help, the PROCEDURE DIVISION of a COBOL program can be read and understood with little more difficulty than might be experienced in reading and understanding a good mystery story. It will be left to the reader to verify that this program is consistent with the definition of the problem previously given and with the flowchart of the problem given in Fig. 11-2. It is also suggested that the reader reconstruct the flowchart from the coding in the PROCEDURE DIVISION. Such an analysis will be presented in the discussion of sample COBOL application 2.

Typical output from the program for application 1 is shown in Fig. 11-7.

## SAMPLE COBOL APPLICATION 2

For our second example we will discuss a COBOL program written to produce a sales report. We shall be given the definition of the problem, the coding of the problem, and from these develop a program flowchart.

COBOL

427

Prepare a program to produce a daily sales report. The input for this problem will be a card file (Fig. 11-8) with the following format:

| CARD COLUMNS USED | INFORMATION CONTAINED |
| --- | --- |
| 1–20 | Item description |
| 21–25 | Invoice number |
| 26–31 | Unit price |
| 32–35 | Quantity |
| 36–80 | Not used |

where

$$\text{Total Item Cost} = (\text{Unit Price}) \times (\text{Quantity})$$

$$\text{Total Cost} = \text{Sum of the Total Item Costs}$$

Output is to be printed and should appear as follows:

| SALES REPORT | | | | |
| --- | --- | --- | --- | --- |
| ITEM DESCRIPTION | INVENTORY NUMBER | UNIT PRICE | QUANTITY | TOTAL |
| XXXXXXXXXXXXXXXXXXXX | XXXXX | $XXXX.XX | XXXX | $XXXXXXXX.XX |
| ↓ | ↓ | ↓ | ↓ | ↓ |
| XXXXXXXXXXXXXXXXXXXX | XXXXX | $XXXX.XX | XXXX | $XXXXXXXX.XX |
| | | | TOTAL SALES | $XXXXXXXXXX.XX |

*Note:* Each X in this illustration represents a digit, letter of the alphabet, or blank in the output report.

The coding in Fig. 11-9 is for sample COBOL application 2 as it would appear written by the programmer DR WM FUORI using the COBOL language.

**Program Flowchart**

To determine what this program is doing, we must direct our attention to the PROCEDURE DIVISION. It is this division of a COBOL program that contains the logical sequence of instructions designed to solve the problem. From our analysis of the PROCEDURE DIVISION, we will construct a flowchart for our second COBOL sample application.

As is customary when flowcharting an application, the flowchart should begin with a terminal symbol:

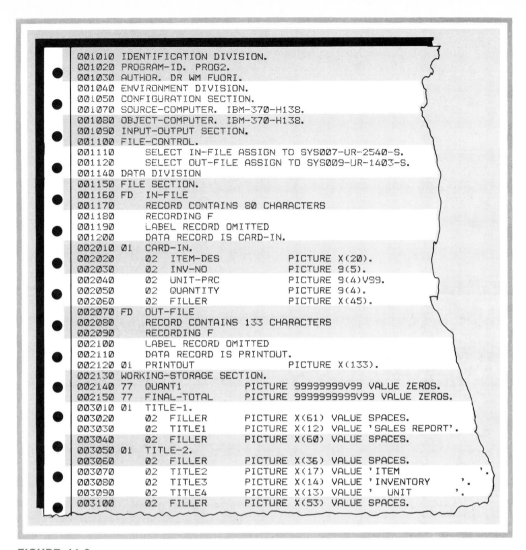

```
001010 IDENTIFICATION DIVISION.
001020 PROGRAM-ID. PROG2.
001030 AUTHOR. DR WM FUORI.
001040 ENVIRONMENT DIVISION.
001050 CONFIGURATION SECTION.
001070 SOURCE-COMPUTER.  IBM-370-H138.
001080 OBJECT-COMPUTER.  IBM-370-H138.
001090 INPUT-OUTPUT SECTION.
001100 FILE-CONTROL.
001110     SELECT IN-FILE ASSIGN TO SYS007-UR-2540-S.
001120     SELECT OUT-FILE ASSIGN TO SYS009-UR-1403-S.
001140 DATA DIVISION
001150 FILE SECTION.
001160 FD  IN-FILE
001170     RECORD CONTAINS 80 CHARACTERS
001180     RECORDING F
001190     LABEL RECORD OMITTED
001200     DATA RECORD IS CARD-IN.
002010 01  CARD-IN.
002020     02  ITEM-DES        PICTURE X(20).
002030     02  INV-NO          PICTURE 9(5).
002040     02  UNIT-PRC        PICTURE 9(4)V99.
002050     02  QUANTITY        PICTURE 9(4).
002060     02  FILLER          PICTURE X(45).
002070 FD  OUT-FILE
002080     RECORD CONTAINS 133 CHARACTERS
002090     RECORDING F
002100     LABEL RECORD OMITTED
002110     DATA RECORD IS PRINTOUT.
002120 01  PRINTOUT            PICTURE X(133).
002130 WORKING-STORAGE SECTION.
002140 77  QUANT1        PICTURE 99999999V99 VALUE ZEROS.
002150 77  FINAL-TOTAL   PICTURE 9999999999V99 VALUE ZEROS.
003010 01  TITLE-1.
003020     02  FILLER    PICTURE X(61) VALUE SPACES.
003030     02  TITLE1    PICTURE X(12) VALUE 'SALES REPORT'.
003040     02  FILLER    PICTURE X(60) VALUE SPACES.
003050 01  TITLE-2.
003060     02  FILLER    PICTURE X(36) VALUE SPACES.
003070     02  TITLE2    PICTURE X(17) VALUE 'ITEM            '.
003080     02  TITLE3    PICTURE X(14) VALUE 'INVENTORY     '.
003090     02  TITLE4    PICTURE X(13) VALUE '  UNIT       '.
003100     02  FILLER    PICTURE X(53) VALUE SPACES.
```

**FIGURE 11-9**

Computer listing of the program for Sample COBOL Application 2

Upon examining the PROCEDURE DIVISION of our sample program, we see that the first instruction is a processing operation: the opening of the input file IN-FILE and the output file OUT-FILE. Adding a processing symbol and an appropriate note within it to our existing terminal symbol, we have the following flowchart:

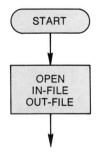

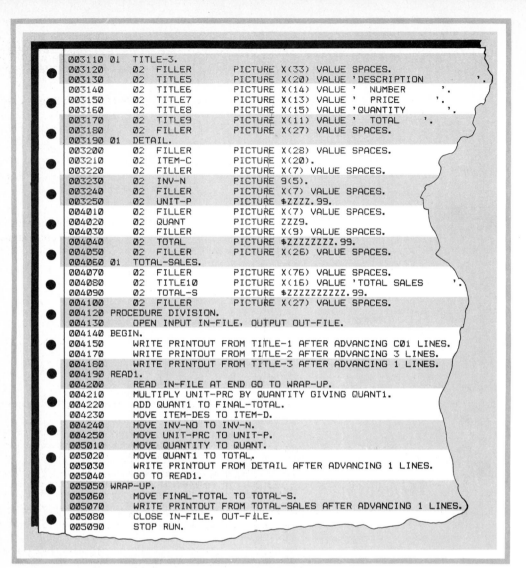

```
003110 01   TITLE-3.
003120     02  FILLER      PICTURE X(33) VALUE SPACES.
003130     02  TITLE5      PICTURE X(20) VALUE 'DESCRIPTION     '.
003140     02  TITLE6      PICTURE X(14) VALUE ' NUMBER      '.
003150     02  TITLE7      PICTURE X(13) VALUE '  PRICE      '.
003160     02  TITLE8      PICTURE X(15) VALUE 'QUANTITY      '.
003170     02  TITLE9      PICTURE X(11) VALUE '  TOTAL   '.
003180     02  FILLER      PICTURE X(27) VALUE SPACES.
003190 01   DETAIL.
003200     02  FILLER      PICTURE X(28) VALUE SPACES.
003210     02  ITEM-C      PICTURE X(20).
003220     02  FILLER      PICTURE X(7) VALUE SPACES.
003230     02  INV-N       PICTURE 9(5).
003240     02  FILLER      PICTURE X(7) VALUE SPACES.
003250     02  UNIT-P      PICTURE $ZZZZ.99.
004010     02  FILLER      PICTURE X(7) VALUE SPACES.
004020     02  QUANT       PICTURE ZZZ9.
004030     02  FILLER      PICTURE X(9) VALUE SPACES.
004040     02  TOTAL       PICTURE $ZZZZZZZZ.99.
004050     02  FILLER      PICTURE X(26) VALUE SPACES.
004060 01   TOTAL-SALES.
004070     02  FILLER      PICTURE X(76) VALUE SPACES.
004080     02  TITLE10     PICTURE X(16) VALUE 'TOTAL SALES    '.
004090     02  TOTAL-S     PICTURE $ZZZZZZZZZZ.99.
004100     02  FILLER      PICTURE X(27) VALUE SPACES.
004120 PROCEDURE DIVISION.
004130     OPEN INPUT IN-FILE, OUTPUT OUT-FILE.
004140 BEGIN.
004150     WRITE PRINTOUT FROM TITLE-1 AFTER ADVANCING C01 LINES.
004170     WRITE PRINTOUT FROM TITLE-2 AFTER ADVANCING 3 LINES.
004180     WRITE PRINTOUT FROM TITLE-3 AFTER ADVANCING 1 LINES.
004190 READ1.
004200     READ IN-FILE AT END GO TO WRAP-UP.
004210     MULTIPLY UNIT-PRC BY QUANTITY GIVING QUANT1.
004220     ADD QUANT1 TO FINAL-TOTAL.
004230     MOVE ITEM-DES TO ITEM-D.
004240     MOVE INV-NO TO INV-N.
004250     MOVE UNIT-PRC TO UNIT-P.
005010     MOVE QUANTITY TO QUANT.
005020     MOVE QUANT1 TO TOTAL.
005030     WRITE PRINTOUT FROM DETAIL AFTER ADVANCING 1 LINES.
005040     GO TO READ1.
005050 WRAP-UP.
005060     MOVE FINAL-TOTAL TO TOTAL-S.
005070     WRITE PRINTOUT FROM TOTAL-SALES AFTER ADVANCING 1 LINES.
005080     CLOSE IN-FILE, OUT-FILE.
005090     STOP RUN.
```

**FIGURE 11-9 continued**

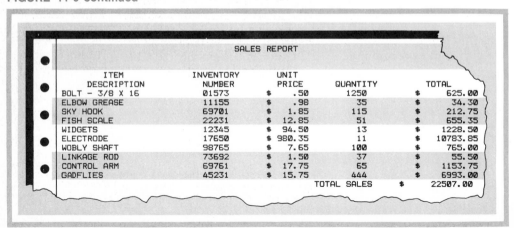

```
                         SALES REPORT


        ITEM           INVENTORY       UNIT
     DESCRIPTION        NUMBER         PRICE       QUANTITY           TOTAL
BOLT - 3/8 X 16         01573      $     .50        1250        $      625.00
ELBOW GREASE            11155      $     .98          35        $       34.30
SKY HOOK                69701      $    1.85         115        $      212.75
FISH SCALE              22231      $   12.85          51        $      655.35
WIDGETS                 12345      $   94.50          13        $     1228.50
ELECTRODE               17650      $  980.35          11        $    10783.85
WOBLY SHAFT             98765      $    7.65         100        $      765.00
LINKAGE ROD             73692      $    1.50          37        $       55.50
CONTROL ARM             69761      $   17.75          65        $     1153.75
GADFLIES                45231      $   15.75         444        $     6993.00
                                             TOTAL SALES   $     22507.00
```

**FIGURE 11-10**

Output for Sample COBOL Application 2

In the next paragraph of the program, we find three consecutive write or output statements which, when flowcharted, give us

Note that in the first of these symbols it refers to ADVANCING C01 LINES. This instructs the computer to advance the paper to the top of the next page and write TITLE-1. This is because C01 is a reserved word known to the compiler that means the top of the next page. Output for Application 2 is shown in Fig. 11-10.

In the next paragraph of the program (READ1), we find 10 instructions consisting of several different types. The first instruction (line 004200) is actually two instructions combined into one, an instruction to read a card together with an instruction to branch to the section of the program called WRAP-UP when all data cards in the input file IN-FILE have been read. In the flowchart, this instruction would appear as follows:

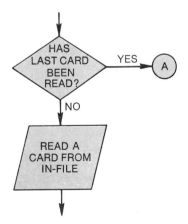

The next seven instructions are simple processing instructions and are symbolized as follows:

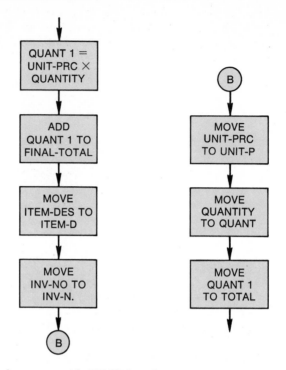

Next in the paragraph READ1 we have an output or write statement followed by a branch instruction back to the beginning of this paragraph. To flowchart these two instructions, we must refer to an instruction previously included in the flowchart (READ IN-FILE AT END GO TO WRAP-UP). This would be accomplished as follows:

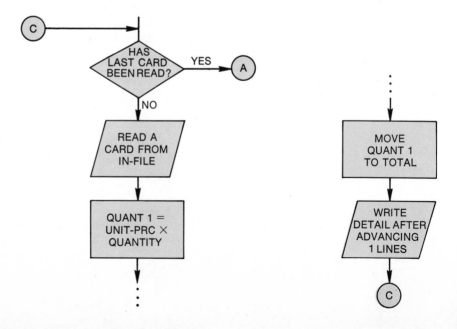

Notice that the last instruction in this paragraph calls for the computer to transfer to READ1, the paragraph label. Yet in the flowchart we transferred, via connector Ⓒ, to the first instruction in the paragraph. This is necessary because there is no flowcharting symbol reserved for holding paragraph names. If we wish, however, we would indicate the paragraph name as follows:

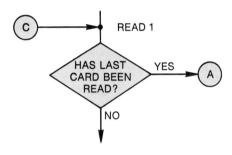

The next paragraph we encounter in the program is called WRAP-UP, a name we have seen before. We have seen it in connection with the first instruction in the READ1 paragraph. You will recall that the flowchart of this instruction (READ IN-FILE AT END GO TO WRAP-UP.) appeared as shown above, where the exit connector

was to connect to the paragraph WRAP-UP. To facilitate this we must begin the paragraph WRAP-UP with the entry connector:

Subsequently in this paragraph we find a processing instruction (MOVE FINAL-TOTAL TO TOTAL-S.), an output statement (WRITE PRINT OUT FROM TOTAL-SALES AFTER ADVANCING 1 LINES.), another processing instruction (CLOSE IN-FILE, OUT-FILE), and finally a terminal operation (STOP RUN.). In the flowchart these instructions would appear as

Figure 11-11 illustrates how this flowchart would appear when all of the parts thus far developed are combined.

It should be emphasized once more that this entire flowchart was constructed from only the PROCEDURE DIVISION of the program. For an individual who is primarily a computer user and not a computer programmer, this is the most meaningful portion of the COBOL program.

To verify your understanding of the previous material, turn to page 439 and take Self-Test 11-4.

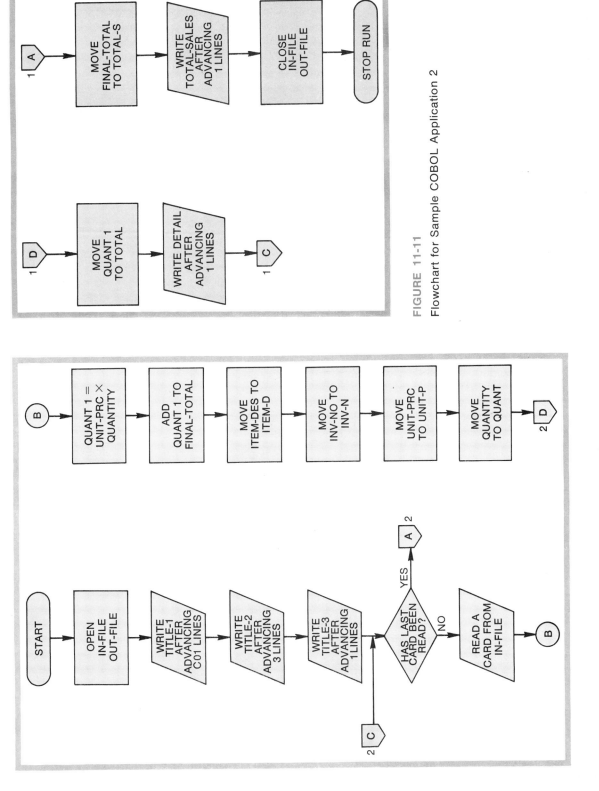

FIGURE 11-11

Flowchart for Sample COBOL Application 2

# focus on the field

### Standards—The Way to Go

**Guidelines for application development.**

## By Phillip Braverman

Do you know that one of the most powerful productivity techniques you can employ is a set of standards for application development?

Standards—or guidelines—are written, usable documents of successful experience. Their use overcomes lost project experience, or word of mouth recollections. Standards are precise descriptions of what needs to be built, how the "products" are to be built, what the products should look like when completed, and the best set of procedures to follow during the development process.

Written standards represent a consistent, effective means of communication between the project team, the users and management.

Without standards, the target is often blurred and difficult to hit. With standards, unlike the confused "Alice in Wonderland," you know where you're going; and you will be able to recognize your destination when you've arrived.

Consider the turkey, *Meleagris Gallopave,* native bird of our land, center of attraction at the holiday table—sandwiches for the next week; maybe soup, too. The turkey gives all on every occasion—a marvelous performer.

Why is the turkey so good each time and so consistent from year to year and place to place? *Because there are standard ways to raise and to cook turkeys.* Call them recipes if you like, but they really are standards, and written ones at that. Every facet of the fowl deed is explained in detail. But that doesn't mean you can't adapt your own special seasoning. What it does mean is that if you follow the standard directions you will complete the project in grand style.

Followed faithfully, and with calibrated equipment, this standard will bring you in on time, on plan, and with user satisfaction (pass the turkey again, please). Consistent application of successful experience time after time. That's what standards can do for you.

Many of us have been involved with enough "turkeys" in our data processing careers to last a lifetime, and suspect that there might be a better way to develop systems. Besides, you can clean up a mess in the kitchen in a few minutes. Cleaning up a mess of a DP project takes considerably longer. Let's look at some examples of standards as they apply to application development.

There are two types of standards used in development: technical standards, such as for structured programming in COBOL, data base design guidelines; and project planning and management standards, such as design phase guidelines, project tracking and project review guidelines. Most of what follows is devoted to the management standards. The terms standards and guidelines are used interchangeably.

Project planning and management standards are aimed at improving the degree of communication between the users, the developers, and management by using experience that has proven successful, is now documented, and is continually improved as a result of management's commitment to maintaining this environment.

A standard for a system design effort might look like this:

1. Describes the purpose of the design phase.
2. Lists the products of the phase, the documentation required.
3. Lists the major tasks to be performed during the phase.
4. Lists the level of detail required for

the design document, such as input/output descriptions, data base descriptions. Describes what each section of the design document is to contain.

5. Lists other standards to be used during the systems design such as for recovery support, data security, audits and controls, HIPO documentation, testing, etc.

6. Lists the management plans to be used during the design process: specifies the project tracking system, change control procedures and project reviews.

7. Describes the sign-offs and approvals that will be needed during and at the completion of the systems design.

8. Defines the terms used in the system design phase.

So what do you do with a collection of standards like these, assuming you had them? You know, if you were given a design project to manage, exactly what products have to be developed—so does DP management and the users. You would know the purpose and objectives of the design effort. So would the users and management. All of you could see if you are meeting, or have met, the predefined objectives.

You will have a list of the major tasks (maybe even a precedence diagram) to help you during the estimating and scheduling process. You will know in advance how the project has to be controlled and who has to approve the work. You have ground rules for controlling change—set in advance. You'll know what detail is required, so that you don't over-produce or fail to produce the appropriate level of detail for the next phase of the project. You'll know what technical standards apply to this project.

You are now more readily able to plan your project and communicate goals and activities to your people.

DISCUSSION QUESTIONS

1. What are standards and what purposes do they serve?

2. What differences exist between technical standards and project planning and management standards? Describe the possible uses of each.

## SELF-TEST 11–1

1. The word "COBOL" is derived from the phrase ———— .

2. COBOL is a common language in that ———— .

3. COBOL is business oriented in that ———— .

4. COBOL is relatively easy to learn because ———— .

5. Documentation of COBOL programs is simpler than with most other languages since in many cases the program itself ———— .

6. COBOL is referred to as a ————-oriented language and utilizes a ———— program to convert a COBOL ———— program into a machine-language or an ———— program.

7. COBOL translator programs are generally supplied by ———— .

8. Before a COBOL source program can be ———— it must be translated into machine language.

9. Every COBOL program must consist of four ———— . They are the ————, ————, ————, and ———— .

10. The four divisions appear in every COBOL program in ———— order.

11. The order in which the divisions appear is ———— .

12. The IDENTIFICATION DIVISION provides _____.
13. The ENVIRONMENT DIVISION provides _____.
14. The DATA DIVISION describes _____.
15. The PROCEDURE DIVISION contains _____.
16. COBOL source statements are first written onto a standardized _____ and then _____.

## SELF-TEST 11–2

1. Before attempting to program any application, the programmer must have a clear and precise _____, which should contain a detailed description of the _____, _____, and _____ requirements.
2. Program information concerning the date written, installation, and security would be found in the _____.
3. The SOURCE-COMPUTER is the computer that will _____ the source program, while the OBJECT-COMPUTER is the computer that will _____ the object program.
4. The only required entry in the IDENTIFICATION DIVISION is the _____ entry, but additional entries will provide more complete _____.
5. The FILE-CONTROL paragraph specifies the _____ to be used to input and output data and the names of the input and output _____.

## SELF-TEST 11–3

1. The DATA DIVISION consists of two sections, the _____ SECTION and the _____ SECTION.
2. The primary purpose of the FILE SECTION is to _____.
3. Data defined in the FILE SECTION are stored in _____ on a medium such as _____.
4. Each file must have a least one _____.
5. Each _____ is associated with an 01-level indicator.
6. Succeeding level numbers beyond the 01 level are used to show _____.
7. An 02 level would be a subdivision or part of an _____-level item.
8. A PICTURE clause is necessary to _____.
9. The entry PICTURE 9(5) describes a field which is _____ and _____ characters long.
10. The character V is used as _____.
11. When a data field contains both alphabetic and numeric characters an _____ is required in the PICTURE clause entry.
12. A FILLER is used to _____.
13. Storage areas for the results of calculations are generally described in the _____ SECTION.
14. Individual data items in the WORKING-STORAGE SECTION are assigned the level number _____.
15. Initial values (*may, may not*) be assigned to 77 level items in WORKING-STORAGE.

1. The instructions in the PROCEDURE DIVISION of a COBOL program are expressed in terms of _____ .
2. Before data can be read or written on the file, the file must be _____ .
3. The instruction which brings data into the computer for processing is the _____ instruction.
4. An unconditional branch instruction in COBOL is coded by a(n) _____ statement.
5. To transmit data from one storage area to another requires a _____ instruction.
6. Normally, execution of instructions will proceed sequentially unless a _____ is encountered.
7. In the phrase AT END GO TO END-OF-JOB from Sample COBOL Application 1, END-OF-JOB is a _____ name.
8. A STOP RUN instruction _____ program execution.
9. One can, without great difficulty, construct a _____ from the PROCEDURE DIVISION of a COBOL program.

**Answers to Self-Tests**

11-1

1. COmmon Business Oriented Language
2. it can be used on many makes and models of computers
3. it makes use of ordinary business terminology
4. it uses easily learned English words and phrases
5. provides a substantial portion of the necessary documentation
6. procedure; translator; source; object
7. the computer manufacturer
8. executed
9. divisions; IDENTIFICATION DIVISION; ENVIRONMENT DIVISION; DATA DIVISION; PROCEDURE DIVISION

10. the same
11. IDENTIFICATION DIVISION; ENVIRONMENT DIVISION; DATA DIVISION; PROCEDURE DIVISION
12. a standard method of identifying the program to the computer
13. information about equipment used to execute the program
14. the input, output, and work areas of the program
15. the instructions in the logical sequence in which they must be executed to attain the desired end results from the given starting data
16. coding form; keypunched or recorded on a computer compatible medium

11-2

1. statement of the problem; input; processing; output
2. IDENTIFICATION DIVISION
3. translate; execute
4. PROGRAM-ID; program documentation
5. equipment; files

11–3

1. FILE; WORKING-STORAGE
2. describe the input and output data files in detail
3. secondary storage; card, tape, disk, drum, data cell
4. record
5. record
6. subdivisions of the record
7. 01

8. describe the length and type of data to be stored
9. numeric; five
10. an implied decimal point
11. X
12. label unused or unreferenced positions in a record
13. WORKING-STORAGE
14. 77
15. may

11–4

1. simple, meaningful English words, statements, and sentences
2. opened
3. READ
4. GO TO

5. MOVE
6. branching statement
7. paragraph
8. terminates
9. program flowchart

## EXERCISES

**11–1**
**True/False**

_____ 1. Every COBOL program must contain four divisions in a specified order.

_____ 2. Of all the COBOL divisions, the DATA DIVISION is the most machine-dependent.

_____ 3. The primary purpose of the FILE SECTION is to describe the input and output data files in detail.

_____ 4. A FILLER is used in the DATA DIVISION of a COBOL program to represent unused or unreferenced positions in a record.

_____ 5. Before any data can be written onto a file, the file must be opened.

_____ 6. Before a COBOL program can be executed, it must be translated into machine language.

_____ 7. The character V in a PICTURE clause refers to an implied decimal point.

_____ 8. Records may not be defined in the WORKING-STORAGE SECTION.

_____ 9. The minimum number of records that a file can contain is one.

_____ 10. The level number 02 may be assigned to a subdivision of an 01 level data item.

_____ 11. An advantage of COBOL is that it reduces retraining and reprogramming costs normally caused by the acquisition of new equipment.

_____ 12. COBOL programs are efficient because they are coded in machine language and do not require translation before they are executed.

_____ 13. COBOL programming has an advantage over many other languages in that it can be easily understood by nonprogramming personnel.

_____ 14. Quotation marks are used to describe the extremities of characters being defined.

_____ 15. The COBOL system consists of a source language together with a translator for converting instructions into machine language.

_____ 16. Instructions directing the computer to read an input file would be found in the PROCEDURE DIVISION.

_____ 17. The name of the programmer and date written are required information in the IDENTIFICATION DIVISION.

_____ 18. A level number used exclusively in the WORKING-STORAGE SECTION is 77.

_____ 19. Instructions in the PROCEDURE DIVISION are executed sequentially unless a branching instruction is encountered.

_____ 20. A GO TO instruction is an example of a conditional branch instruction.

_____ 21. The DATA DIVISION describes only the data read from or written onto files.

_____ 22. The VALUE clause may be used in the WORKING-STORAGE SECTION of the DATA DIVISION only.

_____ 23. The ENVIRONMENT DIVISION does not contain information about the translating computer.

_____ 24. The PROCEDURE DIVISION is divided into the CONFIGURATION SECTION and the INPUT-OUTPUT SECTION.

_____ 25. COBOL programs written for one computer system are able to run on similar computer systems with only minor modifications.

**11-2** 1. A GO TO statement is an example of a(n) _____ branch.

**Fill-in** 2. Initial values may be assigned to variables that are described in the _____ SECTION of the _____ DIVISION.

3. The PICTURE clause that would describe an input field consisting of a five-digit number with one assumed decimal place would be _____ .

4. The only required entry in the IDENTIFICATION DIVISION is the _____ entry.

5. COBOL is an abbreviation for _____ .

6. The four divisions of a COBOL program in the order in which they must appear are _____ .

7. The DATA DIVISION of a COBOL program consists of the _____ and _____ SECTIONS.

8. If one were to construct a program flowchart from a COBOL program, one would refer principally to the _____ DIVISION.

9. The _____ statement is used to transfer data from one location in storage to another.

10. Each _____ in a COBOL program is assigned the level number 01.

1. What is the purpose of each of the following?
   a. PICTURE clause
   b. COMPUTE
   c. GO TO
   d. WRITE
   e. MOVE
   f. OPEN
   g. STOP RUN

2. Examine the sample DATA DIVISION shown and answer the associated questions.

```
DATA DIVISION.
FILE SECTION.
FD    SALES-FILE
      RECORDING MODE F
      LABEL RECORDS ARE OMITTED
      RECORD CONTAINS 80 CHARACTERS
      DATA RECORD IS SALES-REGISTER.
   01 SALES-REGISTER.
      02  COMPANY-NAME     PICTURE X(30).
      02  ACCOUNT-NO       PICTURE 9(5).
      02  AMOUNT-SOLD      PICTURE 9(6)V99.
      02  DATE.
      03  MONTH            PICTURE 9(2).
      03  DAY              PICTURE 9(2).
      03  YR               PICTURE 9(2).
      02  FILLER           PICTURE X(31).
```

   a. _____ The name of the file is _____.
   b. _____ The name of the record is _____.
   c. _____ The data record contains _____ characters.
   d. _____ _____ positions of the record are set aside for alphanumeric information.
   e. _____ There are _____ unused or unreferenced positions in the record.

3. Examine the sample PROCEDURE DIVISION shown and answer the associated questions.

```
PROCEDURE DIVISION.
BEGIN.
      OPEN INPUT SALES-FILE, OUTPUT SALES-LIST.
CALC-RTN.
      READ SALES-FILE AT END GO TO FINISH.
      MOVE ACC-NO TO ACC-NO-OUT.
      MOVE SALESMAN TO SALESMAN-OUT.
      MULTIPLY AMOUNT-OF-SALE BY .06 GIVING
      COMMISSION. IF COMMISSION > 500 MOVE
      500 TO COMMISSION.
      WRITE SALES-REPORT. GO TO START.
FINISH.
      CLOSE SALES-FILE, SALES-LIST.
      STOP RUN.
```

**a.** _____ How many times will the OPEN instruction be executed?

**b.** _____ An example of a paragraph name is _____.

**c.** _____ Which statement is executed prior to the STOP RUN statement?

**d.** _____ Which statement transfers control to CLOSE SALES-FILE, SALES-LIST. statement?

**e.** _____ Assuming there are 10 input records, how many output records will be written?

**f.** _____ _____ is the highest amount a salesman can receive as a commission for an account.

4. Use your own data names to code the DATA DIVISION entries for the following card input record:

cc   1–25   employee name (alphabetic)
cc   26–29  not used
cc   30–36  year to date earning with dollars and cents
cc   37–39  not used
cc   40–43  hourly wage with dollars and cents
cc   44     not used
cc   45–47  hours worked with one decimal place
cc   48–80  not used

_Note:_ Decimal positions are implied.

5. Construct a program flowchart from the following COBOL PROCEDURE DIVISION instructions:

```
PROCEDURE DIVISION.
BEGIN
        OPEN INPUT IN-FILE, OUTPUT OUT-FILE.
        MOVE ZEROES TO TOTAL.
CALC-RTN.
        READ IN-FILE AT END GO TO EXIT.
        IF AMOUNT > 100 MULTIPLY AMOUNT
        BY .05 GIVING DISCOUNT ELSE
        MULTIPLY AMOUNT BY .04 GIVING
        DISCOUNT.
        ADD DISCOUNT TO TOTAL.
        SUBTRACT DISCOUNT FROM AMOUNT
        GIVING NET.
        MOVE ACCOUNT-NO TO ACCT-NO-OUT.
        MOVE AMOUNT TO AMOUNT-OUT.
        MOVE NET TO NET-OUT.
        WRITE PRINT-OUT.
        GO TO START.
EXIT.   MOVE TOTAL TO TOTAL-OUT.
        WRITE PRINT-OUT-1.
        DISPLAY 'END OF JOB'.
        CLOSE IN-FILE, OUT-FILE.
        STOP RUN.
```

6. Briefly distinguish between the FILE SECTION and the WORKING-STORAGE SECTION of the DATA DIVISION.

7. Discuss COBOL with respect to its application in business-oriented problems:
   a. How does it aid documentation?
   b. How does it relate to nonprogrammer personnel?
   c. How does it relate to the training of potential programmers and analysts?
   d. What possible disadvantages might be encountered with the structure of the language?
   e. How does it compare with other computer languages you might be familiar with?
8. Discuss the purpose of each of the COBOL divisions. Which are dependent on the particular machine to be used?
9. Determine how the output would appear after having been edited by the indicated PICTURE.

# appendix: IBM® AMERICAN NATIONAL STANDARD COBOL Reserved Words

No word in the following list should appear as a programmer-defined name. The keys that appear before some of the words, and their meanings, are:

(xa)  before a word means that the word is an IBM extension to American National Standard COBOL.

(xac) before a word means that the word is an IBM extension to both American National Standard COBOL and CODASYL COBOL.

(ca)  before a word means that the word is a CODASYL COBOL reserved word not incorporated in American National Standard COBOL or in IBM American National Standard COBOL.

(sp)  before a word means that the word is an IBM function-name established in support of the SPECIAL-NAMES function.

(spn) before a word means that the word is used by an IBM American National Standard COBOL compiler, but not this compiler.

(asn) before a word means that the word is defined by American National Standard COBOL, but is not used by this compiler.

| | | | | | |
|---|---|---|---|---|---|
| | ACCEPT | | AFTER | | MERIC-EDITED | | AREA |
| | ACCESS | | ALL | | ALTER | | AREAS |
| | ACTUAL | | ALPHABETIC | | ALTERNATE | | ASCENDING |
| | ADD | (ca) | ALPHANU- | | AND | | ASSIGN |
| (asn) | ADDRESS | | MERIC | (xa) | APPLY | | AT |
| | ADVANCING | (ca) | ALPHANU- | | ARE | | AUTHOR |

(xac) BASIS
BEFORE
BEGINNING
BLANK
BLOCK
BY

(xa) CALL
(xa) CANCEL
(xac) CBL
(xa) CD
CF
CH
(xac) CHANGED
(xa) CHARACTER
CHARACTERS
(asn) CLOCK-UNITS
CLOSE
(asn) COBOL
CODE
COLUMN
(spn) COM-REG
COMMA
COMP
(xa) COMP-1
(xa) COMP-2
(xa) COMP-3
(xa) COMP-4
COMPUTA-
TIONAL
(xa) COMPUTA-
TIONAL-1
(xa) COMPUTA-
TIONAL-2
(xa) COMPUTA-
TIONAL-3
(xa) COMPUTA-
TIONAL-4
COMPUTE
CONFIGURA-
TION
(sp) CONSOLE
(ca) CONSTANT
CONTAINS
CONTROL
CONTROLS
COPY
(xac) CORE-INDEX
CORR
CORRESPOND-
ING
(xa) COUNT
(sp) CSP
CURRENCY
(xac) CURRENT-
DATE
(spn) CYL-INDEX
(spn) CYL-OVER-
FLOW
(sp) C01

(sp) C02
(sp) C03
(sp) C04
(sp) C05
(sp) C06
(sp) C07
(sp) C08
(sp) C09
(sp) C10
(sp) C11
(sp) C12

DATA
(xa) DATE
DATE-COM-
PILED
DATE-WRIT-
TEN
(xa) DAY
DE
(xac) DEBUG
(ca) DEBUG-CON-
TENTS
(ca) DEBUG-ITEM
(ca) DEBUG-LINE
(ca) DEBUG-SUB-1
(ca) DEBUG-SUB-2
(ca) DEBUG-SUB-3
(ca) DEBUG-NAME
(ca) DEBUGGING
DECIMAL-
POINT
DECLARA-
TIVES
(xac) DELETE
(xa) DELIMITED
(xa) DELIMITER
DEPENDING
(xa) DEPTH
DESCENDING
(xa) DESTINATION
DETAIL
(ca) DISABLE
(xac) DISP
DISPLAY
(xac) DISPLAY-ST
(ca) DISPLAY-n
DIVIDE
DIVISION
DOWN

(xac) EJECT
ELSE
(xa) EMI
(ca) ENABLE
END
END-OF-PAGE
(xa) ENDING
ENTER
(xac) ENTRY
ENVIRON-
MENT

(xa) EOP
EQUAL
(ca) EQUALS
ERROR
(xa) ESI
(xa) ETI
EVERY
EXAMINE
(ca) EXCEEDS
(xac) EXHIBIT
EXIT
(spn) EXTENDED-
SEARCH

FD
FILE
FILE-CON-
TROL
FILE-LIMIT
FILE-LIMITS
FILLER
FINAL
FIRST
FOOTING
FOR
FROM

GENERATE
GIVING
GO
(xac) GOBACK
GREATER
GROUP

HEADING
a HIGH-VALUE
HIGH VALUES
(ca) HOLD

I-O
I-O-CONTROL
(xac) ID
IDENTIFICA-
TION
IF
IN
INDEX
(ca) INDEX-n
INDEXED
INDICATE
(ca) INITIAL
INITIATE
INPUT
INPUT-OUTPUT
(xac) INSERT
(ca) INSPECT
INSTALLA-
TION
INTO
INVALID
IS

JUST
JUSTIFIED

KEY
(ca) KEYS
LABEL
(xac) LABEL-
RETURN
LAST
LEADING
(xac) LEAVE
LEFT
(xa) LENGTH
LESS
(ca) LIBRARY
LIMIT
LIMITS
(ca) LINAGE
(ca) LINAGE-
COUNTER
LINE
LINE-
COUNTER
LINES
(xa) LINKAGE
LOCK
LOW-VALUE
LOW-VALUES
(ca) LOWER-
BOUND
(ca) LOWER-
BOUNDS

(spn) MASTER-
INDEX
MEMORY
(ca) MERGE
(xa) MESSAGE
MODE
MODULES
(xac) MORE-LABELS
MOVE
MULTIPLE
MULTIPLY

(xac) NAMED
NEGATIVE
NEXT
NO
(xac) NOMINAL
NOT
NOTE
(spn) NSTD-REELS
NUMBER
NUMERIC
(ca) NUMERIC-
EDITED

OBJECT-COM-
PUTER
(ca) OBJECT-PRO-

GRAM
OCCURS
OF
OFF
(ca) OH
OMITTED
ON
OPEN
OPTIONAL
OR
(xac) OTHERWISE
OUTPUT
(ca) OV
(xa) OVERFLOW

PAGE
PAGE-
COUNTER
PERFORM
PF
PH
PIC
PICTURE
PLUS
(xa) POINTER
POSITION
(xac) POSITIONING
POSITIVE
(ca) PREPARED
(xac) PRINT-
SWITCH
(ca) PRINTING
(ca) PRIORITY
PROCEDURE
(ca) PROCEDURES
PROCEED
PROCESS
(ca) PROCESS
PROCESSING
(xa) PROGRAM
PROGRAM-ID

(xa) QUEUE
QUOTE
QUOTES

RANDOM
(ca) RANGE
RD
READ
(xac) READY
(xa) RECEIVE
RECORD
(xac) RECORD-OVER-

FLOW
(xa) RECORDING
RECORDS
REDEFINES
REEL
(ca) REFERENCES
RELEASE
(xac) RELOAD
REMAINDER
REMARKS
RENAMES
(xac) REORG-CRITE-
RIA
REPLACING
REPORT
REPORTING
REPORTS
(xac) REREAD
RERUN
RESERVE
RESET
RETURN
(xac) RETURN-CODE
REVERSED
REWIND
(xac) REWRITE
RF
RH
RIGHT
ROUNDED
RUN

(ca) SA
SAME
SD
SEARCH
SECTION
SECURITY
SEEK
(xa) SEGMENT
SEGMENT-
LIMIT
SELECT
(ca) SELECTED
(xa) SEND
SENTENCE
(xa) SEPARATE
SEQUENTIAL
(xac) SERVICE
SET
SIGN
SIZE
(xac) SKIP1
(xac) SKIP2
(xac) SKIP3

SORT
(xac) SORT-CORE-
SIZE
(xac) SORT-FILE-
SIZE
(ca) SORT-MERGE
(xac) SORT-MES-
SAGE
(xac) SORT-MODE-
SIZE
(xac) SORT-RETURN
SOURCE
SOURCE-COM-
PUTER
SPACE
SPACES
SPECIAL-
NAMES
STANDARD
(xac) START
STATUS
STOP
(xa) STRING
(xa) SUB-QUEUE-1
(xa) SUB-QUEUE-2
(xa) SUB-QUEUE-3
SUBTRACT
SUM
(ca) SUPERVISOR
(xa) SUPPRESS
(ca) SUSPEND
(xa) SYMBOLIC
SYNC
SYNCHRO-
NIZED
(sp) SYSIN
(spn) SYSIPT
(spn) SYSLST
(sp) SYSOUT
(spn) SYSPCH
(sp) SYSPUNCH
(sp) S01
(sp) S02

(xa) TABLE
TALLY
TALLYING
TAPE
(ca) TERMINAL
TERMINATE
(xa) TEXT
THAN
(xac) THEN
THROUGH

THRU
(xa) TIME
(xac) TIME-OF-DAY
TIMES
TO
(xac) TOTALED
(xac) TOTALING
(xac) TRACE
(xac) TRACK
(xac) TRACK-AREA
(xac) TRACK-LIMIT
(xac) TRACKS
(xa) TRAILING
(xac) TRANSFORM
TYPE

(ca) UNEQUAL
UNIT
(xa) UNSTRING
UNTIL
UP
UPON
(ca) UPPER-BOUND
(ca) UPPER-
BOUNDS
(spn) UPSI-0
(spn) UPSI-1
(spn) UPSI-2
(spn) UPSI-3
(spn) UPSI-4
(spn) UPSI-5
(spn) UPSI-6
(spn) UPSI-7
USAGE
USE
USING

VALUE
VALUES
VARYING

WHEN
WITH
WORDS
WORKING-
STORAGE
WRITE
(xac) WRITE-ONLY
(spn) WRITE-VER-
IFY

ZERO
ZEROES
ZEROS

# A SYSTEMS
# APPROACH

12345

INTRODUCTION

WHAT IS A BUSINESS SYSTEM?

OBJECTIVES OF A SYSTEM STUDY

SYSTEMS ANALYSIS AND DESIGN

**Feasibility Study**

Initialization

Selection of Objectives

Detailed Analysis

Resource Allocations

Conclusions

**Modify the Existing System**

**Developing a New System**

DEVELOPING A SYSTEM DESIGN

**Investigation**

**Hypothesis**

**Implementation**

FOCUS ON THE FIELD

SELF-TESTS

EXERCISES

# CHAPTER 12

# Systems Analysis

## INTRODUCTION

The study of "systems" is by no means a new or even recent endeavor. Systems have been in use for thousands of years. The Egyptians employed a form of a bookkeeping system over 5000 years ago for keeping their accounts, while Phoenician astronomers studied systems of stars for the purpose of making predictions. Humans have sought, from the beginning of time, to find relationships, to generalize these relationships, and to explain what they can see, hear, touch, smell, and reason.

All human history has been a continuing enlargement of this theme: Meaningful and durable relationships must be uncovered if we are to expand our knowledge and successfully administer our affairs. The scientific method of investigation, which necessitates such meaningful and durable relationships for its results, is systems analysis in the broadest sense.

In this chapter, however, we will only concern ourselves with those systems which are of direct and immediate concern to a business in the processing of information to produce meaningful results for management. That is, systems analysis will refer to the analysis of business systems.

Systems today are essential to the operation of any part of a business. They must be made to function at peak efficiency if a business is to survive. But a system can function only as effectively as users such as the accountant, business manager, and other responsible individuals within the company make it function. To make a system function at maximum capacity demands more of its users than that they have a superficial knowledge of how to use the system.

All too often, managers are told that they only need to know how to access required information, thus making them ignorant of the operations of the system as a whole. In accepting such advice, these managers are, in essence, relinquishing a substantial part of the control of the organization to the system's designers and operators.

It is therefore essential that early in their careers, managers and potential managers be made to understand clearly what a system is, what its objectives are, what kinds of systems there are, what goes into their creation and maintenance, what their costs and benefits are, and how to analyze and evaluate systems. It is to provide such an understanding that this and subsequent chapters are presented.

Upon completing this chapter you should be able to:

- Describe a business system
- List the objectives of a system study
- Discuss what a feasibility study is and when it should be undertaken
- Describe the steps generally involved in a feasibility study
- Describe the three stages in developing a system
- Define the following terms:

| | |
|---|---|
| Analysis | Investigation |
| Business systems | Modifying an existing |
| Conclusions | system |
| Developing a new system | Pilot study |
| Feasibility study | Purpose of systems study |
| Hypothesis | Resource allocations |
| Implementation | Selection of objectives |
| Initialization | Systems |

## WHAT IS A BUSINESS SYSTEM?

A business system may be defined as a combination of personnel, equipment, and other facilities operating as a unit according to a set of procedures designed to record and control the actions and activities connected with a business.

Prior to the advent of the computer, a business could survive even though it did not merge and correlate all phases of its activities into a unified whole, but today this is no longer possible. A good system is the key to the efficient operation of each and every part of a business. If a business is to outdistance and outlast its competitors, its operations must be based on carefully planned and operationally current systems.

Modern business systems accept input data, move it methodically through a preplanned series of procedures to a computer, where it is used to create needed reports, to update various records, to make routine decisions automatically, or to provide management with current and meaningful information on which to base its decisions. These systems must be flexible enough to adapt to changes in the structure of the business or the market it serves. They must be able to interact with one another in a productive and meaningful way. The systems which control the prime functions of a business are similar to the systems which, within the human being, work together to keep the body operating efficiently and effectively.

Examples of systems commonly found in business include

1. Accounts payable
2. Personnel accounting
3. Payroll
4. Accounts receivable
5. Inventory

Systems Analysis

Complex systems such as these certainly were not the result of chance but were developed as the result of careful and detailed investigations. The first of these investigations must be directed toward determining, clearly and precisely, what the objectives of the system study are.

To verify your understanding of the previous material, turn to page 461 and take Self-Test 12-1.

## OBJECTIVES OF A SYSTEM STUDY

A complete and detailed systems analysis can take many months to develop and cost thousands of dollars. In light of this, there can be little doubt that there is a need to establish the objectives of the system analysis before such substantial energies or monies are expended. These objectives may be broad, long-range expectations, or they may be short-range plans. In either case, they will have one overall objective in common—to increase the effectiveness and efficiency of an operation or procedure. This objective can be met by developing new procedures or by improving existing procedures so as to obtain new and better information for management, to increase the effectiveness of operations, and, where possible, to reduce operating expenses. However, to make a complete system analysis, these general statements must be converted into definite steps to be followed. These steps will be discussed in detail later.

Basically, the overall objective of increased effectiveness can be satisfied in one or more of the following ways:

1. Improved service to the customer or user of the system
2. Improved quantity, quality, depth, and form of information provided to management
3. Increased speed and accuracy in the processing of data and the preparation of reports
4. Improved coordination between the various operating units and associated personnel
5. Improved overall operating efficiency by making possible more speedy action on management decisions
6. Eliminating the conflicting or overlapping services
7. Reduced inventory and other working-capital requirements

## SYSTEMS ANALYSIS AND DESIGN

Once the objectives of the system have been determined, the analyst can proceed with his investigation to determine whether the existing system, be it manual, mechanical, punched-card, or computerized, is adequate or whether this system should be modified, updated, or replaced. Such an analysis is termed a feasibility study.

**Feasibility Study**

A complete and effective feasibility study would require an overall study of the entire organization. Before initiating such a study, the management of the organization should be apprised of the fact that a sufficiently detailed, well-planned, and well-executed feasibility study is both expensive and time-consuming. Management should also be made aware that such a study can be beneficial to the organization regardless of the study's outcome. For example, should the study reveal that the existing system is sufficient and appropriate for the organization's needs and therefore should not be changed or replaced, substantial time and money can be saved for the organization in not needlessly attempting to develop a replacement system. Also, management could be assured that, for their purposes, the existing system is the most efficient and competitive possible. The size and complexity of a feasibility study necessitates that it be broken down into several less comprehensive steps. Although these steps may differ in name, they will be similar in content to the following five steps:

1. Initialization
2. Selection of objectives
3. Detailed analysis
4. Resource allocations
5. Conclusions

Initialization. In this phase of the study, contacts should be made with employees associated with the existing system, from the lowest-level employee through management personnel, in order to develop a clear understanding of the advantages and disadvantages of the existing system as well as to point out any unsolved problems. For future analysis, a study team should be formed, consisting of at least one member from each of these areas. The first task of this team will be to determine the present and future requirements of the system, the extent of available equipment and methods relating to this system, and what expenditures of personnel, time, and money can be anticipated to complete the feasibility study.

Selection of Objectives. In this phase of the study, the system specifications and objectives should be written down in detail, accompanied by a realistic timetable for the completion of the feasibility study. Krauss[1] suggests that the answers to the questions below will help the analyst determine this information.

[1]Leonard I Krauss, *Administering and Controlling the Company Data Processing Function.* Englewood Cliffs, N.J.: Prentice-Hall, Inc., pages 51–52.

## Management

1. What are the past and future objectives?
2. What is the general attitude?
3. What is the underlying philosophy?
4. What organizational changes are planned?
5. What are the unfulfilled information needs?
6. How receptive is management to new techniques or change?

## Procedures

1. What work is performed?
2. In what sequence does the work take place?
3. Who performs the functions?
4. How many people are needed?
5. When is the function performed?
6. What equipment is used?
7. Is the function needed?
8. What inputs and outputs are involved?
9. How much volume is there—average, peak, growth?
10. How much time is required for the functions?
11. How often is the work done?
12. What controls are required?
13. What are the turnaround-time requirements?
14. What "business rules" apply to each function?

## Cost

1. How much does the present system cost?
2. How much is spent on forms and supplies?
3. What are the costs for carrying inventory or receivables awaiting collection?
4. What are the personnel costs?
5. What overhead is charged?

## Effectiveness

1. Does the current system do what was intended?
2. What are the strong points?
3. What are the disadvantages?
4. What effects would expansion have?
5. Is the current output useful?
6. How much inefficiency and duplication of effort exists?
7. What interdepartment relationships exist?

There are several ways to go about obtaining the answers to these and other questions. Three of the most common fact-gathering techniques which are currently used to obtain information about the present system and future needs are as follows:

1. Interviewing
2. Reviewing historical records
3. Sampling and estimating

Interviewing is probably the most productive of the three and usually begins with top management to obtain broad background information; then with middle or first-line management, who provide the details; and, finally, the individual workers are questioned. One must bear in mind that the lowest-graded worker can often point out the imperfections in the existing system and occasionally will even suggest worthwhile remedies. Interviewing techniques will be discussed in greater detail when we discuss developing a system design.

The degree to which historical records can be beneficial is greatly dependent on the nature and rate of growth of the business. All too often the analyst will discover that the records are too poorly kept or too out of date to serve as predictors with any degree of certainty. In these cases, the records are better put aside and their absence compensated for by a more in-depth analysis of other source data.

It is often helpful to gather sample data from which estimates or projections can be made which will serve either to confirm or to cast doubt on conclusions reached by other means. However, this technique should be used cautiously, as substantial errors are possible if one is not experienced and knowledgeable concerning its use.

Detailed Analysis.   In this phase, the present and past systems used by the company are examined in comparison to other companies that have instituted such studies. Careful consideration should be given to the relationship between the dollar cost of the systems study and tangible savings and benefits, not only with regard to profits but with respect to savings in space, time, experience gained, increased competitive potential, and so on.

The relationship between the system under investigation and other independent and interdependent systems within the company should also be determined. In determining this relationship, each of the systems should be analyzed and compared with the remaining systems concerning their functional design as opposed to their organizational arrangements.

Resource Allocations.   An account should be taken of all the company's resources, including such items as manpower, money, time, and space. For example, a hypothetical list of proposed system costs and benefits is given in Fig. 12-1. Included should be a detailed statement concerning whether or not each of these resources is being efficiently utilized.

Conclusions.   A written report incorporating the study team's findings and recommendations should be submitted to management. It is

| PROPOSED SYSTEM COSTS | PROPOSED SYSTEM BENEFITS |
|---|---|
| **Hardware**<br>Basic processor<br>Terminals<br>Storage and input/output<br>Communications<br>Facilities<br>Equipment maintenance<br><br>**Operating Expenses**<br>Programmers to maintain the system<br>Equipment operators<br>Data entry and media preparers<br>Data collectors<br>Data control and correction<br>Electricity, heating, and air conditioning<br>Cards, paper, tapes, etc.<br><br>**Developmental Costs**<br>Hiring and training programmers and analysts<br>Salaries of programmers and analysts<br>Salaries of additional study team or developmental personnel<br>Disruption of normal operations<br>Retraining of displaced personnel<br>Establishment of new files and/or database(s) | **Decreased Operating Costs**<br>Fewer people<br>Less inventory<br>Fewer penalties for late delivery or payment<br>Reduced spoilage of goods<br>Lower transportation or purchasing costs for material<br>Fewer shortages to interrupt production<br>Better scheduling of production<br>More efficient use of equipment<br><br>**Increased Revenues**<br>Ability to handle more customers with existing facilities<br>More customers by faster or more dependable service<br>Higher price or more customers from better quality of product |

**FIGURE 12-1**

Hypothetical list of proposed system costs and benefits

important to support these recommendations in detail, making certain to highlight any anticipated benefits in addition to pointing out the degree of uncertainty and risks inherent in the recommendations.

Such a feasibility study could have only two possible outcomes. The first possible outcome is that the present system is as good as or superior to any other system thus far proposed or evaluated. In this case the study would be discontinued for the immediately foreseeable future. At such time as new developments should arise, the feasibility study could be reinitiated.

The second possible outcome would be that the present system is not the most effective and efficient system for the company's needs. In such a case, two possible alternatives could be suggested as a result of the feasibility study: Modify the existing system or develop a new system.

**Modify the Existing System**   Inexpensive modifications to the existing system are often sufficient for the user's needs. A simple modification such as the standardizing of invoice layouts that had previously varied from one department to another within the company would, for example, lower the cost of the forms, simplify personnel training, and reduce possible errors in using and understanding these forms. Modification of the existing system could also include the replacement of manual methods by mechanical or computerized methods or the replacement of existing equipment by more sophisticated and more efficient equipment.

**Developing a New System**   To develop a new system is a long and tedious procedure and will be discussed in detail in the next section.

To verify your understanding of the previous material, turn to page 461 and take Self-Test 12-2.

## DEVELOPING A SYSTEM DESIGN

The developing of a system can be reduced to three fundamental stages: the investigation stage, the hypothesis stage, and the implementation stage (Fig. 12-2).

FIGURE 12-2

Steps in a system design

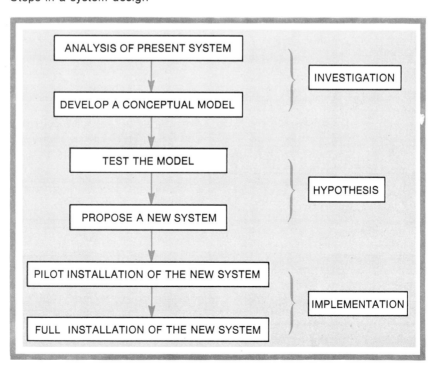

**Investigation**     The first phase of any system investigation is to acquire a detailed understanding of the existing system. A great deal of this information should have been revealed in the feasibility study, but it will be restated for emphasis.

The investigation stage is a period of intensive data collection and interviewing. A substantial amount of written material must be collected in this process and generally takes one or more of the following forms:

1. Representative input and output data
2. Practical examples of the existing system's malfunctions, if any
3. Reports and commentaries indicating previous studies of, or attention given to, the same or similar problems

Equally as important as written materials is the interview. Many items can be determined from an interview that would be almost impossible to obtain from written documents. However, one must approach the interview with caution, since interviews can easily become confused, redundant, and time-consuming. The interviewer must make every effort to eliminate any bias that might be injected as a result of the position and personality of the person being interviewed. He must also be careful to avoid the common pitfalls that can occur in interviewing. Some of these common errors are

1. Interrupting the story to insert your own ideas and views
2. Allowing the direction of the interview to be diverted onto nonproductive paths
3. Allowing blanket statements and broad generalizations to obscure the facts
4. Leaving the interview only half understanding an issue or problem
5. Allowing oneself to be overpowered by the person being interviewed and end up as the interviewed instead of the interviewer
6. Allowing oneself to become involved in operational problems, thus distracting one's attention from the prime purpose of information gathering
7. Asking leading questions that can be answered with a "yes" or "no," as very often this kind of question calls for an opinion and not fact
8. Failure to take notes or record the results of the interview.

After all interviews have been completed and their results have been assembled, the conceptual model will begin to take shape. The conceptual model is the analyst's first idea concerning how to attack the problem and concerning the manner in which the system should be redesigned. The analyst should be careful not to attempt to draw conclusions or to attempt to solve the problem during this stage, but to make a concerted effort simply to collect data.

**Hypothesis**     Upon completion of the analysis of the existing system and the development of a conceptual model (investigation stage), the analyst must test the conceptual model and propose a new system (hypothesis stage).

The conceptual model to be tested can appear in many forms. If it were to appear in a mathematical form, for example, its analysis would be reasonably routine; however, the problem does not usually appear this way. Therefore, there remains only one effective means to evaluate the model. This means is simply to expose the model to its potential users for their analysis and comments. This should be done as early as possible after the completion of the investigation stage. The problem becomes even more difficult in the case of a new system, where the potential users have had little or no previous exposure to this or a previous, but similar, system. In such cases it is desirable to test subsystems of the overall system separately as well as testing the overall operation of the system in any way feasible. It is important to verify that the subsystems are compatible and can function together to produce the desired results. The unstructured or nonmathematical nature of most business systems must be given careful consideration in designing the testing format to be utilized. This should be considered in much the same way as it will be in the design of the system itself.

**Implementation**     If possible, a pilot implementation study should be performed, as this type of study has the distinct advantage of allowing the system in miniature to operate under battle conditions. This means that any defect can be corrected or any changes made prior to the making of any large-scale commitments. In the analysis of this pilot study, the analyst must realize that it is difficult, if not impossible, to design a completely optimal system. Even if one were able to develop such a system, changes in input or output requirements might necessitate that the analyst settle with a system design which is somewhat less optimum. The system designer must realize that his or her role is simply to improve the existing process to the greatest extent *practically* possible in the shortest possible time. Otherwise, a great deal of time can be needlessly expended by the analyst in an attempt to produce the optimum system, not realizing that, in so doing, the completion date of the system is being postponed and the company is losing the benefit of the use of the new system.

"All right, let's keep it moving—keep your punch cards handy for quick processing."

Once the pilot study has been made to perform satisfactorily, it can be expanded, step by step, until it covers the full operational scope for which the system was designed.

The system approach that you have just studied closely follows the scientific method. It requires that the system be carefully and methodically analyzed functionally and operationally, and that it consider suitable alternatives. It also dictates that the problem be attacked in an orderly way, first by investigation, then by the establishing of a reliable hypothetical model of the problem, and finally by a careful and thorough testing phase.

To verify your understanding of the previous material, turn to page 462 and take Self-Test 12-3.

## Successful Systems Are Designed by Users

### By George U. Isaacs     and     Roger E. Olson

Experience has shown that there is a need for extensive user involvement in any significant information systems project. Excellent systems can be designed and installed without much involvement, but they are rarely implemented or used effectively.

This is especially true in manufacturing organizations planning to install integrated management systems encompassing materials management, production and inventory control, master scheduling, capacity planning and loading, shop floor control and so on. Such systems represent a major, often traumatic, departure from the tried and true methods of the past. Complete dependence and trust must be placed on computer-generated information. Unless they are designed from the bottom up, by foremen, supervisors and plant management, no amount of "selling" can convince the users that the systems can be relied upon and trusted. They will seek to prove that the systems don't work. Their efforts will eventually be rewarded and the systems will fail.

In order to provide the structure or framework needed, a task force of user managers or their representatives is formed to design and implement the systems. The task force involves people responsible for all key functions—plant management, marketing, customer service production scheduling, inventory management, finance and so on. It is a user task force, led by a user manager, not a data processing manager.

For a task force to be successful, it is necessary to bring each member up to the level of understanding required to evaluate systems alternatives. This is accomplished through formal and informal education and training sessions. The formal sessions cover such subjects as: sales forecasting, master scheduling, inventory management, material requirements planning, product structuring techniques, capacity planning and loading, production planning and control, shop floor control and data processing concepts.

The first phase, Project Initiation and Planning, establishes the foundation and framework through which users are able to conduct the project. An outside management consultant conducts a user "Needs and Wants" survey, structures a customized education course and presents it.

Shortly after completing the education seminar, a brainstorming session is conducted with a representative group of user managers. During this session the users prioritize their company's information needs. Later, the prioritized needs are presented to a top management steering committee for approval.

Once the priorities are approved, the consultant helps organize the user task force and guides it through the steps required to plan, design, develop and install the user's systems. As the project progresses and the user task force gains experience, the need for the consultant decreases. After about a year, the consultant comes in only once a month primarily to monitor progress and resolve any problems that may have developed. After two years, the consultant has typically worked himself out of a job.

To ensure that users accept responsibility for the success of "their" systems, it is essential that data processing does not take over the project. Therefore, the data processing manager or a representative is assigned to the task force as the data processing team leader and reports to the task force manager.

Yet, the data processing team's contribution is different in many respects. The user teams design and implement the systems while the data processing team provides the resources and technical expertise the users need to do their jobs.

Throughout the project there is a clear definition of responsibility. Any disputes or conflicts are resolved by the task force manager and backed up by the steering committee. Users are held accountable for ensuring that the system design meets their needs and that, when developed to their specifications, the systems will work.

Data processing is held accountable for quality control and assuring that the hardware and software meets the user's design specifications. Users are responsible for implementing the systems and using them to produce the benefits they have defined. The task force manager is responsible for the project as a whole and must ensure that each team member complete his or her tasks on schedule and within budget.

By sharing project responsibilities for design, development and implementation among a task force, it is possible to implement systems in less than half the time normally required.

In order to maintain the integrity of the "user designed systems" approach, it is important to ensure that the consultant does not take over the project. This is accomplished by appointing the task force manager early in the project. Once appointed, the consultant works through the task force manager who coordinates and supervises the consultant's activities.☐

DISCUSSION QUESTIONS

1. Why is it essential to have user involvement in any systems project?

2. What is the first step in getting the user involved? Where and how else should users be involved in a systems project?

## SELF-TEST 12–1

1. A _____ may be defined as a combination of personnel, equipment, and other facilities operating as a unit according to a set of procedures designed to record and control the actions and activities connected with a business.

2. The modern business system utilizes computers to _____ .

3. A system must be flexible enough to adapt to _____ .

4. Five examples of business systems are _____ .

5. The common overall objective of all systems analysis is _____ .

6. The first step in evaluating a system is to _____ .

## SELF-TEST 12–2

1. A _____ is used by the analyst to determine whether the existing system is adequate.

2. A complete and effective feasibility study would require an overall study of _____ .

3. An integral part of a feasibility study is the selecting of the objective of the system and establishing of _____ .

4. The five steps generally required in a feasibility study are _____ .

5. The _____ step of a feasibility study involves contact with employees in order to understand _____ .

6. In collecting data for the feasibility study the analyst may utilize _____ , _____ , and _____ techniques.

7. It is often _____ to update the existing system than to develop a new system.

8. In the _____ phase of the feasibility study, the relationship between the system under investigation and other independent and interdependent systems should be determined.


## SELF-TEST 12–3

1. The three stages in developing a system design are _____, _____ and _____.

2. The _____ stage is concerned with analyzing the present system and _____.

3. The hypothesis stage of the system development includes _____ and _____.

4. In employing the interview technique, an interviewer must take every precaution to eliminate any _____ that might be interjected as a result of the position and personality of the person being interviewed.

5. The ideal form of a conceptual model is _____.

6. A _____ installation is a miniaturized version of the planned system designed to test the system under fire on a small scale.

7. The _____ stage of system development is concerned with developing a pilot study.

8. A system study is based on the _____ method.


**Answers to Self-Tests**

12–1

1. business system

2. create needed reports, make decisions automatically, update various records, and provide management with current and meaningful information on which to base its decisions

3. the changes in the structure of the business or in the market it serves

4. accounts payable, personnel accounting, payroll, inventory, and accounts receivable

5. to increase the effectiveness of the operation or procedure

6. determine what the specific objectives of the system are


12–2

1. feasibility study

2. the entire organization

3. a realistic timetable for the completion of the feasibility study

4. initialization, selection of objectives, detailed analysis, resource allocations, and conclusions

5. initialization; the relative advantages, disadvantages, and unsolved problems associated with the existing system

6. interviews; review of historical records; sampling and estimating

7. less expensive and tedious

8. detailed analysis

12–3
1. investigation; hypothesis; implementation
2. investigation; developing a conceptual model
3. testing the model; proposing a new system
4. bias
5. a mathematical model
6. pilot
7. implementation
8. scientific

## EXERCISES

_____ 1. A detailed understanding of the existing system is a necessary part of any system investigation.

_____ 2. In an interview, it is essential that the person being interviewed be made to feel at ease, even if this means that all problems might not be thoroughly discussed.

_____ 3. The first step in evaluating a system is to determine whether or not the existing system can be updated, or to determine whether or not a new system should be designed.

_____ 4. The common overall objective of all systems analyses is to accomplish the existing job more inexpensively.

_____ 5. All existing systems within a business should be reviewed periodically.

_____ 6. It is recommended that the analyst draw as many conclusions as possible during the investigation stage.

_____ 7. Systems analysis is a scientific method of investigation that seeks meaningful and durable relationships.

_____ 8. Leading questions that call for opinions should not be used in an interview.

_____ 9. Minor system modifications are very often sufficient for the user's needs and should always be considered in a feasibility study.

_____ 10. It is a bad practice for an interviewer to discuss his or her own ideas during an interview.

_____ 11. The ideal form that a conceptual model can take is a mathematical one.

_____ 12. A system must be flexible enough to adapt to the changes in the structure of the business or the market it serves.

_____ 13. Historical records are reliable sources of information to be used in the selection of objectives.

_____ 14. Note taking can be distracting and therefore should never be done during an interview.

_____ 15. The testing of a conceptual model and the proposing of a new system is known as the hypothesis stage.

_____ 16. The least productive method of obtaining information pertaining to the present system and future needs is through the interview.

_____ 17. The factor of primary importance in the evaluation of a system is the determining of specific objectives.

___ **18.** Modifications to existing systems are costly.

___ **19.** In an interview, it is best to let some problems go so that the person being interviewed will not be upset.

___ **20.** The primary aim of a systems study is to increase the efficiency and effectiveness of the system. Sampling and estimating techniques should be used cautiously as substantial errors are possible if one is not experienced in using this technique.

___ **21.** If the outcome of a feasibility study is to make no changes in the existing system, the study should be immediately redone by another team.

___ **22.** The initialization phase is the first step in a feasibility study.

___ **23.** Users need only know how to access information from a system.

___ **24.** The report of a study team is generally submitted to management.

___ **25.** In the initialization phase of a feasibility study, communication should take place only with top-level management.

**12–2**
**Multiple-choice**

___ **1.** A systems analyst need not
  **a.** be familiar with the business being examined
  **b.** know the uses and limitations of a computer
  **c.** have a logical reasoning ability
  **d.** none of the above
  **e.** (b) and (c) only

___ **2.** The stages in developing a system do not include
  **a.** feasibility
  **b.** investigation
  **c.** hypothesis
  **d.** implementation
  **e.** none of the above

___ **3.** A request for a systems investigation should include
  **a.** price and time
  **b.** scope and boundary
  **c.** address and location
  **d.** scope and cost
  **e.** none of the above

___ **4.** A conceptual model is generally evaluated
  **a.** mathematically
  **b.** by actual use
  **c.** by exposure to the potential users for analysis and comments
  **d.** by computer
  **e.** none of the above

___ **5.** Which of the following questions should an interviewer avoid asking the manager of a shipping department?
  **a.** Do you believe the XYZ form is adequate for your use?
  **b.** Why is the battery information block used on form XYZ?
  **c.** How many persons do you employ in the crating department?
  **d.** When are the steam buckets wrapped and bagged?
  **e.** What organizational changes do you plan next year?

1. A complete and effective _____ would require an overall study of the entire organization.

2. The steps generally required in a feasibility study are: _____

3. The stages in developing a system design are _____.

4. The _____ stage in developing a new system is concerned with analyzing the present system and developing a conceptual model.

5. A _____ is a miniaturized version of the planned system designed to test the system under fire on a small scale.

6. A system study is based on the

_____.

7. The _____ phase is the first step in a feasibility study.

8. The part of the system study where new ideas are proposed is the _____ stage.

9. The _____ stage of a system development is concerned with developing a pilot study.

A. Pilot installation

B. Investigation, hypothesis, implementation

C. Initialization

D. Scientific method

E. Hypothesis

F. Initialization, selection of objectives, detailed analysis, resource allocations, conclusions

G. Feasibility study

H. Investigation

I. Implementation

1. Describe and justify the importance of each of the five basic steps involved in the feasibility study.

2. Name and describe some common business systems about which you have read or have been associated.

3. As an interviewer, would you accept the following answers in an interview or continue the questioning? Why?
   a. There is no need for the w-234 form in this department.
   b. That operation requires 700 straphangers per week.
   c. We have 14 midget sanders, 27 rod benders, and 3 salami slicers in our manufacturing operation.
   d. Right now, we hand sort the XYZ form by date and enter the number of items, cost, and color for each article into form XYZ-2. Management is investigating the use of a machine sorter, and I understand that we should have one next quarter.

4. Several fact-gathering techniques are used to obtain information about present and future needs. List and discuss three of these techniques.

5. The report of the study team is presented to management. List and discuss several items that might be in this report.

6. Name and discuss the three basic stages in the development of a system.

7. Why should management be involved in the design and analysis of a system? Explain.

8. How does planning a system differ from planning a program? How is it the same?

INTRODUCTION
FORM DESIGN
PUNCHED CARD AND CRT LAYOUT AND DESIGN
CODING OF INPUT
**Block Code**
**Sequence Code**
**Faceted Code**
DATA FILES
SYSTEM FLOWCHART
SYSTEM TESTING
SYSTEM DOCUMENTATION
FOCUS ON THE FIELD
SELF-TESTS
EXERCISES

# Systems Considerations

## INTRODUCTION

In this chapter we will discuss the more important of those items which the manager and potential manager will find helpful in using and understanding his company's systems and with which the systems analyst must be concerned in designing and implementing a system. Specifically, we will discuss form design, card and CRT layout and design, coding of input, data files, system flowcharts, system testing, and system documentation.

Upon completion of this chapter you should be able to:

- Describe the procedure used to determine whether a form is appropriate or not
- Describe the major sections of a form
- Describe the card design process
- List and describe the principal input coding schemes
- Distinguish between dynamic and reference files
- Describe a procedures manual
- Define the following terms:

| | |
|---|---|
| Block code | Reference file |
| Direct-access file | Sequence code |
| Dynamic file | Sequential file |
| Faceted code | System documentation |
| Form design | System flowcharting |
| Input coding | symbols |
| Punched card design | System testing |

## FORM DESIGN

The analyst is often faced with the task of examining current or designing new forms and form-handling procedures. By periodically examining existing forms, unused and obsolete forms can be uncovered and subsequently modified, combined, simplified, or eliminated. Such decisions should be made in an attempt to satisfy one or more of the following general objectives:

1. The reduction of printing, recording, and distribution costs
2. The reduction or elimination of unnecessary paperwork
3. The combining and simplifying of forms and form-handling procedures

While this analysis is being conducted, verification can be made that all existing forms have been properly classified and indexed by content, type of use, and source and destination of all copies.

Each form should be specifically examined to determine, for example, whether or not it clearly indicates its purpose, commands attention, and allows space for the inclusion of the data. A form should also

1. Contain a specific amount and kind of information
2. Make entering the required information easy
3. Make using the data it contains easy
4. Be reproduced as economically as possible
5. Be designed to minimize the possibility of error
6. Be related to other forms and to other documents used for the form in question
7. Be designed as concisely and clearly as possible
8. Be related to the characteristics of the machines or the equipment on which it will be used
9. Facilitate the operation for which it is designed

More often, however, the analyst is called on by a department to design a completely new form. Before actual work can be started on the creation of the new form, the analyst must consult the concerned department to determine answers to certain basic but standard questions. Among these one would expect to find the following questions:

1. Will this form replace any existing form(s)?
2. What necessary information will be contained on this form?
3. What source document contains this information?
4. Is this information presently available on existing machine-readable media?
5. How was this information previously gathered and reported?
6. Is it possible to modify an existing form to include the required information?

The analyst, in consultation with appropriate management personnel from the affected department, would then compile and study the answers to the above questions. Based on this analysis, a joint decision would be rendered concerning the necessity and advisability of creating a new form. Should a new form be justified, the analyst could then turn to the matter of the actual design and layout of the new form. It is advisable that the analyst or form designer chosen for this task have a working knowledge of the equipment on which the form is to be used, the considerations and problems involved in the printing of forms, and the cost factors involved in the production of forms.

Forms are generally subdivided into three sections:

1. Introductory
2. Main body
3. Conclusion

*INTRODUCTION*                                                                    *Yes*    *No*

    1. Is the title clearly and concisely stated?      \_\_\_\_ \_\_\_\_

    2. Is the company or agency identified?      \_\_\_\_ \_\_\_\_

    3. Are general instructions reduced to the minimum?      \_\_\_\_ \_\_\_\_

    4. Is the file or reference data properly placed for the type of file to be used?      \_\_\_\_ \_\_\_\_

*MAIN BODY*

    1. Does the form read left to right?      \_\_\_\_ \_\_\_\_

    2. Are there writing lines?      \_\_\_\_ \_\_\_\_

    3. Are related vertical columns clearly separated?      \_\_\_\_ \_\_\_\_

    4. Can the reading lines be followed without confusion?      \_\_\_\_ \_\_\_\_

    5. Are the writing lines adequate for the load?      \_\_\_\_ \_\_\_\_

    6. Are lines to be filled in by typewriting spaced to conform to typewriter spacing?      \_\_\_\_ \_\_\_\_

    7. Is the vertical alignment on forms to be typewritten such that clerks can use the typewriter tabular-stop device?      \_\_\_\_ \_\_\_\_

    8. Does the form provide larger spaces for handwritten data than typewritten data?      \_\_\_\_ \_\_\_\_

    9. If the form is to take information from or pass information to another form, does it show items in the same order as the other?      \_\_\_\_ \_\_\_\_

    10. Does the form have all recurring items printed so that only variables need to be filled in?      \_\_\_\_ \_\_\_\_

    11. Have all fact-gathering data been included?      \_\_\_\_ \_\_\_\_

    12. Have the data been so arranged that backtracking is unnecessary?      \_\_\_\_ \_\_\_\_

*CONCLUSION*

    1. Has space been provided for signature, title, and date?      \_\_\_\_ \_\_\_\_

    2. Has space been provided for approval signature, title, and date when required?      \_\_\_\_ \_\_\_\_

    3. Is the identification form number in the proper place for filing, binding, or reordering?      \_\_\_\_ \_\_\_\_

*GENERAL*

    1. Will the form fit window or other envelopes which may be used?      \_\_\_\_ \_\_\_\_

    2. Is the form the correct size for filing or binding?      \_\_\_\_ \_\_\_\_

    3. Is the form printed on the size and weight of paper that is most economical?      \_\_\_\_ \_\_\_\_

    4. Is a revised form sufficiently different from the older form?      \_\_\_\_ \_\_\_\_

    5. Does the form make use of color as an aid to identification, reference, and prevention of eyestrain?      \_\_\_\_ \_\_\_\_

    6. Does the form make use of combination forms and carbon copies where possible?      \_\_\_\_ \_\_\_\_

    7. Have unnecessary carbon copies been eliminated?      \_\_\_\_ \_\_\_\_

All items checked "Yes" need no further consideration. The items with a "No" require investigation and/or revision.

**FIGURE 13-1**

Form evaluation checklist

"Actually, it's just a microcomputer system in a big rack. But I had to justify the software costs somehow."

The introductory material is generally placed at the top of the form and contains information concerning how the form is to be prepared as well as the name and number of the form. The main body of the form should contain the information for which the form was designed, and the conclusion of the form should provide room for the signature and title of authorizing persons, as well as providing room for the date of the authorized signing.

To make certain that no items have been overlooked in the design of the form, the analyst or form designer should have a checklist similar to the one presented in Fig. 13-1. Those items which are checked with a "yes" represent items which have been satisfactorily presented or which do not apply. Those items checked with a "no" represent items which will require further analysis and/or revision.

Figure 13-2 illustrates some typical form designs.

**FIGURE 13-2**

Typical form designs

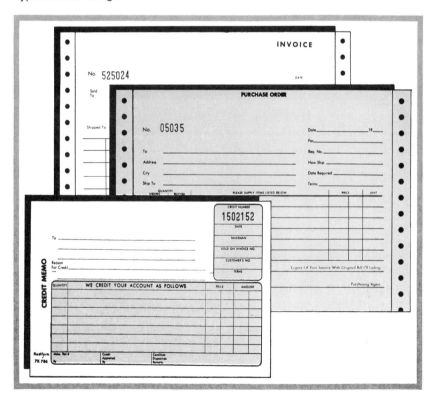

# PUNCHED CARD AND CRT LAYOUT AND DESIGN

Punched card or CRT (cathode ray tube) design can be defined as a technique for determining where and in what form data are to be punched into cards or keyed into a terminal for maximum processing efficiency. At first glance, this would appear to be a very simple and unimportant task. However, this is not at all the case. The design of a card or terminal input can seriously affect the data-entry and programming operations.

Well-planned and carefully designed input can be used in the production of numerous reports. Poorly designed input, however, can increase the possibility of keying errors, in addition to causing the creation of redundant, repetitive, and inefficient programs.

Punched card or CRT design begins with a determination of what accounting, management, or statistical reports are to be prepared in part or whole from these input data. Not until this has been accomplished can an analyst turn to the actual data that are to be recorded. A series of questions whose answers should reveal the required information concerning these data is as follows:

1. What input data are necessary for each report desired?
2. What source document(s) contains these input data?

FIGURE 13-3

Card layout forms

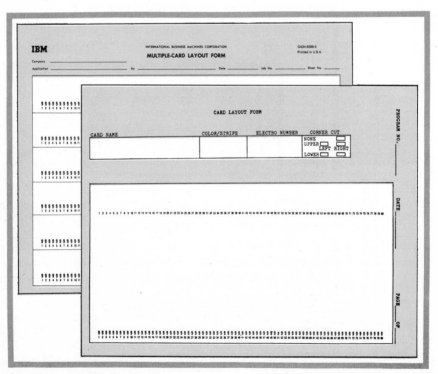

3. Are these input data presently available on a computer-acceptable medium or database?
4. What are possible sources of additional data needed but not contained on the above source document(s)?
5. What additional information must be recorded to identify the source of the data?
6. What are the optimum field sizes for the required input data?
7. Which fields can be coded for storage efficiency, and which must remain uncoded for immediate visual interpretation?
8. Is the data record to be a master, detail, or summary record?

Figure 13-3 illustrates two of the *card layout* forms that are available to aid the analyst with the physical design and layout of a punched card. Similar forms are available for the design of CRT input records. With forms such as these and the information previously gathered, the analyst can complete the design.

To verify your understanding of the previous material, turn to page 484 and take Self-Test 13-1.

## CODING OF INPUT

A code can be described as a system of symbols for representing data. A code provides a substitute name, in the form of a set of arbitrary characters, for the actual names or numbers.

There are several reasons why input data are coded. Among the more important of these reasons are:

1. *Save space on the input media.* For example, if one were to classify individuals by sex, one would have two categories: male and female. By assigning the code 1 to the category male and the code 0 to the category female, the two categories can be represented by exactly one character, as opposed to the previous possibility of four or six characters. And the 1–0 coded categories convey exactly the same amount of information as did the original male–female categories.
2. *Processing and storage advantages.* In some computers it is easier and faster to compare and store numeric quantities than it is alphabetic or alphanumeric quantities. In such machines, nonnumeric input data would be represented by a numeric code.
3. *File security.* By coding information contained in classified files, it affords them some degree of content security.
4. *Remote entry speed and accuracy.* In the case that data are entered via terminals, input data transmission can be speeded up with decreased errors if concise data coding is employed to represent the data with fewer coded characters. Computer output responses will also be faster for the same reason.
5. *Sorting and information retrieval.* The coding of input data facilitates the sorting of the data and limited information retrieval.

Systems Considerations

Determining the actual coding system involves two basic steps. The first step is to determine the classification scheme that is to be used to discriminate between the different types of data. The second step, based on the number of classifications and possible subclassifications, is to determine the type of code that is to be employed. It then only remains to determine specifically what coding scheme will be utilized. Let us now examine each of these steps in greater detail.

A classification scheme is one in which data are systematically divided into classes or groups so that like or similar items are combined. Depending upon the use of the data, individual group members can be further divided according to their fundamental properties or characteristics. Establishing an efficient and complete classification scheme will often form the basis for sorting and limited information retrieval.

The next step is to determine the type of code to be used. There are three general types:

1. Numeric: a code based on numbers only
2. Alphabetic: a code based on letters only
3. Alphanumeric: a code based on numbers, letters, and possibly some special characters

**Block Code**  The actual scheme chosen will depend greatly on the classification scheme. For example, suppose that we must determine a scheme for coding 63 items classified into four groups, respectively, containing 8, 11, 32, and 12 items each.

A simple two-digit decimal code could be

| GROUP | CODE NUMBERS ALLOCATED | UNUSED CODE NUMBERS IN GROUP |
|-------|------------------------|------------------------------|
| 1 | 01–17 | 9 |
| 2 | 18–37 | 9 |
| 3 | 38–78 | 9 |
| 4 | 79–99 | 9 |

This scheme is called a **two-digit block code** and nicely fills our immediate need, as well as providing room for expansion within each group. In this scheme, the two-digit block codes are arbitrarily assigned depending on the number of items in each group and the total number of items to be represented.

**Sequence Code**  However, if the 63 items had been classified into nine groups, respectively, containing 5, 6, 8, 5, 9, 7, 9, 6, and 8 items each, a possible scheme might be

| GROUP | CODED NUMBERS ALLOCATED | UNUSED CODE NUMBERS IN GROUP |
|---|---|---|
| 1 | ①0 – ①9 | 5 |
| 2 | ②0 – ②9 | 4 |
| 3 | ③0 – ③9 | 2 |
| 4 | ④0 – ④9 | 5 |
| 5 | ⑤0 – ⑤9 | 1 |
| 6 | ⑥0 – ⑥9 | 3 |
| 7 | ⑦0 – ⑦9 | 1 |
| 8 | ⑧0 – ⑧9 | 4 |
| 9 | ⑨0 – ⑨9 | 2 |
| 10 | unused | 10 |

This type of code is called a **sequence code.** In a sequence code, each digit represents a subclassification of the preceding digit.

For example, the code 84 could mean a recliner chair:

This coding scheme offers some advantages over the block code. To illustrate one such advantage, let us assume that we wish to produce a report indicating the number of chairs of each type currently in our inventory. If a sequence code such as the one described above were employed, it would only be necessary to direct the computer to select out those items whose two-digit code begins with an 8. To accomplish the same thing employing a two-digit block code, at the very least, it would be necessary to provide the computer with the code number of the first chair listed and the code number of the last chair listed and to direct it to select all items with numbers greater than or equal to the first number and less than or equal to the second number. However, if chairs were not assigned consecutive block numbers, it would have been necessary to input to the computer the block number for each type of chair in the inventory.

**Faceted Code**   Other coding schemes make use of significantly placed letters and/or digits. Each letter or digit in the code represents a particular characteristic of the item. For example, CT 30 CB could be a code for **C**hair **T**ype **30** with **C**hrome legs and a **B**lue seat. This type of scheme is called a **faceted code** since each component or part of the total code describes a different facet of the item it represents.

As you can see, there are many types of codes that can be used. The job of the analyst in coding input is to determine which code is most advantageous in what particular situation. His decision should attempt to satisfy, as closely as possible, each of the following conditions:

1. Code must be adaptable to automated processing.
2. Code must be as compact as possible.
3. Code must be flexible enough to allow for future additions and changes.
4. Code must allow for easy encoding and decoding.

## DATA FILES

A **file** is a collection of related records treated as a unit. That is, a set of accessible records similar to one another in purpose, form, and content. Files can be broadly classified according to their degree of activity as **dynamic** (very active) or **reference** (relatively inactive) files.

The storage medium used for a particular file is determined by several factors:

1. Activity of the file
2. Access speeds required
3. Manner in which transactions arrive to update file
4. Volume of data in the file
5. Frequency with which records are added to or deleted from the file

If the file is an active one and is to be randomly accessed, for example, a **direct-access** medium would be appropriate.

In such a case, the file would be maintained on either magnetic disk, magnetic drum, or mass storage system. The fastest of these is the magnetic drum, the least expensive the mass storage system, and the magnetic disk is average in cost and speed with a large storage capacity.

If, on the other hand, the data input to update the file will be in sequence and available in batches or groups, a **sequential** medium can be used. For some time magnetic tape has been the most commonly used sequential medium. This is because of its low cost and relatively fast processing speeds when dealing with large-volume sequential files. However, in recent years disk storage systems have become available

that can be economically applied to the processing of sequential files. Only time will tell whether or not they will virtually replace the magnetic tape as the principal sequential medium. In the case of the microcomputer, the diskette has already established itself as the principal sequential and direct-access medium. One must realize, however, that the file-processing capabilities of these systems limit their application to relatively small or low-volume files.

The manner in which the data are organized on the file is quite technical and generally within the exclusive province of the systems analyst. Therefore we will not discuss this further.

To verify your understanding of the previous material, turn to page 484 and take Self-Test 13-2.

## SYSTEM FLOWCHART

We have learned that a flowchart is a means of visually presenting the flow of data through an information-processing system, the operations performed in the system, and the sequence in which these operations are performed. We have discussed in detail how the program flowchart is used to describe the sequence of operations which must be performed to obtain a computerized solution to a particular problem. What we have not discussed, however, is that there is another type of flowchart—the **system flowchart.** And, as we found the program flowchart useful in understanding a computer program, we will find the system flowchart to be even more useful in understanding a computerized system.

A system flowchart pictorially describes the flow of data through all parts of a system. Figures 13-4 and 13-5 illustrate the standard system flowchart symbols together with a description of each symbol.

Actual operations to be performed are briefly described with the major emphasis being placed on the media involved and the work stations through which they must pass. As a result, much of a systems flowchart consists of symbols depicting these documents and operations. For this reason, document and operational symbols were designed so that when used in a system flowchart, they are meaningful

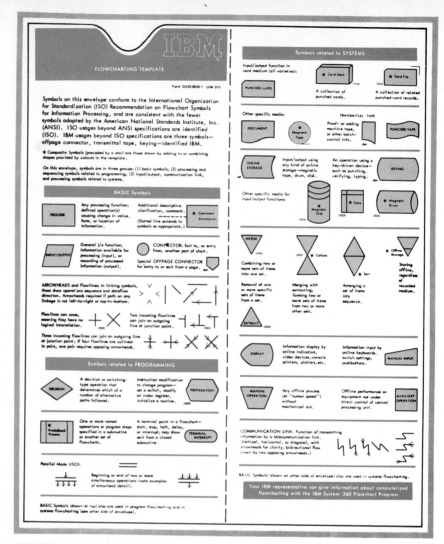

**FIGURE 13-4**

Annotated flowcharting template symbols

without comment or text. Therefore, when a note is placed within a flowcharting symbol, the flowchart takes on specific application meaning. For example, the document symbol

represents any kind of paper documents and reports, including source documents and ledgers. And yet, the document symbol and note

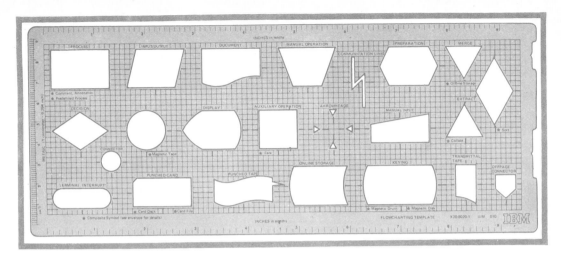

**FIGURE 13-5**

Flowcharting template

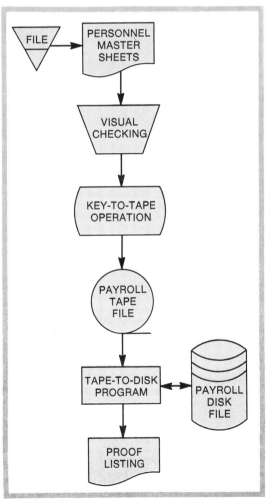

**FIGURE 13-6**

System flowchart for the creation of a payroll master disk file

479

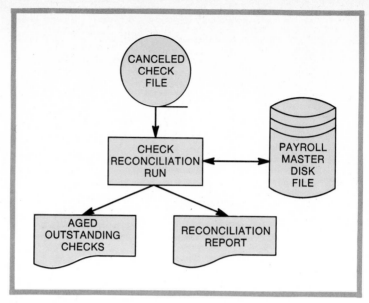

FIGURE 13-7

System flowchart for bank reconciliation report

tell the reader much more. They indicate specifically the document—deduction authorization form—and the area of application—payroll system. Figure 13-6 illustrates a system flowchart describing the creation of a sequential payroll master disk file from payroll master source documents. Other system flowcharts are illustrated in Figs. 13-7, 13-8, and 13-9.

To verify your understanding of the previous material, turn to page 485 and take Self-Test 13-3.

## SYSTEM TESTING

A system must be thoroughly tested before it is placed into actual operation. The testing process involves analysts, programmers, management, auditors, and individual user departments and generally consists of three phases.

In the first phase, the lead programmer on the project must test each of the program segments separately and in combinations. Program test data and verified output should be included in the final program documentation. When all program testing and documenting has been

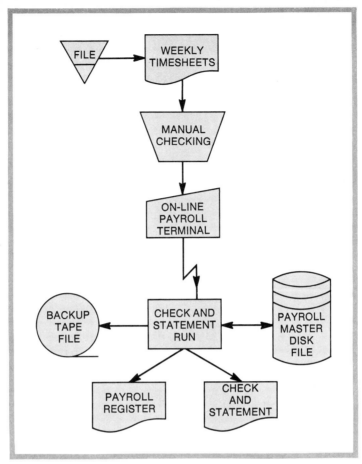

FIGURE 13-8

System flowchart for a payroll check and statement run

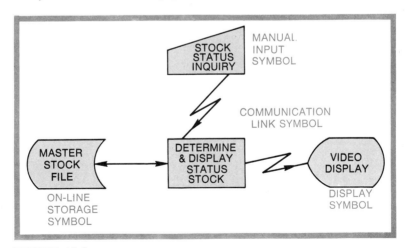

FIGURE 13-9

System flowchart for an online inquiry

completed, the lead programmer forwards a complete set of fully tested and documented programs to the project analyst.

In the second phase of the system test, the analyst checks program flowcharts and decision tables against original specifications. He will subject the programs to actual data as well as data with planted errors to verify that they will be detected should they arise in actual use. When he has thoroughly examined and reviewed the logic of each subsystem, the flow of information through the system, and the overall system, he will gather together systems test data or actual data and create special test files.

In the third and final phase, the entire system is tested utilizing actual machines and employees. The system is tested down to the most minute detail. Forms are checked, schedules are checked, operating instructions are verified, and the movement of data and results are tested. In cases where there is no existing automated system to test against, individual departments may ask or be asked to check the accuracy of the system's output manually. If a company auditor is available, he or she should be consulted from time to time throughout this process, as the system may be audited by noncompany data-processing auditors at a future date.

The system is now ready to be put into actual use. This, of course, requires that all files be first created and then tested before the changeover takes place.

Once the system has been implemented, it must be constantly tested and improved if it is to remain efficient and effective. A system can be thought of as a living thing, requiring that it be constantly nurtured and cared for if it is to survive and grow.

"Why did you turn off my power? I paid my bill. See? Here's my canceled check."

## SYSTEM DOCUMENTATION

A system cannot be completely effective unless it is adequately documented. It should be documented as it is being created. That is, at various stages or intervals in the system development, status reports should be prepared for those management personnel for whom the system is being designed. Such reports would include flowcharts, decision tables, output or report forms, and other documents thus far developed. Also included would be any problems encountered, suggested solutions, and resulting schedule revisions. In this way management is kept abreast of the system's progress so that where necessary, they can offer criticisms or suggest change while it is still economically and physically possible to make these changes without it being necessary to revise the entire system. These progress reports provide an excellent basis on which to build additional documentation.

Instructions and narrative descriptions must be prepared for every phase and part of the system, including system logic, timings, user instructions, instructions for operations personnel in the data-processing center, and instructions concerning the transmission of data and results. Much of this can be incorporated into a **procedures manual.** This manual stipulates the relationship between personnel in the application areas affected by the system and the data-processing center. It should relate, in detail, exactly what procedures must be employed by the user to operate the system efficiently and effectively.

To verify your understanding of the previous material, turn to page 485 and take Self-Test 13-4.

# focus on the field

## "Data System"—A New Concept

A new term, "data system," has come on the scene. It is a concept designed to give a more comprehensive approach to developing new applications faster and making them even more productive for the end users they serve.

Data system is a larger concept than data base/data communications (db/dc) because it uses more than data base software merged with a data communications management system.

A data system environment also includes data administration and data delivery products, a number of interactive tools to help end users solve problems, and a growing list of application products.

IBM's data administration product, the DB/DC Data Dictionary, enables a data system user to establish a single authoritative source of all data definitions and cross-relationships. The data dictionary, for example, makes it easy to find out what data elements are used by each program and which users will be affected by a proposed change in a data base. It's a particu-larly useful tool for the auditor who may want to analyze specific usage patterns.

IBM's data delivery products can help the programming process of converting data into useful information for end users. They include application generators such as the Application Development Facility (ADF) and the Development Management System (DMS).

APL, Interactive Instructional System (IIS) and PLANCODE are typical of a number of online interactive tools used in a data system to help end user professionals solve problems.

To round out the expanded concept of a data system there is a large and growing list of DL/1-based application programs that address such areas as manufacturing, health care, personnel and finance. To support key data system products IBM is introducing the new System Installation Productivity Option-Extended (System IPO-E), to help ease implementation and maintenance of data system products.

In brief, a data system means more efficient administration of the data base through a data dictionary, as well as improved delivery of that data to end users through easy-to-use application development tools.

DISCUSSION QUESTIONS

1. What is entailed in a data system?
2. What advantages does a data system have over a database system?

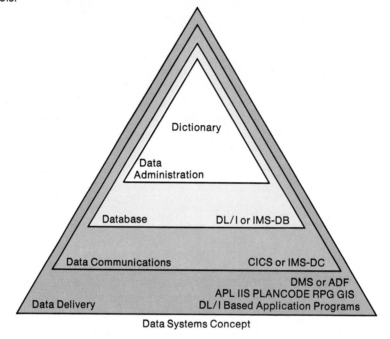

Data Systems Concept

## SELF-TEST 13–1

1. Existing forms should be periodically _____.
2. Objectives to be used when examining forms are _____.
3. Forms are generally subdivided into three sections: _____, _____, and _____.
4. The design of a card or teminal input can seriously affect the _____ and _____ operations.
5. _____ forms are used as an aid to the analyst in the physical design and layout of punched cards.
6. Card design begins with the determining or what _____ will be prepared in part or whole from the input data.
7. All input data fields (_are, are not_) coded for storage efficiency.

## SELF-TEST 13–2

1. Analysts often make use of _____ to conserve space on a card layout as well as to reduce keypunching errors.
2. Some of the more significant reasons why data are coded are _____ .
3. Three codes employed in coding data are _____ , _____ , and _____ .
4. A file is defined as _____ .
5. Files are classified according to their degree of activity as _____ or _____ files.
6. A very active file can also be called a _____ file.
7. The storage medium used for a given file is based on _____ .
8. Dynamic files generally use a _____ medium, while reference files use a _____ medium.

## SELF-TEST 13–3

1. A system flowchart visually shows _____ .
2. Flowcharts consist of two general types: _____ and _____ .
3. Standard flowcharting symbols are used with _____ flowcharts.
4. The shape of the system flowchart symbol indicates the _____ to be performed while the _____ within the symbol conveys more specific information about that particular case.

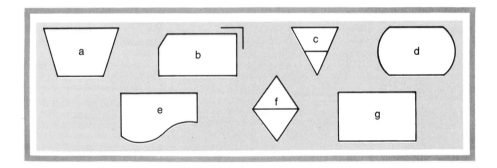

5. The system flowcharting symbols shown above are used to represent (a)_____ , (b) _____ , (c)_____ , (d) _____ , (e)_____ , (f)_____ , and (g)_____ .
6. Which of these symbols would be used to indicate a machine-verifying operation?
7. Which of these symbols would represent a computer program that is to be keypunched?

8. What symbol is used for comments?
9. The merge and extract symbols are ———— and ————.
10. The symbol and note to represent a master payroll tape file is ————.
11. The symbol ⟋⟍ is a ———— symbol.


## SELF-TEST 13–4

1. Before a system is considered operational, it must go through three phases of ————.
2. The first phase of testing a system deals with ————.
3. The second phase for testing a system includes ————.
4. The final phase of testing of a system involves ————.
5. System documentation is necessary to ————.
6. Documentation reports would include such items as ————.
7. The ———— stipulates the relationship between personnel in the applications areas affected by the system and data-processing center.


**Answers to Self-Tests**

13–1

1. examined and unused or obsolete ones modified, combined, simplified, or eliminated

2. cost reduction, eliminating unnecessary paper work, reduction of form handling

3. introduction; main body; conclusion
4. data entry; programming
5. Card layout
6. reports
7. are not

13–2

1. coded data

2. to save space and keypunching errors, for more efficient processing and storage security, for faster input speeds from terminals, to facilitate sorting and information retrieval

3. block code; sequence code; faceted code

4. a collection of related records treated as a unit
5. dynamic; reference
6. dynamic
7. activity of the file, access speeds required, how the file update data will be received, and the volume of data in the file
8. direct-access; sequential

13-3

1. the flow of data through the system, the operations performed in the system, and the sequence in which the operations are performed
2. program flowcharts; system flowcharts
3. both program and system
4. operation; note
5. (a) manual operation; (b) card file; (c) offline storage; (d) keying operation; (e) document; (f) sort; (g) processing function
6. symbol d

7. symbol e
8.
$$- - - -\;\boxed{\text{COMMENT OR ANNOTATION SYMBOL}}$$
9.
▽     △
MERGE    EXTRACT
10.
MASTER PAYROLL FILE
11. communications link

13-4

1. testing

2. testing the computer programs using simulated data to verify the output

3. the checking of program flowcharts and decision tables against original specifications and testing programs using actual data

4. actual machines and employers who check its performance under operational conditions
5. keep management abreast of current developments and to explain the workings of the system to users and other concerned individuals
6. flowcharts, decision tables, output or report forms, etc.
7. procedures manual

# EXERCISES

13-1
**True/False**

_____ 1. Terminal input design can seriously affect data-entry and programming operations.

_____ 2. How a form is folded and its final size are important general considerations in form design and evaluation.

_____ 3. When designing a form, space should be provided for the date and the signature of the person filling out the form.

_____ **4.** If a card is designed properly, it is possible that it will serve as input for several reports.

_____ **5.** When designing a code, one must allow for future additions and/or changes.

_____ **6.** Systems analysts should not be concerned with form-handling procedures.

_____ **7.** Forms are generally subdivided into three sections: introductory, main body, and conclusion.

_____ **8.** The principal medium use with microcomputers for the storage of sequential and direct-access files is the diskette.

_____ **9.** A system flowchart is a pictorial description of the flow of data through the system.

_____ **10.** The code BR72G, which represents a book rack, 7 shelves by 2 bays, gray in color, is an example of a faceted code.

_____ **11.** Symbols used in system flowcharting are generally the same as those used in program flowcharting.

_____ **12.** Field size is a relatively unimportant consideration in card design.

_____ **13.** Coding of data can aid information retrieval.

_____ **14.** The first step in coding data is to determine a classification scheme to discriminate between the different types of data.

_____ **15.** A file is a collection of related records.

_____ **16.** Existing forms should be periodically examined and unused or obsolete forms modified, combined, simplified, or eliminated.

_____ **17.** Dynamic files generally use a sequential access device while reference files utilize direct access devices.

_____ **18.** Card or terminal design begins with determining what reports will be prepared from the input data.

_____ **19.** In a sequence code, each digit of the number 4731 could represent specific information.

_____ **20.** Magnetic disk storage systems are currently used to store sequential files.

_____ **21.** New forms should not resemble old forms so that there will be no confusion.

_____ **22.** Card and CRT design is a very simple and relatively unimportant task.

_____ **23.** A classification scheme is one which groups data pertaining to similar or like items.

_____ **24.** Bright red is a good color for a form because it attracts attention.

_____ **25.** Before designing a new form, other information sources should be checked to make sure that the information needed from the form is not already available.

_____ **1.** System documentation generally does not include
    **a.** progress reports
    **b.** decision tables
    **c.** report forms
    **d.** problems encountered
    **e.** none of the above

_____ **2.** Conversion of a numeric grading system into an alphabetic grading system is an example of
    **a.** alphabetic coding
    **b.** block coding
    **c.** sequence coding
    **d.** faceted coding
    **e.** all of the above

_____ **3.** Which of the following need not be considered in the design of a form by an analyst?
    **a.** minimize the possibility of error
    **b.** command attention
    **c.** be dissimilar to other forms
    **d.** (a) and (c) only
    **e.** none of the above

_____ **4.** Which of the following are not system flowcharting symbols? (1) punched card (2) punched tape (3) processing (4) document (5) keying operation (6) input/output
    **a.** (2) and (3)
    **b.** (2) and (5)
    **c.** (3) and (6)
    **d.** all of the above
    **e.** none of the above

_____ **5.** Punched card or CRT design necessitates that the analyst be concerned with
    **a.** using the largest field sizes possible
    **b.** size of the card
    **c.** information to be recorded to identify the source of the data
    **d.** all of the above
    **e.** none of the above

**1.** Some of the objectives one aims for when designing a form are _____.

**2.** Forms are generally subdivided into the following sections: _____.

**A.** Cost reduction, elimination of unnecessary paperwork, reduction of form handling

**B.** Block, sequence, faceted

**C.** Dynamic, reference

**D.** Introductory, main body, conclusion

3. Considerations that must be given to a card design include: _____ .

4. _____ is used to conserve space on a card layout as well as to decrease the possibility of keypunching errors.

5. Codes employed in coding data include _____ .

6. Files are classified according to the degree of activity as _____ .

7. A symbol used to indicate a machine verifying operation is _____ .

8. A symbol used to facilitate comments is _____ .

9. A symbol used to indicate a merge operation is _____ .

10. A symbol used to represent a tape file is _____ .

11. A symbol used to represent a communications link is _____ .

12. A symbol used to represent an output document is _____ .

13. A symbol used to represent a sort operation is _____ .

14. A symbol used to represent a manual operation is _____ .

15. A symbol used to represent an offline storage operation is _____ .

16. A symbol used to represent a magnetic disk file is _____ .

17. A symbol used to represent an online keyboard is _____ .

18. A symbol used to represent online video, console, printer, plotter, etc. devices is _____ .

19. A symbol used to represent a file maintained on magnetic drum is _____ .

E. Data coding

F. Keypunching, programming

G.

H.

I.

J.

K.

L.

M.

N.

O.

P.

Q.

R.

S.

1. List and discuss several of the questions that the designer of a form should have to answer after completion of his or her study.

2. List and discuss several reasons for coding input data.

3. Discuss the similarities and differences between the systems flowchart and the program flowchart.

4. Justify the reasoning behind the three-phase testing of a new system.

5. What are some of the reasons for documenting a system?

6. What is a procedures manual? What does it contain?

7. How does system documentation differ from program documentation? Explain.

INTRODUCTION

WHAT IS AN INFORMATION SYSTEM?

OFFLINE INFORMATION SYSTEMS

ONLINE INFORMATION SYSTEMS

ONLINE REAL-TIME INFORMATION SYSTEMS

MULTIPROGRAMMING/MULTIPROCESSING INFORMATION SYSTEMS

TIME-SHARING INFORMATION SYSTEMS

INTEGRATED INFORMATION SYSTEMS

MANAGEMENT INFORMATION SYSTEMS

DISTRIBUTED DATA PROCESSING

**Computing Systems**

**Networks**

**Data Communications/Teleprocessing**

FOCUS ON THE FIELD

SELF-TESTS

EXERCISES

# CHAPTER 14

# Information Systems

## INTRODUCTION

Today's business manager cannot possibly assimilate the deluge of facts and figures which confront him or her daily. Although surrounded by data, a manager often lacks the necessary information which he or she must have readily available to function effectively. Relevant and essential information must be able to be retrieved quickly and selectively. Thus, businesses have turned to information systems in an attempt to provide relevant information to appropriate personnel, in appropriate form, and at the appropriate time.

Upon completing this chapter you should be able to:

- Determine the difference between an online and an offline information system
- Describe the various types of information systems
- State the advantages and disadvantages of the various types of information systems
- Describe the two principal types of distributed data-processing systems
- List and describe the principal components of a teleprocessing system
- Describe the most common types of communication lines
- Define the following key terms:

| | |
|---|---|
| Batch or sequential | Multiprogramming |
| Centralized computing system | Offline |
| Communication line | Online |
| Communications network | Online real-time |
| Conversational mode | Remote batch-processing |
| Database | mode |
| Decentralized computing system | Ring network |
| Distributed computing system | Simplex line |
| Duplex line | Software |
| Facts vs information | Spider network |
| Half-duplex line | Star network |
| Information system | Telecommunications |
| Integrated information system | Teleprocessing |
| Management information system | Terminal |
| Modem | Time-sharing |
| Multiprocessing | Transmission control unit |

# WHAT IS AN INFORMATION SYSTEM?

An information system can be defined as the interacting of humans and machine which, under human control, gathers data and disseminates information. Such a system has as its major objective the providing of information to its user. To accomplish this, data must be evaluated, analyzed, and processed to produce meaningful and useful information on which management can base future decisions. *Unprocessed facts and figures are data, not information.* Information systems have been classified according to various criteria. They have been classified according to system response time, or the elapsed time from data input or inquiry to the output of usable information; according to the number of users or programs which can be serviced simultaneously; and according to the degree of integration of the separate data-processing systems within a company. These are some of the common means that have been used to classify information systems. Some of these classification schemes overlap, resulting in the fact that particular information systems can be included in one or more classifications. Some of the more common classifications of information systems include

1. Offline
2. Online
3. Online real-time
4. Multiprogramming
5. Multiprocessing
6. Time-sharing
7. Integrated
8. Management
9. Distributed data-processing

To verify your understanding of the previous material, turn to page 518 and take Self-Test 14-1.

# OFFLINE INFORMATION SYSTEMS

In Chapter 4 we described an offline operation as one in which the input/output devices or auxiliary equipment are not under the direct control of the computer. It is the use of offline operations that characterizes an offline information system. In such a system, input data or transactions are generally collected into groups or batches and sorted into sequence before being submitted to the computer for processing. If these transactions are to be processed against a master file, they are sorted into the same sequence as the master file before processing, and subsequently processed in that order.

The fact that, in an offline information system, input is batched and sequenced prior to processing has led to the more commonly used names **batch processing** and **sequential processing.**

Batch processing accounts for a large portion of the work performed in today's business installations. This is simply for reasons of economy. Processing a large volume of data through the computer generally results in lower processing costs per record than processing the transactions as they occur. Therefore, transactions are collected until

such time as it is most convenient and economically feasible to process them. This means, of course, that there may be a time delay of minutes, hours, or even days between the time the transaction occurs and its eventual processing. For this reason, batch processing is utilized for those applications in which this delay does not reduce the usefulness of the resulting information. In instances where the batched input data are on cards, for example, special offline conversion devices can be utilized to transcribe the data from cards to a faster and more efficient medium, such as magnetic tape, before it is processed. The results of the processing can then be output for the computer to an offline device, and then converted to the desired output medium.

There are, however, certain inherent disadvantages in batch processing:

1. In certain instances the time required to prepare the batched input could drastically reduce the value of the resulting information.
2. The necessity of arranging input data and master files into sequential order prior to processing is both expensive and time-consuming.
3. Other computer users must often wait a substantial period of time for access to the computer if it is involved in a batch run.
4. Inquiries concerning the status of a particular account are time-consuming because of the required sequential file organization.
5. Batch systems require very precise scheduling to make the most efficient use of the central processing unit.
6. Master files are only completely up to date immediately after a batch-processing run.
7. Batch processing results in peak-load requirements, resulting at times in the necessity to operate the system around the clock to produce both special and routine reports. To eliminate such peak-load periods, many organizations have installed oversized systems to handle the peak load at costs far in excess of the overall productivity realized.

**To verify your understanding of the previous material, turn to page 518 and take Self-Test 14-2.**

## ONLINE INFORMATION SYSTEMS

An online information system is one in which the terminal or input/output devices are directly tied to and controlled by the central processing unit and where these devices are capable of direct two-way communications with the central processing unit (Fig. 14-1). As one

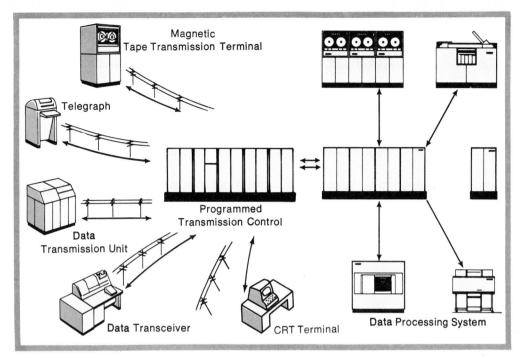

FIGURE 14-1

Online computer system

might imagine, such a system would necessitate reasonably fast response times to facilitate effective two-way communications between the user and the central processing unit.

In an online system, as data become available, they can be input to the system immediately, thus simplifying the precise scheduling procedure required of an offline or batch system.

In addition, with a capability for processing transactions almost immediately, data files can be kept up to date. This then allows for much easier processing of inquiries and guarantees more accurate inquiry responses than is generally possible with a batch system. The central processing unit, in an online system, is in control from the point of origin of the input without human intervention.

However, there are also disadvantages associated with an online system:

1. An online system is usually more expensive to operate than a batch system.
2. If data arrive in large quantities, the slow operating speeds of input/output devices as compared to the processing speeds attainable by the central processing unit cause the CPU to be idling, or waiting for data to process, a great deal of the time. This can be both time-consuming and expensive.
3. An online reporting system occupies the processing system a good deal of the available time, thus limiting its use for processing other applications.

To verify your understanding of the previous material, turn to page 518 and take Self-Test 14-3.

## ONLINE REAL-TIME INFORMATION SYSTEMS

An online system is not always a real-time system, but a real-time system must consist of equipment with an online capability. To be a real-time system, the time delay between the creation of data to be processed and the actual processing of these data must be "insignificant." Whether this time delay is short enough to be insignificant is determined by the needs of the user. That is, if information reaches management in sufficient time and in an appropriate form for management to make required decisions, then we have a real-time situation.

A real-time system with the capability of providing instantaneous access to any and all data would be neither realistic nor economical, since much of the data utilized in the operations of a business need only be made accessible to management periodically.

In real-time systems, time delays can range from fractions of a second when necessary to several days where allowable. For example, for a computer system in control of an atomic reactor, a real-time response might be limited to a fraction of a second, while in looking up a purchase order in a real-time accounts payable system, a response time of 1 or 2 seconds would easily qualify as real-time.

As was the case with an online information system, an online real-time information system must also be capable of effectively handling direct two-way communications between the terminal devices and the central processing unit. The response times associated with an online system are, however, generally significantly longer than could be tolerated in an online real-time system. Each user must have access to any *required* online data stored within the computer system and should be able to alter these data as though the computer was serving him individually and exclusively. Let us consider how an online real-time system might be utilized in a typical sales application. In such a system, each sales office would be equipped with terminals capable of communicating inquiries directly to the computer and capable of displaying the computer response. To place an order, the salesman would enter the pertinent information about the proposed order, via a terminal, to the computer. Within a matter of seconds, the system would respond through the terminal with complete information concerning the cost, availability, and status of the item ordered. If the item is in stock, a purchase order would be created and the sales office informed of planned shipping information. Simultaneously the system would update the inventory files and issue a reorder notice for the item if the stock on hand is below the reorder point. If the item is temporarily out of stock or has been discontinued, the sales office would be notified of this fact as well as when a new shipment is expected or what substitute item is currently available. And this entire process could be accomplished in a matter of seconds.

As in the above example, real-time systems provide for the constant and almost instantaneous updating of all files. Real-time systems, such as the one described, consist of five major components:

*prime necessity*

1. A **computer** to accept, process, and output data in the required format to the user in minimal time
2. The **software** or composite of all routines and programs necessary to operate the system
3. The **terminals** which will accept user input or inquiries and produce or display system output
4. A **communication network** to link the terminals with the computer
5. The **database** which consists of large-volume, randomly accessible files required for the processing of input or inquiries

Such a system is proving more and more to be essential to provide management with timely, up-to-the-minute information concerning the operations of the business.

The main disadvantage of an online real-time system is the tremendous expense associated with such a system. Both the hardware and software costs associated with the system exceed those associated with online or batch systems.

Continual improvements in hardware design are providing more efficient random-access storage devices and improved communications equipment at lower costs, thus increasing the reliability and economic feasibility of utilizing online real-time processing in more and more areas of application.

To verify your understanding of the previous material, turn to page 518 and take Self-Test 14-4.

## MULTIPROGRAMMING/MULTIPROCESSING INFORMATION SYSTEMS

Often the terms "multiprogramming" and "multiprocessing" are confused because of the similar appearance and sound of the two terms. However, there is a substantial difference between the meaning of these two systems.

A multiprogramming system is one that has the capability of executing two or more programs concurrently utilizing one central processing unit. Hence the name multiprogramming. A multiprogramming system generally consists of one central processing unit and several input/output units. While one program is concerned with an input/output operation, the central processing unit can be performing an arithmetic or logic operation associated with another program. While one program requires a search of a disk file to locate a needed record, for example, requiring conceivably as much as a half-second, a large-

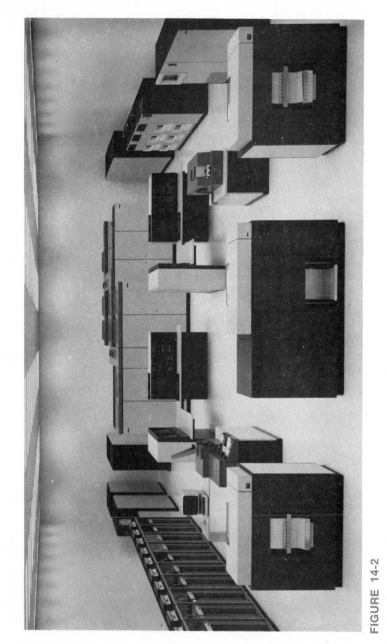

FIGURE 14-2

Multiprocessing system consisting of two IBM 370 Model 168 Processors

scale modern computer could be performing hundreds or thousands of operations on other programs being processed concurrently. This multi-programming capability makes it possible for the computer to juggle or "swap" several jobs back and forth within its memory and mass data-storage facilities. In so doing, the output or productivity of a computer can, literally, be multiplied by a factor of 5 or 10. The proper operation of a multiprogramming system requires a supervisory program or "supervisor," usually provided by the computer manufacturer with its hardware. One of the prime functions of this program is to determine in what order the programs will be processed as well as performing other essential control functions.

A multiprocessing system, on the other hand, is one that utilizes two or more interconnected central processing units at the same time to solve problems (Fig. 14-2). In this manner, several programs can be processed independently and simultaneously. Each processor has direct access to the system's memory, and each processor can perform computations and request input or output on individual programs stored in the system's memory.

To verify your understanding of the previous material, turn to page 518 and take Self-Test 14-5.

## TIME-SHARING INFORMATION SYSTEMS

An exact definition is difficult, as there are almost as many definitions as there are operational time-sharing systems. However, there are three basic characteristics that serve both to identify and to explain the meaning of time sharing: multiprogramming, online interaction, and real-time response. A time-shared information system must have the capability to provide a number of users with simultaneous access to one computer, thus sharing the available computer time. In such a system it is possible to reduce **idle time**—the time that the central processing unit is available for use but is not being used—by having the computer solve more than one problem at a time.

There are two basic modes of time-shared processing:

1. Conversational mode
2. Remote batch-processing mode

To say that a computer system is operating in the conversational mode simply means that real-time human–machine communications are maintained and that the computer system is being used extensively to support and service remote terminals. In this mode, each statement or request input by the user through a terminal is immediately processed and an appropriate reply sent back to the terminal. In this mode, the user may communicate great distances via telephone lines from the terminal to the computer. The language called BASIC was developed for this type of application. In this mode, the user may also call out previously written programs for the immediate processing of current input data.

Some of the advantages of time-shared processing in a conversational mode are

1. Immediate response to inquiries
2. Ease of learning to use remote terminals
3. Relatively low cost of terminal operation
4. Availability of the efficient and easily used language BASIC
5. Terminals can be installed virtually anywhere

"Actually, I didn't even *want* aluminum siding, but an automatic dialing machine sold it to my automatic answering machine."

A time-sharing information system operating in the remote batch-processing mode is also concerned with the shared use of a computer by several users concurrently. Terminals used in this system are quite different from those employed by a conversational time-sharing system, usually consisting of unsophisticated input/output devices such as a card reader and printer, and are often connected online to a small computer. This small computer is utilized as a remote terminal. In this manner, relatively inexpensive computers can be utilized to perform the time-consuming input/output operations while feeding a much larger, faster, and more expensive computer. That is, the larger, faster computer can concern itself principally with the processing of data fed to it by the smaller computer terminals.

However, the major disadvantage of such a system is that telephone lines are not suitable for communicating data from a computer terminal to the central computer; this makes it necessary for such computer terminals to be within close proximity and directly wired to the main computer.

A time-sharing information system can be equally beneficial to the large corporation as to the small business. However, when contemplating a time-sharing system, a business must be certain of its operational benefits before expending the 50% to 100% additional dollars that a time-shared information system could cost as compared to the cost of any of the previously mentioned information systems.

In the large corporation, such a system could provide for remote terminals in the office of all decision-making management personnel. From a terminal located hundreds or thousands of miles from the computer, a corporate executive could analyze a previously constructed corporate model concerning possible courses of action in a given situation. In a matter of moments a response could be received, in the form of displays on a cathode ray tube (similar in appearance to a commer-

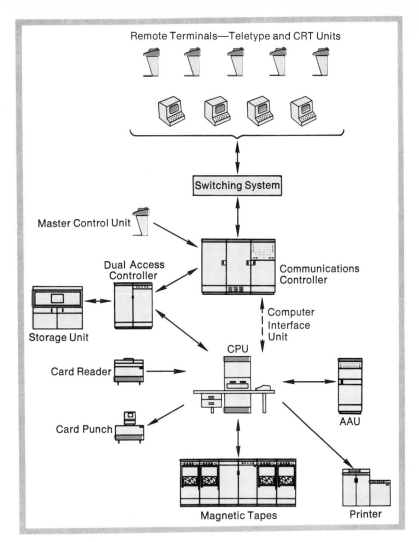

Remote Terminals—Teletype and CRT Units

Switching System

Master Control Unit

Dual Access Controller

Communications Controller

Storage Unit

Computer Interface Unit

CPU

Card Reader

AAU

Card Punch

Magnetic Tapes

Printer

**FIGURE 14-3**

A typical time-sharing system configuration

cial television set), or in printed form, containing detailed information concerning available alternatives. Armed with this information, the executive would be able to weigh the consequences of each alternative and select the most desirable course of action.

Equally important, however, is the fact that this entire process could have taken place without interrupting, in any way, the operations of numerous possible other corporate terminal users accessing the same computer and without an awareness on the part of any one user that he or she is not the only user of the computer.

Today many small business concerns are turning to service bureaus to buy time in a time-shared system. In this way the small user would have storage space made available in a centrally stored computer data bank or database. When operating a terminal a user would be totally unaware if he or she was the only user at that time or if there were 20 or 50 other users using the system at the same time. However, each user would have the computing power of a very large and expensive system available at only a fraction of the cost of maintaining the system, since he or she is sharing both the use and expense of the system with the other users.

Time-shared systems, although individually quite different in complexity, cost, and capabilities, possess certain common features:

1. Simultaneous operation: A time-sharing system must be capable of supporting many online terminals simultaneously.

2. Rapid response times: A time-sharing system must have response times which do not exceed several seconds. Response time includes the time required to transmit the inquiry from the terminal to the computer, processing time at the computer, the time required to locate and make ready for use any file records or data needed to answer the inquiry, and the time required to transmit the information back to the terminal.

3. Independent operations: A time-sharing system must provide the capability for each terminal to operate independently of every other terminal. System facilities must be capable of being used by any one user or shared with other users.

4. Flexibility: A time-sharing system should be flexible enough to handle, separately and simultaneously, a wide variety of applications ranging from the handling of online inquiries to offline processing.

5. Security controls: A time-sharing system must provide some degree of internal control to protect one user's programs and data from being accessed, used, changed, or destroyed by any unauthorized user.

A typical time-sharing system configuration is shown in Fig. 14-3.

**To verify your understanding of the previous material, turn to page 519 and take Self-Test 14-6.**

## INTEGRATED INFORMATION SYSTEMS

An integrated information system is one in which separate but related systems within a business are functionally united through the use of common data (Fig. 14-4). These data are recorded only once, generally at their source of origin, and are utilized directly by the processing systems in existing departments within the business. This minimizes the need to convert these data into different coded forms and minimizes the need to record or copy them onto different media, thus avoiding duplication of files.

Input recording devices used in an integrated information system include punched paper tape, magnetic tape, and transaction or point-of-data recorders.

Among the advantages of an integrated information system are

1. All departments within the business having access to the most up-to-date records

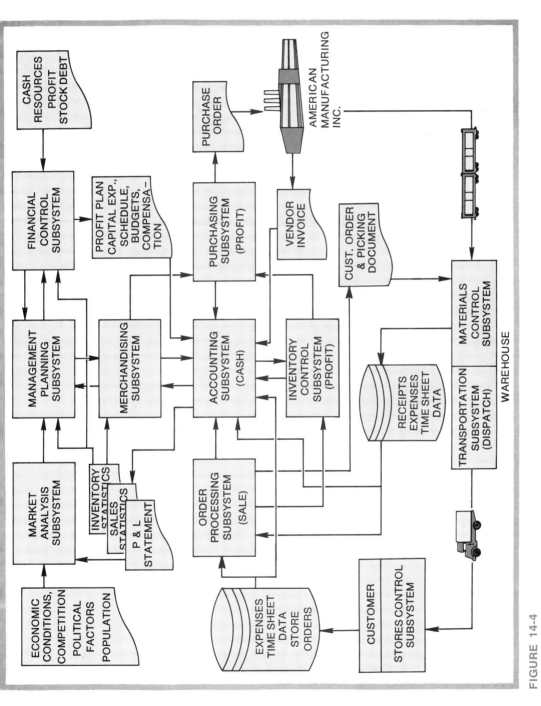

**FIGURE 14-4**

Integrated information and control system for the distribution industry

2. Reductions in the expense, time, and effort otherwise expended in duplicating input records

3. Increased overall speeds of processing transactions, updating files, and so on

4. Reduction in the amount of manual data handling required

**To verify your understanding of the previous material, turn to page 519 and take Self-Test 14-7.**

## MANAGEMENT INFORMATION SYSTEMS

There is little agreement concerning what a total or management information system (MIS) is supposed to be. However, it is possible to define a management information system in terms of what it should accomplish. In this context, a management information system can be described as an information system that can provide all levels of management with information essential to the running of the business. This information must be as relevant, timely, accurate, complete, and concise as is economically feasible. More specifically, a management information system should accomplish the following:

1. A database which is constantly kept current and accessible. This would necessitate the accurate updating of any and all conceivable files or data banks affected by any transaction occurring anywhere in the company and within an acceptable time span. Transaction data can be input either through an on-site input unit or through a remote data-collection station.

2. Automatic issuance of periodic information and reports in sufficient detail so as to allow management to take appropriate action.

3. Capability of producing special reports on demand.

4. Capability of accepting and answering real-time inquiries for information in greater scope or depth than issued in periodic reports. Such inquiry responses would incorporate any transactions which might have occurred since the last periodic report.

5. An efficient output communication network capable of disseminating management commands and decisions to appropriate output stations.

6. A self-checking feature to indicate a system failure or breakdown.

7. A built-in warning system to immediately inform the appropriate level of management of any out-of-line situations as they occur. This is often called **exception reporting**. In exception reporting, the computer reports only those situations when the actual results obtained differ from the management projected results.

8. Automatic comparison of transaction results with predetermined criteria and the automatic issuance of corresponding action instructions predefined policy limits. Such action instructions might include, for example, an instruction to order certain items of stock depleted by a transaction or an instruction to inform a particular customer that he has exceeded his credit limit.

Today, for most businesses, such a system is a management dream but not a reality. There are very few such systems actually in operation, although more and more are being implemented. By today's standards, this is the ultimate in automated information systems, and as costs decrease and the understanding of such a system by management increases, it is not unreasonable to assume that the number of organizations implementing management information systems will increase greatly.

To verify your understanding of the previous material, turn to page 519 and take Self-Test 14-8.

## DISTRIBUTED DATA PROCESSING

**Computing Systems**  Until the concept of distributed data processing (DDP), data processing was either centralized or decentralized. A **centralized computing system** provides advantages in both resource sharing and management control (see Fig. 14-6). The centralized facilities offer shared benefits to all users. Each user has access to a larger computer system with its associated peripherals and software support than would be possible with separate or dedicated computer systems. In addition, data-processing personnel resources can also be shared. This alone can be critically important as computer specialists such as systems programmers, communications specialists, and database administrators are difficult to find and, when available, very expensive.

FIGURE 14-5

Components of a typical distributed data processing system

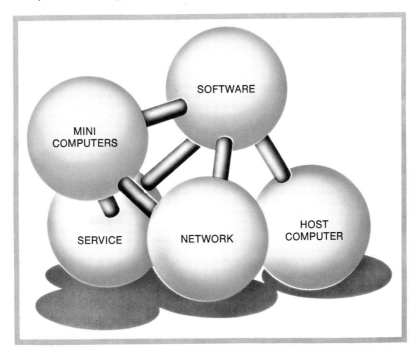

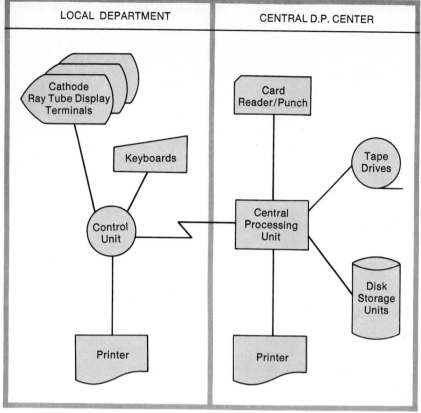

**FIGURE 14-6**

Centralized computing system

In addition to shared resources, a centralized computing system offers more effective management control. This permits closer coordination and communication among key personnel as well as sharing of facilities-oriented elements such as security and backup. More carefully detailed standards and procedures can be established at a centralized facility and are available to all users of the system. However, users of such systems must make compromises as are dictated by scheduling requirements to equalize the load and eliminate any peak-load situations.

A **decentralized computing system** provides strengths in the areas where centralized support is weak, but it possesses certain unique weaknesses of its own (see Fig. 14-7). The principal strengths of a decentralized computing system lie in the area of departmental or individual end-user support. In addition, departmental control is enhanced and support can be directed specifically to an individual department's needs. Support requirements of a decentralized system are, of course, less than those of a centralized system, as the user base is generally smaller and typically more homogeneous.

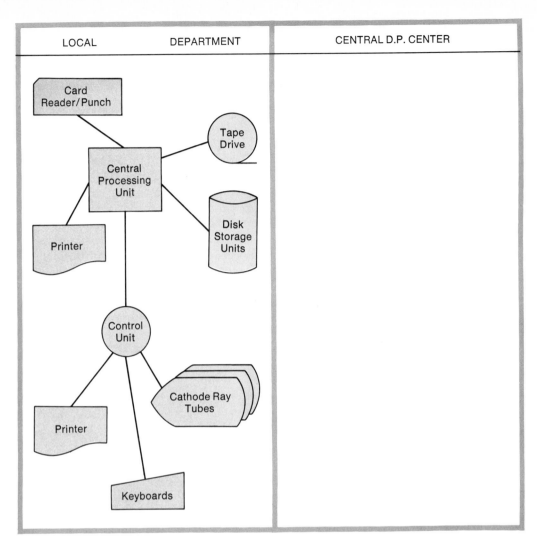

| LOCAL | DEPARTMENT | CENTRAL D.P. CENTER |

Card Reader/Punch

Tape Drive

Central Processing Unit

Printer

Disk Storage Units

Control Unit

Cathode Ray Tubes

Printer

Keyboards

**FIGURE 14-7**

Decentralized computing system

There is no question that availability is certainly enhanced, as there are no other users on the system. Thus there is less contention for the system's resources. Response times can possibly be improved because of the smaller number of users and decreased system complexity. System overhead is thus reduced. However, unless there are redundant resources available, there can be problems should a critical component malfunction and remain out of service for any period of time. Thus backup is required, and individual facility backup solutions can be more expensive than concentrating the backup in a central system. In addition, personnel and system resources are duplicated and are not always shared easily across departmental boundaries to provide backup support or to balance available capacity. One reason for this is that management control is limited when the facilities are dispersed.

"You'll have to forgive Howard. He was just *positive* you were bringing the floppy disk he ordered last week."

A **distributed data-processing** system, however, combines the advantages of both the centralized and decentralized computing systems. DDP emanates from a central host-supported base (see Fig. 14-8). As with any centralized system, this facilitates the sharing of the central resources, which include system resources such as the central processing unit, the host database, as well as personnel resources. In a distributed data-processing environment, tasks such as design and program development are by necessity centralized. Strong management control must be maintained at the host, while the distributed sites are monitored and controlled from the central facility. The hardware, software, and application support status of each site are known centrally. In addition, growth from a centralized site in a controlled manner permits the distributed sites to use existing applications software.

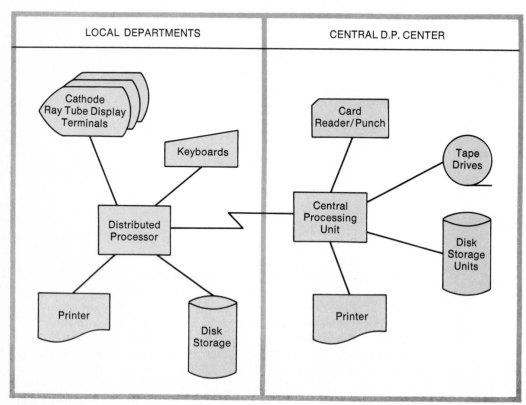

**FIGURE 14-8**

Distributed data processing system

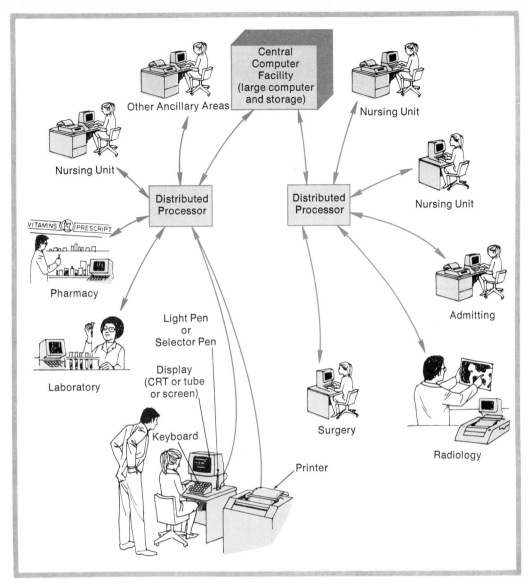

Central Computer Facility (large computer and storage)

Other Ancillary Areas

Nursing Unit

Nursing Unit

Distributed Processor

Distributed Processor

Nursing Unit

VITAMINS PRESCRIPT

Pharmacy

Admitting

Laboratory

Light Pen or Selector Pen

Display (CRT or tube or screen)

Keyboard

Surgery

Radiology

Printer

**FIGURE 14-9**

Typical hospital distributed data processing system

While taking advantage of the features of a centralized system, a distributed data-processing system also provides the user with additional functions and data. For example, many of the benefits of a decentralized computing system are realized by the users. Even though the total data processing environment may be complex and sophisticated, the individual distributed sites present a more structured and simpler environment. Fewer tasks and transactions are required to be handled at each of the distributed sites. Availability of resources and response times is enhanced. If the DDP system is appropriately designed, the remote sites can have a certain degree of independence from the host so that local operations can proceed uninterrupted for reasonable periods of time even in the event that the central facilities are unavailable.

Research has shown that response time can be greatly improved in both quantity and quality in a distributed data-processing environment. Not only are response times better, but they may also be more consistent and predictable. These factors are often more important than absolute response time alone. User control is also enhanced in a distributed data-processing environment. Both automated and manual interfaces tend to be more precisely defined. The user then has the degree of control and responsibility commensurate with the degree of data and functions available at the user's site.

**FIGURE 14-10**

Star or spider network

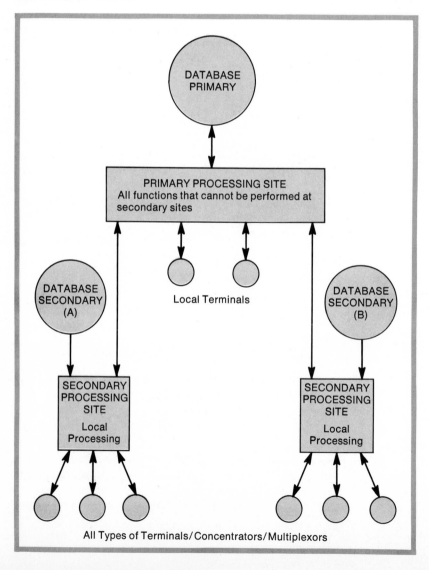

A typical hospital distributed data-processing system is shown in Fig. 14-9.

**Networks** There are two general configurations of distributed data-processing systems, the star or spider network and the ring network.

The **star** or **spider network** utilizes a host computer to which several remote computer systems are attached. In such a system all communications must be routed through the host computer before being routed to the appropriate satellite processing system. Such a system is illustrated in Fig. 14-10.

The **ring network** consists of several computer systems interconnected by a single communications line with no one system acting as host computer. Communications can take place directly between the satellite systems. Such a system is illustrated in Fig. 14-11. This is not to imply that these are the only type of networks in use or that the advantages of each type of network cannot be combined into more sophisticated network. Combination systems such as the one illustrated in Fig. 14-12 are in use. But, by and large, distributed data-processing systems are of the two types listed.

Most current distributed data-processing systems require some form of communications system for transmitting data between the host computer and its terminal or satellites and between satellites. Let us briefly examine the concepts of such a communication system.

FIGURE 14-11

Ring network

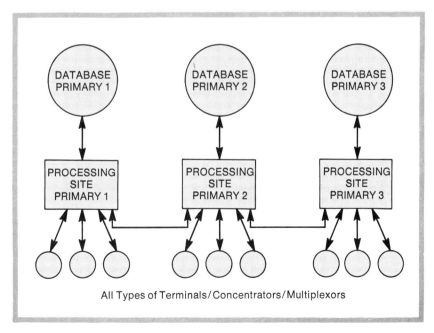

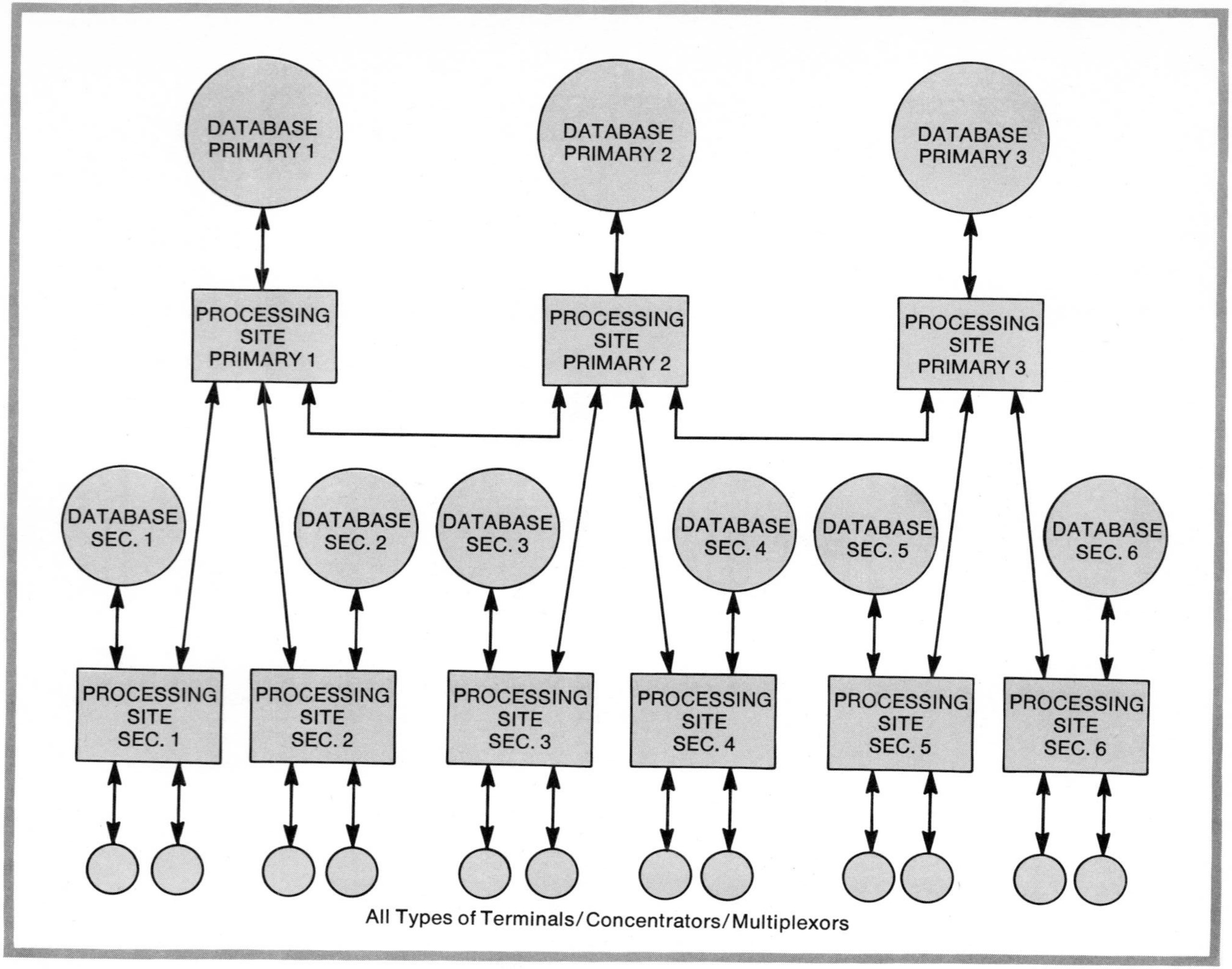

All Types of Terminals/Concentrators/Multiplexors

**FIGURE 14-12**
Combination ring and star network

**Data Communications/ Teleprocessing**

Every business with complex activities in one central location or with activities at several remote or satellite locations must provide for a system of data communications. Early communication systems utilized existing telephone and telegraph line to communicate data between the central computer and its satellites. This facilitated the communicating of large volumes of data without concern for weather or traffic conditions, which could otherwise cause significant delays. This kind of data communications has come to be known as **telecommunications**. The processing of data utilizing telecommunications is commonly referred to as **teleprocessing.**.

A typical teleprocessing system consists of five principal components:

1. Terminal: capable of input/output operations with or without a processing capability
2. Modem: to convert the data to and from a form suitable for telecommunications
3. Communications line: to carry the data to and from the computer and the terminal or between terminals
4. Transmission control unit: for decoding and verifying the transmitted data as well as separating the data received from several terminals into separate data elements
5. Multiplexor channel: to communicate the data to and from the CPU of the central computer

Communication lines used in teleprocessing are generally of three types: simplex, half-duplex, and duplex. A **simplex line**, like a one-way street, can carry information in one direction only. A **half-duplex line**, on the other hand, can facilitate communications in both directions, but only in one direction at a time. Users of citizens band radios have used this method of communicating for some time. A **duplex** or **full-duplex line**, as it is sometimes called, can carry information in both directions at the same time.

Today, communication lines are available from common carrier communication services such as American Telephone and Telegraph and Western Union that can transmit data at rates from below 100 bits per second to well over one megabit (1,000,000 bits) per second. For example, Satellite Business Systems (SBS), a satellite owned by IBM, Aetna, and COMSAT (Communications Satellite Corporation) jointly, can relay data at a rate of over 40 megabits per second.

The technical details of how data are encoded, transmitted, and decoded are beyond the scope of our presentation. However, should you desire this information, it can generally be obtained from any of the common carrier communication services.

To verify your understanding of the previous material, turn to page 519 and take Self-Test 14-9.

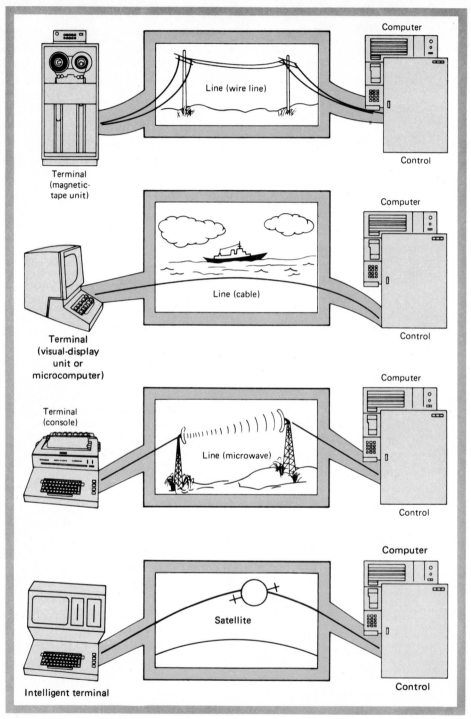

FIGURE 14-13

Examples of communication lines

# it's truly amazing

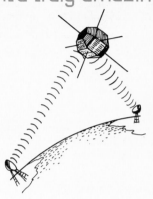

The SBS (Satellite Business Systems) satellite can relay messages at a rate of 40 million bits per second. It would take approximately one-half million people talking simultaneously to equal this rate.

# focus on the field

## Retailing

**Distributed processing key to retailers in 1980s**

Distributed information processing (DIP), with store-based micro and minicomputers networked to give instant aid in stock replenishment decisions, will be the competitive edge for retailers in the next decade.

What's more, according to Joseph Mallory of the Booz-Allen & Hamilton consulting firm, hardware is finally approaching the point where its essential, widespread use is technically and economically feasible. "We're moving into a new era that should be called an entirely new period in the history of mankind," said Mallory at the National Retail Merchants Association's annual EDP conference in Houston, TX, last fall. "It may be called the information revolution, when information technology is beginning to catch up with other fundamental technology.

"We're talking about every store in the mid-1980s having the option of an IBM-370/158-class machine, with more storage than you could ever think about using, for something like $20,000," he said. All this, he added is what makes distributed information processing really possible on the grand scale that is necessary to be truly effective.

Most urgent help is needed by the beleaguered "buyer," who according to Booz-Allen & Hamilton studies, makes an average 146,500 stock replenishment decisions a month. The biggest and most costly problem in retailing is stock replenishment, Mallory said. That means having the right items in the right stores at the right time and in appropriate quantities.

### DISCUSSION QUESTIONS

1. What kind of computers and systems will be used by retailers in the next decade?

2. What is the biggest and most costly problem that distributed processing is expected to alleviate?

## SELF-TEST 14-1

1. A(n) _____ can be defined as the interacting of humans and machines which, under human control, gathers data and disseminates information.
2. Unprocessed facts and figures are_____ , not_____ .
3. Some of the more common classifications of information systems are_____ .

## SELF-TEST 14-2

1. An_____ information system is one that is characterized by input/output or auxiliary equipment not under direct control of the computer and the collecting of data into groups before being submitted to the computer for processing.
2. A name associated with offline processing is_____ processing.
3. Batch processing *(is, is not)* used in applications where an up-to-date master file is needed at all times.
4. The main advantage of offline or batch processing is that_____ .
5. Some of the disadvantages of offline or batch processing are_____ .

## SELF-TEST 14-3

1. An online information system is one that is characterized by_____ .
2. In an online information system transactions can be_____ .
3. Utilization of an online information system will generally result in more up-to-date _____ than are possible with a _____ system.
4. Some of the disadvantages of an online information system are_____ .

## SELF-TEST 14-4

1. In a real-time information system, the time delay between a request for information and the actual delivery of this information is considered "insignificant" if_____ .
2. A_____ is the device commonly used to enter inquiries into an online real-time information system.
3. The response times associated with an online system are generally _____ than associated with an online real-time system.
4. In an online real-time system, each user must have access to any required online _____ stored within the system as though the computer was providing individual, exclusive service.
5. Real-time systems consist of five major components:_____ , _____ , _____ , _____ , and_____ .
6. The main disadvantage of an online real-time information system is_____ .

## SELF-TEST 14-5

1. A_____ system has the capability of executing two or more programs concurrently utilizing one central processing unit.

2. A multiprogramming capability makes it possible for the computer to _____ several jobs back and forth within its memory and data storage facilities.

3. The proper operation of a multiprogramming system requires a _____, usually provided by the computer manufacturer.

4. One of the prime functions of the supervisory program or "supervisor" in a multiprogramming environment is to determine _____.

5. A multiprogramming system can facilitate maximum usage of the _____.

6. A _____ system makes use of two or more interconnected central processing units.

## SELF-TEST 14-6

1. The three basic characteristics of a time-sharing information system are _____, _____, and _____.

2. _____ and _____ are the two basic modes of time-shared processing.

3. Time-shared information systems generally employ _____ as a means of communication between remote terminals and the central processing unit.

4. The language _____ was designed for use with time-sharing systems.

5. A _____ system often utilizes a small computer as a remote terminal, thus freeing the main computer to concern itself with _____.

6. A major advantage that time-sharing information systems offer to the small business is _____.

7. Common features of time-sharing systems are _____.

## SELF-TEST 14-7

1. An integrated information system is one in which separate but related systems are functionally united through _____.

2. The use of common data minimizes the need to _____, thus avoiding duplication of files.

3. Advantages of an integrated information system are _____.

## SELF-TEST 14-8

1. A management information system can be generally described as _____.

2. A management information system should maintain a database that is _____ and _____.

3. Exception reporting is _____.

4. Essential requirements of a management information system are _____.

## SELF-TEST 14-9

1. Prior to distributed data-processing systems, computer systems were either _____ or _____.

2. The two types of distributed data-processing networks are _____.

3. The processing of data utilizing telecommunications is referred to as _____ .

4. The three types of communications lines are _____ .

5. A _____ communication line is capable of two-way communications, but only in one direction at a time.

**Answers to Self-Tests**

14–1

1. information system

2. data; information

3. offline, online, multiprogram- ming, multiprocessing, time-sharing, integrated, manage-ment, and distributed data-processing

14–2

1. offline

2. batch or sequential

3. is not

4. it is so economical

5. time loss in preparing input batches, necessity to arrange input data and master files into sequence prior to processing, locking out of other users while a batch run is in progress, in-quiries are time-consuming, necessity for precise scheduling of computer usage on the part of operations personnel, and files are not always current be-cause of peak-load require-ments

14–3

1. input/output devices that are directly tied to and controlled by the CPU and are capable of two-way communications with the CPU

2. input to the system immediately

3. data files; batch

4. it is usually more expensive than batch processing, it gen-erally cannot handle large quantities of input or output at any one time, it occupies the CPU a great deal of the time, thus limiting its use for process-ing other applications

14–4

1. it reaches management in suf-ficient time and in an appro-priate form for use in making required decisions

2. terminal

3. significantly longer

4. data

5. computer; software; terminals; communications network; data-base

6. the tremendous associated ex-pense

14–5

1. multiprogramming

2. juggle or swap

3. supervisory program

4. in what order the programs will be processed

5. central processing unit

6. multiprocessing

14-6

1. multiprogramming; online interaction; real-time response

2. conversational; remote batch processing

3. telephone lines

4. BASIC

5. remote batch processing; the processing of data fed to it by the smaller computer terminal

6. the capability of a large-scale computer at a cost which is reasonable to the small user

7. simultaneous operation of many terminals, rapid response times, independent operation of terminals, flexibility, and security controls

14-7

1. the use of common data

2. copy or record data onto different media

3. common access to up-to-date

files, reduction in cost, time, and effort of duplicating records, increased overall processing speeds, reduced manual data handling

14-8

1. an information system that can provide all levels of management with information essential to the running of the business

2. current; accessible

3. where the system is designed to report any conditions that occur and are exceptions or out of line from what was anticipated

4. a database that is always cur-

rent and accessible, automatic issuance of periodic information and reports, capability of producing special reports on demand, real-time inquiry capability, efficient output communications network, a system self-checking feature, a built-in warning system to inform management of any unexpected occurrences, capability to issue routine instructions based on predefined conditions

14-9

1. centralized; decentralized

2. star or spider and ring

3. teleprocessing

4. simplex, half-duplex, and duplex or full-duplex

5. half-duplex

## EXERCISES

**14-1**
**True/False**

_____ 1. An information system can be defined as an interacting of humans and machine which, under human control, gathers data and disseminates information.

_____ 2. Exception reporting is where the system is designed to report any conditions that occur and are exceptions or out of line from what was anticipated.

_____ 3. The use of common data in an integrated information system minimizes the need to copy or record data onto different media.

_____ 4. The language BASIC was originally designed for use with time-sharing information systems.

_____ 5. In a real-time information system, the time delay between a request for information and the delivery of this information is considered "insignificant" if it occurs within a few seconds.

_____ 6. A characteristic of an online information system is input/output devices that are directly tied to the CPU.

_____ 7. A multiprocessing system has the capability of executing two or more programs concurrently utilizing one CPU.

_____ 8. Time-shared information systems generally employ telephone lines for communications when operating in a conversational mode.

_____ 9. The magnetic tape storage medium is often used when batch processing.

_____ 10. Because of their increased costs, time-sharing systems are generally limited to large companies.

_____ 11. Management information systems are generally used by top management only.

_____ 12. Conversational mode simply means that the computer is being used extensively to support and service remote terminals.

_____ 13. Batch processing necessitates immediate input of data, not just when it is economically feasible.

_____ 14. The terms "multiprogramming" and "multiprocessing" are synonymous.

_____ 15. Terminals for use with a time-sharing system must be installed near the CPU.

_____ 16. Time-shared systems offer certain common features such as simultaneous operation and rapid response time.

_____ 17. Multiprogramming efficiency is dependent on the supervisory program.

_____ 18. The terminals employed in a time-shared system operating in the remote-batch mode are the same as those employed in a conversational mode.

_____ 19. Both management information systems and integrated information systems require an extensive database.

_____ 20. With the use of a batch system, precise scheduling is no longer needed to use the CPU efficiently.

_____ 21. A time-shared information system allows many users to access one computer simultaneously.

_____ 22. Programs run on an online system occupy the system most of the time, thus limiting its use for processing other applications.

_____ 23. In a multiprogramming environment, a computer is able to juggle or swap several jobs back and forth between its memory and secondary storage facility.

_____ 24. In response to an inquiry for the current price of IBM stock, the price is displayed at the stockbroker's desk in up to 3 seconds. This would be considered a real-time system.

25. Time-sharing users could possibly pirate information from competitors in the same system unless proper security precautions were taken.

26. A large department store which inventories, reorders, adjusts sales commissions, computes tax, etc. from a database being updated by sales information is using an integrated information system.

27. In an offline information system, input data generally need not be sequenced before they are submitted for processing.

28. For many purposes, a time-sharing system could be considered to be operating in real time.

29. Computer control of a space mission must operate in a real-time mode.

30. A major disadvantage of a remote batch time-sharing system is that telephone lines are generally not suitable for communicating data from the terminal to the central computer over great distances at high speed.

**14-2**
**Multiple-choice**

1. A system in which I/O devices and auxiliary equipment are not under the direct control of the computer are classified as
   a. batched-process systems
   b. sequential-process systems
   c. offline systems
   d. continuous-process systems
   e. none of the above

2. Around-the-clock operation is sometimes necessary during peak loads, which are prevalent in
   a. offline systems
   b. online systems
   c. time-sharing systems
   d. all of the above
   e. none of the above

3. The information system best suited for small, active businesses with a large inventory would be
   a. offline
   b. online
   c. online real-time
   d. time-sharing
   e. none of the above

4. Time-sharing can be economically justifiable for
   a. large businesses with several locations across the country
   b. large businesses located in one city only
   c. small businesses with large computer needs
   d. all of the above
   e. (a) and (b) only

5. BASIC is a computer language developed for
   a. online systems

b. online real-time systems
c. time-sharing systems
d. multiprogramming systems
e. none of the above

_____ 6. A requirement of an integrated information system is
a. a large, common database
b. separate but related systems
c. common type input/output devices
d. all of the above
e. (a) and (b) only

_____ 7. Time spent by the CPU's waiting to process data
a. is called waiting time
b. no longer exists with modern computer systems
c. is not charged to the user
d. is called idle time
e. none of the above

_____ 8. In a multiprogramming system it is possible to reduce idle time by
a. shutting off the computer between jobs
b. having the computer solve more than one problem concurrently
c. there is no way of reducing idle time
d. batching data
e. none of the above

**14-3** 1. The two basic modes of time-shared processing are _____ and _____ .

**Fill-in** 2. A characteristic of an _____ information system is that transactions can be input to the system as they occur.

3. An offline information system is also called a _____ information system.

4. A _____ program is required for the proper operation of a multiprogramming system.

5. One of the main advantages of an offline information system is that it is generally more _____ than other types of information systems.

6. Features of a time-shared information system include _____ .

7. Two characteristics of the database associated with a management information system are that it is _____ and _____ .

8. The major components associated with a real-time information system are _____ .

9. A _____ device is commonly used to enter inquiries into an online real-time information system.

10. The basic characteristics of a time-shared information system are _____ .

**14-4** 1. Discuss several of the more common classifications of information systems.

**Problems** 2. List and discuss the major differences between an offline information system and an online information system

3. What is meant by a real-time system?

4. What are the advantages and disadvantages of a real-time system?

5. Discuss the following statement: "An online information system is not always a real-time information system, but a real-time information system must consist of equipment with an online capability."

6. Define and discuss the terms "multiprogramming" and "multiprocessing." Indicate their similarities and differences.

7. What are the characteristics of a timed-shared information system?

8. What do you think are the main reasons for the rapid growth of time-sharing information systems?

9. Compare time-sharing in a conversation mode with time-sharing in a remote batch mode.

10. Describe the characteristics of a management information system.

11. Discuss the relationship between an integrated information system and a management information system.

12. Why do you think there are so few currently operational management information systems?

13. Give examples from your own experience of uses for each of the information systems discussed in this chapter.

INTRODUCTION

FUNDAMENTAL ACCOUNTING SYSTEMS

PAYROLL SYSTEM

Objectives

Payroll Master File

Weekly Attendance Time Card

Earnings File

Deduction Authorizations

Bank Reconciliation File

Payroll Audit Register

Payroll Register

Check and Earnings Statement

Bank Reconciliation Report

Deduction Registers

Tax Reports

Management Reports

FOCUS ON THE FIELD

SELF-TESTS

EXERCISES

# CHAPTER 15

# Business Systems

## INTRODUCTION

When computers were first introduced on the business scene in the early 1950s, they served as a replacement for the tabulating machine and were therefore programmed to perform repetitive and routine calculations. As the advantages and versatility of the computer became more apparent to management, the areas of computer applications were expanded from the performing of simple computations to the handling of business accounting functions, until today the computer has become an integral part of every phase of the operations of a business, a **total-systems concept.** Previously separate and autonomous functions of the business entity, such as payroll and inventory, have been combined into and work harmoniously together as, a total system. One could say that the business organization is one large, all-encompassing total system. This large or total system, then, is a composite of many smaller and interrelated systems. Each system is responsible for carrying out a major accounting function within the business enterprise, in addition to working in concert with other systems to function as a total system. This concept is illustrated in Fig. 15-1. If you were to carefully examine the individual systems which comprise the total system, you will discover that they represent the major accounting functions required to control the operations of a business no matter how large or small that business might be. In view of the importance of these systems to the overall operations of the business entity, it should be quite clear that a basic knowledge of the purpose and objectives of these systems is essential to any individual intending to enter the business world as an accountant, business manager, or in any other position of responsibility. Therefore, in this chapter we will discuss one of these systems in detail—a payroll system.

Upon completing this chapter you should be able to:
- Describe the nature and purpose of a payroll system
- List the required and optional reports contained in such a system
- Describe each of the reports produced by a payroll system
- Name the fundamental accounting systems
- Define the following terms:
  Bank reconciliation report     Deduction registers
  Check and earnings     Management reports
     statement     Payroll audit register

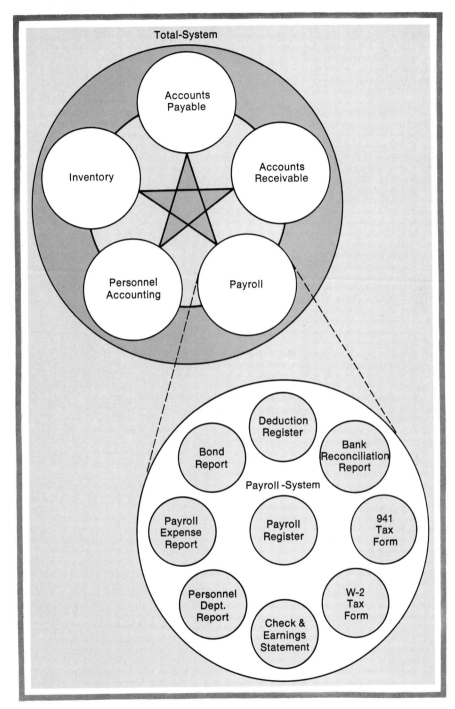

FIGURE 15-1

A total business system and its major subsystems

Payroll register                     Tax reports
Payroll system                       Total system concept

## FUNDAMENTAL ACCOUNTING SYSTEMS

We can see from Fig. 15-1 that the five basic systems within a business entity are

1. Payroll
2. Accounts payable
3. Accounts receivable
4. Inventory
5. Personnel accounting

We will now review the output and procedures inherent in a typical payroll system. This system is somewhat simplified, less sophisticated and more card-oriented than those presently in use in many business organizations. In using this simplified approach, however, the components and functions commonly found in such a system will be illustrated in a clearer and more easily understood manner. To this end, the detailed documentation that would normally be required as an integral part of the design and programming of this system has also been omitted. However, to tie together and more clearly illustrate previously discussed concepts and procedures, some of the documentation associated with the development of the deduction register in a payroll system has been provided in the Appendix at the end of this chapter. It is suggested that this material be reviewed following the discussion of the deduction register.

To verify your understanding of the previous material, turn to page 546 and take Self-Test 15-1.

## PAYROLL SYSTEM

Today, organizations of all sizes employ the paycheck as the means of remunerating their employees for services rendered. The production of the paycheck and associated reports might seem to be a simple task, but in practice it is as involved as any of the other business systems.

Employees have bills to pay and depend on receiving their checks on time and for the correct amount. Considerations must also be made in such a system for special cases such as advanced payment of salaries for employees going on trips or vacations and for correction of any errors that might occur anywhere in the process. In addition, careful consideration should be given to what should be done in the event that the computer should fail before or during the preparation of employee checks. In many companies consideration must be given to a second or

"About our prospects for that merger, it says: 'you have a snowball's chance in ....'"

executive payroll run. Since check forms usually contain a statement limiting the amount to which the check can be drawn, special check forms must be used for the larger executive salaries. And the job of preparing the payroll for an organization becomes increasingly difficult as the number of persons employed increases.

Therefore, it should be apparent that a payroll system is far from a trivial system; in fact, it is a complex one.

The advantages of an automated payroll system are

1. Expensive and time-consuming clerical operations can be drastically reduced, if not eliminated entirely.
2. Accounting and analytical reports can be produced in great detail and as a byproduct of the payroll preparation.
3. Federal and state reports can be routinely produced by the computer, eliminating the peak workloads normally associated with their preparation.
4. Departmental payroll expense reports and comparisons of the expended amounts with budget amounts can be prepared easily and with sufficient dispatch to render them useful.
5. Payroll expense summary reports as well as current period and year-to-date employee earning comparisons can be easily prepared as scheduled, providing management with up-to-the-minute data concerning the company's payroll expenses.

Let us now examine, in detail, the specific objectives of a payroll system and how these objectives can be satisfied.

**Objectives**    The general objective of a payroll system is to perform certain required accounting functions and to produce associated reports. To accomplish this general objective, the following specific objectives must be reached.

1. Preparation of the payroll audit
2. Preparation of the payroll register
3. Preparation of the check and earnings statement
4. Preparation of the bank reconciliation report
5. Preparation of the deduction registers
6. Preparation of the tax reports
7. Preparation of the management reports

To prepare the reports and maintain the records stated above, one must determine the original documents and files from which required information can be secured. This required information would include such items as

1. Employee name
2. Employee number
3. Employee position, description, and code
4. Social Security number
5. Department/service assigned
6. Authorized deductions and amounts
7. Regular hours worked and rate
8. Overtime hours worked and rate
9. Expense account number charged

Much of this information, if not all, is available from one or more of the following sources:

1. Payroll master file
2. Weekly attendance time cards
3. Earnings file
4. Deduction authorizations
5. Reconciliation file

**Payroll Master File**  All pertinent information about each employee is contained on this file. In many companies the payroll master file is used in their payroll systems and also used in their personnel accounting system, since much of the information contained in this file is required by each of the systems. This file generally contains employee information such as

| | |
|---|---|
| Branch store where employed | Date of birth |
| Department | Sex |
| Employee number | Marital status |
| Employee name | Actual dependents |
| Employee home address | Education |
| Salary code | Military service or status |
| Base salary | Physical condition code |
| Scheduled hours | Date employed |
| City withholding | Special skills codes |
| State withholding | Dependents declared for tax purposes |
| Federal withholding | FICA deduction |
| Accumulated sick days | Accumulated federal withholding |
| Accumulated vacation days | Accumulated state withholding |
| Accumulated earnings | Accumulated city withholding |
| Hourly rate | Disability deduction |

|                    |                        |
|--------------------|------------------------|
| Accumulated FICA   | Medical deduction      |
| Bond deduction     | Credit union deduction |
| Bond denomination  | Union dues deduction   |
| Bond balance       | Quarterly gross        |

Depending upon the company, the payroll master file may be significantly more or less detailed than the one illustrated.

This file is utilized for the preparation of almost every report associated with a payroll system and must therefore be updated weekly if not more often.

**Weekly Attendance Time Card**
Attendance and time records are the basis of payroll computations in any payroll system. The maintenance of these records is required of every business by the Federal Fair Labor Standards Act.

The source of data for these records is the weekly attendance time sheet or time card. Time cards can be of the type illustrated in Fig. 15-2 or any of several other types used by business concerns. Regardless of the method used, the following basic information will be required:

1. Employee number
2. Employee name
3. Hours worked

Exception attendance records are also prepared for employees who worked other than standard hours or shifts.

**Earnings File**
This file contains the information about an employee necessary for the printing of his paycheck and statement. It also contains data necessary for the reconciling of outstanding checks. This file is created from the payroll master file and weekly attendance data.

**Deduction Authorizations**
Deduction authorization forms similar to that given in Fig. 15-3 are used by an organization to determine the voluntary deduction an employee desires made. A separate deduction card must be keypunched for each employee-authorized deduction. These deduction cards are then used to update the payroll master file.

**Bank Reconciliation File**
This file consists of information relative to unreconciled checks. It is processed with the earnings file to reconcile returned checks. Information concerning any unreconciled check for a given pay period is taken from the earnings file for that pay period and is used to update the bank reconciliation file.

**Payroll Audit Register**
At the end of each week, the employee attendance records and exception attendance records are input into the computer together with control cards prepunched with departmental budget controls for employee position code counts and hours. Unusual conditions such as missing attendance records or over-budget conditions are printed out

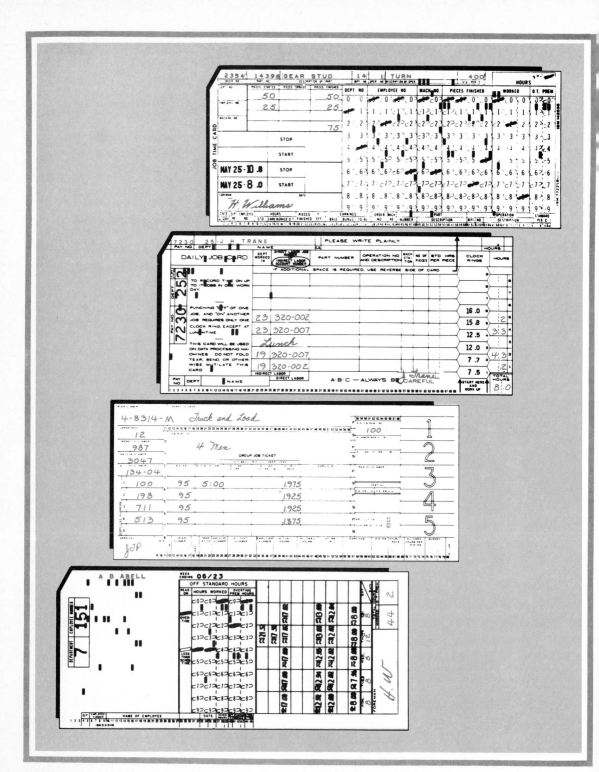

**FIGURE 15-2**

Sample time cards

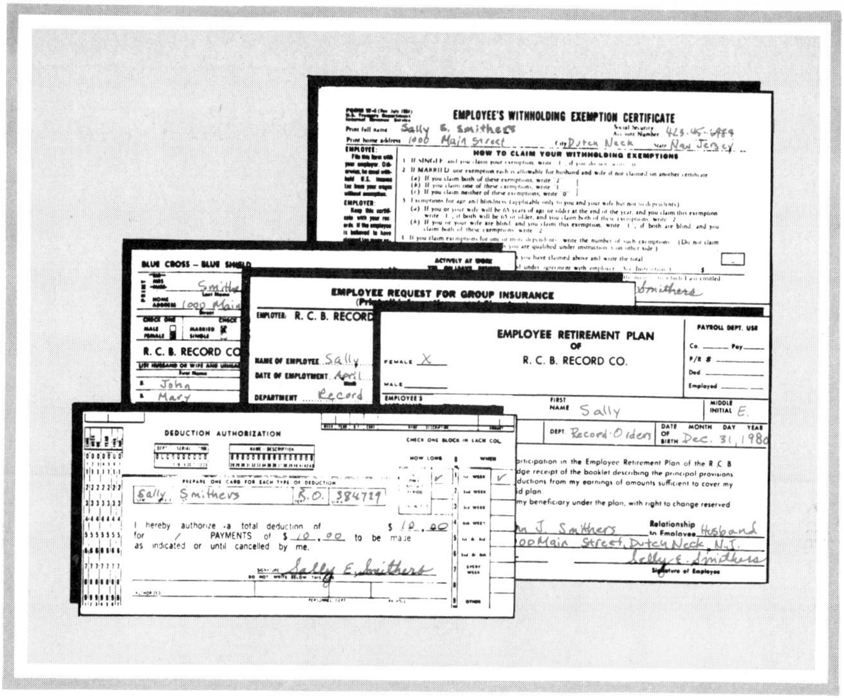


FIGURE 15-3

Sample deduction authorization forms

(Figs. 15-4 and 15-5). When management approval is given, the remainder of the payroll procedures can commence.

**Payroll Register** The payroll register is a report that shows in detail the earnings and deductions of all employees (Figs. 15-6 and 15-7). It is produced

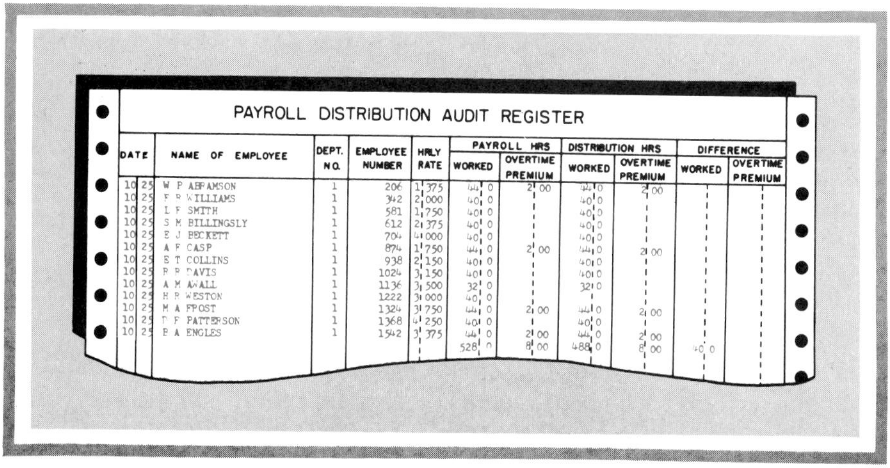

PAYROLL DISTRIBUTION AUDIT REGISTER

| DATE | | NAME OF EMPLOYEE | DEPT. NO. | EMPLOYEE NUMBER | HRLY RATE | PAYROLL HRS WORKED | PAYROLL HRS OVERTIME PREMIUM | DISTRIBUTION HRS WORKED | DISTRIBUTION HRS OVERTIME PREMIUM | DIFFERENCE WORKED | DIFFERENCE OVERTIME PREMIUM |
|---|---|---|---|---|---|---|---|---|---|---|---|
| 10 | 25 | W P ABRAMSON | 1 | 206 | 1 375 | 44 0 | 2 00 | 44 0 | 2 00 | | |
| 10 | 25 | F R WILLIAMS | 1 | 342 | 2 000 | 40 0 | | 40 0 | | | |
| 10 | 25 | L F SMITH | 1 | 581 | 1 750 | 40 0 | | 40 0 | | | |
| 10 | 25 | S M BILLINGSLY | 1 | 612 | 2 375 | 40 0 | | 40 0 | | | |
| 10 | 25 | E J BECKETT | 1 | 704 | 4 000 | 40 0 | | 40 0 | | | |
| 10 | 25 | A F CASP | 1 | 874 | 1 750 | 44 0 | 2 00 | 44 0 | 2 00 | | |
| 10 | 25 | E T COLLINS | 1 | 938 | 2 150 | 40 0 | | 40 0 | | | |
| 10 | 25 | R R DAVIS | 1 | 1024 | 3 150 | 40 0 | | 40 0 | | | |
| 10 | 25 | A M AWALL | 1 | 1136 | 3 500 | 32 0 | | 32 0 | | | |
| 10 | 25 | H R WESTON | 1 | 1222 | 3 000 | 40 0 | | | | | |
| 10 | 25 | M A FROST | 1 | 1324 | 3 750 | 44 0 | 2 00 | 44 0 | 2 00 | | |
| 10 | 25 | D F PATTERSON | 1 | 1368 | 4 250 | 40 0 | | 40 0 | | | |
| 10 | 25 | B A ENGLES | 1 | 1542 | 3 375 | 44 0 | 2 00 | 44 0 | 2 00 | | |
| | | | | | | 528 0 | 8 00 | 488 0 | 8 00 | 40 0 | |

FIGURE 15-4

Payroll audit register showing an error

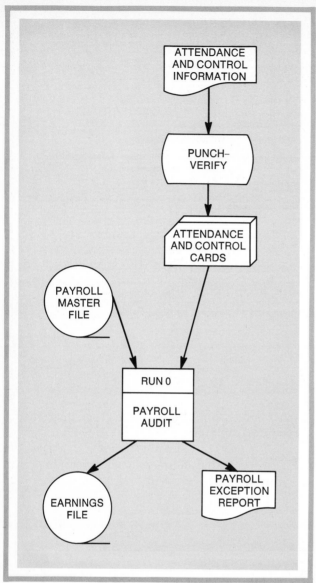

**FIGURE 15-5**

Flowchart of payroll audit run

from the earnings file. Control totals are produced for verification of payroll calculations and payroll account cash requirements.

When the payroll register has been approved, the check and earnings statement can be run.

**Check and Earnings Statement**   Checks and earnings statements are produced from the earnings file after the payroll register has been verified (Figs. 15-8 and 15-9). The forms used are preprinted and perforated vertically down the center. One side is the payroll check, and the other the earnings statement. As the checks and earnings statements are printed, a reconciliation file

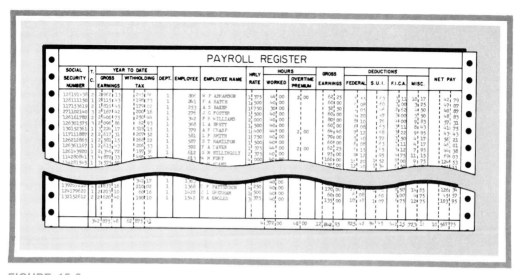

FIGURE 15-6

Typical payroll register

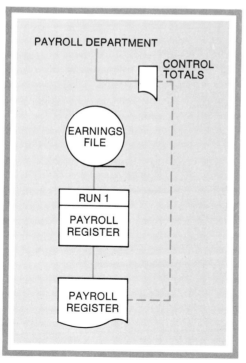

FIGURE 15-7

Flowchart of payroll register run

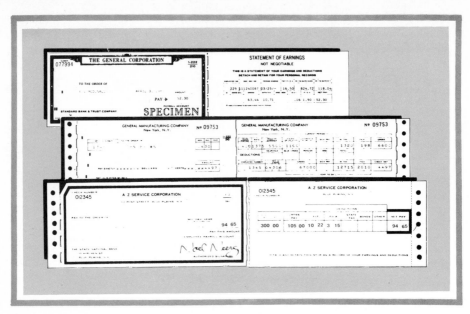

**FIGURE 15-8**

Sample payroll checks and earnings statements

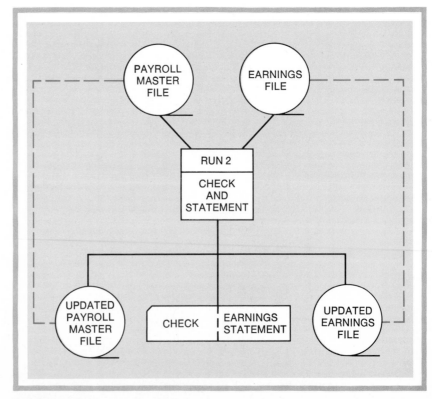

**FIGURE 15-9**

System flowchart for check and earnings statement run

is also created and the check numbers are added to the earnings file. In addition, year-to-date figures are updated on the payroll master file.

**Bank Reconciliation Report**   As the checks are processed by the bank, a file is generally created which is returned to the company together with the canceled checks. This bank file is then matched against the reconciliation file (data concerning old, unreconciled checks) and the earnings file (data concerning the current pay period checks). Outstanding checks are listed on the bank reconciliation report together with the totals of matched and unmatched checks. Unreconciled checks from the current pay period are also added to the reconciliation file (Fig. 15-10).

**Deduction Registers**   After the earnings file has been used to prepare the check and statement, it is again used to prepare the various deduction registers. One register can be prepared for all types of voluntary deductions, or one register can be prepared for each type of voluntary deduction allowable (Figs. 15-11 and 15-12). These deduction registers may then be used as records for outside individuals or organizations such as banks and insurance associations.

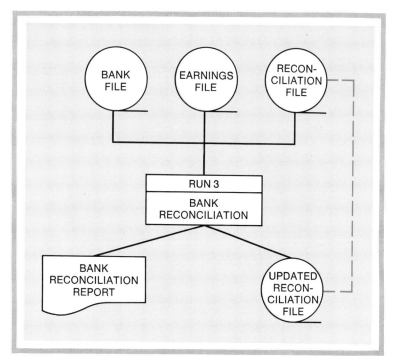

FIGURE 15-10

Flowchart of bank reconciliation report

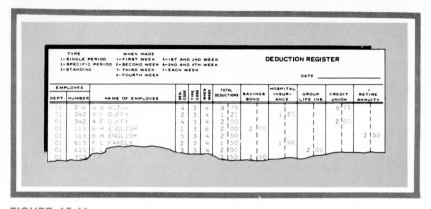

FIGURE 15-11

Sample payroll deduction register

Some of the documentation generated during the design and programming of this subsystem is illustrated in the Appendix at the end of this chapter.

**Tax Reports**    Tax reports are generated from the payroll master file and contain cumulative totals of taxable earnings, FICA deductions, and federal and state withholding taxes (Figs. 15-13 and 15-14). These are generally prepared quarterly or annually and include such reports as the federal W2 and 941 forms.

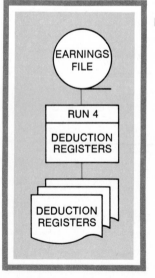

FIGURE 15-12

Flowchart of deduction register run

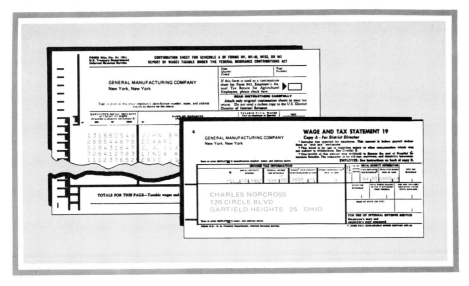

FIGURE 15-13

Sample tax reports

**Management Reports**   As we mentioned earlier, one of the advantages of a computerized payroll system is that many detailed and timely reports can be prepared for management as a spinoff of the basic payroll runs (Fig. 15-15). Such reports in the hands of management can facilitate a careful and fruitful evaluation of the organization which would otherwise be impos-

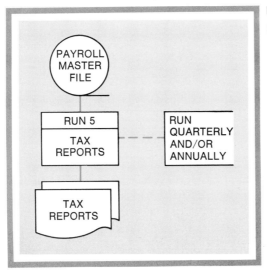

FIGURE 15-14

Flowchart of tax report run

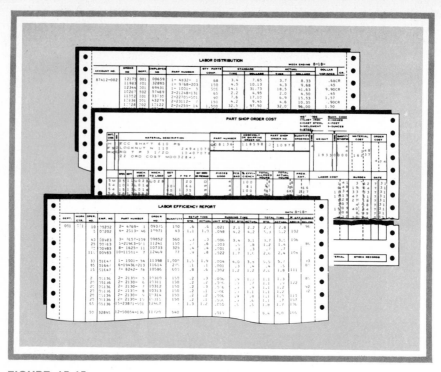

**FIGURE 15-15**

Representative management reports

"I think I forgot to tell the computer that Bambi is a Great Dane."

sible. Reports which, if desired by management, can be easily provided as the result of an automated payroll system might include

1. Labor cost analysis: This report would contain a cost breakdown per item produced in terms of materials used, manhours expended, and so forth.

2. Employee daily performance record: Such a report might be provided for department heads and would include an analysis of time expended and output produced by employees. Such a report would be useful when considering employees for increases in salary and responsibility.

3. Absentee ratio by department: This report would inform management at a glance if there were any departments with exceptionally good or exceptionally bad attendance records. Appropriate action could then be taken swiftly and effectively.

4. Departmental expense ratio report: This report would inform management of the ratio of supervisory to nonsupervisory personnel. This information could then be matched against the department output record to determine if the department is appropriately staffed or administratively top-heavy.

These are only some of the many reports that management might request *and get* quickly and easily as the result of an automated payroll system.

To verify your understanding of the previous material, turn to page 546 and take Self-Test 15-2.

# focus on the field

## An Outside Auditor Looks In
### by Thomas McCarty

Are you ready for the new auditor? No longer recognized by his green eye shade, today's trained specialist is technically qualified and he is no longer likely to become confused by technical terms. In fact, he is armed with a few terms of his own, stemming from development of new and innovative approaches to auditing in a computer environment.

Auditors of years past may have been satisfied to form their auditing opinions by holding discussions with the accounting and operations people, and rely on various tests and procedural reviews, but in today's computer-oriented business environment that's not enough. Now, a whole new set of analytical techniques have been created that focus on the role the computer plays in a company's financial systems. So the next time an outside accountant comes around to do "risk analysis" in preparation for developing "transaction flow analysis flow charts," which guide him in developing the scope of his "predictive auditing" and "compliance testing," you know the auditor has arrived.

This article is intended to provide insight into how an outside auditor looks at your systems. Hopefully, it will also renew your awareness of the importance of internal controls. Perhaps the best way to think about the importance of internal controls is in the words of the renowned philosopher, "Murphy," who said:

- If there is a possibility of several things going wrong, the one that goes wrong first will do the most damage.
- If everything seems okay, something obviously has been overlooked.
- It is impossible to make anything fool-proof because fools are so ingenious.

If your internal controls are in place before the audit, you can sit back and relax when the auditors arrive. Here is an outsider's view of why the auditors are there, what they will be doing and how it will affect you the person responsible for your computer systems' effectiveness.

### Who They Are

Each company that has publicly traded stock is required to obtain an independent audit of its financial statements. Privately held companies also obtain audits, either as a result of requirements imposed by a third party, such as a bank, or simply to protect the owners' interest and assure them that the financial statements fairly reflect the company's financial position and results of operations. In addition, suggestions for improving procedures, internal controls and reporting are important byproducts.

Typically, audits are performed by representatives of public accounting firms—certified public accountants. The audit is performed by one or more staff members, supervised by a manager under the overall direction of a partner in the firm. Increasingly, the audit team is supplemented by computer specialists who are typically part of the accounting firm's consulting division.

The auditors' visit to the dp center is a part of their overall review of the company's internal controls. And they use many techniques to evaluate accuracy of a company's books and records. Consider accounts receivable, for example. In a very small company, with manual systems and low volumes, it might be possible for the auditors to completely verify account balances by confirming with each customer that the amount shown on the monthly statement accurately represents the amount receivable from the customers. In this way, the auditors could obtain 100 percent satisfaction that the accounts receivable balance in the company's accounts is accurate. However, in a more realistic situation, volumes do not permit such an exhaustive examination; hence, the auditors must find other ways of assuring accuracy.

Professional standards require the auditors to assess a company's internal controls and then, based on that evaluation, to determine the work necessary to verify the account balances. If a company appears to have strong internal controls, the auditors might rely on contacting a small sample of accounts by mail. However, if the internal controls are weak, the auditors may elect to circularize a large number of customers as well as to perform various accuracy tests.

The auditors want to determine if transactions are properly authorized, if there are physical safeguards over financial data, if transactions are accurately processed and if there are procedures to insure that financial data is substantiated and properly evaluated. To meet these objectives, the auditors interview various data processing personnel and review documentation and physical resources. Their discussions with management and staff generally cover the following areas:

- Organization and management of departments
- Application systems development
- Application systems maintenance
- Computer operations
- Data control and data entry

In more specific terms, the auditors will discuss the flow of data and the input, processing, and output controls in the system.

### What They Usually Find

There are any number of systems control weaknesses common to small business systems. In general, the auditors are most concerned with problems in the application areas that could affect the computer reports that are the basis for the financial statements. For example, consider the accounts receivable trial balance which supports the company's accounts receivable balance. The trial balance identifies each customer and the amount owed. The auditor is concerned that this is a full and complete listing and that the amounts owed and the aging of those amounts is accurate. The following examples illustrate processing errors that might occur if controls are inadequate:

- The total accounts receivable trial balance does not equal the accounts receivable account in the general ledger. Not all customers appear on the trial balance.
- There are mathematical errors in the calculations of invoice amounts.
- Inaccurate prices are used in the invoicing.
- Payments are applied to the wrong customer.
- There is no invoice register nor copies of invoices which support the amounts on the trial balance.

There are many other instances of control deficiencies. It is left to the auditor to focus on the causes of these problem areas and this is the thrust of the evaluation.

The auditor typically has a checklist of commonly used control techniques that serves as a starting point for evaluating system controls. The checklist is likely to be organized in the following manner:

- Organization and management of the EDP department. This item relates to the techniques used to define and communicate the department's structure, policies and procedures that reasonably assure that personnel perform their duties correctly and procedures and controls are followed. Also, it focuses on the extent to which there is a division of responsibilities among operations, programming and user personnel. Strict separation of duties help minimize errors and reduce the risk of deliberate fraud by any one person.
- Data entry and control. Techniques should be used that assure only approved input is accepted by the data processing department. These include a data control function, input/output logs, reconciliation of control totals and others. As on-line systems are of increasing concern, the auditor looks for controls that protect against accidental or deliberate access to unauthorized programs or files. They also check for a reporting mechanism to monitor the system utilization.
- Input controls. For each application being reviewed, the auditor is interested in the techniques used to assure that all the input is accepted for processing. These include batch controls, input control logs, prenumbered documents and cancelled source documents. Input controls within the computer system include various validation or editing techniques such as check digits, reasonableness tests, valid account number tables and the use of reference files. Procedures should ensure that errors are corrected and resubmitted.

The increasing use of terminals introduces many new concerns. The terminals should be secured when not in use; control passwords should be in place for access to the system; and access authorization tables should restrict terminals and/or individuals only for certain transactions.

- Processing controls. All systems should include techniques to determine that transactions are processed against an appropriate record on a master file. These include verification against the master file before processing, approved signatures on maintenance transaction, reports which show the before-and-after contents of fields being changed, and programs that develop control totals.
- Output controls. Reports should be scrutinized by responsible personnel to determine overall reasonableness. Also, there should be appropriate audit trail reports, and control totals should be available for reconciliation.

## After It's Over

The auditor's final report renders a conclusion regarding the company's financial records. Typically a supplemental but less formal report is prepared that includes other observations and recommendations. This supplemental report typically would include any comments and suggestions that relate to the data processing area. Such comments would normally be reviewed with the data processing manager prior to the final report going to top management. □

## DISCUSSION QUESTIONS

1. What is the purpose of an audit and what does an auditor look for in an audit?
2. What do auditors generally find?

## SELF-TEST 15–1

1. The term *total system* as it applies to a business organization is _____.
2. The individual systems within a total system comprise _____.
3. The five basic systems within a total system are _____, _____, _____, _____, and _____.

## SELF-TEST 15–2

1. The principal input for payroll computations is the _____.
2. Some of the reports that must be prepared in connection with a payroll system are _____.
3. The _____ serves to identify any unusual conditions prior to the printing of the payroll register and checks and statements.
4. The payroll register is a report that lists _____.
5. The _____ is the basic input from which the various tax reports are created.
6. The two most common tax reports are the _____ and the _____.

**Answers to Self-Tests**

15–1

1. a composite of many smaller and interrelated systems
2. the major accounting functions required to control the operations of a business
3. accounts receivable; accounts payable; payroll; inventory; personnel accounting

15–2

1. weekly time card
2. payroll audit, payroll register, check and earnings statement, bank reconciliation report, deduction registers, tax reports, and management reports
3. payroll audit
4. the earnings and deductions of all employees
5. payroll master file
6. W2; 941

## EXERCISES

**15–1 True/False**

_____ 1. Time cards may take the form of mark-sensed punched cards.
_____ 2. The earnings file of a payroll system is created from the payroll master file and weekly attendance time cards.
_____ 3. Subsystems of a total system usually deal with the primary accounting functions of a business.
_____ 4. The W2 is a required earnings statement issued by the company on a semiannual basis.
_____ 5. The term "total system" refers to a composite of many smaller and interrelated systems.
_____ 6. The individual systems within a total system represent the major accounting functions required to control the operations of a business.

_____ 7. The term "total system" as it pertains to a business refers to a system that is made up of many smaller subsystems.

_____ 8. One register can be prepared for all voluntary deductions, or one register can be prepared for each type of voluntary deduction.

_____ 9. A labor cost analysis might include such information as materials used and man-hours expended.

_____ 10. The earnings file is used in the preparation of the check and statement.

_____ 11. During the preparation of the payroll register, control totals are produced for verification of payroll calculations and cash requirements.

_____ 12. The reconciliation file is produced at the time the deduction register is being printed.

_____ 13. The earnings file is needed for the preparation of the deduction register.

_____ 14. The payroll register is a report that lists all exceptions found during the payroll audit.

_____ 15. Details concerning earnings and deductions, gross pay, and tax withheld for all employees are shown in the payroll audit register.

**15–2**

**Multiple-choice**

_____ 1. Advantages of a payroll system include
   **a.** reduced clerical operations
   **b.** production of detailed reports
   **c.** elimination of peak workload periods
   **d.** more timely production of management reports
   **e.** all of the above

_____ 2. Data required in a payroll system are available from
   **a.** payroll master file
   **b.** time cards
   **c.** earnings file
   **d.** reconciliation file
   **e.** all of the above

_____ 3. Reports that can be produced by an automated payroll system if desired by management do not include
   **a.** labor cost analysis
   **b.** employee daily performance records
   **c.** absentee ratios by department
   **d.** department expense ratios
   **e.** none of the above

_____ 4. Typical business systems include
   **a.** payroll
   **b.** accounts payable
   **c.** accounts receivable
   **d.** personnel accounting
   **e.** all of the above

_____ 5. The database for a payroll system does not include
   **a.** authorized deductions and amounts
   **b.** Social Security number

c. employee job descriptions

d. time cards

e. none of the above

**15-3**  **1.** Two mandatory tax reports are _____ .

**Fill-in**  **2.** Three specific objectives of a payroll system are _____ .

**3.** The _____ report shows in detail the earnings and deductions of all employees.

**4.** The _____ and _____ files are used to reconcile checks returned from the bank.

**5.** The earnings file is principally used to _____ .

**6.** _____ records are the initial source of data for payroll computation.

**15-4**  **1.** From the knowledge that you have gained from this and preceding chapters, discuss what type of equipment would be needed to implement a payroll system for a medium-sized company.

**Problems**

**2.** Would a payroll system lend itself efficiently to a tape system, a disk system, or a card system?

**3.** What source documents are used in a payroll system?

**4.** Discuss the various management reports that would be produced from a payroll system.

**5.** What specific operations are required in a payroll system in order to obtain an employee's gross pay and tax deductions?

**6.** Salesmen operating on a commission basis receive a specific percentage of their sales. What information would be required and where would it be input to produce a file of total sales by salesmen for use in the payroll system?

**7.** Where and how would the file produced in Problem 6 be incorporated into the payroll system?

# appendix: APPENDIX SAMPLE ITEMS USED IN SYSTEM DOCUMENTATION

## DESCRIPTION

The Deduction Register Report (P004) generates a listing of all employee's earnings, withholdings, and itemized deductions for the pay period. In addition, it provides a summary report of the entire payroll; itemizing all the voluntary deductions.

Input to the program is the Current Earnings File. The date that the report is run must also be input to the program by the operator prior to processing the Earnings File.

Output from the program will be forwarded to the Payroll Department for audit and control considerations. Normally, this report is run after each payroll has been completed.

TITLE PAGE

| | |
|---|---|
| SYSTEM | PAYROLL |
| PROGRAM NAME | DEDUCTION-REGISTER |
| PROGRAM NUMBER | P004 |
| PROGRAMMER | T. M. Taylor, Ext. 384 |
| USER | Payroll Department, Ext. 493 |
| DATE WRITTEN | June 18, 1980 |
| PROJECT SUPERVISOR | William M. Fuori, Ext. 406 |
| | |
| SCHEDULE | Weekly (Thursday) |
| ESTIMATED TIME | 15 Minutes |
| CONTROLS | Visual comparison with previous pay period totals. Internal and external tape label checks. |
| | |
| SECURITY | Proprietary to Payroll dept. & designated recipients |
| PURPOSE | Generate Deduction Register & Summary from Earnings File |

INPUT

(1) EARNINGS-FILE

Reel Label: EARNINGS-P000E
Data Records: EARNINGS-REC
Estimated Volume: 350 records (1 reel)
Sequence: Numeric by Employee Number
Tape Labels: Standard volume, header, and trailer
Record Length: 127 Characters
Blocking Factor: 5

OUTPUT

(1) DEDUCTION-REGISTER

Form Used: General purpose 6 lines/inch, 4 ply paper
Estimated Volume: 15 pages
Post Processing Requirements: Burst & collate
Carriage Control Tape: P004

DISTRIBUTION

(2) SUMMARY

Form Used: General purpose 6 lines/inch, 4 ply paper
Estimated Volume: 1 page
Post Processing Requirements: None
Carriage Control Tape: P004
Original and 3 copies to Payroll Dept. Copy 3 returned to Data Processing following review and validation.

REMARKS

NCC Form 1888

SYSTEM FLOWCHART
DEDUCTION REGISTER REPORT

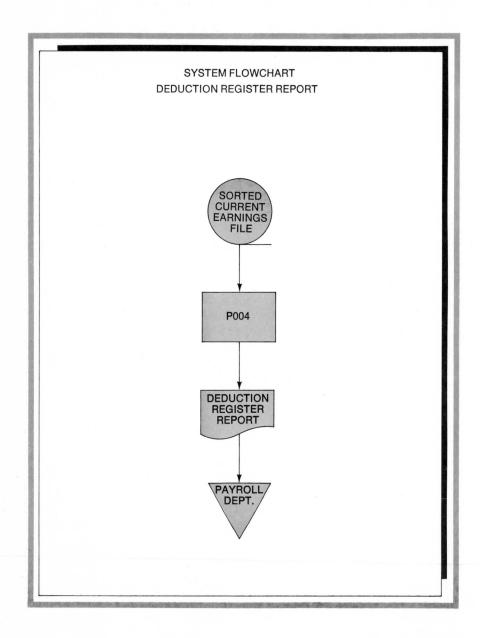

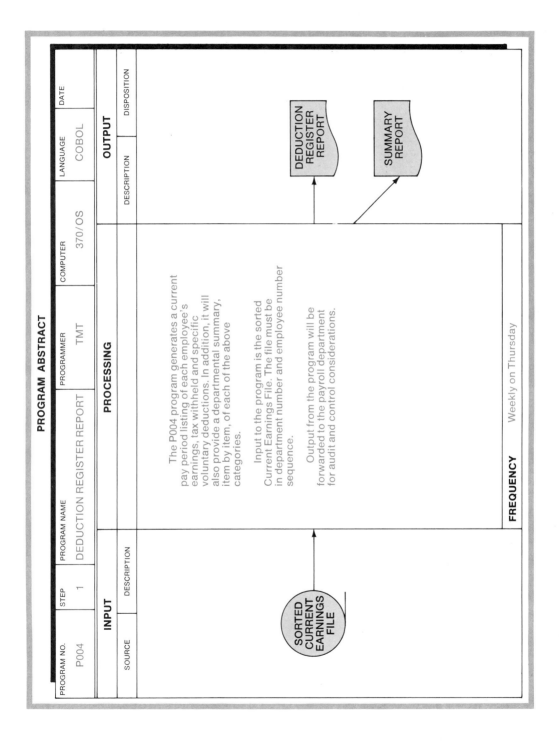

# PROGRAM ABSTRACT

| PROGRAM NO. | STEP | PROGRAM NAME | PROGRAMMER | COMPUTER | LANGUAGE | DATE |
|---|---|---|---|---|---|---|
| P004 | 1 | DEDUCTION REGISTER REPORT | TMT | 370/OS | COBOL | |

## INPUT

| SOURCE | DESCRIPTION |
|---|---|

SORTED CURRENT EARNINGS FILE

## PROCESSING

The P004 program generates a current pay period listing of each employee's earnings, tax withheld and specific voluntary deductions. In addition, it will also provide a departmental summary, item by item, of each of the above categories.

Input to the program is the sorted Current Earnings File. The file must be in department number and employee number sequence.

Output from the program will be forwarded to the payroll department for audit and control considerations.

## OUTPUT

| DESCRIPTION | DISPOSITION |
|---|---|

DEDUCTION REGISTER REPORT

SUMMARY REPORT

**FREQUENCY** Weekly on Thursday

551

| PROJECT: | Payroll | | APPLICATION: | Payroll System | |
|---|---|---|---|---|---|

| FILE NAME: Earnings–File | | FILE NO: 1134-76 |
|---|---|---|

| OTHER NAME(S): | RUN NAME: PAY-DED | RUN NO: |
|---|---|---|

| OUTPUT FROM: Check and Earnings Statement | INPUT TO: P003, P004 |
|---|---|

ACTIVITY % OF RECORDS: 100    LAYOUT NO:    FORM NO:

| MEDIA: | AVG. VOL. | NUMBER | PER | PERIOD | MAX. VOL. | SAME PERIOD |
|---|---|---|---|---|---|---|

TIME DUE IN/OUT:    PROJECTED VOL. (5 YRS.):

| DISTRIBUTION: | NO. OF COPIES | USE |
|---|---|---|

CONTENTS    TOTAL NO. OF CHAR: AVG. 127    MAX.

| FIELD NO. | FIELD NAME | SORT SEQ. | NO. OF CHAR. AVG. | NO. OF CHAR. MAX. | A/N | PROCESSING |
|---|---|---|---|---|---|---|
| 1 | Employee No. | 1 | 6 | | | 999999 |
| 2 | Employee Name | | 20 | | A | |
| 3 | Dept. No. | 2 | 1 | | N | |
| 4 | Social Security No. | | 9 | | N | 999999999 |
| 5 | Check No. | | 5 | | N | 99999 |
| 6 | Hours Worked | | 5 | | N | 999v99 |
| 7 | Rate Per Hour | | 4 | | N | 99v99 |
| 8 | Gross Pay | | 8 | | N | 999999v99 |
| 9 | Net Pay | | 8 | | N | 999999v99 |
| 0 | Med. Deduction | | 5 | | N | 999v99 |
| 1 | Union Dues Deduction | | 5 | | N | 999v99 |
| 2 | Credit Union Deduction | | 5 | | N | 999v99 |
| 3 | FICA Deduction | | 5 | | N | 999v99 |
| 4 | State Tax W/H | | 5 | | N | 999v99 |
| 5 | Federal Tax W/H | | 6 | | N | 9999v99 |
| 6 | Sick Days Taken | | 2 | | N | 99 |
| 7 | Vacation Days Taken | | 2 | | N | 99 |
| 8 | Year/Date FICA | | 5 | | N | 999v99 |
| 9 | Year/Date State Tax | | 6 | | N | 9999v99 |
| 0 | Year/Date Fedl. Tax | | 7 | | N | 99999v99 |
| 1 | Year/Date Gross Earnings | | 8 | | N | 999999v99 |

| DATE: 5/12/80 | ANALYST: TMT | SOURCE: | PAGE 1 OF 2 |
|---|---|---|---|

(SP–1)    TEAM LOR:    DATE:

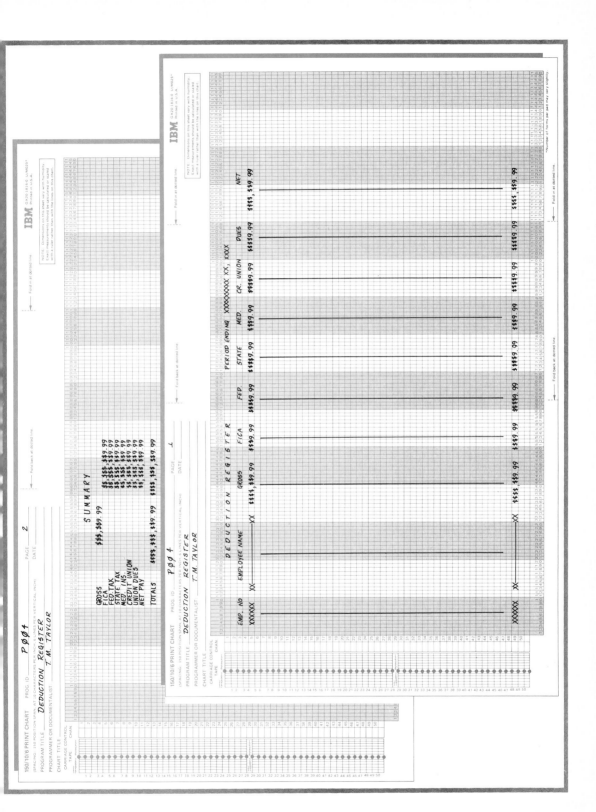

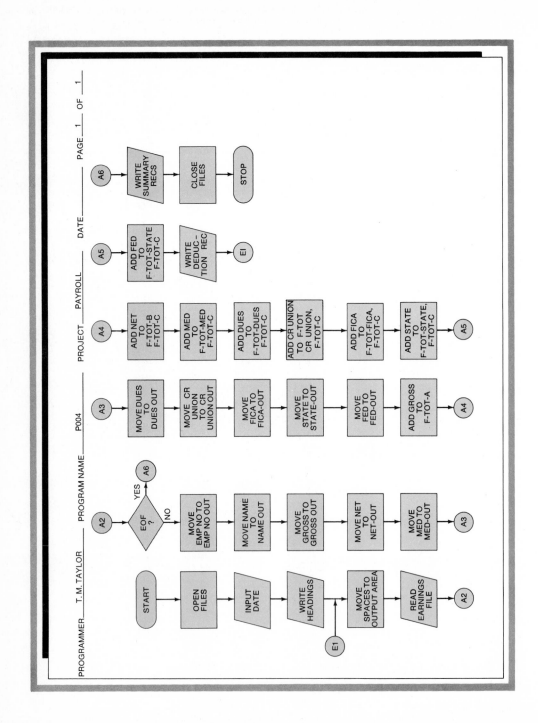

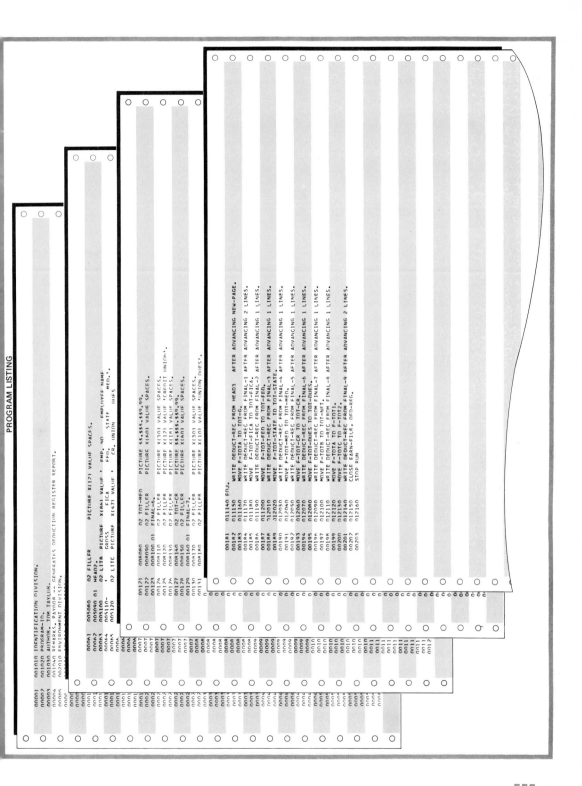

```
101000RALPH JOHNSON    4126385991    00000000000003R46200029264002000000000000000020000010730059250000280001015022008299500
053R46R
102000PETER PHILIPS    2138648290    0800000450003600000295610020000250000000018720061R003499000026208008852004599990
05040000
103000JAMES KERR    1144873895    0810002500020375000176R600200000000000001059000560013740000148170007840019236O
02R0250
104000ESTER KESSLER    3193721843    0R000036000288000002551800200000000000001497000540015310000209580007560021434O
0403200
105000JOHN LOPEZ    1125384203    00000000000576920004364100200000000000000299902192008660000419860305980121240O
0R07692
106000SHIRLEY MOORE    2126378592    0R000060000480000003439100200000250000000024960186500879800034944026110012317200
0672000
107000MATHEW LANE    4134812641    0000000000192308001134292000000000250000000000000001R256039760000040560125584055666400
269230R
108000MARK ADAMS    11R7381R59    0R00007500006000000048426002000025000000000000010810027110020115134003794029599960
0R40000
109000ADA PERRY    2142873R90    0800003440002752000023444002000000000000014310030302124200020034004242002899880
0291200
110000JOHN PERRONE    3126033008    0R000034400027520000234440020000000000000014310030302142000021420000340042002998R0
03R5280
111000ETHEL SILVER    2127048592    0000002500020000000167R20020000000000000010400024301735000210401372432556735 2
0R05280
112000JOHN STEWART    1134521859    00000000009615400074633000000000000000000051220163990000040568081708022957 70
6020135
113000WILLIAM SIEGAL    4166385242    0R0000450003600000264040020000250000000000001872011670061070000261380163480 854980
1346154
114000SALLY RENDER    2174395388    0000000009550076400056230020002000025000000000001060156140004056005784021859 60
0504000
115000STEPHEN RELLO    3192623854    0000000000115385008271400000000000000000007936024735000040560111104034629 00
1069600
116000RODNEY AXLER    4177618550    0800005000040000003253900200025000000250000000020800079200413900030120011088005794 60
1615385
117000ROBERT RACH    2170700111    08500045000393750003261002000025000000200472006380036390000286580089320050946O
0560000
118000MAE RADER    3182398742    00000000000538460004238400200000000000027990156400684990000393810218960096613O
0551250
119000MAUREEN WEST    4142385910    0R0000250002000000157760020000000000000140004450022539000073000063300035516O
0755846
120000COLLINS REID    1144543877    0R00003440027520002140402000000000000014310062700385800020344008778005301 20
0280000
121000JOSEPH MOLONEY    2149738941    0R0000265000212000001681900200000000000000011020038500269440001542800539000377160
03R52R0
122000PHILIP OLSEN    2167824187    0R000075000060000005175100200025000000000000013600066433000640283000034994012418006479 20
029600
123000NORMAN MONACO    1152822381    0R0000600004000000397890020000000000000104004450029544000154500062300013560
0R40000
124000THOMAS MOHERN    1134185996    0800002500020000001536100200000000000000001040004450056000623000041356O
0672000
125000THOMAS GONER    3134185996
02R0000
ABNORMAL EOJ EXIT
```

SAMPLE OUTPUT

## D E D U C T I O N   R E G I S T E R
### PERIOD ENDING

| EMP. NO | EMPLOYEE NAME | GROSS | FICA | FED. | STATE | MED. | CR. UNION | DUES | NET |
|---|---|---|---|---|---|---|---|---|---|
| 101000 | RALPH JOHNSON | $384.62 | $20.00 | $59.25 | $10.73 | $2.00 | $0.00 | $0.00 | $292.64 |
| 102000 | PETER PHILIPS | $360.00 | $18.72 | $34.99 | $6.18 | $2.00 | $0.00 | $2.50 | $295.61 |
| 103000 | JAMES KERR | $203.75 | $10.59 | $13.74 | $0.56 | $2.00 | $0.00 | $0.00 | $176.86 |
| 104000 | ESTER KESSLER | $288.00 | $14.97 | $15.31 | $0.54 | $2.00 | $0.00 | $0.00 | $255.18 |
| 105000 | JOHN LOPEZ | $576.92 | $29.99 | $86.60 | $21.92 | $2.00 | $0.00 | $0.00 | $436.41 |
| 106000 | SHIRLEY MOORE | $480.00 | $24.96 | $87.98 | $18.65 | $2.00 | $0.00 | $2.50 | $343.91 |
| 107000 | MATHEW LANE | $1,923.08 | $0.00 | $397.60 | $182.56 | $0.00 | $0.00 | $0.00 | $1,342.92 |
| 108000 | MARK ADAMS | $600.00 | $0.00 | $88.32 | $22.92 | $2.00 | $0.00 | $2.50 | $484.26 |
| 109000 | ADA PERRY | $208.00 | $10.81 | $21.14 | $2.71 | $2.00 | $0.00 | $0.00 | $171.34 |
| 110000 | JOHN PERRONE | $275.20 | $14.31 | $21.42 | $3.03 | $2.00 | $0.00 | $0.00 | $234.44 |
| 111000 | ETHEL SILVER | $275.20 | $14.31 | $21.42 | $3.03 | $2.00 | $0.00 | $0.00 | $234.44 |
| 112000 | JOHN | | | $17.35 | | | | $0.00 | $167.82 |
| 113000 | WILL | | | | | | | | |
| 114000 | SALL | | | | | | | | |
| 115000 | STEP | | | | | | | | |
| 116000 | RODN | | | | | | | | |
| 117000 | ROBE | | | | | | | | |
| 118000 | MAE | | | | | | | | |
| 119000 | MAIR | | | | | | | | |
| 120000 | COLI | | | | | | | | |
| 121000 | JOSE | | | | | | | | |
| 122000 | PHIL | | | | | | | | |
| 123000 | NORM | | | | | | | | |
| 124000 | THOM | | | | | | | | |
| 125000 | THOM | | | | | | | | |

### S U M M A R Y

| | |
|---|---|
| GROSS | $12,313.57 |
| FICA | $328.13 |
| FED. TAX | $1,871.50 |
| STATE TAX | $530.00 |
| MED. INS. | $44.00 |
| CREDIT UNION | $0.00 |
| UNION DUES | $20.00 |
| NET PAY | $9,519.94 |
| TOTALS | $12,313.57      $12,313.57 |

# Glossary of Data-Processing Terms

APPENDIX A

A

*absolute coding

Coding that uses machine instructions with absolute addresses. Synonymous with specific coding.

†acceleration time

The elapsed time between the interpretation of tape read or write instructions and the transfer to or from tape and internal storage.

*access arm

A part of a disk storage unit that is used to hold one or more reading and writing heads.

*access time

1. The time interval between the instant at which data are called for from a storage device and the instant delivery begins.
2. The time interval between the instant at which data are requested to be stored and the instant at which storage is started.

*accounting machine

1. A keyboard actuated machine that prepares accounting records.
2. A machine that reads data from external storage media, such as cards or tapes, and automatically produces accounting records or tabulations, usually on continuous forms.

*accuracy

The degree of freedom from error, that is, the degree of conformity to truth or to a rule. Accuracy is contrasted with precision. For example, four-place numerals are less precise than six-place numerals, nevertheless a properly computed four-place numeral might be more accurate than an improperly computed six-place numeral.

*acoustic delay line

A delay line whose operation is based on the time of propagation of sound waves in a given medium. Synonymous with sonic delay line.

†acronym

A word formed from the first letter or letters of the words in a name, term, or phrase, for example, SAGE from semiautomatic ground environment, and ALGOL from algorithmic language.

*adder

1. A device whose output is a representation of the sum of the quantities represented by its inputs.
2. See **half-adder.**

*Definitions preceded by an asterisk are reproduced with permission from American National Standards **Vocabulary for Information Processing**, X3.12-1970, copyright 1970 by the American National Standards Institute, copies of which may be purchased from the American National Standards Institute at 1430 Broadway, New York, N.Y. 10018.

†IBM definition.

**\*address**
1. An identification, as represented by a name, **label,** or number, for a **register,** location in **storage,** or any other **data** source or destination such as the location of a station in a communication network.
2. Loosely, any part of an **instruction** that specifies the location of an **operand** for the instruction.

**\*address format**
1. The arrangement of the **address parts** of an **instruction.** The expression "plus-one" is frequently used to indicate that one of the addresses specifies the location of the next instruction to be executed, such as one-plus-one, two-plus-one, three-plus-one, four-plus-one.
2. The arrangement of the parts of a **single address,** such as those required for identifying **channel, module, track,** etc. in a disc system.

**†addressing**

The means whereby the originator or control station selects the unit to which it is going to send a message.

**\*address register**

A register in which an address is stored.

**†add time**

The time required for one addition, not including the time required to get and return the quantities from storage.

**\*algorithm**

(‡SC1) A prescribed set of well-defined rules or **processes** for the solution of a problem in a finite number of steps, e.g., a full statement of an arithmetic procedure for evaluating sin x to a stated **precision.** Contrast with **heuristic.**

**†allocate**

To grant a resource to, or reserve it for, a job or task.

**\*alphabetic code**

(SC1) A code whose code set consists only of letters and associated special characters.

**\*alphameric**

Same as **alphanumeric.**

**\*alphanumeric**

Pertaining to a character set that contains letters, digits, and usually other characters such as punctuation marks. Synonymous with **alphameric.**

**\*alphanumeric character set**

A **character set** that contains **letters, digits,** and usually other **characters.**

**\*alphanumeric code**

(SC1) A **code** whose **code set** consists of **letters, digits,** and associated **special characters.**

**ALU**

See **arithmetic logic unit.**

**\*analog**
1. (SC1) Pertaining to representation by means of continuously variable physical quantities.
2. Contrast with **digital.**
3. See **network analog.**

**\*analog computer**
1. (SC1) A computer in which analog representation of data is mainly used.
2. A computer that operates on analog data by performing physical processes on these data. Contrast with **digital** computer.

**\*AND**

A logic operator having the property that if P is a statement, Q is a statement, R is a statement . . . , then the AND of P, Q, R . . . is true if all statements are true, false if any statement

---

†SC1 identifies definitions that have been discussed, and agreed upon at meetings of the International Organization For Standardization Technical Committee 97/Subcommittee 1.

is false. P and Q is often represented by $P \cdot Q$, PQ, $P \wedge Q$. Synonymous with logical multiply.

argument

A simple variable or numeric quantity that is required by a function.

arithmetic logic unit (ALU)

A computational subsystem that performs the mathematical and logical operations of a digital computer. A basic element of a central processing unit.

arithmetic operation

Any of the fundamental operations of arithmetic, for example, the binary operations of addition, subtraction, multiplication, and division, and the unary operations of negation and absolute value.

*arithmetic unit

The unit of a computing system that contains the circuits that perform arithmetic **operations.**

*arm

See **access arm.**

array

See **table.**

*artificial intelligence

The capability of a device to perform functions that are normally associated with human intelligence, such as reasoning, learning, and self-improvement. Related to **machine learning.**

artificial language

A **language** based on a set of prescribed rules that are established prior to its usage.

*ASCII (American National Standard Code for Information Interchange, X3.4-1968)

The standard **code,** using a coded **character set** consisting of 7-bit coded characters (8 bits including **parity check**), used for information interchange among **data processing systems,** communications systems,

and associated equipment. Synonymous with USASCII.

*assemble

To prepare a **machine language program** from a symbolic language program by substituting **absolute operation codes** for symbolic operation codes and **absolute** or relocatable addresses for **symbolic addresses.**

*assembler

A computer program that assembles.

*asynchronous computer

(SC1) A computer in which each event or the performance of each operation starts as a result of a signal generated by the completion of the previous event or operation, or by the availability of the parts of the computer required for the next event or operation. Contrast with **synchronous computer.**

*automatic

(SC1) Pertaining to a process or device that, under specified conditions, functions without intervention by a human operator.

*automatic computer

A **computer** that can perform a sequence of **operations** without intervention by a human **operator.**

*automation

1. (SC1) The implementation of processes by **automatic** means.
2. The theory, art, or technique of making a process more **automatic.**
3. The investigation, design, development, and application of methods of rendering processes **automatic,** self-moving, or self-controlling.
4. (SC1) The conversion of a procedure, a process, or equipment to **automatic** operation.

*auxiliary operation

An **offline operation** performed by equipment not under control of the **central processing unit.**

auxiliary storage

See **secondary storage.**

## B

**\*background processing**

The **automatic** execution of lower priority **computer programs** when higher priority programs are not using the system resources. Contrast with **foreground processing.**

**\*base**

1. A reference value.
2. A number that is multiplied by itself as many times as indicated by an exponent.
3. Same as **radix.**
4. See **floating-point base.**

**\*batch processing**

1. Pertaining to the technique of executing a set of computer programs such that each is completed before the next program of the set is started.
2. Pertaining to the sequential input of computer programs or data.
3. Loosely, the execution of computer programs serially.

**\*BCD**

**Binary-coded decimal notation.**

**\*binary**

1. Pertaining to a characteristic or property involving a selection, choice, or condition in which there are two possibilities.
2. Pertaining to the **number representation system** with a **radix** of two.
3. See **Chinese binary, column binary, row binary.**

**\*binary cell**

A **storage cell** of one **binary digit** capacity, e.g., a single bit **register.**

**\*binary code**

A **code** that makes use of exactly two distinct characters, usually 0 and 1.

**\*binary-coded decimal notation**

**Positional notation** in which the individual **decimal digits** expressing a **number** in **decimal notation** are each represented by a **binary numeral,** e.g., the number twenty-three is represented by 0010 0011 in the 8-4-2-1 type of binary-coded decimal notation and by 10111 in **binary notation.** Abbreviated BCD.

**\*binary digit**

1. In **binary notation,** either of the characters, 0 or 1.
2. See equivalent binary digits. Abbreviated **bit.**

**\*binary element**

A constituent element of data that may take either to two values or states.

**binary notation**

Fixed radix notation where the radix is two. For example, in binary notation the numeral 111 represents the number $1 \times 2$ squared plus $1 \times 2$ to the first plus $1 \times 2$ to the zero power, that is, seven.

**\*binary number**

Loosely, a binary numeral.

**\*binary numeral**

A binary representation of a number, e.g., "101" is a binary numeral and a "V" is the equivalent Roman numeral.

**†binary to decimal conversion**

Conversion of a binary number to the equivalent decimal number, that is, a base two number to a base ten number.

**\*bit**

1. A binary digit.
2. Same as **Shannon.**
3. See check bit, information bits, parity bit, sign bit.

**black box**

A generic term used to describe an unspecified device which performs a special function or in which known inputs produce known outputs in a fixed relationship.

**\*blank**

A part of a **medium** in which no **characters** are recorded.

**\*block**

1. A set of things, such as **words, characters,** or **digits** handled as a unit.
2. A collection of contiguous **records** recorded as a unit. Blocks are separated by **block gaps** and each block may contain one or more records.
3. A group of bits, or n-ary digits, **transmitted** as a unit. An encoding procedure is generally applied to the group of bits or n-ary digits for error-control purposes.
4. A group of contiguous characters recorded as a unit.
5. See **input block.**

**\*block diagram**

A diagram of a **system,** instrument, or **computer** in which the principal parts are represented by suitably associated geometrical figures to show both the basic functions and the functional relationships among the parts. Contrast with **flowchart.**

**\*block gap**

An area on a data medium used to indicate the end of a **block** or **record.**

**blocking**

Combining two or more records into one block.

**\*block length**

A measure of the size of a **block,** usually specified in units such as **records, words, computer words,** or **characters.**

**\*boolean**

1. Pertaining to the **process** used in the algebra formulated by George Boole.
2. Pertaining to the operations of **formal logic.**

**\*boolean operator**

A logic operator each of whose **operands** and whose result have one to two values.

**\*bootstrap**

A technique or device designed to bring itself into a desired state by means of its own action, e.g., a machine **routine** whose first few instructions are sufficient to bring the rest of itself into the computer from an input device.

**\*branch**

1. A set of instructions that are executed between two successive decision instructions.
2. To select a branch as in (1).
3. A direct path joining two nodes of a network or graph.
4. Loosely, a conditional jump.

**buffer**

A **routine** or **storage** used to compensate for a difference in rate of flow of **data,** or time of occurrence of events, when transmitting data from one device to another.

**\*bug**

A **mistake** or **malfunction.**

**\*burst**

1. To separate continuous-form paper into discrete sheets.
2. In data transmission, a sequence of **signals** counted as one unit in accordance with some specific criterion or measure.

**\*business data processing**

1. (SC1) Use of automatic data processing in accounting or management.
2. Data processing for business purposes, e.g., recording and summarizing the financial transactions of a business.
3. Synonymous with administrative data processing.

**\*byte**

A sequence of adjacent binary digits operated upon as a unit and usually shorter than a computer word.

C

**\*calculator**

1. (SC1) A **data processor** especially suitable for performing arithmeti-

cal **operations** which requires frequent intervention by a human **operator.**

2. Generally and historically, a device for carrying out logic and arithmetic digital operations of any kind.

†**card code**

The combinations of punched holes which represent characters (letters, digits, etc.) in a punched card.

*__card column__

A single line of **punch positions** parallel to the short edge of a 3¼ by 7⅜ inch **punched card.**

*__card deck__

Same as **deck.**

*__card row__

A single line of **punch positions** parallel to the long edge of a 3¼ by 7⅜ inch **punched card.**

†**card-to-tape**

Pertaining to equipment which transfers information directly from punched cards to punched or magnetic tape.

*__cathode ray storage__

An **electrostatic storage** device that utilizes a cathode ray beam for access to the **data.**

**cathode ray tube display**

1. A device that presents data in visual form by means of controlled electron beams. (Abbreviated "CRT display".)

2. The data display produced by the device as in (1).

*__central processing unit__

(SC1) A unit of a **computer** that includes the circuits controlling the interpretation and execution of **instructions.** Synonymous with **main frame.** Abbreviated CPU.

*__chain printer__

A printer in which the type slugs are carried by the links of a revolving chain.

*__channel__

1. A path along which **signals** can be sent, e.g., **data** channel, **output** channel.

2. The portion of a **storage medium** that is accessible to a given reading or writing station, e.g., **track, bank.**

3. In communication, a means of one way transmission. Several channels may share common equipment. For example, in frequency multiplexing carrier systems, each channel uses a particular frequency band that is reserved for it. Contrast with **circuit.**

4. See **input channel, output channel.**

*__character__

A **letter, digit,** or other **symbol** that is used as part of the organization, control, or representation of **data.** A character is often in the form of a spatial arrangement of adjacent or connected strokes.

*__character printer__

A device that prints a single **character** at a time. Contrast with **line printer.**

*__character recognition__

The identification of graphic, phonic, or other **characters** by **automatic** means. See **magnetic ink character recognition, optical character recognition.**

*__character set__

A set of unique representations called characters, e.g., the 26 letters of the English alphabet, O and I of the Boolean alphabet, the set of signals in the Morse code alphabet, the 128 characters of the ASCII alphabet.

**character string**

A linear sequence of characters.

*__check bit__

A **binary check digit,** e.g., a **parity bit.**

**Chinese binary**

See **column binary.**

**\*circuit**

In communications, a means of two-way communication between two points, comprising associated "go" and "return" channels.

**\*clock**

1. A device that generates periodic **signals** used for synchronization.
2. A device that measures and indicates time.
3. A **register** whose content changes at regular intervals in such a way as to measure time.

**\*closed subroutine**

A **subroutine** that can be stored at one place and can be linked to one or more calling **routines.** Contrast with **open subroutine.**

**\*COBOL**

(COmmon Business Oriented Language) A **business data processing** language.

**\*code**

(SC1) A set of unambiguous rules specifying the way in which **data** may be represented, for example, the set of correspondences in the standard code for information interchange.

**\*collating sequence**

An ordering assigned to a set of items, such that any two sets in that assigned order can be collated.

**\*column**

1. A vertical arrangement of characters or other expressions.
2. Loosely, a digit place.

**column binary**

Pertaining to the binary representation of data on punched cards in which adjacent positions in a column correspond to adjacent bits of data. (Synonymous with **Chinese binary.**)

**COM**

See **computer output microfilm.**

**\*common field**

A field that can be accessed by two or more independent routines.

**communication**

Transmission of intelligence between points of origin and reception without alteration of sequence or structure of the information content.

**\*communication link**

The physical means of connecting one location to another for the purpose of transmitting and receiving data.

**\*compile**

To prepare a machine language program from a computer program written in another programming language by making use of the overall logic structure of the program, or generating more than one machine instruction for each symbolic statement, or both, as well as performing the function of an assembler.

**\*compiler**

A program that compiles.

**\*complement**

A **number** that can be derived from a specific number by subtracting it from a second specified number. For example, in **radix notation,** the second specified number may be a given power of the **radix** or one less than a given power of the radix. The negative of a number is often represented by its complement.

**\*computer**

1. (SC1) A **data processor** that can perform substantial computation, including numerous arithmetic or logic operations, without intervention by a human **operator** during the **run.**
2. A device capable of solving problems by accepting data, performing described operations on the data, and supplying the results of these operations. Various types of computers are calculators, digital computers, and analog computers.

**\*computer code**
A **machine code** for a specific **computer.**

**\*computer instruction**
A **machine instruction** for a specific **computer.**

**computer output microfilm (COM) device**
A peripheral device capable of recording computer output on photosensitive film (microfilm or microfiche) in microscopic form.

**\*computer program**
A series of **instructions** or **statements,** in a form acceptable to a **computer,** prepared in order to achieve a certain result.

**computer statement**
The CPU and associated peripheral equipment which function as a unit.

**\*computer word**
A sequence of **bits** or **characters** treated as a unit and capable of being **stored** in one **computer location.** Synonymous with **machine word.**

**\*concurrent**
Pertaining to the occurrence of two or more **events** or activities within the same specified interval of time. Contrast with **consecutive, sequential, simultaneous.**

**\*connector**
1. (SC1) On a **flowchart,** the means of representing the convergence of more than one **flowline** into one, or the divergence of one flowline into more than one. It may also represent a break in a single flowline for continuation in another area.
2. A means of representing on a **flowchart** a break in a line of flow.

**\*consecutive**
Pertaining to the occurrence of two **sequential** events without the intervention of any other such event. Contrast with **concurrent, sequential, simultaneous.**

**\*console**
That part of a **computer** used for communication between the **operator** or **maintenance** engineer and the computer.

**†constant**
A fixed or invariable value or data item. See **figurative constant.**

**\*control panel**
A part of a computer console that contains manual controls.

**control total**
A sum resulting from the addition of a specified field from each record in a group of records, used for checking machine, program, and data reliability.

**control unit**
In a digital computer, those parts that effect the retrieval of instructions in proper sequence, the interpretation of each instruction, and the application of the proper signals to the arithmetic unit and other parts in accordance with this interpretation.

**conversational mode**
Communication between a terminal and the computer in which each entry from the terminal elicits a response from the computer and vice versa.

**\*core**
See **magnetic core, multiple aperture core.**

**CPS**
"Characters per second" or "cycles per second", depending on context.

**\*CPU**
**Central Processing Unit.**

**\*CRT display**
Cathode Ray Tube display.

**\*cryotron**
A device that makes use of the effects of low temperatures on conductive materials such that small magnetic field changes can control large current changes.

**\*cybernetics**

(SC1) That branch of learning which brings together theories and studies on communication and control in living organisms and machines.

**\*cycle**

1. An interval of space or time in which one **set** of **events** or phenomena is completed.
2. Any set of **operations** that is repeated regularly in the same **sequence.** The operations may be subject to variations on each repetition.

**D**

**\*data**

1. (SC1) A representation of facts, concepts, or **instructions** in a formalized manner suitable for communication, interpretation, or processing by humans or automatic means.
2. Any representations such as **characters** or **analog** quantities to which meaning is or might be assigned.
3. See **input data, numeric data.**

**\*data bank**

A comprehensive collection of **libraries** of data. For example, one line of an invoice may form an **item,** a complete invoice may form a **record,** a complete **set** of such records may form a **file,** the collection of inventory control files may form a **library,** and the libraries used by an organization are known as its data bank.

**database**

A set of logically related files organized in such a way that data access is improved and redundancy or duplication is minimized.

**data item**

The name for an individual member of a set of data denoted by a data element. For example, the data item "Tuesday" is a member of the set denoted by the data element "weekday".

**database management system**

A software system for managing the storage, access, updating, and maintenance of a database.

**\*data medium**

1. (SC1) The material in or on which a specific physical variable may represent **data.**
2. (SC1) The physical quantity which may be varied to represent **data.**

**data name**

An identifier that names unambiguously an item of data.

**\*data processing**

(SC1) The execution of a systematic sequence of **operations** performed upon **data.** Synonymous with **information processing.**

**data processing cycle**

The combined functions of input, processing, and output.

**†data processing system**

A network of machine components capable of accepting information, processing it according to a plan, and producing the desired results.

**\*data processor**

(SC1) A device capable of performing **data processing,** including desk **calculators, punched card machines,** and **computers.** Synonymous with **processor(1).**

**data set**

1. The major unit of data storage and retrieval in the operating system, consisting of a collection of data in one of several prescribed arrangements and described by control information to which the system has access.
2. A device which performs the modulation/demodulation and control functions necessary to provide compatability between business machines and communications facilities.

**\*debug**

To detect, locate, and remove **mistakes** from a **routine** or **malfunctions** from a **computer.** Synonymous with **troubleshoot.**

**\*decimal**

1. Pertaining to a characteristic or property involving a selection, choice, or condition in which there are ten possibilities.
2. Pertaining to the **number representation system** with a **radix** of ten.
3. See **binary-coded decimal notation.**

**\*decimal digit**

In **decimal notation,** one of the **characters** 0 thru 9.

**\*decimal notation**

A **fixed radix notation** where the **radix** is ten. For example, in decimal notation, the **numeral 576.2 represents the number** $5 \times 10$ squared plus $7 \times 10$ to the first power plus $6 \times 10$ to the zero power plus $2 \times 10$ to the minus 1 power.

**\*decision**

A determination of future action.

**\*decision table**

A **table** of all contingencies that are to be considered in the description of a problem, together with the actions to be taken. Decision tables are sometimes used in place of **flowcharts** for problem description and documentation.

**\*deck**

1. A collection of **punched cards.** Synonymous with **card deck.**
2. See **tape deck.**

**\*decode**

To apply a set of unambiguous rules specifying the way in which **data** may be restored to a previous representation, i.e., to reverse some previous **encoding.**

**\*delay**

The amount of time by which an event is retarded.

**\*destructive read**

A read process that also erases the data from the source.

**\*detail file**

Same as **transaction file.**

**\*digit**

A **symbol** that represents one of the nonnegative integers smaller than the radix. For example, in **decimal notation,** a digit is one of the **characters** from 0 to 9. Synonymous with **numeric character.**

**\*digital**

1. (SC1) Pertaining to **data** in the form of **digits.**
2. Contrast with **analog.**

**\*digital computer**

1. (SC1) A **computer** in which **discrete** representation of **data** is mainly used.
2. A **computer** that operates on **discrete data** by performing arithmetic and logic processes on these data. Contrast with **analog computer.**

**\*direct access**

1. Pertaining to the process of obtaining **data** from, or placing data into, **storage** where the time required for such access is independent of the **location** of the data most recently obtained or placed in storage.
2. Pertaining to a **storage** device in which the **access time** is effectively independent of the location of the **data.**
3. Synonymous with random access(1).

**\*disc**

Alternate spelling for disk. See **magnetic disc.**

**\*disk**

Alternate spelling for disc. See **magnetic disc.**

diskette

See **floppy disk.**

*display
1. A visual presentation of data.
2. See **cathode ray tube display.**

distributed data processing (DDP) system
A system consisting of a host or central computer system and database together with one or more satellite processing sites. The two general configurations of DDP systems are the star and ring networks. Limited data communications can occur between the host and satellite sites or directly between satellite sites providing for a company wide communication and processing system.

†DOS
Disk operating system.

*double precision
Pertaining to the use of two computer words to represent a number.

†double punch
More than one numeric punch in any one column of an IBM card.

†downtime
The time interval during which a device is **malfunctioning.**

*drum
See **magnetic drum**

*dump
1. To copy the contents of all or part of a **storage,** usually from an internal storage into an external storage.
2. A process as in (1).
3. The **data** resulting from the process as in (1).

duplex
A communication link that is capable of transmitting data in two directions at the same time.

†duplexed system
A system with two distinct and separate sets of facilities, each of which is capable of assuming the system function while the other assumes a standby status. Usually both sets are identical in nature.

*duplicate
To **copy** so that the result remains in the same physical form as the source, e.g., to make a new **punched card** with the same pattern of holes as an original punched card. Contrast with **copy.**

*dynamic storage
A device **storing data** in a manner that permits the data to move or vary with time such that the specified data are not always available for recovery. **Magnetic drum** and **disc** storage are nonvolatile dynamic storage. An **acoustic delay line** is a volatile dynamic storage.

*dynamic storage allocation
A **storage allocation** technique in which the location of **computer programs** and **data** is determined by criteria applied at the moment of need.

E

*EAM
**Electrical Accounting Machine.**

*edit
To modify the form or **format** of **data,** e.g., to insert or delete **characters** such as page numbers or decimal points.

*EDP
**Electronic Data Processing.**

*eleven-punch
A punch in the second **row** from the top, on a **Hollerith punched card.** Synonymous with **x-punch.**

*emulate
To imitate one **system** with another such that the imitating system accepts the same **data,** executes the same **programs,** and achieves the same results as the imitated system. Contrast with **simulate.**

encode
To convert data to a coded form.

*ENQ
The **enquiry character.**

**\*enquiry character**
A **communication control character** intended or use as a request for a response from a remote station. The response may include station identification and, if required, the type of equipment in service and station status. Abbreviated ENQ.

**EPROM**
An acronym for Erasable Programmable Read Only Memory—a special PROM that can be erased under high intensity ultraviolet light and reprogrammed.

**\*error message**
An indication that an **error** has been detected.

**\*error range**
The difference between the highest and lowest **error** values.

**\*exclusive OR**
A logic operator having the property that if P is a statement and Q is a statement, then P exclusive OR Q is true if either but not both statements are true, false if both are true or both are false. P exclusive OR Q is often represented by P $\oplus$ Q, P $\not\forall$ Q.

**†execute**
To carry out an instruction or perform a routine.

**†expression**
A source-language combination of one or more operations.

**†extent**
The physical locations on input-output devices occupied by, or reserved for, a particular data set.

**†external storage**
A storage device outside the computer which can store information in a form acceptable to the computer, for example, cards and tapes.


**F**

**feasibility study**
1. One of the initial steps in a systems study to determine whether the existing system, be it manual, mechanical, punched card, or computerized, is adequate or whether it should be modified, up-dated, or replaced.
2. Usually the initial procedures and criteria for determination of suitability, capability, and compatibility of computer systems to various firms or organizations. A preliminary systems analysis of potential cost savings and increased problem solving capability as a result of the procurement of the first or a different computer.

**\*feedback loop**
The components and processes involved in correcting or controlling a system by using part of the output as input.

**\*ferrite**
An iron compound frequently used in the construction of magnetic cores.

**\*field**
1. In a **record,** a specified area used for a particular category of **data,** e.g., a group of card columns used to represent a wage rate, a set of **bit** locations in a **computer word** used to express the **address** of the **operand.**
2. See **common field.**

**\*figurative constant**
A preassigned, fixed, **character string** with a preassigned, fixed, **data name** in a particular **programming language.**

**\*file**
A collection of related **records** treated as a unit. For example, one line of an invoice may form an **item,** a complete invoice may form a **record,** the complete set of such records may form a file, the collection of inventory control files may form a **library,** and the libraries used by an organization are known as its **data bank.**

*file layout

The arrangement and structure of **data** in a **file,** including the **sequence** and size of its components. By extension, a file layout might be the description thereof.

*file maintenance

The activity of keeping a **file** up to date by adding, changing, or deleting **data.**

firmware

Instructions or data stored in a fixed or "firm" way, usually on a ROM, PROM, or EPROM as opposed to instructions or data stored in the RAM memory. Contrast with **software** and **hardware.**

†first generation computer

A computer utilizing vacuum tube components.

fixed-length record

Pertaining to a file in which all records are constrained to be of equal, predetermined length. (Contrast with **variable-length record.)**

*fixed storage

**Storage** whose contents are not alterable by **computer instructions,** e.g., **magnetic core** storage with a lockout feature, photographic disc. Synonymous with **nonerasable storage, permanent storage, read-only storage.**

floating-point base

In floating-point representation, the fixed positive integer that is the understood base of the power. (Synonymous with **"floating-point radix".)**

floating-point radix

Same as **floating-point base.**

*floating-point representation

A **number representation system** in which each **number,** as represented by a pair of **numerals,** equals one of those numerals times a power of an implicit fixed positive integer **base** where the power is equal to the implicit base raised to the **exponent** represented by the other numeral.

| Common Notation | A Floating Point Representation |
|---|---|
| 0.0001234 or $(0.1234) \times (10^{-3})$ | 1234-03 |

floppy disk

A flexible oxide-coated mylar disk (diskette) that is stored in a protective envelope. Floppy disks provide low-cost direct access storage for mini- and microcomputer systems.

*flowchart

(SC1) A graphical representation for the definition, analysis, or solution of a problem, in which **symbols** are used to represent **operations, data,** flow, equipment, etc. Contrast with **block diagram.**

flowchart symbol

(SC1) A **symbol** used to represent **operations, data,** flow, or equipment on a **flowchart.**

*flowline

(SC1) on a flowchart, a line representing a connecting path between flowchart symbols, e.g., a line to indicate a transfer of data or control.

*foreground processing

The automatic execution of the computer programs that have been designed to preempt the use of the computing facilities. Usually a real time program. Contrast with **background processing.**

*format

1. The arrangement of data.
2. See **address format.**

FORTRAN

(FORmula TRANslating system) A language primarily used to express computer programs by arithmetic formulas.

function

A process that is performed on a number or character string.

function subprogram

A subprogram that returns a single value result. The two principal types are library and user-defined functions.

## G

†gang-punch

To punch all or part of the information from one punched card into succeeding cards.

*general purpose computer

(SC1) A **computer** that is designed to handle a wide variety of problems.

## H

*half-adder

A combinational logic element having two outputs, S and C, and two inputs, A and B, such that the outputs are related to the inputs according to the following table.

| input | | output | |
|---|---|---|---|
| A | B | C | S |
| 0 | 0 | 0 | 0 |
| 0 | 1 | 0 | 1 |
| 1 | 0 | 0 | 1 |
| 1 | 1 | 1 | 0 |

S denotes "Sum Without Carry," C denotes "Carry." Two half-adders may be used for performing binary addition.

half-duplex

A communication link that is capable of transmitting data in two directions, but only in one direction at a time.

*half-word

A contiguous sequence of **bits** or **characters** which comprises half a **computer word** and is capable of being addressed as a unit.

*hardware

(SC1) Physical equipment, as opposed to the **computer program** or method of use, e.g., mechanical, magnetic, electrical, or electronic devices. Contrast with **software.**

*header card

A card that contains **information** related to the **data** in cards that follow.

*heuristic

Pertaining to exploratory methods of problem solving in which solutions are discovered by evaluation of the progress made toward the final result. Contrast with **algorithm.**

*hexadecimal

Same as **sexadecimal.**

hierarchy plus input-processing-output

A design and documentation tool used to

1. State the functions to be accomplished by the program (or system).
2. Provide an overall structure or hierarchy by which the individual functions of the program (or system) can be understood.
3. Provide a visual description of the input to be used and the output produced by each function.

HIPO

See **hierarchy plus input-processing-output**

*Hollerith

Pertaining to a particular type of **code** or **punched card** utilizing 12 **rows** per **column** and usually 80 columns per card.

host computer

The central or controlling computer in a multiple computer network or distributed data processing system.

*hybrid computer

(SC1) A **computer** for **data processing** using both **analog** representation and **discrete** representation of **data.**

## I

*identity unit

An n-**input** unit that yields a specified **output signal** only when all n-input signals are alike.

*idle time

That part of **available time** during which the **hardware** is not being used. Contrast with **operating time.**

*inclusive OR

Same as OR.

**\*inconnector**

In **flowcharting,** a connector that indicates a continuation of a broken **flowline.** Contrast with **outconnector.**

**\*index**

1. An ordered reference list of the contents of a **file** or **document** together with **keys** or reference notations for identification or location of those contents.
2. To prepare a list as in (1).
3. A **symbol** or a **numeral** used to identify a particular quantity in an **array** of similar quantities. For example, the terms of an array represented by $X_1, X_2, \ldots, X_{100}$ have the indexes $1, 2, \ldots, 100$ respectively.
4. To move a machine part to a predetermined position, or by a predetermined amount, on a **quantized** scale.
5. See **index register.**

**indexed sequential**

A means of organizing data on a direct access storage device. An index is established to show where the data records are stored. Any desired data record can thus be accessed from the device by consulting the index(es). Data records can also be accessed sequentially or serially.

**\*index register**

A **register** whose content may be added to or subtracted from the **operand address** prior to or during the execution of a **computer instruction.** Synonymous with **b box.**

**\*information**

(SC1) The meaning that a human assigns to data by means of the known conventions used in their representation.

**\*information bits**

In telecommunications, those bits which are generated by the data source and which are not used for error control by the data transmission system.

**\*information retrieval**

(SC1) The methods and procedures for recovering specific information from stored data.

**information system**

The interacting of man and machine which, under man's control gathers data and disseminates information.

**\*information theory**

The branch of learning concerned with the likelihood of accurate transmission or communication of messages subject to transmission failure, distortion, and noise.

**inline processing**

The processing of data in random order, not subject to preliminary editing or sorting.

**\*input**

1. Pertaining to a device, process, or **channel** involved in the insertion of **data** or states, or to the data or states involved.
2. One, or a sequence of, **input states.**
3. Same as **input device.**
4. Same as **input channel.**
5. Same as **input process.**
6. Same as **input data.**
7. See **manual input, real time input.**

**\*input area**

An area of **storage** reserved for **input.** Synonymous with **input block.**

**\*input block**

Same as **input area.**

**\*input channel**

A **channel** for impressing a state on a device or **logic element.** Synonymous with input(4).

**\*input data**

**Data** to be processed. Synonymous with input(6).

**\*input device**

The device or collective set of devices used for conveying **data** into another device. Synonymous with input(3).

*input/output

Pertaining to either **input** or **output,** or both.

*input process

1. The process of receiving **data** by a device.
2. The process of transmitting data from **peripheral equipment,** or external **storage,** to internal storage.
3. Synonymous with input(5).

instruction

A **statement** that specifies an **operation** and the values or locations of its **operands.** In this context, the term "instruction" is preferable to the terms "command" or "order" which are sometimes used synonymously. "Command" should be reserved for electronic signals, and "order" should be reserved for sequence, interpolation, and related usage.

*instruction register

A register that stores an instruction for execution.

interactive programming language

A programming language which facilitates communication between user and computer on a conversational basis.

*interface

A shared boundary. An interface might be a **hardware** component to link two devices or it might be a portion of **storage** or **registers accessed** by two or more **computer programs.**

*internal storage

Addressable **storage** directly controlled by the **central processing unit** of a **digital computer.**

*interpreter

1. A **computer program** that **translates** and executes each **source language** statement before translating and executing the next one.
2. A device that prints on a **punched card** the **data** already punched in the card.

*inter-record gap

(See **record gap.**)

I/O

An abbreviation for input/output.

J

*job

A specified group of tasks prescribed as a unit of work for a **computer.** By extension, a job usually includes all necessary **computer programs, linkages, files,** and **instructions** to the **operating system.**

*job control statement

A **statement** in a **job** that is used in identifying the job or describing its requirements to the **operating system.**

K

*K

1. An abbreviation for the prefix kilo, i.e., 1000 in decimal notation.
2. Loosely, when referring to storage capacity, two to the tenth power, 1024 in decimal notation.

*key

1. One or more characters within an item of data that are used to identify it or control its use.

*keypunch

A keyboard actuated device that punches holes in a card to represent data.

L

*label

One or more **characters** used to identify a **statement** or an **item** of **data** in a **computer program.**

*language

A set of representations, conventions, and rules used to convey information.

*latency

The time between the completion of

the interpretation of an **address** and the start of the actual transfer from the addressed **location.** Latency includes the **delay** associated with access to **storage devices** such as **magnetic drums** and **delay lines.**

**\*library**
1. A collection of organized **information** used for study and reference.
2. A collection of related **files.** For example, one line of an invoice may form an **item,** a complete invoice may form a file, the collection of inventory control files may form a library, and the libraries used by an organization are known as its **data bank.**
3. See **program library.**

**library function**
A function subprogram available on the program or system library for general use.

**line printer**
A device that prints all characters of a line as a unit. Contrast with **character printer.**

**literal**
A symbol or quantity in a source program that is itself data, rather than a reference to data.

**load**
In programming, to enter data into storage or working registers.

**\*load-and-go**
An operating technique in which there are no stops between the loading and execution phases of a program and which may include assembling or compiling.

**\*logical file**
A collection of one or more **logical records.**

**\*logical record**
A collection of **items** independent of their physical environment. Portions of the same logical **record** may be located in different physical records.

**\*loop**
1. A **sequence** of **instructions** that is executed repeatedly until a terminal condition prevails.
2. See **feedback loop.**

## M

**machine-code**
An operation code that a machine can recognize and execute.

**†machine-independent**
Pertaining to procedures or programs created without regard for the actual devices which will be used to process them.

**\*machine instruction**
An instruction that a machine can recognize and execute.

**\*machine language**
A language that is used directly by a machine.

**\*machine learning**
(SC1) The ability of a device to improve its performance based on its past performance. Related to artificial intelligence.

**\*magnetic card**
A card with a magnetic surface on which **data** can be **stored** by selective magnetization of portions of the flat surface.

**\*magnetic core**
A configuration of magnetic material that is, or is intended to be, placed in a spatial relationship to current-carrying conductors and whose magnetic properties are essential to its use. It may be used to concentrate an induced magnetic field as in a transformer induction coil, or armature, to retain a magnetic polarization for the purpose of **storing** data, or for its nonlinear properties as in a **logic element.** It may be made of such material as iron, iron oxide, or ferrite and in such shapes as wires, tapes, toroids rods, or thin film.

**\*magnetic disc**

A flat circular plate with a magnetic surface on which **data** can be **stored** by selective magnetization of portions of the flat surface.

**\*magnetic drum**

A right circular cylinder with a magnetic surface on which **data** can be **stored** by selective magnetization of portions of the curved surface.

**\*magnetic ink**

An ink that contains particles of a magnetic substance whose presence can be detected by magnetic sensors.

**\*magnetic ink character recognition**

The machine recognition of characters printed with magnetic ink. Contrast with optical character recognition. Abbreviated MICR.

**\*magnetic storage**

A storage device that utilizes the magnetic properties of materials to store data, e.g., magnetic cores, tapes, and films.

**\*magnetic tape**

1. A tape with a magnetic surface on which **data** can be **stored** by selective polarization of portions of the surface.
2. A tape of magnetic material used as the constituent in some forms of **magnetic cores.**

**\*magnetic thin film**

A layer of magnetic material, usually less than one micron thick, often used for logic or storage elements.

**\*main frame**

(SC1) Same as **central processing unit.**

**\*main storage**

The general-purpose **storage** of a **computer.** Usually, main storage can be **accessed** directly by the operating **registers.** Contrast with **auxiliary storage.**

**†major total**

The result when a summation is ter-

minated by the most significant change of group.

**\*management information system**

1. (SC1) Management performed with the aid of **automatic data processing.** Abbreviated **MIS.**
2. An **information system** designed to aid in the performance of management **functions.**

**\*manual input**

1. The entry of **data** by hand into a device.
2. The data entered as in (1).

**†mark-sense**

To mark a position on a punched card with an electrically conductive pencil, for later conversion to machine punching.

**\*mark sensing**

The electrical sensing of manually recorded conductive marks on a nonconductive surface.

**†mass storage (online)**

The storage of a large amount of data which is also readily accessible to the central processing unit of a computer.

**\*mass storage device**

A device having a large storage capacity, e.g., magnetic disc, magnetic drum.

**\*master file**

A file that is either relatively permanent or that is treated as an authority in a particular job.

**\*match**

To check for identity between two or more items of data.

**\*mathematical model**

A mathematical representation of a process, device, or concept.

**matrix**

A mathematical term for an array or table.

**\*medium**

The material, or configuration thereof, on which data are recorded, e.g., paper tape, cards, magnetic tape. Synonymous with **data medium.**

*merge

To combine **items** from two or more similarly ordered sets into one set that is arranged in the same order. Contrast with **collate.**

*MICR

**Magnetic Ink Character Recognition.**

microcomputer

A small but complete computer system, consisting of hardware and software whose main processing part is a microprocessor.

microfiche

A sheet of photosensitive film about 4 inches by 6 inches on which the images of computer output may be recorded. A single sheet of microfiche is capable of recording over 250 pages of computer output.

microprocessor

1. A simple computer on a chip.
2. The central processing unit of a microcomputer.
3. An integrated circuit that can perform a variety of operations in accordance with a set of instructions.

†microsecond

One-millionth of a second.

†millisecond

One-thousandth of a second.

minicomputer

A digital computer that is characterized by higher performance than a microcomputer, more versatility, and a wide selection of available programming languages, operating systems and application software.

†minor total

The result when a summation is terminated by the least significant change of group.

*mnemonic symbol

A **symbol** chosen to assist the human

memory, e.g., an abbreviation such as "mpy" for "multiply."

*monadic operation

An opration on one operand, e.g., negation. Synonymous with **unary operation.**

†monolithic integrated circuit

A class of integrated circuits wherein the substrate is an active material, such as the semiconductor silicon.

*monitor

Software or hardware that observes, supervises, controls, or verifies the operations of a system.

*multiple aperture core

A **magnetic core** with two or more holes through which wires may be passed and around which magnetic flux may exist. Multiple aperture cores may be used for **nondestructive reading.**

*multiplex

To **interleave** or simultaneously **transmit** two or more messages on a single **channel.**

*multiprocessing

1. Pertaining to the simultaneous execution of two or more **computer programs** or **sequences** of **instructions** by a **computer** or **computer network.**
2. Loosely, **parallel processing**

*multiprocessor

A **computer** employing two or more processing units under integrated control.

*multiprogramming

Pertaining to the **concurrent** execution of two or more **programs** by a **computer.**

N

nanosecond

One-billionth of a second.

network

A system of interacting computer systems and terminals.

**\*network analog**

The expression and solution of mathematical relationships between variables using a circuit or circuits to represent these variables.

**network, ring**

A network consisting of several computer systems interconnected by a single communications line with no one system acting as host computer. Communications can take place directly between the satellite systems.

**network, spider**

See **network, star.**

**network, star**

A network in which all communications must be routed through the host or central computer before being routed to the appropriate satellite processing system.

**\*nines complement**

The **radix-minus-one** complement in **decimal notation.**

**†nominal (rated) speed**

Maximum speed or data rate of a device or facility which makes no allowance for necessary delaying functions, such as checking, tabbling, etc.

**\*nondestructive read**

A **read** process that does not **erase** the **data** in the source. Abbreviated NDR.

**\*number**

1. A mathematical entity that may indicate quantity or amount of units.
2. Loosely, a **numeral.**

**\*number representation system**

An agreed set of **symbols** and rules for **number representation.** Synonymous with **numeral system, numeration system.**

**\*number system**

Loosely, a **number representation system.**

**\*numeration system**

Same as **number representation system.**

**\*numerical analysis**

The study of methods of obtaining useful quantitative solutions to problems that have been expressed mathematically, including the study of the errors and bounds on errors in obtaining such solutions.

**\*numerical control**

(SC1) Automatic control of a process performed by a device that makes use of all or part of numerical data generally introduced as the operation is in process.

**\*numeric character**

Same as **digit.**

**\*numeric code**

(SC1) A code whose code set consists only of digits and associated special characters.

**numeric data**

Data represented by numeric characters and some special characters.

**\*numeric data code**

A code consisting only of numerals and special characters.

## O

**\*object code**

**Output** from a **compiler** or **assembler** which is itself executable **machine code** or is suitable for processing to produce executable machine code.

**\*object language**

Same as **target language.**

**\*object program**

A fully **compiled** or **assembled program** that is ready to be **loaded** into the **computer.** Synonymous with target program. Contrast with **source program.**

**\*OCR**

**Optical character recognition.**

**\*octal**

1. Pertaining to a characteristic or property involving a selection, choice or condition in which there are eight possibilities.

**2.** Pertaining to the **number representation system** with a **radix** of eight.

*offline

Pertaining to equipment or devices not under control of the **central processing unit.**

*offline storage

**Storage** not under control of the **central processing unit.**

†on-demand system

A system from which information or service is available at time of request.

†one-for-one

A phrase often associated with an assembly routine where one source language instruction is converted to one machine language instruction.

*ones complement

The **radix-minus-one complement** in **binary notation.**

*online

**1.** Pertaining to equipment or devices under control of the **central processing unit.**

**2.** Pertaining to user's ability to interact with a **computer.**

*openended

Pertaining to a process or system that can be augmented.

*open subroutine

A subroutine that is inserted into a routine at each place it is used. Synonymous with **direct insert subroutine.** Contrast with closed subroutine.

*operand

That which is operated upon. An operand is usually identified by an address part of an instruction.

*operating system

(SC1) **Software** which controls the execution of **computer programs** and which may provide scheduling **debugging,** input/output control, accounting, **compilation storage** assignment, **data** management, and related services.

*operating time

That part of available time during which the hardware is operating and assumed to be yielding correct results. It includes development time, production time, and makeup time.

*operation

**1.** A defined action, namely, the act of obtaining a result from one or more operands in accordance with a rule that completely specifies the result for any permissible combination of operands.

**2.** The set of such acts specified by such a rule, or the rule itself.

**3.** The act specified by a single **computer instruction**

**4.** A **program** step undertaken or executed by a **computer,** e.g., addition, multiplication, **extraction,** comparison, **shift, transfer.** The operation is usually specified by the **operator** part of an instruction.

**5.** The event of specific action performed by a **logic element.**

*operation code

A **code** that represents specific operations. Synonymous with **instruction code.**

*optical character recognition

The machine identification of printed **characters** through use of light-sensitive devices. Contrast with **magnetic ink character recognition.** Abbreviated **OCR.**

*optical scanner

**1.** A device that scans optically and usually generates an analog or digital signal.

**2.** A device that optically scans printed or written data and generates their digital representations.

*OR

**1.** A logic **operator** having the property that if P is a statement, Q is a statement, R is a statement, . . . then the OR of P, Q, R, . . . , is true if at least one statement is true, false if all statements are false. P OR Q is often represented by P + Q, P ∨ Q. Synonymous with inclusive OR, boolean add, logical add. Contrast with **exclusive OR.**

2. The abbreviation for **Operations Research.**

3. See **exclusive OR, inclusive OR.**

**OS**

Operating system, q.v.

*\*outconnector*

In **flowcharting,** a **connector** that indicates a point at which a **flowline** is broken for continuation at another point. Contrast with **inconnector.**

*\*output*

1. (SC1) Pertaining to a device, **process,** or **channel** involved in an **output process,** or to the data or states involved.

2. One, or a sequence of, **output states.**

3. Same as **output device.**

4. Same as **output channel.**

5. Same as **output process.**

6. Same as **output data.**

7. See **real time output.**

*\*output area*

An area of **storage** reserved for **output.**

*\*output channel*

A **channel** for conveying **data** from a device or **logic element.** Synonymous with output(4).

*\*output process*

(SC1) The **process** of delivering **data** by a system, subsystem, or device. Synonymous with output(5).

*\*overflow*

1. That portion of the result of an **operation** that exceeds the capacity of the intended unit of **storage.**

2. Pertaining to the generation of overflow as in (1).

3. Contrast with **underflow.**

†*overlap*

To do something at the same time that something else is being done; for example, to perform input/output

operations while instructions are being executed by the central processing unit.

*\*overlay*

The technique of repeatedly using the same blocks of internal **storage** during different stages of a **program.** When one **routine** is no longer needed in storage, another routine can replace all or part of it.

**P**

*\*parallel*

1. Pertaining to the **concurrent** or **simultaneous** occurrence of two or more related activities in multiple devices or **channels.**

2. Pertaining to the simultaneity of two or more **processes.**

3. Pertaining to the simultaneous processing of the individual parts of a whole, such as the **bits** of a **character** and the characters of a **word,** using separate facilities for the various parts.

4. Contrast with **serial.**

*\*parallel operation*

Pertaining to the **concurrent** or **simultaneous** execution of two or more **operations** in devices such as multiple arithmetic or logic units. Contrast with **serial operation.**

*\*parallel processing*

Pertaining to the **concurrent** or **simultaneous** execution of two or more **processes** in multiple devices such as **channels** or processing units. Contrast with **multiprocessing, serial processing.**

*\*parallel transmission*

In **telecommunications,** the **simultaneous transmission** of a certain number of **signal** elements constituting the same telegraph or **data** signal. For example, use of a **code** according to which each signal is characterized by a combination of three out of twelve frequencies simultaneously transmitted over the **channel.** Contrast with **serial transmission.**

*parity bit

A **check bit** appended to an **array** of **binary digits** to make the sum of all the binary digits, including the check bit, always odd or always even.

*parity check

A **check** that tests whether the number of ones (or zeros) in an **array** of **binary digits** is odd or even. Synonymous with **odd-even check.**

*patch

1. To modify a **routine** in a rough or expedient way.
2. A temporary electrical connection.

*pattern recognition

The identification of shapes, forms, or configurations by **automatic** means.

*peripheral equipment

(SC1) In a data processing system, any unit of equipment, distinct from the central processing unit, which may provide the system with outside communications.

†physical record

A record from the standpoint of the manner or form in which it is stored, retrieved, and moved—that is, one that is defined in terms of physical qualities.

†PL/I

Programming Language/I, a high level programming language.

*plugboard

A perforated board into which plugs are manually inserted to control the operation of equipment. Synonymous with **control panel**(2).

†point-to-point transmission

Transmission of data directly between two points without the use of any intermediate terminal or computer.

*positional notation

(SC1) A **numeration system** in which a **number** is represented by means of an ordered **set** of **digits,** such that the value contributed by each digit depends upon its position as well as upon its value. Synonymous with **positional representation.**

*predefined process

A process that is identified only by name and that is defined elsewhere.

*preventive maintenance

**Maintenance** specifically intended to prevent **faults** from occurring during subsequent **operation.** Contrast with **corrective maintenance.** Corrective maintenance and preventive maintenance are both performed during **maintenance time.**

†primary storage

The main internal storage.

*printer

See **chain printer, character printer, line printer**

*problem description

1. (SC1) In **information processing,** a statement of a problem. The statement may also include a description of the method of solution, the procedures and **algorithms,** etc.
2. A statement of a problem. The statement may also include a description of the method of solution, the solution itself, the transformations of **data** and the relationship of procedures, data, constraints, and environment.

*problem oriented language

A **programming language** designed for the convenient expression of a given class of problems.

*procedure oriented language

A programming language designed for the convenient expression of procedures used in the solution of a wide class of problems.

*process

A systematic **sequence** of **operations** to produce a specified result. See **input process, output process, predefined process.**

**\*processor**

1. In **hardware,** a **data processor.**
2. In **software,** a **computer program** that includes the **compiling, assembling, translating,** and related functions for a specific **programming language, COBOL** processor, **FORTRAN** processor.
3. See **data processor, multiprocessor.**

**\*program**

1. (SC1) A series of actions proposed in order to achieve a certain result.
2. Loosely, a **routine.**
3. To design, write, and test a program as in (1).
4. Loosely, to write a **routine.**
5. See **computer program, object program, source program, target program.**

**\*program library**

A collection of available computer programs and routines.

**\*programmer**

(SC1) A person mainly involved in designing, writing and testing **computer programs.**

**\*programming**

(SC1) The design, the writing, and testing of a **program.**

**\*programming language**

A **language** used to prepare **computer** programs.

**PROM**

An acronym for Programmable Read Only Memory. A memory that is programmed by a special electronic programming device. Once programmed, it functions as ROM.

**pseudocode**

An imitation computer code. It is used in place of symbols or a flowchart to describe the logic of a program. It employs the basic structures utilized in structured programming.

**\*punch**

A perforation, as in a **punched card** or paper tape.

**\*punched card**

1. A card **punched** with a pattern of holes to represent **data.**
2. A card as in (1) before being **punched.**

**\*punched tape**

A tape on which a pattern of holes or cuts is used to represent **data.**

### Q

**queue**

(Noun). A waiting line formed by items in a system waiting for service; for example, customers at a bank teller window or messages to be transmitted in a message switching system. (verb). To arrange in, or form, a queue.

**\*queued access method**

Any access method that automatically synchronizes the **transfer** of **data** between the **program** using the access method and **input/output** devices, thereby eliminating delays for input/output **operation.**

### R

**\*radix**

(SC1) In **positional representation,** that integer, if it exists, by which the **significance** of the **digit place** must be multiplied to give the significance of the next higher digit place. For example, in **decimal notation,** the radix of each place is ten; in a **biquinary code,** the radix of the fives place is two. Synonymous with **base**(3).

**\*radix complement**

(SC1) A **complement** obtained by subtracting each **digit** from one less than its **radix,** then adding one to the least **significant digit,** executing all **carries** required, e.g., **tens comple-**

ment in **decimal notation, twos complement** in **binary notation.** Synonymous with **true complement.**

**\*radix-minus-one complement**

A **complement** obtained by subtracting each **digit** from one less than the **radix,** e.g., **nines complement** in **decimal notation, ones complement** in **binary notation.** Synonymous with **diminished radix complement.**

**RAM**

An acronym for Random-Access Memory. Data can be written into and read out of RAM and can be changed at any time by a new write operation. RAM is the main memory of a microcomputer.

**\*random access**

1. Same as **direct access.**
2. In COBOL, an **access mode** in which specific **logical records** are obtained from or placed into a **mass storage file** in a nonsequential manner.

**random access device**

A device in which the access time is effectively independent of the location of the data. (Synonymous with "**direct access device.**")

**\*range**

1. The **set** of values that a quantity or **function** may assume.
2. The difference between the highest and lowest value that a quantity or **function** may assume.
3. See **error range.**

**\*read**

1. To acquire or interpret data from a storage device, a data medium, or any other source.
2. See **destructive read, nondestructive read.**

**\*real time**

1. Pertaining to the actual time during which a physical **process** transpires.
2. Pertaining to the performance of a computation during the actual

time that the related physical **process** transpires, in order that the results of the computation can be used in guiding the physical process.

**\*real time input**

**Input data** inserted into a **system** at the time of generation by another system.

**\*real time output**

**Output data** removed from a **system** at time of need by another system.

**\*record**

1. A collection of related **items** of **data,** treated as a unit, for example, one line of an invoice may form a record; a complete set of such records may form a **file.**
2. See **logical record, variable-length record.**

**\*record gap**

An area on a **data medium** used to indicate the end of a **block** or **record.** Synonymous with **inter-record gap.**

**\*recording density**

The number of **bits** in a single linear **track** measured per unit of length of the recording **medium.**

**\*record layout**

The arrangement and structure of **data** in a **record,** including the **sequence** and size of its components. By extension, a record layout might be the description thereof.

**†reel**

A mounting for a roll of tape.

**\*register**

A device capable of storing a specified amount of data, such as one **word.**

**\*relocate**

In **computer programming,** to **move** a **routine** from one portion of **storage** to another and to adjust the necessary **address** references so that the routine, in its new **location,** can be executed.

**\*remote access**

Pertaining to communication with a **data processing** facility by one or more stations that are distant from that facility.

**†report generation**

A technique for producing complete machine reports from information which describes the input file and the format and content of the output report.

**†reproduce**

To prepare a duplicate of stored information, especially for punched cards, punched paper tape, or magnetic tape.

**†reproducer**

A device which will duplicate, in one card, all or part of the information contained in another card.

**†rewind**

To return a magnetic or paper tape to its beginning.

**\*roll-in**

To restore in **main storage, data** which had previously been **transferred** from main storage to **auxiliary storage.**

**\*roll-out**

To record the contents of **main storage** in **auxiliary storage.**

**ROM**

An acroynm for Read-Only Memory. Nonerasable, permanently programmed memory. Programs stored in ROM are sometimes referred to as **firmware.**

**\*rounding error**

An **error** due to **roundoff.** Contrast with **truncation error.**

**\*roundoff**

To delete the least **significant digit** or digits of a **numeral,** and to adjust the part retained in accordance with some rule.

**\*routine**

(SC1) An ordered set of **instructions**

that may have some general or frequent use.

**row binary**

Pertaining to the binary representation of data on cards in which adjacent positions in a row correspond to adjacent bits of data; for example, each row in an 80-column card may be used to represent 80 consecutive bits of two 40-bit words.

**RPG**

Report program generator.

**\*run**

A single, continuous performance of a **computer program** or **routine.**

## S

**simplex**

A communication link that is capable of transmitting data in one direction only. Contrast with **half-duplex** and **duplex.**

**\*scheduled maintenance**

Maintenance carried out in accordance with an established plan.

**secondary storage**

A storage device in addition to the main storage of a computer; e.g., magnetic tape, disk, drum, or card. Secondary storage usually holds much larger amounts of data with slower access times than primary storage.

**second generation computer**

A computer utilizing solid state components.

**seek**

To position the access mechanism of a direct access device at a specified location.

**selector**

A device for directing electrical input pulses onto one of two output lines, depending upon the presence or absence of a predetermined accompanying control pulse.

†sequencing

Ordering in a series or according to rank or time.

*sequential

Pertaining to the occurrence of **events** in time **sequence,** with little or no simultaneity or overlap of events. Contrast with **concurrent, consecutive, simultaneous.**

*sequential computer

A **computer** in which **events** occur in time **sequence,** with little or no simultaneity or overlap of events.

*sequential control

A mode of **computer operation** in which **instructions** are executed in an implicitly defined **sequence** until a different sequence is explicitly initiated by a **jump instruction.**

*sequential operation

Pertaining to the performance of **operations** one after the other.

*serial

1. Pertaining to the **sequential** or **consecutive** occurrence of two or more related activities in a single device or **channel.**
2. Pertaining to the **sequencing** of two or more **processes.**
3. Pertaining to the **sequential processing** of the individual parts of a whole, such as the **bits** of a **character** or the characters of a **word,** using the same facilities for successive parts.
4. Contrast with **parallel.**

*serial access

1. Pertaining to the **sequential** or **consecutive transmission** of **data** to or from **storage.**
2. Pertaining to the **process** of obtaining **data** from or placing **data** into **storage,** where the **access time** is dependent upon the **location** of the data most recently obtained or placed in storage. Contrast with **direct access.**

*serial computer

1. A computer having a single arithmetic and logic unit.
2. A computer some specified characteristic of which is serial, e.g., a computer that manipulates all bits of a word serially. Contrast with **parallel computer.**

*serial processing

Pertaining to the sequential or consecutive execution of two or more processes in a single device such as a channel or processing unit. Contrast with **parallel processing.**

†serial transfer

A transfer of data in which elements are transferred in succession over a single line.

*serial transmission

In **telecommunications, transmission** at successive intervals of **signal** elements constituting the same telegraph or **data** signal. The **sequential** elements may be transmitted with or without interruption, provided that they are not transmitted **simultaneously.** For example, telegraph transmission by a time divided **channel.** Contrast with **parallel transmission.**

*service routine

A **routine** in general support of the **operation** of a **computer,** e.g., an **input-output, diagnostic, tracing,** or **monitoring routine.** Synonymous with **utility routine.**

*sexadecimal

1. Pertaining to a characteristic or property involving a selection, choice, or condition in which there are sixteen possibilities.
2. Pertaining to the **numeration system** with a **radix** of sixteen.
3. Synonymous with **hexadecimal.**

*Shannon

A unit of measurement of quantity of information equal to that contained in a message represented by one or the other of two equally probable, exclusive, and exhaustive states.

**\*sharing**

See **time sharing.**

**\*sign bit**

A **binary digit** occupying the **sign position.**

**\*significance**

(SC1) In **positional representation,** the factor, dependent on the **digit place,** by which a **digit** is multiplied to obtain its additive contribution in the representation of a **number.** Synonymous with **weight.**

**\*significant digit**

A **digit** that is needed for a certain purpose, particularly one that must be kept to preserve a specific **accuracy** or **precision.**

**\*sign position**

A **position,** normally located at one end of a **numeral,** that contains an indication of the algebraic sign of the **number.**

**simplex mode**

Operation of a communication channel in one direction only, with no capability for reversing.

**\*simulate**

1. (SC1) To represent certain features of the behavior of a physical or abstract **system** by the behavior of another system.
2. To represent the functioning of a device, **system,** or **computer program** by another, e.g., to represent the functioning of one **computer** by another, to represent the behavior of a physical system by the execution of a computer program, to represent a biological system by a **mathematical model.**
3. Contrast with **emulate.**

**\*simultaneous**

Pertaining to the occurrence of two or more **events** at the same instant of time. Contrast with **concurrent, consecutive, sequential.**

**†simultaneous transmission**

Transmission of control characters or data in one direction while infor-

mation is being received in the other direction.

**\*single-address**

Pertaining to an **instruction format** containing one **address part.** Synonymous with **one-address.**

**\*single factor**

A **number** used as a multiplier, so chosen that it will cause a set of quantities to fall within a given **range** of values. To scale the **values** 856, 432, −95, and −182 between −1 and +1, a scale factor of $\frac{1}{1000}$ would be suitable.

**software**

A set of programs, procedures, rules and possibly associated documentation concerned with the operation of a data processing system. For example, compilers, library routines, manuals, circuit diagrams.

**\*solid state component**

A component whose **operation** depends on the control of electric or magnetic phenomena in solids, e.g., a transistor, crystal diode, **ferrite** core.

**\*sort**

1. To segregate items into groups according to some definite rules.
2. Same as **order.**

**\*sorter**

A person, device, or **computer routine** that **sorts.**

**\*source language**

The **language** from which a **statement** is translated.

**\*source program**

A **computer program** written in a **source language.** Contrast with **object program.**

**\*SP**

The **space character.**

**\*space**

1. A site intended for the **storage** of **data,** e.g., a site on a printed page or a **location** in a **storage medium.**
2. A basis **unit** of area, usually the size of a single **character.**

3. One or more **space characters.**

4. To advance the **reading** or **display position** according to a prescribed **format,** e.g., to advance the printing or display position horizontally to the right or vertically down. Contrast with **backspace.**

*special character

A **graphic character** that is neither a **letter,** nor a **digit,** nor a **space character.**

*special purpose computer

(SC1) A **computer** that is designed to handle a restricted class of problems.

*spot punch

A device for **punching** one hole at a time.

*statement

1. In **computer programming,** a meaningful expression or generalized **instruction** in a **source language.**

2. See **job control statement.**

*static storage

**Storage** other than **dynamic storage.**

†station

One of the input or output points of a communications system; for example, the telephone set in the telephone system or the point where the business machine interfaces the channel on a leased private line.

*storage

1. Pertaining to a device into which data can be entered, in which they can be held, and from which they can be retrieved at a later time.

2. Loosely, any device that can store data.

3. Synonymous with **"memory."**

*storage allocation

1. The assignment of **blocks** of **data** to specified blocks of **storage.**

2. See **dynamic storage allocation.**

*storage capacity

The amount of **data** that can be contained in a **storage device.**

*storage cell

An elementary **unit** of **storage,** e.g., a **binary cell,** a **decimal** cell.

*storage device

A device into which **data** can be inserted, in which they can be retained, and from which they can be retrieved.

*storage protection

An arrangement for preventing access to **storage** for either **reading,** or **writing,** or both. Synonymous with **memory protection.**

*stored program computer

(SC1) A **computer** controlled by internally stored **instructions** that can synthesize, **store,** and in some cases alter instructions as though they were **data** and that can subsequently execute these instructions.

*string

A linear sequence of entities such as characters or physical elements.

structured programming

A technique for designing and writing computer programs which have a definite form and are therefore more easily understood by the programmer and anyone else who needs to read and understand them.

†summary punch

(Noun). A card-punching machine which can be connected to an accounting machine to punch totals or balance cards. (verb). To punch summary information in cards.

†supervisor

A routine or routines executed in response to a requirement for altering or interrupting the flow of operation through the central processing unit, or for performance of input/output operations, and, therefore, the medium through which the use of resources is coordinated and the flow of operations through the central processing unit is maintained. Hence, a control routine that is executed in supervisor state.

**\*symbolic address**

An **address** expressed in **symbols** convenient to the **computer programmer.**

**\*symbolic coding**

**Coding** that uses **machine instructions** with **symbolic addresses.**

**\*synchronization pulses**

Pulses introduced by **transmitting** equipment into the receiving equipment to keep the two equipments operating in step.

**\*synchronous computer**

(SC1) A **computer** in which each **event,** or the performance of any basic **operation,** is constrained to start on, and usually to keep in step with, **signals** from a **clock.** Contrast with **asynchronous computer.**

**\*syntax**

1. The structure of expressions in a **language.**
2. The rules governing the structure of a **language.**

**\*system**

1. (SC1) An assembly of methods, **procedures,** or techniques united by regulated interaction for forming an organized whole.
2. (SC1) An organized collection of men, **machines,** and methods required to accomplish a **set** of specific **functions.**


T

**table**

A collection or arrangement of data in fixed form for ready reference, frequently as stored in consecutive storage locations or written in the form of a grid consisting of rows and columns.

**\*tape deck**

Same as tape unit.

**\*tape to card**

Pertaining to equipment or methods that transmit data from either

magnetic tape or punched tape to punched cards.

**\*tape unit**

A device containing a **tape drive,** together with **reading** and **writing heads** and associated controls. Synonymous with **tape deck, tape station.**

**\*target language**

The **language** to which a **statement** is **translated.** Synonymous with **object language.**

**\*target program**

Same as **object program.**

**\*telecommunications**

Pertaining to the **transmission** of **signals** over long distances, such as by telegraph, radio, or television.

**†teleprocessing**

A form of information handling in which a data processing system utilizes communications facilities. (Originally an IBM trademark.)

**†teletype**

Trademark of Teletype Corporation, usually referring to a series of different types of teleprinter equipment such as tape punches, reperforators, page printers, etc., utilized for communications systems.

**†teletypewriter**

Generic term referring to the basic equipment made by Teletype Corporation and to teleprinter equipment.

**\*temporary storage**

In **programming, storage locations** reserved for intermediate results. Synonymous with **working storage.**

**\*tens complement**

The **radix complement** in **decimal notation.**

**\*terminal**

A point in a **system** or communication network at which **data** can either enter or leave.

**†third generation computer**

A computer utilizing SLT components.

*three-address
>Pertaining to an **instruction format** containing three **address parts.**

†throughput
>A measure of system efficiency; the rate at which work can be handled by a system.

†tie line
>A private-line communications channel of the type provided by communications common carriers for linking two or more points together.

tie truck
>A telephone line or channel directly connecting two branch exchanges.

time sharing
>Participation in available computer time by multiple users, via terminals. Characteristically, the response time is such that the computer seems dedicated to each user.

top-down program design
>A technique for designing a program (or system) according to its major functions and breaking these functions down into small subfunctions.

TOS
>Tape Operating System.

trailer record
>A record which follows one or more records and contains data related to those records.

*transaction file
>A **file** containing relatively transient **data** to be processed in combination with a **master file.** For example, in a payroll application, a transaction file indicating hours worked might be processed with a master file containing employee name and rate of pay. Synonymous with **detail file.**

†transistor
>A small solid-state, semiconducting device, ordinarily using germanium, that performs nearly all the functions of an electronic tube, especially amplification.

†translator
>1. A device that converts information from one system of representation into equipment information in another system of representation. In telephone equipment, it is the device that converts dialed digits into call-routine information.
>2. A routine for changing information from one representation or language to another.

*true complement
>Same as **radix complement.**

*truncate
>To terminate a computational process in accordance with some rule, e.g., to end the evaluation of a power series at a specified term.

*truncation error
>An **error** due to truncation. Contrast with **rounding error.**

†turnaround time
>1. The elapsed time between submission of a job to a computer center and the return of results.
>2. The actual time required to reverse the direction of transmission from send to receive or vice versa when using a half-duplex circuit. For most communications facilities, there will be time required by line propagation and line effects, modem timing, and machine reaction. A typical time is 200 milliseconds on a half-duplex telephone connection.

*twelve-punch
>A **punch** in the top row of a **Hollerith punch card.** Synonymous with **y-punch.**

*twos complement
>The **radix complement in binary notation.**

†typebar
>A linear type element containing all printable symbols.

*type font
>Type of a given size and style, e.g., 10-point Bodoni Modern.

## U

**\*unary operation**
Same as **monadic operation.**

**\*underflow**
Pertaining to the condition that arises when a machine computation yields a nonzero result smaller than the smallest nonzero quantity that the intended **unit** of **storage** is capable of storing. Contrast with **overflow.**

**\*unit**
1. A device having a special **function.**
2. A basic element.
3. See **arithmetic unit, central processing unit, control unit, identity unit, tape unit.**

**†unit record**
Historically, a card containing one complete record. Currently, the punched card.

**†update**
To modify a master file with current information according to a specified procedure.

**\*USASCII**
Same as **ASCII.**

**†user**
Anyone utilizing the services of a computing system.

**user-defined function**
A function defined in an application program and generally not available as a library function.

**\*utility routine**
Same as **service routine.**

## V

**\*variable**
A quantity that can assume any of a given **set** of values.

**\*variable-length record**
Pertaining to a **file** in which the **records** are not uniform in length.

**†verifier**
A device similar to a card punch used to check the inscribing of data by rekeying.

**\*verify**
1. To determine whether a transcription of **data** or other **operation** has been accomplished accurately.
2. To **check** the results of **keypunching.**

**†voice-grade channel**
A channel suitable for transmission of speech, digital or analog data, or facsimile, generally with a frequency range of about 300 to 3000 cycles per second.

**†volume**
The portion of a single unit of storage media which is accessible to a single read/write mechanism.

## W

**†wait condition**
As applied to tasks, the condition of a task such that it is dependent on an event or events in order to enter the ready condition.

**\*word**
A character string or a bit string considered as an entity.

**\*word length**
A measure of the size of a word, usually specified in units such as characters or binary digits.

**word processing**
A systematic method for the handling of document production and the associated administrative support function.

**\*working storage**
Same as **temporary storage.**

**\*write**
To record **data** in a **storage device** or a data **medium.** The recording need not be permanent, such as the writing on a **cathode ray display device.**

## X

*x-punch
>  Same as **eleven-punch.**

## Y

*y-punch
>  Same as **twelve-punch.**

## Z

*zero suppression
>  The elimination of nonsignificant zeros in a **numeral.**

*zone punch
>  A **punch** in the eleven, twelve, or zero row of a **punched card.**

# Computer Number Systems

## INTRODUCTION

We have learned that computers deal extensively with numbers and numerical quantities. It is also true that internally computers operate on numbers and numerical quantities which are represented in a form other than in the traditional decimal number system. It is, therefore, appropriate that we briefly analyze number systems.

## WHAT IS A NUMBER SYSTEM?

Before we can discuss the different number systems used in modern-day computers, we must first answer the question: What is a number system?

Briefly stated, a number system is a method for representing quantities of physical items. The method is a very simple one which is based on and dependent upon a fixed set of weights. To understand this concept, let us consider the hypothetical example of a butcher who sells meat by the pound, employing a simple balance scale (Fig. B-1). Let us assume that the butcher has available nine weights each of 1 pound, 10 pounds, and 100 pounds. Given the above, how could the butcher weigh out 208 pounds of beef?

First, he could select a combination of available weights which together would equal 208 pounds. This could be accomplished with two 100-lb weights, no 10-lb weights, and eight 1-lb weights:

$$2\ 100\text{-lb.} + 0\ 10\text{-lb} + 8\ 1\text{-lb}$$

The butcher might then write down the combinations as

$$2\text{--}0\text{--}8$$

for the sake of brevity, realizing that each of these digits represents the quantity of weights used in decreasing order of value. That is, the 2 refers to the number of 100-lb weights, the 0 refers to the number of 10-lb weights, and the 8 refers to the number of 1-lb weights. As the butcher became more familiar with this system, he may even denote the same total as 208, omitting the dashes (Fig. B-2).

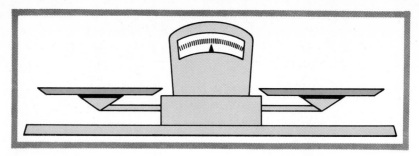

Simple balance scale

And we recognize this to be the decimal notation for 208. We also know it to be

$$(2 \times 100) + (0 \times 10) + (8 \times 1)$$

which we shall refer to as the **expanded form** of the number. Therefore, we have the relationship that

$$208 = (2 \times 100) + (0 + 10) + (8 \times 1)$$

In a similar manner, any decimal number could be represented by a combination of weights, related in that the smallest weight is one (1) and successive weights are found by multiplying 10 times the previous weight. That is,

$$1, 10 \times 1, 10 \times (10 \times 1), 10 \times (10 \times (10 \times 1)), \text{ etc.}$$

or

$$1, \quad 10, \quad\quad 100, \quad\quad\quad 1000, \quad\quad \text{etc.}$$

Since deca means ten, and the weights in this system result from multiplications by 10, this system became known as the base 10 or decimal system. This kind of a system is also termed a **positional** or **place-value number system** in that the actual value of a specific digit in a number is determined by (1) the place that the digit holds in the number and

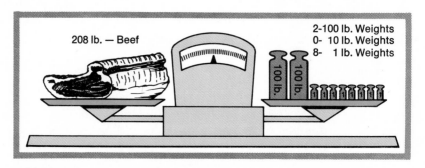

208 lb. — Beef

2-100 lb. Weights
0- 10 lb. Weights
8- 1 lb. Weights

FIGURE B-2
Weighing out 208 pounds on a simple balance scale

COMPUTER NUMBER SYSTEMS

(2) by the value of the digit itself. In the number 30303, for example, there are three 3's, each having a different value since each is associated with a different place or weight. Writing out the expanded form of this number, we have

$$30303 = (3 \times 10{,}000) + (0 \times 1{,}000) + (3 \times 100) + (0 \times 10) + (3 \times 1)$$

It is now more easily seen that the position of the first 3 gives it a total value of 30,000, while the position of the second 3 give it a total value of 300, and similarly the position of the third 3 gives it a total value of 3.

We can now more clearly understand our number system and why it is called a positional or place-value number system and why it is given the name decimal number system.

It should also be clear that the decimal number system has two distinctive features: (1) the 10 digits, 0, 1, 2, 3, 4, 5, 6, 7, 8, and 9 and (2) weights which are derived from multiplication by 10.

## THE BINARY NUMBER SYSTEM

Let us now consider a place-value number system with only the two digits 0 and 1 and with a set of weights derived from multiplications by 2. We will call this number system the **binary** or **base 2** number system. The weights would then be explicitly determined as follows:

| ... | $2 \times 16$ | $2 \times 8$ | $2 \times 4$ | $2 \times 2$ | $2 \times 1$ | 1 |
|-----|------|-----|-----|-----|-----|---|
| ... | 32 | 16 | 8 | 4 | 2 | 1 |

With these weights, the decimal number 13 could be represented as follows:

$$13 = (1 \times 8) + (1 \times 4) + (0 \times 2) + (1 \times 1)$$

You will note that each positional weight is determined by multiplying 2 times the previous one, since the base of this system is 2 (see Table B-1).

As an additional example, let us consider the binary representation of the decimal number 43. What we need to do, then, is to select a com-

| BINARY WEIGHTS | DECISION TO ACCEPT OR REJECT | CUMULATIVE TOTAL |
|----------------|------------------------------|------------------|
| 128 | No | 0 |
| 64 | No | 0 |
| 32 | Yes | 32 |
| 16 | No | 32 |
| 8 | Yes | 40 |
| 4 | No | 40 |
| 2 | Yes | 42 |
| 1 | Yes | 43 |

| DECIMAL VALUE | | | VALUE IN BINARY NUMBER SYSTEM | | | | | | |
| --- | --- | --- | --- | --- | --- | --- | --- | --- | --- |
| 100 | 10 | 1 | 64 | 32 | 16 | 8 | 4 | 2 | 1 |
| | | 1 | | | | | | | 1 |
| | | 2 | | | | | | 1 | 0 |
| | | 3 | | | | | | 1 | 1 |
| | | 4 | | | | | 1 | 0 | 0 |
| | | 5 | | | | | 1 | 0 | 1 |
| | | 6 | | | | | 1 | 1 | 0 |
| | | 7 | | | | | 1 | 1 | 1 |
| | | 8 | | | | 1 | 0 | 0 | 0 |
| | | 9 | | | | 1 | 0 | 0 | 1 |
| | 1 | 0 | | | | 1 | 0 | 1 | 0 |
| | 1 | 1 | | | | 1 | 0 | 1 | 1 |
| | 1 | 2 | | | | 1 | 1 | 0 | 0 |
| | 1 | 3 | | | | 1 | 1 | 0 | 1 |
| | 1 | 4 | | | | 1 | 1 | 1 | 0 |
| | 1 | 5 | | | | 1 | 1 | 1 | 1 |
| | 1 | 6 | | | 1 | 0 | 0 | 0 | 0 |
| | 1 | 7 | | | 1 | 0 | 0 | 0 | 1 |
| | 1 | 8 | | | 1 | 0 | 0 | 1 | 0 |
| | 1 | 9 | | | 1 | 0 | 0 | 1 | 1 |
| | 2 | 0 | | | 1 | 0 | 1 | 0 | 0 |
| | 2 | 1 | | | 1 | 0 | 1 | 0 | 1 |
| | 2 | 2 | | | 1 | 0 | 1 | 1 | 0 |
| | 2 | 3 | | | 1 | 0 | 1 | 1 | 1 |
| | 2 | 4 | | | 1 | 1 | 0 | 0 | 0 |
| | 2 | 5 | | | 1 | 1 | 0 | 0 | 1 |
| | 2 | 6 | | | 1 | 1 | 0 | 1 | 0 |
| | 2 | 7 | | | 1 | 1 | 0 | 1 | 1 |
| | 2 | 8 | | | 1 | 1 | 1 | 0 | 0 |
| | 2 | 9 | | | 1 | 1 | 1 | 0 | 1 |
| | 3 | 0 | | | 1 | 1 | 1 | 1 | 0 |
| | 3 | 1 | | | 1 | 1 | 1 | 1 | 1 |
| | 3 | 2 | | 1 | 0 | 0 | 0 | 0 | 0 |
| | 3 | 3 | | 1 | 0 | 0 | 0 | 0 | 1 |
| | 3 | 4 | | 1 | 0 | 0 | 0 | 1 | 0 |
| | 3 | 5 | | 1 | 0 | 0 | 0 | 1 | 1 |
| | 3 | 6 | | 1 | 0 | 0 | 1 | 0 | 0 |
| | 3 | 7 | | 1 | 0 | 0 | 1 | 0 | 1 |
| | 3 | 8 | | 1 | 0 | 0 | 1 | 1 | 0 |
| | 3 | 9 | | 1 | 0 | 0 | 1 | 1 | 1 |
| | 4 | 0 | | 1 | 0 | 1 | 0 | 0 | 0 |

bination of binary weights which, when added together, equal but do not exceed 43. Summarizing, we have

$$43 = (1 \times 32) + (0 \times 16) + (1 \times 8) + (0 \times 4) + (1 \times 2) + (1 \times 1)$$

Using the place-value notation previously discussed, we have

$$101011 = (1 \times 32) + (0 \times 16) + (1 \times 8) + (0 \times 4) + (1 \times 2) + (1 \times 1)$$

But 101011 could be misinterpreted as meaning one hundred one thousand eleven. To eliminate this confusion, one inserts a small 2 just after, and slightly below, the rightmost digit of the number to denote that it is a binary or base 2 number. Consistent with this notation, any nondecimal number will contain a small digit to the right of, and just below, its rightmost digit. Decimal numbers are written as usual, without any such digit to indicate the base in which the number is written. The above binary number would then be written

$$101011_2$$

Given a number in this notation, it is a simple matter to determine what its equivalent would be in the decimal or base 10 number system. This is accomplished by assigning to each digit in the binary number its appropriate weight. We begin by assigning the weight of 1 to the rightmost or **low-order** bit (binary digit). Each subsequent digit is assigned a weight equal in value to twice or double the weight assigned to the previous digit.

For the binary number $101011_2$, this procedure would appear as follows:

| Binary digits | 1 | 0 | 1 | 0 | 1 | $1_2$ |
|---|---|---|---|---|---|---|
| Weights | 32 | 16 | 8 | 4 | 2 | 1 |
| Decimal value | 32 + | 0 + | 8 + | 0 + | 2 + | 1 = 43 |

As an added illustration, let us determine the decimal equivalent of the binary number $101011010_2$:

| Binary digits | 1 | 0 | 1 | 0 | 1 | 1 | 0 | 1 | $0_2$ |
|---|---|---|---|---|---|---|---|---|---|
| Weights | 256 | 128 | 64 | 32 | 16 | 8 | 4 | 2 | 1 |
| Decimal value | 256 + | 0 + | 64 + | 0 + | 16 + | 8 + | 0 + | 2 + | 0 = 346 |

At this point, we realize that we can represent a given quantity of objects using either the decimal or binary number systems just as we can have the same value of money in two different currencies. And as we would have to understand the French monetary system to do business in France, so must we have a working knowledge of the binary number system to do business with an individual who calculates in binary.

You ask, who calculates in binary? The answer is, no person, but a thing, a computer. Computers, in general, operate in binary, and to understand the working of a computer one must understand the binary number system. As was illustrated above, a number expressed in the binary number system can also be expressed in the decimal system. Similarly, there is a correspondence between the numbers in any one number system and the numbers in any other number system. Therefore, as long as the basic rules of arithmetic are observed, the result of any calculation or series of calculations will lead to equivalent results.

**Hexadecimal Number System**  In addition to utilizing the binary number system, computers also make use of the **base 16** or **hexadecimal number system.** A unique relationship between the binary number system and the hexadecimal number system makes it suitable for use in a computer. This relationship will become apparent later.

In dealing with the hexadecimal number system, a new problem arises. We know that there should be 16 digits but we are only familiar with the 10 decimal digits 0, 1, 2, 3, 4, 5, 6, 7, 8, and 9. Therefore, we must create 6 additional symbols to represent the 6 additional hexadecimal digits. Traditionally, the symbols chosen and their representations are A, B, C, D, E, and F, where A = 10, B = 11, C = 12, D = 13, E = 14, and F = 15. The 16 basic hexadecimal digits then are 0, 1, 2, 3, 4, 5, 6, 7, 8, 9, A, B, C, D, E, and F.

Let us now consider the hexadecimal number $3B_{16}$. To convert such a number to its decimal equivalent we proceed as we have in the past with binary conversions. That is, we express $3B_{16}$ in the expanded form utilizing the 16 hexadecimal digits and the hexadecimal weights. The hexadecimal weights are determined as follows:

| ... | $16 \times 256$ | $16 \times 16$ | $16 \times 1$ | 1 |
|-----|-----------------|----------------|---------------|---|
| ... | 4096 | 256 | 16 | 1 |

Employing these weights, we see that the hexadecimal number $3B_{16}$ becomes

$$3B_{16} = (3 \times 16) + (B \times 1)$$

and since B = 11, we have

$$3B_{16} = (3 \times 16) + (11 \times 1) = 59$$

Let us consider the slightly more involved problem of determining the decimal equivalent of $15A_{16}$:

| Hexadecimal digits | 1 | 5 | $A_{16}$ |
|--------------------|------|-----|----------|
| Weights | 256 | 16 | 1 |
| Decimal value | 256 + | 80 + | A  = 346 (since A = 10) |

Thus,

$$15A_{16} = 346$$

But we have seen the number 346 before. We have seen this number to be equivalent to the binary number $101011010_2$. We have, therefore, that

$$346 = 15A_{16} \text{ and } 346 = 101011010_2$$

Examining these two representations for the decimal number 346, we see a very interesting and unique relationship. That is,

| 1 | 5 | A | (Hexadecimal equivalent of 346) |
|------|------|------|---------------------------------|
| 0001 | 0101 | 1010 | (Binary equivalent of 346) |

| DECIMAL VALUE | | | HEXADECIMAL VALUE | | |
|---|---|---|---|---|---|
| 100 | 10 | 1 | 256 | 16 | 1 |
| | | 1 | | | 1 |
| | | 2 | | | 2 |
| | | 3 | | | 3 |
| | | 4 | | | 4 |
| | | 5 | | | 5 |
| | | 6 | | | 6 |
| | | 7 | | | 7 |
| | | 8 | | | 8 |
| | | 9 | | | 9 |
| | 1 | 0 | | | A |
| | 1 | 1 | | | B |
| | 1 | 2 | | | C |
| | 1 | 3 | | | D |
| | 1 | 4 | | | E |
| | 1 | 5 | | | F |
| | 1 | 6 | | 1 | 0 |
| | 1 | 7 | | 1 | 1 |
| | 1 | 8 | | 1 | 2 |
| | 1 | 9 | | 1 | 3 |
| | 2 | 0 | | 1 | 4 |
| | 2 | 1 | | 1 | 5 |
| | 2 | 2 | | 1 | 6 |
| | 2 | 3 | | 1 | 7 |
| | 2 | 4 | | 1 | 8 |
| | 2 | 5 | | 1 | 9 |
| | 2 | 6 | | 1 | A |
| | 2 | 7 | | 1 | B |
| | 2 | 8 | | 1 | C |
| | 2 | 9 | | 1 | D |
| | 3 | 0 | | 1 | E |
| | 3 | 1 | | 1 | F |
| | 3 | 2 | | 2 | 0 |
| | 3 | 3 | | 2 | 1 |
| | 3 | 4 | | 2 | 2 |
| | 3 | 5 | | 2 | 3 |

Starting from the units, or low-order, side of each number, you will notice that a group of four binary digits is equal to one hexadecimal digit. That is,

$$0001_2 = (0 \times 8) + (0 \times 4) + (0 \times 2) + (1 \times 1) = 1_{16}$$
$$0101_2 = (0 \times 8) + (1 \times 4) + (0 \times 2) + (1 \times 1) = 5_{16}$$
$$1010_2 = (1 \times 8) + (0 \times 4) + (1 \times 2) + (0 \times 1) = A_{16}$$

In general, conversions from one system to another are not this simple. The exception in this case is due to the fact that there is a whole-power relationship between these bases:

$$2^4 = 2 \times 2 \times 2 \times 2 = 16$$

Simple and rapid conversions, such as the one illustrated, will exist between numbers when the bases in which the numbers are represented have such a whole-power relationship. Moreover, the relationship between the number of digits in one system which corresponds to one digit in the other system will exactly match the relationship between their bases. That is, since four 2's must be multiplied together to produce one 16, four binary digits will be required to equal one hexadecimal digit. A complete list of all hexadecimal-to-binary digits is given in Table B-3.

Let us consider two additional examples.

1. $1011010111011001_2 = ?$ (hexadecimal equivalent)

| 1011 | 0101 | 1101 | 1001 | (binary number) |
|------|------|------|------|-----------------|
| B(11) | 5 | D(13) | 9 | (hexadecimal equivalent) |

Therefore, $1011010111011001_2 = B5D9_{16}$.

2. $13A4F_{16} = ?$ (binary equivalent)

| 1 | 3 | A(10) | 4 | F(15) | (hexadecimal number) |
|------|------|------|------|------|----------------------|
| 0001 | 0011 | 1010 | 0100 | 1111 | (binary equivalent) |

Eliminating leading zeros, we have

$$13A4F_{16} = 10011101001001111_2$$

**TABLE B-3**
Binary-to-hexadecimal Conversions

| BINARY DIGITS | HEXADECIMAL DIGITS |
|:-------------:|:------------------:|
| 0000 | 0 |
| 0001 | 1 |
| 0010 | 2 |
| 0011 | 3 |
| 0100 | 4 |
| 0101 | 5 |
| 0110 | 6 |
| 0111 | 7 |
| 1000 | 8 |
| 1001 | 9 |
| 1010 | A |
| 1011 | B |
| 1100 | C |
| 1101 | D |
| 1110 | E |
| 1111 | F |

Let us begin our analysis by considering a hypothetical situation. Suppose that we have a child seated at a table with 25 pencils, several pieces of string, and a small box placed on the table in front of him.

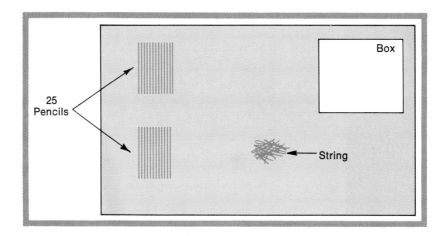

Let us also suppose that we instruct the child to perform a series of simple steps.

Step 1. Pick up two pencils and tie them together. Repeat this tying process until either all pencils have been tied into bundles of two pencils each, or until only one pencil remains unbundled on the table. If one pencil remains, place it in the box.

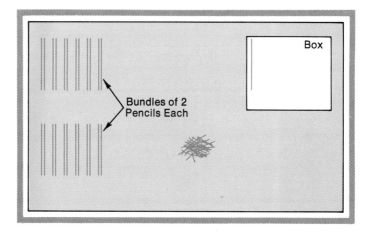

Step 2. Pick up two bundles and tie them together. Repeat this tying process until either all previous bundles have been tied into larger bundles or until only one small bundle remains. If one small bundle remains, place it in the box.

Step 3. Repeat step 2. This would result in

Step 4. Repeat step 2. This would result in

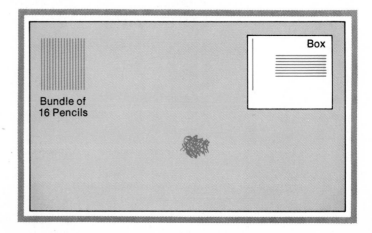

Step 5. Repeat step 2. This would result in

You may ask: What does such a process have to do with number systems? To answer this question, let us examine the results of each step in a somewhat less elaborate form.

| | PENCILS ON THE TABLE | DISCARDS INTO THE BOX |
|---|---|---|
| Initially | 25 unbundled pencils | |
| After step 1 | 12 bundles, 2 pencils each | 1 unbundled pencil |
| After step 2 | 6 bundles, 4 pencils each | 0 bundles, 2 pencils each |
| After step 3 | 3 bundles, 8 pencils each | 0 bundles, 4 pencils each |
| After step 4 | 1 bundle, 16 pencils | 1 bundle, 8 pencils |
| After step 5 | 0 bundles, 32 pencils | 1 bundle, 16 pencils |

Since, at the end of this process, there are no individual pencils or bundles of pencils on the table, it follows that all the original 25 pencils have been discarded into the box. Therefore, if we sum the number of pencils discarded at each step, we should have all the original pencils, or 25 pencils:

$$
\begin{array}{ll}
\text{1 unbundled pencil} & = \text{ 1 pencil} \\
\text{0 bundles, 2 pencils each} & = \text{ 0 pencils} \\
\text{0 bundles, 4 pencils each} & = \text{ 0 pencils} \\
\text{1 bundle, 8 pencils} & = \text{ 8 pencils} \\
\text{1 bundle, 16 pencils} & = \text{16 pencils} \\
\hline
\textit{Total} & = \text{25 pencils}
\end{array}
$$

Or, stated in a slightly different manner,

$$25 = (1 \times 16) + (1 \times 8) + (0 \times 4) + (0 \times 2) + (1 \times 1)$$

But we also recognize this to be the expanded form of the binary number $11001_2$.

If we examine the steps leading to this result, we will see that this bundling process is, in actuality, a division process, or **algorithm.** This process is illustrated below.

$$
\begin{array}{rl}
2\overline{)25} & \\
12 & \text{remainder 1} \\
2\overline{)12} & \\
6 & \text{remainder 0} \\
2\overline{)6} & \\
3 & \text{remainder 0} \\
2\overline{)3} & \\
1 & \text{remainder 1} \\
2\overline{)1} & \\
0 & \text{remainder 1}
\end{array}
$$

Combining steps, we have

$$
\begin{array}{rl}
2\overline{)25} & \\
2\overline{)12} & 1 \\
2\overline{)6} & 0 \\
2\overline{)3} & 0 \\
2\overline{)1} & 1 \\
0 & 1
\end{array}
$$

We also see that the remainders from this division process, recorded from the bottom to the top, reveal that

$$25 = 11001_2$$

Similarly, by repeatedly dividing by 16 until a quotient of zero is obtained, and recording the remainders from the bottom to the top, one can determine the base 16 or hexadecimal equivalent of 28:

$$
\begin{array}{rl}
16\overline{)28} & \text{remainders} \\
16\overline{)1} & 12 = C \\
0 & 1
\end{array}
$$

Therefore, $28 = 1C_{16}$. Let us consider the more involved exercise of determining the hexadecimal equivalent of 37469:

$$
\begin{array}{rl}
16\overline{)37469} & \\
16\overline{)2341} & 13 = D \\
16\overline{)146} & 5 \\
16\overline{)9} & 2 \\
0 & 9
\end{array}
$$

Therefore, $37469 = 925D_{16}$. It is recommended, however, in cases such as this, where the division is reasonably extensive, that the division steps be done with the aid of a calculator or off to the side using long division. In this way, unnecessary division errors can be avoided.

We have seen that this **remainder system,** or **division algorithm,** applies to problems of converting decimal numbers to equivalent binary and hexadecimal numbers. The division algorithm is also applicable to converting decimal numbers to equivalent numbers in any other number system.

# Answers to End-of-Chapter Exercises

APPENDIX C

## CHAPTER 1

### 1–1 True/False Exercises (Page references are given for all "False" questions.)

| | | | |
|---|---|---|---|
| **1.** F (page 17) | **7.** T | **13.** F (page 8) | **19.** F (page 18) |
| **2.** T | **8.** T | **14.** T | **20.** F (page 10) |
| **3.** T | **9.** F (page 14) | **15.** T | **21.** T |
| **4.** T | **10.** T | **16.** F (page 17) | **22.** T |
| **5.** T | **11.** T | **17.** T | **23.** T |
| **6.** F (page 19) | **12.** T | **18.** T | **24.** F (page 8) |

### 1–2 Multiple-choice Exercises

| | | | |
|---|---|---|---|
| **1.** e | **3.** d | **5.** e | **7.** d |
| **2.** b | **4.** a | **6.** e | **8.** c |

## CHAPTER 2

### 2–1 True/False Exercises (Page references are given for all "False" questions.)

| | | | |
|---|---|---|---|
| **1.** F (page 36) | **6.** T | **11.** T | **16.** F (page 49) |
| **2.** T | **7.** T | **12.** T | **17.** F (page 54) |
| **3.** T | **8.** T | **13.** T | **18.** T |
| **4.** F (page 54) | **9.** T | **14.** T | **19.** F (page 40) |
| **5.** F (page 39) | **10.** F (page 52) | **15.** F (page 48) | **20.** F (page 49) |

### 2–2 Multiple-choice Exercises

| | | | |
|---|---|---|---|
| **1.** a | **4.** b | **7.** b | **10.** e |
| **2.** d | **5.** e | **8.** e | |
| **3.** e | **6.** e | **9.** e | |

# CHAPTER 3

## 3-1 True/False Exercises (Page references are given for all "False" questions.)

| | | | |
|---|---|---|---|
| **1.** T | **8.** F (page 90) | **15.** T | **22.** F (page 82) |
| **2.** T | **9.** F (page 79) | **16.** F (page 75) | **23.** T |
| **3.** T | **10.** F (page 72) | **17.** T | **24.** T |
| **4.** T | **11.** T | **18.** F (page 94) | **25.** T |
| **5.** T | **12.** T | **19.** T | |
| **6.** T | **13.** T | **20.** T | |
| **7.** T | **14.** F (page 96) | **21.** F (page 79) | |

## 3-2 Multiple-choice Exercises

| | | | |
|---|---|---|---|
| **1.** b | **3.** e | **5.** c | **7.** e |
| **2.** b | **4.** c | **6.** d | **8.** e |

# CHAPTER 4

## 4-1 True/False Exercises (Page references are given for all "False" questions.)

| | | | |
|---|---|---|---|
| **1.** T | **8.** T | **15.** T | **22.** T |
| **2.** T | **9.** T | **16.** T | **23.** T |
| **3.** F (page 136) | **10.** T | **17.** T | **24.** T |
| **4.** T | **11.** T | **18.** F (page 127) | **25.** F (page 128) |
| **5.** T | **12.** T | **19.** T | |
| **6.** T | **13.** F (page 126) | **20.** F (page 149) | |
| **7.** F (page 132) | **14.** T | **21.** T | |

## 4-2 Fill-in Exercises

| | |
|---|---|
| **1.** row; row; column; column | **6.** sequential |
| **2.** punched paper; magnetic | **7.** essential |
| **3.** character | **8.** cathode ray tube |
| **4.** computer output microfilm | **9.** on-line |
| **5.** slower or less | **10.** direct-access storage device |

# CHAPTER 5

## 5-1 True/False Exercises (Page references are given for all "False" questions.)

| | | | |
|---|---|---|---|
| **1.** T | **8.** T | **15.** T | **22.** T |
| **2.** T | **9.** F (page 189) | **16.** T | **23.** T |
| **3.** T | **10.** T | **17.** T | **24.** T |
| **4.** T | **11.** T | **18.** T | **25.** F (page 167) |
| **5.** F (page 161) | **12.** T | **19.** F (page 161) | |
| **6.** F (page 172) | **13.** F (page 163) | **20.** F (page 175) | |
| **7.** T | **14.** F (page 181) | **21.** T | |

## 5-2 Fill-in Exercises

1. access time
2. laser
3. primary; secondary
4. control; arithmetic/logic; storage
5. pages

## 5-3 Multiple-choice Exercises

1. d
2. c
3. d
4. e
5. e
6. e
7. a
8. b

# CHAPTER 6

## 6-1 True/False Exercises (Page references are given for all "False" questions.)

1. T
2. T
3. F (page 204)
4. F (page 208)
5. F (page 204)
6. T
7. T
8. F (page 217)
9. T
10. F (page 218)
11. F (page 218)
12. F (page 203)
13. F (page 208)
14. F (page 218)
15. T
16. T
17. F (page 211)
18. T
19. T
20. F (page 212)
21. F (page 208)
22. T
23. T
24. T
25. T

## 6-2 Multiple-choice Exercises

1. d
2. b
3. d
4. c
5. d
6. c
7. b
8. e

# CHAPTER 7

## 7-1 True/False Exercises (Page references are given for all "False" questions.)

1. T
2. T
3. T
4. T
5. F (page 243)
6. T
7. F (page 238)
8. F (page 264)
9. T
10. F (page 251)
11. T
12. T
13. T
14. T
15. T
16. T
17. F (page 261)
18. F (page 266)
19. F (page 266)
20. T
21. T
22. F (page 275)
23. T
24. F (page 235)
25. F (page 266)
26. T
27. F (page 269)
28. T
29. F (page 247)
30. T

## 7-2 Matching Exercise

1. D
2. K, O, L
3. F
4. H
5. E
6. G
7. I
8. A
9. L, M
10. P
11. J, N, M
12. C
13. B

# CHAPTER 8

## 8–1 True/False Exercises (Page references are given for all "False" questions.)

| | | | |
|---|---|---|---|
| **1.** T | **6.** F (page 290) | **11.** T | **16.** T |
| **2.** T | **7.** T | **12.** T | **17.** T |
| **3.** F (page 289) | **8.** T | **13.** F (page 294) | **18.** F (page 292) |
| **4.** T | **9.** T | **14.** T | **19.** T |
| **5.** T | **10.** T | **15.** T | **20.** T |

## 8–2 Multiple-choice Exercises

| | | | |
|---|---|---|---|
| **1.** e | **3.** e | **5.** a | **7.** d |
| **2.** e | **4.** a | **6.** d | **8.** e |

## 8–3 Fill-in Exercises

1. program
2. manufacturer
3. input/output, control, arithmetic, logical, and specification
4. the American National Standards Institute
5. compilers
6. debugging
7. operational
8. sequential
9. coding or syntax; logic

# CHAPTER 9

## 9–1 True/False Exercises (Page references are given for all "False" questions.)

| | | | |
|---|---|---|---|
| **1.** T | **9.** T | **17.** T | **25.** F (page 331) |
| **2.** F (page 331) | **10.** F (page 325) | **18.** F (page 334) | **26.** T |
| **3.** T | **11.** T | **19.** T | **27.** T |
| **4.** F (page 331) | **12.** F (page 328) | **20.** T | **28.** F (page 336) |
| **5.** T | **13.** F (page 336) | **21.** T | **29.** F (page 330) |
| **6.** F (page 334) | **14.** F (page 326) | **22.** T | **30.** F (page 326) |
| **7.** T | **15.** T | **23.** F (page 329) | |
| **8.** T | **16.** F (page 327) | **24.** F (page 327) | |

## 9–2 Multiple-choice Exercises

| | | | |
|---|---|---|---|
| **1.** a | **3.** b | **4.** b | **5.** e |
| **2.** a | | | |

### 9-3 Fill-in Exercises

1. 5; 15
2. less than or equal to
3. BYE or GOODBYE
4. exponentiation (↑ or **), multiplication (*), division (/), addition (+), and subtraction (−)
5. letter; letter followed by a digit
6. batch; interactive
7. integer
8. Beginner's All-purpose Symbolic Instruction Code
9. exponentiation; **
10. the value of the quantity to be printed is negative

## CHAPTER 10

### 10-1 True/False Exercises (Page references are given for all "False" questions.)

1. F (page 374)
2. T
3. T
4. F (page 379)
5. T
6. T
7. F (page 359)
8. T
9. F (page 360)
10. T
11. T
12. T
13. F (page 364)
14. F (page 367)
15. F (page 373)
16. T
17. T
18. T
19. F (page 384)
20. T

### 10-2 Matching Exercises

1. r
2. m
3. b
4. u
5. v
6. g
7. l
8. a
9. w
10. q
11. j
12. f
13. x
14. e
15. c
16. t
17. h
18. i
19. k
20. n
21. d
22. s
23. o
24. p

## CHAPTER 11

### 11-1 True/False Exercises (Page references are given for all "False" questions.)

1. T
2. F (page 414)
3. T
4. T
5. T
6. T
7. T
8. F (page 424)
9. T
10. T
11. T
12. F (page 413)
13. T
14. T
15. T
16. T
17. F (page 418)
18. T
19. T
20. F (page 426)
21. F (page 420)
22. T
23. F (page 419)
24. F (page 419)
25. T

## 11–2 Fill-in Exercises

1. unconditional

2. WORKING-STORAGE; DATA

3. 9999V9

4. PROGRAM-ID

5. COmmon Business Oriented Language

6. IDENTIFICATION DIVISION, ENVIRON-
   MENT DIVISION, DATA DIVISION, and
   PROCEDURE DIVISION

7. FILE and WORKING-STORAGE

8. PROCEDURE

9. MOVE

10. record

# CHAPTER 12

## 12–1 True/False Exercises (Page references are given for all "False" questions.)

| | | | |
|---|---|---|---|
| 1. T | 8. T | 15. T | 22. T |
| 2. F (page 458) | 9. T | 16. F (page 455) | 23. F (page 450) |
| 3. F (page 452) | 10. T | 17. T | 24. T |
| 4. F (page 452) | 11. T | 18. F (page 457) | 25. F (page 453) |
| 5. T | 12. T | 19. T | |
| 6. F (page 458) | 13. F (page 455) | 20. T | |
| 7. T | 14. F (page 458) | 21. F (page 456) | |

## 12–2 Multiple-choice Exercises

| | | | |
|---|---|---|---|
| 1. d | 3. d | 4. c | 5. a |
| 2. a | | | |

## 12–3 Matching Exercise

| | | | |
|---|---|---|---|
| 1. G | 4. H | 6. D | 8. E |
| 2. F | 5. A | 7. C | 9. I |
| 3. B | | | |

# CHAPTER 13

## 13–1 True/False Exercises (Page references are given for all "False" questions.)

| | | | |
|---|---|---|---|
| 1. T | 8. T | 15. T | 22. F (page 472) |
| 2. T | 9. T | 16. T | 23. T |
| 3. T | 10. T | 17. F (page 476) | 24. F (page 470) |
| 4. T | 11. F (page 478) | 18. T | 25. T |
| 5. T | 12. F (page 473) | 19. T | |
| 6. F (page 468) | 13. T | 20. T | |
| 7. T | 14. T | 21. T | |

## 13–2 Multiple-choice Exercises

| | | | |
|---|---|---|---|
| 1. a | 3. e | 4. c | 5. c |
| 2. b | | | |

### 13-3 Matching Exercise

| | | | |
|---|---|---|---|
| 1. A | 6. C | 11. H | 16. Q |
| 2. D | 7. N | 12. K | 17. S |
| 3. F | 8. J | 13. I | 18. R |
| 4. E | 9. O | 14. G | 19. P |
| 5. B | 10. M | 15. L | |

## CHAPTER 14

### 14-1 True/False Exercises (Page references are given for all "False" questions.)

| | | | |
|---|---|---|---|
| 1. T | 9. T | 17. T | 25. T |
| 2. T | 10. F (page 503) | 18. F (page 502) | 26. T |
| 3. T | 11. F (page 506) | 19. T | 27. F (page 495) |
| 4. T | 12. T | 20. F (page 496) | 28. T |
| 5. F (page 498) | 13. F (page 496) | 21. T | 29. T |
| 6. T | 14. F (page 499) | 22. T | 30. T |
| 7. T | 15. F (page 501) | 23. T | |
| 8. T | 16. T | 24. T | |

### 14-2 Multiple-choice Exercises

| | | | |
|---|---|---|---|
| 1. c | 3. c | 5. c | 7. d |
| 2. a | 4. d | 6. d | 8. b |

### 14-3 Fill-in Exercises

1. conversational; remote batch
2. online
3. batch or sequential processing
4. supervisor
5. economical
6. simultaneous operation of many terminals, rapid response times, independent operation of terminals, flexibility, and security controls
7. current; accessible
8. computer software, terminals, communication network, and database
9. terminal
10. multiprogramming, online interaction, and real-time response

## CHAPTER 15

### 15-1 True/False Exercises (Page references are given for all "False" questions.)

| | | | |
|---|---|---|---|
| 1. T | 5. T | 9. T | 13. T |
| 2. T | 6. T | 10. T | 14. F (page 535) |
| 3. T | 7. T | 11. T | 15. F (page 533) |
| 4. F (page 540) | 8. T | 12. F (page 539) | |

## 15–2 Multiple-choice Exercises

1. e    3. e    4. e    5. d
2. e

## 15–3 Fill-in Exercises

1. W2 and 941
2. preparation of the payroll audit, preparation of the check and earnings statement, and the bank reconciliation report
3. payroll register
4. earnings and bank reconciliation
5. produce and check and statement
6. Attendance and time

# INDEX

## A

Abacus, 36, *37*, 63
ABC computer, 49, 64
Access mechanism, magnetic
     disk, *209*
Access time, 170, 559
Accounts payable, 530
Accounts receivable, 530
Action entry, 259-61
Action stub, 259-61
Adding machines, early, *39*
Address, 165, 560
Aiken, Howard H., 45-47, 64
Algorithm, 218, 604, 605
Alphabetic characters, 76, *78*
Alphabetic field, 79, 80
Alphanumeric field, 79, 80
American National Standards
     Institute, Inc., 181, 135
American Standard Code for
     Information Interchange,
     175, 181-82, 188
"Analytical Engine," 39-40, *41*, 63
ANSI (*see* American National
     Standards Institute, Inc.)
Apple Computer, Inc., *191*, 192
Arithmetic/logic unit, 161, *162*,
     163
ASCII (*see* American Standard
     Code for Information
     Interchange)
Assembly system, 292
Atanasoff, John, 49
Audio devices, 103-4, 148-49
Automatic computation, early
     history, 63-64
Auxiliary storage (*see* Secondary
     storage)

## B

Babbage, Charles, 39-42, 63
     analytical engine, 39-40, *41*, 63
     difference engine, 39, *40*, 63
Base, of a number system, 594-95
Base sixteen (hexadecimal) table,
     *559, 600*
Base two (binary) table, 596
BASIC:
     arithmetic operations, 336
     batch, 324
     branch statements, 340-45
     constants, 327-28
     dialing up the computer, 324-25
     expression, 336-38
     file processing, 384-88
     format, 326
     functions and subprograms,
          381-84
     general form, 329-30
     instructions and commands:
          ABS(X), 381
          BYE, 326
          CLOSE, 386
          computed GO TO, 362-64
          DATA, 364-65
          DEF, 382
          DELETE, 326
          DIM, 373
          END, 334
          FOR/NEXT, 359-61
          GET, 386
          GOODBYE, 326
          GOSUB, 383-84
          GO TO, *340*, 341
          IF/THEN, 342-44
          INPUT, 333-34
          INT(X), 381

BASIC (*Contd.*)
     LET, 338-40
     LIST, 325
     LIST n, 325
     MAT INPUT, 380
     MAT PRINT, 379-80
     MAT READ, 379
     NEW, 325
     OLD, 325
     OPEN, 385
     PRINT, 330-33
     PRINT/TAB, 369
     PRINT/USING, 369-71
     PUT, 385
     READ, 364-65
     READY, 325
     REMARK, 327
     RESTORE, 366
     RETURN, 384
     RND(X), 381
     RUN, 325
     SGN(X), 381
     SQR(X), 381
     STOP, 325, 362
     SAVE, 326
     interactive language, 296-97,
          324
     library functions, 375, 381
     line numbers, 326
     looping, 344
     matrices, 377-80
     printed line format, 332
     reference summary, 399-409
     relational comparisons, 342
     remarks, 326
     rules for printing numbers, 331
     sample programs, *335, 339, 345,
          360, 361, 363, 365, 368, 375,
          376, 378, 383, 388*

BASIC (*Contd.*)
  semicolon, 366-67
  simple variable, 328
  string variable, 328-29
  string variables, comparison of, 342-44
  subprograms, 383
  system commands, 325-26
  table handling, 372-80
  user-defined functions, 382-83
  UWBIC, 324
  variables and variable names, 328-29
Batch processing, 495-96
BCD (*see* Binary Coded Decimal)
Beginner's All-purpose Symbolic Instruction Code (*see* BASIC)
Binary Coded Decimal, 82-83, *85*, 175-80, 188
Binary number system, 174, 595-97
  as proposed by von Neumann, 48-49
  why used with computers, 174-75, 597
Binary-to-decimal, 597
Binary-to-hexadecimal, 598-600
Bit, 166
Block, magnetic tape, 203, *205*
Block code, 474
Block diagram (*see* Flowchart)
Bubble memory, (*see* Magnetic bubble memory)
Buffer, 186
Burks, Arthur W., 47
Burrough's Corp., 55
Business data processing, 9
Business systems, 451-52
Byte, 180, *181*

**C**

Calcomp, plotter, *152, 153*
Calculating, 9, 13-14
Card column, 76
Card field, 79-81
Card layout and design, 472-73
Card punch, 83, *87*
Card punching, 83-84, 109-15
Card reading and punching devices, 119-26
Card-to-tape, 137-39

Card verifying, 113-15
Carrol, John M., 55
Cartridge, mass storage system, 213, *214*
Cathode ray tube, 61, *65, 142, 146*
Census tabulator, 44, *45*
Central processing unit, 161-74
  arithmetic/logic unit, 161, 163
  control unit, 161-63
  storage unit, 161, 163-74
Chain printer, 130-32, *134*
Channel:
  multiplexor, 186, *187, 188*, 515
  selector, 186, *187*
Character, 76
Charged-coupled device (*see* Storage, charged-coupled)
Character printers, 128-30
Character readers, 97-101
Character recognition, 97-101
Check bit, 177, *178*, 181, 203
Classifying, 9, 10, *13*
COBOL:
  advantages, 412-13
  CODASYL Committee, 412
  Common Business Oriented Language, 412
  flowcharing a program, 427-35
  program structure, 413-14
    Data Division, 414, 420-24
    Environment Division, 414, 419-20
    Identification Division 414, 418-19
    Procedure Division, 414, *415*, 424-427
  reading a program, 424-27
  reserved words, 418, 444-46
  sample program, 416-27
CODASYL (*see* Conference on Data Systems Languages)
Coding errors, 298-99
Coding input, 473-76
Coding programs, 288-98 (*see also* Chapter 9, 10, and 11)
Collator, 89-90
COM (*see* Computer output microfilm)
Common Business Oriented Language (*see* COBOL)
Communication lines, 515, *516*
Communications network, 499
Compiler, 293, 298
Computer:
  ABC, 49, 64

Computer (*Contd.*)
  applications, 8, 19, *20, 21, 22*, 27
  crime, 25
  Cray I, 8, 175
  EDSAC, 49, 64
  EDVAC, 64
  ENIAC, 49, 64
  generations, 51-57, 64
  history, summary, 63-64
  IAS, 64
  MARK I, *46*, 47, 64
  microcomputer, 61-66, 188-92
  minicomputer, 57-61
  number systems, 48-49, 593-600
  in society, 24, 26
  soluble problems, 17-22
  stored-program, 49
  UNIVAC I, 49-51, 64
  uses, 8, 18-24
Computer output microfilm, 147-48
Computer program (*see* Programming)
Condition entry, 259-61
Condition stub, 259-61
Conference On Data Systems Languages, 412
Connectors, flowchart, 241-44
Constant, BASIC, 327-28
Control instruction, 288
Control unit:
  of central processing unit, 161-63
  input/output, 188
  transmission, 515
Conversational time-shared processing, 501-2
Core, ferrite, 163-68, *169, 172*
CPU (*see* Central processing unit)
Cray I, 8, 175
Crime, computer, 25
CRT (*see* Cathode ray tube)
Cylinder, magnetic disk, 209

**D**

Data, coding of input, 473-76
Database, 220-21, *222-23*, 499
  management system, 220
  on-line real-time information system, 499
Data cell, 211-12, *213*

Data division, COBOL, 414, 420-24
Data entry (*see* Chapter 3)
Data files, 215-20, 476-77
Data Processing:
  basic functions, 17
  business, 9
  cycle, *16,* 17
  definition, 8
  history (*see* Chapter 2)
  operations, 9-17
  scientific, 9
Debugging, 298-301
Decimal number system, 593-95
Decimal-to-binary, 601-4
Decimal-to-hexadecimal. 601-5
Decision symbol, flowchart, 239-41
Decision Data Corp., 115
Decision table, 256-64
  physical form, *259*
  purpose, 256
  reading and interpreting, 261-62
  sample program, *263*
Deck, punched card, 79
Definable, 18
Density, 209
Diagnostics, 292, 293
"Difference Engine," 39, *40,* 63
Digit punching area, 78
Digital Broadcasting Corp., 25
Digital Equipment Corp., *190*
Digits:
  binary, 595
  decimal, 594-95
  hexadecimal, 598
Direct-access, 140-41, 206-15
Direct file organization, 218-19
Disk:
  floppy, 92-93
  packs, 210, *214*
  storage devices, 140, 208-11
  tracks, 208, *209*
Diskette, 92
Distributed data processing information system, 507-14
Divisions, COBOL, 414-15, 418-27
Documentation:
  program, 301-13
  system, 482-83, 548
Doubleword, 180, *181*
Do-until structure, 269, *274*

Do-while structure, 268-69, *271, 272, 274*
Drum storage devices, 140, 206-8
Dump, 180
Duplex line, 515
Duplicating, 83-84, 111

**E**

EBCDIC (*see* Extended Binary Coded Decimal Interchange Code)
Eckert, Presper, 49
EDSAC, 49
Eighty column card, *45,* 76-81
Electro-optical storage (*see* Laser memory)
ENIAC, 49
Environment Division, COBOL, 414, 419-20
EPROM, 189-90
Errors, programming, 298-301
Exception reporting, 506
Execution, program, 298-301
Expanded form, 594
Expression, BASIC, 336-38
Extended Binary Coded Decimal Interchange Code, 175, *179,* 180-81, *182,* 188
  hex notation, 181

**F**

Faceted code, input coding, 476
Feasibility study, 453-57
Ferrite core (*see* Core, ferrite)
Field, 79-81
File:
  choice of storage media, 216-17
  data, 476-77
  definition, 216
  organizational considerations, 217
  organizations, 215-20
    direct, 218-19, 476
    indexed sequential, 219-20
    sequential, 217-18, 476
    used in payroll system, 532-33
File protect ring, 204, *206*
First generation computers, 51, *52, 54,* 64

Five-channel code, paper tape, *135*
Fixed-length tape records, *205*
Floppy disk, 92-93
Flowchart:
  developing of a counter, 253, *255*
  developing of a sum, 247-51, *255*
  functions and flowlines, 235
  illustrations, *245, 254, 257-59, 287*
  initialization, 248, *255*
  looping, 250, *255*
  notes, 236
  plan of attack, 244
  symbols, 235, *237,* 238-44, *478*
  system, 477-80, *481*
  template, *237, 479*
  vs pseudocode, 269
  Worksheet, *287, 288*
Formula translator (*see* FORTRAN)
Forms design, 468-71
FORTRAN, 293, *296*
Fourth generation computers, 54-57, 64
Full duplex line, 515
Fullword, 180, *181*

**G**

Generation, computer, 51-57
Gigabyte, 212
Glossary, 559-91
Goldstine, Herman H., 47
Graphic display device (*see* Visual display device)

**H**

Half duplex line, 515
Halfword, 180, *181*
Hardware, 51
Hexadecimal:
  notation, 181
  number system, 598-600
Hexadecimal-to-binary, 598-600
Hexadecimal-to-decimal, 598
Hierarchy chart, 264, *265*
Hierarchy plus input-processing-output, 264-66
  hierarchy chart, 264, *265*

Hierarchy plus (*Contd.*)
input-process-output chart, 264, *265*
objectives, 264
HIPO (*see* Hierarchy plus input-processing-output)
Hollerith, Herman, 43-44, 64
Hollerith code, *45, 78*
vs BCD code, 175-76
vs EBCDIC, *179*, 180
Honeywell:
intelligent terminal, *95*
display station, *145*
series 200 computer, 144
teller register, 144

**I**

IBG (*see* Interblock gap)
IBM:
hardware devices:
029 Card punch, *87*
360 Computer system, *55*
370 Computer system, *56, 58*
701 Computer, 64
1054 Paper tape reader, *135*
1055 Paper tape punch, *135*
1092 Programmed keyboard, *142*
1401 Computer, *53*
1428 Alphameric optical reader, *120*
1627 Plotter, *151*
2301 Magnetic drum, *207*
2305 Fixed head storage module, *210*
2321 Data cell drive, model 1, *212*
2400 Series magnetic tape units, *138*
2540 Card read punch, *120, 125*
2671 Paper tape reader, *135*
2822 Control unit, *135*
2841 Storage control, *211*
3211 Printer, *120*
3275 Display station, 146
3344 Direct access storage facility, *211*
3348 Data module, *210*
3350 Disk storage device, *208*
3410 Magnetic tape unit, *120*
3420 Magnetic tape unit, *138*
3780 Remote job processing terminal, *143*

IBM (*Contd.*)
3800 Laser printer, *130*
3850 Mass storage system, 212, *214*
3851 Mass storage facility, 212
3890 OCR document processor, *100*
4341 Processor, *181*
5100 Portable computer, *60*, 61
7770 Audio response unit, 148-49
teller register, *144*
96-column punched card, 81-85
Standard punched card, *45*, 76-81
System/3, 81
Identification Division, COBOL, 414, 418-19
If-then-else structure, 267-68, *270, 271, 273*
Impact printers:
character-at-a-time, 128-30
line-at-a-time, 130-32
Indexed sequential file organization, 219-20
Information, as opposed to data, 5, 495
Information systems:
classifications, 495
distributed data processing, 507-14
integrated, 504-6
management, 506-7
multiprocessing, 499-501
multiprogramming, 499-501
off-line, 495-96
on-line, 496-97
on-line real-time, 498-99
time-sharing, 501-4
definition and purpose, 495
Input, function, *16*, 17
Input data, coding of, 473-76
Input devices (*see* Input/Output, devices)
Input media (*see* Punched card, Magnetic tape, Paper tape)
Input/Output:
devices:
audio, 103-4, 148-49
direct-access, 140-41, 206-15
film, 147-48
graphic, 146, 149-51, *152, 153*
punched card, 119
summary of, 122-23

Input/Output (*Contd.*)
tape, 134-40, 203-6
terminals, 141-46
flowchart symbol, 238
media, 122-23
Input-process-output chart, 264, *265*
Instructions, types, 288
Integer constant, BASIC, 327
Integrated information system, 504-6
Intel Magnetics Corp., 172
Interactive language, 289, 296-98
Interblock gap, 203-4, 208
International Business Machines Corporation (*see* IBM)
Interpreter, 88
Interpreting, 81, 88
Inventory system, 530
ISAM (*see* Indexed sequential file organization)

**J**

Jacquard, Joseph Marie, 39
Justifiable, 17-18
Justified, left- and right-, 79-80

**K**

Kemeny, John G., 324
Keyboard devices, 143-44
Keypunch (*see* Card punch)
Key-to-disk, 91-93
Key-to-tape, 90-91
Kodak Corp.:
Komstar 200 microimage processor, *148*
microfiche, *147*
microfilm cartridge, *147*
Kurtz, Thomas E., 324

**L**

Language:
interactive, 289, 296-98
machine, 51, 52, 54, 288-91
problem-oriented, 54, 289, 295-96, *297*
procedure-oriented, 54, 288, 292-95
symbolic, 52, 54, 288, 291-92
Laser memory, 55, 170

Laser printer, 126
Left-justified, 79-80
Light pen, 146
Literal, BASIC, 330-31
Logical instruction, 288
Logical record, 75
Logic errors, 299-301
Loom, by Jacquard, 39

## M

Machine Arithmétique, 36-37
Machine language, 51, 52, 54,
    288-91
Magnetic card storage, 211-12, *213*
Magnetic disk, 208-11
    disk pack, 210-11
    storage devices, 140
Magnetic drum, 140, 206-8
Magnetic ink character
    recognition, 97-98, 99
Magnetic tape:
    block, 203, *205*
    capacity, 137
    cassette devices, 139-40
    compared with punched card,
        *204*
    density, 137
    devices, 136-40
    disadvantages, 139
    file protect ring, 204, *206*
    key-to-disk, 92
    key-to-tape, 90-91
    tracks, 203
Management, exception
    reporting, 506
Management information
    systems, 506-7
Mark I computer, *46,* 47
Mass storage system, 212-15
Mauchly, John W., 49
Media, input or output, 17
Memory:
    charged-coupled, 172-73
    comparative costs, *172*
    core, 163-68, *169*
    general, 163-65
    laser, 55, 170
    magnetic bubble, 55, 57, *59,*
        170-72
    metal-oxide semiconductor
        (MOS), 169-70
    monolithic, 54, *56*
    transistor, 51-52
    vacuum tube, 47, 51

Memory (*Contd.*)
    virtual storage concept 55,
        173-74
MICR (*see* Magnetic ink
        character recognition)
Microcomputer, 61-66, 188-92
    EPROM, 189-90
    PROM, 189, 298
    RAM, 189
    ROM, 189
Microfiche, 147
Microfilm, 147
Microprocessor, 61-65
Minicomputer, 57-61
Modem, 57-61
Monolithic storage, 54, *56*
MOS integrated circuit memory,
        169-70, *172*
Multiple-record block, *205*
Multiplexor channel, 186, *187,*
        *188,* 515
Multiprocessing, 499-501
Multiprogramming, 499-501

## N

Nanosecond, 10, *165*
Network:
    combination, *514*
    ring, *513*
    star or spider, *512,* 513
Nine-track tape, 203
Ninety-six column card, 81-86
    vs standard 80-column card,
        81-82
Nondecimal numbers, notation,
        597
Number:
    expanded form, 594
    exponential form, 328
    integer, 327
    real, 327
Number system:
    binary, 48-49, 174, 595-97
    concept of, 593-95
    conversions:
        binary-to-decimal, 597
        binary-to-hexadecimal,
            598-600
        decimal-to-binary, 601-4
        decimal-to-hexadecimal,
            601-5
    decimal, 593-95
    hexadecimal, 598-600
    place-value, 594-95

Number System (*Contd.*)
    positional, 594-95
Numeric characters, 76, *78*
Numeric field, 79, 80

## O

Objectives, system study, 452
    feasibility study, 453-57
Object program, 419
OCR (*see* Optical character
        recognition)
Odd parity, 177
Off-line information processing
        system, 495-96
OMR (*see* Optical mark readers)
On-line information system,
        496-97
On-line real-time information
        system, 498-99
Optical character recognition,
        100-101
Optical mark readers, 98
Output functions, *16,* 17
Overlapped processing, 184-88

## P

Paper tape, 134-36
    used with terminals, 136
Parity, 177
    bits, 177, 181 (*see also* Check
        bit)
Pascal, Blaise, 36, 293
Payroll system:
    advantages, 531
    bank reconciliation report, 539
    check and statement, 536, *538*
    data required, 532-33
    deduction registers, 539-40
    documentation, 548-57
    files, 532-33
    management reports, 541-43
    payroll audit register, 533-34,
        *535*
    payroll register, 535-36, *537*
    sources of data, 532
    specific objectives, 531
    tax reports, 540, *541*
Peripheral devices, 119
Place-value number system,
        594-95
Plotters, 149-51, *152, 153*
Positional number system, 594-95

Primary storage, 163-74
Printers:
  chain, 130-32
  character, 128-30
  drum, 130-32, *134*
  impact, 128-32
  laser, *126*, 134
  line, 130-32
  nonimpact, 132-34
  print wheel, 130-32, *133*
  wire matrix, 128-30, *132*
  xerographic, 132
Problem analysis, 286
Problem-oriented language, 54,
  289, 295-96, *297*
Procedure division, COBOL, 414,
  *415*, 424-27
Procedure-oriented language, 54,
  288, 292-95 (*see also*
  Chapter 11)
Procedures manual, 303-13, 483
Processing:
  flowchart symbol, 238-39
  function, *16*, 17
Processor, 292
Program flowchart, 268-88 (*see*
  *also* Chapter 7)
Program loop, 250
Programming:
  coding and execution, 288-98
  debugging, 298-301
  documentation, 301-13
  errors, 298-301
  flowchart, 286-88 (*see also*
    Chapter 7)
  preparation for, 285
  problem analysis, 286
  program testing, 301
Programming languages:
  ADA, 312-13
  BASIC (*see* Chapter 9 and 10)
  COBOL (*see* Chapter 11)
  FORTRAN 293, *296*
  interactive, 289, 296-98
  machine, 51, 52, 54, 288-91
  PASCAL, 293
  PL/I, 293
  problem-oriented, 54, 289, 295-
    96, *297*
  procedure-oriented, 54, 288,
    292-95
  RPG, 295-96, *297*
  symbolic, 52, 54, 288, 291-92
PROM, 189, 298
Pseudocode, 269-73, *274*

Punched card:
  advantages and disadvantages,
    81
  design, 472-73
  96-column, 81-85
  processing machines, 85-90
  punching of, 83-84, 109-115
  readers and punches, 119-26
  standard 80-column, *45*, 76-8↓
  unit record, *43*, 44, 75
  verifying of, 113-15
Punched card operations, 83-84,
  109-115
Punched paper tape (*see* Paper
  tape)

**R**

Radio Shack:
  Quickprinter II, 130, *132*
  TRS-80, *65*, 190, *191*
RAM, 189
Random-access devices:
  data cell, 211-12, *213*
  magnetic disk, 140, 208-11
  magnetic drum, 140, 206-8
  mass storage system, 212-215
Reader punch, 119-26
Read-write head, 207, 208, *209*
Real constant, BASIC, 327-28
Record:
  logical, 75
  unit, *43*, 44, 75
Recording, 9-10, *11*
Reference summary, BASIC,
  399-409
Register, in arithmetic/logic unit,
  163
Remote batch time-shared
  processing, 502
Reptitive, criteria for
  computerized solution, 17,
  18
Reporting, data processing
  operation, 9, 17
Reproducer, 86-88
Ribicoff, Abraham, 25
Right-justified, 79-80
Ring network, 513
ROM, 189
RPG, 295-96, *297*
Rule entry, 259-61
Run manual (*see* Procedures
  manual)

**S**

Scheutz, George, 42
Scientific data processing, 9
Scientific method, in systems
  design, 459
Secondary storage, 183-84
Second generation computers, 51-
  52, *53*, *54*, 64
Sector, magnetic disk, 209
Selector channel, 186, *187*
Sequence code, input coding,
  474-76
Sequence structure, 267, *270*, *272*,
  *273*
Sequential:
  files, 203-6
  processing, 495-96
Sequential file organization,
  217-18
Seven-bit alphanumeric code (*see*
  Binary Coded Decimal)
Seven-track tape, 203
Sharpe, W.F., 324
Shift count, 327
Simplex line, 515
Single record block, *205*
Society, computers in, 24-26
Software, 499
Sorter, 89
Sorting, 9, 12-13, *14*, 89
Special characters, *45*, 76, *78*
Specification instructions, 288
Speech recognition system, 103-4
Spider network, *512*, 513
Star network, *512*, 513
Storage:
  American Standard Code for
    Information Interchange,
    175, 181-82
  auxiliary, 183
  Binary Coded Decimal, 175-80
  binary form, 174-75
  charged-coupled, 172-73
  core, 163-68, *169*
  Extended Binary Coded
    Decimal Interchange Code
    *179*, 180-81, *182*
  laser, 55, 170
  magnetic bubble, 55, 57, *59*,
    170-72
  magnetic card, 211-212, *213*
  magnetic disk, 208-211
  magnetic drum, 207-208
  magnetic tape, 203-4

Storage (*Contd.*)
monolithic, 54, *56*
MOS, 169-70
primary, 163-74
primary vs secondary, *184*
secondary, 183-84
unit, 161, *162*, 163-74
virtual, 55, 173-74
Stored program, 49, 164
Summarizing, data processing
operation, 9, 10-12
Symbolic language, 52, 54, 288,
291-92
Syntax error, 298-99
System:
business, 451-52 (*see also*
Chapter 15)
design, 457-59
documentation, 482-83
feasibility study, 453-57
flowchart, 477-80
fundamental accounting, 530
importance of to business, 528
information, 495-514
overall objectives, 452
procedures manual, 303-13, 483
proposed cost and benefits, *456*
testing, 480-82
total, 528, *529*
System flowchart, 477-80

**T**

Tabulating Machine Company,
44
Tape:
magnetic, 136-40
paper, 134-36
Telecommunications, 515

Teleprocessing, 515
Teletype Corp.:
4210 Magnetic tape data
terminal, *137*
Model 4500 terminal, *94*
terminal, *131*
Terminals, 93-97, 141-46, 499, 515
intelligent, 94-95
interactive, 93-94
point-of-sale, 95-97
Terminal, flowchart symbol, 244
Third generation computers, 52-
54, *55*, 64
Tier, 81, *82, 83*
Time-sharing information
system, 501-4
Total-system concept, 528, *529*
Top-down program design, 264-74
HIPO, 264-66
structured programming,
266-74
Track:
disk, 208, *209*
drum, *206*
tape, 252
Transistorized computers, 51-52

**U**

United States Census Bureau, 43
Unit-record, *43*, 44, 75
UNIVAC Division of Sperry Rand
Corp.:
Card reader, *121*
UNIVAC I, 49-51
716 Card reader subsystem, *124*
1801 Verifying punch, *115*
Universal Product Code, 96, *97*

University of Washington BASIC
Interpretive Compiler, 324

**V**

Vacuum tube computers, 47, 51
Variable, BASIC, 328-29
Variable length tape records, *205*
Verifying, 113-15
Virtual storage, 55, 173-74
Visual display devices, 144-46
Voice input/output, 103-4, 148-49
Volume data or calculations,
criteria for computerized
solution, 18
Von Neumann, John, 47-49, 64

**W**

Wang Laboratories:
minicomputer, *60*
word processing, *23*
Wheel printer, 130-32, *133*
Wire matrix printer, 128-30, *132*
Word, 180
Word processing, 23-24

**X**

Xerographic printer, 132
Xerox:
Laser printer, *126*, 132

**Z**

Zone punching area, 78